Praise for *The Anarchy*

A Finalist for the Cundill History Prize

"As William Dalrymple shows in his rampaging, brilliant, passionate history, *The Anarchy*, the East India Co. was the most advanced capitalist organization in the world . . . Mr. Dalrymple gives us every sword-slash, every scam, every groan and battle cry. He has no rival as a narrative historian of the British in India. *The Anarchy* is not simply a gripping tale of bloodshed and deceit, of unimaginable opulence and intolerable starvation. It is shot through with an unappeasable moral passion."
—*The Wall Street Journal*

"Superb . . . a vivid and richly detailed story . . . The greatest virtue of this disturbingly enjoyable book is perhaps less the questions it answers than the new ones it provokes about where corporations fit into the world, both then and now . . . Dalrymple's book [is] worth reading by everyone." —*The New York Times Book Review*

"Gripping . . . Drawing richly from sources in multiple languages, *The Anarchy* is gorgeously adorned with luminous images representing a range of perspectives . . . Delightful passages abound, including of the duel between Warren Hastings and Philip Francis, Shah Alam as 'the sightless ruler of a largely illusory empire,' and action-packed scenes of battle . . . Dalrymple has taken us to the limit of what page-turning history can be and do." —*Los Angeles Review of Books*

"A great story told in fabulous detail with interesting, if at times utterly rapacious or incompetent, characters populating it." —NPR.org

"An energetic page-turner that marches from the counting house on to the battlefield, exploding patriotic myths along the way . . . Dalrymple's spirited, detailed telling will be reason enough for many readers to devour *The Anarchy*. But his more novel and arguably greater achievement lies in the way he places the company's rise in the turbulent political landscape of late Mughal India." —*The Guardian*

"How timely [*The Anarchy*] feels, how surprisingly of the moment . . . It serves as a reminder that early capitalism was just as perverse, predatory, and single-minded in its pursuit of profit as its much-derided late-model equivalent." —*The Daily Beast*

"William Dalrymple, the most versatile chronicler of India past and present, distilled another complex yet highly topical history into *The Anarchy*, a bloodcurdling account of the East India Co.'s ascent to imperial dominance, full of implications for corporate behavior today." —Maya Jasanoff, *The Wall Street Journal*

"A well-known historian both in his native Britain and his adoptive India . . . Dalrymple has influenced the scholarly as well as the popular understanding of South Asian history through his use of both European and Indian sources, thus uniting the halves of a previously bisected whole." —*The New York Review of Books*

"Splendid . . . Dalrymple's book is an excellent example of popular history—engaging, readable, and informative." —*National Review*

"William Dalrymple's *The Anarchy* makes sense of the East India Co. and the political and economic conditions that enabled its curious ascent . . . [Dalrymple] navigates the teeming current of events smoothly, here gliding forward, there slowing to study the view." —*Air Mail*

"[*The Anarchy*] compelled my admiration . . . In William Dalrymple's deft hands we have an epic tale. It's very strong stuff." —Paul Kennedy, *The Wall Street Journal*

"Mr. Dalrymple sails through this story in fine style . . . The reader will find plenty that echoes in modern India." —*The Economist*

"[Dalrymple] has been at the forefront of the new wave of popular history, consistently producing work that . . . engages with a wider audience through writerly craft, an emphasis on characters and their agency, evocative description of place and time, and the inclusion of long-neglected perspectives. [*The Anarchy*]'s real achievement is to take readers to an important and neglected period of British and South

Asian history, and to make their trip there not just informative [but] colorful." —*The Observer*

"The author is a marvelous storyteller. By quoting extensively from the company's own voluminous records, private letters, and diaries, Persian-language sources, eyewitness accounts penned by an insightful local historian, and other reports, Dalrymple creates a 'you are there' environment for the reader that makes the book hard to put down." —*Washington Independent Review of Books*, Favorite Books of 2019

"Dalrymple recounts the remarkable history of the East India Company from its founding in 1599 to 1803 when it commanded an army twice the size of the British Army and ruled over the Indian subcontinent . . . It's a hell of a story." —Marginal Revolution

"[An] expert account of the rise of the first great multinational corporation." —*Kirkus Reviews*

THE ANARCHY

In Xanadu: A Quest
City of Djinns: A Year in Delhi
From the Holy Mountain: A Journey in the Shadow of Byzantium
The Age of Kali: Indian Travels and Encounters
White Mughals: Love and Betrayal in Eighteenth-Century India
Begums, Thugs & White Mughals: The Journals of Fanny Parkes
The Last Mughal: The Fall of a Dynasty, Delhi 1857
Nine Lives: In Search of the Sacred in Modern India
Return of a King: The Battle for Afghanistan
Princes and Painters in Mughal Delhi, 1707–1857
(with Yuthika Sharma)
The Writer's Eye
The Historian's Eye
Koh-i-Noor: The History of the World's Most Infamous Diamond
(with Anita Anand)
Forgotten Masters: Indian Painting for the East India Company 1770–1857

THE ANARCHY

The East India Company, Corporate
Violence, and the Pillage of an Empire

WILLIAM DALRYMPLE

BLOOMSBURY PUBLISHING

NEW YORK · LONDON · OXFORD · NEW DELHI · SYDNEY

BLOOMSBURY PUBLISHING
Bloomsbury Publishing Inc.
1385 Broadway, New York, NY 10018, USA

BLOOMSBURY, BLOOMSBURY PUBLISHING, and the Diana logo
are trademarks of Bloomsbury Publishing Plc

First published in 2019 in Great Britain
First published in the United States 2019
This edition published 2021

Copyright © William Dalrymple, 2019
Maps and illustrations © Olivia Fraser, 2019

ISBN: HB: 978-1-63557-395-4; PB: 978-1-63557-580-4; EBOOK: 978-1-63557-433-3

Library of Congress Cataloging-in-Publication Data is available.

2 4 6 8 10 9 7 5 3 1

Typeset by Newgen KnowledgeWorks Pvt. Ltd., Chennai, India
Printed and bound in the U.S.A.

To find out more about our authors and books visit
www.bloomsbury.com and sign up for our newsletters.

Bloomsbury books may be purchased for business or promotional use.
For information on bulk purchases please contact Macmillan Corporate and
Premium Sales Department at specialmarkets@macmillan.com.

A commercial company enslaved a nation comprising two hundred million people.

Leo Tolstoy, Letter to a Hindu, 14 December 1908

Corporations have neither bodies to be punished, nor souls to be condemned, they therefore do as they like.

Edward, First Baron Thurlow (1731–1806), the Lord Chancellor during the impeachment of Warren Hastings

Contents

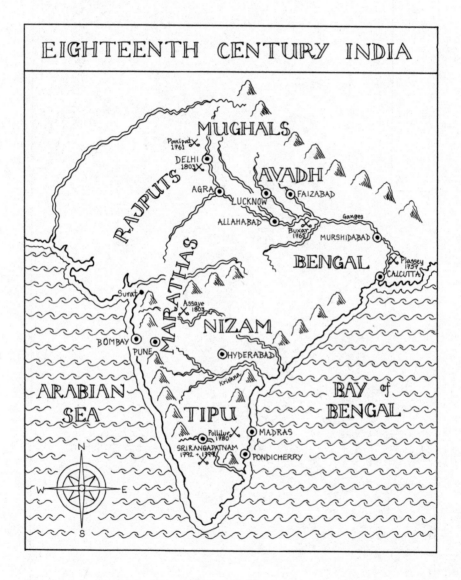

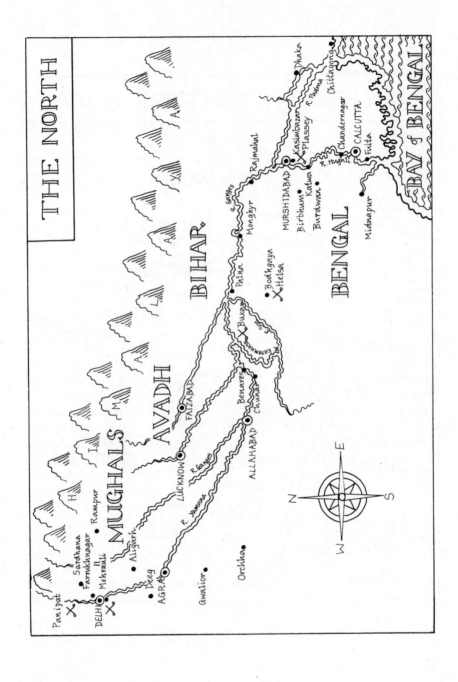

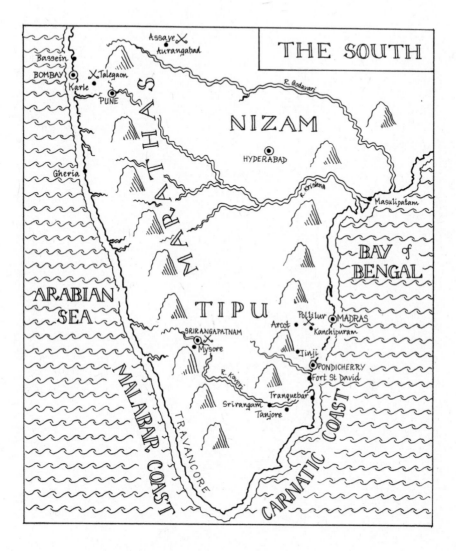

Dramatis Personae

Robert Clive, 1st Baron Clive

1725–74

East India Company accountant who rose through his remarkable military talents to be Governor of Bengal. Thickset, laconic, but fiercely ambitious and unusually forceful, he proved to be a violent and ruthless but extremely capable leader of the Company and its military forces in India. He had a streetfighter's eye for sizing up an opponent, a talent at seizing the opportunities presented by happenchance, a willingness to take great risks and a breathtaking, aggressive audacity. It was he who established the political and military supremacy of the East India Company in Bengal, Bihar and Orissa, and laid the foundations for British rule in India.

Warren Hastings

1732–1818

Scholar and linguist who was the first Governor of the Presidency of Fort William, the head of the Supreme Council of Bengal and the de facto first Governor General of India from 1773 to 1785. Plain-living, scholarly, diligent and austerely workaholic, he was a noted Indophile who in his youth fought hard against the looting of Bengal by his colleagues. However his feud with Philip Francis led to him being accused of corruption and he was impeached by Parliament. After a long and very public trial he was finally acquitted in 1795.

Philip Francis

1740–1818

Irish-born politician and scheming polemicist, thought to be the author of *The Letters of Junius*, and the chief opponent and antagonist of Warren Hastings. Wrongly convinced that Hastings was the source of all corruption in Bengal, and ambitious to replace him as Governor General, he pursued Hastings from 1774 until his death. Having failed to kill Hastings in a duel, and instead receiving a pistol ball in his own ribs, he returned to London where his accusations eventually led to the impeachment of both Hastings and his Chief Justice, Elijah Impey. Both were ultimately acquitted.

Charles Cornwallis, 1st Marquess Cornwallis

1738–1805

Having surrendered British forces in North America to a combined American and French force at the Siege of Yorktown in 1781, Cornwallis was recruited as Governor General of India by the East India Company to stop the same happening there. A surprisingly energetic administrator, he introduced the Permanent Settlement, which increased Company land revenues in Bengal, and defeated Tipu Sultan in the 1782 Third Anglo-Mysore War.

Richard Colley Wellesley, 1st Marquess Wellesley

1760–1842

Governor General of India who conquered more of India than Napoleon did of Europe. Despising the mercantile spirit of the East India Company, and answering instead to the dictates of his Francophobe friend Dundas, President of the Board of Trade, he used the East India Company's armies and resources successfully to wage the Fourth Anglo-Mysore War, which ended with the killing of Tipu Sultan and the destruction of his capital in 1799, then the Second Anglo-Maratha War, which led to the defeat of the armies of both Scindia and Holkar in 1803. By this time he had expelled the last French units from India and given the East India Company control of most of the subcontinent south of the Punjab.

Colonel Arthur Wellesley
1769–1852

Governor of Mysore and 'Chief Political and Military Officer in the Deccan and Southern Maratha Country', he helped defeat the armies of Tipu in 1799 and those of the Marathas in 1803. Later famous as the Duke of Wellington.

Gerald, 1st Viscount Lake
1744–1808

Lord Lake, who liked to claim descent from the Arthurian hero Lancelot of the Lake, was not a man who admired diplomacy: 'Damn your writing,' he is alleged to have cried at an army bookkeeper. 'Mind your fighting!' Although sixty years old, and a veteran of the Seven Years War and the American War of Independence, where he fought against Washington at Yorktown, he was famous for his boyish charm and immense energy, often rising at 2 a.m. to be ready to lead the march, blue eyes flashing. He was Wellesley's very capable Commander in Chief and in 1803 was put in charge of defeating the Maratha armies of Hindustan in the northern theatre of operations.

Edward Clive, 1st Earl of Powis
1754–1839

Son of Robert Clive ('Clive of India'), he was the notably unintelligent Governor of Madras

2. THE FRENCH

Joseph-François Dupleix
1697–1764

Governor General of the French establishments in India, who lost the Carnatic Wars in southern India to the young Robert Clive.

Michel Joachim Marie Raymond
1755–98

Mercenary commander of the French Battalion in Hyderabad.

General Pierre Cuiller-Perron

1755–1834

Perron was the son of a Provençal weaver who succeeded the far more capable Benoît de Boigne as Commander of Scindia's regiments. He lived with his troops a hundred miles to the south-east of Delhi in the great fortress of Aligarh, but in 1803 betrayed his men in return for a promise by the Company to let him leave India with his life savings.

3. THE MUGHALS

Alamgir Aurangzeb

1618–1707

Charmless and puritanical Mughal Emperor, whose overly ambitious conquest of the Deccan first brought Mughal dominions to their widest extent, then led to their eventual collapse. His alienation of the Empire's Hindu population, and especially the Rajput allies, by his religious bigotry accelerated the collapse of the Empire after his death.

Muhammad Shah Rangila

1702–48

Effete Mughal aesthete whose administrative carelessness and lack of military talent led to his defeat by the Persian warlord Nader Shah at the Battle of Karnal in 1739. Nader Shah looted Mughal Delhi, taking away with him the Peacock Throne, into which was embedded the legendary Koh-i-Noor diamond. He returned to Persia, leaving Muhammad Shah a powerless king with an empty treasury and the Mughal Empire bankrupt and fractured beyond repair.

Ghazi ud-Din Khan, Imad ul-Mulk

1736–1800

The teenage megalomaniac grandson of Nizam ul-Mulk, 1st Nizam of Hyderabad. He first turned on and defeated his patron, Safdar Jung, in 1753, then blinded, imprisoned and finally murdered his Emperor, Ahmad Shah, in 1754. Having placed Alamgir II on the throne in his stead, he then tried to capture and kill the latter's son, Shah Alam, and finally assassinated his own puppet Emperor in 1759. He fled Delhi after the rise of the Afghan Najib ud-Daula, who succeeded him as effective Governor of Delhi.

Alamgir II
1699–1759
The son of the Emperor Jahandar Shah, and the father of Shah Alam II, he was taken out from the Salatin Cage and made puppet Emperor by Imad ul-Mulk in 1754, only to be assassinated on his orders in Feroz Shah Kotla in 1759, four years later.

Shah Alam
1728–1806
Handsome and talented Mughal prince whose life was dogged by defeat and bad luck but who showed an extraordinary determination through horrific trials. As a boy he had seen Nadir Shah ride into Delhi and loot it. He later escaped Imad ul-Mulk's attempt to assassinate him and survived repeated battles with Clive. He fought the Company at Patna and Buxar, awarded the Diwani to Clive at Allahabad and defied Warren Hastings by his cross-country trek back to Delhi. There, with Mirza Najaf Khan, against all the odds he nearly succeeded in rebuilding the empire of his ancestors; only to see it vanish like a mirage after the premature death of that last great Mughal general. Finally, at his lowest point, the Emperor was assaulted and blinded by his psychotic former favourite, Ghulam Qadir. Despite these trials he never gave up, and only briefly – after the rape of his family and his blinding by the Rohillas – did he allow himself to give way to despair. In the most adverse circumstances imaginable, that of the Great Anarchy, he ruled over a court of high culture, and as well as writing fine verse himself he was a generous patron to poets, scholars and artists.

4. THE NAWABS

Aliverdi Khan, Nawab of Bengal
1671–1756
Aliverdi Khan, who was of mixed Arab and Afshar Turkman stock, came to power in 1740 in Bengal, the richest province of the Mughal Empire, in a military coup financed and masterminded by the immensely powerful Jagat Seth bankers. A cat-loving epicure who loved to fill his evenings with good food, books and stories, after defeating the Marathas he created in Murshidabad a strong and dazzling Shia court culture, and a stable political, economic and political centre which was a rare island of calm and prosperity amid the anarchy of Mughal decline.

Siraj ud-Daula, Nawab of Bengal

1733–57

Grandson of Aliverdi Khan and the man whose attack on the East India Company factories in Kasimbazar and Calcutta began the Company's conquest of Bengal. Not one of the many sources for the period – Persian, Bengali, Mughal, French, Dutch or English – has a good word to say about Siraj: according to Jean Law, who was his political ally, 'His reputation was the worst imaginable.' The most damning portrait of him, however, was painted by his own cousin, Ghulam Hussain Khan, who had been part of his staff and was profoundly shocked by the man he depicts as a serial bisexual rapist and psychopath: 'His character was a mix of ignorance and profligacy,' he wrote.

Mir Jafar, Nawab of Bengal

c. 1691–1765

An uneducated Arab soldier of fortune originally from the Shia shrine town of Najaf, he had played his part in many of Aliverdi's most crucial victories against the Marathas, and led the successful attack on Calcutta for Siraj ud-Daula in 1756. He joined the conspiracy hatched by the Jagat Seths to replace Siraj ud-Daula with his own rule, and soon found himself the puppet ruler of Bengal at the whim of the East India Company. Robert Clive rightly described him as 'a prince of little capacity'.

Mir Qasim, Nawab of Bengal

d. 1763

Mir Qasim was as different a man as could be imagined from his chaotic and uneducated father-in-law, Mir Jafar. Of noble Persian extraction, though born on his father's estates near Patna, Mir Qasim was small in frame, with little military experience, but young, capable, intelligent and, above all, determined. He conspired with the Company to replace the incompetent Mir Jafar in a coup in 1760 and succeeded in creating a tightly run state with a modern infantry army. But within three years he ended up coming into conflict with the Company and in 1765 what remained of his forces were finally defeated at the Battle of Buxar. He fled westwards and died in poverty near Agra.

Shuja ud-Daula, Nawab of Avadh

1732–74

Shuja ud-Daula, son of the great Mughal Vizier Safdar Jung and his successor as Nawab of Avadh, was a giant of a man. Nearly seven feet tall, with oiled moustaches that projected from his face like a pair of outstretched eagle's wings, he was a man of immense physical strength. By 1763, he was past his prime, but still reputedly strong enough to cut off the head of a buffalo with a single swing of his sword, or lift up two of his officers, one in each hand. His vices were his overweening ambition, his haughty self-importance and his inflated opinion of his own abilities. This was something that immediately struck the urbane intellectual Ghulam Hussain Khan, who regarded him as a slight liability, every bit as foolish as he was bold. Shuja, he wrote, 'was equally proud and ignorant ...' He was defeated by the Company at the Battle of Buxar in 1765 and replaced by Clive back on the throne of Avadh, where he ruled until the end of his life as a close ally of the EIC.

5. THE ROHILLAS

Najib Khan Yusufzai, Najib ud-Daula
d. 1770
Former Yusufzai Pashtun horse dealer who served the Mughals as a cavalry commander, but deserted to Ahmad Shah Durrani during his invasion of 1757. He became Ahmad Shah's Governor of Delhi, based for the final part of his career in his eponymous capital of Najibabad, near Saharanpur, until his death in 1770.

Zabita Khan Rohilla
d. 1785
Rohilla chieftain who fought at Panipat and rebelled repeatedly against Shah Alam. He was the son of Najib ud-Daula and the father of Ghulam Qadir.

Ghulam Qadir Khan Rohilla
c. 1765–1787
Ghulam Qadir was the son of Zabita Khan Rohilla. He was captured by Shah Alam at the fall of Ghausgarh in 1772 and taken back to Delhi where he was brought up as an imperial prince in Qudsia Bagh. Some sources indicate that he was a favurite of Shah Alam and may even have become his catamite. In 1788, possibly in revenge for offences at this time, he attacked Delhi, looted the Red Fort, tortured and raped the imperial household and blinded Shah Alam. He was eventually captured and himself tortured to death by the Maratha troops of Mahadji Scindia.

6. THE SULTANS OF MYSORE

Haidar Ali

d.1782

Officer in the Mysore army who overthrew the Wadyar Rajas of Mysore in 1761 and seized power in their place. Having learned modern infantry warfare by observing French tactics, he offered strong resistance to the East India Company, gaining his most notable victory alongside his son Tipu Sultan at Pollilur in 1780.

Tipu Sultan

1750–99

Warrior Sultan of Mysore, who defeated the East India Company in several campaigns, most notably alongside his father Haidar Ali at the Battle of Pollilur in 1780. He succeeded his father in 1782 and ruled with great efficiency and imagination during peace, but with great brutality in war. He was forced to cede half his kingdom to Lord Cornwallis's Triple Alliance with the Marathas and Hyderabadis in 1792 and was finally defeated and killed by Lord Wellesley in 1799.

7. THE MARATHAS

Chhatrapati Shivaji Bhonsle

d. 1680

Maratha war leader who carved out a kingdom in the Deccan from the ruins of the Adil Shahi Sultanate of Bijapur and then fought against the Mughal Empire, which had conquered Bijapur in 1686. Having turned himself into the nemesis of the Mughal Emperor Aurangzeb, he built forts, created a navy and raided deep into Mughal territory. He was crowned Chhatrapati, or Lord of the Umbrella, at two successive coronation ceremonies at Raigad towards the end of his life in 1674.

Nana Phadnavis

1742–1800

Pune-based statesman and minister to the Peshwas, known as 'the Maratha Machiavelli'. He was one of the first to realise that the East India Company posed an existential threat to India and tried to organise a Triple Alliance with the Hyderabadis and the Sultans of Mysore to drive them out, but failed to carry the project through to its conclusion.

Tukoji Holkar

1723–97

Dashing Maratha chieftain who survived the Battle of Panipat to become the great rival of Mahadji Scindia in north India.

Mahadji Scindia

1730–94

Maratha chieftain and statesman who was the most powerful Indian ruler in northern Hindustan for twenty years, from the 1770s onwards. Badly wounded at the Battle of Panipat in 1761, he limped for the rest of his life and became hugely fat, but he was a shrewd politician who took Shah Alam under his wing from 1771 onwards and turned the Mughals into Maratha puppets. He created a powerful modern army under the Savoyard General Benoît de Boigne, but towards the end of his life his rivalry with Tukoji Holkar and his unilateral peace with the East India Company at the Treaty of Salbai both did much to undermine Maratha unity and created the conditions for the final Company victory over the Marathas nine years after his death.

Peshwa Baji Rao II

1775–1851

The Last Peshwa of the Maratha Empire, who ruled from 1795–1818. When he first succeeded to the *musnud* he was slight, timid, unconfident-looking boy of twenty-one with a weak chin and a downy upper lip. He quickly showed himself comprehensively unequal to the challenge of holding together the different factions that made up his Maratha power base, and the treaty he signed with the East India Company at Bassein in 1802 led to the final unravelling of the great Maratha Confederacy.

Daulat Rao Scindia

1779–1827

When Mahadji Scindia died in 1794, his successor, Daulat Rao, was only fifteen. The boy inherited the magnificent army that Benoît de Boigne trained up for his predecessor, but he showed little vision or talent in its deployment. His rivalry with the Holkars and failure to come together and create a common front against the East India Company led to the disastrous Second Anglo-Maratha War of 1803. This left the East India Company the paramount power in India and paved the way for the British Raj.

Jaswant Rao Holkar
1776–1811
Jaswant Rao was the illegitimate son of Tukoji Holkar by a concubine. A remarkable war leader, he showed less grasp of diplomacy and allowed the East India Company fatally to divide the Maratha Confederacy, defeating Scindia first and then forcing him into surrender the following year. This left the Company in possession of most of Hindustan by the end of 1803.

Introduction

One of the very first Indian words to enter the English language was the Hindustani slang for plunder: *loot*. According to the *Oxford English Dictionary*, this word was rarely heard outside the plains of north India until the late eighteenth century, when it suddenly became a common term across Britain. To understand how and why it took root and flourished in so distant a landscape, one need only visit Powis Castle in the Welsh Marches.

The last hereditary Welsh prince, the memorably named Owain Gruffydd ap Gwenwynwyn, built Powis Castle as a craggy fort in the thirteenth century; the estate was his reward for abandoning Wales to the rule of the English monarchy. But its most spectacular treasures date from a much later period of English conquest and appropriation.

For Powis is simply awash with loot from India, room after room of imperial plunder, extracted by the East India Company (EIC) in the eighteenth century. There are more Mughal artefacts stacked in this private house in the Welsh countryside than are on display in any one place in India – even the National Museum in Delhi. The riches include hookahs of burnished gold inlaid with empurpled ebony; superbly inscribed Badakhshan spinels and jewelled daggers; gleaming rubies the colour of pigeon's blood, and scatterings of lizard-green emeralds. There are tiger's heads set with sapphires and yellow topaz; ornaments of jade and ivory; silken hangings embroidered with poppies and lotuses; statues of Hindu gods and coats of elephant armour. In pride of place stand two great war trophies taken after their owners had been defeated and killed: the palanquin Siraj ud-Daula, the Nawab of Bengal, left behind when he fled the battlefield of Plassey, and the campaign tent of Tipu Sultan, the Tiger of Mysore.

Such is the dazzle of these treasures that, as a visitor last summer, I nearly missed the huge framed canvas that explains how all this loot came to be here. The picture hangs in the shadows over a doorway in a wooden chamber at the top of a dark, oak-panelled staircase. It is not a masterpiece, but it does repay close study. An effete Indian prince, wearing cloth of gold, sits high on his throne under a silken canopy. On his left stand scimitar- and spear-carrying officers from his own army; to his right, a group of powdered and periwigged Georgian gentlemen. The prince is eagerly thrusting a scroll into the hands of a slightly overweight Englishman in a red frock coat.

The painting shows a scene from August 1765, when the young Mughal emperor Shah Alam, exiled from Delhi and defeated by East India Company troops, was forced into what we would now call an act of involuntary privatisation. The scroll is an order to dismiss his own Mughal revenue officials in Bengal, Bihar and Orissa and replace them with a set of English traders appointed by Robert Clive – the new governor of Bengal – and the directors of the Company, whom the document describes as 'the high and mighty, the noblest of exalted nobles, the chief of illustrious warriors, our faithful servants and sincere well-wishers, worthy of our royal favours, the English Company'. The collecting of Mughal taxes was henceforth subcontracted to a powerful multinational corporation – whose revenue-collecting operations were protected by its own private army.

The Company had been authorised by its founding charter to 'wage war' and had been using violence to gain its ends since it boarded and captured a Portuguese vessel on its maiden voyage in 1602. Moreover, it had controlled small areas around its Indian settlements since the 1630s.[1] Nevertheless, 1765 was really the moment that the East India Company ceased to be anything even distantly resembling a conventional trading corporation, dealing in silks and spices, and became something altogether much more unusual. Within a few months, 250 company clerks, backed by the military force of 20,000 locally recruited Indian soldiers, had become the effective rulers of the richest Mughal provinces. An international corporation was in the process of transforming itself into an aggressive colonial power.

By 1803, when its private army had grown to nearly 200,000 men, it had swiftly subdued or directly seized an entire subcontinent. Astonishingly, this took less than half a century. The first serious territorial conquests began in Bengal in 1756; forty-seven years later, the Company's reach extended as far north as the Mughal capital of Delhi, and almost all of India south of that city was by then effectively ruled from a boardroom in the City of London. 'What honour is left to us?' asked a Mughal official, 'when we have to take orders from a handful of traders who have not yet learned to wash their bottoms?'[2]

We still talk about the British conquering India, but that phrase disguises a more sinister reality. It was not the British government that began seizing great chunks of India in the mid-eighteenth century, but a dangerously unregulated private company headquartered in one small office, five windows wide, in London, and managed in India by a violent, utterly ruthless and intermittently mentally unstable corporate predator – Clive. India's transition to colonialism took place under a for-profit corporation, which existed entirely for the purpose of enriching its investors.

At the height of the Victorian period in the mid-nineteenth century there was a strong sense of embarrassment about the shady, brutal and mercantile way the British had founded the Raj. The Victorians thought the real stuff of history was the politics of the nation state. This, not the economics of corrupt corporations, they believed was the fundamental unit of study and the real driver of transformation in human affairs. Moreover, they liked to think of the empire as a *mission civilisatrice*: a benign national transfer of knowledge, railways and the arts of civilisation from West to East, and there was a calculated and deliberate amnesia about the corporate looting that opened British rule in India.

A second picture, this one commissioned from William Rothenstein to be painted onto the walls of the House of Commons, shows how successfully the official memory of this process was spun and subtly reworked by the Victorians. It can still be found in St Stephen's Hall, the echoing reception area of the Westminster Parliament. The painting was part of a series of murals entitled *The Building of Britain*. It features what the Hanging Committee at the time regarded as the highlights and turning points of British history: King Alfred defeating the Danes in 877, the parliamentary union of England and Scotland in 1707, and so on.

The fresco in this series that deals with India shows another image of a Mughal prince sitting on a raised dais, under a canopy. Again, we are in a court setting, with bowing attendants on all sides and trumpets blowing, and again an Englishman is standing in front of the Mughal. But this time the balance of power is very different.

Sir Thomas Roe, the ambassador sent by James I to the Mughal court, is shown before the Emperor Jahangir in 1614 – at a time when the Mughal empire was still at its richest and most powerful. Jahangir inherited from his father Akbar one of the two wealthiest polities in the world, rivalled only by Ming China. His lands stretched through most of India, all of what is now Pakistan and Bangladesh, and most of Afghanistan. He ruled over five times the population commanded by the Ottomans – roughly 100 million people – and his subjects produced around a quarter of all global manufactures.

Jahangir's father Akbar had flirted with a project to civilise India's European immigrants, whom he described as 'an assemblage of savages', but later dropped the plan as unworkable. Jahangir, who had a taste for exotica and wild beasts, welcomed Sir Thomas Roe with the same enthusiasm he had shown for the arrival of the first turkey in India, and questioned Roe closely on the oddities of Europe. For the committee who planned the House of Commons paintings, this marked the beginning of British engagement with India: two nation states coming into direct contact for the first time. Yet, as the first chapter of this book shows, British relations with India actually began not with diplomacy and the meeting of royal envoys, but with a trade mission led by Captain William Hawkins, a bibulous Company sea dog who, on arrival in Agra, accepted a wife offered to him by the emperor and merrily brought her back to England. This was a version of history the House of Commons Hanging Committee chose to forget.

In many ways the East India Company was a model of commercial efficiency: one hundred years into its history, it had only thirty-five permanent employees in its head office. Nevertheless, that skeleton staff executed a corporate coup unparalleled in history: the military conquest, subjugation and plunder of vast tracts of southern Asia. It almost certainly remains the supreme act of corporate violence in world history.

Historians propose many reasons for the astonishing success of the Company: the fracturing of Mughal India into tiny, competing states; the military edge that Frederick the Great's military innovations had given the European Companies; and particularly the innovations in European governance, taxation and banking that allowed the Company to raise vast sums of ready money at a moment's notice. For behind the scarlet uniforms and the Palladian palaces, the tiger shoots and the polkas at Government House always lay the balance sheets of the Company's accountants, with their ledgers laying out profit and loss, and the Company's fluctuating share price on the London Stock Exchange.

Yet perhaps the most crucial factor of all was the support that the East India Company enjoyed from the British Parliament. The relationship between them grew steadily more symbiotic throughout the eighteenth century until eventually it turned into something we might today call a public–private partnership. Returned nabobs like Clive used their wealth to buy both MPs and parliamentary seats – the famous Rotten Boroughs. In turn, Parliament backed the Company with state power: the ships and soldiers that were needed when the French and British East India Companies trained their guns on each other.

For the Company always had two targets in its sights: one was the lands where its business was conducted; but the other was the country that gave it birth, as its lawyers and lobbyists and MP shareholders slowly and subtly worked to influence and subvert the legislation of Parliament in its favour. Indeed, the East India Company probably invented corporate lobbying. In 1693, less than a century after its foundation, the EIC was discovered for the first time to be using its own shares for buying parliamentarians, annually shelling out £1,200 a year to prominent MPs and ministers. The parliamentary investigation into this, the world's first corporate lobbying scandal, found the EIC guilty of bribery and insider trading, and led to the impeachment of the Lord President of the Council, and the imprisonment of the Company's Governor.

Although its total trading capital was permanently lent to the British state, when it suited, the East India Company made much of its legal separation from the government. It argued forcefully, and successfully, that the document signed by Shah Alam in 1765 – known as the

Diwani – was the legal property of the Company, not the Crown, even though the government had spent an enormous sum on naval and military operations protecting the EIC's Indian acquisitions. But the MPs who voted to uphold this legal distinction were not exactly neutral: nearly a quarter of them held Company stock, which would have plummeted in value had the Crown taken over. For the same reason, the need to protect the Company from foreign competition became a major aim of British foreign policy.

The transaction depicted in the painting was to have catastrophic consequences. As with all such corporations, then as now, the EIC was answerable only to its shareholders. With no stake in the just governance of the region, or its long-term well-being, the Company's rule quickly turned into the straightforward pillage of Bengal, and the rapid transfer westwards of its wealth.

Before long the province, already devastated by war, was struck down by the famine of 1769, then further ruined by high taxation. Company tax collectors were guilty of what was then described as the 'shaking of the pagoda tree' – what today would be described as major human rights violations committed in the process of gathering taxes. Bengal's wealth rapidly drained into Britain, while its prosperous weavers and artisans were coerced 'like so many slaves' by their new masters.

A good proportion of the loot of Bengal went directly into Clive's pocket. He returned to Britain with a personal fortune, then valued at £234,000, that made him the richest self-made man in Europe. After the Battle of Plassey in 1757 – a victory that owed as much to treachery, forged contracts, bankers and bribes as it did to military prowess – he transferred to the EIC treasury no less than £2.5 million* seized from the defeated rulers of Bengal – unprecedented sums at the time. No great sophistication was required. The entire contents of the Bengal treasury were simply loaded into one hundred boats and floated down the Ganges from the Nawab of Bengal's palace in Murshidabad to Fort William, the Company's Calcutta headquarters. A portion of the proceeds was later spent rebuilding Powis.

The painting of Clive and Shah Alam at Powis is subtly deceptive: the painter, Benjamin West, had never been to India. Even at the time,

---

* £262.5 million today.

a reviewer noted that the mosque in the background bore a suspiciously strong resemblance 'to our venerable dome of St Paul'. In reality, there had been no grand public ceremony. The transfer took place privately, inside Clive's tent, which had just been erected on the parade ground of the newly seized Mughal fort at Allahabad. As for Shah Alam's silken throne, it was in fact Clive's armchair, which for the occasion had been hoisted on to his dining-room table and covered with a chintz bedspread.

Later, the British dignified the document by calling it the Treaty of Allahabad, though Clive had dictated the terms and a terrified Shah Alam had simply waved them through. As the contemporary Mughal historian Ghulam Hussain Khan put it: 'A business of such magnitude, and which at any other time would have required the sending of wise ambassadors and able negotiators, and much negotiation and contention with the ministers, was done and finished in less time than would usually have been taken up for the sale of a jack-ass, or a beast of burden, or a head of cattle.'[3]

Before long the EIC was straddling the globe. Almost single-handedly it reversed the balance of trade, which from Roman times on had led to a continual drain of Western bullion eastwards. The EIC ferried opium east to China, and in due course fought the Opium Wars in order to seize an offshore base at Hong Kong and safeguard its profitable monopoly in narcotics.

To the West it shipped Chinese tea to Massachusetts, where its dumping in Boston harbour triggered the American War of Independence. Indeed, one of the principal fears of the American Patriots in the run-up to the war was that Parliament would unleash the East India Company in the Americas to loot there as it had done in India. In November 1773, the Patriot John Dickinson described EIC tea as 'accursed Trash', and compared the potential future regime of the East India Company in America to being 'devoured by Rats'. This 'almost bankrupt Company', he said, having been occupied in wreaking 'the most unparalleled Barbarities, Extortions and Monopolies' in Bengal, had now 'cast their Eyes on America, as a new Theatre, whereon to exercise their Talents of Rapine, Oppression and Cruelty'.[4]

By 1803, when the EIC captured the Mughal capital of Delhi, and within it, the sightless monarch, Shah Alam, sitting blinded in his ruined palace, the Company had trained up a private security force of around 200,000 – twice the size of the British army – and marshalled more firepower than any nation state in Asia.

A mere handful of businessmen from a distant island on the rim of Europe now ruled dominions that stretched continuously across northern India from Delhi in the west to Assam in the east. Almost the entire east coast was in the Company's hands, together with all the most strategic points on the west coast between Gujarat and Cape Comorin. In just over forty years they had made themselves masters of almost all the subcontinent, whose inhabitants numbered 50 to 60 million, succeeding an empire where even minor provincial nawabs and governors ruled over vast areas, larger in both size and population than the biggest countries of Europe.

The EIC was, as one of its directors admitted, 'an empire within an empire', with the power to make war or peace anywhere in the East. It had also by this stage created a vast and sophisticated administration and civil service, built much of London's Docklands and come close to generating nearly half of Britain's trade. No wonder that the EIC now referred to itself as 'the grandest society of merchants in the Universe'.

Yet, like more recent mega-corporations, the EIC proved at once hugely powerful and oddly vulnerable to economic uncertainty. Only seven years after the granting of the Diwani, when the Company's share price had doubled overnight after it acquired the wealth of the treasury of Bengal, the East India bubble burst after plunder and famine in Bengal led to massive shortfalls in expected land revenues. The EIC was left with debts of £1.5 million and a bill of £1 million* in unpaid tax owed to the Crown. When knowledge of this became public, thirty banks collapsed like dominoes across Europe, bringing trade to a standstill.

In a scene that seems horribly familiar to us today, this corporation had to come clean and ask for a massive government bailout. On 15 July 1772, the directors of the East India Company applied to the Bank of England for a loan of £400,000. A fortnight later, they returned, asking for an additional £300,000. The bank raised only £200,000.** By August, the directors were whispering to the government that they would actually need an unprecedented sum of a further £1 million. The official report the following year, written by Edmund Burke, foresaw that the EIC's financial problems could, potentially, 'like a mill-stone, drag [the government] down into an unfathomable abyss ... This cursed

---

* £157.5 million and £105 million today.

** £400,000 = £42 million; £300,000 = £31.5 million; £200,000 = £21 million today.

Company would, at last, like a viper, be the destruction of the country which fostered it at its bosom.'

But the East India Company really was too big to fail. So it was that the following year, in 1773, the world's first aggressive multinational corporation was saved by one of history's first mega-bailouts – the first example of a nation state extracting, as its price for saving a failing corporation, the right to regulate and severely rein it in.

This book does not aim to provide a complete history of the East India Company, still less an economic analysis of its business operations. Instead it is an attempt to answer the question of how a single business operation, based in one London office complex, managed to replace the mighty Mughal Empire as masters of the vast subcontinent between the years 1756 and 1803.

It tells the story of how the Company defeated its principal rivals – the nawabs of Bengal and Avadh, Tipu Sultan's Mysore Sultanate and the great Maratha Confederacy – to take under its own wing the Emperor Shah Alam, a man whose fate it was to witness the entire story of the Company's fifty-year-long assault on India and its rise from a humble trading company to a fully fledged imperial power. Indeed, the life of Shah Alam forms a spine of the narrative which follows.

It is now the established view that, contrary to the writings of earlier generations of historians, the eighteenth century was not a 'Dark Age' in India. The political decline of the Mughal imperium resulted, rather, in an economic resurgence in other parts of the subcontinent, and much recent academic research has been dedicated to deepening our understanding of that proposition.[5] All this brilliant work on regional resurgence does not, however, alter the reality of the Anarchy, which undoubtedly did disrupt the Mughal heartlands, especially around Delhi and Agra, for most of the eighteenth century. As Fakir Khair ud-Din Illahabadi put it, 'disorder and corruption no longer sought to hide themselves and the once peaceful realm of India became the abode of Anarchy (*dâr al-amn-i Hindûstân dâr al-fitan gasht*). In time, there was no real substance to the Mughal monarchy, it had faded to a mere name or shadow.'[6]

Given the reality of the Anarchy is something recorded not just by a few disconsolate Mughal gentlemen like Fakir Khair ud-Din and Ghulam Hussain Khan, but by every single traveller in the period, I believe that the process of revisionism may have gone a little too far. From Law and Modave to Pollier and Franklin, almost all eyewitnesses of late eighteenth-century India remark, over and over again, on the endless bloodshed and chaos of the period, and the difficulty of travelling safely through much of the country without a heavily armed escort. Indeed, it was these eyewitnesses who first gave currency to the notion of a Great Anarchy.

The Company's many wars and its looting of Bengal, Bihar and Orissa, particularly between the 1750s and 1770s, hugely added to this disruption, and in regions very far from Delhi. This is the reason I have given this book its title. There is clearly a difficult balance to be struck between the fraught, chaotic and very violent military history of the period, and the long-term consolidation of new political, economic and social formations of the kind that Richard Barnett and my old Cambridge professor Chris Bayly did so much to illuminate. I am not sure anyone has yet worked out how these different levels of action and analysis fit together, but this book is an attempt to square that circle.

The Anarchy is based mainly on the Company's own voluminous miles of records. The documents from its head office, and the despatches of its Indian operatives to the directors in Leadenhall Street, now fill the vaults of the British Library in London. The often fuller and more revealing records of the Company's Indian headquarters in Government House and Fort William, Calcutta, can today be found in the National Archives of India (NAI) in New Delhi, and it is there that I have concentrated my research.

The eighteenth-century records in the NAI are, however, much more elusive than those of their well-catalogued nineteenth-century collections, and for the first weeks I struggled even to locate most of the indexes, something that was eventually cracked by the NAI's brilliant and ever-patient Jaya Ravindran and Anumita Bannerjee, who between them scoured the back rooms and stores until they succeeded in finding them. The rewards were remarkable. Within weeks I was holding in my hands the original intelligence report from Port Lorient that led to the Company ordering the Governor, Roger Drake, to rebuild the walls of Calcutta, the *casus belli* that first provoked Siraj ud-Daula, as well as Clive's initial despatch from the battlefield of Plassey.

These English-language Company records I have used alongside the excellent Persian-language histories produced by highly educated Mughal historians, noblemen, *munishis* and scribes throughout the eighteenth century. The best of these, the *Seir Mutaqherin*, or *Review of Modern Times* by the brilliant young Mughal historian Ghulam Hussain Khan, is by far the most perceptive Indian source for the period, and has been available in English since the 1790s. But many other equally revealing Persian-language histories of the time remain both untranslated and unpublished.

These I have used extensively with the assistance of my long-term collaborator Bruce Wannell, whose superb translations of more obscure sources such as the *Ibrat Nama*, or *Book of Admonition* of Fakir Khair ud-Din Illahabadi, or the *Tarikh-i Muzaffari* of Mohammad Ali Khan Ansari of Panipat, produced over many months while staying in his tent in the garden of my Mehrauli goat farm, have been transformative for this project, as has been his unrivalled knowledge of both eighteenth-century India and the wider Islamic world. I am particularly grateful to Bruce for the time he spent in the MAAPRI Research Institute in Tonk, Rajasthan, translating a previously unused biography of Shah Alam, the *Shah Alam Nama* of Munshi Munna Lal, and for his discussions in Pondicherry with Jean Deloche, which ultimately resulted in his exquisite renderings of several previously untranslated and largely unused eighteenth-century French sources, such as the memoirs of Gentil, Madec, Law and especially the wonderful *Voyages* of the Comte de Modave, an urbane friend and neighbour of Voltaire from Grenoble, who casts a sophisticated, sardonic and perceptive eye on the eighteenth-century scene, from the wide boulevards of Company Calcutta to the ruins of Shah Alam's decaying capital in Delhi.

Over six years of work on the Company I have accumulated many debts. Firstly, my thanks are also due to Lily Tekseng for her months of slog, typing out the manuscripts I dug up in the Indian National Archives, and my sister-in-law Katy Rowan and Harpavan Manku, who performed a similar task in London, both battling successfully with the copperplate of the Company's official records and the private correspondence of Clive, Hastings, Cornwallis and Wellesley. I am also thankful to Aliya Naqvi and Katherine Butler Schofield for their beautiful renderings of Shah Alam's own verse.

Many friends read through successive drafts of this book and to them I am particularly grateful: Peter Marshall, Rajat Datta, Robert Travers, Najaf Haider, Lakshmi Subramanian, Jean-Marie Lafont, Nonica Datta, Sonal Singh, Vijay Pinch, Mahmood Farooqui, Yashashwini Chandra, Narayani Basu, Katherine Butler Schofield, Mala Singh, Rory Fraser, Sam Miller, Gianni Dubbini, Jeremy Parkinson, Riya Sarkar, Chiki Sarkar, Jayanta Sengupta, Adam Dalrymple and Nandini Mehta.

Many others have given invaluable assistance. In India, B. N. Goswamy, Ebba Koch, Momin Latif, John Fritz, George Michel, Shashi Tharoor, Chander Shekhar, Jagdish Mittal, Diana Rose Haobijam, Navtej Sarna, Tanya Kuruvilla, S. Gautam, Tanya Banon and Basharat Peer. Particular thanks are due to Lucy Davison of Banyan – by far the best travel agency in India, who ably organised logistics for research trips along the Carnatic coast, to Srirangapatnam, to Tonk, through the Deccan to Pune, and perhaps most memorably of all to Calcutta and Murshidabad during Durga Puja.

In Pakistan: Fakir Aijazuddin, Ali Sethi, Hussain and Aliya Naqvi and Abbas of the Punjab Archives who generously got me access to Persian and Urdu sources.

In the US: Muzaffar Alam, Maya Jasanoff, Ayesha Jalal, Ben Hopkins, Nile Green, Sanjay Subramanyam, Durba Ghosh, Elbrun Kimmelman and Navina Haidar.

In Britain: Nick Robbins, Saqib Baburi, Ursula Sims-Williams, Jon Wilson, Malini Roy, Jerry Losty, John Falconer, Andrew Topsfield, Linda Colley, David Cannadine, Susan Stronge, Amin Jaffer, Anita Anand, Ian Trueger, Robert Macfarlane, Michael Axworthy, David Gilmour, Rory Stewart, Charles Allen, John Keay, Tommy Wide, Monisha Rajesh, Aarathi Prasad, Farrukh Husain, Charles Grieg, Rosie Llewellyn-Jones, Richard Blurton, Anne Buddle, Sam Murphy, Henry

Noltie, Robert Skelton, Francesca Galloway, Sam Miller, Shireen Vakil, Zareer Masani, Tirthankar Roy, Brigid Waddams, Barnaby and Rose Rogerson, Anthony and Sylvie Sattin, Hew, Jock and Rob Dalrymple and the late, and much missed, Chris Bayly whose Cambridge lectures more than thirty years ago first got me interested in the complexities of eighteenth-century India.

I have been lucky as ever to have as my agent the incomparable David Godwin, and my brilliant publishers at Bloomsbury: Alexandra Pringle, Trâm-Anh Doan, Lilidh Kendrick, Emma Bal, Richard Charkin, Yogesh Sharma, Meenakshi Singh, Faiza Khan, Ben Hyman and especially my editor for over thirty years, Mike Fishwick. I should also like to thank Vera Michalski at Buchet Chastel and in Italy the incomparable Roberto Calasso at Adelphi.

My lovely family, Olivia, Ibby, Sam and Adam have kept me sane and happy during the long six years it took to bring this book into being. Olive in particular has been a rock, both emotionally and as guiding force behind this project, my first and best editor as well as my ever-patient, ever-generous, ever-loving partner in life. To them, and to my beloved parents, both of whom died during the writing of this book, I owe my greatest debt. My father in particular was convinced I would never finish this book and indeed he never lived to see the final full stop, dying the day after Christmas when I was still two chapters from its completion. But it was he who taught me to love history, as well as how to live life, and I dedicate this book to his memory.

William Dalrymple
North Berwick–Chiswick–Mehrauli,
March 2013–June 2019

I

1599

On 24 September 1599, while William Shakespeare was pondering a draft of *Hamlet* in his house downriver from the Globe in Southwark, a mile to the north, barely twenty minutes' walk across the Thames, a motley group of Londoners was gathering in a rambling, half-timbered building lit by many-mullioned Tudor windows.[1]

Even at the time the meeting was recognised as historic, and notaries were present with ink and quill to keep a record of the unusually diverse cross section of Elizabethan London that came that day to the Founders' Hall, off Moorgate Fields.[2] At the top of the social scale, hung with his golden chain of office, there was the stout figure of the Lord Mayor himself, Sir Stephen Soame, robed in scarlet fustian. He was accompanied by two of his predecessors in office and several senior Aldermen of the City – buttery Elizabethan burghers, their white-bearded faces nestling in a feathery tangle of cambric ruffs.[3] The most powerful of these was the gravely goateed, ermine-trimmed and stovepipe-hatted figure of Sir Thomas Smythe, Auditor of the City of London, who had made a fortune importing currants from the Greek islands and spices from Aleppo. A few years earlier 'Auditor Smythe' had helped form the Levant Company as a vehicle for his trading voyages; this meeting was his initiative.[4]

Besides these portly pillars of the City of London were many less exalted merchants hopeful of increasing their fortunes, as well as a scattering of ambitious and upwardly mobile men of more humble estate, whose professions the notaries dutifully noted down: grocers, drapers and haberdashers, a 'clotheworker', a 'vintener', a 'letherseller' and a 'skinner'.[5] There were a few scarred soldiers, mariners and bearded adventurers from the docks at Woolwich and Deptford, surf-battered sea dogs, some of whom had fought against the Spanish Armada a decade earlier, all doublets and gold earrings, with their sea dirks tucked discreetly into their belts. Several of these deckhands and mizzen-masters had seen action with Drake and Raleigh against Spanish treasure ships in the warmer waters of the Caribbean, and now described themselves to the notaries, in the polite Elizabethan euphemism, as 'privateers'. There was also a clutch of explorers and travellers who had ventured further afield: the Arctic explorer William Baffin, for example, after whom the polar bay was named. Finally, also taking careful notes, was the self-described 'historiographer of the voyages of the East Indies', the young Richard Hakluyt, who had been paid £11 10s* by the adventurers for compiling all that was then known in England about the Spice Routes.[6]

Such a varied group would rarely be seen under one roof, but all had gathered with one purpose: to petition the ageing Queen Elizabeth I, then a bewigged and painted woman of sixty-six, to start up a company 'to venter in the pretended voiage to ye Est Indies and other Ilands and Cuntries thereabouts there to make trade ... by buying or bartering of suche goodes, wares, jewelles or merchaundize as those Ilands or Cuntries may yeld or afforthe ... (the whiche it maie please the Lorde to prosper)'.[7]

Smythe had gathered 101 of the richer merchants two days earlier and pressed them to commit to individual subscriptions ranging from £100 to £3,000 – considerable sums in those days. In all Smythe raised £30,133 6s. 8d.** This the investors did by drawing up a contract and adding their contribution in the subscription book 'written with there owne

---

* About £1,200 today.

** The modern equivalences of these sums are: £100 to £3,000 = £10,000 to £300,000 today; £30, 133 6s. 8d. = over £3 million today.

hands', so they declared, 'for the honour of our native country and for the advancement of trade and merchandise within this realm of England'.

It is always a mistake to read history backwards. We know that the East India Company (EIC) eventually grew to control almost half the world's trade and become the most powerful corporation in history, as Edmund Burke famously put it, 'a state in the guise of a merchant'. In retrospect, the rise of the Company seems almost inevitable. But that was not how it looked in 1599, for at its founding few enterprises could have seemed less sure of success.

At that time England was a relatively impoverished, largely agricultural country, which had spent almost a century at war with itself over the most divisive subject of the time: religion.[8] In the course of this, in what seemed to many of its wisest minds an act of wilful self-harm, the English had unilaterally cut themselves off from the most powerful institution in Europe, so turning themselves in the eyes of many Europeans into something of a pariah nation. As a result, isolated from their baffled neighbours, the English were forced to scour the globe for new markets and commercial openings further afield. This they did with a piratical enthusiasm.

Sir Francis Drake set the tone. Drake had made his name in the early 1560s as a buccaneer raiding Spanish mule trains laden with silver on their way from mine to port along the Panama isthmus. With some of the profits of these raids, Drake had set off in 1577 on his three-year circumnavigation of the globe in the *Golden Hinde*. This was only the third time a global voyage had ever been attempted, and it was made possible by developments in compasses and astrolabes – as well as by worsening relations with Spain and Portugal.[9]

Drake had set sail in 'great hope of gold [and] silver … spices drugs, cochineal', and his voyage was sustained throughout by intermittent raids on Iberian shipping. Following his capture of a particularly well-laden Portuguese carrack, Drake returned home with a cargo 'very richly fraught with gold, silver, pearls and precious stones', valued at over

£100,000,* one of the most profitable of all the voyages of discovery. This harrying and scavenging off the earlier and richer Iberian empires that then controlled South and Central America was licensed by the Crown and was essentially a form of Elizabethan state-sanctioned organised crime controlled by the oligarchs of Whitehall and Charing Cross. When Drake's rival, Sir Walter Raleigh, and his crew returned from a similar raid, they were immediately denounced by the Spanish ambassador as 'Pirates, pirates, pirates'.[10]

Many of those the Spanish ambassador would also have considered pirates were present that day in the Founders' Hall. The Company's potential investors knew that this group of mariners and adventurers, whatever their talents as freebooters, had to date shown little success in the more demanding skills of long-distance trade or in the art of planting and patiently sustaining viable colonies. Indeed, compared to many of their European neighbours, the English were rank amateurs at both endeavours.

Their search for the legendary North West Passage to the Spice Islands had ended disastrously, not in the Moluccas, as planned, but instead on the edge of the Arctic Circle, with their galleons stuck fast in pack ice, their battered hulls punctured by icebergs and their pike-wielding crew mauled by polar bears.[11] They had also failed at protecting their infant Protestant plantations in Ireland which were under severe attack in 1599. English attempts to bully their way into the Caribbean slave trade had come to nothing, while attempts to plant an English colony in North America had ended in outright disaster.

In 1584 Sir Walter Raleigh had founded the first British settlement on Roanoke Island, south of Chesapeake Bay, in an area he named Virginia, after his monarch. But the colony survived barely a year and was abandoned by June 1586 when the relief fleet arrived to find the settlement deserted. A shipload of eager new colonists jumped ashore to find both the stockade and the houses within completely dismantled and nothing to indicate the fate of the settlers except a single skeleton – and the name of the local Indian tribe, CROATOAN, carved in capital letters into a tree. There was simply no sign of the 90 men, 17 women and 11 children whom Raleigh had left there only two years earlier. It was as if the settlers had vanished into thin air.[12]

* Over £10 million today.

Even the two most experienced mariners and Eastern explorers in London, both of whom were present in the Founders' Hall, had arrived back from their travels with little more than wonderful tales to show for their efforts, and with neither crews nor cargoes intact.

Ralph Fitch was the first. In 1583 he had set out from Falmouth on the *Tyger*. Sent to the East to buy spices by Auditor Smythe's new Levant Company, Fitch had gone overland from the Levantine coast via Aleppo, but had only got as far as Hormuz before he was arrested as a spy by the Portuguese. From there he was sent in chains to Goa where they threatened to subject him to the *strappado* – the Inquisition's answer to bungee jumping, where a man was dropped from a height attached to a rope. The bone-jarring jerk when the rope halted his rapid descent was said to be even more exquisitely agonising than the rack, the Elizabethans' own preferred form of torture.

Fitch was helped to escape by Fr Thomas Stevens, an English Jesuit long based in Goa, who stood surety for him, and he duly succeeded in travelling through the rich Sultanates of the Deccan to the sixteenth-century Mughal capital of Agra, and hence, via Bengal, to the Moluccas.[13] On his return to London three years later, he regaled the city with his traveller's tales and became such a celebrity that his ship was mentioned by Shakespeare in *Macbeth*: 'her husband is to Aleppo gone, master o' th' *Tiger*'. But while Fitch brought back many enticing details of the pepper trade, he had arrived home with no actual pepper.[14]

The Levant Company's next attempt to break into the spice trade, this time by the sea route, was even more of a disaster. Sir James Lancaster's 1591 voyage into the Indian Ocean was the first English attempt to reach the East via the Cape. Both its funding, and its armed shipping, was provided by Auditor Smythe and his Levant Company. But in the event, only one of Lancaster's four ships, the *Edward Bonaventure*, made it back from the Indies, and that on a skeleton crew. The last survivors, five men and a boy, worked it home with its cargo of pepper which they had earlier looted from a passing Portuguese ship. Lancaster himself, marooned on the Comoro Islands with the rest of his crew after he was shipwrecked during a cyclone, finally found his way home in 1594. On the way he had been stuck in the doldrums, ravaged by scurvy, lost three ships and seen almost all his fellow crew members speared to death by angry islanders. It was lucky that the Levant Company had deep pockets, for the voyage was a devastating financial failure.[15]

In contrast to these ragged buccaneers, their more sophisticated Portuguese and Spanish rivals had been busy for over a century establishing profitable and cosmopolitan empires that ranged across the globe – empires whose massive imports of New World gold had turned Spain into the richest country in Europe, and given Portugal control of the seas and spices of the East, so bringing it in a close second place. Indeed, the only rival of the Iberians, gallingly for the English, was the tiny and newly independent republic of Holland, whose population was less than half that of England, and which had thrown off the rule of Spain only twenty years earlier, in 1579.

It was the recent astonishing success of the Dutch that had brought this diverse group of Londoners together. Three months earlier, on 19 July, Admiral Jacob Corneliszoon van Neck of the Dutch Compagnie Van Verre – the Company of Distant Lands – had successfully returned from Indonesia with a vast cargo of spices – 800 tons of pepper, 200 tons of cloves and great quantities of cinnamon and nutmeg. The voyage made an unprecedented 400 per cent profit: 'There never arrived in Holland ships so richly laden,' wrote one envious Levant Company observer.[16]

By August, following this 'success of the viage performed by the Dutche nation', English merchants had begun discussing the possibilities of setting up a company to make similar voyages to buy spices not, as before, from Middle Eastern middlemen, who trebled the price as their commission, but instead direct from the producers, half the way around the world, in the East Indies. The prime movers in this initiative were again Smythe's cabal of Levant Company merchants who realised, as one wrote from the Greek island of Chios, that this Dutch 'trading to the Indies has clean overthrown our dealings to Aleppo'.[17]

The final straw was when the Dutch sent a delegation to London to try to buy up English shipping for further voyages eastwards. This was too much for the pride of Elizabethan London. The Amsterdam Agents, waiting in the Old Steelyard of the Hamburg Company, were told, 'Our merchants of London have need of all our ships and none to sell to the Dutch. We ourselves intend forthwith to have trade with the East Indies.'[18] The meeting at the Founders' Hall was the direct result of that retort. As they told Elizabeth's Privy Council in their petition, they were moved 'with no less affection to advance the trade of their native country than the Dutch merchants were to benefit their commonwealth ... For the honour of our native country and the advancement of trade ... to set forth a voyage this present year to the East Indies.'[19]

Fully one-quarter of the subscribers to the voyage, and seven of the original fifteen directors of the enterprise, were the Levant Company grandees. They feared, with reason, that the Dutch had ruined their existing investment in the spice trade, and they provided not only one-third of the subscription, but also many of the ships and the offices where the initial meetings took place. 'The Company of Merchants of London trading to the East Indies' was thus originally an outgrowth of the Levant Company and a mechanism for its shareholders to extend its existing trade to the Far East by developing the sea route, and to raise as much new capital as possible.[20]

This was the reason Smythe and his associates had decided to found a new company, and open it to any subscriber who would contribute, rather than merely extend the remit of their existing monopoly. For, unlike the Levant Company, which had a fixed board of fifty-three tightly knit subscribers, the EIC was from the very first conceived as a joint stock corporation, open to all investors. Smythe and his associates had decided that, because of the huge expenses and high risks involved, 'a trade so far remote cannot be managed but by a joint and united stock'.[21] Costs were, after all, astronomically high. The commodities they wished to buy were extremely expensive and they were carried in huge and costly ships that needed to be manned by large crews and protected by artillery masters and professional musket-men. Moreover, even if everything went according to plan, there would be no return on investment for several years.

The idea of a joint stock company was one of Tudor England's most brilliant and revolutionary innovations. The spark of the idea sprang from the flint of the medieval craft guilds, where merchants and manufacturers could pool their resources to undertake ventures none could afford to make individually. But the crucial difference in a joint stock company was that the latter could bring in passive investors who had the cash to subscribe to a project but were not themselves involved in the running of it. Such shares could be bought and sold by anyone, and their price could rise or fall depending on demand and the success of the venture.

Such a company would be 'one body corporate and politick' – that is, it would be a corporation, and so could have a legal identity and a form of corporate immortality that allowed it to transcend the deaths of individual shareholders, 'in like manner', wrote the legal scholar William Blackstone, 'as the River Thames is still the same river, though the parts which compose it are changing every instance'.[22]

Forty years earlier, in 1553, a previous generation of London merchants had begun the process of founding the world's first chartered joint stock company: the Muscovy Company, or to give it its full and glorious title, The Mysterie and Companie of the Merchant Adventurers for the Discoverie of Regions, Dominions, Islands and Places Unknown.[23] The original aim was to explore an idea first mooted by classical geographers, who believed their world to be an island, surrounded by an ocean, which meant there had to be a northern route to the spices and gold of the Far East as well as that by the Cape – and that passage would be free from all Iberian rivalry.

Although the Muscovy Company directors soon came to the conclusion that the northern route did not exist, in the process of looking for it they discovered, and successfully traded along, a direct overland route with Persia via Russia. Before Ottoman Turkish conquests cut the road in 1580, they sent out six successful voyages to Isfahan and the other great bazaar towns of the region, and managed to post a respectable profit.[24]

In 1555, the Muscovy Company was finally granted its royal charter laying out its privileges and responsibilities. By 1583 there were chartered Venice and Turkey companies, which merged in 1592 to become the Levant Company. The same year the slave-trading Sierra Leone Company was founded. The East India Company was thus following a fairly well-trod path, and its royal charter should have come through without complication. Moreover, the Queen wanted to keep the City on her side in case of a threatened rebellion by the unruly Robert Devereux, Earl of Essex, and she proved surprisingly receptive to the petition.[25]

But almost immediately orders came from the court of the Privy Council suspending both the formation of the Company and the preparations for the voyage. The peace negotiations with Spain which had followed the death of King Philip II in 1598 were progressing, and their lordships, 'thinking it more beneficiall ... to enterteyne a peace, than that the same should be hindered' by a quarrel, made the decision that the adventurers should 'proceade noe further in this matter for this yere'.

The merchants, none of whom were from the nobility, and so had little standing or influence at court, had no option but to wait. For twelve months it looked as if the ambitious idea of founding an English company to trade with the East would remain just that – a midsummer dream.

It was only when the Spanish peace talks foundered in the summer of 1600 that the Privy Council had a change of heart and felt confident enough to stress the universal freedom of the seas and the right of all nations to send ships wherever they wished. Almost exactly a year after the petition had been drafted, on 23 September 1600, the subscribers were finally given the go-ahead: 'It was her Majesty's pleasure', they were told, 'that they shuld proceade in ther purpose ... and goe forward in the said viage.'[26]

On 31 December 1600, the last day of the first year of the new century, the 'Governor and Company of Merchants of London trading to the East Indies', a group of 218 men, received their royal charter.[27]

This turned out to offer far wider powers than the petitioners had perhaps expected or even hoped for. As well as freedom from all customs duties for their first six voyages, it gave them a British monopoly for fifteen years over 'trade to the East Indies', a vaguely defined area that was soon taken to encompass all trade and traffic between the Cape of Good Hope and the Strait of Magellan, as well as granting semi-sovereign privileges to rule territories and raise armies. The wording was sufficiently ambiguous to allow future generations of EIC officials to use it to claim jurisdiction over all English subjects in Asia, mint money, raise fortifications, make laws, wage war, conduct an independent foreign policy, hold courts, issue punishment, imprison English subjects and plant English settlements. It was not without foundation that a later critic and pamphleteer complained that the Company had been granted monopoly on 'near two-third parts of the trading World'.[28] And though it took two and a half centuries for the potential to be realised, the wording of the EIC's charter left open from the beginning the possibility of it becoming an imperial power, exercising sovereignty and controlling people and territory.[29]

In the intervening year, the merchant adventurers had not been idle. They had been to Deptford to 'view severall shippes', one of which, the *May Flowre*, was later famous for a voyage heading in the opposite direction.[30] Four vessels had been bought and put into dry dock to be refitted. Given that time was of the essence, a barrel of beer a day was authorised 'for the better holding together of the workmen from running from ther worke to drinke'. What was intended as the Company's 900-ton flagship, a former privateering vessel, specifically built for raiding Spanish shipping in the Caribbean, the *Scourge of Malice* was renamed the *Red Dragon* so that it might sound a little less piratical.

Before long the adventurers had begun to purchase not only shipping, but new masts, anchors and rigging, and to begin constructing detailed inventories of their seafaring equipment – their 'kedgers', 'drabblers', 'all standard rigging and running ropes', 'cables good and bad, a mayne course bonnet very good' and '1 great warping hauser'. There was also the armament they would need: '40 muskets, 24 pikes ... 13 sackers, 2 fowlers, 25 barrelles of powder' as well as the 'Spunges, Ladles and Ramers' for the cannon.[31]

They also set about energetically commissioning hogsheads to be filled with 'biere, 170 tonnes, 40 tonnes of hogshed for Porke, 12 tonnes drie caske for Oatemeal, one tonne dryie caske for mustard seed, one tonne dry caske for Rice ... bisket well dryed ... good fish ... very Dry' as well as '120 oxen' and '60 Tons of syder'. Meanwhile, the financiers among them began to collect £30,000* of bullion, as well as divers items to trade on arrival – what they termed an 'investment' of iron, tin and English broadcloth, all of which they hoped would be acceptable items to trade against Indonesian pepper, nutmeg, cloves, mace, cardamom and the other aromatic spices and jewels they hoped to bring home.[32]

There was one last hiccup. In February 1601, the presiding genius of the nascent Company, Auditor Smythe, was briefly incarcerated in the Tower of London on a charge of complicity in the rebellion of the hot-headed Earl of Essex.[33] Nevertheless, only two months after the formal granting of their charter, on 13 February 1601, the refitted *Red Dragon* slipped its Woolwich moorings and glided through the cold February

---

* Over £3 million today.

Thames fog, followed closely by its three smaller escorts, the *Hector*, the *Susan* and the *Ascension*. In command again was the stern but now-chastened figure of Sir James Lancaster. Lancaster had learned several lessons from his previous adventures and brought along lemon juice to administer to his crew to prevent scurvy, and enough armament – no less than thirty-eight guns – to take on any competition he might encounter en route.[34]

The voyage got off to an almost comically bad start. As they were leaving the Thames estuary, the wind dropped and for two months the fleet stood humiliatingly becalmed in the Channel, within sight of Dover. But the wind eventually picked up and by September the fleet had rounded the Cape, where it stopped in for provisions. Wishing to indicate to the waiting tribesmen that he wanted to buy meat, Lancaster, showing a linguistic aptitude that would come to distinguish English imperialism, 'spake to them in cattel's language ... moath ['moo'] for kine and oxen, and baah for sheep'. They then headed on to Mauritius where, on the shore, they found a series of carvings on a rock. It was not good news: five Dutch ships had recorded their visit only five months earlier.[35]

It was not until June 1602 that Lancaster's fleet made it to Acheh and began to negotiate with the Sultan for his spices. Shortly afterwards the crew spied a Portuguese carrack. Lancaster had been advised to conduct his men 'in a merchantlike course', but was also authorised to indulge in piracy against Spanish or Portuguese ships should 'an opportunity be offered without prejudice or hazard'. He did not hesitate.

A year later, on 1 June 1603, rumours began to filter into London via France that the Company's first fleet had returned safely into European waters. But it was not until 6 June that Lancaster finally anchored on the south coast at the Downs, 'for which thanked be Almightie God who hath delivered us from infinite perils and dangers'.[36] This time Lancaster had brought back all four of his vessels, intact and fully loaded. He was carrying no less than 900 tons of pepper, cinnamon and cloves, much of it taken from the Portuguese carrack, which along with more spices bought in Acheh made the voyage an impressive 300 per cent profit.

It would be the first of fifteen more EIC expeditions that would set out over the next fifteen years. But the truth was that this was small fry compared with what the Dutch were already achieving on the other side of the Channel. For in March 1602, while Lancaster was still in the

Moluccas, the different Dutch East India Companies had all agreed to amalgamate and the Dutch East India Company, the VOC (Vereenigde Oostindische Compagnie), had received its state monopoly to trade with the East. When the Amsterdam accountants had totted up all the subscriptions, it was found that the VOC had raised almost ten times the capital base of the English EIC, and was immediately in a position to offer investors a 3,600 per cent dividend.[37]

Compared to this, the English Company was for many years an extremely modest venture, and one with relatively limited ambitions. For all the initial excitement at the Founders' Hall, the merchants had raised only a relatively paltry £68,373 capital, as opposed to the Dutch who had by then pulled together a magnificent £550,000* for their rival venture. Since then, further Dutch subscriptions had poured in, while the English Company had, on the contrary, found it difficult to squeeze out even what the initial subscribers had promised.

In October 1599 the Company records contain the first complaints about the 'slacknes of many of the contributors who had sett down ther names' but had 'hitherto brought in noe moneys'. A few months later the directors began to threaten more severe sanctions against those who had failed to deliver on their promises at the Founders' Hall. On 11 January 1600 they 'ordered that any brother of this fellowship who shall ... have fallen into breach of any of ye ordinances ... then such person shall be committed to prison there to remaine duringe ye pleasure of ye generalitie'. A warrant was then issued for four persons to be committed to Marshalsea unless they paid up in four days.

The result of this inadequate funding was a small company with small fleets, and no permanent capital of its own, merely individual subscriptions for individual voyages. The English at this stage simply did not have the deep financial pockets of the Dutch. Moreover, Virginia and the New World had increasingly captured the imagination of the richer English nobles, not least because it seemed a more affordable and less risky option: the offer of ten shillings for a plot of 100 fertile acres in Virginia was a far more attractive option than £120** for ten volatile shares in East India stock. For the time being the EIC could hope for

---

* The modern equivalences of these sums are: £68,373 = £7,179,165 today; £550,00 = over £57 million today.

** £12,600 today.

no more than becoming very minor players in one of the richest, most sophisticated and competitive markets in the world.[38]

Nor, with the serious risks involved, was the Company attracting the calibre of applicant it needed to make a success of its difficult venture. 'It is not uncommon to have them out of Newgate [prison], as several have confessed', reads one early Company letter complaining about the quality of its recruits, 'however those we can keep pretty much in order. But of late we have had some from [the lunatic asylum of] Bedlam.'[39] Already reports had come of Company servants 'dangerously disordering themselves with drink and whores', while another letter begs that the directors attempt to recruit 'civill, sober men' and that 'negligent or debauched persons or common drunkards should be discarded'.[40]

Many more voyages set off throughout the early seventeenth century, mostly generating modest profits, but from the first the EIC was unable to prevail against better armed, better financed and more skilfully sailed fleets of Dutch East Indiamen. 'Theis [Dutch] buterboxes are groanne soe insolent,' complained one East India captain, 'that yf they be suffered but a whit longer, they will make claims to the whole Indies, so that no man shall trade but themselves or by thear leave; but I hoope to see their pride take a falle.'[41] It was not, however, the Dutch whose pride was to be dented. In 1623, the English factory (trading station) at Amboina in the Moluccas was attacked by the Dutch VOC troops and ten Englishmen were tortured and killed. This opened several decades of conflict between England and Holland in which, despite occasional successes, the English consistently came off worse. At one point a Dutch fleet even sailed up the Thames and attacked Sheerness, destroying the ships in Chatham and Rochester dockyards.[42]

After several more bruising encounters, the EIC directors decided they had little option but to leave the lucrative Spice Islands and their aromatic spice trade to the Dutch and focus instead on less competitive but potentially more promising sectors of the trade of Asia: fine cotton textiles, indigo and chintzes.

The source of all three of these luxuries was India.

On 28 August 1608, Captain William Hawkins, a bluff sea captain with the Third Voyage, anchored his ship, the *Hector*, off Surat, and so became the first commander of an EIC vessel to set foot on Indian soil.[43]

India then had a population of 150 million – about a fifth of the world's total – and was producing about a quarter of global manufacturing; indeed, in many ways it was the world's industrial powerhouse and the world's leader in manufactured textiles. Not for nothing are so many English words connected with weaving – chintz, calico, shawl, pyjamas, khaki, dungarees, cummerbund, taffetas – of Indian origin.[44] It was certainly responsible for a much larger share of world trade than any comparable zone and the weight of its economic power even reached Mexico, whose textile manufacture suffered a crisis of 'de-industrialisation' due to Indian cloth imports.[45] In comparison, England then had just 5 per cent of India's population and was producing just under 3 per cent of the world's manufactured goods.[46] A good proportion of the profits on this found its way to the Mughal exchequer in Agra, making the Mughal Emperor, with an income of around £100 million,* by far the richest monarch in the world.

The Mughal capitals were the megacities of their day: 'They are second to none either in Asia or in Europe,' thought the Jesuit Fr Antonio Monserrate, 'with regards either to size, population, or wealth. Their cities are crowded with merchants, who gather from all over Asia. There is no art or craft which is not practised there.' Between 1586 and 1605, European silver flowed into the Mughal heartland at the astonishing rate of 18 metric tons a year, for as William Hawkins observed, 'all nations bring coyne and carry away commodities for the same'.[47] For their grubby contemporaries in the West, stumbling around in their codpieces, the silk-clad Mughals, dripping in jewels, were the living embodiment of wealth and power – a meaning that has remained impregnated in the word 'mogul' ever since.

By the early seventeenth century, Europeans had become used to easy military victories over the other peoples of the world. In the 1520s the Spanish had swept away the vast armies of the mighty Aztec Empire in a matter of months. In the Spice Islands of the Moluccas, the Dutch had recently begun to turn their cannons on the same rulers they had earlier traded with, slaughtering those islanders who rode out in canoes

---

* Over £10,000 million today.

to greet them, burning down their cities and seizing their ports. On one island alone, Lontor, 800 inhabitants were enslaved and forcibly deported to work on new Dutch spice plantations in Java; forty-seven chiefs were tortured and executed.[48]

But as Captain Hawkins soon realised, there was no question of any European nation attempting to do this with the Great Mughals, not least because the Mughals kept a staggering 4 million men under arms.[49] When, in 1632, the Emperor discovered that the Portuguese had been building unauthorised fortifications and 'dwellings of the utmost splendour and strength' in Hughli in Bengal, as well as flouting Mughal rules by making forced conversions to Christianity, he commanded that the Portuguese settlement should be attacked and the Portuguese expelled.

The city fell to the Mughal armies within days and the attempts of the inhabitants to escape down the Ganges were thwarted by a boom ingeniously thrown across the river. Four hundred of the captured Portuguese prisoners 'along with the idols of those erroneous infidels' were then sent off to Agra to beg for mercy. Those who refused were 'divided [as slaves] among the amirs', according to the *Padshahnama*, 'or held in prison and tortured. Most of them perished.' There was nothing the Portuguese Viceroy of Goa could do about this.[50]

With this in mind, the Company realised that if it was to trade successfully with the Mughals, it would need both partners and permissions, which meant establishing a relationship with the Mughal Emperor himself. It took Hawkins a year to reach Agra, which he managed to do dressed as an Afghan nobleman. Here he was briefly entertained by the Emperor, with whom he conversed in Turkish, before Jahangir lost interest in the semi-educated sea dog and sent him back home with the gift of an Armenian Christian wife. The mission achieved little, and soon afterwards another EIC fleet, captained by Sir Henry Middleton, was driven away from the Surat anchorage of Suvali – or 'Swally Hole' as the English mangled it – by local officials who ordered him to leave after threats from the Portuguese residents in the port.[51]

A new, more impressive mission was called for, and this time the Company persuaded King James to send a royal envoy. The man chosen was a courtier, MP, diplomat, Amazon explorer, Ambassador to the Sublime Porte and self-described 'man of quality', Sir Thomas Roe.[52] In 1615 Roe finally arrived in Ajmer, bringing presents of 'hunting dogges' – English mastiffs and Irish greyhounds – an English state

coach, some Mannerist paintings, an English virginal and many crates
of red wine for which he had heard Jahangir had a fondness; but Roe
nevertheless had a series of difficult interviews with the Emperor. When
he was finally granted an audience, and had made his obeisance, Roe
wanted immediately to get to the point and raise the subject of trade
and preferential customs duties, but the aesthete Emperor could barely
conceal his boredom at such conversations.

Jahangir was, after all, an enormously sensitive, curious and
intelligent man: observant of the world around him and a keen collector
of its curiosities, from Venetian swords and globes to Safavid silks, jade
pebbles and even narwhal teeth. A proud inheritor of the Indo-Mughal
tradition of aesthetics and knowledge, as well as maintaining the Empire
and commissioning great works of art, he took an active interest in goat
and cheetah breeding, medicine and astronomy, and had an insatiable
appetite for animal husbandry, like some Enlightenment landowner of
a later generation.

This, not the mechanics of trade, was what interested him, and there
followed several months of conversations with the two men talking at
cross purposes. Roe would try to steer the talk towards commerce and
diplomacy and the firmans (imperial orders) he wanted confirming
'his favour for an English factory' at Surat and 'to establish a firm and
secure Trade and residence for my countrymen' in 'constant love and
pease'; but Jahangir would assure him such workaday matters could
wait, and instead counter with questions about the distant, foggy island
Roe came from, the strange things that went on there and the art which
it produced. Roe found that Jahangir 'expects great presents and jewels
and regards no trade but what feeds his insatiable appetite after stones,
riches and rare pieces of art'.[53]

'He asked me what Present we would bring him,' Roe noted.

I answered the league [between England and Mughal India] was yet
new, and very weake: that many curiosities were to be found in our
Countrey of rare price and estimation, which the king would send,
and the merchants seeke out in all parts of the world, if they were
once made secure of a quiet trade and protection on honourable
Conditions.

He asked what those curiosities were I mentioned, whether I meant
jewels and rich stones. I answered No: that we did not thinke them

fit Presents to send backe, which were first brought from these parts, whereof he was the Chiefe Lord ... but that we sought to find things for his Majestie, as were rare here, and vnseene. He said it was very well: but that he desired an English horse ... So with many passages of jests, mirth, and bragges concerning the Arts of his Countrey, he fell to ask me questions, how often I drank a day, and how much, and what? What in England? What beere was? How made? And whether I could make it here. In all which I satisfied his great demands of State ...[54]

Roe could on occasion be dismissively critical of Mughal rule – 'religions infinite, laws none' – but he was, despite himself, thoroughly dazzled. In a letter describing the Emperor's birthday celebrations in 1616, written from the beautiful, half-ruined hilltop fortress of Mandu in central India to the future King Charles I in Whitehall, Roe reported that he had entered a world of almost unimaginable splendour.

The celebrations were held in a superbly designed 'very large and beautifull Garden, the square within all water, on the sides flowres and trees, in the midst a Pinacle, where was prepared the scales ... of masse gold' in which the Emperor would be weighed against jewels.

Here attended the Nobilitie all sitting about it on Carpets until the King came; who at least appeared clothed, or rather laden with Diamonds, Rubies, Pearles, and other precious vanities, so great, so glorious! His head, necke, breast, armes, above the elbowes, at the wrists, his fingers each one with at least two or three Rings, are fettered with chaines of dyamonds, Rubies as great as Walnuts – some greater – and Pearles such as mine eyes were amazed at ... in jewells, which is one of his felicityes, hee is the treasury of the world, buyeing all that comes, and heaping rich stones as if hee would rather build [with them] than wear them.[55]

The Mughals, in return, were certainly curious about the English, but hardly overwhelmed. Jahangir greatly admired an English miniature of one of Roe's girlfriends – maybe the Lady Huntingdon to whom he wrote passionately from 'Indya'.[56] But Jahangir made a point of demonstrating to Roe that his artists could copy it so well that Roe could not tell copy from original. The English state coach was also admired, but Jahangir had the slightly tatty Tudor interior trim immediately upgraded with Mughal cloth of gold and then again showed off the skills of the Mughal *kar-khana* by having the entire coach perfectly copied, in little over a week, so his beloved Empress, Nur Jahan, could have a coach of her own.[57]

Meanwhile, Roe was vexed to discover that the Mughals regarded relations with the English as a very low priority. On arrival he was shoved into a substandard accommodation: only four caravanserai rooms allotted for the entire embassy and they 'no bigger than ovens, and in that shape, round at the top, no light but the door, and so little that the goods of two carts would fill them all'.[58] More humiliatingly still, his slightly shop-soiled presents were soon completely outshone by those of a rival Portuguese embassy who gave Jahangir 'jewels, Ballests [balas spinels] and Pearles with much disgrace to our English commoditie'.[59]

When Roe eventually returned to England, after three weary years at court, he had obtained permission from Jahangir to build a factory (trading station) in Surat, an agreement 'for our reception and continuation in his domynyons' and a couple of imperial firmans, limited in scope and content, but useful to flash at obstructive Mughal officials. Jahangir, however, made a deliberate point of not conceding any major trading privileges, possibly regarding it as beneath his dignity to do so.[60]

The status of the English at the Mughal court in this period is perhaps most graphically illustrated by one of the most famous images of the period, a miniature by Jahangir's master artist, Bichitr. The conceit of the painting is how the pious Jahangir preferred the company of Sufis and saints to that of powerful princes. This was actually not as far-fetched as it might sound: one of Roe's most telling anecdotes relates how Jahangir amazed the English envoy by spending an hour chatting to a passing holy man he encountered on his travels:

> a poor silly old man, all asht, ragd and patcht, with a young roague attending on him. This miserable wretch cloathed in rags, crowned with feathers, his Majestie talked with about an hour, with such familiaritie and shew of kindnesse, that it must needs argue an humilitie not found easily among Kings ... He took him up in his armes, which no cleanly body durst have touched, imbracing him, and three times laying his hand on his heart, calling him father, he

left him, and all of us, and me, in admiration of such a virtue in a heathen Prince.[61]

Bichitr illustrates this idea by showing Jahangir centre frame, sitting on a throne with the halo of Majesty glowing so brightly behind him that one of the putti, caught in flight from a Portuguese transfiguration, has to shield his eyes from the brightness of his radiance; another pair of putti are writing a banner reading 'Allah Akbar! Oh king, may your age endure a thousand years!' The Emperor turns to hand a Quran to a cumulus-bearded Sufi, spurning the outstretched hands of the Ottoman Sultan. As for James I, in his jewelled and egret-plumed hat and silver-white Jacobean doublet, he is relegated to the bottom left corner of the frame, below Jahangir's feet and only just above Bichitr's own self-portrait. The King shown in a three-quarter profile – an angle reserved in Mughal miniatures for the minor characters – with a look of vinegary sullenness on his face at his lowly place in the Mughal hierarchy.[62] For all the reams written by Roe on Jahangir, the latter did not bother to mention Roe once in his voluminous diaries. These awkward, artless northern traders and supplicants would have to wait a century more before the Mughals deigned to take any real interest in them.

Yet for all its clumsiness, Roe's mission was the beginning of a Mughal–Company relationship that would develop into something approaching a partnership and see the EIC gradually drawn into the Mughal nexus. Over the next 200 years it would slowly learn to operate skilfully within the Mughal system and to do so in the Mughal idiom, with its officials learning good Persian, the correct court etiquette, the art of bribing the right officials and, in time, outmanoeuvring all their rivals – Portuguese, Dutch and French – for imperial favour. Indeed, much of the Company's success at this period was facilitated by its scrupulous regard for Mughal authority.[63] Before long, indeed, the Company would begin portraying itself to the Mughals, as the historian Sanjay Subrahmanyam has nicely described it, as 'not a corporate entity but instead an anthropomorphized one, an Indo-Persian creature called *Kampani Bahadur*'.[64]

On his return to London, Roe made it clear to the directors that force of arms was not an option when dealing with the Mughal Empire. 'A warre and traffic,' he wrote, 'are incompatible.' Indeed he advised against even fortified settlements and pointed out how 'the Portuguese many rich residences and territoryes [were] beggaring' their trade with unsupportable costs. Even if the Mughals were to allow the EIC a fort or two, he wrote, 'I would not accept one … for without controversy it is an errour to affect garrisons and land warrs in India.' Instead he recommended: 'Lett this be received as a rule, that if you will seek profit, seek it at sea and in a quiett trade.'[65]

To begin with, the Company took his advice. Early EIC officials prided themselves on negotiating commercial privileges, rather than resorting to attacking strategic ports like the more excitable Portuguese, and it proved to be a strategy that paid handsome dividends. While Roe was busy charming Jahangir, another Company emissary, Captain Hippon, was despatched on the *Globe* to open the textile trade with the eastward-facing Coromandel coast and to establish a second factory at Masulipatnam, the port of the Mughal's great Deccani rivals, the diamond-rich Sultanate of Golconda, where could be bought the finest jewels and chintz in India.[66] A third factory dealing mainly with the trade in saltpetre – the active ingredient in gunpowder – opened shortly afterwards in Patna.

This trade in jewels, pepper, textiles and saltpetre soon resulted in even better returns than the Dutch trade in aromatic spices: by the 1630s the EIC was importing £1 million of pepper from India which, in a dramatic reversal of centuries of trading patterns, it now began exporting to Italy and the Middle East, through its sister the Levant Company. Thirty years later they were importing a quarter of a million pieces of cloth, nearly half of them from the Coromandel.[67] Losses were still heavy: between 1601 and 1640, the Company sent a total of 168 ships eastwards; only 104 arrived back again.[68] But the Company's balance sheets grew increasingly profitable, so much so that investors from around Europe began for the first time queuing up to buy EIC stock. In 1613 the subscription for the First Joint Stock raised £418,000. Four years later, in 1617, the subscription to Second Joint Stock pulled in a massive £1.6 million,*

---

* The modern equivalences of these sums are: £1 million = £105 million today; £418,000 = nearly £44 million today; £1.6 million = £168 million today.

turning the EIC for the first time into a financial colossus, at least by English standards.[69] The success of the EIC in turn stimulated not only the London docks but also the nascent London stock exchange. By the middle of the century half of those who were elected to the elite Court of Aldermen of the City of London were either Levant Company traders or EIC directors, or both.[70] One Company member, the early economic theorist Thomas Mun, wrote that the Company's trade was now 'the very *touchstone* of the Kingdom's prosperity'.[71]

It was not until 1626 that the EIC founded its first fortified Indian base, at Armagon, north of Pulicat, on the central Coromandel coast. It was soon crenellated and armed with twelve guns. But it was quickly and shoddily constructed, in addition to which it was found to be militarily indefensible, so was abandoned six years later in 1632 with little regret; as one factor put it, 'better lost than found'.[72]

Two years later, the EIC tried again. The head of the Armagon factory, Francis Day, negotiated with the local governor of what was left of the waning and fragmented South Indian Vijayanagara empire for the right to build a new EIC fort above a fishing village called Madraspatnam, just north of the Portuguese settlement at San Thome. Again, it was neither commercial nor military considerations which dictated the choice of site. Day, it was said, had a liaison with a Tamil lady whose village lay inland from Madraspatnam. According to one contemporary source Day 'was so enamoured of her' and so anxious that their 'interviews' might be 'more frequent and uninterrupted' that his selection of the site of Fort St George lying immediately adjacent to her home village was a foregone conclusion.[73]

This time the settlement – soon known simply as Madras – flourished. The Naik (governor) who leased the land said he was anxious for the area to 'flourish and grow rich', and had given Day the right to build 'a fort and castle', to trade customs free and to 'perpetually Injoy the priviledges of minatag[e]'. These were major concessions that the more powerful Mughals to the north would take nearly another century to yield.

Initially, there were 'only the French padres and about six fishermen, soe to intice inhabitants to people the place, a proclamation was made … that for a terme of thirty years' no custom duties would be charged. Soon weavers and other artificers and traders began pouring in. Still more came once the fort walls had been erected, 'as the tymes are turned upp syde downe', and the people of the coast were looking for exactly the security and protection the Company could provide.[74]

Before long Madras had grown to be the first English colonial town in India with its own small civil administration, the status of a municipality and a population of 40,000. By the 1670s the town was even minting its own gold 'pagoda' coins, so named after the image of a temple that filled one side, with the monkey deity Hanuman on the reverse, both borrowed from the old Vijayanagara coinage.[75]

The second big English settlement in India came into the hands of the Company via the Crown, which in turn received it as a wedding present from the Portuguese monarchy. In 1661, when Charles II married the Portuguese Infanta, Catherine of Braganza, part of her dowry, along with the port of Tangier, was the 'island of Bumbye'. In London there was initially much confusion as to its whereabouts, as the map which accompanied the Infanta's marriage contract went missing en route. No one at court seemed sure where 'Bumbye' was, though the Lord High Chancellor believed it to be 'somewhere near Brazil'.[76]

It took some time to sort out this knotty issue, and even longer to gain actual control of the island, as the Portuguese governor had received no instructions to hand it over, and so understandably refused to do so. When Sir Abraham Shipman first arrived with 450 men to claim Bombay for the English in September 1662, his mission was blocked at gunpoint; it was a full three years before the British were finally able to take over, by which time the unfortunate Shipman, and all his officers bar one, had died of fever and heatstroke, waiting on a barren island to the south. When Shipman's secretary was finally allowed to land on Bombay island in 1665, only one ensign, two gunners and 111 subalterns were still alive to claim the new acquisition.[77]

Despite this bumpy start, the island soon proved its worth: the Bombay archipelago turned out to have the best natural harbour in South Asia, and it quickly became the Company's major naval base in Asia, with the only dry dock where ships could be safely refitted during the monsoon. Before long it had eclipsed Surat as the main centre of EIC operations on the west coast, especially as the rowdy English were becoming less and less welcome there: 'Their private whorings, drunkenesse and such like ryotts ... breaking open whorehouses and rackehowses [i.e. arrack bars] have hardened the hearts of the inhabitants against our very names,' wrote one weary EIC official. Little wonder that the British were soon being reviled in the Surat streets 'with the names of Ban-chude* and Betty-chude† which my modest language will not interpret'.[78]

Within thirty years Bombay had grown to house a colonial population of 60,000 with a growing network of factories, law courts, an Anglican church and large white residential houses surrounding the fort and tumbling down the slope from Malabar Hill to the Governor's estate on the seafront. It even had that essential amenity for any God-fearing seventeenth-century Protestant community, a scaffold where 'witches' were given a last chance to confess before their execution.[79] It also had its own small garrison of 300 English soldiers, '400 Topazes, 500 native militia and 300 Bhandaris [club-wielding toddy-tappers] that lookt after the woods of cocoes'. By the 1680s Bombay had briefly eclipsed Madras 'as the seat of power and trade of the English in the East Indies'.[80]

Meanwhile, in London, the Company directors were beginning to realise for the first time how powerful they were. In 1693, less than a century after its foundation, the Company was discovered to be using its own shares for buying the favours of parliamentarians, as it annually shelled out £1,200 a year to prominent MPs and ministers. The bribery, it turned out, went as high as the Solicitor General, who received £218, and the Attorney General, who received £545.** The parliamentary investigation into this, the world's first corporate lobbying scandal, found the EIC guilty of bribery and insider trading and led to the impeachment of the Lord President of the Council and the imprisonment of the Company's Governor.

Only once during the seventeenth century did the Company try to use its strength against the Mughals, and then with catastrophic consequences. In 1681 the directorship was taken over by the recklessly aggressive Sir Josiah Child, who had started his career supplying beer

---

* Lit: 'Sister-fucker'.

† Lit: 'Daughter-fucker'. Yule, incidentally, includes both terms in Hobson-Jobson. He avoids giving direct translations of these still popular Hindustani endearments, saying merely that 'Banchoot and Beteechoot [are] terms of abuse which we should hesitate to print if their odious meanings were not obscure "to the general". If it were known to the Englishmen who sometimes use the words we believe there are few who would not shrink from such brutality.'

** The modern equivalences of these sums are: £1,200 = £126,000 today; £218 = £22,890 today; £545 = £57,225 today.

to the navy in Portsmouth, and who was described by the diarist John Evelyn as 'an overgrown and suddenly monied man ... most sordidly avaricious'.[81] In Bengal the factors had begun complaining, as Streynsham Master wrote to London, that 'here every petty Officer makes a pray of us, abuscing us at pleasure to Screw what they can out of us'. We are, he wrote, 'despised and trampled upon' by Mughal officials. This was indeed the case: the Nawab of Bengal, Shaista Khan, made no secret of his dislike of the Company and wrote to his friend and maternal nephew, the Emperor Aurangzeb, that 'the English were a company of base, quarrelling people and foul dealers'.[82]

Ignorant of the scale of Mughal power, Child made the foolish decision to react with force and attempt to teach the Mughals a lesson: 'We have no remedy left,' he wrote from the Company's Court in Leadenhall Street, 'but either to desert our trade, or we must draw the sword his Majesty has Intrusted us with, to vindicate the Rights and Honor of the English Nation in India.'[83] As a consequence, in 1686 a considerable fleet sailed from London to Bengal with 19 warships, 200 cannons and 600 soldiers. 'It will,' Child wrote, 'become us to Seize what we cann & draw the English sword.'[84]

But Child could not have chosen a worse moment to pick a fight with the Emperor of the richest kingdom on earth. The Mughals had just completed their conquest of the two great Deccani Sultanates of Bijapur and Golconda and seemed also to have driven the Marathas back into the hills whence they had come. The Mughal Empire had thus emerged as the unrivalled regional power, and its army was now able to focus exclusively on this new threat. The Mughal war machine swept away the English landing parties as easily as if it were swatting flies; soon the EIC factories at Hughli, Patna, Kasimbazar, Masulipatnam and Vizagapatam had all been seized and plundered, and the English had been expelled completely from Bengal. The Surat factory was closed and Bombay was blockaded.

The EIC had no option but to sue for peace and beg for the return of its factories and hard-earned trading privileges. They also had to petition for the release of its captured factors, many of whom were being paraded in chains through the streets or kept fettered in the Surat castle and the Dhaka Red Fort 'in insufferable and tattered conditions ... like thiefs and murders'.[85] When Aurangzeb heard that the EIC had 'repented of their irregular proceedings' and submitted to Mughal authority, the Emperor left the factors to lick their wounds for a while, then in 1690 graciously agreed to forgive them.

It was in the aftermath of this fiasco that a young factor named Job Charnock decided to found a new British base in Bengal to replace the lost factories that had just been destroyed. On 24 August 1690, with 'ye rains falling day and night', Charnock began planting his settlement on the swampy ground between the villages of Kalikata and Sutanuti, adjacent to a small Armenian trading station, and with a Portuguese one just across the river.

Job Charnock bought the future site of Calcutta, said the Scottish writer Alexander Hamilton, 'for the sake of a large shady tree', an odd choice, he thought, 'for he could not have found a more unhealthful Place on all the River'.[86] According to Hamilton's *New Account of the East Indies*: 'Mr *Channock* choosing the Ground of the Colony, where it now is, reigned more absolute than a *Rajah*':

> The country about being overspread with *Paganism*, the Custom of Wives burning with their deceased Husbands is also practised here. Mr *Channock* went one Time with his guard of Soldiers, to see a young widow act that tragical Catastrophe, but he was so smitten with the Widow's Beauty, that he sent his guards to take her by Force from her Executioners, and conducted her to his own Lodgings. They lived lovingly many Years, and had several children. At length she died, after he had settled in *Calcutta*, but instead of converting her to *Christianity*, she made him a Proselyte to *Paganism*, and the only Part of *Christianity* that was remarkable in him, was burying her decently, and he built a Tomb over her, where all his Life after her Death, he kept the anniversary Day of her Death by sacrificing a Cock on her Tomb, after the *Pagan* Manner.[87]

Mrs Charnock was not the only fatality. Within a year of the founding of the English settlement at Calcutta, there were 1,000 living in the settlement but already Hamilton was able to count 460 names in the burial book: indeed, so many died there that it is 'become a saying that they live like Englishmen and die like rotten sheep'.[88]

Only one thing kept the settlement going: Bengal was 'the finest and most fruitful country in the world', according to the French traveller François Bernier. It was one of 'the richest most populous and best cultivated countries', agreed the Scot Alexander Dow. With its myriad weavers – 25,000 in Dhaka alone – and unrivalled luxury textile production of silks and woven muslins of fabulous delicacy, it was by the end of the seventeenth century Europe's single most important supplier of goods in Asia and much the wealthiest region of the Mughal Empire, the place where fortunes could most easily be made. In the early years of the eighteenth century, the Dutch and English East India Companies between them shipped into Bengal cargoes worth around 4.15 million rupees* annually, 85 per cent of which was silver.[89]

The Company existed to make money, and Bengal, they soon realised, was the best place to do it.

It was the death of Aurangzeb in 1707 that changed everything for the Company.

The Emperor, unloved by his father, grew up into a bitter and bigoted Islamic puritan, as intolerant as he was grimly dogmatic. He was a ruthlessly talented general and a brilliantly calculating strategist, but entirely lacked the winning charm of his predecessors. His rule became increasingly harsh, repressive and unpopular as he grew older. He made a clean break with the liberal and inclusive policies towards the Hindu majority of his subjects pioneered by his great-grandfather Akbar, and instead allowed the *ulama* to impose far stricter interpretations of Sharia law. Wine was banned, as was hashish, and the Emperor ended his personal patronage of musicians. He also ended Hindu customs adopted by the Mughals such as appearing daily to his subjects at the *jharoka* palace window in the centre of the royal apartments in the Red Fort. Around a dozen Hindu temples across the country were destroyed, and in 1672 he issued an order recalling all endowed land given to Hindus and reserved all future land grants for Muslims. In 1679 the Emperor reimposed the *jizya* tax on all non-Muslims that had been abolished by Akbar; he also executed Teg Bahadur, the ninth of the gurus of the Sikhs.[90]

While it is true that Aurangzeb is a more complex and pragmatic figure than some of his critics allow, the religious wounds Aurangzeb

* £54 million today.

opened in India have never entirely healed, and at the time they tore the country in two.* Unable to trust anyone, Aurangzeb marched to and fro across the Empire, viciously putting down successive rebellions by his subjects. The Empire had been built on a pragmatic tolerance and an alliance with the Hindus, especially with the warrior Rajputs, who formed the core of the Mughal war machine. The pressure put on that alliance and the Emperor's retreat into bigotry helped to shatter the Mughal state and, on Aurangzeb's death, it finally lost them the backbone of their army.

But it was Aurangzeb's reckless expansion of the Empire into the Deccan, largely fought against the Shia Muslim states of Bijapur and Golconda, that did most to exhaust and overstretch the resources of the Empire. It also unleashed against the Mughals a new enemy that was as formidable as it was unexpected. Maratha peasants and landholders had once served in the armies of the Bijapur and Golconda. In the 1680s, after the Mughals conquered these two states, Maratha guerrilla raiders under the leadership of Shivaji Bhonsle, a charismatic Maratha Hindu warlord, began launching attacks against the Mughal armies occupying the Deccan. As one disapproving Mughal chronicler noted,

---

* According to the eminent historian Ishwari Prasad, of the Allahabad School, Aurangzeb was a 'bigoted Sunni intolerant of all forms of dissent', see I. Prasad, *The Mughal Empire*, Allahabad, 1974, p. 612. Jadunath Sarkar painted a very similar portrait over five volumes: Jadunath Sarkar, *History of Aurangzeb*, London, 1912–24. In recent years, there has been an effort to make over Aurangzeb's reputation as a bigot and to fact-check some of the more extreme claims made against him. The most interesting contribution was by Katherine Butler Brown, who pointed out that, far from ending musical production in the Empire, the reign of Aurangzeb actually produced more musical writing than the previous hundred years. See 'Did Aurangzeb ban Music?', *Modern Asian Studies*, vol. 41, no. 1 (2007), pp. 82–5. Also fascinating, though more controversial, was Audrey Truschke's *Aurangzeb: The Man and the Myth*, New Delhi, 2017, which turned the unfortunate American Sanskritist into a major hate figure of the Hindutva right wing. Munis D. Faruqui is working on a major new study of Aurangzeb, but in the meantime his *Princes of the Mughal Empire 1504–1719* (Cambridge, 2012) is full of illuminating insights on Aurangzeb. My own view is that, while Aurangzeb is certainly a more complex figure than his detractors allow, and that it is true that early in his career he did protect Brahmins, patronise Hindu institutions and Hindu noblemen, and that he consulted with Hindu astrologers and physicians to the end, he was still an unusually cold, ruthless and unpleasant character, and his aggression and charmlessness did do much to undermine the empire he worked so hard to keep together.

'most of the men in the Maratha army are unendowed with illustrious birth, and husbandmen, carpenters and shopkeepers abound among their soldiery'.[91] They were largely armed peasants; but they knew the country and they knew how to fight.

From the sparse uplands of the western Deccan, Shivaji led a prolonged and increasingly widespread peasant rebellion against the Mughals and their tax collectors. The Maratha light cavalry, armed with spears, were remarkable for their extreme mobility and the ability to make sorties far behind Mughal lines. They could cover fifty miles in a day because the cavalrymen carried neither baggage nor provisions and instead lived off the country: Shivaji's maxim was 'no plunder, no pay'.[92] One Jacobean traveller, Dr John Fryer of the EIC, noted that the 'Naked, Starved Rascals' who made up Shivaji's army were armed with 'only lances and long swords two inches wide' and could not win battles in 'a pitched Field', but were supremely skilled at 'Surprising and Ransacking'.[93]

According to Fryer, Shivaji's Marathas sensibly avoided pitched battles with the Mughal's army, opting instead to ravage the centres of Mughal power until the economy collapsed. In 1663, Shivaji personally led a daring night raid on the palace of the Mughal headquarters in Pune, where he murdered the family of the Governor of the Deccan, Aurangzeb's uncle, Shaista Khan. He also succeeded in cutting off the Governor's finger.[94] In 1664, Shivaji's peasant army raided the Mughal port of Surat, sacking its richly filled warehouses and extorting money from its many bankers. He did the same in 1670, and by the Marathas' third visit in 1677 there was not even a hint of resistance.

In between the last two raids, Shivaji received, at his spectacular mountain fastness of Raigad, a Vedic consecration and coronation by the Varanasi pandit Gagabhatta, which was the ritual highlight of his career. This took place on 6 June 1674 and awarded him the status of the Lord of the Umbrella, *Chhatrapati*, and legitimate Hindu Emperor, or *Samrajyapada*. A second Tantric coronation followed shortly afterwards, which his followers believed gave him special access to the powers and blessings of three great goddesses of the Konkan mountains:

Sivaji entered the throne room with a sword and made blood sacrifices to the *lokapalas*, divinities who guard the worlds. The courtiers attending the ceremony were then asked to leave while auspicious mantras were installed on the king's body to the accompaniment of music and the chanting of samans. Finally he mounted his lion throne, hailed by cries of 'Victory' from the audience. He empowered the throne with the mantras of the ten Vidyas. Through their power, a mighty splendour filled the throne-room. The Saktis held lamps in their hands and lustrated the king, who shone like Brahma.[95]

Aurangzeb dismissed Shivaji as a 'mountain rat'. But by the time of his death in 1680, Shivaji had turned himself into Aurangzeb's nemesis, leaving behind him a name as the great symbol of Hindu resistance and revival after 500 years of Islamic rule. Within a generation, Maratha writers had turned him into a demi-god. In the *Sivabharata* of Kaviraja Paramananda, for example, Shivaji reveals himself to be none other than Vishnu-incarnate:

I am Lord Vishnu,
Essence of all gods,
Manifest on earth
To remove the world's burden!
The Muslims are demons incarnate,
Arisen to flood the earth,
With their own religion.
Therefore I will destroy these demons
Who have taken the form of Muslims,
And I will spread the way of *dharma* fearlessly.[96]

For many years the Mughal army fought back steadily, taking one Deccan hillfort after another, and for a while it looked like the imperial forces were slowly succeeding in crushing Maratha resistance as methodically as they did that of the Company. On 11 March 1689, the same year that the Emperor crushed the Company, Aurangzeb's armies captured Sambhaji, the eldest son and successor of Shivaji. The unfortunate prince was first humiliated by being forced to wear an absurd hat and being led into durbar on a camel. Then he was brutally tortured for a week. His eyes were stabbed out with nails. His tongue was cut out and his skin flayed with tiger claws before he was savagely put to death. The body was then thrown to the dogs while his head was stuffed with straw and sent on tour around the cities of the Deccan before being hung on the Delhi Gate.[97] By 1700, the Emperor's siege trains had taken the Maratha capital, Satara. It briefly seemed as if Aurangzeb had finally gained victory over the Marathas, and, as the great Mughal historian Ghulam Hussain Khan put it, 'driven that restless nation from its own home and reduced it to taking shelter in skulking holes and in fastnesses'.[98]

But in his last years, Aurangzeb's winning streak began to fail him. Avoiding pitched battles, the Marathas' predatory cavalry armies adopted guerrilla tactics, attacking Mughal supply trains and leaving the slow, heavily encumbered Mughal columns to starve or else return, outmanoeuvred, to their base in Aurangabad. The Emperor marched personally to take fort after fort, only to see each lost immediately his back was turned. 'So long as a single breath of this mortal life remains,' he wrote, 'there is no release from this labour and work.'[99]

The Mughal Empire had reached its widest extent yet, stretching from Kabul to the Carnatic, but there was suddenly disruption everywhere. Towards the end it was no longer just the Marathas: by the 1680s there was now in addition a growing insurgency in the imperial heartlands from peasant desertion and rebellion among the Jats of the Gangetic Doab and the Sikhs of the Punjab. Across the Empire, the landowning zamindar gentry were breaking into revolt and openly battling tax assessments and attempts by the Mughal state to penetrate rural areas and regulate matters that had previously been left to the discretion of hereditary local rulers. Banditry became endemic: in the mid-1690s the Italian traveller Giovanni Gemelli Careri complained that Mughal India did not offer travellers 'safety from thieves'.[100] Even Aurangzeb's son Prince Akbar went over to the Rajputs and raised the standard of rebellion.

These different acts of resistance significantly diminished the flow of rents, customs and revenues to the exchequer, leading for the first time in Mughal history to a treasury struggling to pay for the costs of administering the Empire or provide salaries for its officials. As military expenses continued to climb, the cracks in the Mughal state widened into, first, fissures, then crevasses. According to a slightly later text, the *Ahkam-i Alamgiri*, the Emperor himself acknowledged 'there is no province or district where the infidels have not raised a tumult, and since they are not chastised, they have established themselves everywhere. Most of the country has been rendered desolate and if any place is inhabited, the peasants have probably come to terms with the robbers.'[101]

On his deathbed, Aurangzeb acknowledged his failures in a sad and defeated letter to his son, Azam:

> I came alone and I go as a stranger. The instant which has passed in power has left only sorrow behind it. I have not been the guardian and protector of the Empire. Life, so valuable, has been squandered in vain. God was in my heart but I could not see him. Life is transient. The past is gone and there is no hope for the future. The whole imperial army is like me: bewildered, perturbed, separated from God, quaking like quicksilver. I fear my punishment. Though I have a firm hope in God's grace, yet for my deeds anxiety ever remains with me.[102]

Aurangzeb finally died on 20 February 1707. He was buried in a simple grave, open to the skies, not in Agra or in Delhi but at Khuldabad in the middle of the Deccan plateau he spent most of his adult life trying,[103] and failing, to bring to heel. In the years that followed his death, the authority of the Mughal state began to dissolve, first in the Deccan and then, as the Maratha armies headed northwards under their great war leader Baji Rao, in larger and larger areas of central and western India, too.

Mughal succession disputes and a string of weak and powerless emperors exacerbated the sense of imperial crisis: three emperors were murdered (one was, in addition, first blinded with a hot needle); the mother of one ruler was strangled and the father of another forced off a precipice on his elephant. In the worst year of all, 1719, four different Emperors occupied the Peacock Throne in rapid succession. According to the Mughal historian Khair ud-Din Illahabadi, 'The Emperor spent years – and fortunes – attempting to destroy the foundations of Maratha power, but this accursed tree could not be pulled up by the roots.'

> From Babur to Aurangzeb, the Mughal monarchy of Hindustan had grown ever more powerful, but now there was war among his descendants each seeking to pull the other down. The monarch's suspicious attitude towards his ministers and the commanders habitual interfering beyond their remit, with short-sighted selfishness and dishonesty, only made matters worse. Disorder and corruption

no longer sought to hide themselves and the once peaceful realm of India became a lair of Anarchy.[104]

On the ground, this meant devastating Maratha raids, leaving those villages under Mughal authority little more than piles of smoking cinders. The ruthlessness and cruelty of these guerrilla raids were legendary. A European traveller passing out of Aurangabad came across the aftermath of one of these Maratha attacks:

When we reached the frontier, we found all put to fire and sword. We camped out next to villages reduced to ashes, an indescribably horrid and distressing scene of humans and domestic animals burned and lying scattered about. Women clutching their children in their arms, men contorted, as they had been overtaken by death, some with hands and feet charred, others with only the trunk of the body recognisable: hideous corpses, some char-grilled, others utterly calcined black: a sight of horror such as I had never seen before. In the three villages we passed through, there must have been some 600 such disfigured human bodies.[105]

Yet if the Marathas were violent in war, they could in times of peace be mild rulers.[106] Another French traveller noted, 'The Marathas willingly ruin the land of their enemies with a truly detestable barbarity, but they faithfully maintain the peace with their allies, and in their own domains make agriculture and commerce flourish. When seen from the outside, this style of government is terrible, as the nation is naturally prone to brigandage; but seen from the inside, it is gentle and benevolent. The areas of India which have submitted to the Marathas are the happiest and most flourishing.'[107] By the early eighteenth century, the Marathas had fanned out to control much of central and western India. They were organised under five chieftains who constituted the Maratha Confederacy. These five chiefs established hereditary families which ruled over five different regions. The Peshwa – a Persian term for Prime Minister that the Bahmani Sultans had introduced in the fourteenth century – controlled Maharashtra and was head of the Confederacy, keeping up an active correspondence with all his regional governors. Bhonsle was in charge of Orissa, Gaekwad controlled Gujarat, Holkar dominated in central India and Scindia was in command of a growing swathe of territory in Rajasthan and north India. The Marathas continued to use Mughal administrative procedures and practices, in most cases making the transition to their rule so smooth it was almost imperceptible.[108]

In the face of ever-growing Maratha power, Mughal regional governors were increasingly left to fend for themselves, and several of these began to behave as if they were indeed independent rulers. In 1724, one of Aurangzeb's favourite generals and most cherished protégés, Chin Qilich Khan, Nizam ul-Mulk, left Delhi without the sanction of the young Emperor Muhammad Shah and set himself up as the regional Governor in the eastern Deccan, defeating the rival Governor appointed by the Emperor and building up his own power base in the city of Hyderabad. A similar process was under way in Avadh – roughly present-day Uttar Pradesh – where power was becoming concentrated in the hands of a Shia Persian immigrant, Nawab Sa'adat Khan, and his Nishapur-born nephew, son-in-law and eventual successor, Safdar Jung. Uncle and nephew became the main power brokers in the north, with their base at Faizabad in the heart of the Ganges plains.[109]

The association of both governors with the imperial court, and their personal loyalty to the Emperor, was increasingly effected on their own terms and in their own interests. They still operated under the carapace of the Mughal state, and used the name of the Emperor to invoke authority, but on the ground their regional governates began to feel more and more like self-governing provinces under their own independent lines of rulers. In the event both men would go on to found dynasties that dominated large areas of India for a hundred years.

The one partial exception to this pattern was Bengal, where the Governor, a former Brahmin slave who had been converted to Islam, Murshid Quli Khan, remained fiercely loyal to the Emperor, and continued annually to send to Delhi half a million sterling of the revenues of that rich province. By the 1720s Bengal was providing most of the revenues of the central government, and to maintain the flow of funds Murshid Quli Khan became notorious for the harshness of his tax-collecting regime. Defaulters among the local gentry would be summoned to the Governor's eponymous new capital, Murshidabad, and there confined without food and drink. In winter, the Governor would order them to be stripped naked and doused with cold water. He then used to 'suspend the zamindars by the heels, and bastinado

[beat] them with a switch'. If this did not do the trick, defaulters would be thrown into a pit 'which was filled with human excrement in such a state of putrefaction as to be full of worms, and the stench was so offensive, that it almost suffocated anyone who came near it … He also used to oblige them to wear long leather drawers, filled with live cats.'[110]

As the country grew increasingly anarchic, Murshid Quli Khan found innovative ways to get the annual tribute to Delhi. No longer did he send caravans of bullion guarded by battalions of armed men: the roads were now too disordered for that. Instead he used the credit networks of a family of Marwari Oswal Jain financiers, originally from Nagaur in Jodhpur state, to whom in 1722 the Emperor had awarded the title the Jagat Seths, the Bankers of the World, as a hereditary distinction. Controlling the minting, collection and transfer of the revenues of the empire's richest province, from their magnificent Murshidabad palace the Jagat Seths exercised influence and power that were second only to the Governor himself, and they soon came to achieve a reputation akin to that of the Rothschilds in nineteenth-century Europe. The historian Ghulam Hussain Khan believed that 'their wealth was such that there is no mentioning it without seeming to exaggerate and to deal in extravagant fables'. A Bengali poet wrote: 'As the Ganges pours its water into the sea by a hundred mouths, so wealth flowed into the treasury of the Seths.'[111] Company commentators were equally dazzled: the historian Robert Orme, who knew Bengal intimately, described the then Jagat Seth as 'the greatest shroff and banker in the known world'.[112] Captain Fenwick, writing on the 'affairs of Bengal in 1747–48', referred to Mahtab Rai Jagat Seth as a 'favourite of the Nabob and a greater Banker than all in Lombard Street [the banking district of the City of London] joined together'.[113]

From an early period, East India Company officials realised that the Jagat Seths were their natural allies in the disordered Indian political scene, and that their interests in most matters coincided. They also took regular and liberal advantage of the Jagat Seths' credit facilities: between 1718 and 1730, the East India Company borrowed on average Rs400,000 annually from the firm.* In time, the alliance, 'based on reciprocity and mutual advantage' of these two financial giants, and the access these

* Over £5 million today.

Marwari bankers gave the EIC to streams of Indian finance, would radically change the course of Indian history.[114]

In the absence of firm Mughal control, the East India Company also realised it could now enforce its will in a way that would have been impossible a generation earlier. Even in the last fraying years of Aurangzeb's reign there had been signs that the Company was becoming less respectful of Mughal authority than it had once been. In 1701, Da'ud Khan, the Governor of the newly conquered Carnatic, complained about the lack of courtesy on the part of the Madras Council who, he said, treated him 'in the most cavalier manner ... They failed to reflect that they had enriched themselves in his country to a most extraordinary degree. He believed that they must have forgotten that he was General over the province of the Carnatic, and that since the fall of the Golconda kingdom they had rendered no account of their administration, good or bad ... Nor had they accounted for the revenues from tobacco, betel, wine et cetera, which reached a considerable sum every year.'[115]

The Company's emissary, Venetian adventurer Niccolao Manucci, who was now living as a doctor in Madras, replied that the EIC had transformed a sandy beach into a flourishing port; if Da'ud Khan was harsh and overtaxed them, the EIC would simply move its operations elsewhere. The losers would be the local weavers and merchants who earned his kingdom lakhs* of pagodas each year through trade with the foreigners. The tactic worked: Da'ud Khan backed off. In this way the EIC prefigured by 300 years the response of many modern corporates when faced with the regulating and taxation demands of the nation state: treat us with indulgence, they whisper, or we take our business elsewhere. It was certainly not the last time a ruler on this coastline would complain, like Da'ud Khan, that the 'hat-wearers had drunk the wine of arrogance'.

Nine years later, the EIC went much further. In response to the seizure of two Englishmen and a short siege by the Mughal Qiladar (fort keeper) of Jinji, the factors of Fort St David, a little to the south of Madras, took up arms. In 1710, they rode out of their fortifications near Cuddalore, broke through Mughal lines and laid waste to fifty-two towns and villages along the Coromandel coast, killing innocent villagers and destroying fields of crops containing thousands of pagodas of rice

* A lakh equals a hundred thousand.

awaiting harvest which, the Governor of Madras proudly reported, 'exasperated the enemy beyond reconciliation'. This was perhaps the first major act of violence by Englishmen against the ordinary people of India. It was two years before the EIC was reconciled with the local Mughal government, through the friendly mediation of the French Governor of Pondicherry. The directors in London approved of the measures taken: 'The natives there and elsewhere in India who have, or shall hear of it, will have a due impression made upon their minds of the English Courage and Conduct, and know that we were able to maintain a War against even so Potent a Prince.'[116]

In Bengal, Murshid Quli Khan had also become disgusted by the rudeness and bullying of the increasingly assertive Company officials in Calcutta and wrote to Delhi to make his feelings plain. 'I am scarce able to recount to you the abominable practices of these people,' he wrote.

> When they first came to this country they petitioned the then government in a humble manner for the liberty to purchase a spot of ground to build a factory house upon, which was no sooner granted but they ran up a strong fort, surrounded it with a ditch which has communication with the river and mounted a great number of guns upon the walls. They have enticed several merchants and others to go and take protection under them and they collect a revenue which amounts to Rs100,000* ... They rob and plunder and carry a great number of the king's subjects of both sexes into slavery.[117]

By this time, however, officials in Delhi were occupied with more serious worries.

Delhi in 1737 had around 2 million inhabitants. Larger than London and Paris combined, it was still the most prosperous and magnificent

---

* Over £1 million today.

city between Ottoman Istanbul and imperial Edo (Tokyo). As the Empire fell apart around it, it hung like an overripe mango, huge and inviting, yet clearly in decay, ready to fall and disintegrate.

Despite growing intrigue, dissension and revolt, the Emperor still ruled from the Red Fort over a vast territory. His court was the school of manners for the whole region, as well as the major centre for the Indo-Islamic arts. Visitors invariably regarded it as the greatest and most sophisticated city in South Asia: 'Shahjahanabad was perfectly brilliant and heavily populated,' wrote the traveller Murtaza Husain, who saw the city in 1731. 'In the evening one could not move one *gaz* [yard] in Chandni Chowk or the Chowk of Sa'adullah Khan because of the great crowds of people.' The courtier and intellectual Anand Ram Mukhlis described the city as being 'like a cage of tumultuous nightingales'.[118] According to the Mughal poet Hatim,

> Delhi is not a city but a rose Garden,
> Even its wastelands are more pleasing than an orchard.
> Shy, beautiful women are the bloom of its bazaars,
> Every corner adorned with greenery and elegant cypress trees.[119]

Ruling this rich, vulnerable empire was the effete Emperor Muhammad Shah – called Rangila, or Colourful, the Merry-Maker. He was an aesthete, much given to wearing ladies' *peshwaz* and shoes embroidered with pearls; he was also a discerning patron of music and painting. It was Muhammad Shah who brought the sitar and the tabla out of the folk milieu and into his court. He also showered his patronage on the Mughal miniature atelier neglected by Aurangzeb and his successors, commissioning bucolic scenes of Mughal court life: the palace Holi celebrations bathed in fabulous washes of red and orange; scenes of the Emperor going hawking along the Yamuna or visiting his walled pleasure gardens; or, more rarely, holding audiences with his ministers amid the flowerbeds and parterres of the Red Fort.[120]

Muhammad Shah somehow managed to survive in power by the simple ruse of giving up any appearance of ruling: in the morning he watched partridge and elephant fights; in the afternoon he was entertained by jugglers, mime artists and conjurors. Politics he wisely left to his advisers and regents; and as his reign progressed, power ebbed gently away from Delhi, as the regional Nawabs began to take their own decisions on all important matters of politics, economics, internal security and self-defence.

'This prince had been kept in the Salim-garh fort, living a soft and effeminate life,' wrote the French traveller and mercenary Jean-Baptiste Gentil, 'and now took the reins of government amid storms of chaos and disorder.'

> He was young and lacked experience and so failed to notice that the imperial diadem he was wearing was none other than the head-band of a sacrificial animal, portending death. Nature lavished on him gentle manners and a peaceful character, but withheld that strength of character necessary in an absolute monarch – all the more necessary at a time when the grandees knew no law other than the survival of the fittest and no rule but that of might is right; and so this unhappy prince became the plaything, one after another, of all those who exercised authority in his name, who recognised that now-empty title, that shadow of a once august name, only when it served to legitimise their unlawful take-over of power. Thus in his reign, they carried out their criminal usurpations, dividing up the spoils of their unfortunate master, after destroying the remnants of his power.[121]

A French eyewitness, Joseph de Volton from Bar-le-Duc, wrote to the French Compagnie des Indes headquarters in Pondicherry giving his impressions of the growing crisis in the capital. According to a digest of his report:

> the poor government of this empire seemed to prepare one for some coming catastrophe; the people were crushed under by the vexations of the grandees ... [Muhammad Shah] is a prince of a spirit so feeble that it bordered on imbecility, solely occupied with his pleasures ... The great Empire has been shaken since some time by diverse rebellions. The Marathas, a people of the Deccan who were at one time tributary, have shaken off the yoke, and they have even had the audacity to penetrate from one end of Hindustan in armed bodies, and to carry out a considerable pillage. The little resistance that they have encountered prefigures the facility with which anyone could seize hold of this Empire.[122]

De Volton was right: as the Maratha armies swept ever further north, even the capital ceased to be secure. On 8 April 1737, a swift-moving warband under the young star commander of the Maratha Confederacy, Baji Rao, raided the outskirts of Agra and two days later appeared at the gates of Delhi, looting and burning the suburban villages of Malcha, Tal Katora, Palam and Mehrauli, where the Marathas made their camp in the shadow of the Qu'tb Minar, the victory tower which marked the arrival of the first Islamic conquerors of India 600 years earlier. The raiders dispersed when news came that Nawab Sa'adat Khan was approaching with his army from Avadh to head them off; but it was nevertheless an unprecedented insult to the Mughals and a blow to both their credibility and self-confidence.[123]

Realising how far things had slipped, the Emperor called for Nizam ul-Mulk to come north to save Delhi: 'the old general had served with distinction under Aurangzeb,' wrote Ghulam Hussain Khan, 'and passed for a wolf that had seen much bad weather, and was much experienced in the ways of the world.'[124] The Nizam obeyed the summons, and gathered an army for the long trek north; but he realised that it was now no easy task to bring the Marathas to heel: 'the resources of the Marathas have doubled since the death of Aurangzeb,' he wrote to the Emperor, 'while the affairs of the Empire, on the contrary, have fallen into disorder. Signs of our decline have become manifest everywhere.'[125] The Mughal accountants would have backed the Nizam on this: by the 1730s the Marathas were collecting 1 million rupees* in tribute from the rich central Indian lands of Malwa alone, funds which were now effectively lost to the Mughals, whose treasury was correspondingly depleted.[126]

The Nizam was right to be apprehensive. On 7 January 1738, Baji Rao's Maratha army surprised the Nizam near Bhopal, encircling and surrounding him. At first, Baji Rao was too intimidated to take on the Nizam's fortified position, but he attacked anyway and, somewhat to the surprise of both sides, defeated the veteran Mughal general. The captive Nizam pledged to get the grant of the governorship of Malwa for Baji Rao, hoping to turn the Maratha poachers into Mughal gamekeepers and co-opt them into the Mughal system.[127] But even as the Nizam was

* £13 million today.

making his way, humiliated, to Delhi, a much more serious threat to the Empire was manifesting itself to the north.

Nader Shah Afshar, born in Persian Khorasan, was the son of a humble shepherd and furrier. He had risen rapidly in the Safavid Persian army due to his remarkable military talents. He was just as tough, ruthless and efficient a figure as Muhammad Shah was artistic and chaotic. The finest pen portrait that survives of Nader was written by an urbane French Jesuit, Père Louis Bazin, who became Nader's personal physician. Bazin both admired and was horrified by the brutal yet commanding man he agreed to take care of: 'In spite of his humble birth, he seemed born for the throne,' wrote the Jesuit. 'Nature had given him all the great qualities that make a hero and even some of those that make a great king':

> His beard, dyed black, was in stark contrast to his hair which had gone completely white; his natural constitution was strong and robust, of tall stature; his complexion was sombre and weather-beaten, with a longish face, an aquiline nose, and a well-shaped mouth but with the lower lip jutting out. He had small piercing eyes with a sharp and penetrating stare; his voice was rough and loud, though he managed to soften it on occasion, as self-interest or caprice demanded ...
>
> He had no fixed abode – his court was his military camp; his palace was a tent, his throne was placed in the middle of weapons, and his closest confidants were his bravest warriors ... Intrepid in combat, he pushed bravery to the limits of rashness, and was always to be found in the midst of danger among his braves, as long as the action lasted ... Yet sordid avarice, and his unheard-of cruelties soon wearied his own people, and the excesses and horrors to which his violent and barbarous character led him made Persia weep and bleed: he was at once admired, feared and execrated ...[128]

In 1732, Nader had seized the Persian throne in a military coup. Shortly afterwards he deposed the last infant Safavid prince, ending 200 years of Safavid rule. Seven years later, in the spring of 1739, he invaded Afghanistan. Even before he had left Isfahan, there were rumours that his real plan was to mount a raid on the treasures of Mughal Delhi, 'to pluck some golden feathers' from the Mughal peacock.[129]

On 21 May, Nader Shah with a force of 80,000 fighting men crossed the border into the Mughal Empire, heading for the summer capital of Kabul, so beginning the first invasion of India for two centuries. The great Bala Hisar of Kabul surrendered at the end of June. Nader Shah then descended the Khyber. Less than three months later, at Karnal, one hundred miles north of Delhi, he defeated three merged Mughal armies – around a million men, some half of whom were fighters – with a relatively small but strictly disciplined force of 150,000 musketeers and Qizilbash horsemen armed with the latest military technology of the day: armour-penetrating, horse-mounted *jazair*, or swivel guns.

Nader Shah's job was certainly made much easier by the increasingly bitter divisions between Muhammad Shah's two principal generals, Sa'adat Khan and Nizam ul-Mulk. Sa'adat Khan arrived late at the Mughal camp, marching in from Avadh long after the Nizam had encamped, but, keen to show off his superior military abilities, decided to ride straight into battle without waiting for his exhausted soldiers to rest. Around noon on 13 February, he marched out of the earthwork defences erected by the Nizam to protect his troops, 'with headlong impetuosity misplaced in a commander', and against the advice of the Nizam, who remained behind, declaring that 'haste is of the devil'.[130] He was right to be cautious: Sa'adat Khan was walking straight into a carefully laid trap.

Nader Shah lured Sa'adat Khan's old-fashioned heavy Mughal cavalry – armoured cuirassiers fighting with long swords – into making a massed frontal charge. As they neared the Persian lines, Nader's light cavalry parted like a curtain, leaving the Mughals facing a long line of mounted musketeers, each of whom was armed with swivel guns. They fired at point-blank range. Within a few minutes, the flower of Mughal chivalry lay dead on the ground. As a Kashmiri observer, Abdul Karim Sharistani, put it, 'the army of Hindustan fought with bravery. But one cannot fight musket balls with arrows.'[131]

Having defeated the Mughals in an initial engagement, Nader Shah then managed to capture the Emperor himself by the simple ruse of inviting him to dinner, then refusing to let him leave.[132] 'Here was an army of a million bold and well-equipped horsemen, held as it were in captivity, and all the resources of the Emperor and his grandees at the disposal of the Persians,' wrote Anand Ram Mukhlis. 'The Mughal monarchy appeared to be at an end.'[133] This was certainly the view of the ambassador of the Marathas, who fled the Mughal camp under cover of darkness and made it back to Delhi by a circuitous route through the jungle, only to leave the same day, heading south as fast as he could. 'God has averted a great danger from me,' he wrote to his masters in Pune, 'and helped me escape with honour. The Mughal empire is at an end, and the Persian has begun.'[134]

On 29 March, a week after Nader Shah's forces had entered the Mughal capital, a newswriter for the Dutch VOC sent a report in which he described Nader Shah's bloody massacre of the people of Delhi: 'the Iranians have behaved like animals,' he wrote. 'At least 100,000 people were killed. Nader Shah gave orders to kill anyone who defended himself. As a result it seemed as if it were raining blood, for the drains were streaming with it.'[135] Ghulam Hussain Khan recorded how, 'In an instant the soldiers getting on the tops of the houses commenced killing, slaughtering and plundering people's property, and carrying away their wives and daughters. Numbers of houses were set on fire and ruined.'[136]

In addition to those killed, many Delhi women were enslaved. The entire quarter around the Jama Masjid was gutted. There was little armed resistance: 'The Persians laid violent hands on everything and everybody; cloth, jewels, dishes of gold and silver were all acceptable spoil,' wrote Anand Ram Mukhlis, who watched the destruction from his rooftop, 'resolving to fight to the death if necessary ... For a long time after, the streets remained strewn with corpses, as the walks of a garden are with dead flowers and leaves. The town was reduced to ashes, and had the appearance of plain consumed with fire. The ruin of its beautiful streets and buildings was such that the labour of years could alone restore the city to its former state of grandeur.'[137] The French Jesuits recorded that fires raged across the city for eight days and destroyed two of their churches.

The massacre continued until the Nizam went bareheaded, his hands tied with his turban, and begged Nader on his knees to spare the inhabitants and instead to take revenge on him. Nader Shah ordered his troops to stop the killing; they obeyed immediately. He did so, however, on the condition that the Nizam would give him 100 crore (1 billion) rupees* before he would agree to leave Delhi. 'The robbing, torture and plundering still continues,' noted a Dutch observer, 'but not, thankfully, the killing.'[138]

---

* £13 billion today.

In the days that followed, the Nizam found himself in the unhappy position of having to loot his own city to pay the promised indemnity. The city was divided into five blocks and vast sums were demanded of each: 'Now commenced the work of spoliation,' remarked Anand Ram Mukhlis, 'watered by the tears of the people ... Not only was their money taken, but whole families were ruined. Many swallowed poison, and others ended their days with the stab of a knife ... In short the accumulated wealth of 348 years changed masters in a moment.'[139]

The Persians could not believe the riches that were offered to them over the next few days. They had simply never seen anything like it. Nader's court historian, Mirza Mahdi Astarabadi, was wide-eyed: 'Within a very few days, the officials entrusted with sequestration of the royal treasuries and workshops finished their appointed tasks,' he wrote. 'There appeared oceans of pearls & coral, and mines full of gems, gold and silver vessels, cups and other items encrusted with precious jewels and other luxurious objects in such vast quantities that accountants and scribes even in their wildest dreams would be unable to encompass them in their accounts and records.'

> Among the sequestered objects was the Peacock Throne whose imperial jewels were unrivalled even by the treasures of ancient kings: in the time of earlier Emperors of India, two crores worth* of jewels were used as encrustation to inlay this throne: the rarest spinels and rubies, the most brilliant diamonds, without parallel in any of the treasure of past or present kings, were transferred to Nader Shah's government treasury. During the period of our sojourn in Delhi, crores of rupees were extracted from the imperial treasuries. The military and landed nobility of the Mughal state, the grandees of the imperial capital, the independent rajas, the wealthy provincial governors – all sent contributions of crores of coined bullion and gems and jewel-encrusted imperial regalia and the rarest vessels as tributary gifts to the royal court of Nader Shah, in such quantities that beggar all description.[140]

Nader never wished to rule India, just to plunder it for resources to fight his real enemies, the Russians and the Ottomans. Fifty-seven days

* £260 million today.

later, he returned to Persia carrying the pick of the treasures the Mughal Empire had amassed over its 200 years of sovereignty and conquest: a caravan of riches that included Jahangir's magnificent Peacock Throne, embedded in which was both the Koh-i-Noor diamond and the great Timur ruby. Nader Shah also took with him the Great Mughal Diamond, reputedly the largest in the world, along with the Koh-i-Noor's slightly larger, pinker 'sister', the Daria-i-Noor, and '700 elephants, 4,000 camels and 12,000 horses carrying wagons all laden with gold, silver and precious stones', worth in total an estimated £87.5 million* in the currency of the time.

In a single swift blow, Nader Shah had broken the Mughal spell. Muhammad Shah Rangila remained on the throne, but, with little remaining credibility or real power, he withdrew from public life, hardly leaving Delhi. As the Mughal historian Warid declared,

> His Majesty, in order to soothe his heart afflicted by sad news, either visited the gardens to look at the newly planted trees, or rode out to hunt in the plains, while the vizier went to assuage his feelings by gazing at the lotuses in some pools situated four leagues from Delhi, where he would spend a month or more in tents, hunting fish in the rivers and deer in the plains. At such times, the Emperor and wazir alike lived in total forgetfulness of the business of the administration, the collection of the revenue, and the needs of the army. No one thought of guarding the realm and protecting the people, while daily the disturbances grew greater.[141]

The old Mughal elite realised that the end was in sight for their entire world. As the poet Hatim wrote:

> Nobles are reduced to the status of grass cutters
> Palace-dwellers do not possess even ruins to give them shelter.
>
> Strange winds seem to blow in Delhi
> The nobles have fled from the cities
>
> Instead owls from the forest have descended on Shahjahanabad,
> And taken up residence in the courtyards of princes.

---

* Around £9,200 million today.

Many observers, like the nobleman Shakir Khan, put the blame on the corruption and decadence of society under Muhammad Shah, and turned to a more austere form of Islam in reaction to the Emperor's careless hedonism: 'At the beginning of this period,' he wrote, 'there was music and drinking, noisy entertainers and crowds of prostitutes, a time of foolery and joking, effeminacy, and chasing after transvestites.'

> All pleasures, whether forbidden or not, were available and the voice of the spiritual authorities grew indistinct, drowned out in the uproar of partying. People got used to vice and forgot to promote what was decent, for the mirrors of their hearts could no longer reflect a virtuous face – so much so, that when the catastrophe happened and society was torn apart, it was no longer capable of being mended.
>
> It soon reached a point where the contents of the private mansions and royal apartments, royal armouries, the royal wardrobe and furniture store, even the pots and pans out of the royal kitchen, the books from the royal library, the instruments from the lodge for royal fanfares and the drum-house, everything from the royal workshops, all were sold to shopkeepers and dealers. Most was used to pay off the arrears of the troops.[142]

This was the moment that the two greatest regional governors, Nizam ul-Mulk and Safdar Jung, ceased to send their tax revenues to Delhi, so worsening the financial crisis of a Mughal state that was now on the verge of complete bankruptcy. The sudden impoverishment of Delhi meant that the administrative and military salaries could no longer be paid, and without fuel, the fire went out of the boiler house of Empire. The regional dynasties of governors consolidated their hold on power, now free from the control of Delhi. In just a few months, the Mughal Empire, built up over 150 years, shattered and fragmented like a mirror thrown from a first-storey window, leaving in its place glinting shards of a mosaic of smaller and more vulnerable successor states.

The days of huge imperial armies, financed by an overflowing treasury, had ended for ever. Instead, as authority disintegrated, everyone took measures for their own protection and India became a decentralised and disjointed but profoundly militarised society. Almost everybody now carried weapons. Almost everybody was potentially a soldier. A military labour market sprang up across Hindustan – one of the most thriving free markets of fighting men anywhere in the world – all up for sale to the highest bidder. Indeed, warfare came to be regarded as a sort of business enterprise.[143] By the end of the eighteenth century, substantial sections of the peasantry were armed and spent part of their year as mercenaries serving in distant locations. Sometimes they moved their family and agricultural bases to take advantage of opportunities for military earnings. Meanwhile, the regional rulers they fought for had to find ways of paying for them and the expensive new armies they needed in order to compete with their rivals. To do this they developed new state instruments of bureaucracy and fiscal reputation, attempting to exercise a much deeper control over commerce and production than the Mughal regime they had replaced.[144]

The most perceptive historian of eighteenth-century India, Ghulam Hussain Khan, could see only horror and anarchy in these developments: 'Then it was,' he wrote, 'that the Sun of Justice and Equity, that had already been verging from the Meridien, inclined downwards, degree by degree, and at last entirely set in the Occident of ignorance, imprudence, violence and civil wars.'

> It is from those times must be dated the sinking of rents, the decrease of husbandry, the distress of the people and their detestation of their Rulers. Nor was anything else thought of, but how to bring money to hand by any means whatever. This and this alone became the utmost ambition of all ranks.
>
> It was in such an enfeebled state of the Empire, that there arose a new sort of men, who so far from setting up patterns of piety and virtue, squandered away the lives and properties of the poor with so much barefacedness, that other men, on beholding their conduct, became bolder and bolder, and practised the worst and ugliest action, without fear or remorse. From those men sprung an infinity of evil-doers, who plague the Indian world, and grind the faces of its wretched inhabitants …
>
> Evils are now arisen to such a height, as render a remedy impossible. It is a consequence of such wretched administrations that every part of India has gone to ruin. So that, comparing the present times with the past, one is apt to think that this world is overwhelmed with darkness.[145]

But what appeared to be the end of an era in Delhi looked quite different in other parts of India, as a century of imperial centralisation gave way to a revival of regional identities and regional governance. Decline and disruption in the heartlands of Hindustan after 1707 was matched by growth and relative prosperity in the Mughal peripheries. Pune and the Maratha hills, flush with loot and overflowing tax revenues, entered their golden age. The Rohilla Afghans, the Sikhs of the Punjab and the Jats of Deeg and Bharatpur all began to carve independent states out of the cadaver of the Mughal Empire, and to assume the mantle of kingship and governance.

For Jaipur, Jodhpur, Udaipur and the other Rajput courts, this was also an age of empowerment and resurgence as they resumed their independence and, free from the tax burdens inherent in bowing to Mughal overlordship, began using their spare revenues to add opulent new palaces to their magnificent forts. In Avadh, the baroque palaces of Faizabad rose to rival those built by the Nizam in Hyderabad to the south. All these cities emerged as centres of literary, artistic and cultural patronage, so blossoming into places of remarkable cultural efflorescence.

Meanwhile, Benares emerged as a major centre of finance and commerce as well as a unique centre of religion, education and pilgrimage. In Bengal, Nadia was the centre of Sanskrit learning and a sophisticated centre for regional architectural and Hindustani musical excellence.

To the south, in Tanjore, a little later, Carnatic music would begin to receive enlightened patronage from the Maratha court that had seized control of that ancient centre of Tamil culture. At the other end of the subcontinent, the Punjab hill states of the Himalayan foothills entered a period of astonishing creativity as small remote mountain kingdoms suddenly blossomed with artists, many of whom had been trained with metropolitan skills in the now-diminished Mughal ateliers, each family of painters competing with and inspiring each other in a manner comparable to the rival city states of Renaissance Italy. In this scenario, Guler and Jasrota stood in for San Gimignano and Urbino, small but wealthy hilltowns ruled by a court with an unusual interest in the arts, patronising and giving refuge to a small group of utterly exceptional artists.

However, the two powers which would make most use of the opportunities presented by the descent of the Mughal heartlands into Anarchy were not Indian at all. In Pondicherry and Madras, two rival

European trading companies, alerted to Mughal weakness and the now deeply divided and fragmented nature of authority in India, began to recruit their own private security forces and to train and give generous wages to locally recruited infantry troops.

As the EIC writer William Bolts later noted, seeing a handful of Persians take Delhi with such ease spurred the Europeans' dreams of conquests and Empire in India. Nader Shah had shown the way.

In the young French settlement of Pondicherry, on the warm, sandy Coromandel coast south of Madras, news of Nader Shah's invasion was being closely followed by the Compagnie des Indes' ambitious and dazzlingly capable new Director General, Joseph-François Dupleix. On 5 January 1739, even before Nader Shah had reached Karnal, Dupleix wrote, 'We are on the eve of a great revolution in this Empire.'

> The weakness of the Mogol government gives ample grounds to believe Nader may very soon be master of this Empire. This revolution if it takes place, can only cause a *grand derangement* to trade. However it can only be advantageous to Europeans.[146]

Dupleix had arrived in India as a young man, and had risen through the ranks as his employer, the French Compagnie des Indes, slowly grew and prospered. For the French had been relatively late to realise the possibilities inherent in trading with India. It was not until 1664 that they had set up a rival to the EIC; eight years later, they had founded Pondicherry, successfully bribing the Marathas to leave it alone on their periodic raids into the Carnatic.

In its first incarnation, the Compagnie lost substantial amounts of money and in 1719 it had to be refounded by the brilliant Lowland Scots financier John Law de Lauriston, who had fled from London to France after a duel and rose to become an adviser to the Regent Orléans. Law combined two small insolvent French Indies companies and raised enough money to make it a going concern. But the Compagnie des

Indes remained permanently underfunded. Unlike the EIC, which was owned by its shareholders, from the beginning the French Compagnie was partially a royal concern, run by aristocrats who, like their king, tended to be more interested in politics than trade; Dupleix was relatively unusual in that he was interested in both.[147]

In 1742, aged nearly fifty, Dupleix moved south from running Chandernagar, the French base in Bengal, to take over as both Governor of Pondicherry and Director General of the Compagnie in India. As one of his first acts he got De Volton, his representative at the Mughal court, to petition the Emperor to make him a Nawab with the rank of 5,000 horse, and to give the French in Pondicherry the right to mint coins. When both wishes were instantly granted, Dupleix began to understand how far Mughal authority had been weakened by Nader Shah's invasion.[148]

He made immediate plans to increase the Compagnie's military capability, and for the first time took the initiative to begin training up locally recruited Tamil-, Malayali- and Telugu-speaking warriors in modern European infantry tactics.[149] By 1746, two regiments of 'cypahes' (sepoys) had been formed, drilled, uniformed, armed and paid in the French manner. As his military commander, Dupleix appointed the talented Charles-Joseph Patissier, Marquis de Bussy, who had just moved from Ile de Bourbon – modern Mauritius – to Pondicherry as military ensign for the French Compagnie. Together the two would take the first steps to entangle the European trading companies in regional post-Mughal politics.

By the time Dupleix arrived in Pondicherry he had already made himself a mercantile fortune, and was keen to add to it. Like many of his British counterparts, he made more money through private trading schemes, often in partnership with Indian traders and moneylenders, than he did from his official salary. He therefore had a strong interest in both Companies remaining neutral as growing Anglo-French rivalry in Europe made war between the two increasingly likely.

France in the 1740s had by far the larger economy, double that of Britain; it also had three times the population and the largest army in Europe. Britain, however, had a much larger navy and was the dominant power on the seas; moreover, since the Glorious Revolution of 1688, it had more advanced financial institutions built with Dutch expertise, and capable of raising large amounts of war finance very quickly. Both sides therefore had reason to believe that they could win a war against the other. Dupleix was keen that none of this should get in the way of his profitable trading operations. Consequently, as soon as news belatedly arrived from Europe that Britain and France had joined the War of Austrian Succession on opposing sides, Dupleix approached his EIC counterpart in Madras, Governor Morse, to assure him that the French in Pondicherry would not be the first aggressors.

Morse would personally have been happy to agree to such a pact of neutrality, but he knew what Dupleix did not: that a Royal Navy squadron had already been despatched eastwards and that it was expected any day. He therefore equivocated and told Dupleix he had no authority to make such a pact. The squadron arrived in February 1745, and promptly attacked and seized a number of French ships, among them one in which Dupleix had a large financial interest.[150]

Dupleix made an attempt to secure compensation from Madras. But after being rebuffed he made the decision to strike back and get redress by force. He summoned a rival squadron from the French naval base at Ile de Bourbon, and sent his chief engineer, a Swiss mercenary named Paradis, to assess the defences of Madras. A month later he wrote to Mauritius that the 'garrison, defences and governor of Madras were, alike, pitiable'. He then set about repairing the walls of Pondicherry with his own funds, while assuring his secretary, Ananda Ranga Pillai, that 'the English Company is bound to die out. It has long been in an impecunious condition ... Mark my words. The truth of them will be brought home to you when you, ere long, find that my prophecy has been realised.'[151]

His reinforcements – around 4,000-strong and including several battalions of highly trained African slave troops and some state-of-the-art siege artillery – arrived in early September. Immediately, Dupleix took the initiative. His new regiments of sepoys and the African and French reinforcements from Mauritius were all sent north on troop transports overnight, supported by eight men-of-war. Landing just to the south of Madras, near St Thomas Mount, they then marched quickly north, moving in to invest the city from the opposite direction to that from which they were expected. In this way they appeared without warning behind the British lines and to the rear of the EIC defences. The siege began on 18 September with such an immense bombardment of mortars that the EIC's nervous chief gunner, Mr Smith, died there and then of a heart attack.

Madras had a garrison of only 300, half of them Indo-Portuguese guards who had no wish to fight and die for their British employers. The other half were an untrained militia of portly, pink-faced British merchants. Within three days, having lost many of his troops to desertion, Governor Morse sought terms. On 20 September, after the loss of only six EIC lives and no French casualties at all, Madras surrendered to the French. Ananda Ranga Pillai gave a rather more colourful version of events in his diaries than the slightly unheroic events perhaps warranted: 'The French,' he wrote, 'hurled themselves against Madras as a lion rushes into a herd of elephants... They captured the Fort, planted their flag on the ramparts, and shone in Madras like the sun which spreads its beams over the whole world.'[152]

The most significant incident in this war, however, took place a month later. The Mughal Nawab of the Carnatic, Anwar ud-Din, was furious with Dupleix for ignoring his orders by attacking Madras without his permission, and then insulting him by refusing to hand over the captured town to his authority. He had no intention of allowing a trading company to defy his rule in this manner, so he sent his son, Mahfuz Khan, with the entire Mughal army of the Carnatic, to punish the French.

On 24 October 1746, on the estuary of the Adyar River, Mahfuz Khan tried to block the passage of 700 French sepoy reinforcements under Paradis. The French beat off an attack by the 10,000 Mughal troopers with the help of sustained musketry, their infantry drawn up in ranks, file-firing and using grapeshot at close quarters in a way that had never before been seen in India. Ananda Ranga Pillai was again an eyewitness. 'M Paradis made a breastwork of Palmyra trees, on the strip of sand next to the sea,' he wrote,

> and formed the soldiers and the sepoys into four divisions. He ordered each to engage a separate body of the enemy. He placed himself at the head of the foremost party. On this, three rockets and four cannon were fired by the Muhammadans. Their contents fell into the river, and caused no damage. The French then opened a volley of musketry on the enemy, killing numbers of them.
>
> The Muhammadans threw down their arms and fled, with dishevelled hair and dress. Some fell dead in the act of flight. The loss thus caused to them was immense. Mafuz Khan also ran on foot, until he reached his elephant, and mounting this, quickly made his escape. He and his troops did not cease their flight until they reached

Kunattur. The rout was general, so much so that not a fly, not a sparrow, not a crow was to be seen in all Mylapore.[153]

Another account – written by the court historian of the Nawabs of the Carnatic – claimed that the French attacked at night and 'since the Nawab's army had not the least suspicion of a night attack, they were unready, so the Mughal army got confused in the darkness'. Whatever the truth, the Battle of Adyar River proved a turning point in Indian history. Only two French sepoys were killed, while Mughal casualties were over 300. For the first time, techniques of eighteenth-century European warfare, developed in Prussia and tested on the battlefields of France and Flanders, had been tried out in India. It was immediately clear that nothing in the Mughal armoury could match their force.

Europeans had long suspected they were superior to the Mughals in tactical prowess, but they had not appreciated how great this advantage had become due to military developments in the previous half-century since 1687 when the pike-wielding Jacobean troops of Sir Josiah Child were quickly overwhelmed by Aurangzeb's Mughal troopers. But the wars of late seventeenth-century Europe had seen rapid development in military tactics, particularly the widespread introduction of flintlock muskets and socket bayonets to replace pikes. The organisation of the infantry into battalions, regiments and brigades made continuous firing and complex battlefield manoeuvres by infantry a possibility. The standard infantry tactic was now a bayonet charge after devastating volley firing, supported by mobile and accurate field artillery. The invention of screws for elevating the guns gave the artillery greater precision and increased the firepower of the foot soldiers, giving them an edge in battle against cavalry. The Battle of Adyar River, the first time these tactics were tried out in India, had shown that a small body of infantry armed with the new flintlock muskets and bayonets, and supported by quick-firing mobile artillery, could now scatter a whole army just as easily as they could in Europe. The lesson was not forgotten. The trained sepoy with his file-firing muskets and hollow squares, and supported by artillery quick-firing grape and canister shot, would be an unstoppable force in Indian warfare for the next century.[154]

Even before witnessing the Battle of Adyar River, Ananda Ranga Pillai had told Dupleix that 1,000 such French soldiers with cannon and mines could conquer all of south India. Dupleix had replied that half that number, and two cannon, would suffice.

In the years that followed, both men would have ample opportunity to test this idea.

In 1749 news came from Europe that the War of the Austrian Succession had ended, and that at the Treaty of Aix-la-Chapelle it had been agreed that Madras should be restored to the EIC.

Peace, however, now proved more elusive: the dogs of war, once let slip, were not easily brought to heel. Rather than disbanding his new sepoy regiments, Dupleix decided to hire them out to his Indian allies, and to use them to gain both land and political influence.

The new Governor of Madras, Charles Floyer, wrote the following year that 'in spite of peace, affairs are more embroiled than ever during the war owing to the artifices of Dupleix, who so hates the English as to be unable to refrain from underhand acts of hostility'.[155] The directors in London agreed that the Company must not again let down its guard: 'Experience has proved that no Regard is paid by the French to the neutrality of the Mogul's Dominions',

> and that were the Country [Mughal] Government willing to protect us, they are not able to do it against the French, who have little to lose, and are prone to violate the Laws of Nations to enrich themselves with plunder … You have orders to make yourselves as secure as you can against the French or any other European Enemy … His Majesty will support the Company in whatever they may think fit to do for their future Security; for though a Peace is now made with France, no one knows how long it may last, and when war breaks out, it is always too late to make Fortifications strong enough to make Defence against an Enterprising Enemy, as happened in Madras.[156]

Soon both the British and the French were intriguing with the different states in the south, covertly offering to sell their military assistance in return for influence, payments or land grants. In 1749, in return for a small trading port, the EIC became involved in its first attempt at what today would be called regime change, taking sides in a succession dispute in the Maratha kingdom of Tanjore. The attempted coup was a miserable failure.

Dupleix, however, had much more success as a military entrepreneur. His clients had to pay for their European weapons and troops in land grants and land revenue collection rights that would enable the French Compagnie to maintain its sepoys and finance its trade from Indian revenues rather than importing bullion from Europe. Dupleix sold his services as a mercenary first to one of the claimants to the throne of the Carnatic, and then, in a much more ambitious move, despatched the Marquis de Bussy to Hyderabad to take sides in the succession crisis that had followed the death of the region's most powerful Mughal overlord, Nizam ul-Mulk, as his sons fought for control of the Nizam's semi-detached fragment of the Mughal Empire. Dupleix was handsomely rewarded for his assistance with a present of £77,500, the high Mughal rank of Mansab of 7,000 horse – the equivalent of a Dukedom in Europe – the rich port of Masulipatnam and a *jagir* (a landed estate) worth £20,000.* Selling the services of his trained and disciplined troops, he soon realised, was an infinitely more profitable business than dealing in cotton textiles.

Dupleix's generalissimo, the Marquis de Bussy, who also made a fortune, could hardly believe the dramatic results his tiny mercenary force achieved as he marched through the Deccan: 'Kings have been placed on the throne with my hands,' he wrote to Dupleix in 1752, 'sustained by my forces, armies have been put to flight, towns taken by assault by a mere handful of my men, peace treaties concluded by my own mediation ... The honour of my nation has been taken to a pinnacle of glory, so that it has been preferred to all the others in Europe, and the interests of the Compagnie taken beyond its hopes and even its desires.'[157]

In reality, however, these were all two-way transactions: weak Indian rulers of fragmented post-Mughal states offered large blocks of territory, or land revenue, to the different European Companies in return for military support. The warfare that followed, which usually involved

---

* The modern equivalences of these sums are: £77,500 = over £8 million today; £20,000 = £2 million today.

very small Company armies, was often incoherent and inconclusive, but it confirmed that the Europeans now had a clear and consistent military edge over Indian cavalry, and that small numbers of them were capable of altering the balance of power in the newly fractured political landscape that had followed the fall of the Mughal Empire.

The Carnatic Wars that rumbled on over the next decade might have had few conclusive or permanent strategic results, but they witnessed the transformation of the character of the two Companies from trading concerns to increasingly belligerent and militarised entities, part-textile exporters, part-pepper traders, part-revenue-collecting land-holding businesses, and now, most profitably of all, state-of-the-art mercenary outfits.

The British observed Dupleix's successes greedily: 'The policy of the Mughals is bad,' wrote one English soldier of fortune, Colonel Mills, 'their army worse; they are without a navy ... the country might be conquered and laid under contribution as easily as the Spaniards overwhelmed the naked Indians of America ...'[158] The new Governor of Madras, Thomas Saunders, agreed: 'The weakness of the Moors is now known,' he wrote, 'and 'tis certain any European nation resolved to war on them with a tolerable force may overrun the whole country.'[159]

Looking back on the Carnatic Wars fifty years later, the urbane Comte de Modave blamed the hubris of his own French compatriots for bringing European rivalries and Anglo-French wars to Indian shores, and, through the pride and vaulting ambition of Dupleix and Bussy, destroying their own chances of a profitable trade.

They did this, he wrote, by forcing their British rivals to throw all their military resources into protecting what had already become far too profitable a trading business to abandon willingly. Writing towards the end of his life, with the benefit of hindsight, the Comte reminisced about where things had gone wrong in the Carnatic half a century earlier. 'The Mughal Empire held together while Aurangzeb reigned,' he wrote, 'and even for some years after he died in the early years of this century.'

For generally beneficial laws have a certain inner strength which allows
them, for a time, to resist the assaults of anarchy. But at last, about
forty years ago, a horrible chaos overtook the Mughal empire: any
spark of good that Aurangzeb had done to promote commerce was
snuffed out. Ruthlessly ambitious Europeans were no less deadly in
these parts, as if Europe and America were too small a theatre of war
for them to devour each other, pursuing chimeras of self-interest, and
undertaking violent and unjust resolutions, they insisted on Asia too
as the stage on which to act out their restless injustices.

The trade of the Mughal Empire was divided at the time between
two national groups, the French and the English; for the Dutch had
by now degenerated into base, avaricious toads squatting on their
heaps of gold and spices, as if in apology for having once grabbed the
empire of the Portuguese, and reducing them to nobodies.

A few passing successes, more apparent than real – for these
came with a series of crushing defeats – dazzled the French and
went to their heads: as if drunk, they now foolishly boasted they
could take over all the trade of India. They were, however, inferior
to the British in naval power, their Company was corrupt and
its leadership grotesquely ignorant, their major undertakings at
sea were all vitiated by causes too easy to guess (and which will
alas endure as long as their monarchy) and therefore always
failing: none of this could puncture their mad hopes of becoming
the dominant power in India. They campaigned complacently, as
if there could be no doubt of their success, and thus, inevitably,
failed to secure what they wanted, and lost even what they might
have kept.

The English were at that time concerned only in developing their
trade from their bases in India, in all security. The administrators of
that Company had never deviated from the fundamental purpose for
which it had been incorporated … It was the ill-judged, scheming
ambitions of the French that roused English jealousy and greed.

For the former, this project of total domination was ruinously
expensive and impossible to achieve, whereas for the latter it was
indeed a tricky undertaking, but one promising great profits. The
French rushed in impetuously, squandering money they could not
afford to replace in mad undertakings; they were met by the English
with implacable steadiness of purpose and constantly replenished

resources, and soon they were working to bring about what we had
dreamed of and waiting for an opportunity to put us out of action,
far from any possibility of causing them any trouble or of challenging
the immense advantages they had secured.[160]

That opportunity manifested itself even as the Carnatic Wars were
grinding to an inconclusive end in the mid-1750s. For it was not just
in India that Anglo-French rivalry was smouldering, ready to reignite
at the slightest spark. Instead the trail of gunpowder which ignited the
next round of Anglo-French conflict began far away from India, on the
frozen borderlands of America and New France – what we today call
Canada – between the great lakes and the headwaters of the Ohio River.

On 21 June 1752, a party of French Indians led by the French
adventurer Charles Langlade, who had a Huron wife and was also
influential among the Seneca, Iroquois and Micmac, led a war party of
240 warriors down Lake Huron, across Lake Erie and into the newly
settled farmlands of British Ohio. Tomahawks at the ready, they fell
on the British settlement of Pickawillany, achieving complete surprise.
Only twenty British settlers managed to muster at the stockade. Of
those, one was later scalped and another ceremonially boiled and the
most delicious parts of his body eaten.[161]

The violent raid spread a sense of instability and even terror among
British traders and settlers as far as New York and Virginia. Within
months, regular French troops, supported by indigenous guides,
auxiliaries and large numbers of Indian warriors were rumoured to
be moving in large numbers into the headwaters of the Ohio Valley,
and on 1 November the Governor of Virginia sent a 21-year-old militia
volunteer north to investigate. His name was George Washington. So
began the first act in what Americans still call the French and Indian
Wars, and which is known in the rest of the world as the Seven Years
War.[162]

This time it would be total war, and properly global, fought on
multiple continents and in ruthless advancement of worldwide British
and French imperial interests. It would carry European arms and
warfare from the Ohio to the Philippines, from Cuba to the coast of
Nigeria, and from the Heights of Abraham outside Quebec to the
marshy flatlands and mango groves of Plassey.

But the part of the globe it would transform most lastingly was India.

An Offer He Could Not Refuse

In early November 1755, an anonymous figure trained a telescope across the wintry estuary of the Scorff and beyond towards the French shipyards at Port Lorient in Brittany. The round sight panned over the wharves and warehouses, past the dry docks and milling quaysides, until finally coming to rest on a flotilla of eleven tall-masted ships – six men-of-war with full battle rigging and five French East Indiamen – all bobbing at anchor, slightly apart from the other shipping, on the seaward edge of the harbour.

The ships were at the centre of a hive of frantic activity: French troops were marching in file over the gangplanks onto the frigates, while wooden dockside cranes slowly swung cannon after cannon aboard. They landed on the quarterdecks, between iron-bound barrels of wine and water, bales of food and pallets loaded with supplies for many months at sea. The observer then began to count the ships, and to note down the supplies and armaments being carried on board, precisely mentioning the different bores of the cannon, the numbers of troops being loaded and carefully assessing how deep in the water each ship was floating.

A neat précis of the resulting intelligence report, written for the attention of the directors of the East India Company, sits today in the vaults of the National Archives of India.[1] For obvious reasons the document does not give the identity of the person who produced the information: it might have been an official in the port, or a merchant from a third country innocently unloading his wares on a neighbouring quayside. But given the detail of the intelligence it contained, and the fact that the writer was able to make enquiries about the destination of the ships and the dates of their probable embarkation, it was unlikely to have been a distant observer out along the coast surveying the port through a spyglass or a passing British privateer risking a trip down the coast south of Brittany, past the heavily guarded French naval bases at Brest and Rochefort and the anchorage of Quiberon Bay in between. The source of the intelligence must have been in the port, amid the milling crowds and embarking marines, carefully observing all the preparations for departure, while casually eliciting information from the sailors, dock workers and warehousemen, perhaps over a glass of brandy in the port's taverns.

Some weeks later, on 13 February 1756, the anxious directors of the East India Company sat in their panelled Council Chamber in Leadenhall Street, carefully studying the report and arguing about its implications. What was clear, they agreed, was that, given the French aggression on America's border, war was now all but inevitable. The flotilla was therefore probably not some stray French Compagnie mission but more likely early evidence of a major French initiative in India. The directors feared that Versailles was now embracing the plan that Dupleix had first dreamed up: the overthrow of the British East India Company and its replacement by its French counterpart. They were also clear that they must not allow this to happen.

After discussing the various options open to them, the directors decided to forward the intelligence to Roger Drake, the Governor of Fort William in Calcutta, to warn him that war was now imminent. There must be no repetition of the loss of Madras a decade earlier. Drake must be vigilant about defence, they warned, as they presumed that the flotilla must be aimed at either Calcutta or Madras, for given 'the present situation of affairs between the British and French nations, it is natural to suppose that the French will aim a blow wherever they can strike the most effectually'.

As our Company may feel the weight of it, especially in Bengal, where the settlement has been deprived of the Military Recruits for some years past, adding to which is the insufficiency of the fortifications at Fort William to defend the settlement against an at all formidable European Force, the Court [of Directors] have thought it necessary to appoint you to take such measures as shall best conduce to the Protection and Preservation of the Company's Estate, Rights and Privileges in Bengal.

They then discussed the details of the intelligence that had just been revealed to them: 'We were informed that [a flotilla of] eleven of the French Company's Ships sailed from Port Lorient about the middle of November, with about three thousand men aboard.'

Six of the largest, being only half-loaded and carrying about sixty guns, of different bores, each intended for a guard of convoy for the other five, which are loaded as usual; these eleven ships, with four that sailed some time before, make already fifteen gone; and it was reported they intended to send some more. But as none were destined for China, it is probable therefore that this armament is intended for the coast of Coromandel or Bengal.

Finally, they delivered precise instructions as to what they now wanted done in response: 'You are to put the settlement in the best posture of defence you can, that you be constantly vigilant, and concert the properest Measures for its Security, in order to which you must claim the assistance of our other Presidencies, whenever you are apprehensive of danger.'

The great point is to render your garrison more respectable, by recruiting it with as many Europeans as will make it fully compleat, which we recommend to your utmost care and attention & effort, in order to which you must press the Select Committee of Fort George [Madras] to cause you to be supplied with as many [troops] as can be spared from thence and Bombay, and you must from time to time acquaint the Commander of His Majesty's Naval and Land forces with your situation and desire their Assistance and Protection whenever it shall appear to be necessary.

We earnestly recommend it to you to take all Prudent Measures you can, to engage your Nabob [the Nawab of Bengal, Aliverdi Khan] to take effectual care to prevent all Hostilities between the subjects of the British and French nations in Bengal, and to preserve Strictest Neutrality in his whole Government. It is so much in his interest that we [protect] ourselves, your applications cannot but be attended with Success, and shall accordingly hope to find the many good effects resulting from such a Pacifick Measure.

Signing off, the directors urged strict confidentiality: 'The most inviolable secrecy must be observed with regard to this information, that it may not, by any means, get to the ears of the French. The Fatal Consequences of a discovery being too obvious to mention. The like secrecy must be observed throughout the whole of your transactions.'[2]

In the event, as is so often the case in dramatic intelligence reports, both ancient and modern, the intelligence turned out to have a fundamental flaw. For all the impressive detail of the report, the flotilla in Port Lorient was not in fact heading to India; indeed no troop-carrying French fleet left for Bengal in 1755, and when one did finally set sail, months later in December 1756, its destination was Pondicherry, not Calcutta.[3] But right or wrong, the report was detailed enough to be credible, and was quickly transmitted from Port Lorient first to London and from there on to Calcutta. On receipt, Governor Drake immediately ordered work to begin on rebuilding and strengthening the city walls, an action explicitly forbidden by the Nawab of Bengal – which in turn quickly set off a chain of events fatal both for the people of Bengal and for the French in India.

Some months before the directors sent the intelligence from Port Lorient to Calcutta, a young politician had been summoned to a meeting in the same East India House Council Chamber. Until a day earlier, this individual had been the MP for a Cornish constituency, a position from which he had just been summarily unseated due to alleged irregularities during the election. The directors did not hesitate to seize their chance. They summoned the thickset, laconic, but fiercely ambitious and unusually forceful young man, and then in formal Council presented Robert Clive with an offer of employment that he could not refuse.

The Company's head office had recently been rebuilt in the current Georgian style, but it was still easily missed by passers-by: flat-fronted and set slightly back from the street behind railings, it was only two storeys tall – significantly lower than the buildings on either side – and a mere five windows wide, an unexpectedly modest structure for what was, after all, now the headquarters of the world's largest, richest and most complex business organisation and which housed a group of directors who exercised political and financial powers second only to the Crown itself.

This anonymity was not accidental. The Company, which had always found it useful to behave with great ostentation in India, had correspondingly found it advantageous to downplay its immense wealth at the London end of its operations. As late as 1621, two decades after its founding, the Company was still operating from the home of Sir Thomas Smythe, its Governor, with a permanent staff of only half a dozen.[4] It was not until 1648 that the Company finally moved to Leadenhall Street, operating from a humble, narrow-fronted house whose first-storey façade was decorated with images of galleons in full sail at sea. In 1698, when a casual passer-by asked who lay within, he was told 'men with deep purses and great designs'.[5]

Soon after East India House was given a Palladian facelift, a Portuguese traveller noted in 1731 that it was 'lately magnificently built, with a stone front to the street; but the front being very narrow, does not make an appearance in any way answerable to the grandeur of the house within, which stands upon a great deal of ground, the offices and storehouses admirably well contrived, and the public hall and committee room scarce inferior to anything of the like nature in the city'.[6] Like so much about the power of the East India Company, the modest appearance of East India House was deeply deceptive.

Inside, beyond the entrance hall, lay the main administrative block: a warren of rooms whose shelves groaned with scrolls, archives, records and registers, and where toiled 300 clerks, notaries and accountants scribbling figures into vast leather-bound ledgers. There were also a number of committee rooms of varying sizes and, grandest of all, the director's boardroom, known as the Council Chamber. Here the most important meetings were held, letters to India drafted, the inward and outward cargoes for the Company's thirty annual sailings discussed, and the sales – which then ran at between £1.25 and £2 million annually – were calculated and evaluated.

From these rooms was run a business that was, by the 1750s, of unprecedented scale and which generated nearly £1 million out of Britain's total £8 million import trade. Sales of tea alone cleared half a million sterling, which represented the import of some 3 million pounds of tea leaves. The rest of the EIC's accounts were made up of sales of saltpetre, silk, gorgeously painted palampores (bed covers) and luxurious Indian cotton cloth, around 30 million square yards of which was now imported annually.[7] The EIC's stock was fixed in 1708 at £3.2 million, a figure which was subscribed to by some 3,000 shareholders, who earned an annual 8 per cent dividend. Every year roughly £1.1 million of EIC stock was bought and sold.[8] The EIC had the deepest of pockets and used this credit to borrow extensively on bond. In 1744, its debts were set at £6 million.* It paid nearly a third of a million pounds annually to the government in customs duties. Two years earlier, in 1754, in return for the loan of 1 million sterling to the government, the EIC's charter had been extended until 1783, so guaranteeing its profitable monopoly on the trade with Asia for at least another thirty years. By eighteenth-century standards, it was an economic giant, the most advanced capitalist organisation in the world.[9]

This was the business whose directors, on 25 March 1755, signed up the thirty-year-old Robert Clive, for the second time. This was something of a surprise to all parties: only eighteen months earlier, Clive had retired from the Company's service having already made in India a substantial fortune by the age of twenty-eight. He had returned to London with the intention of entering politics and quickly used his wealth to buy a rotten borough. Nothing, however, had worked out for him at Westminster: the previous day, Clive 'by a most unusual proceeding', had been ejected from the House of Commons after

---

* The modern equivalences of these sums are: £1.25 and £2 million = £130 million and £210 million today; £1 million = £105 million; £8 million = £840 million; £3.2 millon = £336 million; £1.1 million = £115 million; £6 million = £630 million.

objections had been raised as to the integrity of the election process in his constituency. Following several weeks of wrangling and horse-trading, a series of political shenanigans by the Tories, who were attempting to collapse the Whig government, had managed to unseat Clive by 207 votes to 183.[10] Having spent much of his new fortune trying to bribe his way into getting elected, this left Clive humiliated, unemployed and out of pocket. A second career in India was Clive's best option to restore his fortune, and so set himself up for a second run at Parliament sometime in the future.

The directors had reason to move so quickly. For Clive, who first went out to India as a humble accountant, had proved to have unexpected talents in a quite different sphere. With no military training and no formal commission, and still only in his mid-twenties, the curt, withdrawn and socially awkward young accountant had been the surprise star of the Carnatic Wars, and the man who as much as anyone had prevented Dupleix from realising his dreams of expelling the EIC from India and establishing the French Compagnie in its place. Now that the French war drums were beginning to beat again in North America, and as both Britain and France began frantically rearming and preparing for another round of conflict, the directors were keen to send Clive back to India at the head of the private army of sepoys that Clive himself had helped recruit, drill and lead into battle.

Robert Clive was born on 29 September 1725 at Styche Hall in the Shropshire village of Moreton Say, into a family of minor provincial country gentry. He had quickly gained a reputation as an unusually unruly and violent child: by the age of seven he had become 'out of all measure addicted to fightin'', according to his worried uncle, 'which gives his temper a fierceness and imperiousness, so that he flies out upon every trifling occasion … I do what I can,' he added, 'to suppress the hero, that I may help forward the more valuable qualities of meekness, benevolence and patience.'[11] The uncle's efforts were entirely in vain: meekness, benevolence and patience remained qualities which eluded Clive throughout his life. Instead, soon after hitting puberty, he had turned village delinquent, running protection rackets around Market Drayton, 'now levying blackmail on anxious shopkeepers trembling for the security of their windows; now turning his body into a temporary dam across the street gutter to flood the shop of an offending tradesman'.[12]

By the time Clive turned seventeen, his father Richard recognised that his son was too morose and difficult for the Church, and far too hot-headed and impatient for the law. Luckily, Richard Clive happened to know a director of the EIC. Robert presented himself at East India House for the first time on 15 December 1742, where he was formally admitted to the most junior rank of 'Writer'. Three months later, on 10 March 1743, he took ship for India.

It was not a very brilliant start. En route, Clive lost much of his baggage off Brazil, then managed to fall overboard and narrowly avoided drowning; he was only spotted by a sailor entirely by chance, fished out and saved. On arrival in Madras he made little impression: unknown, unremarkable and without the necessary introductions, he led a solitary life, occasionally quarrelling with his fellow writers and getting into fights. 'Dour, aloof and withdrawn', on one occasion he behaved so badly to the Secretary at Fort St George that the Governor made him formally apologise. He was lonely, homesick and miserable. Before long he had developed a profound hatred for India that never left him. 'I have not enjoyed one happy day since I left my native country,' he wrote home at the end of his first year, as he gradually sank into a deep depression. Within a year, in the absence of any better outlet, he turned his innate violence on himself and attempted suicide.

None of his letters from Madras contain a word about the wonders of India, and he gives no hint of the sights he saw; nor does he seem to have made any attempt to learn the languages. He had no interest in the country, no eye for its beauty, no inquisitiveness about its history, religions and ancient civilisations, and not the slightest curiosity about its people whom he dismissed as universally 'indolent, luxurious, ignorant and cowardly'.[13] 'I think only of my dear Native England,' he wrote home in 1745. What he did have, from the beginning, was a streetfighter's eye for sizing up an opponent, a talent at seizing the opportunities presented by happenchance, a willingness to take great risks and a breathtaking audacity. He was also blessed with a reckless bravery; and, when he chose to exercise it, a dark personal magnetism that gave him power over men.

It was only during the French attack and conquest of Madras in 1746 that Clive's talents became apparent. He was in Madras when Dupleix's forces took the town. Refusing to give his word that he would not bear arms against the French, he slipped out of the town at night, in disguise, managed to dodge French patrols and made it on foot to the other, smaller British stronghold on the Coromandel coast, Fort St David. Here he was trained to fight by Stringer Lawrence, a bluff, portly John Bull, known as 'the Old Cock', who had seen action against the French at Fontenoy and Bonnie Prince Charlie's Jacobites on Culloden Moor. The two terse and plain-spoken men worked well together, and Lawrence was the first to spot Clive's potential. By the time Dupleix began leasing out his sepoy regiments to his client Nawabs in the late 1740s, Clive was showing promise in what he called 'the military sphere', steadily rising in the ranks to become the lieutenant of a Company of Foot, and demonstrating the aggressive chutzpah and a willingness to take risks that would distinguish him throughout his life.

It was at this point, under the tutelage of Stringer Lawrence, that the Madras authorities began to imitate the French initiative and for the first time started training up their own sepoys – at first mainly Telugu-speakers – and drilling them to fight in infantry formations, supported by mobile European field artillery. For many years, the sepoys numbered only a few hundred and did not even have proper uniforms; what fighting they did was initially tentative and amateurish: 'How very ignorant we were of the art of war in those days,' wrote Clive in the mid-1750s, looking back at his performance in the early years of the Carnatic Wars.

On 26 August 1751, Clive first made his name when he volunteered to march through torrential monsoon rains to relieve the siege of Arcot, the capital of the Nawabs of the Carnatic, with only a small force of 200 Europeans and 300 sepoys. Clive surprised the French and their allies by attacking in the middle of a thunderstorm, and soon raised the Nawab's Mughal colours from the gates. His victory gave the first indication that the Company could manage a successful military campaign in India, either against Indian troops, who had until then often defeated them, or against the French, who only a few years before had been the first to demonstrate the possibilities of modern infantry and field artillery techniques over Indian cavalry armies. It was a crucial moment in the rising confidence of the Company in India.[14]

Professional military pundits sniffed at the amateur soldier and carped that they 'envied him for his good luck but could not admire him for his knowledge of the military art'.[15] But Clive's record of success spoke for itself. The use of speed and surprise was to remain his favourite strategy as a soldier. War in eighteenth-century India was often a slow, gentlemanly and formal affair, as much a sophisticated chess game as an act of aggression: bribes and negotiation usually played a more important role than formal assaults; armies could be bought off, or generals turned and made to break with their paymasters. Clive was happy to play these games when it suited him, but as often as not broke with these conventions, attacking when least expected and with as much ruthlessness and offensive force as possible, making forced marches in monsoon rains, laying down unexpected ambushes and attacking at night or in thick fog.

Clive's greatest success came in 1752 when he beat off a threatened attack on Madras. He and Stringer Lawrence then went on the offensive and managed to win a series of small engagements around the Carnatic, securing Arcot and Trichinopoly for the British and their tame Nawab, Muhammad Ali. The French began to run out of money and failed to pay their Indian troops.[16] On 13 June 1752, the French commander, Jacques Law, a nephew of the founder of the French Compagnie, surrendered to Clive and Lawrence outside the magnificent island temple of Srirangam, the ancient centre of Tamil Vaishnavism. Seven hundred and eighty-five French and 2,000 Compagnie sepoys were made prisoners of war.

It was a crushing blow to Dupleix's ambitions: according to his secretary, Ananda Ranga Pillai, when he heard the news Dupleix 'could neither attend mass nor eat his dinner'. Soon afterwards, Dupleix was sacked, arrested and sent back to France in disgrace.[17] Clive, in contrast, returned to Madras a hero. In a letter of congratulation, Clive's father urged him quickly to gather what wealth he could in India: 'As your conduct and bravery is become the publick talk of the nation,' he wrote, 'this is the time to increase your fortune, [and to] make use of the present opportunity before you quit the Country.'[18] Clive needed no encouragement. As a reward for his success he was given the lucrative position of Quartermaster in the Commissary, a post which earned him the huge sum of £40,000* in commissions in a very short period.

On 18 February 1753 Clive impulsively married the formidable Margaret Maskelyne, sister of Nevil, the Astronomer Royal, in St Mary's,

---

* Over £4 million today.

Fort St George.* The following month, on 23 March, the couple set sail for England on the *Bombay Castle*. They had no wish ever to return to India. On his arrival in London, Clive quickly paid off his family debts – his father Richard allegedly commented, 'So Bob's not a boobie after all' – and spent large sums trying to enter Parliament. But despite successfully buying a Cornish rotten borough, his political career was quickly wrecked on the shoals of inter-party intrigue, and after only eighteen months he found that he needed to return and make a second fortune in India.

With a major French offensive thought to be imminent, his services were badly needed. Reflecting his odd position, strung between the Company's Civil and Military services, Clive rejoined in the senior position of Deputy Governor of Madras, and was also given a military rank in the army: a local commission as a royal lieutenant colonel, effective only in India.[19] Egged on by the Company, ministers had now become alarmed at the level of force the French were building up in India and the fact that the British could not begin to match it. This was a matter of personal concern for many MPs, as a large number had invested their savings in East India stock.[†] Lord Holderness, the government minister who took the closest interest in India, told his colleague Lord Albemarle that the British government must never accept 'a decisive superiority of force in the hands of the French in that part of the world'. The decision was soon made to send out a squadron of Royal Navy warships under Admiral Watson to support the EIC's own private army, along with some regular British army troops in order to match the regiment believed to have been sent by

* The Reverend Nevil Maskelyne was, of course, the villain of Dava Sobel's bestseller *Longitude: The Story of a Lone Genius Who Solved the Greatest Scientific Problem of His Time*, London, 1995. Here Maskelyne is painted, as one critic put it, as 'a dull but jealous and snobbish Cambridge-trained cleric, whose elitism and privileging of astronomy over mechanical inventiveness prejudice him against the Yorkshire-born and Lincolnshire-bred [hero of the book, John] Harrison. He is jealous, petty and obstructive, putting potential personal gain over disinterested judgement.'

† As well as generous stock dividends, the other very valuable thing that the directors and the servants in India had to offer was, of course, patronage: that is, appointments to lucrative places in India for the connections of politicians. This was another major reason for MPs to rally around the EIC and send the fleets of the Royal Navy and regiments of British army troops to protect it.

the French.[20] Clive followed it a month later in a separate flotilla. In his pocket was a Royal Commission to take charge of the troops on arrival in India.

It was an entirely random set of political circumstances that wrecked Clive's ultimate ambition to become a politician, destroying his fortune and forcing him back into the arms of the Company. But it was a piece of happenchance that had immense and wide-ranging repercussions. It was Clive's particular qualities of extreme aggression and devil-may-care audacity that drove the events of the next few months, and which directly led to one of the oddest events in world history: a trading company based in one small building in the City of London defeating, usurping and seizing power from the once-mighty Mughal Empire.

'Calcutta,' wrote Clive a few years later, 'is one of the most wicked places in the Universe ... Rapacious and Luxurious beyond conception.'[21]

In September 1755, as Clive's ship, the *Stretham*, neared India, the British bridgehead in Bengal was unrecognisable from the muddy trading station founded by Job Charnock only sixty years earlier. Charnock's daughter-in-law was still living in Calcutta, but there was very little else that the town's founder would now recognise.[22]

Since Charnock's death, Calcutta had quickly grown to become the jewel among the Company's overseas trading stations: it was by far the EIC's most important trading post in India and the major source of British textile imports. Indeed, 60 per cent of all EIC exports from Asia were now passing through Calcutta.[23] To pay for these exports, the EIC sent out annually to Bengal £180,000,* 74 per cent of it in the form of gold and silver bullion.[24]

As a result of these huge flows of cash, the city had been transformed: its fortifications, wharves and honeycomb of warehouses now straggled three miles down the silt banks of the river, towards the jungles of

---

* Nearly £19 million today.

the Sunderbans, its flat skyline dominated by the low ramparts of Fort William, and a number of grand new 'Grecian' buildings: Roger Drake's Governor's House, a school, the playhouse, St Anne's Protestant church, St Nazareth for the Armenians, a hospital, the jail, the grand tank for the drinking water and an increasingly well-stocked burial ground for the dead.

Calcutta probably now contained around 200,000 people – though some wilder estimates put the figure at almost double that – of whom around a thousand were Europeans. The city's docks were as busy and bustling as its bazaars, and twice as many ships now visited it every year as docked at its Mughal rival, Hughli, a little upstream. The Calcutta punch houses were always full of captains and their crews of boatswains, mates and pilots, drinking away their sorrows before heading to Calcutta's notorious brothels.

Set back from the riverfront, the European houses in Calcutta were usually large, comfortable and airy buildings, painted bright white, with wide verandas, stable blocks and large gardens. Even at the best of times, town planning was never one of Calcutta's more obvious virtues: Mrs Jemima Kindersley thought the city looked 'as awkward a place as can be conceived, and so irregular that it looks as if all the houses had been thrown up in the air, and fallen down again by accident as they now stand: people keep constantly building; and everyone who can procure a piece of ground to build a house upon consults his own taste and convenience, without any regard to the beauty or regularity of the town'.[25] Chaotic it may have been, but it was also extremely prosperous.

The profits from Calcutta's trade were huge and still growing, but what really attracted Indians to this foreign-owned Company town was the sense that it was safe and secure. Throughout the 1740s, while the Carnatic Wars were raging in the south, the Marathas had attacked Bengal with horrifying violence, killing what the Dutch VOC chief in Bengal estimated to be as many as 400,000 civilians.[26] In 1750, Bhaskar Pandit, a general of the Maratha leader Bhonsle, invaded Bengal again, this time with 20,000 cavalry. They carried out night raids, pillaging the Nawab's camp, and destroyed the convoys which brought provisions for his army. The Marathas followed a scorched-earth policy, burning the neighbouring villages to prevent grain from reaching the enemy. The Nawab's soldiers were thus denied food, conveyance and their own baggage, and so rendered ineffective, something the Company factors graphically described in their letters home.[27] Vaneshwar Vidyalankar, the Pandit of the Maharaja of Bardwan, wrote that the Marathas 'are niggard of pity, slayers of pregnant women and infants, of Brahmans and the poor, fierce of spirit, expert in robbing the property of everyone and committing every sinful act. They created a local cataclysm and caused the extirpation of the people of Bengal villages like an [ominous] comet.'[28]

The Bengali poet Ganga Ram in his *Maharashta Purana* gave a fuller picture of the terror they inspired. 'The people on earth were filled with sin,' he wrote, 'and there was no worship of Rama and Krishna. Day and night people took their pleasure with the wives of others.' Finally, he wrote, Shiva ordered Nandi to enter the body of the Maratha king Shahu. 'Let him send his agents, that sinners and evil doers be punished.'[29] Soon after:

> The Bargis [Marathas] began to plunder the villages and all the people fled in terror. Brahmin pandits fled, taking with them loads of manuscripts; goldsmiths fled with the scales and weights; and fishermen with their nets and lines – all fled. The people fled in all directions; who could count their numbers?
>
> All who lived in villages fled when they heard the name of the Bargis. Ladies of good family, who had never before set a foot on a road fled from the Bargis with baskets on their heads. And land owning Rajputs, who had gained their wealth with the sword, threw down their swords and fled. And sadhus and monks fled, riding on litters, their bearers carrying their baggage on their shoulders; and many farmers fled, their seed for next year's crops on the backs of their bullocks, and ploughs on their shoulders. And pregnant women, all but unable to walk, began their labour on the road and were delivered there.
>
> There were some people who stood in the road and asked of all who passed where the Bargis were. Everyone replied – I have not seen them with my own eyes. But seeing everyone flees, I flee also.
>
> Then suddenly the Bargis swept down with a great shout and surrounded the people in their fields. They snatched away gold and silver, rejecting everything else. Of some people they cut off the hand, of some the nose and ears; some they killed outright. They dragged away the most beautiful women, who tried to flee, and tied ropes to their fingers and necks. When one had finished with a

woman, another took her, while the raped women screamed for help. The Bargis after committing all foul, sinful and bestial acts, let these women go.

After looting in the fields, they entered the villages and set fire to the houses. Bungalows, thatched cottages and temples, they burned them all, large and small. They destroyed whole villages and roamed about on all sides plundering. They bound some people, with their hands behind their backs, others they threw to the ground and while they were on their backs on the ground, kicked them with shoes. They constantly shouted, 'Give us rupees, give us rupees, give us rupees.' When they got no rupees, they filled their victims' nostrils with water, or drowned them in tanks. When they demanded money and it was not given to them, they would put a man to death … Bungalows, thatched-roofed houses, Vishnu-*mandapas*, they burned them all, large and small … Every Brahman or Vaishnava or *sannyasi* whom they saw they killed, and they slaughtered cows and women by the hundreds.[30]

What was a nightmare for Bengal turned out to be a major opportunity for the Company. Against artillery and cities defended by the trained musketeers of the European powers, the Maratha cavalry was ineffective.[31] Calcutta in particular was protected by a deep defensive ditch especially dug by the Company to keep the Maratha cavalry at bay, and displaced Bengalis now poured over it into the town that they believed offered better protection than any other in the region, more than tripling the size of Calcutta in a decade. According to a Kashmiri soldier named Abdul Karim, who visited Bengal during this period, the Marathas made a point of not attacking any of the different European strongholds along the Hooghly: 'The European soldiers are superior to those of any other country,' he wrote, 'of which the Marathas are so sensible that although Calcutta abounds with all kinds of Europe merchandise, and it has no fortifications, whilst the number of European inhabitants is but inconsiderable, and the Marathas swarm like ants or locusts, they have never made any attempt upon that quarter, from the dread that Europeans would unite their forces for mutual defence. The Europeans excel in the use of cannon and muskets.'[32]

Among the refugees were those who would go on to found some of the city's most illustrious dynasties such as Nabakrishna Deb and

Ramdulal Dey.[33] But it was not just the protection of a fortification that was the attraction. Already Calcutta had become a haven of private enterprise, drawing in not just Bengali textile merchants and moneylenders, but also Parsis, Gujaratis and Marwari entrepreneurs and business houses who found it a safe and sheltered environment in which to make their fortunes.[34] This large Indian population also included many wealthy merchants who simply wanted to live out of the reach of the Nawab's taxation net. Others took advantage of the protection of the British fleet to make trading expeditions to Persia, the Gulf and eastwards through the Strait of Malacca to China.[35] The city's legal system, and the availability of a framework of English commercial law and formal commercial contracts, enforceable by the state, all contributed to making it increasingly the destination of choice for merchants and bankers from across Asia.[36]

As a result, by 1756 the city had a fabulously diverse and polyglot population: as well as Bengalis, and Hindu and Jain Marwari bankers, there were Portuguese, Armenians, Persians, Germans, Swedes and Dutch, some – judging by an early census – with sophisticated and sometimes bizarre skills: watch- and clockmakers, painters, pastry cooks, goldsmiths, undertakers and wig fabricators.

The Black Town – the Indian section of Calcutta, with its countless temples and mosques and bustling vegetable markets – was even more chaotic, dirty and swampy than the White Town. Nevertheless, visitors from other parts of Asia wrote of the settlement with great admiration. According to one Persian traveller, a learned Sayyid named Abdul Lateef Shushtari, 'Calcutta has replaced Hoogly which is now frequented only by Dutch ships. [White Town] contains many 2–3 storey houses of stone or brick and stucco, painted and coloured like marble.'

Houses stand on the road and allow passers-by to see what is happening inside; at night camphor candles are burned in upper and lower rooms, which is a beautiful sight. There is no fear of robbers nor highwaymen, no one challenges you where you are going nor where you have come from; all the time, big ships come from Europe and China and the New World filled with precious goods and fine cloths, so that velvets and satins, porcelains and glassware have become commonplace. In the harbour at Calcutta there are constantly over

1000 large and small ships at anchor, and the captains fire cannons to signal arrival or departure ...[37]

Whatever their many vices, wrote Shushtari, the English welcomed and rewarded talent: 'the English have no arbitrary dismissal,' he noted, 'and every competent person keeps his job until he writes his own request for retirement or resignation. More remarkable still is that they take part in most of the festivals and ceremonies of Muslims and Hindus, mixing with the people. They pay great respect to accomplished scholars of whatever sect.'

Intermarriage, he wrote, was common, though the Indian women who took European partners were, he maintained, rarely respectable: 'The women of people with no future, of corrupt Muslims, of evil Hindus, who of their own desire enter into the bonds of wedlock with the English, they do not interfere with their religion nor compel them to leave purdah veiling; when any son born of the union reaches the age of 4, he is taken from his mother and sent to England to be educated.'

The Englishmen shave their beards and moustaches, and twist hair into pig-tails. They scatter a white powder to make their hair look white, both men and women do this, to lessen the difference between old and young. Neither men nor women remove pubic hair, accounting comely to leave it in its natural state. And indeed, most European women have no body-hair, and even if it does occur, it is wine-coloured, soft and extremely fine.

By reason of women going unveiled, and the mixed education of boys and girls in one school-house, it is quite the thing to fall in love, and both men and women have a passion for poetry and compose love poems. I have heard that well-born girls sometimes fall in love with low-born youths and are covered in scandal which neither threats nor punishment can control, so their fathers are obliged to drive them out of the house. The streets are full of innumerable such once-well-bred girls sitting on the pavements.

Brothels are advertised with pictures of prostitutes hung at the door, the price of one night written up with the furnishings required for revelry ... As a result of the number of prostitutes, *atashak* [gonorrhoea] – a severe venereal disease causing a swelling of the scrotum and testicles – affects people of all classes. It spreads from

one to another, healthy and infected mixed together, no one holding
back – and this is the state of even the Muslims in these parts![38]

Shushtari was not alone in being suspicious of Calcutta's rakish English
inhabitants. They had come east with just one idea: to amass a fortune
in the quickest possible time, and most had little interest in either the
mores of the country they were engaged in trade with, or indeed in the
social niceties of that which they had left behind. The many Company
servants and soldiers who arrived annually in Calcutta – typically,
penniless younger sons of provincial landed families, Scots who had lost
their estates or their fortunes (or both) in the Jacobite 1745 uprising,
squaddies recruited from the streets of the East End, down-at-heel
Anglo-Irish landowners and clergymen's sons – were all prepared to
risk their lives and travel thousands of miles to the impossible climate
of Bengal's undrained marsh and steaming jungle, hazarding what was
very probably an early death for one reason: if you survived there was
no better place in the world to make your fortune.

For Calcutta was a city where great wealth could be accumulated in a
matter of months, then lost in minutes in a wager or at the whist table.
Death, from disease or excess, was a commonplace, and two-thirds of
the Company servants who came out never made it back – fewer still
in the Company's army, where 25 per cent of European soldiers died
each year.[39] The constant presence of mortality made men callous: they
would mourn briefly for some perished friend, then bid drunkenly
for his effects – his horses and buggies, his inlaid ivory Vizagapatam
furniture, even his Bengali *bibis*.[40] This meant the city tended to be full
of young men: Roger Drake, for example was only thirty when he was
appointed Governor.

Most found that Calcutta was an expensive town to live in: keeping a
decent house in Bengal at this time cost around £1,000 per annum* and
almost all of Calcutta's European inhabitants were to some extent in
debt to Indian moneylenders.[41] On 3 January 1754, a young Scot, Stair
Dalrymple, fresh from North Berwick, wrote home to his MP father Sir
Hew that, 'everything here is double the price it is at home. With the
best economy in the world it is impossible but to be extravagant. No
sooner did I arrive here than my ears were stain'd with this melancholy

---

* £105,000 today.

truth, of which I have been told by all the Gentlemen in the place. Nothing is what you imagined it to be ... I have built many castles in the air.' With 'good economy' he thought he might be able to make his annual salary pay for six months' living expenses. Earlier he had written, 'I expect to be here fifteen or twenty years at least. In that time I may be made Governour. If not that, I may make a fortune which will make me live like a gentleman.'[42]

Amid all these frantic attempts at money-making, Drake's Calcutta Council had forgotten one major consideration: the importance of maintaining the city's defences. The fort walls were visibly crumbling, the guns rusting and new buildings had encroached on all sides of the battlements, in several cases looking down over the fortifications. Moreover, there was only a very limited militia to call up in case of attack: around 260 soldiers and officers, only one-quarter of whom were actually British – the rest were Portuguese, Italian, Swiss and Scandinavian mercenaries. The experiments made in Madras during the Carnatic Wars of training up the local warrior castes as sepoys had not yet been introduced to Bengal. As Captain David Renny reported, 'Calcutta is as deficient of military stores, as it is of soldiers':

> we have no good gun carriages. There are neither small arms nor cartouch boxes enough for the militia ... The Company wrote out by the *Delawar* last year, to put the place in a better state of defence, but they were not in cash for such works, there was no proper Engineer, and tho money if wanted could be borrow'd, yet that is what our Company is extremely averse to. Ammunition is in the utmost bad order, no Cartridges of any kind ready: the small quantity of Grape[shot] in store, had lyen by so long, that it was destroy'd by the Worms; no shells filled nor Fuses prepared for small or great ... We have but a small quantity of [gun] powder, and the greatest part of that damp.[43]

The French were well aware of these weaknesses. Jean Law, the brother of Jacques who was defeated by Clive in the Carnatic Wars, was the director of the French factory at Kasimbazar, the commercial centre on the southern edge of the Bengali capital, Murshidabad. He wrote how Calcutta's 'fort was small, and rather badly constructed and without a moat. Its walls are overlooked by many houses and its garrison was ... far too few to defend it.'[44]

In London, the directors were also anxiously aware of this obvious
vulnerability, and as war with France loomed ever closer they sent out
an additional fifty-nine cannon to Calcutta, and again advised the
Council to begin work on strengthening fortifications immediately. In
1756 they wrote to ask Drake whether any work had been completed in
upgrading the defences, urging that he quickly make whatever repairs
were necessary, ideally with the approval of the Nawab, Aliverdi Khan,
'or at least with such connivance of the Nawab's officers as you shall
judge effectual as their consent'. It was not just the French threat that
concerned them. 'The death of the Nawab is an event that may on
account of his great age be daily expected and it is highly probable that
it may be attended with great confusion and troubles in the province
before another can be securely seated; we therefore recommend to
you whenever it happens, to take all prudent measures to preserve our
possessions, effects and privileges.'[45]

It was some weeks later in 1756 that the repairs and rebuilding
actually began, and Drake ignored his instructions to seek the Nawab's
permission, having been advised by William Watts, who ran the English
factory of Kasimbazar, that 'it is far from being certain that he [Aliverdi]
will take any notice of our making Calcutta defensible ... though we
may be assured that his previous leave [to make repairs] could not be
obtained without a considerable sum of money. Your Honour should
therefore determine to set about fortifying without applying for leave.'[46]

But the Nawab's intelligence service was more efficient than either
Drake or Watts realised. Within days, the old Nawab, Aliverdi Khan,
had received a full account of Drake's repair programme and summoned
his grandson and heir apparent to discuss the proper response to this
attempt to subvert Mughal authority by these impudent merchants.
The grandson's name was Siraj ud-Daula.

The city of Murshidabad, the capital of late Mughal Bengal, lay
three days' sailing from Calcutta up the Bhagirathi, one of the two
headstreams of the Ganges.

Along with the great weaving centre of Dhaka, it was one of two cities in Bengal that in 1756 was still substantially larger than Calcutta; indeed, according to some estimates its population was roughly comparable to that of London. From it, Nawab Aliverdi Khan ran what was by far the richest province of the Mughal Empire, though how far that empire still existed in more than name in 1756 was now a matter of debate. The Nawab had ceased to send the annual revenue payments to Delhi after the onset of the Maratha invasions in the 1740s, and although those invasions had now ceased the revenue payments to Delhi had not resumed.

Aliverdi Khan, who was of mixed Arab and Afshar Turkman stock, had come to power in 1740 in a military coup financed and masterminded by the immensely powerful Jagat Seth bankers, who controlled the finances of Bengal. The Jagat Seths could make or break anyone in Bengal, including the ruler, and their political instincts were usually as sharp as their financial ones. In this case, as so often, the Seths had chosen their man well: Aliverdi proved to be a popular and cultured ruler; he was also an extremely capable one. It was his bravery, persistence and military genius which had succeeded in keeping the Maratha invasions at bay, something few other Mughal generals had ever succeeded in doing. He managed this partly by simple military efficiency, but also by ruthless cunning: in 1744, he lured Bhaskar Pandit and his Maratha officers into negotiations, and used the occasion to have his Afghan general, Mustafa Khan, assassinate the entire Maratha leadership in the tent where the peace negotiations were to take place.

In Murshidabad, Aliverdi Khan created a strong and dazzling Shia court culture, and a stable political, economic and political centre which was a rare island of calm and prosperity amid the anarchy of Mughal decline. Many talented Mughal émigrés – soldiers, administrators, singers, dancers and painters – migrated here from the increasingly turbulent and violent streets of Shahjahanabad. As a result, under Aliverdi's rule Murshidabad became one of the great centres of the late Mughal arts.[47]

The celebrated Delhi artists Dip Chand and Nidha Mal led an émigré painting atelier where the Murshidabad court artists soon developed an instantly recognisable regional style, with the wide expanse of the Ganges invariably running smoothly in the background. Many of these images displayed a wonderful new naturalism that rejoiced in bustling riverside village landscapes full of temples and mosques, shaded by mango and kadambar groves, while farmers with ploughs and traders with scales wandered past, bowing to dreadlocked, tiger-skin-clad holy men. To one side passed nobles on caparisoned elephants and princes in palanquins. All the while, up and down a riverbank dotted with the tall fans of Palmyra palms, fishing canoes and Company sloops slipped past the gorgeously gilt and sickle-shaped royal Murshidabad harem barges as they plied their way across the Bhagirathi to the Mughal gardens of Khushbagh.[48]

In one of these court miniatures, painted no later than 1755, Aliverdi's son-in-law Shahamat Jang enjoys an intimate musical performance by a troupe of hereditary musicians, or *kalawants*, from Delhi, who were clearly regarded as prize acquisitions because they are all named and distinctively portrayed. Seated waiting to sing on the other side of the hall are four exquisitely beautiful Delhi courtesans, again all individually named.[49]

Among the many who emigrated from the ruined streets of Delhi at this time was the Nawab's cousin, the brilliant young Mughal historian Ghulam Hussain Khan, for whom Aliverdi Khan was a great hero. In the *Seir Mutaqherin*, or *Review of Modern Times*, his great history of eighteenth-century India, by far the most revealing Indian source for the period, Ghulam Hussain paints an attractive portrait of a cat-loving epicure who loved to fill his evenings with good food, books and stories: 'His attention was so intensely given to maintaining the peace and security of his subjects, and of the farmers especially, that none of them can be said to have been so much at ease on their father's knees or their mother's lap':

> He understood the arts, was fond of exquisite performances, and never failed to show his regard to the artistes, knowing how to reward those who excelled in the arts. Fond of the pastime of witty conversation, he was himself excellent company; so far as to be equalled by hardly any of his contemporaries. A prudent, keen general and a valorous soldier, there are hardly any virtues or qualifications he did not possess ...
>
> Aliverdi himself never smoked, but he drank coffee and it was distributed around ... [After his morning's work was done] he amused himself for a full hour with conversation, with hearing verses, reading poetry or listening to some pleasing story; to which we must add some occasional orders which he would give about

[a recipe for] some dish or other, which was always dressed in his presence, to the care of which was appointed some person freshly come from Persia or any other country renowned for good cookery; for he was fond of good eating, and had a very delicate taste.

Sometimes he ordered the meat, spice, and other necessities to be brought in his presence, and he gave orders to his cooks, often directing them, sometimes inventing some new method of proceeding ... After dinner, he retired to his bedroom to take a nap, at which time the story-tellers and bed watchmen attended and did their office.[50]

Aliverdi's other great passion was white Persian cats, and the French and English in Bengal competed to find him the most beautiful specimens from around the world, a present always guaranteed to win them favour.[51] Aliverdi had occasionally pressed the European Companies for substantial contributions to the defence of Bengal against the Marathas, much to their displeasure; but in general they appreciated the peace and prosperity safeguarded by his strong rule. He in turn was aware of the wealth and other benefits that the trading companies brought to his realm: 'merchants are the kingdom's benefactors,' he believed, 'their imports and exports are an advantage to all men.'[52]

On one occasion Aliverdi Khan told his elderly general, Mir Jafar Khan, that the Europeans were like a hive of bees, 'of whose honey you might reap benefit, but if you disturbed their hive they would sting you to death'.[53] He advised his generals not to antagonise them: 'What wrong have the English done me that I should wish them ill?' He told one headstrong Afghan officer: 'Look at yonder plain covered with grass; should you set fire to it, there would be no stopping its progress; and who is the man then that shall put out the fire that shall break forth at sea, and from thence come upon land? Beware of lending an ear to such proposals again, for they will produce nothing but evil.'[54]

In retrospect, Bengalis came to remember the last years of Aliverdi Khan as a golden age, which all subsequent epochs failed to match: the country was rich and flourishing – Bengal's revenues had risen by 40 per cent since the 1720s – and one single market near Murshidabad was said alone to handle 650,000 tons of rice annually.[55] The region's export products – sugar, opium and indigo, as well as the textiles produced by its 1 million weavers – were desired all over the world, and, since the defeat of the Marathas, the state enjoyed a period of great peace. In 1753, an Englishman wrote that merchants could send bullion from one end of Bengal to another 'under the care frequently of one, two or three peons only'.[56] For Ghulam Hussain Khan, as for many members of the court, there was only one cloud on the horizon: Aliverdi Khan's grandson and heir apparent, Siraj ud-Daula.

Not one of the many sources for the period – Persian, Bengali, Mughal, French, Dutch or English – has a good word to say about Siraj: according to Jean Law, who was his political ally, 'His reputation was the worst imaginable.'

This young man of average height, aged about 24 or 25 years old … was noted for indulgence in all kinds of debauchery and for his revolting cruelty. The women of the Gentiles [Hindus] are in the habit of bathing in the Ganges. Siraj was informed by his henchmen of those who were of some beauty. He would send his henchmen in small boats to carry them off while they were still in the water. He had been seen many times, when the river was in flood, to intentionally ram the ferry boats to jolt them, or make them spring a leak, in order to experience the cruel pleasure of frightening a hundred or more people – men, women and children – many of whom would not know how to swim and would be certain to perish by drowning.

If it was necessary to get rid of some minister or noble, Siraj would volunteer his services. Aliverdi Khan, who could not bear to hear the cries of those being executed, would in the meantime retire to some garden or house outside the city. People trembled at the mere mention of his name. Such was the dread he inspired … This thoughtless young man had no real talent for government. He ruled only by inspiring fear, but at the same time he was known to be the most cowardly of men.

He was by nature rash, but lacking in courage, was stubborn and irresolute. He was quick to take offence, even at the most minor infractions, and sometimes for no apparent reasons. He displayed all the fluctuations which a tumult of opposed passions can produce in a weak temperament, was treacherous at heart, rather than in spirit, without faith or trust in anyone, and with no regard for the oaths which he swore and violated with equal facility. The only excuse that can be offered in his favour was that, ever since his infancy, the prospect of sovereignty had always been held out to the young man. With scant education, he learned no lessons that could have taught him the value of obedience.[57]

The most damning portrait of him, however, was painted by his own cousin, Ghulam Hussain Khan, who had been part of his staff and was profoundly shocked by the man he depicts as a serial bisexual rapist and psychopath: 'His character was a mix of ignorance and profligacy,' he wrote. 'The grandees and commanders had already conceived a dislike to the prince on account of his levity, his harsh language and the hardness of his heart':

This Prince ... made a sport of sacrificing to his lust almost every person of either sex to which he took a fancy, or else he converted them without scruple into so many objects of the malignity of his temper, or the frolics of his inconsiderate youth ... He neglected and daily insulted those ancient commanders that had served so faithfully and so bravely Aliverdi Khan, so that intimidated now by his grandson's character and foul language, they did not dare to open their mouths, or even take breath in his presence. Most of them, shocked at the dishonourable expressions made use of in speaking to them, and incensed at the insolence of the upstarts that had taken possession of his mind, were so far from offering advice upon the posture of affairs that they were generally ill-intentioned and wished to see his downfall, while he made it a point not to ask anyone's opinions.

As for himself, Siraj was ignorant of the world, and incapable of taking a reasonable line of action, being totally destitute of sense and penetration, and yet having a head so obscured with the smoke of ignorance, and so giddy and intoxicated with the fumes of youth and power and dominion, that he knew no distinction between good and bad, nor betwixt vice and virtue. His imprudence was so great that, in the middle of a military expedition, he would set daggers in the hearts of his bravest and ablest commanders by his harsh language, and his choleric disposition. Such usage naturally rendered them regardless, and utterly neglectful ... In time he became as hated as Pharaoh. People on meeting him by chance used to say, *God save us from him!*[58]

Siraj's most serious error was to alienate the great bankers of Bengal, the Jagat Seths. The Seths' machinations had brought Aliverdi to power, and anyone who wanted to operate in the region did well to cultivate their favour; but Siraj did the opposite to the two men of the family who were now in charge of the banking house, Mahtab Rai, the current holder of the title Jagat Seth, and Swaroop Chand, his first cousin, who had been accorded the title 'Maharaja' by Aliverdi Khan. In the early days of his rule, when he wished to arm and equip a force to take on his cousin in Purnea, Siraj ordered the bankers to provide Rs30,000,000;* when Mahtab Rai said it was impossible, Siraj struck him.[59] According to Ghulam Hussain Khan, 'Jagat Seth, the principal citizen of the capital, whom he had often used with slight and derision, and whom he had mortally affronted by sometimes threatening him with circumcision, was in his heart totally alienated and lost [to Siraj's regime].'[60] It was an easily avoided mistake, and one that he would later come to regret.

Yet for all this, Siraj had a strange hold on his grandfather. The old man had had no sons of his own, only three daughters, and after the death from smallpox of his only other grandson, Siraj's elder brother, all his hopes rested on the survivor. The two men could not be more different: Aliverdi Khan was wise and disciplined, while his grandson was an ignorant debauchee; yet still Aliverdi's love knew no bounds. According to Ghulam Hussain Khan, even when Siraj had revolted against Aliverdi in 1750 and seized the town of Patna, the fond grandfather had insisted on forgiving him, writing to him 'in the terms of an impassionate lover, who has supplicated the favour of his shewing once more that beloved face of his to an alienated old man, whose sole delight in his old age centred in that enjoyment'.[61]

For some time there was hope that Aliverdi Khan might see sense and appoint as successor his generous and popular son-in-law, Nawazish Khan, who was married to his eldest daughter, Ghasiti Begum, and who according to the consensus of the court would have been the perfect choice; but instead, in 1754, Siraj was formally named his heir.

By 1755, this had become a matter of real concern, for it was clear to everyone that the eighty-year-old Nawab, stricken with dropsy, was nearing the end. The Company was especially anxious about this as they had failed to cultivate Siraj and instead concentrated on befriending Nawazish Khan

* £390 million today.

and his wife, who Siraj had now come to hate. The French, in contrast, had played their cards more cleverly and Jean Law hoped that this might give them a distinct advantage in Bengal when Aliverdi finally died. The English were 'convinced by the violence of Siraj's character, and the hatred which he inspired, that he would never become Subedar.'

> They never approached him, nor had they ever petitioned for his assistance in their affairs. On the contrary they had avoided all communication with him. It was well known that on several occasions they had refused him entry to their factory at Kassimbazaar, and their houses in the countryside. Siraj ud-Daula, rowdy and ignorant, was known to smash furniture, if it pleased him, and carry off whatever caught his fancy. But Siraj was incapable of forgetting any injury or slight which he might have received. So long before the death of Aliverdi Khan, it was well known that Siraj ud-Daula was annoyed with the English.
>
> On the other hand, he was rather partial towards us [the French]. As it was in our interest to humour him gently, we had always received him at our factory with a thousand courtesies, far more than he merited, and we sought his intervention in all important matters. This was achieved by sending him presents from time to time. This helped in maintaining cordial relations between us.[62]

In March 1756, Aliverdi Khan's health worsened markedly, and he lay half paralysed with a severe attack of dropsy. It was around this time that the old Nawab received a report from visitors from the Mughal south of how the Europeans had behaved in the Carnatic Wars five years earlier. In particular he had been told about the way they had turned from being useful tools in the hands of the Mughal Nawabs of the Carnatic to overmighty puppet masters, creating and discarding rival rulers at their whim. The news 'made a great impression on his mind,' wrote Ghulam Hussain Khan, 'for he knew with how sparing a hand Providence had bestowed on Siraj ud-Daula his share of knowledge and prudence; and he was full sensible of the manner in which he would govern and on what bad terms he already was with the military officers and how prone he seemed to be to fall out with the English of Calcutta. He used to assure in full company that as soon as he should be dead, and Siraj ud-Daula succeed him, the hat-men would possess themselves of all the shores of India.'[63]

So when reports came in, shortly afterwards, that the EIC had been caught red-handed making unauthorised repairs, and in some places completely rebuilding the walls of Calcutta, Aliverdi summoned Siraj and determined to write to both the English and the French, telling them both to dismantle their fortifications completely. The French sent back a tactful reply, and by distributing bribes to the Mughal officials at Chandernagar were able to get around knocking down their substantial new walls. But Governor Drake, whose fortifications were in reality much more modest, only managed to make matters worse by writing back to the Nawab what was taken to be an insolent and defiant reply, questioning the ability of the Nawab to protect his subjects and suggesting that the English were preparing to carry into Bengal their wars against the French that had already wreaked so much havoc in the Carnatic: 'We cannot think of submitting to a demand of so unprecedented a nature,' wrote Drake.

> For this century past we have traded in his [the Nawab's] dominions, and have been protected and encouraged by the several subahs, always have paid obedience to their orders, that it gave us concern to observe that some enemies had advised his Excellency, without regard to truth, that we were erecting new fortifications ... He must have been acquainted of the great loss our Company sustained by the capture of Madras by the French, that there was an appearance of a war between our nations, that, therefore, we were repairing our walls which were in danger of being carried away by the river [floods], and that we were not otherwise erecting new works.[64]

In response, Aliverdi turned one last time to diplomacy, and sent as his agent Narayan Singh, who he tasked with talking Drake into proper obedience and to explain to him the place and status of merchants in a Mughal kingdom, and to outline the consequences if the Company were to continue defying his will.

The old Nawab's final days were spent watching cockfights and giving advice to his grandson to follow where possible the path of conciliation: 'As the prosperity of the state depends on union and cooperation,' he said, 'and its ruin on quarrel and opposition, if your rule is to be based on agreement and obedience, it is necessary that you should remain firm in following my manners and ways, so that to the end of your life you will remain safe from the dominance of your enemies. But if you take the path of quarrel and hostility, it is very likely that this state will so decline from its good name that for a long period grief and regret will prevail.'[65]

Aliverdi Khan died on 9 April 1756, at 5 a.m. He was buried that day, next to his mother in the Khushbagh. That same evening Siraj ud-Daula attacked the palace of his aunt Ghasiti Begum, killed or disarmed her household troops and seized all her money and jewellery.

The following month, on 22 May, Siraj was marching towards Purnea with thousands of men and 500 elephants to attack a cousin he saw as another potential rival, when he met his grandfather's agent, Narayan Singh, who was returning from his mission to Calcutta angry and humiliated. He told the new Nawab that Drake had had him seized and expelled from the city without so much as an audience. ' "What honour is left to us," he asked, "when a few traders, who have not yet learned to wash their bottoms, reply to a ruler's order by expelling the envoy?" Siraj ud-Daula, on hearing such words, with a vast force, turned back and in one night's march came and alighted at the back of the English factory at Kasimbazar.'[66]

The EIC factory closed its gates and primed the cannon on the battlements with grapeshot; for several days there was a standoff, with the factory first blockaded then besieged, and the factors divided on whether to offer military resistance with the few troops and limited weaponry they had at hand, or to meekly submit to Siraj ud-Daula. Initially, there were only 300 Mughal cavalry ringing the factory, but every day the number of troops increased until, on 3 June, Siraj appeared in person with a body of troops that the anxious factors estimated at 30,000.[67] They in contrast numbered only 200. Eventually, William Watts, the Chief Factor, after receiving advice from various friends in the Bengal court that the Nawab would be magnanimous if offered unconditional surrender, decided upon the latter course.

According to an English eyewitness report, 'Upon Mr Watts' going before the Nabob, with his hands across and a handkerchief wrapt round his wrists, signifying himself his slave and prisoner, he [Siraj] abused him very much.'[68] Watts was made to hug the Nawab's feet, and cry: '*Tomar ghulam, tomar Ghulam*' – 'I am your slave, your slave.'

Upon opening the Factory gates, the enemy immediately entered in great numbers, and demanded the keys of the godowns [warehouses] both publick and private; they no sooner took possession of the arms and ammunition, but they behaved in a most insolent manner, threatening the gentlemen to cut off their ears, slit their noses and chabuck [whip] them, with other punishments, in order to extort compliance from them … Then he [Siraj] ordered all the Europeans out of the Factory, and put them under a strong guard. All the prisoners were sent to Murshidabad Cutcherry [gaol], and put in irons, where they remained.[69]

Among those captured, plundered and shackled was a young, 24-year-old apprentice factor named Warren Hastings. The commander of the surrendered garrison, Lieutenant Elliott, rather than endure such insults, humiliation and imprisonment, chose instead to blow out his own brains.[70]

On 28 May, during the middle of the siege, Siraj ud-Daula had sent off an Armenian intermediary to Calcutta with a last series of demands for Drake, telling him, 'if the English are contented to remain in my country they must submit to having their forts razed, their ditches filled in, and trade upon the same terms as they did in the time of Nawab Murshid Quli Khan; otherwise I will expel them entirely out of the provinces of which I am Subah [Governor] … I am fully determined to reduce that nation to the above mentioned conditions …'[71] What Siraj wanted was for the British to behave as the Armenians had done for centuries: to trade in the province as a subject merchant community, relying not on their own fortifications but on the protection of the Mughal governor.

Drake did not even bother to reply, so the day after the surrender of Kasimbazar factory, Siraj ud-Daula marched off with his army, now 70,000-strong, to conquer Calcutta, and bring its overmighty merchants to heel.

As Siraj ud-Daula was marching south to exert his authority on the Company, 1,000 miles inland another young Mughal prince, also in his early thirties and whose destiny would also be fatally entangled with that of Clive and the Company, was trying to exert his authority in the

The first subscription list of 101 well-fleeced London names gathered by 'Auditor Smythe' for 'the voiag to the Easte Indes', on 22 September 1599, two days before the first public meeting at the Founder's Hall, Moorgate Fields.

Sir Thomas 'Auditor' Smythe, the founder of the East India Company, in 1616.

Sir James Lancaster, who commanded the Company's first voyage in 1601, shown five years earlier, on his return from his first disastrous voyage east.

Sir Thomas Roe, the ambassador of James I who led Britain's first official diplomatic mission to India in 1615.

Jahangir as the Millennial Sultan Preferring the Company of Sufis, by Bichitr. Jahangir is sitting enthroned with the halo of majesty glowing so brightly behind him that one of the putti has to shield his eyes from his radiance; another pair of putti are writing a banner reading 'Allah-o Akbar! Oh king, may your age endure a thousand years!' The Emperor turns to hand a Quran to a sufi, spurning the outstretched hands of the Ottoman Sultan. James I, meanwhile, is relegated to the bottom corner of the frame, below Jahangir's feet, and only just above Bichitr's own self-portrait. The King shown in a three-quarter profile – an angle reserved in Mughal miniatures for the minor characters – with a look of vinegary sullenness on his face at his lowly place in the Mughal hierarchy.

New East India House, the East India Company headquarters in London's Leadenhall Street, after its early eighteenth-century Palladian facelift. A Portuguese traveller noted in 1731 that it was 'lately magnificently built, with a stone front to the street; but the front being very narrow, does not make an appearance in any way answerable to the grandeur of the house within'. Like so much about the power of the East India Company, the modest appearance of East India House was deeply deceptive.

East India Company ships at Deptford, 1660.

Headquarters of the Dutch East India Company at Hughli by Hendrik van Schuylenburgh, 1665.

Fort William, Calcutta, by George Lambert and Samuel Scott, 1731.

The severe and puritanical Mughal Emperor Alamgir Aurangzeb, whose overly ambitious conquest of the Deccan first brought Mughal dominions to their widest extent, then led to the eventual collapse of the Empire, painted c. 1653.

Below is his nemesis, the Maratha warlord Shivaji Bhonsle, shown at the end of his life c. 1680. Shivaji built forts, created a navy and raided deep into Mughal territory. He was crowned *Chhatrapati*, or Lord of the Umbrella, at two successive coronation ceremonies at his remote stronghold of Raigad in 1674.

The Persian warlord Nader Shah was the son of a humble shepherd and furrier. He rose rapidly in the Safavid army due to his remarkable military talents, before deciding to take over the Kingdom and then 'pluck some golden feathers from the Mughal peacock'.

Nader Shah with the effete aesthete Emperor Muhammad Shah Rangila, whom the Persian relieved of his entire treasury, including the Peacock Throne, into which was embedded the great Koh-i-Noor diamond. The sudden impoverishment of Delhi after Nader's departure meant that the administrative and military salaries could no longer be paid, and, without fuel, the fire went out of the boiler house of Empire.

A Mughal prince, probably the young Shah Alam, on the terrace of the Red Fort being entertained by dancing girls, c. 1745, just after the time of Nader's Shah invasion.

Aerial view down over the Red Fort, c. 1770.

A Leisurely Ride, by Nainsukh. In the aftermath of the fall of Mughal Delhi, the imperial artists fanned out across the Empire, and elegant masterpieces such as this began to be painted in courts as remote as Guler and Jasrota in the Himalayan foothills.

Europeans Besiege a City. As Mughal authority disintegrated, everyone took measures for their own protection and India became a decentralised and disjointed but profoundly militarised society. European mercenaries were much in demand for their military skills, especially as artillerymen.

A scene at a Murshidabad shrine.

Above the Hughli near Murshidabad.

The palaces of Faizabad.

Aliverdi Khan came to power in 1740 in Bengal in a military coup financed by the powerful Jagat Seth bankers. A cat-loving epicure who loved to fill his evenings with good food, books and stories, after defeating the Marathas he created in Murshidabad a stable political, economic and political centre which was a rare island of prosperity amid the anarchy of Mughal decline.

Above, Aliverdi Khan is shown hawking, and below, a little older, he awards a turban jewel, or *sarpeche*, the Mughal badge of office, to his nephew, while his grandson, Siraj ud-Daula, looks on.

Left and right: Siraj ud-Daula with his women. 'This prince made a sport of sacrificing to his lust almost every person of either sex to which he took a fancy,' wrote his cousin, the historian Ghulam Hussain Khan.

Aliverdi's son-in-law, Shahmat Jang, enjoys an intimate musical performance by a troupe of hereditary musicians, or *kalawants*, from Delhi. These were clearly regarded as prize acquisitions because they are all named and distinctively portrayed. Seated waiting to sing on the other side of the hall are four exquisitely beautiful Delhi courtesans, again all individually named.

Siraj ud-Daula rides off to war.

The brilliant historian Ghulam Hussain Khan. The Nawab's cousin was among the many who emigrated from the ruined streets of Delhi at this time. His *Seir Mutaqherin, or Review of Modern Times*, his great history of eighteenth-century India, is by far the most revealing Indian source for the period.

Robert Clive in command at
the Battle of Plassey, 1757.

Mir Jafar Khan was an
uneducated Arab soldier of
fortune who had played his
part in many of Aliverdi's most
crucial victories against the
Marathas, and led the successful
attack on Calcutta for Siraj
ud-Daula in 1756. He joined the
conspiracy hatched by the Jagat
Seths to replace Siraj ud-Daula,
and found himself the puppet
ruler of Bengal at the whim of
the East India Company. Robert
Clive rightly described him as 'a
prince of little capacity'.

The Young Robert Clive, c. 1764, one year before Buxar. Laconic, but fiercely ambitious and unusually forceful, he was a violent but extremely capable leader of the Company and its military forces in India. He had a streetfighter's eye for sizing up an opponent, a talent at seizing the opportunities presented by happenchance and a willingness to take great risks.

Jat stronghold of Hansi, some hundred miles to the west of Delhi. The prince, an affable and humane intellectual and litterateur, 'good to the point of weakness', according to the Comte de Modave, was not really cut out for a punitive expedition, and his passage was marked by rather less success than that of the ruthless and bloodthirsty Siraj ud-Daula.[72]

Prince Ali Gauhar, Shah Alam, was a tall, handsome, well-built man gifted with all the charm, sensitivity and learning that Siraj ud-Daula lacked. He was no soldier, but he was an exceptional poet in several languages; it was in this field, rather than in the arts of war, that his interests lay, even though he was personally renowned as courageous in battle and a fine swordsman.

Jean Law, who wrote so scathingly of Siraj ud-Daula, came close to describing the young Shah Alam as a perfect prince: 'He is above average height with attractive features, but a surprisingly dark complexion,' he wrote.

> The Shahzada has had the best education and has benefited greatly from it. All that I observed seemed favourable. He is well versed in the Oriental tongues, and in history. He is familiar with the Arabic, Persian, Turki and Hindustani languages. He loves reading and never passes a day without employing some hours in it ... He is of an enquiring mind, naturally gay and free in his private society, where he frequently admits his principal military officers in whom he has confidence. I have often had this honour.[73]

It was the Prince's ill fate that he was born during an era when naked aggression and brute force seemed to yield more reliable results than either charm or conciliation. As he put it himself,

> through the perfidiousness of the nobility and vassals, this anarchy has arisen, and everyone proclaims himself a sovereign in his own place, and they are at variance with one another, the strong prevailing over the weak ... His Majesty's sacred heart is exceedingly disturbed to reflect that if he does not vindicate the honour of his own family and Empire, it will lessen his dignity in the eyes of those who follow appearances alone ... In this age of delusion and deceit, His Majesty places no dependence on the services or professions of loyalty of anyone.[74]

Since the dramatic contraction of the Empire during the reign of Muhammad Shah Rangila two decades earlier, the hinterlands of Shahjahanabad had succumbed to a feral, dog-eat-dog disorder, where every village was now a self-sufficient, fortified republic, at war with its neighbours. As the Mughals gave little or no assistance to these village republics in times of trouble and invasion, the villagers saw no reason to pay their taxes. The prince's job, according to the *Shah Alam Nama*, was 'to chastise those villainous Rajas who had stepped outside of the pale of obedience and those Zamindars who, out of the darkness of their hearts, had turned rebellious, so that they should be reprimanded and brought in line'.[75] It did not work out quite like that. When the prince tried to get Hansi to submit and pay its dues, the townsmen merely shut their gates, then attacked and robbed his camp under cover of darkness.

Shah Alam had been born in the Red Fort, a grandson of the Emperor Bahadur Shah I. He was brought up and educated in the prince's 'cage' – the salatin quarters of the Red Fort where the princes were raised in some comfort, but with no freedom to leave their prison. He was only twelve when Nader Shah rode into Delhi and looted the Mughals of almost all their treasures; and he grew up constantly aware of what his dynasty had lost to the Persians, Afghans and Marathas, and the urgent need to rebuild. But in 1753, rather than coming together and fighting back, the Mughals had destroyed themselves yet again in a new civil war which brought to a close any foreseeable hope of an imperial recovery.

Following a court conspiracy against him, the Vizier Safdar Jung, Nawab of Avadh, had battled it out in the streets of Delhi with his former protégé, the sixteen-year-old Imad ul-Mulk, the teenage megalomaniac grandson of Nizam ul-Mulk. The civil war between the old vizier and his teenage replacement raged across the suburbs of the city for six months, from March to November, with the old and new cities of Delhi held by rival factions. The fighting reduced the space between them to ruins. The poet Sauda wrote that the danger of assault was now always present in Delhi so that even in the middle of Shahjahanabad, men would go out fully armed in the evening to *mushairas* [poetry recitals] as though they were heading into battle: 'See the perverted justice of the age!' he wrote. 'The wolves roam free: the shepherds are in chains.'[76]

The new vizier had been brought up by his puritan father, Ghazi ud-Din, with great strictness and austerity, spending his days under the care of tutors and mullahs, and on the Friday Muslim Sabbath with the company of only eunuchs. He was never allowed to mix with children of his own age or attend performances by musicians and dancing girls. The result was precocious intellectual achievement; but this was undermined by unbounded ambition and profound amorality that led to his turning on all who helped him, starting with his patron Safdar Jung.

The latter had earlier intervened to save Imad's family estates on the death of his father and had him appointed at the age of sixteen to the important court position of imperial paymaster.[77] 'To all appearances, the young Imad ul-Mulk was a handsome young man with a charming and amiable manner,' wrote Jean Law. 'Safdar Jung regarded him like his own son and could scarcely have imagined he was actually nursing a serpent at his breast.'

> His natural charm and talent enabled him to achieve complete domination over the mind of the Emperor ... and he had absolutely no scruples with respect to honour when it was a question of attaining his objective and was quite ready to sacrifice his benefactor ... His conduct was marked only by an extreme cunning and revolting cruelty. He is always seen with a rosary in his hands, but his apparent piety was like that of Aurangzeb – nothing but sheer hypocrisy. Piety is most to be feared when it is carried to excess. Barely confirmed in his appointment as Vizier, he now plotted against all who had served him best.[78]

Safdar Jung's Old Delhi stronghold – the area around Purana Qila – was looted and destroyed, never to recover. According to Ghulam Hussain Khan, 'Old Delhi, which used to be even wealthier and more populous than the new city, Shahjahanabad, was plundered and sacked so thoroughly that an infinity of people lost their consorts and children, and were totally ruined, besides numbers that were massacred.'[79] Eventually he had no option but to retreat back to Avadh. Safdar Jung never recovered, and 'his shock and grief at his fall sent him to an early grave' less than a year later.[80]

Having successfully conspired to bring down his first benefactor, Safdar Jung, at the tender age of sixteen, at seventeen Imad ul-Mulk decided to depose his other great patron, the Emperor himself. Emperor Ahmad Shah Gurgani and his mother, the Qudsia Begum, were found hiding in the garden in front of the Rang Mahal of the Red Fort. They were both thrown into prison, and Imad ul-Mulk had their eyes slit with hot needles. In Ahmad Shah's place, Imad ul-Mulk chose as his puppet the 55-year-old Alamgir II, who had no experience of government and who he knew he could control. From the beginning Alamgir was, as Law put it, 'more slave than king'.[81]

So it was at the age of twenty-six that Shah Alam, the eldest son of Alamgir II, suddenly found himself freed from the salatin 'cage' and appointed the heir apparent of the crumbling Empire. He was given the titles Ali Gauhar and Shah Alam, Exalted of Lineage, Lord of the World, and forced to take an interest in politics as well as his first and most personal passion of poetics. But it was still literature that lay at the heart of his world. Under the pen name 'Aftab', the prince became a prolific and respected author in Urdu, Persian, Punjabi and especially Braj Bhasha, in which language he wrote copious, passionate odes to Lord Krishna, Shiva and to goddesses Kali and Sarasvati; many of his works were later gathered at his own request in a *diwan* (collection) he entitled the *Nadirat-i-Shahi*. He also later composed a *dastan* romance entitled the *Aja'ib al-Qasas*.[82] Shah Alam was a Sufi by inclination. In contrast to his father, the Emperor Alamgir II, a strict puritan who followed the narrow path of the new Emperor Aurangzeb, Shah Alam believed that God could be found not in the rituals of the mosque, but in all the wonders of God's creation:

> Don't waste your time in the mosque and the Ka'ba, oh Mullah,
> Go and search for the footprints of the divine beloved everywhere.

Throughout his life, Shah Alam was a particular devotee of the great Sufi Qu'tb ud-Din Baktiar Khaki, whose shrine was in the middle of the Mughal monsoon resort of Mehrauli. Steeped in Sufi literature and thought, his verses often make the link between the earthly fecundity of the monsoon, the season of joy, love and longing, and the Sufi spirituality of his favourite saint. His favourite *raag*, or musical mode, was the now lost monsoon *raag*, Raag Gaund, which was designed to be sung in the rains and to evoke its many pleasures:

> Oh the season for meeting my dear has come!
> The frog, peafowl, and cuckoo are calling; the koyal is crying.

The rains and the waters, the thunder roars and the clouds gather,
now our eyes are longing to drink
The lightning flashes and shakes my very life; my dear, how will you
sleep?[83]
The great beauty of the green earth pleases, and the clouds circle
all around
This pauper makes his pilgrimage to beg a boon of lord Qu'tb
ud-Din.[84]

Yet amid these Sufi reveries, the prince was becoming increasingly fearful of the very man who had just brought his father to power. The Vizier Imad ul-Mulk, nearly a decade his junior, made no secret of his jealousy of the handsome Crown Prince: according to the *Shah Alam Nama*, Imad ul-Mulk, 'whose heart was full of malice and deceit, could never tolerate anybody else enjoying success. The immense popularity of the Prince was not something that he countenanced with any pleasure. In fact, it displeased him greatly. He set about scheming and plotting. His evil ways caused a discord in the whole realm. The thorn of his tyranny created mayhem in the garden of the kingdom and his dark soul brought desolation in the realm.'[85]

So when, in the middle of Ramadan, at the height of the April heats, Imad ul-Mulk summoned Shah Alam back from his expedition to Hansi, larding him with flattery and saying he wished to honour him in the Red Fort, the prince was understandably suspicious. He was particularly nervous as in truth it was not just taxes he had been collecting in Hansi. According to the Mughal chronicler Khair ud-Din, 'The Emperor resented the almighty airs and graces of Imad ul-Mulk and even more so his own dependence on him, so he began cultivating anyone at court who was in any way alienated from him. Within a short time, relations between them became patently acrimonious, which led to disorder and corruption in the body politic.'

The Emperor gave leave to Shah Alam to come out of the Red Fort, ostensibly to re-establish royal authority in Hansi and the surrounding districts to gather taxes, while secretly giving him instructions to raise a sizeable army in order to counter any hostile intentions on the part of Imad ul-Mulk, and to use his brave and devoted warriors to take the wind out of that wretch's sails.[86]

The prince slowly returned to Delhi, anxiously considering his options, stopping to camp at several Mughal gardens on the way and making a pilgrimage to pray at his favourite shrine in Mehrauli. Several friends at court had ridden out to Haryana to warn him to be very careful, telling him that he was walking into a trap. They told him that Imad ul-Mulk, far from wishing to honour him, actually intended instead to cast him back into the salatin 'cage' from which he had been so recently released, as soon as he stepped inside the Red Fort. All the while, Imad ul-Mulk continued his charm offensive, sending messages of welcome and friendship, and 'large trays of cooked delicacies, pots of flowers and boxes of paan', telling him he was waiting to receive him in the Red Fort.[87] But the prince, increasingly suspicious, sidestepped the ambush and instead took up residence in the great mansion of Ali Mardan Khan on the northern edge of the city, part of which had once been used as a library by the Sufi prince Dara Shukoh.[88]

'Imad al-Mulk pretended to make friends with the Prince and continued to flatter him,' wrote Khair ud-Din. 'Eventually Shah Alam decided to make it look as if he had swallowed these deceptively flattering proposals.'

> As Imad ul-Mulk had suggested, he sent off some of his troops to his revenue-estates, to put them in order, and to gather taxes to pay the troops' salaries. But his most reliable followers he kept by his side. He stationed the infantry and cavalry guards in his service and posted jezail-marksmen and musketeers on the battlements, tower-bastions and the fortified entrance gateway, where he installed rocket operators and watchmen.
>
> For a fortnight Imad ul-Mulk tried to lull him into a false sense of security; then one day, he announced that he would ride out with a company on a pious visit to the shrine of Qadam Sharif, the Prophet's Footstep [just to the north of where the prince was staying]. There was little water in the Jumna, so they approached the mansion of Ali Mardan Khan across the fording place of the river, and through the markets towards the main entrance gateway. They surrounded it from all four directions, like a ring surrounds a finger. Stationing his own troops around the perimeter of Ali Mardan Khan's mansion, ostensibly as a guard of honour, Imad ul-Mulk then ordered his men to take the Prince into custody. The troops attacked the mansion from all sides,

some breaking through the walls, others climbing onto the roofs and firing their muskets down into the courtyards. Some of the Prince's companions offered a desperate resistance and were mown down.[89]

According to Ghulam Hussain Khan, the prince 'had only a few men left with him, but these were determined and resolute'.

Mounting their horses, they advanced on the back part of the house, where there was a certain breach in the wall which looked down on the river, and falling unexpectedly on their enemies, they in a moment cut their passage through them, strewing the ground with their dead. The Prince slew two men with his own hands, and he behaved throughout the whole action with so much personal prowess and heroic conduct, that the heroes of old times would have bit the finger of astonishment had they witnessed his valour. The enemies ashamed to see their prey ready to escape, crowded after them and pursued hotly. In this extremity that intrepid troop turned about, rushed upon their pursuers, raising their swords as if they were battle-standards and put the foremost to flight, killing many of them.[90]

By evening, numbers were beginning to tell against the prince: he had only 400 companions, while Imad ul-Mulk had over 1,500 troops, including sixty European mercenaries equipped with the latest muskets; the prince's troops, in comparison, were mainly armed with 'the lance, the sabre and the bow'.[91]

'Then Mir Jafar and Ali Azam Khan, who were among the bravest, spoke to the Prince to fire him up to fight his way out, resolving':

Let us be ready for death and make a sudden attack on the enemy. If successful, we will break many skulls and necks, and make our escape; otherwise, we will go down in the annals of the brave with eternal honour. The Prince was seated, listening eagerly, and, roused by his companions' words, rose with a few fearless fighters to enter the fray, fighting heroically, cutting down many of the enemy. His companions' bravery came to the rescue in the midst of the cut and thrust: rapidly and skilfully, they began their escape from the melee.

But on the way out of the gully, their enemies crowded around them, wounded the Prince's horse, and tried their utmost to get hold of the Prince's person. Ali Azam Khan, with his accustomed bravery, called out to the Prince: 'Shah Alam you are destined one day to be a resource to an infinity of people, and your life is therefore more precious today than ours. Run forward and gain some distance; I will undertake meanwhile to stop the enemy until you have outdistanced them. I will fight and clear a passage for your escape, even at the cost of my life!' So saying, he jumped off his horse and stood bravely fighting manifold enemies like a roaring lion; wounded many times over, at last he fell to the ground.

By this time, the Prince had ridden on some way out of the town and passed out of the grasp of his enemies; he eventually reached the military camp of his [Maratha] friend, Athil Rao, who lauded his bravery and ordered tents erected for the Prince and his companions. After entertaining the Prince and his party for some days, he accompanied them eastwards to Farrukhabad, where he was offered a tribute-gift of 3 lakhs Rupees.* The Prince passed on to the territories of the Rohillas, who hastened to welcome the royal party, providing hospitality as custom required.[92]

The prince waited at Farrukhabad for a few days hoping that more of his supporters would join him. Knowing now that Imad ul-Mulk would stop at nothing to have him killed, the prince decided not to return to Delhi but instead he 'resolved to move East so that he could take charge of Bengal and Bihar [Purab] which were prosperous and rich provinces'.[93] These he resolved to try to take back from the control of the Nawab governors who had stopped sending their proper dues to Delhi. 'This world,' he announced, 'is like a garden of flowers interspersed with weeds and thorns, I shall therefore resolve to root out the bad that the faithful and good among my people may rest in quietness.'[94]

The prince fully expected the uncertainty and pain of the life of the exile, and 'turned his face to the path of the wilderness in sole reliance on God'. He was not optimistic about his chances but was determined to do what he could to regain his inheritance. Yet as soon as word

* Almost £4 million today.

spread of his bravery in Delhi, and it became known that a new young, popular and dashing Mughal prince was intent on heading eastwards to restore the Empire and end the half-century of anarchy, followers began to travel across Hindustan to join this new Akbar.

What was at first just a trickle grew into a torrent and then a flood; before long the prince found himself being supported by many old Mughal families whose fortunes had been wrecked by half a century of civil war. According to Ghulam Hussain Khan, within a few months of his leaving Delhi nearly 30,000 troops had rallied to his standard. Among these was Ghulam Hussain's own father, whom the queen, Zinat Mahal, Shah Alam's mother, had secretly sent from the Red Fort to act as his adviser: 'The Prince had with him several persons of character and distinction, all attached to his fortune; but all in as much distress as their master.'

On the Imperial Prince first coming out of Shahjahanabad, his circumstances were initially so distressing and his poverty so complete, that few would think of assisting him or following his fortunes. Everyone was, besides, in dread of the Vizier Imad ul-Mulk's resentment ... But my father undertook to prepare some field equipage with some other necessaries, and to bring into his service, on the fame of this expedition, and in the hopes of bettering their fortunes, as many disbanded Mughal soldiers as they could persuade to join them.

As soon as it became certain that Shah Alam intended an expedition into the provinces of Bihar and Bengal, and that he was imminently coming to Azimabad [Patna], there was not an inhabitant who on the strength of the good government which they had formerly experienced from the Prince's ancestors, did not pray for victory to him, and for prosperity to his undertaking. They seemed to have but one mouth and one heart on that subject, though not one of them had yet received any favour from him, or tasted the crumbs that might have fallen from the table of His Goodness.[95]

But in truth, Shah Alam was already too late. The Bengal he was heading to was in the process of being changed for ever by a new force in Indian politics: the East India Company and, in particular, the machinations of Robert Clive.

3

Sweeping With the Broom of Plunder

Siraj ud-Daula led his troops down to Calcutta at far greater speed than anyone imagined possible. Mughal armies were usually notoriously slow-moving, often managing no more than three miles a day; but Siraj urged his forces forward, making some 130 miles in ten days despite the drenching tropical heat of a Bengali June.

Governor Drake believed for several days after the fall of the Kasimbazar factory that the new Nawab was merely bluffing and would never dare to attack Fort William. So poor was his intelligence that he continued to think this even as Siraj's forces were nearing his outer defences. Before the Company's Council at Calcutta had managed even to discuss any coherent defence strategy, the first of Siraj's troops were sighted on 13 June approaching the northern suburbs near Dumdum, and advancing steadily towards the Maratha Ditch.

Drake was not just incompetent, he was also deeply unpopular. According to William Tooke, one of the Calcutta civilians who volunteered to join the town militia, Drake was such a divisive figure that it was practically impossible for him to organise a coherent defence: 'Mr Drake's conduct of late years had without doubt been very blameable,' he wrote, carrying on 'that indiscreet (not to say any worse) affair with his sister, is a circumstance that can never be forgiven him; for the crime was not only itself bad, but after that, every man of character and good sense shunned and avoided him, which was the cause of his running after and keeping very indifferent company, and of committing a thousand little meannesses and low actions, far unbecoming any man, much more a Governour.'[1]

Nor was Drake's military commander, Colonel Minchin, any more reassuring. As one survivor later wrote, 'Touching the military capacity of our commandant, I am a stranger. I can only say we were either unhappy in his keeping it to himself if he had any, as neither I, nor I believe anyone else, was witness to any part of his conduct that spoke or bore the appearance of his being the commanding military officer.'[2]

Watts estimated that Siraj was marching on Calcutta with a force of around 70,000. Against these Drake could field 265 uniformed Company troops and an armed but untrained militia of 250 civilians, a grand total of 515 men in arms.[3] Of these 'there were about 100 Armenians who were entirely useless, and then there was a number among the militia boys and slaves who were not capable of holding a musket, so that in fact our garrison did not consist of more than 250 fighting men, officers included'.[4] In such a situation, grovelling apologies and negotiations would probably have been the wisest strategy. Instead, Drake began, belatedly, to build a series of batteries guarding the principal crossing places over the Maratha Ditch.

The idea of demolishing some of the buildings encroaching upon and overlooking the Fort was mooted, but quickly rejected. According to the account of Captain Grant, the Adjutant General, 'Such was the levity of the times that severe measures were not esteemed necessary':

Our Intelligence of the Nabob's Motions, and numbers, was always very uncertain, and we could never be thoroughly persuaded that he would advance against our Batterys. The most we imagined was that he would form a Blockade and Cut off our Provision until we came to an accommodation …

So little credit was then given, and even to the very last day, that the Nabob would venture to attack us, that it occasion'd a general grumbling to leave any of the European Houses without [the outer perimeter of the defences]. And should it be proposed by any Person to demolish as many Houses as would be necessary to make the Fort defensible, his opinion would have been thought Ridiculous, even had there been sufficient time to execute such a work or powder sufficient to blow them up.[5]

The 'levity of the times' began to dissipate when Siraj ud-Daula arrived in person on 16 June and directed his heavy artillery to begin firing into the town. The first two attempts by Mughal forces to cross the Ditch were driven off with heavy casualties. But by evening, twenty of the defenders were dead and 'just before dark, the whole body [of the Mughal advance guard had] inclined southward, and successfully crossed the Ditch that surrounds the Black Town, the extent of it being so great, and passable in all parts, that it was impossible to do anything to interrupt them'.[6]

The following day, the Black Town was comprehensively looted: 'vast numbers entered our bounds, plundering and setting fire to every house, and by the evening the whole town was surrounded ... Several thousands this night got into the great bazaar where they murdered every person they met and plundered and set fire to all the houses.'[7] The garrison did not make the slightest effort to protect the Black Town or offer shelter in the fort to the terrified inhabitants. No wonder, then, that by the second day all the Indian support staff had defected, leaving the garrison without lascars to pull the guns, coolies to carry shot and powder, carpenters to build batteries and repair the gun carriages, or even cooks to feed the militia.

On the morning of the 18th, the Mughal advance was repulsed in tough house-to-house street fighting to the north of the Fort, but Siraj's troops were still making steady progress advancing forward in the east. There, at 3 p.m., Company forces were impelled to retreat from their stronghold at the gaol, with heavy losses: 'the small party bravely defended it for six hours, till most of the men being wounded, were obliged to retire.' By the evening, the Mughals had also broken through the Company lines near the Great Tank. The northern and south-west batteries were now both in danger of being cut off and so were quickly abandoned. All Company forces were now compelled to withdraw to the inner line of defence, the Fort itself: 'The next thing considered of was a disposition for the Defence of the Fort, which was all that was left us now to maintain,' wrote Captain Grant.

Few expected that the Batterys would have been so suddenly quitted, and most people foresaw that the fall of them would be attended with fatal consequences. For the Enemy's getting possession of the houses contiguous to the Fort and the Church would command the Bastions and Ramparts, so that it would be impossible to stand at the Guns, exposed to the small arms of such a multitude as would occupy those, especially as the parapets of the [Fort's] bastions were very low, and the embrasures so wide that they hardly afforded any shelter. We had sandbags, which might in some measure supply this defect, but we were so abandon'd by all sorts of labourers that we could not get them carried upon the ramparts. And our Military and Militia were so harassed for want of rest and refreshment, that it was at first impossible to get them to do anything.[8]

A late-night Council of War established that there was a maximum of three days' ammunition left, and that the soldiers were already exhausted and in many cases drunk: 'Half our men in liquor, no supplies of provisions or water sent out, the drum beat to arms three different times on alarm of the enemy being under the walls, but hardly a man could be got up onto the ramparts.'[9]

'Now for the first time we began to look upon ourselves in a dangerous way,' wrote David Renny of the militia.

We were in a very distressed condition … It is almost impossible to conceive the confusion there was in the Fort there being at least two thousand women and children, nor was there any method to prevent these coming in as the military and militia declared they would not fight unless their families were admitted in the factory. The Enemy began now to fire warmly upon the Fort from all quarters. Our garrison began to murmur for want of provisions having not a single cook in the Fort, notwithstanding there had been several lodged there on purpose to dress their provisions. The whole Garrison was quite fatigued having been under arms great part of the preceding night. Many of the military and militia having got liquor begun to be very mutinous and under no command, having drawn bayonets on several of their officers.

It was now thought necessary to send our ladies on board some of the ships, which was accordingly done. About 12 o'clock [midnight] news was brought us that the Enemy were going to storm the Fort there being ladders preparing close under the range of godowns [warehouses] to the southward. Immediately every person repaired to the curtain [wall] where we heard them at work. Orders were now given to beat to arms but none of the Armenians or Portuguese appeared, having hid themselves in different parts of the Fort. We threw some hand Grenades down amongst the Enemy, which soon dislodged them.[10]

The following day, the 19th, resistance began to give way to outright panic. The Nawab's principal general, Mir Jafar Ali Khan, pressed forward with his assault and by noon, when it became known there was only two days' supply of ammunition left, the majority of the Council argued in favour of abandoning the Fort altogether and retreating to the ships anchored in the river. By 2 p.m., while the Council were still debating their plans for withdrawal, a cannonball burst through the Council Chamber and the meeting broke up 'with the utmost clamour, confusion, tumult and perplexity'.[11] Morale had now hit rock bottom and despairing drunkenness had broken out everywhere. Soon after lunchtime, there began a chaotic evacuation.

As flights of fire arrows poured into the Fort and onto the shore, one ship, the *Dodally*, headed upriver without orders, to avoid catching fire. The other vessels began to do the same. Thinking the ships were departing without them, the waiting women and children took fright, ran out of the Fort and stampeded down to the shore in an attempt to board and save themselves. All the boats were filled to overcapacity and several capsized.

At that point, 'many of the gentlemen on shore, who perhaps never dreamt of leaving the factory before everybody else did, immediately jumped into such boats as were at the factory and rowed to the ships. Among those who left the factory in this unaccountable manner were the Governor Mr Drake ... [and] Commandant Minchin ... This ill-judged circumstance occasioned all the uproar and misfortune which followed.'[12] Within an hour, all the ships had weighed anchor and began drifting slowly downstream towards the jungles of the Sunderbans, and the coast beyond.

'Finding that matters went hard with him,' wrote Ghulam Hussain Khan, 'Mr Drake abandoned everything and fled, without so much as giving notice to his countrymen.'

He took shelter on board of a ship, and with a small number of
friends and principal persons, he disappeared at once. Those who
remained, finding themselves abandoned by their chief, concluded
their case must be desperate, yet preferring death to life, they fought
it out, until their powder and ball failing at last, they bravely drank
up the bitter cup of death; some others, seized by the claws of destiny,
were made prisoners.[13]

The remaining garrison hoped to escape on the *Prince George*, which was
still anchored a little upriver. But early the following morning, the ship
ran aground at low tide, and could not be budged. 'Finding all Retreat
cut off, the remaining defenders shut the Gates and were resolved to sell
their lives as dear as they could, and fought like mad men.'[14]

Under the command of the Dublin-born John Zephaniah Holwell,
the roughly 150 remaining members of the garrison who had failed to
make their escape continued the resistance for one more morning. But
the Mughal troops attacked fiercely and, just as Captain Grant had
predicted, Mir Jafar sent his sharpshooters with their long-barrelled
jezails onto the flat parapet of the church tower and the houses
overlooking the ramparts, 'which being loftier than the walls, and
commanding all the bastions, galled us so badly with shot that no man
could stand them, they killing or wounding all that appeared in sight,
wounding most of our Officers, several of whom after dyed of wounds.
The surviving officers were obliged to exert themselves, pistol in hand,
to keep the soldiers to their quarters.'[15]

By mid-afternoon, many more of the defenders were dead, and those
that lived were 'exhausted of strength and vigour'. With only a hundred
fighters left on the ramparts, 'about 4 o'clock in the afternoon, the
Enemy called out to us not to fire, in consequence to which Holwell
shewed a flag of truce, and gave orders for the garrison not to fire'.

Upon which the Enemy in vast numbers came under our walls, and
at once began to set fire to the windows and Gates of the Fort which
were stopt up with bales of cotton and cloth, and began to break
open the Fort Gate, scaling our walls on all sides. This put us in the
utmost confusion, some opening the back gate and running into the
river, others to take possession of a boat that lay ashore half afloat and
half dry. It was so full in an instant that she could not be got off.[16]

Inside the Fort, Siraj's forces were now beginning to loot: 'The factory was in a few minutes filled with the enemy,' recalled John Cook, 'who without loss of time began plundering everything they could set their hands on; we were rifled of our watches, buckles, buttons &c but no farther violence used to our persons. The bales of broadcloth, chests of coral, plate and treasure laying in the apartments of the gentlemen who resided in the factory were broke open, and the Moors were wholly taken up in plundering.'[17]

That evening, having 'swept the town of Calcutta with the broom of plunder', Siraj ud-Daula was brought in his litter to visit his new possession.[18] He held a durbar in the centre of the Fort where he announced that Calcutta was to be renamed Alinagar, after Imam Ali – appropriately for a prominent city in a Shia-ruled province. He then appointed one of his Hindu courtiers, Raja Manikchand, to be the Fort Keeper of Alinagar and ordered the demolition of Government House, whose beauty he admired, but considered it worthy to be 'the dwelling of Princes rather than merchants', apparently mistaking it for the private property of the detested Drake.[19] 'Siraj ud-Daula seemed astonished to find so small a garrison,' remembered one of the prisoners, 'and immediately enquired for Mr Drake, with whom he appeared much incensed. Mr Holwell was carried to him with his hands bound, and upon complaining of that usage, the Nabob gave orders for loosing his hands and assured him upon the faith of a soldier that not a hair of our heads should be hurt.'[20] He then offered thanksgiving prayers for his success in battle, and was carried out to his tents.

So far, the surrendered garrison had been treated unusually well by Mughal standards: there had been no immediate enslavement, no summary executions, no impaling, no beheading and no torture, all of which would have been, in the Mughal scheme of things, quite routine punishments for rebellious subjects. It was only after Siraj had left that things began to fall apart.

Many in the Company's garrison were still blind drunk, and in the early evening one intoxicated soldier who was being stripped of his goods became incensed and promptly pulled out a pistol and shot his Mughal plunderer dead. Immediately the tone changed. All the survivors were herded into a tiny punishment cell, eighteen feet long by fourteen feet ten inches wide, with only one small window, little air and less water. The cell was known as the Black Hole. There, according to the Mughal chronicler Yusuf Ali Khan, the officers 'confined nearly 100 Firangis who fell victim to the claws of fate on that day in a small room. As luck would have it, in the room where the Firangis were kept confined, all of them got suffocated and died.'[21]

The numbers are unclear, and much debated: Holwell, who wrote a highly coloured account of the Black Hole in 1758, and began the mythologising of the event, wrote that one woman and 145 Company men were shoved inside, of whom 123 died.[22] This was clearly an exaggeration. The most painstaking recent survey of the evidence concludes 64 people entered the Black Hole and that 21 survived. Among the young men who did not come out was the nineteen-year-old Stair Dalrymple from North Berwick, who only two years earlier had been complaining of Calcutta's cost of living and dreaming of becoming Governor.

Whatever the accurate figures, the event generated howls of righteous indignation for several generations among the British in India and 150 years later was still being taught in British schools as demonstrative of the essential barbarity of Indians and illustrative of why British rule was supposedly both necessary and justified. But at the time, the Black Hole was barely remarked upon in contemporary sources, and several detailed accounts, including that of Ghulam Hussain Khan, do not mention it at all. The Company had just lost its most lucrative trading station, and that, rather than the fate of its feckless garrison, was what really worried the Company authorities.[23]

The full scale of the disaster represented by the fall of Calcutta became apparent in the weeks that followed.

Everyone soon realised that it changed almost everything: William Lindsay wrote to the future historian of the Company, Robert Orme, that it was 'a scene of destruction and dissolution ... and makes me tremble when I think of the consequences that it will be attended with, not only to every private Gentlemen in India but to the English nation in General. I hardly think all the force we have in India will be sufficient to resettle us here into any footing of security, we now being almost as much in want of everything as when we first settled here.'[24]

It was not just a loss of lives and prestige, the trauma and the humiliation that horrified the Company authorities, it was above all an economic body blow for the EIC, which could only send its share price into a possibly terminal decline: 'I would mention what the Company has lost by this melancholy affair,' wrote Captain Renny. 'But it is impossible, for though the present loss is immense, yet it will be still more in the consequences, if not immediately resettled.'

> The cargoes now expected from England will remain unsold, the ships remain at a great expense of demurrage, the same will be repeated next season. The articles of saltpetre and raw silk which we cannot well be without must now be bought at a high price from the Dutch, French, Prussians and Danes, so must Dacca muslins ... to the great loss of the revenue.
>
> The different parts of India will also severely feel the loss of Calcutta, for if I am not mistaken the Coast of Coromandel and Malabar, the Gulf of Persia and Red Sea, nay even Manila, China and Coast of Affrica were obliged to Bengal for taking off their cotton, pepper, drugs, fruits, chank, cowrees, tin too &c: as on the other hand they were supplied from Bengal with what they could not well be without, such as raw silk and its various manufactures, opium, vast quantities of cotton cloth, rice, ginger, turmerick, long pepper &c. and all sorts of other goods.[25]

News of the fall of Kasimbazar, and a first request for military assistance, reached Madras on 14 July. It was a full month later, on 16 August, that the news of Siraj ud-Daula's successful attack on Fort William finally arrived. In normal circumstances, Madras would probably have sent a delegation to Murshidabad, negotiations would have taken place, apologies and assurances would have been issued, an indemnity would have been paid and trading would have carried on as before, to the benefit of both sides. But on this occasion, due not to good planning so much as chance, there was another option.

For, as fate would have it, Robert Clive and his three regiments of Royal Artillery had just arrived on the Coromandel Coast at Fort St

David, south of Madras, aboard Admiral Watson's flotilla of fully armed and battle-ready men-of-war. The force was intended to take on the French, not the Nawab of Bengal, and in the discussions that followed several members of Madras Council argued that the fleet should stay in the Coromandel and continue to guard against the French flotilla believed sent from Port Lorient. This was expected any day, along with news of the outbreak of war, and a strong case was made by several Council members that, having lost one major trading station, it would be an act of extreme carelessness on the part of the Company to risk losing a second.

Moreover, Admiral Watson, as a loyal servant of the Crown, initially saw his role to defend British national interests against the French, not to defend the Company's economic interests from local potentates. But Clive was not going to miss his big chance, especially as he had just lost substantial sums invested both directly in Bengal and indirectly in Company stock. He forcefully, and ultimately successfully, argued for a more aggressive course of action, eventually winning over the other Council members, and persuading Watson to come with him, along with all four of his battleships and a frigate. Watson's one insistence was to wait until the onset of the monsoon in early October, after which the French were less likely to risk sailing into open waters, and he would have several months' grace in which to re-establish British interests in Bengal without leaving the Coromandel criminally undefended.[26]

Within a few weeks, a triumphant Clive was able to write to his father: 'This expedition, if attended by success, may enable me to do great things. It is by far the grandest of my undertakings. I go with great forces and great authority.' His masters in Leadenhall Street he addressed in a rather more measured and less egotistical manner: 'Honourable Gentlemen,' he wrote. 'From many hands you will hear of the capture of Calcutta by the Moors, and the chains of misfortunes which have happened to the Company in particular and to the nation in general.'

Every breast seems filled with grief, horror and resentment ... Upon this melancholy occasion, the Governour and Council thought proper to summon me to this place. As soon as an expedition was resolved upon, I offered my services which at last was accepted, and I am on the point of embarking on board His Majesty's squadron with a fine body of Europeans, full of spirit and resentment for the insults and barbarities inflicted on so many British subjects. I flatter myself that this expedition will not end with the retaking of Calcutta only, and that the Company's estate in these parts will be settled in a better and more lasting condition than ever.[27]

The Select Committee at Madras also shared Clive's ambitions: 'The mere retaking of Calcutta should, we think, be by no means the end of the undertaking,' they wrote to the directors in London in early October. 'Not only should [the EIC's Bengal] settlements and factories be restored, but all their privileges established in full, and ample reparation made for the loss they have lately sustained; otherwise we are of the opinion it would have been better that nothing had been attempted, than to have added the heavy charge of this armament to their former loss, without securing their colonies and trade from future insults and exactions.'[28]

Two months were filled with detailed planning, refitting ships, loading cannon and preparing stores. The relief force consisting of 785 European troops, 940 sepoys and 300 marines, a greater naval and military force than had ever before been gathered together by the British in India, eventually set sail on 13 October. But the same strong monsoon winds that Watson knew would prevent the French from venturing out of port came close to sinking the entire expedition. As it was, the fleet was immediately scattered. Some ships were blown as far south as Sri Lanka, and even Watson's flagship, the *Kent*, took six weeks to reach the point where Clive was able to see the waters of the Bay of Bengal take on the distinctive colour of Ganges silt.[29]

It was not until 9 December that the first ships of the task force, taking advantage of low tides, turned into the Hughli. By this stage half of Clive's soldiers had already succumbed to various diseases, including an outbreak of scurvy. Six days later, the *Kent* dropped anchor at Fulta, where the survivors of the Calcutta debacle had taken shelter on the edge of a malarial swamp, and where just under half of the ragged refugees had already died of fever and were now buried in the alluvial Sunderbans silt.[30]

Two more of Watson's ships turned up soon after; while waiting for the remaining two, the *Marlborough* and *Cumberland*, which carried the bulk of the expedition's artillery and troops, Clive wrote to Raja Manikchand, the new Fort Keeper of Alinagar-Calcutta. He announced that he had come with a force of unprecedented size – 'a larger military force than has ever appeared in Bengal' and that 'we are come to demand satisfaction'. But Clive's threats had little effect. As Ghulam Hussain Khan commented, 'the British were then known in Bengal only as merchants', and no one at court 'had any idea of the abilities of that nation in war, nor any idea of their many resources in a day of reverse'.[31]

With no reply forthcoming, and disease weakening his ranks by the day, on 27 December Clive's expedition cast anchor and sailed slowly upriver, still two ships short. They glided silently past coconut groves and through tangled mangrove swamps thick with lotus leaves and full of huge bats and tigers. As they approached the first serious obstacle, the Fort of Budge Budge, whose heavy guns commanded a bend in the river, they disembarked the sepoys, who had a tough march of sixteen hours, wading sometimes breast-high through water, at other times stumbling through jungle or marshy paddy.[32]

Towards sunset, as they drew near the Fort, Raja Manikchand sprung an ambush, appearing suddenly out of the jungle, attacking from an unexpected direction and achieving complete surprise. The confused skirmish lasted an hour, with high casualties on both sides. Clive was rattled, and was on the verge of ordering a retreat. But the rapid file firing of the army's new Brown Bess muskets, supported by field artillery, worked its dark magic. As Clive's nephew Edward Maskelyne recorded, the Mughals 'were much alarmed at the smartness of our fire, and startled at the appearance of the cannon which they thought it impossible for us to have transported over the ground we had marched the preceding night. Their loss is computed at 200 killed and wounded, 4 Jemidars and 1 elephant killed, and their commander [Raja Manikchand] shot thro the turban.'[33]

When Manikchand retired, Watson's ships were free to unleash broadsides on the Fort, which quickly silenced the Mughal guns. As the troops were being unloaded to begin the ground attack, 'one Strahan, a common sailor, belonging to the *Kent*', having drunk too much rum, staggered up the bank, waded over the moat and 'took into his head to scale a breach that had been made by the cannon of the ships'. Here he was confronted by the garrison, 'at whom he flourished his cutlass, and fired his pistol. Then having given out three loud huzzas, he cried out,

"The place is mine." His comrades rushed to save him and the garrison quickly melted into the night.[34]

The fleet then proceeded further up the river, and two more of Siraj's forts were abandoned without a fight.

As dawn broke on 2 January 1757, the squadron came within sight of Fort William. The marines were landed and a single broadside unleashed on the defences. There was a brief exchange of fire, leaving nine men dead, before Manikchand again withdrew: 'The senseless governor of the place,' wrote Ghulam Hussain Khan, 'intimidated by so much boldness, and not finding in himself courage enough to stand an engagement, thought it prudent to decline a nearer approach, and he fled with all his might. The English general [Clive], seeing the enemy disappearing, took possession of the factory and the fort, raised everywhere his victorious standards, and sent the refugee gentlemen, everyone to his ancient abode, and everyone to his own home.'[35]

People waved. One man hung a Union Jack from a tree;[36] but as the sun rose, the full scale of the devastation became apparent: Government House, St Anne's church and the grand mansions lining the river were all burned-out shells, rising jagged from the loot-littered riverfront like blackened, shattered teeth from a diseased gum. The wharves were derelict; inside the mansions, the gorgeous Georgian furniture, family paintings and even harpsichords had been burned as firewood where they stood in the middle of what had once been drawing rooms. A small mosque had been erected in the eastern curtain wall of the fort.[37]

Nevertheless, by eight o'clock on the morning of 2 January 1757, this shattered and half-ruined Calcutta was back in the hands of the Company.

On 3 January, Clive declared war on Siraj ud-Daula in the name of the Company; Watson did the same in the name of the Crown. It was the first time that the EIC had ever formally declared war on an Indian prince: 'The chess board of time presented a new game,' noted Ghulam Husain Salim's account, *Riyazu-s-salatin*.[38]

Characteristically, Clive went straight onto the offensive. On 9
January, while the inhabitants repaired their homes, and the engineers
began to rebuild the fortifications of Fort William, finally demolishing
all the buildings which overlooked its walls, Clive and Watson set
off in the *Kent* to attack Siraj ud-Daula's principal port, Hughli
Bandar, to exact a violent revenge for the destruction of Calcutta. On
arrival, they raked the ghats of Hughli with grapeshot, then landed
the grenadiers at four o'clock in the evening, seizing the area around
the fort. At 2 a.m., under a full moon, they scaled the fortifications
with siege ladders. Once inside, they made 'themselves masters of the
place, in less than an hour, with little or no loss, effecting a prodigious
slaughter' of the sleeping garrison. Then they set about looting and
burning the port 'the better to distress the enemy, the more to alarm
the province, and to work upon Siraj's governing passion, Fear. Orders
were given for burning the houses, and for destroying, particularly,
all the magazines on both sides of the river.'[39] Then looting parties
fanned out, seizing weapons and burning several villages and their
granaries as they went. By evening, they were back behind the walls
of Fort William.

Two weeks later, on the 23rd, having gathered together another
enormous army 60,000-strong, Siraj ud-Daula again descended on
Calcutta. As before, he moved at speed. On 4 February, Clive was
surprised by the news that Siraj and his forces were already camping
in a pleasure garden on the northern outskirts of Calcutta, just to
the north of the walls. Two senior Company negotiators were sent at
his invitation to speak with him, but Siraj treated them 'with such a
Mixture of Haughtiness and Contempt, as gave little Hopes of their
making any great progress in their Business'.[40] The men were invited
to return the following day 'to parley', but did not do so, anticipating
a trap. Instead, Clive again fell back on his favourite tactic from his
Carnatic days: a surprise night attack.

Acting with his usual decisiveness, Clive 'went immediately on board
Admiral Watson's ship, and represented to him the necessity of attacking
the Nabob without delay; and desired the assistance of four or five
hundred sailors, to carry the ammunition and draw the artillery; which
he [Watson] assented to. The sailors were landed about one o'clock in
the morning. About two, the troops were under arms, and about four
they marched to the attack of the Nabob's camp.'[41]

The new day, 5 February 1757, dawned with a thick, early morning winter fog billowing off the river. Silently, 'we marched with 470 rank & file, 800 sepoys, 6 field pieces, 1 Howitzer & 70 of the train, besides a body of seamen, half of whom were employed in drawing the guns, whilst the other half bore arms,' wrote Edward Maskelyne in his journal.

> At day break, we arrived close to the Nabobs camp before we were challenged, when we received a brisk fire, which was returned by our advance sepoys. The enemy retreated, and we pursued our march through their camp undisturbed till reaching the center of it. Here a body of 300 horses appeared in the fog within 10 yards of the battalion and we gave them two [volleys of] fire by platoons and such havock was made amongst them, that by all accounts not above 13 escaped. After this their whole army began to surround us in great bodies which obliged us to keep them at a distance by a constant fire of musquetry and artillery. We were full 2 hours in marching thro their camp, several charges being made on our rear by the horses; tho not with equal courage to their first.[42]

By 11 a.m., Clive's force had returned dispirited to the city, having lost nearly 150 men, including both Clive's aide-de-camp and his secretary, both of whom were killed by his side: 'It was the warmest service I ever yet was engaged in,' Clive wrote to this father, 'and the attack failed in its main object' – capturing or killing the Nawab.[43] Clive was unsure whether the manoeuvre had been a success or a failure, but suspected the latter. Their guides had got lost in the fog and they had narrowly failed to attack the royal enclosure, shooting wildly into the gloom, unclear if they were hitting or missing their targets. They had also lost two cannon, which they had to leave behind, stuck in the mud of the Nawab's camp. What they had no idea of was the terror they inspired in Siraj ud-Daula, who only narrowly escaped with his life. Around 1,500 of his Murshidabad infantry were not so lucky, nor were 600 cavalry and four elephants. Ghulam Hussain Khan related how the attack looked from the Mughal point of view: 'They put out their boats about two in the morning,' he wrote, 'and rowed towards the extremity of the enemy camp, where they remained waiting during the latter part of the night.'

At about the dawn of day they landed at the back of the army, and entered the camp, where they leisurely commenced a hot fire, which being repeated by those in the boats, rendered musket balls as common as hail stones, so that vast numbers of men and horses, which happened to be exposed to it, were slain and wounded. Dost Mohammad Khan, who was not only the principal commander, but a man of great personal valour, and one of those most attached to Siraj ud-Daula, was wounded and disabled. Numbers of other officers underwent the same fate; and it is reported that the design was no less than to lay hold of Siraj himself, and to carry him away.

Luckily for him there fell such a foul fog and mist, of the kind called in Hindian a *cohessa*, and it occasioned such a darkness, that the two men [Clive and Siraj], though ever so close, could not distinguish each other. This darkness made them mistake their way, and missed Siraj ud-Daula's private enclosure, so that this Prince narrowly escaped. It was observed of the English that they marched steadily, with order and deliberation, as if it had been a review day, firing endlessly on every side, until they arrived at the front of the camp, from whence they returned leisurely to their posts and fortified houses, without suffering the loss of a single man.[44]

Quite unknown to Clive at the time, his night attack was in fact a decisive turning point. Terrified by the unexpected nature of the assault, Siraj struck camp and retreated ten miles that morning. The following day he sent an ambassador with proposals for peace. Even before the night attack, he had been aware of the damage done to the Bengal economy by the destruction of Calcutta, and he was prepared to be a little generous. But on 9 February he signed the Treaty of Alinagar, which granted almost all the Company's main demands, restoring all the existing English privileges and freeing all English goods of taxes, as well as allowing the Company to keep their fortifications and establish a mint. His only insistence was that Drake be removed – 'Tell Roger Drake' not to 'disturb our affairs' – something the Company was more than happy to grant.[45]

The following day, Siraj ud-Daula began his march back to Murshidabad, leaving Clive and Watson astonished at their own success. Clive was ready to return to Madras, having fulfilled all his war aims with minimum cost and casualties: as he wrote to his father on

23 February: 'I expect to return very shortly to the coast, as all is over here.'[46]

For his part, however, Watson reported to the Crown, not the Company, and for him things had just become a great deal more complicated.[47] A few days earlier, he had been officially notified of the outbreak of what future generations would call the Seven Years War. Around the world, from Quebec to the Senegal River, from Ohio to Hanover, Minorca to Cuba, hostilities were now finally breaking out between Britain and France in every imperial theatre. Watson's instructions arrived in a packet from London, with an official copy of the declaration of war and a letter from the Admiralty directing 'all officers under the King to distress the enemy as far as it is in their power'.[48]

Watson was unequivocal about what he now needed to do: attack the French, wherever they were to be found. And in the case of Bengal, that meant starting by attacking the French colony of Chandernagar, twenty miles upstream.

Relations between the authorities in Chandernagar and Calcutta had always been surprisingly cordial: after the fall of Calcutta, the French in Chandernagar had been generously hospitable to the Company refugees as they fled Siraj ud-Daula, reserving their anger only for Drake and his Council: 'Their shameful flight covers all Europeans with a disgrace which they will never wipe out in this count,' wrote the French Governor, M. Renault. 'Everyone curses, detests, abhors them ... In short, whatever one may say, these gentlemen, especially Mr Drake, will never free themselves from such infamy, and Mr Drake will never deprive his nation of the right to hang him and all his Council.'[49]

Given this, the French were quick to reach out to their British counterparts after the recapture of the city, seeking a local neutrality in case of the outbreak of war. Calcutta responded warmly, and negotiations began. It was Watson who broke them off on 6 March, just hours before the treaty of neutrality was to be signed. According to Jean Law, the Admiral took the stand 'that the Chandernagar authorities were not empowered to make treaties, and therefore he had declined to sign the draft. The truth, however, was that on the very day fixed for the signing, the Admiral was informed that his two lost and long-awaited ships had arrived at the mouth of the Ganges, and it was this news that made him change his mind. The English army now set off to march towards Chandernagar, while the missing ships prepared to sail up the Ganges.'50

On 8 March, Clive began his march at the head of a small army which had now swelled to 2,700. He took his time, taking three days to cover the twenty miles separating the two rival trading stations. Two days later, the Nawab wrote Clive a letter which the latter took as giving Siraj's assent for an attack on the French. This was in return for an EIC promise of military assistance should Bengal be attacked by the Afghan monarch Ahmed Shah Durrani, who had just seized Delhi on the first of what were to be seventeen annual raids on north India, and who was said to be planning a looting expedition eastwards. By the 12th, Clive had encamped two miles from Chandernagar and called upon the French to surrender. The French declined to do so.

Chandernagar had, like Calcutta, recently outgrown all its rival settlements to become the prime French trading post in the East. Also like Calcutta, it was vulnerable to attack, less from the land, for its Fort d'Orléans, built on the principles of Sébastien de Vauban, was a much more impressive fortification than Fort William; but its defences against assaults from the river were far less formidable. Renault was aware of this, and as soon as war broke out he sank four ships and ran a boom and several chains around them to block the British warships from coming close to the vulnerable eastern face of his fort.

Early on the morning of 23 March, Clive stormed and took the principal French battery commanding the river. From that point on, Admiral Watson took over and it was to sea power, not Clive's land forces, that most casualties fell. The French, who had only 700 men to defend their fort, fought bravely in their burning, disintegrating buildings, with no possibility of relief.

It was again Clive's nephew who left the best record of the taking of Chandernagar in his journal: 'The *Kent* & *Tyger* were all this time getting up the river,' wrote Edward Maskelyne, 'in the passage of which they were greatly retarded by the French having sunk four ships in the channel.'

This difficulty was at last removed [once the chains and booms had been cut away] & the two ships drew near the fort, but before they got within musquet shot, the French from 16 guns made great havoc. When the broadsides began to fire the enemy soon quitted their guns for they lost 150 officers in two hours, & the faces of two bastions were in the meantime brought to the ground, so that the Monsieurs hung out a flag & surrendered at discretion.

[Before they did so] the quarter-deck of the *Kent* was cleared of every man but the Admiral [Watson] & pilot, Captain Speke, and all the officers being killed or wounded, as were about 150 men in both ships. The *Tyger* suffered vastly in seamen & the *Kent* both in officers & sailors. Captain Speke has his leg sadly mauled & his son Billy has lost one of his with part of his thigh by the same shot. That charming young fellow Perreau was shot through the head, and Second Lieutenant Hayes lost his thigh and is since dead.

As we [land forces] were under cover of houses we suffered little, though we greatly incommoded the enemy in reverse by our shot and shells. It must be owned considering all things that the Messieurs made a good defence, though the Fort held out only 2 hours after the ships came before it.

'Perhaps you will hear of few instances where two ships have met with greater damage than the *Kent* and *Tyger* in this engagement,' wrote one of the surviving sailors. 'We have never yet obtained a victory at so dear a rate.'[51]

The destruction within the Fort was every bit as severe as that on deck. By sunset, all five of the French 24-pounder guns had been blasted off their mounts, 'the walls of d'Orléans were in ruins, the gunners almost all killed, and the men were being shot down by musketeers from the roofs of neighbouring houses and the tops of the masts and rigging of the ships. In a single day's fighting, the French lost two Captains and two hundred men killed and wounded.'[52]

The capture of Chandernagar was a body blow to the entire French presence in India. As Jean Law noted, 'with the fall of Chandernagar, the gate to the entire country was thrown open to the English, a gate that opened onto the road of glory and riches. By the same event, the principal place of commerce of the French Company, the sole port where our ships could shelter, was now closed for a long time. A flourishing colony was destroyed and many honest people in French India were ruined. Indeed, I saw myself ruined.'[53]

While the battle was taking place, Siraj ud-Daula remained in an agony of indecision: wishing to help the French against the British, but not daring to give the Company any excuse to break their treaty with him. At one point he sent a relief force towards Chandernagar, hesitated, and then withdrew it. A day later, making the best of a fait accompli, he sent a message to Clive telling of his 'inexpressible pleasure' at his victory. With the message he sent a present.

'Now taking the cotton wool of recklessness from the ear,' recorded the *Riyazu-s-salatin*, the young Nawab tried to win the friendship of Clive with a gift of two leopards 'extremely good at catching deer'. But it was now much too late. 'For the arrow of fate cannot be parried by the shield of effort once God's decree has already passed another way.'[54]

As April drew to a close, Clive and Watson began to pack up and prepare their troops to leave Bengal for the Coromandel, nervous at how long they had left Madras undefended and open to a French attack. There the whole Bengal campaign would have ended, but for the hatred and disgust now felt for Siraj ud-Daula by his own court, and especially Bengal's all-powerful dynasty of bankers, the Jagat Seths.

Siraj ud-Daula's flight from Calcutta after Clive's night attack, followed by the humiliation of the Treaty of Alinagar, had broken the spell of fear with which Siraj had kept his court cowed. He had alienated many of his grandfather's old military commanders, particularly the veteran general Mir Jafar Ali Khan, an Arab soldier of fortune originally from the Shia shrine town of Najaf in modern Iraq. Mir Jafar had played his part in many of Aliverdi's most crucial victories against the Marathas, and had most recently led the successful attack on Calcutta. But having taken the town and defeated the Company in battle, he had then been sidelined, and the governorship given instead to a Hindu rival, Raja Manikchand. He and his brothers-in-arms from the Maratha Wars, 'commanders of merit, as well as of old standing, all deserving the

utmost regard, were tired of living under such an administration,' wrote
Ghulam Hussain Khan, 'and wished no better than to be rid of such a
government by Siraj ud-Daula's death'.

> So that whenever they chanced to perceive any appearance of
> discontent anywhere, or any hatred against the government, they
> would send secret messages to the party, with exhortations to contrive
> some mode of deliverance, under promise of their being most
> heartily supported. Mir Jafar Khan, as the most considerable and the
> most injured of the malcontents, was the foremost amongst them.
> Jagat Seth had secretly promised to support him vigorously; and
> they formed together a confederacy ... Other disaffected grandees
> joined together in the scheme of overthrowing Siraj ud-Daula, whose
> character of ferocity and thoughtlessness kept them in continual
> alarms, and whose fecklessness of temper made them tremble.[55]

The plotters' first plan had been to support Aliverdi Khan's daughter,
Ghasiti Begum, but Siraj had moved so quickly against her at his
succession that that plan had never got off the ground. A second scheme
had revolved around supporting Siraj's cousin, Shaukat Jung of Purnea,
'a subahdar to the taste of Jagat Seth and the chief Moors and Rajas',
but the latter had proved even less dependable than Siraj.[56] He went
into battle against his psychotic cousin in such a cloud of opium that he
was 'incapable of holding up his head' or to do more 'than listen to the
songs of his women ... so alighted from his elephant ... and was totally
out of his senses when a musquet-ball, lodging into his forehead, made
him return his soul to its maker'.[57]

Only now that Clive had demonstrated his military capacity in taking
back Calcutta, then seizing Chandernagar, did the plotters decide to
reach out to the Company as a third option, hoping to harness the
EIC's military forces for their own ends. William Watts, who had just
returned to the looted English factory of Kasimbazar under the terms of
the Treaty of Alinagar, was the first to hear these murmurs of discontent.
From the EIC's factory on the southern edge of Murshidabad he became
aware of the mutterings of the disaffected nobles at court and hints of a
possible coup, so he sent his Armenian agent, Khwaja Petrus Aratoon,
to investigate. The answer came back that Mir Jafar, in his position as
paymaster of the Bengal army, was prepared to offer the Company the

vast sum of 2.5 crore* rupees if they would help him remove the Nawab. Further investigation revealed that the scheme had wide backing among the nobility but that Mir Jafar, an uneducated general with no talent in politics, was simply a front for the real force behind the coup – the Jagat Seth bankers. 'They are, I can confirm, the *originators* of the revolution,' wrote Jean Law many months later. 'Without them the English would never have carried out what they have. The cause of the English had become that of the Seths.'[58]

Watts passed on the offer to Clive, who was still encamped outside Chandernagar and who had also, quite independently, begun to hear rumblings about a possible palace revolution. On 30 April 1757, Clive first mentioned in writing the scheme with which his name would henceforth be for ever associated. Writing to the Governor of Madras, he observed that Siraj ud-Daula was behaving in an even more violent way than usual – 'twice a week he threatens to impale Mr. Watts … in short he is a compound of everything that is bad, keeps company with none but his menial servants, and is universally hated and despised.'

> This induces me to acquaint you that there is a conspiracy carrying on against him by several of the great men, at the head of whom is Jagat Seth himself. I have been applied to for assistance, and every advantage promised that the Company can wish. The Committee are of the opinion that it should be given as soon as the Nabob is secured. For my part, I am persuaded that there can be neither peace nor security while such a monster reigns.
>
> Mr Watts is at Murshidabad and has many meetings with the great men. He desires that our proposals may be sent, and that they only wait for them to put everything into execution; so that you may very shortly expect to hear of a Revolution which will put an end to all French expectations of ever settling in this country again …[59]

The bankers and merchants of Bengal who sustained Siraj ud-Daula's regime had finally turned against him and united with the disaffected parts of his own military; now they sought to bring in the mercenary troops of the East India Company to help depose him. This was

---

* A crore equals 10 million, £325 million today.

something quite new in Indian history: a group of Indian financiers plotting with an international trading corporation to use its own private security force to overthrow a regime they saw threatening the income they earned from trade.[60] This was not part of any imperial masterplan. In fact, the EIC men on the ground were ignoring their strict instructions from London, which were only to repulse French attacks and avoid potentially ruinous wars with their Mughal hosts. But seeing opportunities for personal enrichment as well as political and economic gain for the Company, they dressed up the conspiracy in colours that they knew would appeal to their masters and presented the coup as if it were primarily aimed at excluding the French from Bengal for ever.*

By 1 May, a Secret Committee made up of senior Company officials in Bengal formally resolved to join the conspiracy: 'The Committee were unanimously of the opinion that there could be no dependence on this Nabob's word, honour and friendship, and that a revolution in the Government would be extremely for the advantage of the Company's affairs.'[61]

The Secret Committee then began to haggle over their terms of service, again using Khwaja Petrus as the intermediary for their coded correspondence. Before long, Mir Jafar and the Jagat Seths had significantly raised their offer, and were now promising the participants Rs28 million, or £3 million sterling – the entire annual revenue of

---

* This is a crucial point. In as far as the EIC, in the shape of its directors, officials and most shareholders, had a corporate will at all, it was for trade yielding maximum profits and a large and steady dividend for themselves and their investors. Since the later seventeenth century, as Philip Stern shows, they certainly welcomed the application of Indian revenues to boosting their commercial capital and, of course, they later enthusiastically welcomed the Bengal revenues secured by Clive. But the directors consistently abhorred ambitious plans of conquest, which they feared would get out of control and overwhelm them with debt. For this reason the great schemes of conquest of the EIC in India very rarely originated in Leadenhall Street. Instead, what conquering, looting and plundering took place was almost always initiated by senior Company individuals on the spot, who were effectively outside metropolitan control, and influenced by a variety of motives ranging from greed, naked acquisitiveness and the urge to get rich quick, to a desire for national reputation and a wish to outflank the French and frustrate their Indian ambitions. This was true throughout the period, as much for Clive and Hastings as for Cornwallis and Wellesley.

Bengal – for their help overthrowing Siraj, and a further Rs110,000 a month to pay for Company troops. In addition, the EIC was to get *zamindari* – landholding – rights near Calcutta, a mint in the town and confirmation of duty-free trade. By 19 May, in addition to this offer, Mir Jafar conceded to pay the EIC a further enormous sum – £1 million* – as compensation for the loss of Calcutta and another half a million as compensation to its European inhabitants.[62]

On 4 June a final deal was agreed. That evening, Khwaja Petrus obtained for Watts a covered harem palanquin 'such as the Moor women are carryed in, which is inviolable, for without previous knowledge of the deceit no one dare look into it'.[63] Within this, the Englishman was carried into Mir Jafar's house to get the signatures of the old general and his son Miran, and to take their formal oath on the Quran to fulfil their part of the treaty obligations.[64] On 11 June, the signed document was back in Calcutta with the Select Committee, who then countersigned it. The next evening, pretending to set off on a hunting expedition, Watts and his men decamped from Kasimbazar and made their escape through the night, down the road to Chandernagar.

On 13 June 1757, a year to the day since Siraj had begun his attack on Calcutta, Clive sent an ultimatum to Siraj ud-Daula accusing him of breaking the terms of the Treaty of Alinagar. That same day, with a small army of 800 Europeans, 2,200 south Indian sepoys and only eight cannon, he began the historic march towards Plassey.

The road from Calcutta to Murshidabad passes through a great planisphere of flat, green floodplains and rice paddy whose abundant soils and huge skies stretch out towards the marshy Sunderbans, the Ganges delta and the Bay of Bengal to the south – a great green Eden of water and vegetation. Amid these wetlands, bullocks plough the rich mud of the rice fields and villagers herd their goats and ducks

---

* The modern equivalences of these sums are: £3 million = £315 million; Rs110,000 = £1,430,000; £1 million = £105 million.

along high raised embankments. Reed-thatched Bengali cottages are surrounded by clumps of young green bamboo and groves of giant banyans, through which evening clouds of parakeets whirr and screech.

In the pre-monsoon heat Clive marched his sepoys along a shaded embankment which led through this vast patchwork of wetlands: muddy paddy of half-harvested rice on one side gave way to others where the young green seedlings had just been transplanted into shimmering squares in the flooded fields. Through all this ran the main waterway of the Bhagirathi on which a small flotilla of wood and bamboo boats – it was now too shallow for Watson's battleships – sailed level with the land forces, providing transport for some of the officers of the European troops, and supplies of food and ammunition for all.

After all the frantic activity and communication of the previous week, as Clive marched north he began to be increasingly nervous about the ominous silence from the plotters. On 15 June, Clive wrote to reassure the Jagat Seths that he remained committed to the terms they had agreed:

As the Nabob has so long delayed the execution of the treaty with the English I am therefore come this way in order to see the articles fulfilled. I hear there are great disturbances in the city. I hope my arrival will put a happy end to them, we are as one, and I shall always listen to your advice. I am now at Culna, and hope to be at Agoa Diep in two days; be assured you may remain in the utmost safety in the city, and that my army shall act in the same manner they have hitherto done, and not plunder the least thing whatever.[65]

He received no reply.

The next day, he wrote again, this time to Mir Jafar: 'I am arrived at Tantesaul near Pattlee. I am in expectation of your news, and shall enter into any measures you desire. Let me hear from you twice a day. I shall not stir from Pattlee till I have news from you.'[66] Again there was no reply. Clive was now becoming suspicious: 'I am arrived at Pattlee with all my forces,' he wrote on the 17th, 'and am very much surprised at not hearing from you. I expect that on the receipt of this you will acquaint me fully with your intentions.'[67]

Despite the silence, he sent a platoon north on the 18th, with orders to take the fort of Katwa, which was seized without opposition. It was here that Mir Jafar was supposed to join the Company forces, but there was no sign of their supposed ally. That afternoon, Clive had a rare crisis of confidence: 'I am really at a loss how to act at the present situation of our affairs,' he wrote back to the Select Committee in Calcutta,

> especially should I receive confirmation by letter of Mir Jafar's resolution to stand neuter [i.e. not engage in the forthcoming battle]. The Nabob's forces at present are said not to exceed 8,000 but a compliance with their demands may easily increase them. If we attack them it must be entrenched and ourselves without any assistance. In this place a repulse must be fateful; on the contrary success may give the greatest advantage ... I beg you will let me have your sentiments how I ought to act at this critical juncture.[68]

Late that night Clive received from Mir Jafar a short and rather ambiguous note: 'On the news of your coming the Nabob was much intimidated and requested at such a juncture that I would stand his friend. On my part, agreeable to the circumstances of the times, I thought it advisable to acquiesce with his request, but what we have agreed on must be done. I have fixed the first day of the moon for my march. God willing I shall arrive.'[69] Clive was initially so relieved to hear anything from Mir Jafar that he replied, more fulsomely than the letter merited: 'I have received your letter which has given me the utmost satisfaction after the great pain I have suffered by your silence.'

> I have sent a party to possess themselves of Katwa town and fort, and shall move with my whole army there tomorrow. I believe I shall march from thence the next day, and hope to be at Moncurra in 2 days, but my motions will in a great measure depend on the advice I receive from you. Write me what you intend to do, and what is proper for me to do. On mutual intelligence depends the success of our affairs, so write me daily and fully. If I meet the Nabob's army what part will you act and how am I to act. This you may be assured of: that I will attack the Nabob within 24 hours after I come in sight of his army. Of all things take care of yourself that you be not arrested by treachery before my arrival.[70]

But the following morning, having reread Mir Jafar's letter, Clive again grew increasingly convinced he was walking into a trap, and wrote angrily to his self-professed ally: 'It gives me great concern that in an affair of so much consequence, to yourself in particular, that you do not exert yourself more.'

> So long as I have been on my march you have not given me the least information what measures it is necessary for me to take, nor do I know what is going forward at Murshidabad. Surely it is in your power to send me news daily. It must be more difficult for me to procure trusty messengers than you. However the bearer of this is a sensible, intelligent man, and in whom I have great confidence. Let me know your sentiments freely by him; I shall wait here till I have proper encouragement to proceed. I think it absolutely necessary you should join my army as soon as possible. Consider the Nabob will increase in strength dayly. Come over to me at Plassey or any other place you judge proper with what force you have – even a thousand horse will be sufficient, and I'll engage to march immediately with you to Murshidabad. I prefer conquering by open force.[71]

On 21 June, Clive called a Council of War to decide whether to continue with the campaign. They were now just one day's march from the mango plantations of Plassey where Siraj ud-Daula's army, swollen to 50,000, had safely entrenched themselves. When Clive presented all his intelligence to his military council, his colleagues voted strongly against continuing the campaign. Clive spent the night racked with indecision, but on waking decided to press on regardless. Shortly after this, a short message arrived from Mir Jafar, apparently saying that he was committing himself to action: 'When you come near, I shall be able to join you.'

To this Clive replied tersely, 'I am determined to risque everything on your account, though you will not exert yourself.'

> I shall be on the other side of the river this evening. If you will join me at Plassey, I will march half way to meet you, then the whole Nabob's army will know I fight for you. Give me leave to call to your mind how much your own glory and safety depends upon it, be assured if you do this, you will be Subah [Governor] of these

provinces, but, if you cannot go even this length to assist us, I call
God to witness the fault is not mine, and I must desire your consent
for concluding a peace with the Nabob.[72]

At six o'clock that evening, having received another brief and ambiguous
letter, he wrote again: 'Upon receiving your letter I am come to a
resolution to proceed immediately to Plassey. I am impatient for an
answer to my letter.'[73]

Clive then ordered his forces forward. The sepoys marched into the
increasingly liquid waterscape where islands of land appeared to float
amid network of streams and rivers and fish-filled, lily-littered *pukhur*
ponds. Towards evening, rising from these ripples, the troops spied
several raised mounds encircled with windbreaks of palm, clumps of
bamboo and tall flowering grasses. On one stood a small wattle village,
with its bullock carts and haystacks, and several spreading banyan trees.
To the other side, enclosed within a meandering oxbow of the Hughli
River, rose the small brick hunting lodge belonging to the Nawab of
Murshidabad, named after the distinctively orange-flowered grove of
palash trees which overlooked it. It was here, at Plassey, in the dark,
about 1 a.m., that Clive took shelter from a pre-monsoon downpour.
His damp troops were less lucky and camped under the shelter of the
thickly planted mango orchards behind his house.

Night passed and morning broke with no further word from Mir
Jafar. At 7 a.m., an anxious Clive wrote threateningly to the general
saying that he would make up with Siraj ud-Daula if Mir Jafar
continued to do nothing and remain silent: 'Whatever could be done
by me I have done,' he wrote. 'I can do no more. If you will come
to Dandpore, I'll march from Plassey to meet you. But if you won't
comply with this, pardon me, I shall make it up with the Nabob.'[74]
Such an eventuality was, however, becoming less and less plausible
by the minute, as the Nawab's forces, in all their magnificent tens of
thousands, emerged from their entrenchment, and began to encircle
the small Company army with a force that outnumbered them by at
least twenty to one.

The storm the night before had cleared the air, and the morning of
22 June dawned bright, clear and sunny. Clive decided to climb onto
the flat roof of the hunting lodge to get a better impression of what he
had taken on. What he saw took him aback: 'What with the number

of elephants, all covered in scarlet embroidery; their horses with their drawn swords glittering in the sun; their heavy cannon drawn by vast trains of oxen; and their standards flying, they made a pompous and fabulous sight.'

In all, Clive estimated that the Nawab had gathered 35,000 infantry, 15,000 cavalry and fifty-three pieces of heavy artillery which was superintended by a team of French experts. With its back to the bends of the Hughli, there was by 8 a.m. no exit for Clive's troops. Whether Mir Jafar lived up to his promises or not, there was now no realistic option but to fight.

At eight a cannonade began and after losing thirty sepoys Clive withdrew his men to shelter under the muddy riverbank bounding the mango grove. There was now a real danger of encirclement. One officer recorded Clive as saying, 'We must make the best fight we can during the day, and at night sling our muskets over our shoulders and march back to Calcutta. Most of the officers were as doubtful of success as himself.'[75] 'They approached at pace,' wrote Clive in his official report, 'and by eight began the attack with a number of heavy cannon, supported by their whole army.'

> They continued to play on us very briskly for Several Hours, during which our situation was of the utmost service to us, being lodg'd in a large Grove, surrounded by good mud Banks. To succeed in an attempt [at seizing] their cannon was next to impossible, as they were planted in a manner round us, and at a considerable distance from each other, we therefore remained quiet in our post, in expectation at best of a successful attack upon their camp during the night.[76]

Then, towards noon, the skies began to darken, thunder boomed and a torrential monsoon storm broke over the battlefield, soaking the men and turning the ground instantly into a muddy swamp. The Company troops made sure to keep their powder and fuses dry under tarpaulins; but the Mughals did not. Within ten minutes of the commencement of the downpour, and by the time Clive had reappeared on the roof of the hunting lodge having changed into a dry uniform, all Siraj's guns had fallen completely silent.

Imagining that the Company's guns would also be disabled, the Nawab's cavalry commander, Mir Madan, gave the order to advance, and 5,000 of his elite Afghan horse charged forward to the Company's right: 'the fire of battle and slaughter, that had hitherto been kept alive under a heap of embers, now blazed out into flames,' wrote Ghulam Hussain Khan.

> But as the nation of Hat-wearers have no equals in the art of firing their artillery and musquetry, with both order and rapidity, there commenced such an incessant rain of balls and bullets, and such a hot-endless firing, that the spectators themselves were amazed and confounded; and those in the battle had their hearing deafened by the continual thunder, and their eyesight dimmed by the endless flashing of the execution.[77]

Among those killed was Mir Madan himself, 'who made great efforts to push to the front, but was hit by a cannon ball in his stomach and died'.[78] 'At the sight of this, the aspect of Siraj ud-Daula's army changed and the artillerymen with the corpse of Mir Madan moved into the tents. It was midday when the people in the tents fled, and gradually the soldiers also began to take to their heels.'[79] At this point, Clive's deputy, Major Kilpatrick, seeing several Mughal batteries being abandoned, in defiance of orders and without permission, advanced to hold the abandoned positions. Clive sent angry messages forward, threatening to arrest Kilpatrick for insubordination; but the act of disobedience won the battle. This was the point, according to Edward Maskelyne, that the tide began to turn: 'Perceiving that many of the enemy were returning to their camp, we thought it a proper opportunity to seize one of the eminences from which the enemy guns had much annoyed us in the morning.'

> Accordingly, the Grenadiers of the first battalion with 2 field pieces and a body of sepoys supported by 4 platoons and 2 field pieces from the 2nd Battalion were order'd to take possession of it, which accordingly they did. Their success encouraged us to take possession of another advanc'd post, within 300 yards of the entrance to the enemy's camp ...[80]

A huge contingent of Mughal cavalry on the left then began to move away down to the banks of the Hughli and left the fighting. This, it turned out, was Mir Jafar, withdrawing just as he had promised.

Following his lead, all the Murshidabad forces were now beginning to fall back. What started as an orderly retreat soon turned into a stampede. Large bodies of Mughal infantry now began to flee: 'On this, a general rout ensued,' wrote Clive in his initial report, which still survives in the National Archives of India, 'and we pursued the enemy six miles, passing upwards 40 pieces of cannon they had abandoned, with an infinite number of hackeries and carriages filled with baggage of all kind.'

> Siraj ud-Daula escaped on a camel, and reaching Murshidabad early the next morning, despatched away what jewels and treasure he conveniently could, and he himself followed at midnight, with only two or three attendants. It is computed there were kill'd of the enemy about 500. Our loss amounted to just 22 killed, and fifty wounded.[81]

The following morning, 24 June, Clive scribbled a strikingly insincere note to Mir Jafar: 'I congratulate you on the victory which is yours not mine,' he wrote. 'I should be glad you would join me with the utmost expedition. We propose marching for now to complete the conquest that God has blessed us with, and I hope to have the honor of proclaiming you Nabob.'[82]

Later that morning, a nervous and tired-looking Mir Jafar presented himself at the English camp, and when the guard turned out in his honour he started back in fear. He was only reassured when he was escorted to Clive's tent and was embraced by the colonel, who saluted him as the new Governor of Bengal. Clive was not planning any treachery: ever the pragmatist, his need to install and use Mir Jafar as his puppet overruled the anger he had felt over the past week. He then advised Mir Jafar to hasten to Murshidabad and secure the capital, accompanied by Watts, who was told to keep an eye on the treasury. Clive followed at a distance with the main army, taking three days to cover the fifty miles to Murshidabad, passing along roads filled with abandoned cannon, broken carriages and the bloated corpses of men and horses.

Clive had been due to enter the city on the 27th, but was warned by the Jagat Seths that an assassination plot was being planned. So it was only on 29 June that Clive was finally escorted into Murshidabad by Mir Jafar. Preceded by music, drums and colours, and escorted by a guard of 500 soldiers, they entered together as conquerors. Mir Jafar was handed by Clive onto the *masnad*, the throne platform, and saluted by him as Governor. He then stated publicly, and possibly sincerely, that the Company would not interfere with his government, but 'attend solely to commerce'.[83] The elderly general 'took quiet possession of the Palace and Treasures and was immediately acknowledged Nabob'.

The pair then went straight to pay their respects to the man who had put both where they were now: Mahtab Rai Jagat Seth. 'I had a great deal of conversation' with the great banker, Clive recorded, 'As he is a person of the greatest property and influence in the three subas [provinces – Bengal, Orissa and Bihar] and of no inconsiderable weight at the Mughal court, it was natural to determine on him as the properest person to settle the affairs of that government. Accordingly, when the new Nawab returned my visit this morning, I recommended him to consult Jagat Seth on all occasions, which he readily assented to.'[84]

As it turned out, the Jagat Seth's goodwill was immediately necessary. There was only about Rs1.5 crore in the treasury – much less than expected, and if Clive and the Company were to be paid their full commission it would have to be through a loan brokered by the great bankers. Clive's personal share of the prize money was valued at £234,000, as well as a *jagir*, a landed estate worth an annual payment of £27,000.* At thirty-three, Clive was suddenly about to become one of the wealthiest men in Europe – but only if the money was actually paid. There followed several tense days. Clive was clearly anxious that Mir Jafar would default on his promises and that again he was in danger of being double-crossed by the old general. Like two gangsters after a heist, Mir Jafar and Clive watched each other uneasily, while the Jagat Seth searched for money: 'Whenever I write to your excellency by the way of complaint, it gives me infinite concern,' wrote Clive to Mir Jafar a week later,

---

* The modern equivalences of these sums are: Rs1.5 crore = about £200 million; £234,000 = almost £25 million; £27,000 = almost £3 million.

and more especially so when it is upon a subject in which I think the English interest suffers. This I am certain of: that anything wrong is foreign to your principles, and the natural goodness of your heart, and if anything be amiss, it must be owing to your ministers. But it is now several days that Mr Watts and Walsh have attended at the treasury to see what was agreed upon between your excellency and the English in presence of Jagat Seth and by his mediation put in execution. But their attendance has been to no manner of purpose, and without your excellency coming to some resolution as to what is to be paid in plate, what in cloth and what in jewels, and give absolute orders to your servants to begin, nothing will be done.

I am very anxious to see the money matters finished, for while they remain otherwise your enemies and mine will always from self-interested principles be endeavouring to create disputes and differences between us, which can only afford pleasure and hope to our enemies. But the English interest and yours is but one, and we must rise or fall together.

Clive characteristically concluded the letter with what could be read as a veiled threat: 'If any accident should happen to you, which God forbid, there will be an end of the English Company. I chose to send your Excellency my thoughts in writing, the subject were of too tender a nature for me to discourse only by word of mouth.'[85]

While Clive waited anxiously for his payment, 'on the insistence of Jagat Seth' Mir Jafar's son, Miran, was scouring Bengal for the fugitive Siraj ud-Daula who had fled the capital, heading upstream 'dressed in mean dress ... attended only by his favourite concubine and eunuch'. Ghulam Hussain Khan wrote how, after Plassey, Siraj 'finding himself alone in the palace for a whole day, without a single friend to unbosom his mind with, and without a single companion to speak to, took a desperate resolution.'

In the dead of night he put Lutf un-Nissa, his consort, and a number of favourites into covered carriages and covered chairs, loaded them with as much gold and as many jewels as they could contain, and taking with him a number of elephants with his best baggage and furniture, he quitted his palace at three in the morning, and fled ...

He went to Bagvangolah, where he immediately embarked on several boats, which are at all times kept ready in that station ...

[Two days later] this unfortunate Prince, already overtaken by the claws of destiny, was arrived at the shore opposite Rajmahal, where he landed for about one hour, with intention only to dress up some khichri [kedgeree – rice and lentils] for himself and his daughter and women, not one of whom had tasted food for three days and nights. It happened that a fakir resided in that neighbourhood. This man, whom he had disobliged and oppressed during his days in power, rejoiced at this fair opportunity of glutting his resentment, and of enjoying revenge. He expressed a pleasure at his arrival; and taking a busy part in preparing some victuals for him, he meanwhile sent an express over the water, to give information to the prince's enemies, who were rummaging heaven and earth to find him out.

Immediately on the advice of Shah Dana – for this was the fakir's name, Mir Qasim [the son-in-law of Mir Jafar] crossed the water, and having got Siraj ud-Daula surrounded with his armed men, they had the pleasure of becoming master of his person, as well as his family and jewels ... The Prince now became a prisoner and was brought back to Murshidabad ... in a wretched condition.

One Mahmedy Beg accepted the commission [to kill Siraj] and two or three hours after the fugitive's arrival, he set out to despatch him. Siraj ud-Daula had no sooner cast his eyes on that miscreant, than he asked whether he was not come to kill him? And the other having answered in the affirmative, the unfortunate prince, on this confession, despaired of his life.

He humbled himself before the Author of all Mercies, asked pardon for his past conduct, and turning to his murderer asked, 'They are not then satisfied with my being willing to retire into some corner, there to end my days with a pension? He had time to say no more; for at this words the butcher smote him repeatedly with his sabre; and some strokes falling on that beauteous face of his, so renowned over Bengal for its regularity and sweetness, the prince sunk to the ground, fell on his face and returned his soul to its maker; and emerged out of this valley of miseries, by wading through his own blood. His body was hacked to pieces, and by strokes without number, and the mangled carcase being thrown across the back of an elephant, was carried throughout the city.[86]

Siraj ud-Daula was only twenty-five years old. Shortly afterwards, Miran wiped out all the women of the house of Aliverdi Khan: 'Around seventy innocent Begums were rowed out to a lonely place into the centre of the Hooghly and their boat sunk.' The rest were poisoned. These bodies were brought together with those which were washed ashore and were buried together in a long line of sepulchres beside the old patriarch in the shady garden of Khushbagh, just across the Hughli from the small market town that today is all that is left of Murshidabad.

One woman, however, was spared. Both Miran and his father asked for the hand of the famously beautiful Lutf un-Nissa. 'But she declined and sent this reply: "having ridden an elephant before, I cannot now agree to ride an ass."'[87]

The same day that the remains of Siraj ud-Daula were paraded through the streets, 7 July, exactly 200 days since the task force had set off up the Hughli to Fulta, Clive finally got his hands on his money. It was one of the largest corporate windfalls in history – in modern terms around £232 million, of which £22 million was reserved for Clive. He immediately despatched his winnings downstream to Calcutta.

'The first fruit of our success was the receipt of Rs75 lakh, nearly a million sterling,* which the Souba paid and was laid on board 200 boats, part of the fleet which attended us in our march up, escorted by a detachment from the army,' wrote Luke Scrafton, one of Clive's assistants.

> As soon as they entered the great river, they were joined by the boats of the squadron, and all together formed a fleet of three hundred boats, with music playing, drums beating, the colours flying, and exhibited to the French and Dutch, whose settlements they passed, a scene far different from what they beheld a year before, when the Nabob's fleet and army passed them, with the captive English, and

---

* £100 million today.

all the wealth and plunder of Calcutta. Which scene gave them more
pleasure, I will not presume to decide.

Clive's winnings in 1757 was a story of personal enrichment very much in
the spirit of the Caribbean privateers who had first founded the Company
157 years earlier: it was all about private fortunes for the officers and
dividends for the Company, about treasure rather than glory, plunder
rather than power. Yet this was only the beginning: in total around
£1,238,575 was given by Mir Jafar to the Company and its servants,
which included at least £170,000 personally for Clive. In all, perhaps
£2.5 million was given to the Company by the Murshidabad Nawabs
in the eight years between 1757 and 1765 as 'political gifts'. Clive himself
estimated the total payments as closer to 'three million sterling'.*[88]
    Clive wrote to his father as he escorted his loot down the Bhagirathi,
telling him that he had brought about 'a Revolution scarcely to be
parallel'd in History'.[89] It was a characteristically immodest claim; but
he was not far wrong. The changes he had effected were permanent
and profound. This was the moment a commercial corporation first
acquired real and tangible political power.[90] It was at Plassey that the
Company had triumphantly asserted itself as a strong military force
within the Mughal Empire. The Marathas who had terrorised and
looted Bengal in the 1740s were remembered as cruel and violent. The
Company's plunder of the same region a decade later was more orderly
and methodical, but its greed was arguably deadlier because it was more
skilful and relentless and, above all, more permanent.[91]
    It initiated a period of unbounded looting and asset-stripping by
the Company which the British themselves described as 'the shaking
of the pagoda tree'.[92] From this point, the nature of British trade
changed: £6 million** had been sent out in the first half of the century,
but very little silver bullion was sent out after 1757. Bengal, the sink into
which foreign bullion disappeared before 1757, became, after Plassey,
the treasure trove from which vast amounts of wealth were drained
without any prospect of return.
    Bengal had always produced the biggest and most easily collected
revenue surplus in the Mughal Empire. Plassey allowed the EIC to

---

* The modern equivalences of these sums are: £1,238,575 = around £130 million; £170,000 =
almost £18 million; £2.5 million = £260 million; £3 million = over £300 million.

** £630 million today.

begin seizing much of that surplus – a piece of financial happenchance that would provide for the Company the resources it would need to defeat a succession of rivals until they finally seized the Mughal capital of Delhi itself in 1803. The Company was now no longer simply one of a number of European trading companies competing for Indian markets and products. Rather, it found that it had become a kingmaker and an autonomous power in its own right. It was not just that the East India Company had assisted in a palace coup for which it had been very well paid. With this victory, the whole balance of power in India had now shifted.

The British had become the dominant military and political force in Bengal. They now suspected that if they grew their army sufficiently they could probably seize any part of the country they took a fancy to, and rule it either directly or through a pliant puppet. Moreover, many Indians were beginning to understand this, too, meaning that the Company would become the focus for the attentions of all the dethroned, dispossessed and dissatisfied rulers, leading to a kaleidoscope of perpetually reforming and dissolving alliances that occurred from this point and which offered the region little prospect of peace or stability.

Indeed, the most immediate effect of Clive's palace coup was to destabilise Bengal. Three months later, in September, Clive had to return to Murshidabad to try and sort out a growing chaos there. Exactions by the Company, gathering arrears of pay of Mir Jafar's troops, military paralysis in the face of rebellions and punitive expeditions using Company sepoys created a growing vortex of violence and unrest. It was becoming abundantly clear that Mir Jafar was not up to the job, and that however many members of Siraj ud-Daula's regime he and Miran purged, there could be little legitimacy for this general who had had his own Nawab murdered and who now sat in what one Company observer called 'a throne warm with the blood of his Lord'.[93]

From now on there would be a slow drift to the Company of troopers, merchants, bankers and civil servants, leaving the Nawabs with nothing more than the shadow of their former grandeur. Clive and his colleagues had intended to do little more than re-establish British trade on a favourable footing and to ensure the accession of a more friendly Nawab. But what they had in fact done was fatally and permanently to undermine the authority of the Nawabs, bringing chaos to what had been up to that point the most peaceful and profitable part of the old Mughal Empire.[94]

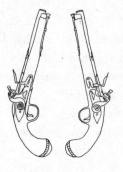

4

A Prince of Little Capacity

Twelve months later, to celebrate the first anniversary of the Plassey Revolution, Mir Jafar paid a state visit to Calcutta.

It was the new Nawab's first visit since he had led the assault on the town as a general of Siraj ud-Daula two years earlier, and his last before Clive would return to London to pursue his parliamentary ambitions. It was therefore as magnificent an affair as the still somewhat battered trading settlement could muster: there was a visit to the theatre, several concerts and a grand ball at the slightly surprising venue of the Calcutta courthouse, where the few women present danced 'until their feet were sore'.

Even more of a surprise was the choice of decoration selected to beautify the halls of justice for the entertainment of the pious Shia Muslim Nawab: 'twelve standing waxwork Venuses', unveiled to the sound of trumpets, horns and kettledrums. 'We have been so much taken up with balls, musick and visits to do honour to the Nabob,' wrote Luke Scrafton, 'that all publick affairs have been totally neglected.'[1]

But behind the external show of friendship between allies, perhaps inevitably, distrust and mutual dislike were now growing between the two rival governments of Bengal. 'Thank God His Excellency is at last gone,' wrote Scrafton a week later. 'He has led me a hell of a life here by the constant attendance I have been obliged to pay to him and his wenches, for he never went twenty yards from his house but they were with him.'[2] Clive, characteristically, was more cutting: the 'humane, generous and honest prince', whose impeccable character he had vouched for to the directors before Plassey, and who he had claimed to honour 'with the same regard as a son has for a father', he now regularly referred to as 'the old fool', while his son Miran was dismissed as 'a worthless young dog'.[3] Indolence, incompetence and opium had changed Mir Jafar, Clive wrote to London. The man he had raised to the throne had now become 'haughty, avaricious, abusive ... and this behaviour has alienated the hearts of his subjects'.[4]

If anyone had changed it was in reality the smugly victorious and now supremely wealthy Clive. Indeed, such was Clive's swaggering self-confidence at this period that he began to show signs of regretting sharing power with the Mughals at all. In despatches to London he flirted with the idea of seizing full and immediate control of Bengal with the now greatly enhanced power of his ever-growing cohort of tightly disciplined sepoy regiments. By the end of 1758 he was dismissively writing to the chairman of the EIC directors, 'I can assert with some degree of confidence that this rich and flourishing kingdom may be totally subdued by so small a force as 2,000 Europeans':

The Moors are indolent, luxurious, ignorant and cowardly beyond all conception ... The soldiers, if they deserve that name, have not the least attachment to their Prince, he can only expect service from them who pays them best; but it is a matter of great indifference to them whom they serve; and I am fully persuaded that after the battle of Plassey I could have appropriated the whole country to the Company and preserved it afterwards with as much ease as Mir Jafar, the present Subah [governor] now does, through the terror of English arms and their influence ...

The power of [the Mughal] Empire is greatly broken by intestine commotions, and perhaps its total ruin has been prevented only by the sums of money sent to Delly [from Bengal] ... You are well acquainted with the nature & dispositions of these Musselmen: gratitude they have none; [they are] bare Men of very narrow conceptions, and have

adopted a system of Politicks more peculiar to this Country than any
other, viz: to attempt everything through treachery rather than force.
Under these circumstances may not so weak a Prince as Mir Jafar be
easily destroyed, or be influenced by others to destroy us? What then
can enable us to secure our present acquisitions, or improve upon
them, but such a force as leaves nothing to the power of Treachery
or Ingratitude?[5]

Even more than the distrust and contempt, what emerges from the
letters of the period is the sense of mutual incomprehension between
these two very different worlds which had now been brought into such
close proximity. Mir Jafar, for example, clearly imagined the Company
to be an individual. When he learned that Clive was returning to
Britain, the packet of presents he sent to his esteemed ally the Company
was accompanied by a courteous Persianate letter addressed to what
Mir Jafar clearly thought was a single sovereign ruler rather than an
impersonal corporate board made up of rich London merchants. In
Warren Hastings' translation from the Persian it expressed Mir Jafar's
'earnest desire to see you ... which exceeds anything that could be
written or spoke ... I proceed to address myself to your heart, the
repository of friendship ... The light of my eyes, dearer than my life, the
Nabob Sabut Jung Bahadur [Clive], is departing for his own country.
A separation from him is most afflicting to me. Despatch him speedily
back to these parts and grant me the happiness of seeing him again
soon.'[6]

The incomprehension was mutual. In London, the directors were
still dimly digesting the news of the overthrow and murder of Siraj
ud-Daula, leading one anxious but inattentive Company director to
ask another, was it true that the recently assassinated Sir Roger Daulat
was a baronet?[7]

What the people of England did understand very clearly was the
unprecedented amount of money – or to use the newly Anglicised
word, loot – that Clive was bringing back with him. Not since Cortés
had Europe seen an adventurer return with so much treasure from
distant conquests.

On 5 February 1760, Clive and his wife Margaret set sail for home on
the *Royal George*, and even before they landed the gossip of the capital
was focusing on the unprecedented wealth that Clive was said to be

shipping home: Edmund Burke speculated in the *Annual Register* that 'it is supposed that the General can realise £1,200,000 in cash, bills and jewels; that his lady has a casket of jewels which are estimated at least at £200,000.* So that he may with propriety be said to be the richest subject in the three kingdoms.'

The true sums were somewhat less than this. Nevertheless, on arrival, the 35-year-old former Governor of Bengal bought the Shropshire estate of Walcott and leased a townhouse in Berkeley Square, the most fashionable part of London's Mayfair. A year later the Clives bought, in addition, the Claremont estate from the Duchess of Newcastle for £25,000, as well as a weekend retreat at Esher and several tracts of surrounding land, which they improved and combined into a single estate for an additional £43,000. They also purchased extensive lands in Co. Clare whose name Clive promptly changed from Ballykilty to Plassey. 'The cost of living rose immediately with the coming of this Croesus,' wrote Horace Walpole, the waspish Whig, in his diary. 'He was all over estates and diamonds ... and if a beggar asks charity, he says, "Friend I have no small brilliants with me."' By this time the rumour mill was in overdrive and the *Salisbury Journal* was reporting that even Lady Clive's pet ferret had a diamond necklace worth over £2,500.**[8]

Meanwhile, the Bengal that Clive had just conquered sank quickly into chaos.

The young Warren Hastings, now the Company's Resident (effectively ambassador) at Murshidabad, had been the first to sound the alarm, urging his boss to stay on and settle the anarchy he had helped unleash. In particular, he cited the growing instability at the Murshidabad court. Just before Clive left, Mir Jafar had been able to pay only three of his army's thirteen months' arrears of pay. As a result the unpaid troops

---

* The modern equivalences of these sums are: £1,200,000 = £126 million; £200,000 = £21 million.

** £25,000 = £2,625,000; £43,000 = £4,515,000; £2,500 = £262,500.

were openly mutinous and some were starving: 'their horses are mere skeletons,' he wrote, 'and their riders little better. Even the Jamadars [officers] are many of them clothed with rags.'⁹ It had taken only three years since Plassey to impoverish what had recently been probably the wealthiest town in India.

Mir Jafar himself certainly bore some of the responsibility for this mess. As with his mentor Clive, Plassey had brought him great personal enrichment, which he did not hesitate to show off, even as his soldiers went hungry: according to Ghulam Hussain Khan, he had always had a taste for fine jewels, but now 'was actually loaded with those glittering things; and he actually wore six or seven bracelets at his wrists, every one of a different species of gem; and he also had hanging from his neck, over his breast, three or four chaplets of pearls, every one of inestimable value ... He at the same time amused himself with listening to the songs and looking at the dances of a number of singers, who he carried with him wherever he went upon elephants.'¹⁰

It was now clear to everyone that Mir Jafar was simply not capable of ruling Bengal: an almost uneducated Arab soldier, he had no political skills and little conception how to run a state or administer its finances. As Clive himself calmly noted before boarding ship with his fortune, Mir Jafar had proved 'a prince of little capacity, and not at all blessed with the talent of gaining the love and confidence of his principal officers. His mismanagement has thrown the country into the greatest confusion.'¹¹ By 1760, three simultaneous rebellions had broken out across his dominions in Midnapur, Purnea and Patna. The Mughal nobility and officers of the army came to be increasingly resentful of the massive tribute that Mir Jafar had so thoughtlessly agreed to pay for Company support in overthrowing Siraj ud-Daula, and which was now daily depriving them of the payments and salaries that sustained the engine of state.

The ever astute and watchful Jagat Seths were among the first to realise they had for once backed a loser, and began to refuse loans for military expeditions to put down the different revolts which had begun to spread across the state like wildfires. To avoid further embarrassments, the bankers announced they were heading off with their families on an extended pilgrimage to the temple of their deity, Parasnath, in the mountains of Jharkhand. When the Nawab ordered his troops to block their way, the Seths called his bluff and forced their way through.

As Mir Jafar stumbled and as his treasury emptied, as intrigue festered in the Murshidabad court and as its military machine seemed locked in paralysis, Mir Jafar's vigorous but violent son Miran turned increasingly vicious. 'His inclination was to oppress and torment people,' wrote Ghulam Hussain Khan, who knew him well. 'He was expeditious and quick-minded in slaughtering people, and in committing murders, having a peculiar knack at such matters, and looking upon every infamous or atrocious deed as an act of prudence and foresight. For him, pity and compassion answered no purpose.'[12]

Miran's first concern was systematically to wipe out what remained of the house of Aliverdi Khan to prevent any counter-coup. He had already sent his henchmen to drown the entire harem of Aliverdi Khan and Siraj ud-Daula. Next came the turn of five of Siraj ud-Daula's closest relatives. His teenage younger brother, Mirza Mehdi, was despatched with especially savage cruelty: 'that unfortunate innocent youth was forced between two of those wooden frames called *takhtahs* [planks], where they conserve shawls and other precious goods; and the ropes having been strained hard at one and the same time, he had been squeezed to death, and it was from that kind of rack that that guiltless soul took its flight to regions of unalterable innocence and eternal repose'.[13] Miran later justified the act by quoting an aphorism of Sa'di: 'killing the snake and keeping its young is not the act of a wise man.'

Other potential rivals, including several favourites of the old regime and two senior ministers of his own court, he either stabbed in durbar, or at the gates of the palace, or despatched 'with a strong dose of poison'. Miran's paranoia grew in proportion to the chaos: the list of potential victims he kept scribbled in a special pocket book soon extended past 300.[14] As Warren Hastings reported to Calcutta when he heard about the mass murder of Siraj's family, 'no argument can excuse or palliate so atrocious a villain, nor (forgive me, Sir, if I add) our supporting such a tyrant'.[15]

But the Company, far from helping Mir Jafar, was actively engaged in undermining the economy which sustained him, so helping wring the neck of the Bengali goose which had been laying such astonishing golden eggs. After Plassey, unregulated private English traders began fanning out across Bengal, taking over markets and asserting their authority in a way that had been impossible for them before the

Revolution. By 1762, at least thirty-three of these private businesses had set themselves up in more than 400 new British trading posts around the province. Here they defied the power of local officials, refusing to pay the few taxes, tolls or customs duties they were still required to pay, as well as encroaching upon land to which they were not entitled. In this manner they ate away at the economy of Bengal like an invasion of termites steadily gnawing at the inside of an apparently sturdy wooden structure.[16]

'They began to trade in articles which were before prohibited, and to interfere in the affairs of the country,' wrote the brilliant but weak young Henry Vansittart, a friend of Hastings who had just taken over from Clive as Governor, and who was attempting, largely in vain, to try and rein in such abuses. 'The Nabob complained very frequently.'[17] Some of these traders operated on a large scale: by 1762–3, Archibald Keir was employing 13,000 men to manufacture 12,000 tons of salt, although the trade was officially out of bounds to any but the Nawab.[18]

Nor was it just Company officials who took advantage of the situation to use force to make a fortune: passes, permissions and sepoys were available to anyone who paid enough to the Company. Mir Jafar made particularly strong complaints about a French merchant who had managed to avail himself of Company *dastaks* (passes) and a battalion of sepoys to impose trade on the people of Assam in 'a very violent and arbitrary manner'.[19] According to his compatriot, the Comte de Modave, M. Chevalier 'took a great stock of salt and other articles to offload in the rich province of Assam, shielded by English passes and an escort of sepoys to safeguard his merchandise. He used this armed escort to facilitate the disposal of his goods, and as soon as he was established in the valley, sent his soldiers to the richest inhabitants, violently forcing them to purchase quantities of salt at prices determined by himself. With the same violence, he disposed of all his other trade goods.'[20]

Modave noted that the further away you went from Calcutta, the worse the situation became: 'A European visiting the upper parts of the Ganges finds mere robbers in charge of Company affairs, who think nothing of committing the most atrocious acts of tyranny, or subaltern thieves whose despicable villainy dishonours the British nation, whose principles of honour and humanity they seem totally to have rejected.'

The morals of this nation, otherwise so worthy of respect, have here become prodigiously depraved, which cannot but cause distress to any decent and thoughtful observer. British soldiers and traders permit themselves all sorts of liberties in the pursuit of private profit or in the hope of impunity. I have seen some so far forget their duty, that they beat to death unfortunate Indians to extract money not owed to them.

The country lies groaning under the Anarchy, laws have no power of sanction, morals are corrupt to the ultimate degree, the people groan under a multitude of vexations, all caused by the decay and confusion into which this once-great empire has fallen, with legitimate rulers having neither credibility nor authority. This rich and fertile land is turning into a desert. It is lost, unless some sudden general revolution restore its ancient splendour.[21]

Again, it fell to the young Warren Hastings, upriver in Murshidabad, to blow the whistle on many of these illicit activities, exposing the unbridled extortion now going on everywhere in the province: 'I beg leave to lay before you a grievance which calls loudly for redress,' he wrote to his friend and ally Vansittart, 'and which will, unless attended to, render ineffectual any endeavours to create a firm and lasting harmony between the Nabob and the Company; I mean the oppressions committed under the sanction of the English name.'

This evil, I am well assured, is not confined to our subjects alone, but is practised all over the country by people falsely assuming the habits of our sepoys, or calling themselves our *gomastas* [agents/managers]. As, on such occasions, the great power of the English intimidates people from making any resistance, so on the other hand the difficulty of gaining access to those who might do them justice, prevents our having knowledge of the oppressions, and encourages their continuance, to the great scandal of our government.

I have been surprised to meet [along the Hughli] with several English flags flying in places which I have passed; and in the river I do not believe there was a boat without one. But whatever title they may have been assumed, I was sure their frequency can bode no good to the Nawab's revenues, or the honour of our nation; but evidently tend to lessen each.[22]

'Nothing will reach the root of these evils,' he added, "till some certain boundary is fix'd between the Nabob's authority and our privilege.'[23]

Hastings was now the rising star of the East India Company's Bengal administration. He had never known either of his parents: his mother had died in childbirth, and his father disappeared to Barbados soon after, where he first remarried, then promptly died. Warren was brought up by his grandfather and educated in a charity school with the poorest children in the Gloucestershire village of Daylesford. At some point he was rescued by an uncle who sent him to London to be educated at Westminster, where he is said to have played cricket with Edward Gibbon, the future historian of Roman decline and fall.* There Hastings quickly excelled as the school's top scholar but was forced to leave, aged only sixteen, when his uncle died. His guardian found him a place as a writer in the Company, and shipped him straight out to Bengal, just in time to become a prisoner of Siraj ud-Daula at the fall of the Kasimbazar factory in 1756.[24]

By then, working as a buyer of silk in the villages around Murshidabad, fluent in Urdu and Bengali, and working hard on his Persian, Hastings had already fallen for his adopted country, which he always maintained he 'loved a little more' than his native one. A portrait from the period shows a thin, plainly dressed and balding young man in simple brown fustian with an open face and a highly intelligent, somewhat wistful expression, but with a hint of sense of humour in the set of his lips. His letters chime with this impression, revealing a diffident, austere, sensitive and unusually self-contained young man who rose at dawn, had a cold bath then rode for an hour, occasionally with a hawk on his arm. He seems to have kept his own company, drinking 'but little wine' and spending his evenings reading, strumming a guitar and working on his Persian. His letters home are full of requests for books.[25] From the beginning he was fierce in his defence of the rights of the Bengalis who had found themselves defenceless in the face of the plunder and exploitation of Company *gomastas* after Plassey: the oppressions of these agents were often so 'scandalous,' he wrote, 'that I can no longer put up with them without injury to my own character … I am tired of

---

* Though the fact that Gibbon was five years younger, born 1737 while Hastings was born 1732, sadly makes this story probably apocryphal.

complaining to people who are strangers to justice, remorse or shame.'[26] Brilliant, hardworking and an unusually skilled linguist, he was quickly promoted to become the Company's Resident at Mir Jafar's court where his job was to try and keep the hapless Nawab's regime from collapse.

This was every day becoming more likely. The absence of taxes and customs duty all added to the financial pressure on the Nawab and led to growing violence in the streets of Murshidabad where the Nawab's hungry sepoys were now taking matters into their own hands. But it also did much to alienate powerful individuals who might otherwise have been tempted to throw in their lot with the Company-backed regime. One of the first victims of the new power equation in Bengal was an influential Kashmiri trader named Mir Ashraf. Mir Ashraf was part of a dynasty of cultured Patna-based merchant princes who had grown rich on the manufacture and trade of saltpetre, derived from the mineral nitrates which appeared naturally in the soils of Bihar. As well as being an important ingredient of gunpowder, it was also used by the Mughals to cool their drinks.

Mir Ashraf's dynasty had good political connections at the Murshidabad court, and until the Battle of Plassey they had found it easy to dominate the saltpetre trade with the support of the Nawab. This irritated their British counterparts, who were unable to compete with the Mir's efficient procurement organisation, and who had for some years been complaining unsuccessfully that he was monopolising all saltpetre stocks and so shutting them out of the market.

Before Plassey, these complaints about Mir Ashraf were simply ignored by Nawab Aliverdi Khan, who dismissed the petitions against his friend by English interlopers as absurdly presumptuous. But within two months of the overthrow of Siraj ud-Daula, the Company's merchants in Patna were not only successfully encroaching upon Mir Ashraf's trade, they actually seized his entire saltpetre stocks by force of arms: in August 1757, a particularly aggressive Company factor named Paul Pearkes, whose name appears in several letters of complaint from Mir Jafar, actually broke into Ashraf's warehouses in an armed attack, using the 170 sepoys stationed to guard the Company's fortified upcountry base, the great Patna factory. His excuse was the patently invented charge that his business rival was sheltering French goods. Pearkes seized all the saltpetre in the warehouse and adamantly refused to return it, despite the intervention of several British officials in Patna.

Only when Mir Ashraf personally appealed to Clive himself was his property restored.[27]

As a result of these abuses, by 1760 both Mir Ashraf and the influential Jagat Seths had turned against the new regime and were actively writing letters to the one force they thought might still be able to liberate Bengal from the encroachments of the Company. This was the new Mughal Emperor, Shah Alam, who since his escape from Delhi had been wandering the Ganges plains, actively looking for a kingdom to rule, and surrounding himself with followers hoping for a return of the old Mughal order.[28]

On 9 February 1760, just four days after Clive had left India, Shah Alam crossed the Karmanasa, the boundary of Mir Jafar's dominions, and announced to his followers that the time had come to retake 'the prosperous and rich province' of Bengal for the Empire. His ultimate aim, he said, was to 'earn the money and revenue required to put down [the psychotic teenage vizier in Delhi] Imad ul-Mulk, and all who were acting against his government'.[29]

But his first goal, encouraged by Mir Ashraf, who used Hindu ascetics to carry his secret messages back and forth, was to take advantage of the growing anarchy in Mir Jafar's dominions to attack his western headquarters, Patna. Within a few days, large numbers of the old Mughal nobility of Bengal had thrown off their allegiance to Mir Jafar and offered their support to the young Emperor in his quixotic quest to rebuild the hollowed-out Mughal imperium.[30]

While Murshidabad had been falling apart, the Mughal capital of Delhi was faring even worse: like some rotting carcass preyed upon by rival packs of jackals, what was left of its riches provided intermittent sustenance to a succession of passing armies, as the city was alternately occupied and looted by Maratha raiders from the south and Afghan invaders from the north.

Throughout these successive occupations, Imad ul-Mulk had some how clung to power in the ruins of Delhi with the backing of the Marathas, sometimes ignoring, sometimes bullying his powerless puppet monarch, Shah Alam's father, Alamgir II. Eventually, on the eve of yet another Afghan invasion by Ahmed Shah Durrani, who was now married to Alamgir's daughter, and who he feared would naturally side with his father-in-law, the vizier decided to rid himself of his royal encumbrance entirely before the latter did the same to him.[31]

According to the account of Khair ud-Din Illahabadi in his *Book of Admonition*, the *Ibratnama*, Imad ul-Mulk finally took action in the early afternoon of 29 November 1759, at the fourteenth-century Firoz Shah's Kotla, south of the Red Fort, overlooking the Yamuna River. 'Imad ul-Mulk mistrusted the King, and equally the minister Khan-i Khanan, whom he knew to be party to the King's secret counsels.'

> So, he first murdered the Khan-i Khanan while he was at his prayers, then he sent to the King the fake news that, 'A wandering dervish from Kandahar has come and settled in the ruins of Firuz Shah's *kûtla*, a wonder-worker definitely worth visiting!' He knew that the pious King had a penchant for visiting fakirs, and that he would not resist an invitation to see one who had come from Ahmad Shah Durrani's homeland.
>
> The King could not contain his eagerness, and immediately set off: when he reached the chamber, he paused at the entrance, and his sword was politely taken from his hand and the curtain lifted: as soon as he was inside, the curtain was dropped again and fastened tight. Mirza Babur, who had accompanied him, saw that the Emperor was in danger and drew his sword to take on the attackers: but he was over-powered by a crowd of Imad al-Mulk's men, disarmed and bundled into a covered litter, then whisked off back to the Salateen prison in the Red Fort.
>
> Meanwhile, some ghoulish Mughal soldiers, who had been awaiting the King's arrival, appeared out of the dark and stabbed the unarmed man repeatedly with their daggers. Then they dragged him out by the feet and threw his corpse down to the sandy river bank below, then stripped it of its coat and under-garments and left it lying naked for six watches before having it taken to be interred in the Mausoleum of the Emperor Humayun.[32]

The news of his father's assassination finally reached Shah Alam three weeks later. The prince was still wandering in the east. His official court chronicle, the *Shah Alam Nama*, paints a picture of the young prince touring the Ganges plains giving titles and promising estates, and trying to gather support rather as a modern Indian politician canvasses for an election: visiting shrines, seeking the blessings of holy men and saints, holding receptions and receiving supporters and recruits.[33]

Shah Alam had no land and no money, but compensated as best he could for this with his immense charm, good looks, poetic temperament and refined manners. The Lord of the Universe may have been unable to enter his own capital, yet there was still some lingering magic in the title, and this penniless wanderer was now widely regarded as the *de jure* ruler of almost all of India, able to issue much-coveted imperial titles.[34] The young Shah Alam proved adept at drawing on the hallowed mystique associated with the imperial person, and the growing nostalgia for the once-peaceful days of Mughal rule. In this way, he managed to collect around him some 20,000 followers and unemployed soldiers of fortune, most of them as penniless and ill equipped as he was. It was as if the value of the royal charisma was growing in importance, even as the royal purse emptied.

Apart from money, what Shah Alam really lacked was a modern European-style infantry regiment, and the artillery which would allow him to besiege walled cities. Shortly before he learned of his father's death, however, fortune brought him a partial solution to both in the person of the dashing fugitive French commander of Scottish extraction, Jean Law de Lauriston. Law had managed to escape from Bengal soon after the twin disasters of the fall of Chandernagar and the Battle of Plassey temporarily ended French ambitions in eastern and northern India. He was still on the run from the Company when he came across the royal camp. He was delighted by what he saw of the ambitious and charming young prince.

Characteristically, Shah Alam did not try to hide the difficulty of his situation from Law. 'Wherever I go I find only pretenders,' he told him, 'nawabs or rajas, who have become accustomed to an independence which suits them so much they have no wish to bestir themselves on my behalf. I have no resources except theirs – unless the heavens declare in my favour by some extraordinary blow. Here, with the whole of Bengal in turmoil, it is just possible that the heavens might intervene in my favour. It might also be the end for me. One can only wait and see.'[35]

Flattered as he was by his royal reception, hard experience made Law sceptical about the new Emperor's chances, particularly given his experience of the Mughal nobility on whom Shah Alam relied.

He confided to the historian Ghulam Hussain Khan, 'I have travelled everywhere from Bengal to Delhi, but nowhere have I found anything from anyone except oppression of the poor and plundering of way-farers.'

> Whenever I wanted that one of these famous potentates like Shuja ud-Daula [the Wazir of Avadh], Imad ul-Mulk or their peers, out of honour and a regard for the regulation of the government, should undertake to put in order the affairs of Bengal and suppress the English, not one of them felt any inclination for the task. They did not once weigh in their minds the shamefulness of their conduct ... The Indian nobles are a set of disorderly, inconsistent blockheads, who exist solely for ruining a world of people.[36]

With him, Law had brought a ragged but determined force of one hundred of the last French troops in north India, and a battle-hardened battalion of 200 highly trained and disciplined sepoys. These troops he now offered to Shah Alam, who accepted with pleasure. On 23 December 1759, at Gothauli near Allahabad, the young Emperor emerged from the royal tents having shut himself away for three days of state mourning for his father.

According to the Mughal historian Shakir Khan, 'On the victorious day of his ascension to the imperial throne, His Sacred Majesty, the Shadow of God, Vice-Regent of the All-Merciful, the Emperor who is a Refuge to all the World, with general support and acclamation, commanded coins to be struck and *khutba* sermons to be given in the name of Shah Alam, King of the World, Warrior, Emperor, Exalted Seed, with the glorious Aureole of Kingship of the ancient Persian Kings, may God grant him eternal rule!'[37]

Soon after, the court artist, Mihir Chand, painted the Shah's dignified accession portrait, and newly minted rupees in the name of Shah Alam were distributed around the camp, as the commanders and army officers came to offer their compliments. 'I was honoured with the office of Mir Atish,' wrote Law, 'that is Master of Mughal Artillery, without actually having any heavy guns, although notionally, all the cannons and firelocks in the Empire were now under my orders':

> Thereafter offices were bestowed upon many other officers. The ceremony was conducted perfectly, accompanied by the sound of music by the *naubat* [trumpet] and artillery salutes ...

The whole country was at this point in flames, torn apart by a multitude of factions. Moreover, the Shah's officers were divided among themselves; there was no uniform command and they had not been paid for months. Money and war materiel were completely lacking ... I had got some bayonets made which were fixed to long poles, and with these I armed about 300 of the Koli tribals who were following us. I made them march in formation behind my regular sepoys, and they greatly augmented our strength. I also added a squadron of about 15 Mughal horsemen, well mounted ... It was not brilliant, but I was now Mir Atish, just as Shah Alam had become Emperor. The idea was everything.[38]

Shah Alam's campaign to recapture Bengal got off to a promising start. The Emperor successfully crossed the Karmanasa, and in durbar formally demanded the homage of the people, landowners and rulers of Bengal, who he commanded to 'remove the cotton wool of negligence from their ears'. Within days, three of the important Bengali zamindars west of the Hughli announced their support, as did two of Mir Jafar's most senior army commanders. All made haste westwards to join the Emperor with their troops.[39]

Shah Alam decided to attack immediately, before Miran and the Company commander Major John Caillaud could arrive with reinforcements from Murshidabad. So on 9 February the Emperor's forces moved forward and at Masumpur, a short distance outside Patna, engaged the Company sepoys commanded by the Governor of Patna, Raja Ram Narain. The battle was fought on the banks of the River Dehva. 'Musket balls were falling from the English line like a storm of hail,' wrote Ghulam Hussain Khan, but the young Emperor's forces attacked first, 'broke the enemy's ranks, and made them turn their backs ...'

As soon as the English fire was silenced, and the enemy was flying, [Shah Alam's commander] Kamgar Khan fell on Ram Narain, who yet stood his ground [on his elephant] with a number of men ...

Ram Narain's army was put to rout, and the Raja himself was obliged to fly for his life. Kamgar Khan ran a spear at him, wounding him grievously ... and he fell speechless inside his howdah, where, luckily for him, he was sheltered by the boards ... Ram Narain appeared senseless, so his driver turned his elephant around and fled ... The Emperor, satisfied with his victory, ordered his music to play in token of rejoicing, but forbore pursuing the vanquished.[40]

Allowing the defeated army to tend their wounded may have been a noble act, but Ghulam Hussain Khan believed it was also a fatal mistake: 'Had the victorious followed their blow, and pursued the vanquished, they would have mastered the city of Patna at once, as there did not remain in it a single soldier; they would have plundered it, and would have finished Ram Narain, who could not move. But as it was ordered by fate that city should be saved, Kamgar Khan contented himself with plundering the flat country outside the walls, and laying it under contribution.'[41]

Part of the British community in Patna fled downriver by boat. But Ram Narain's army remained quite safe within the city for, once the gates had been shut, the Emperor simply did not have the necessary artillery or siege equipment to attempt a storming of the walls.

Exaggerated rumours of the Emperor's victory soon reached Murshidabad where it threw the court into panic, and where Mir Jafar, aware of the extreme instability of his regime, fell into deep despair.[42] In the event, however, it proved a short-lived victory. Less than a week later, Major Caillaud and Miran marched into Patna, relieved the garrison, then marched out to confront the Emperor's force. Caillaud commanded one wing, Miran the other, and it was upon his cavalry that the Emperor's troops first fell.

'The enemy came on with much spirit,' wrote Caillaud afterwards, 'though with some irregularity, and in many separate bodies, after the Eastern manner of fighting.'[43]

Miran's army shattered at the force of the charge: 'Without minding his high rank and conspicuous station,' wrote Ghulam Hussain Khan, 'Miran was struck with a panic and turned around; he fled, followed reluctantly by his commanders, who called in vain for him to return.' He was followed by the Emperor's bowmen who surrounded the elephant and fired into his howdah: 'One arrow hit Miran, breaking his teeth; and whilst he was carrying his hand thither, another arrow lodged in his neck.' But Caillaud's highly disciplined Company sepoys held their ground, formed a square and attacked the flank and rear of the Mughal army at short range, with all the force of the musketry at their command. The effect was devastating. Hundreds were killed. Soon, it was the turn of the Emperor's troops to flee.

But Shah Alam had not come so far from Delhi to give up now. Sending his baggage and artillery back to the camp under the care of Law, he took the bold step of gathering a small body of his elite, lightly equipped Mughal cavalry under Kamgar Khan. Instead of retreating he pressed onwards, heading east, cross-country. 'He resolved to leave the enemy behind,' wrote Ghulam Hussain Khan, 'and by cutting his way through the hills and mountains, to attack the undefended city of Murshidabad, where he hoped he would possess himself of Mir Jafar's person, and of the wealth of so rich a capital.'[44]

The speed and courage shown by Shah Alam's small force took the Company by surprise. It was several days before Caillaud realised what the Emperor had done and where he was heading and was in a position to assemble a crack cavalry force to begin the pursuit.

Meanwhile, with three days' lead, the Emperor and Kamgar Khan, in the words of the *Tarikh-i Muzaffari*, 'thinking it was essential to move by the most rapid route available, crossed over several high passes rapidly and clandestinely, passing with forced marches steep mountains and narrow, dark clefts before heading southwards, down through the Bengal plains, passing Birbhum and eventually reaching the district of Burdwan'. There the Raja, who was an uncle of Kamgar Khan, had already declared for Shah Alam and risen in revolt against Mir Jafar.[45]

It was here, midway between Murshidabad and Calcutta, that the imperial army made the mistake of pausing for three days, while they rested and gathered more recruits, money and equipment from among the disaffected nobility of Bengal. As a relieved Caillaud himself wrote afterwards, 'Either from irresolution or some dissention among his commanders, he [Shah Alam] committed an unpardonable and capital error in hesitating to attack the old Nabob immediately, while the two armies were still divided. The delay completely ruined his design, at first so masterly concerted, and till then with so much steadiness carried on.'[46]

As with the failure to keep up momentum after the victory outside Patna, it gave Shah Alam's opponents time to catch up and regroup. By the time the Emperor had ordered his now slightly larger force to head north from Burdwan, Miran and Caillaud had managed to catch them up, and on 4 April effected a junction with Mir Jafar's small army. Together, they now blocked the road to Murshidabad.

The vital element of surprise was now completely lost. Mir Jafar's combined force lined up at Mongalkote, on the banks of the Damodar River. Here they commanded the crossing place and prevented the Emperor from moving the final few miles north to take the city. Had Shah Alam headed straight to Murshidabad without diverting south to Burdwan he would have found it all but undefended. As it was, a week later further reinforcements were still arriving for Mir Jafar: 'all these forces, with the English military contingent, turned to confront the Emperor's army encamped on the opposite bank.'

> Seeing such overwhelming enemy forces lined up on the bank of the Damodar, and realising that he could not now make the crossing and confront them with any hope of success, the Emperor decided he had no option but to return to Patna. Mir Jafar, seeing himself suddenly victorious, sent a military force to chase the retreating Emperor; however Kamgar Khan and the others kept the pursuing enemy busy, alternately with fighting and fleeing, and thus managed to get their troops and possessions back safely to Patna, where they were reunited with the sepoys of M. Law.[47]

It had been a bold, imaginative and very nearly successful strike. But the game was almost up. The people of Bihar, who had welcomed Shah Alam so enthusiastically a few months before, were now tired of hosting a large, undisciplined and losing army. According to Ghulam Hussain Khan, people initially loved the idea of the return of the good order of Mughal government, but instead they 'experienced from his unruly troops, and from his disorderly generals, every act of oppression and extortion imaginable; and, on the other hand, they saw every day what a strict discipline the English officers of those days did observe, and how amongst them that travelled, [the officers] carried so strict a hand upon their troops, as to suffer not a blade of grass to be touched; then indeed the scales were turned and when the Prince made his second expedition into those parts, I heard people load him with imprecations, and pray for victory to the English army.'[48]

After several months of dwindling fortunes, and deserting troops, the final defeat of the Emperor's army took place at the Battle of Helsa, near Bodhgaya, the site of the Buddha's Enlightenment, on 15 January 1761. Here the imperial army was finally cornered by several battalions of red-coated sepoys.

The night before the battle, Law dined for the last time with the Emperor – 'a very private affair, the atmosphere was very relaxed, and there were none of the usual constraints of etiquette and ceremony. I told him frankly that our situation was very bad. The Prince then opened up his heart about the misfortunes that had continued to dog him, and I tried to persuade him that, for the sake of his own security and peace, it might be better if he turned his gaze in some direction other than Bengal. "Alas!" he said, "what will they say if I retreat? Contempt will be added to the indifference with which my subjects already regard me."'[49]

Early the following morning, the Company troops took the initiative, moving rapidly forward from their entrenchments, 'cannonading as they marched'. A well-aimed ball from a 12-pounder killed the mahout of the Emperor's elephant. Another stray shot wounded the elephant itself, which careered off the field, carrying the Emperor with it.[50] Meanwhile, Mir Jafar, reverting to his usual devious tactics, had managed with large bribes to corrupt Shah Alam's commander, Kamgar Khan, as well as several other courtiers in his retinue, 'who soon crossed sides and joined the forces of the Nawab', reported the French soldier of fortune Jean-Baptiste Gentil. 'After that, there could be no doubt about the outcome. The general and the courtiers all took to their heels, taking with them the greater part of the Mughal army. Monsieur Law de Lauriston, who was in charge of the royal artillery, in spite of his bravery, military skill and all his efforts, could do nothing to stop them, and the French officer was taken prisoner.'[51]

Ghulam Hussain Khan gives a moving account of Law's brave last stand and his determination, having seen the Emperor deserted by all, and betrayed even by his commander-in-chief, to battle to the death: 'M. Law, with a small force, and the few pieces of artillery that he could muster, bravely fought the English, and for some time he managed to withstand their immense numerical superiority. The handful of troops that followed M. Law, discouraged by the flight of the Emperor and tired of the wandering life they had hitherto led in his service, turned about and fled. M. Law, finding himself abandoned and alone, resolved not to turn his back; he bestrode one of the guns, and remained firm in that posture, waiting for the moment of death.'[52]

Moved by Law's bravery, the Company commander, John Carnac, dismounted, and without taking a guard, but bringing his most senior staff officers, walked over on foot, and pulling their 'hats from their heads, they swept the air with them, as if to make him a salaam', pleading with Law to surrender: 'You have done everything that can be expected from a brave man, and your name shall undoubtedly be transmitted to posterity by the pen of history,' he begged. 'Now loosen your sword from your loins, come amongst us, and abandon all thoughts of contending with the English.'

Law answered that if they would 'accept this surrendering himself just as he was, he had no objections; but that as to surrendering himself with the disgrace of his being without a sword, it was a shame he would never submit to; and that they must take his life if they were not satisfied with the condition. The English commanders, admiring his firmness, consented to his surrendering himself in the manner he wished to; after which the Major shook hands with him, in their European manner, and every sentiment of enmity was instantly dismissed from both sides.'[53]

Later, in the Company camp, the historian was appalled by the boorishness of Mir Jafar's Murshidabad soldiers who began to taunt the captured Law, asking 'where is the Bibi [Mistress] Law now?'

> Carnac was furious at the impropriety of the remark: 'This man,' he said, 'had fought bravely, and deserves the attention of all brave men; the impertinences which you have been offering him may be customary amongst your friends and your nation, but cannot be suffered in ours, for whom it is a standing rule never to offer injury to a vanquished foe.' The man whom had taunted Law, checked by this reprimand, held his tongue and did not answer a word. He went away much abashed, and although he was a commander of

importance ... No one spoke to him any more, or made a show of standing up at his departure.

The incident caused Ghulam Hussain Khan to pay a rare compliment to the British, a nation he regarded as having wrecked his motherland:

This reprimand did much honour to the English; and it must be acknowledged, to the honour of these strangers, that their conduct in war and battle is worthy of admiration, just as, on the other hand, nothing is more becoming than their behaviour to an enemy, whether in the heat of action, or in the pride of success and victory.[54]

On 2 July 1761, Miran, the 'abominable', murderous, debauchee son of Mir Jafar, was killed – allegedly by a chance sudden strike of lightning while returning from the campaign against Shah Alam. According to John Caillaud, who was present in the camp, 'the young nabob, was lying asleep in his tent at midnight. Though singular in itself, yet no very extraordinary circumstances attended the event. He was struck dead in the middle of a violent storm, by a flash of lightning. The fire pierced through the top of the tent, struck upon his left breast, and he perished in the flame.'[55]

The event, however, occurred on precisely the anniversary of Miran's mass murder of the harem of Siraj ud-Daula and from the beginning there were rumours that his death was the result of divine intervention – or, alternatively, that it was not an accident at all, and that Miran had been murdered. The most probable candidate was said to be a bereaved concubine who had lost a sister to Miran's murderous tendencies, and who was then said to have covered up her revenge by setting fire to the tent.[56]

Many rejoiced at the death of this bloodthirsty and amoral prince; but for his father, Mir Jafar, it was the last straw. As the Company demanded prompt payment of all his debts, and as his subjects and troopers revolted against him, the old man had relied more and more on the grit and resolution of his son. Without him, Mir Jafar went to pieces. 'He had at no time been in his right senses,' commented Ghulam Hussain Khan, 'but he now lost the little reason that remained to him. The affairs of the army, as well as the government being entirely abandoned to chance, fell into a confusion not to be described.'[57]

But Mir Jafar had a son-in-law, Mir Qasim, as different a man as could be imagined from his chaotic and uneducated father-in-law. Of noble Persian extraction, though born on his father's estates near Patna, Mir Qasim was small in frame, with little military experience, but young, capable, intelligent and, above all, determined.[58]

Warren Hastings was the first to spot his unusual qualities; he was also the first to make clear to Calcutta the urgent need to bring in a new administration to Murshidabad if Bengal was to remain governable. Mir Qasim's 'education has been suitable to his noble birth,' he wrote, 'and there are few accomplishments held requisite for those of highest Rank which he does not possess in an eminent degree. He has given many proofs of his integrity, a capacity for business, and a strict adherence to his Engagements. He is generally respected by the Jamadars [officers] & Persons of Distinction in this Province, and I have seen Letters addressed to him from the Principal Zamindars of Bihar, filled with expressions of the highest respect for this character, and their earnest desire to be under his Government.'[59]

Mir Qasim was duly sent down to Calcutta to meet the new Governor, Henry Vansittart. During the interview he came up with a sophisticated scheme both to solve the Company's financial problems and to repay the Murshidabad debt, by ceding to the Company Burdwan, Midnapur and Chittagong – sufficient territories to pay for the upkeep of both armies. Vansittart was impressed, and decided to back a coup, or second revolution, to put Mir Qasim on the throne in place of his father-in-law. A series of large bribes, including a cash payment of £50,000 to Vansittart personally, and £150,000* to be distributed among his council, cemented the deal.[60]

Meanwhile, on 10 July 1761, matters came to a head in Murshidabad, giving the Company both the excuse and the perfect cover for their second coup: 'The army, demanding their pay which had come into arrears for some years, finally mutinied in a body', recorded the *Riyazu-s-salatin*.

---

* The modern equivalences of these sums are: £50,000 = over £5 million; £150,000 = almost £16 million.

'The mutineers surrounded the palace, pulling their officers from their horses and palanquins, climbing the palace walls and throwing masonry down on palace servants. Then they besieged the Nawab in his Chihil Sutun palace, and cut off supplies of food and water.'

> Mir Qasim, in concert with Jagat Seth, conspired with the English chiefs ... brought Mir Jafar out from the Fort, placed him in a boat, and sent him down to Calcutta [as if to rescue him and saying it was for his own safety]. At the same time, Mir Qasim entered the fort, mounted the *musnud* [throne] and issued proclamations of peace and security in his own name.[61]

Mir Jafar was given an escort, led by the ubiquitous Major Caillaud, 'to protect his person from the insults of the people, and he was permitted to take with him women, jewels, treasure and whatever else he thought proper'.[62] As he was rowed downstream, finally realising that he had been not so much rescued as deposed, a baffled Mir Jafar begged to be allowed to appeal to his patron, Clive: 'The English placed me on the *musnud*,' he said. 'You may depose me if you please. You have thought proper to break your engagements. I will not break with mine. I desire you will either send me to Sabut Jung [Clive], for he will do me justice, or let me go to Mecca.'[63]

But the elderly, failing former Nawab, now of no further use to the Company, was allowed neither of his preferred options. Instead he was given a modest townhouse in north Calcutta, and an equally modest pension, and for several months was kept under strict house arrest. The second revolution engineered by the Company, this time against their own puppet, turned out to be even smoother than the first, and completely bloodless.

But the man they had just put in charge of Bengal would prove to be less easy to bully than Mir Jafar. As the *Tarikh-i Muzaffari* succinctly put it, 'Mir Qasim quickly succeeded in achieving a degree of independence from the English that is now hard to imagine.'[64]

Even Warren Hastings, who greatly admired Mir Qasim's abilities, was surprised by the speed with which he turned matters around.

The new Nawab first quickly dispersed the mutinous sepoys of Murshidabad by paying them from his own treasury. He then applied himself to sorting out finances and surprised everyone with his administrative skills: 'Mir Qasim Khan was very skilled in extracting information and in analysing written reports and accounts,' wrote the historian Mohammad Ali Khan Ansari of Panipat. 'He embarked immediately on the project of bringing the land of Bengal back into some sort of order.'

> He called in the state accountants and tax-gatherers, examining their accounts closely to find out any peculation committed by functionaries of the previous regime. He had Raja Ram Narain [the Governor of Patna, who had helped defeat Shah Alam] brought in for questioning and demanded to see the revenue accounts for Bihar. Any sums claimed to have been made as payments for army salaries were inspected by his tax-gatherers, whom he sent to check the actual numbers of soldiers present, and to correct the record accordingly. After this, Raja Ram Narain, accused on several counts, was imprisoned. Some 15 lakhs rupees* of the Raja's personal wealth was confiscated, together with his jewels.[65]

At first, Mir Qasim struggled to pay the money he owed the British, despite these seizures. He increased taxes to almost double what they had been under Aliverdi Khan, successfully raising Rs30 million** annually – twice the Rs18 million gathered by the regime before Plassey.[66] Meanwhile, the new Nawab began to develop a coherent strategy to deal with the British: he decided more or less to abandon lower Bengal to the Company, but worked to keep their influence at a minimum elsewhere. He also established a highly centralised military state, which he sustained by seizing the property and treasure from any officials he suspected of corruption: 'he pursued with vexations anyone suspected of harbouring wealth and any who held even the slightest enmity towards himself, immediately taking over their hidden riches. In this manner, gold flowed in plenty into the treasury of Mir Qasim Khan.'[67]

* Almost £20 million today.

** £390 million today.

In accordance with his restructuring plan, Mir Qasim decided to leave his uncle in charge of Murshidabad, which he thought too vulnerable to interference from Calcutta, and to rule instead from Bihar, as far as possible from the Company's headquarters. He first moved to Patna, occupying the fort apartments vacated by the now imprisoned Raja Ram Narain. Here he briefly set up court, until the hostility and interference of the Company's aggressive Chief Factor there, William Ellis, prompted him to move a little downstream to the old Mughal fortress of Monghyr where he could not be spied on by the Company.

At Monghyr he continued to reform the finances. He ordered the Jagat Seths to join him, marched them over from Murshidabad under guard and confined them to the fort. There he forced them to pay off both the Nawab's outstanding obligations to the Company and the arrears of the Murshidabad troops.

The better to enforce his will, and also, implicitly, to protect him from the Company, he then reformed his army. The 90,000 troops Mir Qasim was supposed to possess on paper turned out to muster less than half that in reality. Incompetent and corrupt generals were dismissed and he began recruiting new troops, forming a fresh force of 16,000 crack Mughal horse and three battalion of European-style sepoys, amounting to around 25,000 infantry.

To drill them in the new European manner he next appointed two Christian mercenaries. The first was Walter Reinhardt, nicknamed Sumru or Sombre, a gloomy and coldly emotionless Alsatian German soldier of fortune. He had been born to a poor farmer with a smallholding on the Moselle in the Lower Palatinate of the Rhine, and had risen to become a mounted *cuirassier* guard in the French army where he had fought with bravery at the Battle of Ittingen. Finding himself in Holland, he had caught a ship to India on a whim, where, according to one of his colleagues, the Comte de Modave, he soon took 'on the habits and indeed the prejudices of this country to such a degree that even the Mughals believe he was born in Hindustan. He speaks nearly all the local languages, but can neither read nor write. Nevertheless, through his staff, he keeps up an extensive correspondence.'[68]

Mir Qasim's second Christian commander was Khoja Gregory, an Isfahani Armenian to whom Mir Qasim gave the title Gurghin Khan, or the Wolf. Ghulam Hussain Khan met him and thought him a remarkable man: 'above ordinary size, strongly built, with a very fair complexion, an aquiline nose and large black eyes, full of fire'.[69] The job of both men was to train up Mir Qasim's forces so that they could equal those of the Company. They also started armaments factories to provide their master with high-quality modern muskets and cannon. Soon Mir Qasim 'was amassing and manufacturing as many guns and flint muskets as he could, with every necessary for war'.[70]

The new Nawab also set up a formidable new intelligence network, with three head spies, each with hundreds of informers under them. Before long, all three of his intelligence chiefs had been executed for their suspected intrigues. Mir Qasim's rule was quickly proving as chilling as it was effective. 'So suspicious a government soon interrupted all social intercourse,' wrote Ghulam Hussain Khan, who was terrified of the new Nawab. 'He was ever prone to the confiscation of properties, confinement of persons, and the effusion of blood ... People accustomed to a certain set of acquaintances and visits, now found themselves under the necessity of living quietly at home.'[71]

Yet the historian still greatly admired the Nawab's extraordinary administrative skills: 'He had some admirable qualities,' he admitted,

> that balanced his bad ones. In unravelling the intricacies of the affairs of Government, and especially in the knotty mysteries of finance; in establishing regular payments for his troops, and for his household; in honouring and rewarding men of merit, and men of learning; in conducting his expenditure, exactly between the extremities of parsimony and prodigality; and in knowing intuitively where he must spend freely, and where with moderation – in all these qualifications he was an incomparable man indeed; and the most extraordinary Prince of his age.[72]

But beyond the efficiency a darker side to the rule of the new Nawab began to emerge. Many men began to disappear. Rich landowners and bureaucrats were summoned to Monghyr, imprisoned, tortured and stripped of their wealth, whether they were guilty of corruption or not: 'Many were executed on a mere suspicion,' wrote Ansari. 'These killings instilled such fear in the hearts of people, that they dared not speak out against him or his policies, and no-one felt safe in their own home.'[73]

After the Battle of Helsa in early January 1761, the Mughal Emperor found himself in the unexpected position of being on the run from the mercenary troops of a once humble trading company.

The redcoats tracked him relentlessly. On 24 January, Major John Carnac wrote to Calcutta telling his masters, 'We have kept following the prince ever since the action, and press so closely upon him that sometimes we find the fires of his camp still burning ... His army must be totally dispersed ... and he reduced so low as to be more an object of pity than fear.'[74]

Yet it was only now, after the Company had defeated Shah Alam, and his army had largely dissolved, that the British began to understand the moral power still wielded by the Emperor. Shah Alam had lost everything – even his personal baggage, writing table and calligraphy case, which had fallen from his howdah when his elephant charged off the battlefield – and he could now offer his followers almost nothing of any practical value. And yet they continued to revere him: 'It is inconceivable how the name of the king merely should prepossess all minds so strongly in his favour,' wrote Carnac. 'Yet so it is that even in his present distressed condition he is held by both Musselmans and Gentoos [Muslims and Hindus] in a kind of adoration.'

Carnac was as skilled a politician as he was a soldier, and noted, perceptively: 'We may hereafter have it in our power to employ this prepossession to our advantage; in the meantime the axe is laid to the root of the troubles which have so long infested this province.'[75]

In the aftermath of his defeat, Shah Alam had also had time to revaluate his position with regard to the Company and realised that both sides had much to offer each other. After all, he had no wish to rule Bengal directly. Ever since the time Akbar made his former Rajput enemy Raja Jai Singh the commander of his army, the Mughals had always had the happy knack of turning their former enemies into useful allies. Perhaps now, Shah Alam seems to have wondered, he could use the British in the same way Akbar used the Rajputs to effect his ends? In the eyes of most Indians the Company lacked any legal right to rule.

It was in Shah Alam's power to grant them the legitimacy they needed. Maybe an alliance could be formed, and British arms could carry him back to Delhi, remove the usurper, Imad ul-Mulk, and restore him to his rightful throne?

On 29 January an emissary from the Emperor arrived in Carnac's camp, with proposals for a settlement. Ambassadors passed backwards and forwards, messages were sent to Calcutta, and eventually, on 3 February, a meeting was arranged in a mango grove near Gaya. Ghulam Hussain Khan was there, as his father had volunteered to act as Shah Alam's intermediary with the British: 'The Emperor was advancing with his troops in battle array towards the English camp, when, about midday, the Major made his appearance with his officers.'

> Pulling off his hat, and putting it under his arm, he advanced in that posture, marching on foot close to the Emperor's elephant; but the monarch commanded him to be mounted. Carnac got on horseback, and taking his station alone, he preceded the Emperor's elephant by about an arrow's shot. My father, on his elephant, followed the Emperor at a small distance, both men leading the imperial troops, all armed and ready.
>
> At the spot where the troops were to encamp, the Emperor, at Major Carnac's request, entered a tent pitched in a garden surrounded by a grove, where were conducted the usual [welcome] ceremonies of paan, ittar and rose-water, while dancing girls and musicians provided entertainment for the evening.[76]

The next day the two armies set off together to Patna. Few from the Company had ever seen a Mughal Emperor, and as news spread of Shah Alam's approach the entire British community in Bihar turned out to see him, joining the throngs lining the streets to catch a glimpse. It was a scene rich with irony: the victors excitedly going out of their way to honour the somewhat surprised vanquished, a man who had spent much of the previous year trying his best to expel them from India. Even the interpreter on this occasion was Archibald Swinton, the man who had chased Shah Alam's elephant from the battlefield at Helsa, and who had then appropriated the Emperor's personal baggage.[77]

Yet both parties recognised that this was a situation which benefited everyone, and played their part in the charade: 'The English were busy turning their factory into an Imperial hall of audience,' noted Ghulam Hussain Khan, 'arranging a couple of those [long] tables where they take their meals, into a Hindostany throne.'

> [Before long,] the hall, being spread and hung with rich stuffs, assumed a very splendid appearance ... The English assembled in great numbers. These, on hearing the Emperor's being on his march, set out on foot with the Major at their head, and after meeting the Monarch, they continued to march on foot, along with his moving throne. The Emperor, having alighted at the gate of the factory, got into the hall, and took his seat on his throne. The English were standing to the right and left of it. The Major made a profound bow and took his seat.[78]

The only person displeased with this turn of events was the newly installed Nawab, Mir Qasim. He feared, with good reason, that now the Company had the Emperor in their clutches, the usefulness of a tame Nawab was diminished, and that the Company might ask to have themselves appointed in his stead. Mir Qasim was right to be anxious on this score: this was indeed an option the Council in Calcutta had weighed up, but decided not to pursue for the time being.[79]

So it was that Mir Qasim finally met his Emperor, the Refuge of the World, sitting on a makeshift throne, within an East India Company opium factory. After some courtly haggling behind the scenes, a deal had been fixed. Mir Qasim duly bowed three times, offering the Emperor his obedience, and made a formal *nazar* [offering] of 1,001 gold coins, 'and a number of trays covered with precious and curious stuffs for apparel, to which he added a quantity of jewels and other costly articles. The Emperor accepted his homage, and honoured him with a chaplet of pearls, and an aigrette of jewels, adorned with black eagle's feathers.'

In Mughal court language this amounted to a formal investiture, confirming Mir Qasim in the Subadhari [governorship] of Bengal, Bihar and Orissa, so ratifying and legalising the Company's two successive revolutions. In return, Mir Qasim announced he would resume Bengal's annual payments to the Mughal Emperor, promising an enormous annual tribute of 2.5 million rupees, which then equated to around

£325,000. Meanwhile, the English settled on the Emperor a daily allowance of Rs1,800.*[80]

Both sides had reason to be happy with the unexpected way events had been resolved. Shah Alam in particular found himself richer than he had ever been, with a steady flow of income that he could only have dreamed of a few weeks earlier. Only in one thing was he disappointed: Shah Alam wanted his useful new ally, the Company, to send a regiment of sepoys immediately, to install him back on his throne in Delhi. Many in the army, and even some in Calcutta, were attracted by the idea of a Delhi expedition; but given the turbulence of the capital, which was currently hosting yet another unwanted visit from the bloodthirsty Afghan monarch, Ahmad Shah Durrani, Vansittart in the end decided to put off any decision about reinstalling the Shah, 'until after the rains'.[81]

Three months later, seeing that he was making no progress with his plan to return home to the Red Fort, an impatient Shah Alam announced his departure. His next port of call, he said, would be Avadh. There he hoped the rich and powerful Nawab Shuja ud-Daula would be more pliable. Mir Qasim was delighted to get rid of the Emperor, and to hasten his departure paid him up front, and in cash, half the promised annual tribute. Nor did the East India Company have any reason to detain the Emperor, having now extracted from him all they needed. On receiving formal letters of submission from all the principal warlords in north India, on 5 June 1761 Shah Alam finally left, heading west towards the border with Avadh.[82]

Major Carnac escorted him to the banks of the Karmanasa with full military honours. The Emperor crossed back into Avadh on 21 June, where he was greeted by Nawab Shuja ud-Daula, whom he formally appointed Vizier of the Mughal Empire. But Shuja, like the British, warned the Emperor about returning to Delhi while the Afghans were still occupying the city. According to the French mercenary Jean-Baptiste Gentil, who was by then working for Shuja: 'The Vizier warned the Emperor about Durrani true intentions.'

These were to utterly destroy the Timurid royal house, once he had all the Timurid Princes in his power – the only one still at liberty

---

* The modern equivalences of these sums are: £325,000 = £34 million; Rs1,800 = £23,400.

being Shah Alam himself. Durrani's plan was to conquer Hindustan, and a Mughal Prince could only be an irritant and a nuisance to that ambition: it was therefore of capital importance, both for the Emperor himself and for Hindustan, that he should not hand himself over to his enemy. Shah Alam appreciated Shuja ud-Daula's good counsel, and politely declined Durrani's invitation to Delhi.[83]

Meanwhile, Bengal was left under the increasingly uneasy joint rule of Mir Qasim and the Company.

Over the next two years, 1761–2, relations between the two rival governments of Bengal became openly hostile. The cause of the steady deterioration was the violent and rapacious way private Company traders increasingly abused their privileges to penetrate the Bengali economy and undermine Mir Qasim's rule.

These private traders regularly arrested and ill-treated the Nawab's officers, making it almost impossible for him to rule. The Nawab, in turn, became increasingly paranoid that William Ellis, the Chief Factor of the English factory in Patna, was actively fomenting a rebellion against him. Ellis had lost a leg at the siege of Calcutta in 1756 and his subsequent hatred for all things Indian made him take a perverse, almost sadistic, pleasure in disregarding Mir Qasim's sovereignty and doing all he could to overrule his nominal independence.

Henry Vansittart believed that Mir Qasim was a man much more sinned against than sinning, and in this he was seconded by his closest ally on the Council, Warren Hastings. Hastings had been fast-promoted to be Vansittart's deputy after making a success of his time as Resident in Murshidabad; he was now being talked about as a possible future Governor. Anxious to make joint Mughal–Company rule a success in Bengal, Hastings had been the first to spot Mir Qasim's capacity for business and now was quick to defend his protégé. 'I never met a man with more candour or moderation than the Nabob,' he wrote. 'Was there but half the disposition shown on our side which he bears to peace, no

subject of difference could ever rise between us ... He has been exposed
to daily affronts such as a spirit superior to a worm when trodden
on could not have brooked ... The world sees the Nabob's authority
publicly insulted, his officers imprisoned, and sepoys sent against his
forts.'[84] He added: 'If our people instead of erecting themselves into
lords and oppressors of the country, confine themselves to an honest
and fair trade, they will everywhere be courted and respected.'[85]

Then, in early February 1762, Ellis took it upon himself to arrest
and imprison in the English factory a senior Armenian official of Mir
Qasim's, Khoja Antoon. Mir Qasim wrote to Ellis complaining that
'my servants are subjected to such insults, my writing can be of no use.
How much my authority is weakened by such proceedings I cannot
describe.' After this Mir Qasim vowed not to correspond any further
with Ellis.[86]

Thereafter, week after week, in long and increasingly desperate Persian
letters, Mir Qasim poured out his heart to Vansittart in Calcutta, but
the young Governor was no Clive, and seemed unable to enforce his
will on his colleagues, particularly those under Ellis in the Patna factory.
Ellis and his men, wrote Mir Qasim in May 1762, 'have decided to
disrupt my rule. They insult and humiliate my people, and from the
frontiers of Hindustan up to Calcutta, they denigrate and insult me.'

And this is the way your gentlemen behave: they make a disturbance all
over my country, plunder the people, injure and disgrace my servants
with a resolution to expose my government to contempt and making
it their business to expose me to scorn. Setting up their colours,
and showing Company passes, they use their utmost endeavours
to oppress the peasant farmers,* merchants and other people of the
country. They forcibly take away the goods and commodities of the
merchants for a fourth part of their value; and by way of violence and
oppression they oblige the farmers to give five rupees for goods that
are worth but one.

The passes† for searching the boats, which you formerly
favoured me with, and which I sent to every chokey [check post],
the Englishmen by no means regard, I cannot recount how many
tortures they inflict upon my subjects and especially the poor people

* *Ryot* in the original text. I have substituted 'farmer' throughout.

† The word in the original text is *dastak*. I have substituted 'pass' throughout.

... And every one of these Company agents has such power, that he imprisons the local collector [the Nawab's principal officer] and deprives him of all authority, whenever he pleases.

Near four or five hundred new [private English] factories have been established in my dominions. My officers in every district have desisted from the exercise of their functions; so that by means of these oppressions, and my being deprived of my [customs] duties, I suffer a yearly loss of nearly twenty-five lakh rupees.* In that case how can I keep clear of debts? How can I provide for the payment of my army and my household? In this case, how can I perform my duties and how can I send the Emperor his due from Bengal?[87]

In April, Vansittart sent Hastings upriver to Monghyr and Patna in an attempt to defuse the growing crisis and restore harmony. On the way, Hastings wrote a series of letters, at once waxing lyrical about the beauty of Bengal, and expressing his horror at the way the Company was responsible for raping and looting it. On arrival in Monghyr, where ducks clustered on the marshes amid 'beautiful prospects', he wrote with eloquence and feeling of 'the oppression carried out under the sanction of the English name' which he had observed in his travels. 'This evil I am well assured is not confined to our dependants alone, but is practised all over the country by people assuming the habit of our sepoys or calling themselves our managers ...'

A party of sepoys who were on the march before us, afforded sufficient proof of the rapacious and insolent spirit of those people when they are left to their own discretion. Many complaints against them were made to me on the road; and most of the petty towns and serais were deserted at our approach, and the shops shut up, from apprehensions of the same treatment from us ... Every man who wears a hat, as soon as he gets free from Calcutta becomes a sovereign prince ... Were I to suppose myself the Nabob I should be at a loss in what manner to protect my own subjects or servants from insult.[88]

In particular, Hastings was critical of Ellis, whose behaviour, he believed, had been 'so imprudent, and his disaffection to the Nabob so

* £32.5 million today.

manifestly inveterate, that a proper representation of it could not fail to draw upon him the severest resentment of the Company'.[89]

In October, Hastings went again to visit Mir Qasim at Monghyr, this time taking Governor Vansittart with him so that he could see what was happening with his own eyes. Both were appalled by what they witnessed and returned to Calcutta determined to end the abuses. But on arrival, the two young men failed to carry their fellow Council members with them. Instead, the majority decided to send one of their most aggressive members, Ellis's friend James Amyatt, to make his own report, to put Mir Qasim in his place and to demand that all Company servants and managers should be entirely exempted from control by the Nawab's government.

Hastings vigorously objected: 'It is now proposed absolving every person in our service from the jurisdiction of the [Nawab's] Government,' he wrote. 'It gives them a full licence of oppressing others ... Such a system of government cannot fail to create in the minds of the wretched inhabitants an abhorrence of the English name and authority, and how would it be possible for the Nawab, whilst he hears the cries of his people, which he cannot redress, not to wish to free himself from an alliance which subjects himself to such indignities?'[90]

As the urbane Gentil rightly noted, 'The English would have avoided great misfortunes when they broke with the Nawab, had they but followed the wise counsel of Mr Hastings – but a few bankrupt and dissipated English councillors, who had got themselves into debt and were determined to rebuild their personal fortunes at whatever public cost, pursued their ambitions and caused a war.'[91]

In December 1762, just as Amyatt was about to leave Calcutta, Mir Qasim made a deft political move. After putting up with Ellis's violence and aggression for two years, the Nawab finally concluded it was time to fight back and resist the encroachments of the Company. He decided to make a stand.

Realising his officials were only rarely successful in forcing armed Company outposts to pay the due taxes and customs duties, he abolished such duties altogether, across his realm, 'declaring that so long as he failed to levy duties from the rich, he would hold back his hand from doing so in the case of the poor'.[92] In this way he deprived the English of their unfair advantage over local traders, even if it meant enormous losses for him personally, and for the solvency of his government.

Shortly afterwards, on 11 March 1763, armed clashes began to break out between Mir Qasim's men and those of the Company. There were scuffles in Dhaka and Jafarganj, where Mir Qasim's representatives, backed now by his new army, began resisting the depredations of the Company managers, frequently facing off against their sepoy escorts; one of Mir Qasim's officials went as far as issuing an order to execute anyone who claimed EIC protection. Two notorious Company managers were raided in their houses; both escaped through the back door, over the wall. At the same time, Mir Qasim's men began stopping British boats across Bengal, blocking the passage of the goods of private Company traders and seizing their saltpetre, opium and betel nut. On one occasion, when some sepoys went to snatch back impounded boats, a scuffle escalated into volleys of shots, leaving several dead. There began to be talk of war.[93]

Then on 23 May, just as Amyatt arrived in Monghyr, intending to force Mir Qasim to revoke his free trade order, a boat that had come with him was seized by Mir Qasim's police as it landed at the ghats: 'She proved to be laden with a quantity of goods,' wrote Ghulam Hussain Khan, 'under which were found [hidden] five hundred fire-locks, destined for the Patna factory. These Gurgin Khan [the Wolf, Mir Qasim's Armenian commander] wished to impound, whilst Mr Amyatt insisted on the boat being dismissed without being stopped or even being searched.'[94]

The standoff continued for some time, and Mir Qasim considered seizing Amyatt. He told him that he had considered himself in a state of war with the Company, and that he saw Amyatt's mission merely as a blind to cover other hostile moves. But 'after a great deal of parley' he 'consented to allow the envoy to leave ... Mr Amyatt, finding it useless to make any further stay, resolved to return [to Calcutta], and took his leave.'[95]

This was the moment that Ellis decided to hatch a plan to seize Patna by force. He had long regarded Hastings and Vansittart as weak and supine in the face of what he called Mir Qasim's 'pretensions'. Now he decided to take matters into his own hands. But Mir Qasim's intelligence service had managed to place spies with the Patna factory, and the Nawab soon came to hear some details of what Ellis was planning. His response was to write a last letter to his former patrons, Hastings and Vansittart: 'Mr Ellis has proceeded to such lengths as to prepare ladders and platforms in order to take the fort at Patna; now you may take whatever measures you think best for the interest of the Company and your own.'[96] Then he sent the Wolf to mobilise his troops.

By this stage, Ellis had at his command 300 Europeans and 2,500 sepoys. On 23 June, the anniversary of Plassey, Surgeon Anderson of the Patna factory wrote in his diary, 'The gentlemen of the factory learned that a strong detachment of [the Wolf's] horse and sepoys were on the march to Patna, so that a war seemed inevitable. They thought it best to strike the first stroke, by possessing themselves of the city of Patna.' The place where they planned their insurrection against Mughal rule was exactly the spot where they had offered their fealty to Shah Alam only eighteen months earlier.

All day on the 24th, frantic preparations were made: bamboo scaling ladders were roped together, arms were stacked and cleaned, powder and shot prepared. The cannon were attached to harness and the horses were made ready. Just after midnight, the sepoys and the Company's own traders took their muskets and paraded, outside the main factory building, under arms.[97]

At one o'clock on the morning of the 25th, the factory gates swung open and Ellis marched his sepoys out of the compound and began his assault on the sleeping city of Patna. The Company and the Mughals were once again at war.

5

Bloodshed and Confusion

The Company sepoys formed into two bodies and fanned out across the town. One group made for the city walls. There they raised their scaling ladders and shinned silently up onto the wall-walks. Quickly and noiselessly they took all the bastions, bayoneting the small parties of sleeping guards that lay draped over their weapons in each *chhatri*-covered turret.

The second party, under Ellis, headed with the artillery down the main street of the Patna bazaar. After a mile or so they began encountering musket fire, intermittent at first, then heavier, from the rooftops and gatehouses of the havelis. But they pressed swiftly on, and just before sunrise blew the fort gates and stormed into the old Mughal fort: 'As they entered the fortress, they fell on the soldiers, half of them asleep, some awake in their improvised sniper-holes,' wrote the historian Mohammad Ali Khan Ansari. 'They killed many, though a few crawled to safety in corners.'

The sepoys then opened the west gate of the citadel and let in the remainder of their forces who were waiting outside. Again they divided into two columns and advanced along the road to the Diwan quarter and its market. The city governor was in the citadel, and as soon as he realised the disaster that was unfolding, rushed with his troops to confront the English, and met them near the bazaar. Here there were heavy casualties on both sides.

In the first moments, one of the Governor's commanders bravely pressed forward and was wounded by a fierce volley of grape shot. The rest of the troops, seeing this, stampeded and fled. The Governor had. no choice but to escape by the Eastern Gate, hoping to reach Mir Qasim in Monghyr and bring him news of the coup. His wounded commander meanwhile managed to reach the [Mughal] Chihil Sutun palace [within the fort] and bar the gate behind him, to sit it out and wait for another day on which to fight.

The English now had the city in their hands. Their army scum – dark, low-caste sepoys from Telengana – set about plundering goods from shops, dispersing across the city, pillaging the homes of innocent citizens.[1]

Finding all opposition at an end except from the citadel, which was now entirely surrounded, Ellis gave his men leave to sack the city thoroughly, 'which turned their courage into avarice, and every one of them thought of nothing but skulking off with whatever they could get'.[2] The Company factors meanwhile headed back to the factory for breakfast. 'Everybody was quite fatigued,' commented Surgeon Anderson, 'having marched through thick blood.'[3]

Unknown to the Company factors, however, just three miles beyond Patna, the fleeing Governor ran into a large body of reinforcements, consisting of four platoons of Mir Qasim's New Army. These the Nawab had sent from Monghyr by forced marches under General Markar, one of his senior Armenian commanders, as soon he was alerted by his spies to the preparations for the imminent coup. 'They marched as fast as they could,' wrote Ghulam Hussain Khan, 'and taking their route by the waterside they reached the city's Eastern gate, which they prepared to assault directly.'

The English, without being dismayed, opened the gate. They placed two cannon upon the bridge that crossed the fosse, and ranging themselves in a line, prepared to receive the enemy. But one of

Markar's men, who had out-marched his commander, put himself at the head of his men and attacked the English with a discharge of rockets and a volley of musketry. He instantly broke the Company line. The English fell back towards their factory, disheartened by their loss. The Governor, animated by this success, exhorted his commanders to pursue them hotly. On hearing of the disaster, the other Company troops who were yet stationed on the towers and ramparts, were confounded, lost their usual courage, and fled on all sides. Victory was declared for Mir Qasim, and the ramparts and towers were cleared and recovered.[4]

The Company troops were soon heavily outnumbered, their discipline broken and their factory surrounded and besieged. As the factory was overlooked by the city walls, it was quickly found to be indefensible. Ellis soon abandoned the position and led his men out through the water gate and 'so managed to embark in a series of barges with around three platoons of their troops, and sailed westward towards the border with Avadh', hoping to escape into neutral territory.

But they did not get far. When they reached Chhapra, their boats were attacked by the *faujdar* of Saran. Shortly afterwards, [Mir Qasim's German commander] Sumru [Walter Reinhardt] also caught up with them, having arrived by forced marches from his encampment at Buxar, along with a few thousand of his sepoys. Surrounded and outnumbered, they had no option but to throw down their arms. All were taken prisoner. Sumru brought the shackled English prisoners to the prison within Monghyr Fort. Mir Qasim then wrote to all his officials and military personnel that every Englishman, wherever found, must be arrested at once.[5]

By the end of the week, of the 5,000 EIC troops in Bihar, 3,000 had been killed, arrested or gone over and joined Mir Qasim's army. Among the dead was the envoy sent by the Calcutta Council, James Amyatt. He had safely reached as far as Murshidabad, when he was attacked in his boat and killed while resisting arrest by the local military governor. 'In spite of his pleas, begging to be sent alive to Mir Qasim to suffer whatever he should decree, at a signal he and his companions were cut to pieces and killed.'[6]

An outraged Mir Qasim wrote to Calcutta complaining that Ellis, 'like a night robber, assaulted the Qila of Patna, robbed and plundered the bazaar and all the merchants and inhabitants, ravaging and slaying from morning to the afternoon ... You gentlemen must answer for the injury which the Company's affairs have suffered; and since you have cruelly and unjustly ravaged the city and destroyed its people, and plundered to the value of hundreds of thousands of rupees, it becomes the justice of the Company to make reparation for the poor, as was formerly done for Calcutta [after its sack by Siraj ud-Daula].'[7]

But it was far too late for that. There was now no going back. Across Bihar and Bengal, the provincial Mughal elite rose as one behind Nawab Mir Qasim in a last desperate bid to protect their collapsing world from the alien and exploitative rule of a foreign trading company. Whether Mir Qasim realised it or not, all-out war was now unavoidable.

A week later, on 4 July 1763, the Council in Calcutta formally declared war on Mir Qasim. As a measure of their cynicism, they voted to put back on the throne his elderly father-in-law, the former Nawab, Mir Jafar. The latter had used his retirement to become a fully fledged opium addict and was now even more befuddled than before. As careless with the state finances as ever, the old Nawab promised to reimburse the Company up to Rs5 million* for the expense of fighting his ambitious son-in-law.

Mir Jafar was carried back to his erstwhile capital by the large Company expeditionary force which left Calcutta three weeks later. It marched out on 28 July, at the muggy height of the Bengali monsoon heat. It consisted of about 850 Europeans and 1,500 sepoys. 'The English, caught more-or-less unprepared, forced their French Prisoners-of-War to serve in the army commanded by Major Adams,' wrote Jean-Baptiste Gentil. 'This officer wasted no time in marching to Murshidabad, which [on 9 July] he subjugated after a battle with the military commander of

---

* £65 million today.

the place at Katwa, near Plassey. The Major arrived outside Rajmahal at the height of the rains, and his army suffered greatly. But he captured the Nawab's artillery and munitions, as well as the food supplies of his camp, and then quickly stormed Rajmahal.'[8]

Making war against the Nawab they had personally installed only five years earlier was not only a political embarrassment for the Company; it was a financial disaster: 'The Company was sinking under the burden of war,' wrote Luke Scrafton, 'and was obliged to borrow great sums of money from their servants at eight per cent interest, and even with that assistance were obliged to send their ships half-loaded to Europe [as they did not have spare bullion to buy the Indian goods to send to London].'[9] But militarily, the campaign against Mir Qasim was a slow but steady success.

It was quickly becoming clear that Mir Qasim's New Army was still not sufficiently well armed or trained to take on the Company's veteran sepoys. The Company was certainly taking much higher casualties than it had done when facing old-fashioned Mughal cavalry armies, but each time the two infantry armies closed it was Mir Qasim's troops who eventually fled. The Company victory at Katwa, where Major Adams ambushed and killed one of Mir Qasim's bravest generals, Mohammad Taki, was followed by a second at Gheria three weeks later: 'After a fierce, heroically courageous struggle, the forces of Mir Qasim Khan were again broken and scattered,' wrote Mohammad Ali Khan Ansari, 'and the breeze of victory fluttered in the flags of the Company.'

> The defeated troops flew as fast as they could, on the wings of haste, falling back into Bihar, to the fortified hilltop Udhua Nullah. Here Mir Qasim Khan, foreseeing such a day, had prepared a strong defensive emplacement. In this remote fortress the torrent flows fast down from the mountains into the Ganges and is very deep; both its banks are wild and thickly forested; there are no roads other than that which goes over the only bridge. This was built by Mir Qasim, who also dug a deep moat, and built above it a strong defensive wall rivalling that of Alexander, connected to the mountains; facing that is a long lake stretching from the mountain to near the Ganges. Mir Qasim had an earthen bridge built across the moat. There was also a road on top of the walls, winding and turning like the curls of a

bride's hair, which gave the only access. For this reason, Mir Qasim placed great reliance on the impregnability of Udhua Nullah and was convinced that the English would never take it, or if so, only after a long struggle. But Fortune had turned her face away from him.[10]

It was here that the remaining 20,000 troops of Mir Qasim's New Army made their last stand. During the first month of the siege, Major Adams' heavy guns made no impression on the fortifications. But lulled into complacency by their spectacular defences, Mir Qasim's generals let their guard down. As Ghulam Hussain Khan put it, 'They trusted so much to the natural strength of that post, and to the impracticability of the enemy forcing the passage, that they became negligent in their duty; for most of the officers that had any money made it a practice on the beginning of the night to gorge themselves with wine, and to pass the remainder of it in looking at the performance of dancing women, or in taking them to their beds.'[11]

Only one of Mir Qasim's generals made any effort to harass their besiegers at the bottom of the hill. This was an energetic and intelligent young Persian cavalry commander who had recently arrived in India from Isfahan. His name was Mirza Najaf Khan, a name that would be long celebrated in Mughal histories. Najaf Khan found local guides and got them to lead a group of his men through the marshes at the base of the hill. 'They left quietly and forded the outflow of the lake. Then at dawn, he made a sudden rush on the English encampment, where the elderly Nawab Mir Jafar was in his tents. They attacked so vigorously that the ranks of his troops were shaken as if by an earthquake.'[12]

Unfortunately for Mir Qasim's defenders, one of the guides was captured, and a week later, on 4 September, he led Major Adams' troops up the same hidden path, through the swampy morass, to the back of the Mughal entrenchments: 'The English managed to find out the route by which Mirza Najaf Khan had arrived to make his surprise dawn attack, and now used the same route themselves,' wrote Ansari. 'They sent one of their platoons of tall young men to carry out this mission.'

In the middle of the darkest night, they negotiated the outflow of the Lake with water up to their chins, carrying their muskets and powder bags aloft. In this way they reached the defensive emplacement, where they put up their ladders and scaled the walls. The defenders, relying on the difficulty of crossing the waters of the nullah and the lake, heedless of their enemies, were fast asleep on their pallets. The English fired and fell on them, killing and wounding many.

In the darkness, Company troops had crowded below in front of the gateway, and as soon as it was forced open, they entered in one rush, and made a slaughter such as on the Day of Judgement, with the cries of the damned rising all around! Many – those who awoke and were not slaughtered in their sleep – in their panic ran to escape over the monsoon-swollen river, and were drowned in the icy, rushing torrent. That night, nearly fifteen thousand men met their end. One hundred cannon were captured.

Najaf Khan managed somehow to escape from the clutches of the English and headed for the mountains; but many more were drowned or shot while crossing the river. One group, led by Sumru, also managed to re-join, after much falling and stumbling, what remained of Mir Qasim's army in Monghyr. The English sounded the victory drums and raised their battle-standard in the conquered camp. This battle came to an end at one and a half hours after day-break.[13]

Mir Qasim was not in the fort that night; he had just left for Monghyr and so lived to fight another day. But he never entirely recovered from the loss of Udhua Nullah. 'He seemed broke in two; he betrayed every mark of grief and affliction, and passed the whole day in the utmost despondency ... He threw himself onto his bed, tossing in a torment of grief, and ceased taking advice from Gurgin Khan.'[14] With few other options, he fell back on Patna, taking his prisoners with him.

Mir Qasim now became obsessed with the idea that he had been betrayed and that his own commanders were working against him. 'He had already tended to vicious cruelty,' wrote Ansari, 'but now, as the star of his good fortune faded, and cracks appeared in his governance, he pushed ever further down the path of brutality.'

Worried and depressed by the succession of defeats, he decided to send his treasures and jewels, as well as his favourite wife, to the great fort at Rohtas, in the company of a few trusted retainers. He let loose all the other women of his harem, simply expelling them onto the streets. These two notorious defeats, and the shocking expulsion of the womenfolk made some of his attendants turn the gaze of their obedience away. But as Mir Qasim's vicious cruelty left no-one any room for independent judgement in words or actions, his authority remained as before. Every day, he allowed more suspicions to crowd into his mind, and finally, gave the order for all his many prisoners to be killed.[15]

In his enveloping paranoia, Mir Qasim first ordered the assassination of Gurgin Khan, the Wolf, his most loyal Armenian commander. To this act of extreme folly and self-harm, Jean-Baptiste Gentil was an eyewitness. 'On the march to Patna,' he wrote, 'the enemies of Mir Qasim persuaded him that he was being betrayed by his minister, Gurgin Khan, who they said had been influenced by his brother, who was held by the English in their camp. The Nawab swore to destroy his faithful minister, calumnied as a traitor. Gurgin Khan was fully aware of these odious schemes.' Gentil writes, 'I always had my tent pitched next to that of the minister and we took our meals together.'

One day when he was late coming for dinner, I was sitting in front of the various dishes sent from the Nawab's kitchen and started to eat from these: the minister entered and stopped me, saying 'What are you doing? Don't you know these could be poisoned? How careless of you, when you know all the calumnies being spread about me and my brother – I have many enemies, take care!' He immediately ordered these dishes to be cleared away, and had others brought to table which had been prepared by less suspect hands.

Half way between Monghyr and Patna an attempt was made to assassinate him. By chance I had had my bed set up in front of his tent because of the heat, so the assassins thought their plot discovered and postponed till the next day, which was a marching day. The minister arrived later than usual because of the bad roads, and called for dinner to be served immediately. As he was crossing the encampment of his cavalry, he was accosted, in the midst of the horses by a Mughal cavalryman who complained of being short of money and that food-stuffs had become un-affordably expensive, even though he had just received his salary.

Gurgin Khan was angered by the man's request for more money, and called out for one of his attendants and the horseman withdrew. I was overcome with heat, and as the minister was now talking of other matters, I left him to find somewhere cooler. I had barely gone thirty steps, when I heard the attendants who had stayed with the minister calling out for help: I turned, and saw the horseman slashing at Gurgin Khan with his sword.

His attendants were unarmed and dressed in light muslin robes, as was the minister: it was already too late to come to his help, as he had received 3 blows quick as lightning: the first severed half his neck, the second slashed through his shoulder-bone, the third gouged his kidneys. The assassin struck him again in the face as he fell to the ground, after tripping on the long horse-tethers while he sought to run to his tent, fifty paces away. As he was wearing only thin light muslin, the sword cut right through. The horseman disappeared as soon as he had struck him.

I ran up and helped to ease the minister onto his palanquin and ordered the bearers to carry him into his tent, where he gestured to be given something to drink: we gave him water, which ran out of the wound in his neck. Seeing me beside him, Gurgin Khan looked fixedly at me, and struck his thigh 3 times, as if to signal that he had fallen victim to calumny, and that I should take care for my own safety.[16]

After that, it was the turn of Raja Ram Narain, the former Governor of Patna, who had fought so bravely against Shah Alam. Raja Ram Narain was a Kayasth, from a Hindu community who served the Mughals as administrators, and who often used to send their children for a Persianate madrasa education. Ram Narain had grown up loving Persian poetry and had been one of the students of Shaikh Muhammad Ali Hazin of Isfahan, arguably the greatest Persian poet of the eighteenth century, who moved as an exile to Benares. Realising that his execution was imminent, Ram Narain wrote a last series of couplets, in the style of his *ustad* (poetic master). These verses of sadness and resignation were once famous in the region:

Enough! My life flickers away, a solitary candle,
Flames from its head, waxy tears flow down its skirts

Your flirtatious beauty, my dark days, all will pass,
A king's dawn, a pauper's evening, all will pass

The garden visitor, the laughing rosebud, both are fleeting
Grief and joy, all will pass.[17]

Shortly after composing these last verses, Raja Ram Narain was shot by Sumru, still shackled in his prison cell, on the orders of Mir Qasim.

The Jagat Seths were next. When Ellis and his companions were arrested, Mir Qasim had carefully examined the private papers of the English which had been captured at the factory. Among these was found a letter from Jagat Seth Mahtab Rai and his cousin Maharaj Swaroop Chand to Ellis, encouraging him to attack the Nawab, and offering to pay the costs of the military campaign. These two brothers had been moved from their house at Murshidabad and rehoused by order of the Nawab in a large haveli in Monghyr, adjoining a magnificent garden, where they were indulged with every luxury. 'The brothers were immensely rich,' wrote Gentil, 'beyond the dreams of avarice, and were by far the richest bankers in the whole of Hindustan.'

> They had provincial governors of Bengal appointed or dismissed with each transfer of money to Delhi. They were accustomed to have everything and everyone yield beneath the weight of their gold; and so they entered into cabals with Ellis, Amyatt and others, as they had done so many times before. But this time they were found out.
>
> Once the Nawab had seen the correspondence, he had them arrested and put in chains. But it was only after the assassination of Gurgin Khan and Ram Narain that Mir Qasim determined to make the Jagat Seth brothers suffer their punishment. I arrived at court at nightfall, and found the Nawab alone with his officer of pleas, who was just presenting a petition in the name of these two unfortunates. They begged to be pardoned, and offered four crores [40 million] of rupees* if he were prepared to grant them their lives and liberty.
>
> At these words, Mir Qasim turned to me and exclaimed: 'Do you hear what this man is suggesting? On behalf of the two brothers?

* £520 million today.

Four crores! If my commanders heard that, they'd run off to set them free, and would without hesitation give me up to them!'

'Don't move!' he added to his officer of pleas, and immediately called for Sumru. The German assassin arrived and the Nawab repeated to him the Jagat Seths' offer, ordering him to kill them both forthwith. At the same time, he forbade all present to leave his tent until Sumru came back to announce that the execution had been carried out. He said he had shot them, still in their chains, with his pistol.[18]

In his crazed despair, on 29 August Mir Qasim wrote one last time to Warren Hastings asking for permission 'to return to his home and hearth with a view to proceeding finally on a pilgrimage to the holy shrines [in other words, to be allowed to retire from office and go on the Haj to Mecca]'.[19]

Hastings was sympathetic to the situation which had driven his protégé to such savagery, but he also realised it was much too late to save him from his own actions: he had now waded too deep in blood. 'The hoarded resentment of all the injuries which he had sustained,' wrote Hastings, 'was now aggravated by his natural timidity and the prospect of an almost inevitable ruin, [which] from this time took entire possession of his mind and drove from thence every principle, till it satiated itself with the blood of every person within reach who had either contributed to his misfortunes or, by connection with his enemies, become the objects of his revenge.'[20]

When Mir Qasim realised that even his former friend was unable to save him, he played his last remaining trump card. He wrote to Major Adams, questioning the legitimacy of the EIC actions and making one final threat: 'For these three months you have been laying waste to the King's country with your forces,' he wrote. 'What authority do you have? But if you are resolved on your own authority to proceed in this business, know for a certainty that I will cut off the heads of Mr Ellis and the rest of your chiefs and send them to you.'[21]

Just before he took Monghyr on 6 October, Adams sent a brief response to the ultimatum: 'If one hair on the heads of the prisoners is hurt,' he wrote, 'you can have no title to mercy from the English, and you may depend on the utmost form of their resentment, and that they will pursue you to the utmost extremity of the earth. And should we, unfortunately, not lay hold of you, the vengeance of the Almighty cannot fail to overtake you, if you perpetrate so horrid an act as the murder of the gentlemen in your custody.'[22]

The evening that Adams' reply reached Mir Qasim, Gentil was called by the Nawab to the tented hall of audience he had pitched in the Patna fort. 'I found the Nawab alone,' he wrote later. 'He had me sit on a small bolster next to his throne and said':

'I wrote warning Major Adams that if he went beyond Rajmahal, I would have all the English prisoners now in my power killed, and I made a solemn oath on the Quran to that effect. He took no notice of my threats, as he has now taken Monghyr and passed beyond it. Surely I must act on my oath? If they take me prisoner, they will surely treat me in the same way. Well, I'll strike first! What do you advise? Don't you think like me?'

Dumbfounded by his suggestion, I did not reply, believing that my silence would more eloquently signify the abhorrence I felt, than any well-reasoned arguments. But Mir Qasim insisted I give him my honest opinion on the matter, so I replied: 'I must tell you that acting on such an oath would be a crime, in the eyes of all nations: a pointless crime, one that would rule out any possibility of peace. If you had killed these Englishmen in the course of a military action, no one would protest – these are the risks run by any fighter in combat. But to murder prisoners, men who are not your enemies in the sense that they cannot do you any harm, who have laid down their arms on the assurance of safety of life and limb given by your officers in your name – that would be a horrible atrocity, unparalleled in the annals of India. Not only should you not harm them in any way, rather you should protect and succour them in all their needs. Besides, you should not vent your hatred of their nation on them, as they might be of use to you!'

'But,' replied the Nawab, 'if I fell into the hands of the English, they would not spare me, they'd have me killed.'

'Never!' I replied. 'Don't believe such a thing: rather they would treat you as they did your father-in-law when they replaced him with you: if they removed you as governor of Bengal, they would grant you the means to live according to your rank.'

'And how could they be of use to me?' the prince asked.

'By choosing two of the most highly respected among them,' I replied, 'and sending them to negotiate peace: I guarantee they would do their utmost to secure terms, and that, having given you their word of honour, they would come back to you to report on negotiations.'

Sumru arrived at that moment and saluted the prince from a distance, then went to take his place; Mir Qasim called him to sit beside him and dismissed me, saying in an irritable tone that my presence would not be required at his council.

I had barely emerged from the Nawab's tent, when Sumru too rose, saluted the Nawab and went to prepare the massacre of the English. A French sergeant of sepoys named Chateau refused to carry out Sumru's orders to kill the English, saying, 'Though, as a Frenchman, I may be an enemy of the English, I am not their executioner: I will have nothing to do with this atrocity!' Sumru had the man put under guard, and went himself to carry out the barbaric orders of his master.[23]

It was seven o'clock in the evening when Sumru and his platoon of armed sepoys arrived at the haveli where the British prisoners were being kept. He first called out Ellis and his deputy Lushington 'who, being acquainted that he had private business with them, went to him, and were instantly cut down'.[24] Sumru then posted his soldiers on the terraces overlooking the central courtyard of the prisoners' lodgings, where they were just finishing their dinner on a long table in the open air. According to the Comte de Modave, who later quizzed Sumru personally about what happened, the assassin claimed that, with a view to saving as many as he could, he 'shouted out several times that if there were any French, Italian, German or Portuguese among them they could leave. But the prisoners did not realise the significance of the question, and as they were eating their supper, shouted back cheerily that they were all English.'[25]

As soon as the dinner was over, and the plates had been cleared away and the servants had withdrawn, Sumru told his troops to take aim.

Then he ordered them to begin firing. He had the marksmen bring
them down with musket shots, then descended to finish off with their
bayonets those who had run to escape; one man who had hidden in the
lavatory trench was executed three days later: 'It is said that the English
prisoners, while they had life, did not lose their spirits, but rather
fought off their executioners, even with wine-bottles and stones', their
knives and forks having been taken from them after dinner.[26] Their 'cut
up and mangled' corpses were then thrown into a well in the courtyard.
Wherever else there were Company servants imprisoned, they were also
killed; only a very few, like the popular Scottish surgeon and aesthete Dr
William Fullarton came out alive, thanks to the personal intervention
of his old friend the historian Ghulam Hussain Khan, with whom he
used to discuss their shared loved of Mughal miniatures.

Forty-five Company servants perished in what came to be known by
the British as the Patna Massacre. In addition to this number, though
rarely referred to in British histories, were 200 of their sepoys who were
killed because they refused to join Mir Qasim's ranks, and who were
being kept in various places under guard by the local military chiefs.[27]

The next morning, Mir Qasim struck his tents and headed for the
Karmanasa, the border with Avadh. With him he took all that he could
retrieve of his wealth and all his remaining troops: some 30,000 of
his battered fighters and 100 million rupees,* carried on 300 treasure
elephants, with more hidden inside purdah carriages – 'numbers of
covered coaches and chairs, which passed for containing some favourite
ladies, but which, in reality, contained nothing but bags of white cloth,
full of gold coin, as well as jewels of high value'.[28] He had with him,
as Gentil put it, 'all the accumulated wealth of Bengal, which he had
extracted from the landholders, who had themselves been pillaging this
rich province since time immemorial'.[29]

Mir Qasim had earlier sent messages ahead to Shuja ud-Daula, the
Nawab of Avadh, and to Shah Alam, who was still staying with him
as his guest, proposing a grand Mughal alliance against the Company.
Now, as Mir Qasim's army neared the border, messengers arrived
responding positively to the overture, bringing a copy of the Quran
'on some blank leaves of which glorious book were written that Prince's
promise of safe conduct, under his own hand and seal'.[30]

* Over £1 million today.

Mir Qasim was delighted. On the march he had taken Gentil aside and told him he no longer trusted any of his own men, and now badly needed new allies. 'While resting in the shade on the march, this Prince told me: "You see all these people? All my troops? The commanders abuse me, because I'm retreating and not leading them against the English – but they're all traitors! If I led them into battle, they wouldn't fight, they'd betray me to the enemy! I know them: they're unprincipled cowards, I can put no trust in them! And now they have too much money: I've had them paid all I owe them, since leaving Patna – 25 million rupees."'*[31]

Only one man spoke out against the proposed alliance – the young Persian cavalry officer, Mirza Najaf Khan, who was the only one of Mir Qasim's commanders to have acquitted himself with honour on the campaign. He pointed out that Shuja ud-Daula had a reputation for treachery, and that he had over the years double-crossed almost everyone he had entered into alliance with: 'Never,' he said, 'put yourself in that prince's power. Retire to the fortress of Rohtas with your family and treasure, and leave the management of the war to me.'[32]

But Mir Qasim chose to ignore the warnings and replied that the waters of Rohtas had never suited him. Instead, on 19 November, he forded the Karmanasa, and crossed into Avadh.

Shuja ud-Daula, son of the great Mughal Vizier Safdar Jung and his successor as Nawab of Avadh, was a giant of a man. Nearly seven feet tall, with oiled moustaches that projected from his face like a pair of outstretched eagle's wings, he was a man of immense physical strength. By 1763, he was past his prime, but still reputedly strong enough to cut off the head of a buffalo with a single swing of his sword, or lift up two of his officers, one in each hand. One hostile Maratha source described him as 'no ordinary man. He is a demon by nature ... who, if he puts his foot on the hind leg of an elephant

* £325 million today.

and seizes its tail, that elephant cannot get away.[33]* Jean Law described him as 'the handsomest person I have seen in India. He towers over Imad ul-Mulk by his figure, and I believe also in qualities of the heart and temperament. He is occupied in nothing except pleasure, hunting and the most violent exercises.'[34]

Shuja was a man's man: impulsive and forthright, he had the capacity – notably rare in eighteenth-century India – to inspire loyalty in his followers. His most obvious vices were his overweening ambition, his haughty self-importance and his inflated opinion of his own abilities. This was something that immediately struck the urbane intellectual Ghulam Hussain Khan, who regarded him as a slight liability, every bit as foolish as he was bold. Shuja, he wrote, 'was equally proud and ignorant':

> He had conceived as high an opinion of his own power, as he had an indifferent one of what his enemies could perform; and he thought himself more than equal to the task of conquering all the three provinces [of Bengal, Bihar and Orissa]. Indeed he had a numerous army with plenty of artillery, great and small, and all the necessary requisites for war; but no real knowledge about the means of availing himself of so much power … Yet he fancied himself a compound of all excellence … [and believed] that asking advice would detract from his own dignity, even if the advisor were an Aristotle …
>
> He was so full of himself, and so proud to have fought by the side of Ahmad Shah Durrani, whom he had taken for his model, that when anyone proposed any advice upon the mode of carrying on the war, he used to cut him short with, 'do not trouble yourself about that; just fight as I bid you!'[35]

Shuja had been delighted with Mir Qasim's suggestion of a grand Mughal alliance against the Company, and had no doubt at all that if he, the exiled Nawab of Bengal and the Emperor Shah Alam were to unite their forces, resources and authority they could, as he told startled

---

* The *Bhausahebanci Bhakar* even tells how Shuja was born in miraculous circumstances when a fakir gave his barren mother a fruit to eat. She promptly 'became fecund and like Kumara Rama and Polika Rama the child was endowed with surpassing strength'. Quoted in Velcheru Narayana Rao, David Shulman and Sanjay Subrahmanyam, *Textures of Time: Writing History in South India 1600–1800*, New York, 2003, pp. 232–3.

peace envoys from the Company shortly afterwards, easily 'reconquer Bengal and expel the English, and – whenever the English come to court as humble petitioners – His Majesty may choose to assign them a suitable outpost from where they may trade. Otherwise my sword will answer your proposals.'[36]

His guest, the Emperor Shah Alam, was less certain. The Company had formally sworn him fealty, and so in his eyes was now an imperial ally, just as Mir Qasim and Shuja were. According to Khair ud-Din Illahabadi, the Emperor was extremely anxious about the consequences of Shuja's ambitions and told him flatly that 'he had previously seen English fighting methods when he was in Bengal, so he now firmly tried to put a stop to the Nawab Vizier's plans, saying':

> 'A fire that has died down should never be stirred into flame. The rulers of Bengal who have fallen out with the English have had a rough time of it. Whoever has dared attack them has not escaped from the rage of their infantry. If 50,000 Hindustani cavalry should face one thousand of their modern sepoy infantry in battle, it is impossible for them to save even their own lives! So, it would be wiser to proceed cautiously in our dealings with these people, and send letters to intimidate them into accepting our peace-proposals. Besides their respect and devotion to our royal person has already been tried and tested, and they will most certainly follow our royal orders.'

The Nawab Vizier had other ideas and countered 'The English have not yet seen the prowess and skill of our heroic commanders – a mere slap from our royal horsemen will wipe out these people!' His Majesty, remembering the loyal service of the English, felt inclined to favour them, but lacking a decisive independence of mind, he could see no other choice than that of following his host, the Nawab Vizier.[37]

Shah Alam and Shuja were on campaign at the opposite end of Avadh, near Orchha in Bundelkhand, when news arrived that the defeated Mir Qasim had crossed the Karmanasa from Bihar. So it was not until the following February, 1764, that Mir Qasim reached his new host and the three Mughal armies finally came together.

'On hearing that the Nawab Vizier [Shuja] was coming to greet him, His Highness of Bengal [Mir Qasim] had tall scarlet tents erected, in which he placed the two Nawabi thrones.'

The cavalry and infantry lined the road for six miles, the officers dressed in their finest scarlet broadcloth jackets and sparkling new flintlocks. The Nawab Vizier descended from his elephant and was greeted by His Highness at the entrance with all pomp and ceremony. They exchanged greetings, and holding hands, mounted the thrones together. His Highness of Bengal sent to His Majesty 21 trays of precious robes and jewels, as well as elephants majestic as mountains. The Nawab Vizier was impressed by the opulence with which Mir Qasim was travelling, and, with all the desire of his enormous appetites, dreamed of extracting from the English huge sums of gold and all the riches of Bengal. He talked gently to his guest and commiserated with his loss, promising help and seconding his demand for the English to return his confiscated provinces. Then Mir Qasim and Shuja ud-Daula went to wait on His Majesty the Emperor, and, sitting on one elephant, like a conjunction of two auspicious constellations, processed into the royal camp.[38]

Over the weeks that followed, the Mughal leaders finessed their plans, while continuing to levy tribute from the courts of Bundelkhand, and raising money for a final joint effort to expel the Company from Bengal. By early March, they were heading eastward again, their numbers swollen by a regiment of French prisoners-of-war who, under the leadership of a Breton soldier of fortune, René Madec, had taken the opportunity to mutiny against the British officers who had press-ganged them, most unwillingly, into Company service. The combined armies 'moved by slow stages, covering the land like ants or locusts'. But it was only on 17 March, when the armies encamped together outside Benares, near the place where Shuja had ordered a bridge of boats thrown across the Ganges, that the full scale of the force became apparent.

Observers estimated that an unprecedented host, over 150,000-strong, had now gathered from across the Mughal Empire. On one side there were the remnants of Mir Qasim's New Army under the leadership of Sumru, whose reputation for cold-blooded ruthlessness had been greatly enhanced by the Patna Massacre. Next to these, ranged along the riverbank, were the magnificent scarlet tents of Shah Alam's Turani Mughal cavalry. Shuja's forces were even more diverse. There were contingents of Persian Qizilbash cavalry in their red felt hats, and 3,000 pigeon-coated and long-booted Afghan Rohillas, who had once fought with Ahmad Shah Durrani; they were mounted on both horse and camels, and armed with large-bore armour-piercing swivel guns. Then there was Madec's regiment of French deserters, still, somewhat ironically, dressed in the uniform of the Company. But perhaps Shuja's most feared crack troops were a large force of 6,000 dreadlocked Hindu Naga sadhus, who fought mainly on foot with clubs, swords and arrows, ash-painted but entirely naked, under their own much-feared Gossain leaders, the brothers Anupgiri and Umraogiri.[39]

The colossal scale of the combined armies bolstered the confidence of the leaders, as did the news of unrest and further mutinies among the Company forces on the other side of the river. Shuja, convinced that a great victory was imminent, wrote to Calcutta as the vizier of the Emperor, with an ultimatum to the EIC. In his letter he cast the Company as ungrateful aliens – unruly and disobedient rebels against the legitimate Mughal order who had usurped 'different parts of the royal dominions ... Hand over all the territory in your possession,' he demanded, 'and cease to interfere with the government of the country. Revert to your proper place [as humble merchants] and confine yourselves to your original profession of trade – or else take the consequences of war.'[40]

But for all that Shuja wrote in Shah Alam's name, the Emperor himself, who had faced the full force of the Company war machine before, remained unconvinced about the expedition. He was not alone. In early April, Shuja took the Emperor and Mir Qasim to meet the most celebrated poet of the age, Shaikh Muhammad Ali Hazin, in Benares, where he had settled after surviving two of the great disasters of his age: first, the terrible sacking of Isfahan by the Afghans in 1722, and then that of Delhi by Nader Shah in 1739. He was now an old man of seventy-two and revered by all.

> When the poet-saint asked Shuja the purpose of his visit, the Nawab Vizier boomed: 'I have firmly decided to make war on the infidel Christians and with God's help will sweep them out of Hindustan!'
>
> Shuja expected to be congratulated by the poet. But the grey-bearded Shaikh merely smiled and said: 'With untrained troops like yours, who mostly haven't learned how to un-sheath their swords or handle a shield properly, who have never seen the face of war close-up on a modern battlefield, where human bodies scatter

and shatter and fall with their livers blown out, you intend to confront the most experienced and disciplined army this country has ever seen? You ask my advice? I tell you it is a shameful folly, and it is hopeless to expect victory. The Firangis are past-masters at strategy ... only if unity and discipline entirely collapses among them will you ever have any chance of victory.'

This good advice was not at all to the liking of the Nawab Vizier, but he refrained from contradicting the aged scholar-Sufi out of respect. When they rose to leave, the Shaikh sighed and said: 'May God help this camel caravan, whose leaders have no idea of what is bad or good for them!'[41]

Within a week, by 26 March, the whole army had crossed the Ganges by the bridge of boats and was now heading in the direction of the much-contested city of Patna: 'The army proved so very numerous that as far as the eye could see it covered the country and plains, like an inundation, and moved like the billows of the sea,' wrote Ghulam Hussain Khan. 'It was not an army but a whole city in motion, and you could have found in it whatever could be had in former times in Shahjahanabad itself, whilst that fair city was the capital and eye of all Hindustan.'[42]

As the massive Mughal army advanced eastwards, Major John Carnac, the Company's warden of the border with Avadh, abandoned his heavy baggage and retreated as fast as he could towards Patna without contesting the crossing of the Karmanasa or offering the slightest resistance. He had only 19,000 troops – the largest army the Company had yet fielded, but one that was dwarfed by the huge host of 150,000 who were now heading fast towards him. He now had less than a fortnight to prepare dykes, entrenchments and state-of-the-art modern artillery defences against his would-be besiegers.[43]

Carnac had faced a wave of mutinies among his exhausted sepoys; but as they closed in on Patna, the cracks within the Mughal forces became apparent, too. Fights broke out between the naked Naga sadhus and the Pathans, with entire platoons coming close to bloodshed. Meanwhile, rumours began to spread among the commanders that Shah Alam was in secret communication with the Company: 'His Majesty was utterly opposed to fighting the English,' wrote Ansari, 'so throughout these campaigns he took no part in deliberations or planning, and during the battles stood by to observe his warring vassals from a distance.'[44]

'There was so little order and discipline amongst these troops,' wrote Ghulam Hussain Khan, 'and so little were the men accustomed to command, that in the very middle of the camp, they fought, killed and murdered each other, and went out a-plundering and a-marauding without the least scruple or the least control. No one would inquire into these matters; and those ungovernable men scrupled not to strip and kill the people of their own army if they chanced to lag behind their main, or to be found in some lonely spot. They behaved exactly like a troupe of highwaymen … carrying away every head of cattle they could discover.'[45] 'The plundering troops were so destructive that within a radius of ten miles they left no trace of prosperity, habitation or cultivation,' added Ansari. 'The common people were reduced to desperation.'[46]

The combined Mughal army finally arrived in front of the walls of Patna on 3 May 1764. At Shuja's insistence, they went straight into battle. His most experienced advisers 'begged the Nawab Vizier to oversee the battle from a distance, near His Majesty the Emperor, seated on his tall elephant from where he could be seen, like the beneficent, magnificent sun. Seeing him brave and calm overseeing the battle would encourage his troops to stay steady and not to lose heart.'

But Shuja, characteristically, would have none of it.

'I am by far the most experienced in war,' he said. 'I cannot be kept standing still in one place, I must have the fleetest horse to reach, immediately, anywhere I am needed by my faithful troops!' So he stationed himself and his crack troops at the front and centre, lining up his men in order. Then with his bravest troops he emerged from behind the cover of outlying buildings and slowly moved towards the English lines. A roar came up from the troops, and the dust from the charging horses' hooves covered both earth and sky. The English lines appeared from a distance like a cloud of red and black, and bullets rained down on the Nawab Vizier's troops like autumn leaves. They fell writhing and bloody in the dust, time after time, in great numbers.[47]

It was the Naga sadhus, 'naked before and behind', who bore the brunt of the fire. They were mown down in their hundreds, but high on their *bhang* (hash-ish), wave after wave kept running on towards the English entrenchments, regardless of the danger. Meanwhile, Mir Qasim and his troops kept their place to the rear, 'standing far off behind the lines of Shuja's troops, and merely observed the military action from a distance'.

The Nawab Vizier sent a message to Mir Qasim, saying: 'I and your colleagues are in the heat of battle – at every moment, before my very eyes, my servants are offering up their lives like moths rushing to a candle-flame, while you do nothing but watch from a distance! Come and join the fight against the English, or if you're incapable of doing that, at least send Sumru with his modern artillery!' But his Bengali Highness appeared rooted to the spot and neither moved himself, nor sent Sumru to assist his ally.

As the day declined, the Gossains and Nagas continued their attack. Then it was the turn of the Rohillas who came to help them at the command of the Nawab Vizier. The battle was fierce, and English artillery fire blinding and terrifying. Skulls split and necks snapped, scattered over the blood-soaked battlefield, like a sward of wild red poppies and tulips. On every side there was deafening gunfire and flashing sword-blades, as if the hand of Fate were slapping the face of Time. But Major Carnac did not lose his nerve, and, like a Curse of Heaven, attacked those stony-hearted troops and left them writhing on the battlefield or despatched them to the Valley of Non-Existence.

The Nawab Vizier was wounded twice by bullets during this action, but paid no attention to his wounds. In the heat of the action, he sent another message, reviling His Bengali Highness, who replied: 'Day has ended, it is time to go home to our tents! We can always resume tomorrow!'

Stranger even than this reply, was the wind: having blown all day westerly from behind Shuja's troops, driving dust and straw into the eyes of the English force, it now suddenly veered and started blowing from the east, blinding the Nawab Vizier's troops with thorns and rubbish, smoke and gunpowder from the battlefield. So it was that Shuja finally had the drums beaten and retired to have his wounds treated, and thought no more of fighting.[48]

The siege of Patna continued for another three weeks, through the intense heat of May. Surprised at the scale of the bloodshed and the savagery of the fighting they had just witnessed, both sides initially kept to their lines. If the battle had been inconclusive, so now was the siege.

Nevertheless, Shuja pressed the Company sepoys closely and put himself continually in danger, so much so that on one occasion, scouting a forward position with just two guards, he was recognised, chased and nearly captured by a Company patrol: 'the Nawab Vizier could see himself falling prisoner into the clutches of his enemies, but, keeping his presence of mind, and tightly controlling the reins of his horse, he retreated at speed, till he had escaped this death-trap'.[49] But for all Shuja's bravery, Carnac's men had had time to build elaborate and well-defended entrenchments, 'that looked very much like a wall vomiting fire and flames'.[50] All Shuja's efforts achieved was to add to his sense of irritation and disgust at the lack of effort being made by his partners, especially Mir Qasim. This was not, he realised, the moment to take action against his guest; but he made note to do so when the occasion arose.

Of all Shuja's allies, only the French adventurer René Madec really exerted himself: 'I now found myself in a position to fight the English,' wrote the Breton, 'and to take revenge for all the wrongs they had done to me and to my fellow countrymen.'

We attacked their entrenchments with an energy they little expected, but they were so well fortified we were unable to storm them during the twenty days that our attacks lasted. The Nawab often exhorted me not to expose myself to such risks, but I followed only my zeal to destroy this nation which had destroyed mine. I strained every nerve to encompass their utter destruction, but was not supported by the others, so not everything on this campaign went according to my plans. At length, the approaching rains forced us to put off our operations till the next season's campaign, and to look for winter quarters.[51]

On 14 June 1764, after three weeks of steady losses and no discernible gains, just as, unknown to Shuja's Mughals, supplies were beginning to run out in the city and the battered and dispirited Carnac was actively considering surrender, Shuja suddenly tired of the siege and beat the kettledrums announcing withdrawal. He marched his troops westwards, through the first of the monsoon downpours, and settled on the banks of the Ganges at the fort of Buxar, close to the border with Avadh. Here he dug in, erected barracks and determined to continue with his invasion of Bengal when the campaign season began again in the autumn, after the festival of Dusshera. The exhausted Company defenders, aware of how narrowly they had been saved from an abject, starving surrender, declined to pursue Shuja's forces.

But, rather than drilling his troops and actively preparing for the coming campaign, Shuja instead 'sank again into a circle of entertainments, pleasures, and amusements, without once bestowing a thought on the necessary quantity of [cannon] balls, or their quality, or that of the powder; and without consulting anyone about the methods of fighting the enemy. He even declined listening to the requests of one of the officers of the artillery who wanted necessaries for their office. Upon all those subjects he was quite careless and inattentive, spending his time instead in playing at dice, in observing the flight of his pigeons, looking at performances of his dance women, and amusing himself with pastimes of all sorts.'[52]

Only in one way did he take decisive action – and that was not against his Company enemies, but instead against his ally Mir Qasim, on whose inactivity he now publicly blamed the failure of the assault on Patna. He called in Mir Qasim's commander, Sumru, and, with promises of wealth and estates, won over the German assassin. He then ordered him to strip the assets of Mir Qasim: 'Sumru and all his troops surrounded His Highness's tent and forcibly removed his treasure-chests. Sumru's soldiers then set up camp with the troops of the Nawab Vizier.'

> These incidents prompted Mir Qasim to give utterance, rather foolishly during his public audience, to some very unflattering remarks about the Nawab Vizier, which were duly reported back by spies. The Nawab Vizier at once ordered his troops to go and arrest His Highness in his camp and bring him back under armed escort.
>
> In the morning the Nawab Vizier's army went to surround His Bengali Highness's tents, loading up whatever they could find in the women's quarters or store-houses. Mir Qasim now despaired, and turned fakir, seeking refuge in a pretended fit of madness. He put on a vermilion red shirt and a hat, left his throne and went to squat on a mat in the middle distance, surrounded by some of his friends, whose wits had also altogether left them, and who also wore bright parti-coloured fools' costumes, dervish-style. The soldiers of the camp pointed at them and hooted in derision. Before long the officer led Mir Qasim out to mount the elephant that had been brought for him, while he himself sat at the back of the howdah. Jeering crowds accompanied them to the Nawab Vizier's encampment, where His Bengali Highness was locked away in the prison appointed for him.[53]

In the space of a few months, Mir Qasim had transformed from being one of the richest and most powerful rulers in India to become Shuja's shackled and penniless prisoner.

Four months later, on 22 October, to the beat of regimental drums, the red coats of the first battalions of Company sepoys could be seen marching along the banks of the Ganges, through a succession of mango groves, closing in on Buxar. Reinforcements of Company sepoys and a single King's regiment had arrived fresh from Calcutta, commanded by one of the most effective British officers in India, a dashing, cool-headed but utterly ruthless 38-year-old Scottish Highlander named Major Hector Munro.

Jean-Baptiste Gentil, who was now in charge of Shuja's infantry, rode straight over to the Nawab and urged immediate action: 'I am well-acquainted with the English and their methods of warfare,' he said. 'You should not under-estimate them. Rather, wake up now, stop indulging in intoxicating pleasures, and get your troops ready!'

> Now that the English have not yet lined up in battle-order, now that the barges have not yet drawn up along the river to unload their weapons and military equipment, now that they are all busy putting up their tents – now is the moment to attack! God Almighty may allow us to defeat and disperse them now. If we wait till they've settled in, it will be difficult to get the upper hand!' But the Nawab Vizier merely laughed and boasted, 'You'd better leave the tactics and strategy of dealing with this lot to me, and to my judgement!'[54]

That night, Shuja sent his women and treasure back to his capital of Faizabad under guard, while his troops slept under arms, alert for the sort of night attack for which the Company was now feared. But no such attack materialised. Shuja's original plan seems to have been to fight a defensive battle from behind the cover of his entrenchments, just as the Company had done before Patna. But during the course of that morning, seeing how far he outnumbered the Company troops, he changed his mind and decided to fight an offensive battle. 'Munro had drawn up his troops in battle order at dawn,' wrote Ansari, 'and started firing his artillery, inflicting much damage on his enemies. This persuaded the Nawab Vizier to change his battle plan, counting it better to come out from behind the earthworks, and fight with his cavalry in the open.'[55]

So it was that Shuja ordered an advance out of his strong defensive position, to the surprise of Munro, who initially did not believe his runners' reports: he could not understand why Shuja would throw away such an immense defensive advantage. Shortly afterwards, Madec's heavy artillery opened up, and was answered by the lighter, more mobile and faster firing cannon of the Company: 'The English and the French, like tigers or leopards, keenly started the struggle,' noted Ansari, 'with flashing swords and blazing guns.'[56]

By nine o'clock, the two armies were lined up facing each other, with a marsh between them, and the wide, flat expanse of the Ganges flanking the Mughal left wing. Shuja's Naga and Afghan cavalry, who had been placed on the right of the Mughal line, opened the battle by swinging around the marsh, wheeling to Munro's rear and attacking the back of the Company's formation, where the Grenadiers were stationed.

Before long, the Company flank had broken and Shuja's cavalry were through the Grenadiers and in among the reserves, slashing left and right: as Lieutenant Gabriel Harper wrote later: 'I fancy had but one or two thousand of the enemy's cavalry behaved as well as those that attacked the Grenadiers, we should have lost the day ... The chance was more than once against us, and I am of the opinion the sepoys would not have been able to stand the cannonade five minutes longer than they did.'[57] But once the Mughal cavalry had broken through, they carried on into the Company camp, where they put to flight the irregular cavalry guarding the baggage, the treasure and the ammunition. Then they promptly dismounted and began to loot. Thereafter they were lost to Shuja's control and played no further part in the battle.

In the end it was, as ever, the superior discipline of the Company's troops that won them the day. Munro liked to remind his troops that 'regular discipline and strict obedience to orders is the only superiority that Europeans possess in this country', and the events that day proved him right.[58] Despite the loss of their baggage and ammunition, Munro's sepoys grimly held their squares, even while suffering unprecedented casualties from the concentrated artillery fire aimed at them from Madec and Sumru's heavy guns.

The first English prisoners now began to be brought bound before Shuja, who assumed he had already won the day. He ordered fanfares of victory to be sounded, whereupon several commanders left their posts to present their compliments. It was Gentil, who was with Shuja in the centre of the Mughal line, who saw with a sinking heart what happened next: 'It seemed as if the English were completely beaten,' he wrote. 'They had lost their ammunition and food stores, as well as all their baggage and their treasury for military expenses.'

Munro, having recognised his own defeat, sent orders for the supply barges to approach the battlefield as soon as possible, as the English army had no option of retreat other than by river. But there was a long delay in carrying out these orders, and meanwhile the Mughal cavalry was busy pillaging the English camp, instead of harrying their enemy and giving the English no respite. Seeing this, Munro, having lost everything, made a desperate charge against the troops on our left wing.[59]

Realising his moment had come, Munro galloped down his line, braving the volleys of shot aimed at him by the Mughal guns, waving his hat and ordering a general advance. 'By this bravura act of desperation,' wrote Gentil, 'Munro became master of the same battlefield which he believed he had been forced to abandon only a few moments earlier.'[60] The Company sepoys 'had already started to retreat,' wrote Madec, 'thinking they were lost. They would all have fled, had they had the means. But it was just because they did not have the means to escape that they plucked up their courage, and, seeing our left wing towards the Ganges under-staffed and unsupported, charged it with a reckless bravery that has few parallels.'[61]

Shuja, unable to believe the sudden change of fortune, held his ground, determined to rally his troops. 'He imagined himself already holding the lovely figure of Victory in his embrace, and suddenly he saw himself, as if in a mirror, choking in the arms of that incubus, Defeat. He remained rooted to the spot, staring disbelievingly at this horrid and sudden transformation.' As the Mughal lines dissolved around him, it was the Naga chieftain Anupgiri, though himself badly wounded in the thigh, who persuaded Shuja ud-Daula to escape: 'This is not the moment for an unprofitable death!' he said. 'We will easily win and take revenge another day.'[62] Resolving to live, Shuja cantered to the bridge of boats he had thrown across the river, while the naked Nagas fought a fierce rearguard action behind him. As soon as Shuja, Sumru and he had all crossed it, the Naga leader ordered it to be destroyed behind him.

This stopped the Company's advance, but also doomed those of his troops who had failed to make it across – notably the brave Naga rearguard. They tried to wade across the mudflats, where they were picked off by the Company sepoys now lining the riverbanks. 'Vast numbers were endeavouring to cross the deep, muddy river that flowed behind the camp,' wrote Ghulam Hussain Khan, 'but they stuck in the mire and lost their lives to the artillery and succession of volleys which the Telingas [sepoys] were endlessly pouring on the flying enemy …'63

Now it was the turn of the Company troops to enrich themselves: 'Everything belonging to the Vizier or his officers, such as tents, furniture, and other property fell prey to the victors,' wrote Ghulam Hussain Khan. 'Numerous shops of bankers, full of silver and gold coin, and tents of merchants, replete with precious stuffs were rifled in an instant. Two hundred pieces of artillery were taken possession of, so that the English troops made an immense booty … God only knows the wealth which must have existed in that army! There were immense riches in that camp, such as might have vied with the very capital of Hindustan.'64

Buxar was a short and confused battle, but a bloody one: Company forces lost 850 killed, wounded or missing, of the 7,000 men they brought to the field – more than an eighth of their total; Mughal losses were many times higher, perhaps as many as 5,000 dead. For a long time the day's outcome was uncertain. But for all this, it was still, ultimately, one of the most decisive battles in Indian history, even more so than the more famous Battle of Plassey seven years earlier.

The three great armies of the Mughal world had come together to defeat the Company and expel it from India. When instead it was the Mughals that were defeated, the Company was left the dominant military force in north-east India. Buxar confirmed the Company's control of Bengal and the coast and opened the way for them to extend their influence far inland to the west. The Company, which had started off as an enterprise dominated by privateers and former Caribbean pirates, had already transformed itself once into a relatively respectable international trading corporation, with a share price so reliable its stock was regarded almost as a form of international currency. Now the Company was transformed a second time, not just as a vehicle of trade operating from a scattering of Indian coastal enclaves, but as the ruler of a rich and expansive territorial empire extending across South Asia.

For this, above all, was the moment this corporate trading organisation succeeded in laying the ground for its territorial conquest of India. A business enterprise had now emerged from its chrysalis, transformed into an autonomous imperial power, backed by a vast army, already larger than that of the British Crown, and was poised now to exercise administrative control over 20 million Indians. A body of merchants had been transformed into the de facto sovereign rulers of much of northern India. As one contemporary observer put it: 'Through many unexpected contingencies, an incorporated society of private traders [has become] a cabinet of Asiatic princes.'[65] The result was what Adam Smith would call 'a strange absurdity' – a Company State.[66]

When, twenty years later, the tea merchant and traveller Thomas Twining stopped his boat trip up the Ganges to visit the now deserted site of the Battle of Buxar, he wrote in his diary that 'here then may be said to terminate the extraordinary series of military achievements which brought the finest parts of Asia under the dominion of British merchants, who first appeared in the character of needy adventurers on the coasts of India. There are, perhaps, few events in history more remarkable than these transactions. Results so disproportionate to the means which produced them seem quite inexplicable.'[67]

Twining had a point. The Company had gambled everything – and won. The Mughal Empire now lay at its feet, comprehensively defeated, and the stage was set for the most extraordinary corporate takeover in history.[68]

In the days following the Company victory at Buxar, the three Mughal confederates that had joined forces suffered very different fates.

In the course of the headlong flight from Buxar, Mir Qasim was freed by Shuja from his imprisonment. But stripped of both his power and his fortune, and hunted by the unforgiving Company for his part in the Patna Massacre, this most capable of rulers never again found a place for himself in the kaleidoscope of eighteenth-century Mughal politics. He drifted across Hindustan and eventually died in poverty on a smallholding near Agra. At his funeral, his children were said to be unable to afford a winding sheet for their father.[69]

Shuja ud-Daula, characteristically, opted for the path of military resistance. As Munro's Company battalions marched deeper into Avadh, he fought a string of mounted guerrilla raids against his pursuers, but was gradually pushed further and further into the margins, shedding his followers, while Major, now General Carnac appropriated Shuja's Faizabad mansion as his personal residence. The Company finally cornered Shuja at the great fortress of Chunar, but he escaped as it was being stormed, to fight, and to lose, one last battle against the Company, at Kora, on 3 May 1765. Thereafter he spent several months on the run across his old dominions, before taking shelter among the Rohilla Afghans of the Doab.

In the end it was his urbane French soldier of fortune, Jean-Baptiste Gentil, who negotiated his surrender that July. Gentil pointed out to the Company that, under British protection, a defeated Shuja could be reinstalled to provide a useful buffer state between the rich lands of Bengal and the lawless anarchy of the contested lands around Delhi, which continued to pass, chaotically and bloodily, between rival Afghan and Maratha armies.

Assured of his life and liberty, Shuja eventually gave himself up. He arrived out of the blue in Munro's camp, sitting in his outsized palanquin with an escort of only 200 horsemen.[70] 'It was about four o'clock in the afternoon,' wrote Gentil, 'and the general was still dining, and, as is the English custom, passing the port after the dessert. The cloud of dust raised by the horses of the Nawab-Vizier's cavalry escort caused the alarm to be raised, the drums sounded, and everyone rushed to their post. But at that moment two runners arrived and announced the Nawab-Vizier's arrival.'[71]

To his surprise Shuja found that 'the English gentlemen took off their hats, and showed all marks of respect, according to the custom of their country and behaved with great affability. They stood before him, closing their hands together [i.e. clapping].'[72] He was reinstated in a reduced version of his old kingdom, under the watchful eye of a British Resident and guarded by a regiment of Company sepoys, for whose presence he had to pay a huge subsidy, in addition to an immense war indemnity of Rs5 million.*[73]

The Emperor Shah Alam, meanwhile, did his best to patch up relations with the Company, with whom he had been in secret correspondence throughout the Buxar campaign. From his point of view, Buxar was

* £65 million today.

a battle fought between three of his servants, all of whom had sworn fealty to the Mughal throne, and was therefore a conflict in which he must remain neutral. Throughout the battle, he remained in his tent, determined to show his disapproval of what he regarded as Shuja's foolishly confrontational strategy.[74]

Shortly after Buxar, as Shuja and his army fled into Avadh to continue their fight, Shah Alam and his Mughal bodyguard lingered near the battlefield and sent out messengers to Munro seeking an accommodation. As had happened after his defeat at Helsa eighteen months earlier, Shah Alam played a deft hand, understanding that he was much more use to the Company as an ally than an enemy.

Shortly after the battle was over, and 'as soon as the Nawab Vizier was seen fleeing along the other side of that river, the Emperor, who was thereby left at liberty, sent for the English, despatching robes of honour for Munro, Mir Jafar and Vansittart, and so opening negotiations. They, finding so fair a pretence for advancing their own affairs, doubled their pace and joined him in a few hours.'[75]

The Emperor wanted the Company to know that Shuja was not his friend, even threatening that if the vizier and the British were to come to terms, 'I will go to Delhi, for I cannot think of returning again into the Hands of a Man who has used me so ill.'[76] Munro, meanwhile, was well aware what a puppet Shah Alam could give to the Company's expansionist ambitions in terms of a Mughal seal of legitimacy: 'To avoid giving any umbrage or jealousy of our power to the King or nobles of the Empire,' he wrote to Calcutta, 'we will have everything done under the Sanction of his Authority, that We may appear as holding our Acquisitions from him, and acting in the War under his Authority.'[77]

Under Company protection, and personally escorted by his former adversary General Carnac, Shah Alam headed first to Benares, and hence to Allahabad, where the Company lodged him in the magnificent old Mughal fort built by his ancestor Akbar at the auspicious confluence of the Yamuna and the Ganges. There he awaited the arrival of the man whom the directors had despatched from London to Calcutta to clean up the mess created by the greed of their unruly servants, on the basis that the best gamekeeper is a former poacher.

This was the now newly ennobled and increasingly portly figure of Robert Clive, Baron Plassey.

News of the war against Mir Qasim and the fact that Bengal was once again 'a scene of bloodshed and confusion' had reached the Company London headquarters in Leadenhall Street in February 1764; tidings of the Patna Massacre followed soon after. There was talk of defeats, mounting military expenses and financial chaos, which in turn produced a panic among investors and a run on the stock market. The Company's share price quickly fell 14 per cent.[78] At a shareholder meeting, one anxious investor proposed Clive's immediate return to Bengal as both Governor and Commander-in-Chief.[79] The shareholders voted through the resolution unanimously.

Since he had arrived back in England, Clive had quickly succeeded in achieving two of his greatest ambitions: a seat in Parliament and a peerage, albeit an Irish one, which was then considered much less grand than one in England, which gave the holder a place in the Westminister House of Lords. He had bought land and collected estates, squabbled with the directors of the Company and quickly got bored: 'We are not so happy in England as you imagine,' he wrote to Carnac in May 1762. 'Many of us envy your way of life in India.'[80] So when he was offered the governorship of Bengal, with unprecedented powers to reform the government and settle Company control over great swathes of Asia, he did not hesitate. At sundown on 4 June 1764, he sailed out of Portsmouth on the *Kent* for his third posting in India. He left his wife and children at the quayside, and was accompanied instead by a French chef, a band of four musicians and twelve dozen chests of champagne.[81]

As ever, Clive's sense of timing – or perhaps his luck – was uncanny. When the *Kent* docked at Madras in April 1765, news was immediately brought on board of Munro's victory at Buxar, the occupation of Avadh and the death of the recently restored Mir Jafar. Aware of the positive effect this would have on the Company's share price, Clive's first action was to write secretly in cipher to his agent in London to mortgage all his property and to buy as many Company shares as possible.[82] Next he wrote to the directors. As ruthless and incisive as ever, he realised how radically this news changed the entire political landscape: 'We have at last arrived at that critical Conjuncture, which I have long foreseen,' he wrote to the chairman of the EIC. 'I mean that Conjuncture which renders it necessary for us to determine whether we can, or shall, take the whole [Mughal Empire] to ourselves.'

> Mir Jafar is dead, and his natural son is a Minor. Shuja Dowla is beat out of his Dominions; we are in possession of them, and it is scarce a hyperbole to say that the whole Empire is in our hands … Can it be doubted that a large Army of Europeans would effectually preserve to us the Sovereignty, as I may call it, not only by keeping in awe the ambition of any Country Prince, but by rending us so truly formidable, that no French, Dutch or other Enemy could ever dare to molest us?
>
> We must indeed become Nabobs ourselves in Fact if not in Name, and perhaps totally without disguise … We must go forward, for to retract is impossible … If riches and stability are the objects of the Company, then this is the method, the only method, we now have for attaining and securing them.[83]

The new Governor finally arrived back in Calcutta on 3 May 1765, exhausted from a voyage which had taken nearly a year. But he knew that before he could rest he must head straight up country to sort out the unstable and potentially explosive power vacuum in Hindustan which had remain unfilled and unresolved since Buxar. 'Peace on a firm and lasting foundation must be established if possible,' he wrote to Carnac. 'And to attain that object, I conclude it will be necessary to march straight up to you at camp, not to continue long there, but to enter into some treaty with the King.'[84] He turned quickly around, and left Calcutta for Allahabad on 25 June.

His first appointment was with Shuja ud-Daula. Clive appreciated the logic of the solution Gentil had first proposed: that rather than taking the whole of Avadh directly under Company administration, a much wiser course would be instead to reinstate a grateful Shuja as the Company's puppet-dependant and milk him of his resources, while nominally taking him under protection.

On 2 August Clive met the penitent Shuja ud-Daula at Benares and told him of these plans. Shuja, who had only three months before faced total ruin, could not believe his luck, and made his personal gratitude and loyalty to Clive abundantly clear. Soon afterwards, a delighted Clive wrote to his Council that 'if due sensibility of favours are received, an open confidence and many other valuable principles are to be found amongst Musalmans, Shuja Dowlah possesses them in a higher degree than we have elsewhere observed in the country.'[85]

Next Clive determined to add a final political flourish of his own. He decided that a small portion of Shuja's former dominions around Allahabad and Kora would be turned over to support Shah Alam as an imperial demesne. Vague promises would be made about supporting the Emperor's long-dreamed-of return to Delhi, while taking in return the offer of financially managing the three rich eastern provinces of the Emperor dominions – Bengal, Bihar and Orissa. This was the granting of what in Mughal legalese was known as the Diwani – the office of economic management of Mughal provinces.

This not only gave a veneer of Mughal legitimacy for the Company's conquests, it also potentially gave the EIC the right to tax 20 million people, and generate an estimated revenue of between £2 million and £3 million a year* – a massive windfall by eighteenth-century standards. Seizing the many riches of Bengal with its fertile paddy fields and rice surpluses, its industrious weavers and rich mineral resources, opened up huge opportunities for the Company and would generate the finance to continue building up the most powerful army in Asia. The vast revenues of Bengal, which had for so long powered the Mughal exchequer, could, Clive knew, make the Company as unassailable as the Mughals had once been – and provide the finance for perhaps, one day, conquering the rest of the country.

Negotiations between Shah Alam's advisers and those of Clive began on 1 August. On the 9th, the Governor's state barge docked at Allahabad fort, where Clive complained of being 'tormented by bugs and flies'. Here, for the first time, he met the young Emperor whose 'grave deportment bordered on sadness'.[86]

Though the main outlines of the deal had already been settled, negotiations continued for three more days, while Shah Alam held out for a larger payment from the Company. It was, for once, Clive who gave way: 'I think 20 [lakh rupees, £26 million today] is more than sufficient [a pension for the Emperor],' he wrote. 'However, as

---

* £210 to £315 million today.

we intend to make use of his Majesty in a very extra-ordinary manner for obtaining nothing less than a *sanad* [formal legal order] for all the revenues of the country, six lakhs of rupees will be scarce worth disobliging the king, if he should make a point of it.'[87] The final terms were agreed on the evening of 11 August.

On the following morning, the 12th, the Emperor was enthroned on a silk-draped armchair, perilously perched upon Clive's dining-room table. The ceremony, which took place inside Clive's tent, did not last long. As Ghulam Hussain Khan puts it: 'A business of such magnitude, as left neither pretence nor subterfuge, and which at any other time would have required the sending of wise ambassadors and able negotiators, as well as much parley and conference with the East India Company and the King of England, and much negotiation and contention with the ministers, was done and finished in less time than would usually have been taken up for the sale of a jack-ass or a beast of burden.'[88]

It was a hugely significant moment: with one stroke of the pen, in return for a relatively modest payment of Rs2.6 million,* and Clive's cynical promise on behalf of the Company to govern 'agreeably to the rules of Mahomed and the law of the Empire', the Emperor agreed to recognise all the Company's conquests and hand over to it financial control of all north-eastern India. Henceforth, 250 East India Company clerks backed by the military force of 20,000 Indian sepoys would now run the finances of India's three richest provinces, effectively ending independent government in Bengal for 200 years. For a stock market-listed company with profit as its main *raison d'être*, this was a transformative, revolutionary moment.

Even though the Company's military power was now placed within a ritualised Mughal framework, the radical change on the ground brought about by what the Company referred to as the Treaty of Allahabad was immediately apparent. As the *Riyazu-s-salatin* noted shortly afterwards: 'The English have now acquired dominion over the three subahs [provinces] and have appointed their own district officers, they make assessments and collections of revenue, administer justice, appoint and dismiss collectors and perform other functions of governance. The sway and authority of the English prevails ... and their soldiers

---

* £325,000, which equals £34 million today.

are quartering themselves everywhere in the dominions of the Nawab, ostensibly as his servants, but acquiring influence over all affairs. Heaven knows what will be the eventual upshot of this state of things.'[89]

In fact, the upshot was very quickly clear. Bengal was now plundered more thoroughly and brutally than ever before, and the youthful Bengal Nawab was left little more than a powerless, ritualised figurehead: 'Nothing remains to him but the Name and the Shadow of Authority' was how Clive put it.[90] He and a succession of his descendants might survive for a time as nominal governors in their vast riverside palaces in Murshidabad, but it was the EIC that now openly ruled, and exploited, Bengal. Clive took great care to distance the EIC from the humdrum affairs of daily administration: even the existing methods of revenue collection were maintained, run out of Murshidabad offices that were still entirely staffed with Mughal officials. But frock-coated and periwigged British officials were now everywhere at the apex of the administrative pyramid, making all the decisions and taking all the revenues. A trading corporation had become both colonial proprietor and corporate state, legally free, for the first time, to do all the things that governments do: control the law, administer justice, assess taxes, mint coins, provide protection, impose punishments, make peace and wage war.

From now on, the land revenues of those portions of India under the Company corporate control were to be conceived simply as gross profits for the EIC which would, as Clive wrote, 'defray all the expenses of the investment [the goods bought for export to London], furnish the whole of the China treasure [the money used to buy tea from China] and answer all the demands of all your other settlements in India, and still leave a considerable balance in your treasury besides'.

Up to now, gold bullion had represented 75 per cent of the EIC's imports to Bengal, and was the source for much of the 'prodigious ancient riches of the province'. But now the Company no longer had to ship anything from Britain in order to pay for the textiles, spices and saltpetre it wished to buy and export: Indian tax revenues were now being used to provide the finance for all such purchases. India would henceforth be treated as if it were a vast plantation to be milked and exploited, with all its profits shipped overseas to London.[91]

As a result, in the words of Richard Becher, the new Company Resident in Murshidabad, 'the first Consideration seems to have been the raising of as large Sums from the Country as could be collected' – in other words simply to secure as large a revenue as possible through land taxes, and then to transfer that surplus to London bank accounts.[92]

For Clive and his shareholders it was another triumph: 'Fortune seems determined to accompany me to the last,' Clive wrote to his friend and biographer, Robert Orme. 'Every object, every sanguine wish is upon the point of being completely fulfilled, and I am arrived at the pinnacle of all that I covet, by affirming the Company shall, in spite of all the envy, malice, faction and resentment, acknowledge they are become the most opulent company in the world.'[93] To Clive's immense personal profit, the value of EIC stock climbed dramatically, nearly doubling in value in eight months.

But for the people of Bengal, the granting of the Diwani was an unmitigated catastrophe. The Nawab was no longer able to provide even a modicum of protection for his people: tax collectors and farmers of revenue plundered the peasantry to raise funds from the land, and no one felt in the least bit responsible for the wellbeing of the ordinary cultivator. Merchants and weavers were forced to work for the Company at far below market rates; they also seized by force textiles made for their French and Dutch rivals. Merchants who refused to sign papers agreeing to the Company's harsh terms were caned or jailed or were publicly humiliated by being made to rub their noses on the ground.[94] A few years later, in 1769, Becher recorded, 'it must give pain to an Englishman to think that since the accession of the Company to the Diwani, the condition of the people of the country has been worse than it was before; yet I am afraid the fact is undoubted. This fine country, which flourished under the most despotic and arbitrary government, is now verging towards ruin.'[95] The economic indicators were all bad, he wrote, and growing daily worse: land revenues had been declining since the Diwani was handed over, coin was short and Bengal's internal trade was shrinking.[96]

Ghulam Hussain Khan, by far the sharpest observer of his time, was quick to realise what this would mean on the ground. Firstly, it signified the effective extinction of his entire social class. The Mughal nobility, whose power had ultimately rested on their expertise as cavalrymen, were now effectively unemployed as the Company replaced them with infantrymen they recruited largely from rural Hindu Rajput and Brahmin backgrounds. Long before anyone else had thought through the full effects of this new corporate colonialism and its infantry warfare, Ghulam Hussain Khan was lamenting the fate of 'the remaining stock of the ancient nobility ... who in these hard times have not one single resource left under the canopy of the Hindostany heaven ... Numbers therefore have already quitted their homes and countries, and numbers unwilling to leave their abodes, have made a covenant with hunger and distress, and ended their lives in poverty in the corner of their cottages.'

He estimated that these changes would throw between 40,000 and 50,000 troopers out of employment across Bengal and Bihar, besides dispersing 'the thousands and thousands of merchants' who followed 'that numerous cavalry'. This is turn had an important economic and civilisational effect: 'The even more numerous artisans whom the noblemen had always kept busy, sometimes in their own houses' found their patrons no longer capable of sustaining them or their in-house *kar-khanás*. Alternative employment was hard to find, for 'the English are now the rulers and masters of the country' and 'because their arts and callings are of no use to the English', the artisans could only thieve or beg.

> As these rulers have all their necessaries from their own country, it follows that the handycraftsmen and artificers of this land suffer constantly, live in distress, and find it difficult to procure a livelihood sufficient to support their lives. For as the English are now the rulers and masters of this country, as well as the only rich men in it, to whom can those poor people look up for offering up their productions of their art, so as to benefit from their expenses? It is only some artificers that can find livelihood with the English, such as carpenters, silversmiths, ironsmiths &c.[97]

Moreover, wrote Ghulam Hussain Khan, the Company's conquests represented an entirely different form of imperial exploitation from anything India had previously experienced. He articulated, long before any other Indian, both what being a subject colony entailed, and how different this strange and utterly alien form of corporate colonialism was to Mughal rule. 'It was quickly observed that money had commenced to become scarce in Bengal,' he wrote. Initially no one knew whether 'this scarcity was owing to the oppressions and exactions committed by the rulers, or the stinginess of the public expenses, or lastly of the vast exportation of coin which is carried every year to the country of England.' But it rapidly became clear that the drain of wealth was real. It soon became common 'to see every year five or six Englishmen, or even more, who repair to their homes with large fortunes. Lakhs upon lakhs have therefore been drained from this country.'[98]

This, he wrote, was quite different from the system of the Mughals, who though also initially outsiders, determined 'to settle forever [in India] and to fix the foot of permanency and residency in this country, with a mind of turning their conquest into a patrimony for themselves, and of making it their property and inheritance':

> These bent the whole strength of their genius in securing the happiness of their new subjects; nor did they ever abate from their effort, until they had intermarried with the natives, and got children and families from them, and had become naturalized. Their immediate successors having learned the language of the country, behaved to its inhabitants as brothers of one mother and one language … [Hindus and Muslims] have come to coalesce together into one whole, like milk and sugar that have received a simmering.[99]

In contrast, he wrote, the British felt nothing for the country, not even for their closest allies and servants. This was why those Indians who initially welcomed the British quickly changed their minds because 'these new rulers pay no regard to the concerns of Hindustanis, and suffered them to be mercilessly plundered, fleeced, oppressed and tormented by those officers of their appointing'.

> The English have a custom of coming for a number of years, and then of going away to pay a visit to their native country, without any of them shewing an inclination to fix themselves in this land. And as they join to that custom another one of theirs, which every one holds as a divine obligation: that of scraping together as much money as they can in this country, and carrying these immense sums to the Kingdom of England; so it should not be surprising that these two customs, blended together, should be ever undermining and ruining this country, and should become an eternal bar to it ever flourishing again.[100]

As Macaulay later put it, the Company looked on Bengal 'merely as a Buccaneer would look on a galleon'.[101] It took five years for the full effects of this regime of unregulated plunder to become apparent; but when it did so the results were unparalleled in their horror. The stage was now set for the great 1770 Bengal famine.

6

Racked by Famine

The monsoon of 1768 brought only the lightest of rains to north-east India. Then the following summer, 1769, no rain fell at all. Instead, the intense heat continued unabated, the rivers dwindled, the tanks dried and the *pukhurs* – the fish ponds at the centre of every Bengali village – turned first to sticky mud, then to dry earth, then to dust.

The Company officials dotted around rural Bengal watched the deepening drought with concern, realising the effect it would have on their revenues: the rice lands had 'so harden'd for want of water that the *ryotts* [farmers] have found difficulty in ploughing and preparing it for the next crop,' wrote one, and the fields of rice, 'parched by the heat of the sun are become like fields of straw'.[1]

The price of rice rose steadily, week by week, until it had multiplied five times. By October, as drought began to turn to famine, 'great dearth and scarcity' was reported at Murshidabad.[2] By November, the farmers were stated 'to be totally incapacitated to cultivate the valuable crops of Cotton and Mulberries ... which usually succeed the rich rice harvest'.[3] A month later, Mohammad Reza Khan, who now ran the Murshidabad administration, reported to Calcutta that things were so desperate that the hungry labourers had begun to 'sell their children to raise money, much less do they spare their effects and cattle. The plough consequently stands still, and numbers of them desert their homes.'[4]

The first to go hungry were the landless 'labourers, the workmen, the manufacturers and people employed in the river [boatmen]' as they 'were without the same means of laying by stores of grain as the husbandmen'.[5] These, the rural artisans and the urban poor, unprotected and with no safety net, were the first to sicken from malnutrition, then, one by one, to begin dying from starvation or disease. By February 1770, when around 70 per cent of the usual rice crop had been lost, and the price of rice was ten times its normal rate, the hunger started to become much more widespread.

James Grant, who was stationed up country, near Rajmahal, reported a growing deprivation in his district: 'In the country, the highway and fields were strewed, in towns, the streets and passages choked with the dying and the dead,' he wrote. 'Multitudes flocked to Murshidabad, [where] 7,000 were daily fed for several months; the same practice was followed in other places; but the good effects were hardly discernible amidst the general devastation ... It was impossible to stir abroad without breathing an offensive air, without hearing the frantic cries, and seeing numbers of different ages and sexes in every state of suffering and death ... At length a gloomy calm succeeded.'[6]

'All through the stifling summer of 1770, the people went on dying,' wrote Sir William Hunter. 'The husbandmen sold their cattle, they sold their implements of agriculture; they devoured their seed grain; they sold their sons and daughters, till at length no buyers of children could be found. They ate the leaves of the trees and the grass of the field; and in June the Resident at the durbar affirmed that the living were feeding off the dead. Day and night a torrent of famished and disease-ridden wretches poured into the great cities ... [so that soon] the streets were blocked up with promiscuous heaps of the dying and the dead.'[7]

By June 1770, the devastation was unfolding across the entire province. Five hundred a day were now dying of starvation in the streets of Murshidabad.[8] Rice was scarce even in Calcutta, where 76,000 died on its streets between July and September. 'The whole province looked like a charnel house,' reported one officer. The total numbers are disputed, but in all perhaps 1.2 million – one in five Bengalis – starved

Shah Alam, seated on a throne overlooking the Ganges, shortly after his proclamation as Emperor in 1759. Shah Alam had no land and no money, but compensated as best he could for this with his immense charm, poetic temperament and refined manners. In this way he managed to collect around him some 20,000 followers and unemployed soldiers of fortune, most of them as penniless and ill-equipped as he was.

Mir Jafar and his son Miran on a hunting expedition. As Mir Jafar stumbled and as his treasury emptied, his vigorous but violent son Miran turned increasingly vicious. 'His inclination was to oppress and torment people,' wrote Ghulam Hussain Khan, who knew him well. 'He was expeditious and quick-minded in slaughtering people, having a peculiar knack at such matters, and looking upon every infamous or atrocious deed as an act of prudence and foresight.'

Mir Jafar (above) and Mir Qasim in 1765. Mir Qasim (right) was as different a man as could be imagined from his chaotic and uneducated father-in-law, Mir Jafar. Of noble Persian extraction, though born on his father's estates near Patna, Mir Qasim was small in frame, with little military experience, but young, capable, intelligent and, above all, determined. He conspired with the Company to replace Mir Jafar in a coup in 1760 and succeeded in creating a tightly run state with a modern infantry army. But within three years he ended up coming into conflict with the Company.

Khoja Gregory was an Isfahani Armenian to whom Mir Qasim gave the title Gurghin Khan, or the Wolf. Ghulam Hussain Khan thought him a remarkable man: 'Above ordinary size, strongly built, with a very fair complexion, an aquiline nose and large black eyes, full of fire.'

Official in Discussion with a Nawab – probably William Fullarton and Mir Qasim, Patna, 1760–65. Fullarton was a popular Scottish surgeon and aesthete and one of very few to survive the Patna massacre. He was saved by the personal intervention of his old friend, the historian Ghulam Hussain Khan.

A Palladian house and garden by the Bengali artist Shaikh Muhammad Amir of Karraya.

The Shaikh's view of Government House and Esplanade Road, Calcutta, from the Maidan. Both seem to have been painted around 1827.

As the Mughal capital collapsed into anarchy, the celebrated Delhi artists Dip Chand and Nidha Mal migrated eastwards to find work in the richer, more stable and cosmopolitan courts of Patna and Lucknow. Here they developed a regional style, with the wide expanse of the Ganges invariably running smoothly between white sandbanks, as boats ply the waterways. Above: The cultured, Patna-based Kashmiri merchant prince Ashraf Ali Khan and his *bibi* Muttubby, experiment with European fashions. Ashraf perches cross-legged on a Regency chair and both of them rest their hookahs on wooden teapoys. Below, Nawab Shuja ud-Daula passes in a grand procession past a line of riverside palaces.

After Buxar, Europeans and their sepoy guards fanned out across India, trading, fighting, taxing and administering the revenues and justice departments. Above: Captain (later Colonel) James Tod rides an elephant, by Chokha, Mewar, 1817.

Hector Munro, c. 1785. Munro was the victor of Buxar and the vanquished at Pollilur.

Madras sepoys, c. 1780.

British Officer in a Palanquin, by Yellapah of Vellore

A Military Officer of the East India Company, Murshidabad, 1765

Robert Clive by Nathaniel Dance, c. 1770. Here Baron Clive of Plassey is shown in portly middle age, very much the man aware of all that he had achieved to establish the political and military supremacy of the East India Company in Bengal, Bihar and Orissa. 'Fortune seems determined to accompany me to the last,' Clive wrote to his friend and biographer Robert Orme. 'Every object, every sanguine wish is upon the point of being completely fulfilled.'

The young Warren Hastings by Tilly Kettle, c. 1772. A thin, plainly dressed and balding young man in simple brown fustian with an open face and somewhat wistful expression, but with a hint of sense of humour in the set of his lips. His letters at this period reveal a diffident, austere, sensitive and self-contained young man who rose at dawn, had a cold bath then rode for an hour, occasionally with a hawk on his arm. He seems to have kept his own company, drinking 'but little wine' and spending his evenings reading, strumming a guitar and working on his Persian.

Shah Alam Conveying the Gift of the Diwani to Lord Clive, by Benjamin West.

Today we would call this an act of involuntary privatisation. The scroll is an order by the Emperor to dismiss the Mughal revenue officials in Bengal, Bihar and Orissa and replace them with a set of English traders appointed by Clive – the new Governor

of Bengal – and the directors of the Company, whom the document describes as 'the high and mighty, the noblest of exalted nobles, the chief of illustrious warriors, our faithful servants the English Company'. The collecting of Mughal taxes was henceforth subcontracted to a multinational corporation – whose revenue-collecting operations were protected by its own private army.

The Mughal Emperor Shah Alam Reviewing the Troops of the East India Company at Allahabad With General Barker, by Tilly Kettle. In 1771, Barker was despatched to Allahabad to try and stop Shah Alam returning to Delhi but found him 'deaf to all arguments'. The Emperor had long found life in Allahabad as a puppet of the Company insupportable, and now he yearned to return home, whatever the risks.

Shuja ud-Daula, Nawab of Avadh, with four Sons, General Barker and Military Officers, by Tilly Kettle. Shuja ud-Daula was a giant of a man. Nearly seven feet tall, with prominent, oiled moustaches, he was a man of immense physical strength. Even in late middle age he was reputedly strong enough to lift up two of his officers, one in each hand. He was defeated by the Company at the Battle of Buxar in 1765 and replaced by Clive back on the throne of Avadh, where he ruled until the end of his life as a close ally of the EIC.

The royal procession of Shah Alam as the Emperor returns to Delhi in 1771. A long column of troops snakes in wide meanders along the banks of the Yamuna, through a fertile landscape. At the front of the procession are the musicians. Then follow the macemen and the bearers of Mughal insignia. Next comes the Emperor himself, high on his elephant and hedged around by a bodyguard. The imperial princes are next, followed

by the many women of the imperial harem in their palanquins and covered carriages;
then the heavy siege guns, dragged by foursomes of elephants. Behind, the main body of
the army stretches off as far as the eye can see.

Ballajee Pundit-
Nanna Furnaveese

Nana Phadnavis, the Pune-based statesman and minister to the Peshwas, known as 'the Maratha Machiavelli'. He was one of the first to realise that the East India Company posed an existential threat to India and tried to organise a Triple Alliance with the Hyderabadis and the Sultans of Mysore to drive them out, but failed to carry the project through to its conclusion.

to death that year in what became one of the greatest tragedies of the province's history.⁹

The famine did not touch the entire province, and in eastern Bihar the situation was slightly better; but in the worst affected districts, fully one-third of all the peasants died, and two-thirds of the old Mughal aristocracy were ruined. Half of all the rural artisans perished. The Hughli was full of swollen bodies, floating slowly downstream to the sea, its banks littered with corpses where 'dogs, jackals, vultures and every bird and beast of prey grew fat and unwieldy on the flesh of man'.¹⁰ 'The oldest inhabitants say they never remembered anything like it,' reported Clive's successor as Governor, Henry Verelst.¹¹

By July 1770, when it was clear that the rains had disappointed for a third year, Mohammad Reza Khan was writing to his masters in Calcutta not only of the vast numbers of dead and dying, but also of the fires sweeping through the tinder of the empty granaries. Disease killed many others, including an outbreak of smallpox which carried away the young Nawab, Saif ud-Daula: 'How can I describe the misery of the people from the severe droughts and the dearness of the grain?' he wrote. 'Lakhs of people are dying daily ... When the whole country is in the grip of a famine, the only remedy is the mercy of God.'¹²

In reality, there were other remedies to hand which did not require divine intervention. Famines had been a baleful feature of Indian history from time immemorial, whenever the rains failed. But for centuries, and certainly by the time of the Mughals, elaborate systems of grain stores, public works and famine relief measures had been developed to blunt the worst effect of the drought. Even now, some of the more resourceful and imaginative Mughal administrators took initiatives to import rice and set up gruel kitchens.¹³

Ghulam Hussain Khan was especially impressed by the work done by Shitab Rai, the new Governor of Patna. Shitab Rai had been the deputy of Raja Ram Narain and had narrowly escaped death when his master was executed by Mir Qasim. Now he showed himself to be the most effective administrator in the region: 'Shitab Rai, melted by the sufferings of the people, provided in a handsome manner for the necessities of the poor, of the decrepit, the old and the distressed,' wrote the historian. 'In that dreadful year, when famine and mortality, going hand in hand, stalked everywhere, mowing down mankind by the thousands, Shitab Rai heard that the grain was a little cheaper, and in greater plenty in Benares, and set apart a sum of thirty thousand rupees,* and directed that the boats and rowers belonging to his household should bring regularly to Patna, three times a month, the grain provided at Benares.'

This grain being landed at Patna was sold at the Benares price, whilst the boats were despatched for another trip; by which management there were always boats landing and boats loading. In this manner, during the whole time the famine lasted, his boats, divided in three squadrons, were constantly employed in bringing corn, which his people sold at the original price, without loading it with the charges, losses and transport, and it was purchased by the hungry, who flocked to his granaries from all parts.

But as there were still vast numbers that could not afford to purchase grain so dear, he ordered them to be divided into four groups, and lodged in four gardens, surrounded by walls, where they were watched, almost as prisoners, by guards, but daily attended as patients by a number of clerks who kept an account of them, and were assisted by a number of servants, who at stated times used to come loaded with victuals ready dressed for the Mussalmen, and with a variety of grain and pulse and a sufficiency of earthen vessels, and of firewood, for the Gentoos [Hindus], and at the same time several ass-loads of small money, beside a quantity of opium, bhang [hashish], tobacco and a variety of other such articles, were distributed severally to each person, according to the kind he was accustomed to use; and this happened every day and without fail.

On the report of such generosity, the English and Dutch [in Patna] took the hint, and on his example, lodged the poor in several enclosures, where they were regularly fed and tended. In this manner, an immense multitude came to be rescued from the jaws of imminent death … But [elsewhere in Bengal] such a proceeding never came to anyone's head. Indeed some who had been appointed overseers of the poor proved so intent on their own interest, that so far from working to procure plenty of grain, they were foremost in the use of violent methods to engross it. Whenever any loaded boat chanced to come to the market, the grain was dragged away by force.[14]

* £390,000 today.

A few Company officials did their best to help the starving. In several places, the hoarding and export of rice was successfully prevented.[15] In Murshidabad, the Resident, Richard Becher, 'opened six centres for the free distribution of rice and other supplies'. He also warned the Calcutta Council about the dire consequences of failing to provide for the starving, and noted that the normally peaceful highways had become unsafe and that highway robberies, once unknown, were now occurring every day as the desperate and needy struggled to find ways to survive.[16] The Governor of Calcutta, John Cartier, also worked hard to alleviate the distress in the Company's capital: he maintained 'a magazine of grain with which they fed fifteen thousand every day for some months, and yet even this could not prevent many thousands dying of want. The streets were crowded with the most miserable objects, and there were 150 dead bodies picked up in a day, and thrown into the river.'[17]

But in many of the worst affected areas, Company efforts to alleviate the famine were contemptible. In Rangpur, the senior EIC officer, John Grose, could only bring himself daily to distribute Rs5* of rice to the poor, even though 'half the labouring and working people' had died by June 1770 and the entire area was being reduced to 'graveyard silence'.[18] Moreover, the Company administration as a whole did not engage in any famine relief works. Nor did it make seed or credit available to the vulnerable, or assist cultivators with materials to begin planting their next harvest, even though the government had ample cash reserves to do so. Instead, anxious to maintain their revenues at a time of low production and high military expenditure, the Company, in one of the greatest failures of corporate responsibility in history, rigorously enforced tax collection and in some cases even increased revenue assessments by 10 per cent.

Platoons of sepoys were marched out into the countryside to enforce payment, where they erected gibbets in prominent places to hang those who resisted the tax collection.[19] Even starving families were expected to pay up; there were no remissions authorised on humanitarian grounds. Richard Becher in Murshidabad was appalled by what he saw and wrote to Calcutta for instructions: 'Am I really quietly to stand by and see them commit the vilest acts of oppression, without being able to render the aggrieved redress?' he asked. 'The creatures of our government enrich themselves at the people's expense, nay even their ruin.'[20] As

* £65 today.

a result of such heartless methods of revenue collection, the famine initially made no impression on Company ledgers, as tax collections were, in the words of Warren Hastings, 'violently kept up to their former standards'.[21] In February 1771, the Council was able to tell the directors in London that 'notwithstanding the great severity of the late famine, and the great reduction of people thereby, some increase [in revenue] has been made'.[22]

The Council argued that they had responsibilities to maintain the defences of Bengal and protect their military gains. They therefore authorised 44 per cent of their £22 million annual budget* to be spent on the army and on the building of fortifications, so rapidly increasing the size of their sepoy regiments to 26,000 sepoys.[23] The only rice they stockpiled was for the use of the sepoys of their own army; there was no question of cuts to the military budget, even as a fifth of Bengal was starving to death.[24]

Moreover, there were persistent reports of individual Company merchants engaging in grain hoarding, profiteering and speculation. At the height of the famine, Mohammad Reza Khan reported to Calcutta that the managers of private Company traders 'monopolize the rice'.[25] According to an anonymous report sent back to England by one such dissident, possibly John Debrit, and published in full in the *Gentleman's Magazine*: 'As soon as the dryness of the season foretold the approaching dearness of rice, our gentlemen in the Company's service, particularly those whose stations gave them the best opportunities, were as early as possible in buying up all they could lay hold of.'

> When the effects of the scarcity became more and more sensible, the Natives complained to the Nabob at Murshidabad, that the English had engrossed all the rice. This complaint was laid before the President and Council by the Nabob's minister who resides in Calcutta; but the interests of the Gentlemen concerned was too powerful at the board, so that the complaint was only laughed at, and thrown out.
>
> Our Gentlemen in many places purchased the rice at 120 and 140 seers for a rupee, which they afterwards sold for 15 seers for a rupee, to the Black [Indian] merchants, so that the persons principally concerned have made great fortunes by it; and one of our writers at

* £2,310 million today.

the Durbar, who was interested therein, not esteemed to be worth 1000 rupees last year, has sent down it is said £60,000* to be remitted home this year.[26]

This unnamed speculator was not alone: in 1770–71, at the height of the Bengal famine, an astounding £1,086,255 was transferred to London by Company executives – perhaps £100 million in modern currency.[27]

By the end of the summer of 1770, the effects of the Company's policies were now so horrific that they could not be avoided by even the richest and most obtuse Company officials locked away in their walled Calcutta mansions. As Debrit told his London audience, 'The Nabob and several of the great men of the country at Murshidabad distributed rice to the poor gratis, until their stocks began to fail, when those donations were withdrawn, which brought many thousands down to Calcutta, in hopes of finding relief amongst us.'

By this time, we were already greatly affected at Calcutta, many thousands falling daily in the streets and fields, whose mangled bodies in that hot season, when at best the air is very infectious, made us dread the consequences of the plague. We had 100 people employed upon the Cutchery on the Company's account with doolys, sledges and bearers, to carry the dead and throw them into the River Ganges.

I have counted from my bed chamber window in the morning forty dead bodies, laying within twenty yards of the wall, besides many hundreds laying in the agonies of death for want, bending double, with their stomachs quite close contracted to their backbones. I have sent my servant to desire those who had strength to remove further off, whilst the poor creatures with their arms extended, have cried out, 'Baba! Baba! My father! My father! This affliction comes from the hands of your countrymen, and I am come here to die, if it pleases God, in your presence. I cannot move, do what you will with me.'

In the month of June, our condition was still worse, with only three seers of rice to be had in the bazaars, and that very bad, which, when bought must be carried home secretly, to avoid being plundered by the famished multitudes on the road. One could not pass the streets without seeing multitudes in their last agonies, crying out as you

---

* The modern equivalences of these sums are: 1,000 rupees = £13,000; £60,000 = over £6 million.

passed, 'My God! My God! Have mercy on me, I am starving,' whilst on other sides, numbers of dead were seen with dogs, jackalls, hogs, vultures and other birds and beasts of prey feeding on their carcases.

It was remarked by the Natives that greater numbers of these animals came down at this time than was ever known, which, upon this melancholy occasion was of great service, as the vultures and other birds take out the eyes and intestines, whilst the other animals gnaw at the feet and hands; so that very little of the body remains for the Cutcherry people to carry to the River; notwithstanding, they had a very hard time of it. I have observed two of them with a dhooly carrying twenty heads and the remains of the carcasses that had been left by the birds of prey, to the river at a time.

At this time we could not touch fish, the river was too full of carcasses, and of those who did eat it, many died suddenly. Pork, ducks and geese also lived mostly on carcasses, so that our only meat was mutton, when we could get it, which was very dear, and from the dryness of the season so poor, that a quarter would not weigh a pound and a half.

Of this I used to make a little broth, and after I had dined, perhaps there were 100 poor at the door waiting for the remains, which I have often sent amongst them cut up into little pieces; so that as many as could might partake of it; and after one had sucked the bones quite dry, and thrown them away, I have seen another take them up, sand and all among them, and another do the same, and then by a third, and so on.[28]

As Bengal lay racked by famine, 'with the greatest part of the land now entirely uncultivated ... owing to the scarcity of the inhabitants', in London, Company shareholders, relieved to see tax revenues maintained at normal levels, and aware that the share price was now higher than it had ever been – more than double its pre-Diwani rate – celebrated by voting themselves an unprecedented 12.5 per cent dividend.[29]

What they did not know was that this was one of the highest points the Company share price would ever reach; and that what lay ahead was an extended period of unprecedented ill fortune for the Company – financial, political and military – that would do immense damage to the EIC both at home and abroad, bringing it close to bankruptcy and complete closure.

Already, by the end of 1771, the mood was beginning to change in London. Word was spreading about the Company's inhumanity in Bengal: the number of dead and dying was simply too vast to hide. Horace Walpole's letters reflected a growing awareness that behind the EIC's vast profits there was something profoundly rotten at work in the Company's Indian operations. 'The groans of India have mounted to heaven,' he wrote, 'where the Heaven-Born General [Clive] will certainly be disavowed.'

> We have outdone the Spaniards in Peru! They were at least butchers on a religious principle, however diabolical their zeal. We have murdered, deposed, plundered, usurped – say what think you of the famine in Bengal, in which three millions perished, being caused by a monopoly of the provisions by the servants of the East India Company? All this is come out, is coming out – unless the gold that inspired these horrors can quash them.[30]

His words were echoed in the House of Lords by the former Prime Minister. William Pitt, Lord Chatham, came from a dynasty whose fortunes were made in India: his father, 'Diamond Pitt', brought back from his governorship of Madras the fortune that had made possible Pitt's career. Pitt did not, however, like to be reminded of this, and now raised the alarm that the EIC was bringing its corrupt practices back from India and into the very benches of the Mother of Parliaments. 'The riches of Asia have been poured in upon us,' he declared at the despatch box, 'and have brought with them not only Asiatic luxury, but, I fear, Asiatic principles of government. Without connections, without any natural interest in the soil, the importers of foreign gold have forced their way into Parliament by such a torrent of private corruptions as no private hereditary fortune could resist.'[31]

In early 1772, the *London Post* published a series of graphic articles exposing the crimes and murders allegedly committed by the Company in India.[32] In April, the *Gentleman's Magazine*, the same publication which had published Debrit's piece on the Bengal famine, warned that the EIC could repeat 'the same cruelties in this island which have disgraced humanity and deluged with native and innocent blood the plains of India ... Down with that rump of unconstitutional power, the East India Company, the imperious company of East India merchants!'[33]

As the year progressed, and as more and more articles, pamphlets and books were published revealing the catastrophic death tolls in Bengal, India became 'part of the daily newspaper diet' of London, and public opinion swung increasingly against the Company, its returned Nabobs in general, and Clive, their most prominent and conspicuous exemplar, in particular.[34] One pamphlet talked of 'Indians tortured to disclose their treasure; cities, towns and villages ransacked; jaghires and provinces purloined; these were the "delights" and the "religions" of the Directors and their servants.'[35] Walpole was now railing loudly about 'the iniquities of our East India Company and its nest of monsters ... and their spawn of nabobs' to any of his correspondents who cared to listen.[36]

That summer, the Company became the focus for much scandalous gossip in London. There was already in print a brilliant satire attacking the directors of the EIC – *Debates in the Asiatic Assembly*. Among its characters were Sir Janus Blubber, Shylock Buffalo, Jaundice Braywell, Sir Judas Venom, Donald Machaggies, Caliban Clodpate, Skeleton Scarecrow and the villainous Lord Vulture, a character clearly modelled on Clive. As the parade of Company grotesques praise Lord Vulture, only one character – George Manly – dares denounce the others as 'a troop of desperate banditti ... a scandalous confederacy to plunder and strip'.

Manly demands that we 'enquire more deeply into ... [Lord Vulture's] avarice and oppression and tyrannical management of our affairs, his inhumanity and breach of order ... Shall we tamely behold all his engines employed in every dark practice of promises and threats, of corruption and prostitution?' Lord Vulture, says Manly, is 'utterly deaf to every sentiment of justice and humanity', and demands that the Company must be rescued from 'the wanton profusion of this insatiable harpy, whose ambition is unparalleled, and whose avarice knows no bounds'.[37]

Then, in June 1772, the Haymarket Theatre, just off Piccadilly Circus, mounted a play, *The Nabob*, newly written by the Haymarket's proprietor, Samuel Foote. In this bawdy satire, Sir Matthew Mite is an obnoxious India-returned parvenu 'Nabob' hoping to use his Bengal loot to marry into an ancient family and corruptly buy election to Parliament for the constituency of Bribe 'em. At one point in the play, Mite's assistant, Touchit, explains the methods by which Mite and his cronies made their fortunes:

> *Touchit:* We cunningly encroach and fortify little by little, till at length, we are growing too strong for the natives, and then we turn them out of their lands, and take possession of their money and jewels.
>
> *Mayor:* And don't you think, Mr Touchit, that is a little uncivil of us?
>
> *Touchit:* Oh, nothing at all! These people are little better than Tartars or Turks.
>
> *Mayor:* No, no, Mr Touchit; just the reverse: it is they who have caught the Tartars in us.[38]

That summer, the attacks on the Company took many forms. Some accused the Company of near-genocide in India; others of corrupting Parliament; others again focused on the social mountaineering of the returned Nabobs, with their dripping Indian diamonds, their newly bought estates and their rotten boroughs. Many raised the valid point that a private corporation enjoying a government trading monopoly ought not to be running an overseas empire: 'Trade and the Sword ought not to be managed by the same people,' wrote Arthur Young in a widely circulated pamphlet. 'Barter and exchange is the business of merchants, not fighting of battles and dethroning of princes.'[39]

One especially powerful attack on the Company's record was published by a returned EIC official, the Scottish philosopher, historian and mercantilist Alexander Dow, who concluded his scholarly translation from the Persian of Ferishta's *History of Hindostan* with an excoriating attack on the Company's rule of Bengal. Humane, informed and well argued, Dow's attack was the product of one individual's appalled anger at the incompetence and barbarism of the Company's tenure of Bengal and is an invaluable eyewitness account by an intelligent insider: 'Bengal, from the mildness of its climate, the fertility of its soil, and the natural industry of the Hindus, was always remarkable for its commerce,' he wrote. 'The balance of trade was against all nations in favour of Bengal, and it was the sink where gold and silver disappeared, without the least prospect of return ... [But since the Company took over] the country was depopulated by every species of public distress.'

> In the space of six years, half the great cities of an opulent kingdom were rendered desolate; the most fertile fields in the world laid waste; and five millions of harmless and industrious people were either expelled or destroyed. Want of foresight became more fatal than innate barbarism; and [the company's servants] found themselves wading through blood and ruin, when their object was only spoil.
>
> A barbarous enemy may slay a prostrate foe, but a civilised conqueror can ruin nations without the sword. Monopolies and an exclusive trade joined issue with additional taxations ... The unfortunate were deprived of the means, whilst the demands upon them were, with peculiar absurdity, increased ... We may date the commencement of the decline from the day on which Bengal fell under the dominion of foreigners; who were more anxious to improve the present moment of their own emolument than to secure a permanent advantage to the nation. With particular want of foresight they began to drain the reservoir without turning into it any stream to prevent it from being exhausted ...

'The Bengal carcase is now bleaching in the wind,' concluded Dow, 'and is almost picked to the bone.'[40]

However, by far the most influential and damaging of the many tracts against the EIC to be published in 1772 was William Bolts' *Considerations on Indian Affairs*.[41] Bolts, who was of Anglo-Dutch origins, had actually been one of the Company's most unscrupulous operators, an associate of William Ellis of Patna, who had been involved in the Company's brutal transactions during the reign of Mir Qasim. But having fallen out with Clive and been expelled forcibly from Bengal for illegal trading, he vowed to bring down the former Governor. He returned to London, where he promptly set himself up as a whistleblower. *Considerations on Indian Affairs* was his attempt to destroy Clive by lifting the lid on the Company's most disreputable transactions in Bengal, many of which Bolts himself had actually had a direct hand in.[42]

Bolts wrote of Company officials 'unjustly imprisoning the natives and black [Indian] merchants and by violence extorting great sums of money from them'. He also mentions the self-mutilation of weavers who 'cut off their own thumbs' in order to prevent them being press-ganged to wind silk in prison-like factory camps.[43] There was no justice available against the perpetrators: 'We behold the impotency of power on this side of the ocean that not one delinquent in India is brought to justice in Europe.'

Bolts' most thought-provoking idea was that the Company's claim to have obtained the Diwani by the Treaty of Allahabad was in fact a legal nonsense, invented by Clive to mask the reality of his military conquests. The Company, he wrote, 'are become sovereigns of extensive, rich and populous Kingdoms, with a standing army of above 60,000 men at their command'. The Nawab of Bengal and Shah Alam were merely 'nominal nabobs ... puppets', dangling at the EIC's whim, and the land held not by law or treaty but 'possessions acquired and held in reality by either violence or usurpation'. This was so because 'no [Mughal] laws or empire [still] exist'. The Company had become 'an absolute government of monopolists' which was impoverishing Bengal and working against long-term British interests. In comparison, wrote Bolts, the Mughal government which preceded the Company Raj was a model of fair-trade principles in its steady encouragement of merchants and artisans.[44]

Bolts' solution was for the Crown to take over Bengal as a government colony, so ending the asset-stripping of the province by a for-profit Company. Throughout, Bolts addressed himself to the King, suggesting that he should assume his rightful position and extend his benign hand to protect his 'subjects in Asia', whether British or Indian.

The book was full of embittered half-truths and false accusations; and many of the worst abuses enumerated were actually the work of Bolts himself, along with his friend Ellis. But *Considerations* was nonetheless hugely influential. It anticipated many later criticisms of Empire, and it broke much new ground in confronting issues which were then novel problems, but later would become much more common: for the first time a writer grappled, for example, with the question of how to deal with a multinational whose tentacles extended well beyond national frontiers. It also asked important questions about containing an over-powerful and unusually wealthy proprietor: what would happen, asked Bolts, if one very rich magnate were to become too wealthy and powerful for a nation state to control? What would happen if someone could buy the legislature and use his wealth to corrupt MPs for his own business ends?

Long extracts were reprinted in the *London Magazine* and as one correspondent warned Warren Hastings, despite its exaggerations and clear prejudices, 'it is swallowed very greedily by the public whose eyes are fixed on the correction of these abuses by the interposition of Parliament'.[45] For Horace Walpole it proved everything he had long suspected about the evils of the Company. Bolts 'carried the accusations home to Lord Clive; and ... represents him as a monster in assassination, usurpation and extortion, with heavy accusations of his monopolizing in open defiance of the orders of the Company ... To such monopolies were imputed the late famine in Bengal and the loss of three million of the inhabitants. A tithe of these crimes was sufficient to inspire horror.'[46]

Bolts concluded his rant with a warning about the financial stability of the Company: 'The Company may be compared to a stupendous edifice,' he wrote, 'suddenly built upon a foundation not previously well examined or secured, inhabited by momentary proprietors and governors, divided by different interests opposed to each other; and who, while one set of them is overloading the superstructure, another is undermining the foundations.'[47]

It proved a prophetic passage. For, only five months later, the EIC's financial foundations gave way in the most spectacular fashion.

On 8 June 1772, a Scottish banker named Alexander Fordyce disappeared from his office, leaving debts of £550,000.* His bank, Neal, James, Fordyce and Down, imploded soon after and declared bankruptcy. Another institution with large investments in Company stock, Douglas, Heron & Company, otherwise known as the Ayr Bank, closed its doors the following week, so initiating a financial crisis that quickly spread across Britain into Europe.

* Nearly £58 million today.

In the week that followed, across the North Sea there were several failures of Dutch banks with speculative holdings in East India Company stock. Ten more banks folded across Europe within a fortnight, twenty more within the month: thirty banks going down like dominoes in less than three weeks.[48]

This had global repercussions, ranging from suicides in Virginia to, closer to home, the bankruptcy of Sir George Colebrooke, the chairman of the East India Company, which did little to restore confidence in his management. The Bank of England had to intervene, but the Bank itself was under threat. 'We are here in a very melancholy Situation: Continual Bankruptcies, universal Loss of Credit, and endless Suspicions,' David Hume wrote to Adam Smith from Edinburgh in June. 'Do these Events any-wise affect your Theory? Or will it occasion the Revisal of any Chapters [of *The Wealth of Nations*]?'[49]

A month later, on 10 July 1772, a packet of bills worth the enormous sum of £747,195, remittances from India sent by Company officials returning home, arrived at India House in Leadenhall Street. There were now real anxieties about the state of EIC finances, as remittances sent for cashing in London between 1771 and 1772 looked to be heading towards the £1.5 million mark.[50] Questions were asked as to whether the EIC should sanction payment of these remittances, but the account committee insisted on honouring the bills, 'as it was alleged that the credit of the Company might be hurt in the severest manner by refusing'.

At the same time, the famine was finally leading to Bengal land revenues falling. Meanwhile, overpriced EIC tea was lying unsold in vast quantities in its London warehouses: unsold stock had risen from around £1 million in 1762 to more than £3 million in 1772. This coincided with military expenses doubling from 1764 to 1770, while the cost of the 12.5 per cent dividend had added nearly £1 million a year* to the EIC expenses. The books were now very far from balancing.[51] In the second half of the year, the Company defaulted first on its annual customs payments, and then on its loan repayments to the Bank of England. As knowledge of the crisis began to circulate, EIC stock plummeted sixty points in a single month. It was shortly after this that

---

* The modern equivalences of these sums are: £747,195 = £78,455,475; £1.5 million = £157 million; £1 million = £100 million; £3 million = £300 million.

the EIC was forced to go cap in hand to the Bank of England requesting a vast loan.[52]

On 15 July 1772, the directors of the Company applied to the Bank of England for a loan of £400,000. A fortnight later, they returned, asking for an additional £300,000. The Bank could raise only £200,000. There were unpaid bills of £1.6 million and obligations of over £9 million, while the Company's assets were worth less than £5 million.[53] By August, the directors were telling the government in confidence that they would actually need an unprecedented bailout of a further £1 million.*

Already the EIC was in deep debt: between 1769 and 1772 the Company had borrowed £5.5 million** from the Bank of England and as the chairman wrote to Warren Hastings in Calcutta, 'our domestic distresses came fast upon us – a general gloom springing from this immense bankruptcy has brought the public credit almost to stagnate, affected our sales in a deep degree and brought the Bank of England (our single resource) to be severely cautious'.[54] The report written by Edmund Burke shortly afterwards painted a picture of Company servants 'separated both from the country that sent them out and from the country in which they are', and foresaw that the EIC's financial problems could potentially 'like a mill-stone, drag [the government] down into an unfathomable abyss … This cursed Company would, at last, like a viper, be the destruction of the country which fostered it at its bosom.'[55]

At the same time it was widely recognised that it was Indian wealth that was now helping propel Britain's economy and that 'the first and most immediate consequence' of the failure of the EIC would be 'national bankruptcy', or what amounted to the same thing, 'a stop to the payment of interest on the national debt'.[56]

The economic and political theorist Thomas Pownall wrote how 'people now at last begin to view those Indian affairs, not simply as financial appendages connected to the Empire; but from the participation of their revenues being wrought into the very frame of our finances … people tremble with horror even at the imagination of the downfall of this Indian part of our system; knowing that it must necessarily involve with its fall, the ruin of the whole edifice of the British Empire'.[57] This

---

* £400,000 = £42 million; £300,000 = £31 million; £200,000 = £21 million; £1.6 million = £168 million; £9 million = £945 million; £5 million = £525 million; £1 million = £105 million.
** £577 million today.

was certainly the view of the King. George III wrote that he believed 'the real glory of this nation' depended on the wealth of India which offered 'the only safe method of extracting this country out of its lamentable situation owing to the load of debt it labours under'.[58]

On 26 November, Parliament was recalled to discuss the East India Company's financial crisis, as well as the now widespread allegations of corruption and malpractice made against individual EIC servants: the contrast between the bankruptcy of the Company and the vast riches of its employees was too stark not to be investigated. There was also a personal element to this: 40 per cent of MPs owned EIC stock and their finances had all been severely damaged by the fall in its value.

It was now increasingly obvious that if Parliament did vote to bail out the Company to the tune of £1.4 million* there would have to be a *quid pro quo*, and a measure of parliamentary supervision of the EIC in return for authorising such an immense loan. It was widely recognised for the first time that the EIC was incapable of reforming its own affairs and that, unless Parliament intervened, Bengal and its vast revenues would be lost.

As William Burrell MP declared: 'Sir, let no gentleman think this is a trivial question of Ministry or Opposition. No sir, it is the state of the Empire; and perhaps upon it depends whether Great Britain shall be the first country in the world, or ruined or undone.'[59]

On 18 December 1772, the directors of the East India Company were summoned to the Houses of Parliament. There they were fiercely examined by General John Burgoyne's Select Committee, which had been set up to investigate EIC abuses in India, and particularly accusations of embezzlement and bribe-taking. Charges of corruption were levelled against several EIC servants, including Clive, who Burgoyne described as the 'oldest, if not principal delinquent'. The Select Committee in its final report calculated that 'presents' worth over £2 million** had been distributed in Bengal

---

* £147 million today.

** £210 million today.

between 1757 and 1765, and said that the 'very great sums of money ... appropriated' by Clive and his henchmen 'to the dishonour and detriment of the state' should be reimbursed to the Crown.[60]

Clive responded on 21 May 1773 with one of his most famous speeches, saying he objected strongly to being treated like 'a common sheep-stealer'. After Plassey, he thundered, 'a great prince was dependent on my pleasure; an opulent city lay at my mercy; its richest bankers bid against each other for my smiles; I walked through vaults which were thrown open to me alone, piled on either hand with gold and jewels! Mr Chairman, at this moment I stand astonished by my own moderation.'

Clive talked powerfully in his own defence for two hours. Making a final plea, 'leave me my honour, take away my fortune', he walked out of the chamber, tears in his eyes, followed by loud and repeated cries of 'Hear, hear!' Entering his carriage, he drove back home, not knowing whether he had 'a sixpence to call his own in the morning'.[61] The debate lasted long into the night, with a growing majority of speakers rising to attack Burgoyne's motion. The Resolution was eventually rendered harmless by a series of amendments and another praising Clive's 'great and meritorious services to this country'. In the end, after an all-night debate, Clive had been cleared by a vote of 95 for censure to 155 for clearing his name.[62]

The Prime Minister, Lord North, may have lost one battle, but he was still determined to bring the EIC to heel. Shortly after Burgoyne's bill of censure had been defeated, he declared, 'I think, sir, it is allowed that Parliament have a right over the East India Company ... Such continual excesses, such frauds at home, oppressions abroad, that all the world may cry out, let it go to the Crown.'[63] His aim was to take all the EIC's Indian territories, and the 20 million Indians who lived there, under the authority of the state. As one MP put it, the House must 'make some attempt to rescue so many unhappy, industrious natives of the country from the yoke of this government they now live under'.[64]

But in this, too, North ultimately failed. The Company enjoyed chartered privileges, guaranteed by the Crown, and its shareholders were tenacious in their defence of them. Moreover, too many MPs owned EIC stock, and the EIC's taxes contributed too much to the economy – customs duties alone generated £886,922* annually – for it to be possible for any government to even consider letting the Company sink. Ultimately, it

---

* Over £93 million today.

was saved by its size: the Company now came close to generating nearly half of Britain's trade and was, genuinely, too big to fail.

In these circumstances, the outlines of the deal between the Company and Parliament soon became clear, and with it the new partnership with the state that would result. The colossal loan of £1.4 million* that the Company needed in order to stave off its looming bankruptcy would be agreed to. But, in return, the Company agreed to subject itself to a Regulating Act, defined by Lord North's India Bill of June 1773, which would bring the EIC under greater parliamentary scrutiny. Parliament would also get to appoint a Governor General who would now oversee not just the Bengal Presidency but those of Madras and Bombay as well.

On 19 June 1773, Lord North's bill passed its final reading by 47 votes to 15. The world's first aggressive multinational corporation was saved by one of history's first mega-bailouts, an early example of a nation state extracting, as its price for saving a failing corporation, the right to regulate and rein it in. But despite much parliamentary rhetoric, the EIC still remained a semi-autonomous imperial power in its own right, albeit one now partially incorporated within the Hanoverian state machinery. In itself, the Regulating Act did little to muzzle the worst excesses of the EIC, but it did create a precedent, and it marked the beginning of a steady process of state interference in the Company that would ultimately end in its nationalisation eighty years later, in 1858.

The man to whom Parliament first gave the job of Governor General was not some political appointment new to India, but a 41-year-old Company veteran. Warren Hastings was one of the most intelligent and experienced of all Company officials, plain-living, scholarly, diligent and austerely workaholic. The same Act also called for three government-appointed councillors to oversee Hastings' work on behalf of Parliament. Among these was a brilliant and widely read but oddly malevolent and vindictive, as well as insatiably ambitious, young parliamentary secretary. Philip Francis was the son of an Irish Protestant clergyman who had been born in Dublin but brought up in London, who, as he wrote, 'set out in life without the smallest advantage of birth or fortune'. Acutely self-conscious of his status as an upwardly mobile outsider, 'ever on his guard against himself', he was a skilled political operator with a love of subterfuge, deviousness and intrigue: he is the prime candidate for the authorship of the letters of

---

* £147 million today.

'Junius', inflammatory essays attacking George III and his ministers, which were published between 1768 and 1772, and widely reprinted in colonial America and continental Europe.[65] It was the failure of Hastings and Francis to work together, and Francis's ambition to get Hastings recalled and himself become the ruler of Bengal in his place – 'this glorious empire which I was sent to save and govern' – that was to lead to many further problems for the Company and effectively paralyse its goverment in India in the years to come.[66]

The other casualty of the Regulating Act and the parliamentary debates which swirled around it was, perhaps surprisingly, Clive himself. Although he was ultimately vindicated by Parliament, he never recovered from the bruising treatment he received at the hands of Burgoyne and his Select Committee. Despite escaping formal censure, he was now a notorious and deeply unpopular figure and widely regarded around the country as Lord Vulture, the monstrous embodiment of all that was most corrupt and unprincipled about the East India Company.

Shortly after the passing of the Regulating Act, Clive set off abroad on the Grand Tour, dining with some of his former Compagnie des Indes adversaries as he passed through France. For a year, he toured the classical sites of Italy, collecting artworks and meeting some of the most powerful and fashionable figures in Europe; but he never recovered his peace of mind. He had always suffered from depression, and twice in his youth had tried to shoot himself. Since then, despite maintaining an exterior of unbroken poise and self-confidence, he had suffered at least one major breakdown. To this burden was now added agonising stomach pains and gout. Not long after his return to England, on 22 November 1774, at the age of only forty-nine, Robert Clive committed suicide in his townhouse in Berkeley Square.

His old enemy Horace Walpole wrote about the first rumours to circulate around London. 'There was certainly illness in the case,' he wrote, 'but the world thinks more than illness. His constitution was exceedingly broken and disordered, and grown subject to violent pains and convulsions. He came to town very ill last Monday. On Tuesday his physician gave him a dose of laudanum, which had not the desired effect. On the rest, there are two stories; one, that the physician repeated the dose; the other that he doubled it himself, contrary to advice. In short, he has terminated at 50, a life of so much glory, reproach, art, wealth, and ostentation!'[67]

The truth was more unpleasant: Clive had actually cut his jugular with a blunt paperknife. He was at home with his wife Margaret, his secretary Richard Strachey and Strachey's wife Jane. Jane Strachey later recorded that after a game of whist, which had been interrupted by Clive's violent stomach pains, Clive walked out of the drawing room 'to visit the water closet'. When after some time he failed to return, Strachey said to Margaret Clive, 'You had better go and see where my Lord is.' Margaret 'went to look for him, and at last, opening a door, found Lord Clive with his throat cut. She fainted, and servants came. Patty Ducarel got some of the blood on her hands, and licked it off.'[68]

Clive's body was removed at the dead of night from Berkeley Square to the village church in Moreton Say where he was born. There the suicide was buried in a secret night-time ceremony, in an unmarked grave, without a plaque, in the same church where he had been baptised half a century earlier.

Clive left no suicide note, but Samuel Johnson reflected the widespread view as to his motives: Clive, he wrote, 'had acquired his fortune by such crimes that his consciousness of them impelled him to cut his own throat'.[69]

On 19 October 1774, the three Crown councillors appointed by the statutes of the Regulating Act, Philip Francis, General Clavering and Colonel Monson, finally docked in Calcutta. They were immediately offended to be given a seventeen-, not a twenty-one-gun salute, and by the 'mean and dishonourable' reception: 'there were no guards, no person to receive us or to show the way, no state.'[70]

Warren Hastings then compounded their sense of grievance by receiving them for luncheon at his house in informal attire: 'surely Mr Hastings might have put on a ruffled shirt,' wrote Philip Francis's brother-in-law and secretary. General Clavering immediately wrote a letter of complaint to London. By the end of an ill-humoured luncheon, Warren Hastings was already considering resigning. The new political dispensation could not have got off to a more unfortunate start.

Worse was to follow. The following day, 20 October, in the first formal business meeting of the new councillors, their first act was to inquire into the recent Rohilla War and to ask why Hastings had lent Company troops to the Company's ally, Shuja ud-Daula of Avadh. Hastings' aim had been to help Shuja stabilise his western frontier by stopping the incursions of the unruly Rohilla Afghans, but Francis rightly pointed out that the Company's troops had effectively been leased out as mercenaries and under Shuja's command had participated in terrible atrocities on the defeated Afghans.

Hastings, always sensitive to criticism, wrote that he could hardly breathe in this air of extreme malice. 'Dark allusions, mysterious insinuations, bitter invective and ironical reflections are weapons to which I have become accustomed,' he wrote soon after.[71] According to a gleeful Francis, 'the sweat ran down Hastings' face, tears gushed from his eyes, he beat his head, and ran about the room in a fit of distraction'.[72] Soon afterwards, Francis was writing to the Prime Minister, Lord North, of his contemptuous estimate of Hastings: 'without denying him some little Talent of the third or fourth order,' he wrote, 'we were all as much deceived with regard to his Abilities and Judgement, as to his other Qualifications. I look back to my own Prepossession in his favour as to a State of Delirium, from which he himself has recovered me ...'[73]

Under the malevolent influence of Clive, who had always distrusted Hastings' Indophilia, Francis had arrived in India already convinced that Hastings was the source of all the evils and corruption of Bengal. As he wrote to his patron, who was then returning from the last leg of his Grand Tour, 'Mr Hastings is the most corrupt of villains.' As for Hastings' only ally on the Council, Richard Barwell, 'he is an ignorant, false, presumptuous blockhead'.[74]

These were views Philip Francis held steadfastly until his death, and from the day of his arrival in Calcutta he worked hard to bring Hastings down, to block all his initiatives and to reverse all the work he had already done. 'Bengal is ruined and Mr H has done it alone,' he wrote within a few weeks of arriving. 'By the next ship I believe we shall send you such an Account of the Internal State, as will make every man in England tremble.'[75] His two fellow councillors, both peppery soldiers, neither very bright, went along with all that Francis suggested, having been won around to his views in the course of the year-long sea voyage to Bengal.

Hastings had every reason to feel aggrieved. Far from being regarded as the incarnation of Company corruption, up to the arrival of Francis, Hastings had been regarded as a man with a spotless reputation. Tall, thin, clean-living, quietly spoken and dryly scholarly, Hastings was one of the few Company servants who had always stood up against the wilder excesses of Company rule. He was also widely admired for his remarkable administrative ability and sheer industry. The artist William Hodges, who travelled up the Ganges with Warren Hastings, remarked on his plain attire, amid the pomp of his colleagues, and noted how firmly he stopped his attendants treating ordinary Indians roughly. He was constantly lending money to friends in distress and he looked after his household with generosity and consideration: his pension list remembered the widow of his very first servant in Kasimbazar and even a blind man who used to sing for him in the streets of Calcutta.[76] Ghulam Hussain Khan, who has little good to say about any British official, wrote a long and singular passage in his history praising Hastings' struggles for justice for ordinary people under Company rule, as well as his personal generosity: 'May the Almighty Bestower of Graces and Favor reward the Governor for having hastened to the assistance of so many afflicted families ... and of listening to the groans and sobs of so many thousands of oppressed ones, who know how to suffer but cannot speak.'[77]

Far more than any of his contemporaries, Hastings was conscious of the many flaws in the Company's regime, and wrote about them tellingly: 'To hold vast possessions, and yet to act on the level of mere merchants, making immediate gain our first principle; to receive an immense revenue without possessing protective power over the people who pay it ... [these] are paradoxes not to be reconciled, highly injurious to our national character ... and bordering on inhumanity.'[78] He was determined to bring about the changes that were needed to make Company rule more just, more effective and more responsible: Company servants, he wrote, were often ignorant of local languages and customs, but Indian petitioners were still powerless to resist their abuses and oppressions. This he believed to be 'the root of all evil which is diffused through every channel of our government'.[79] 'God forbid,' he wrote as he left to take up the Governor Generalship, 'that the government of this fine country should continue to be a mere chair for a triennial succession of indigent adventurers to sit and hatch private fortunes in.'[80]

Between his appointment, in February 1772, and the coming of Francis and the other councillors two and a half years later, Hastings had already done much to overhaul and reform the worst aspects of Company rule in Bengal. On arrival in Calcutta, he had been appalled by the mess he had inherited: 'The new government of the Company consists of a huge heap of undigested materials, as wild as chaos itself,' he wrote. 'The powers of the government are undefined; the collection of revenue, the provision of the investment, the administration of justice (if it exists at all), the care of the police, are all huddled together, being exercised by the same hands, though most frequently the two latter offices are totally neglected for the want of knowing where to have recourse to them.'[81]

He got quickly to work, beginning the process of turning the EIC into an administrative service. Hastings' first major change was to move all the functions of government from Murshidabad to Calcutta. The fiction that Bengal was still being ruled by the Nawab was dispensed with and the Company now emerged as the undisguised ruler: 'Calcutta is now the capital of Bengal,' he wrote, 'and every Office and trust of the province issues from it … It was time to establish the Line of the Company's Power, & habituate the People, and the Nabob to their Sovereignty.'[82] Yet Hastings wished to retain and revive the existing Mughal system and operate it through Indian officials, only with the office of the Governor General and his Council replacing that of the Nawab. He even went as far as proposing that no Europeans should be permitted to live outside Calcutta, except at a few select factories connected with the Company's trade.

Throughout 1773, Hastings worked with extraordinary energy. He unified currency systems, ordered the codification of Hindu laws and digests of Muslim law books, reformed the tax and customs system, fixed land revenue and stopped the worst oppression being carried out on behalf of private traders by the local agents. He created an efficient postal service, backed a proper cartographical survey of India by James Rennell and built a series of public granaries, including the great Gola at Patna, to make sure the famine of 1770–71 was never repeated.[83]

The Tibetan adventurer and diplomat George Bogle met Hastings around this time and described him as 'a man who is in every way fitted for the station he holds. He possesses a steadiness, and at the same time a moderation of character; he is quick and assiduous in business, and has a fine style of language, a knowledge of the customs and dispositions of the natives, whose tongue he understands, and, although not affable, yet of the most ready of access to all the world. During his administration many abuses have already been reformed and many useful regulations have been established in every department of government.'[84]

Underlying all Hastings' work was a deep respect for the land he had lived in since his teens. For, unlike Clive, Hastings genuinely liked India, and by the time he became Governor spoke not only good Bengali and Urdu but also fluent court and literary Persian. He even sang 'Hindoostanee airs'. His letters, including some written to his friend Samuel Johnson, reveal a deep affection for India and Indians quite absent from the openly racist letters of Clive: 'Our Indian subjects,' wrote Hastings, 'are as exempt from the worst propensities of human nature as any people upon the face of the earth, ourselves not exempted. They are gentle, benevolent, more susceptible to gratitude for kindness shewn them than prompt to vengeance for wrongs sustained, abhorrent of bloodshed, faithful and affectionate in service and submissive in legal authority.'[85] Hastings particularly disliked the haughty way Company servants dealt with Indians and the tone they often took: 'There is a fierceness in the European manners, especially among the lower sort, which is incompatible with the gentle temper of the Bengalee, and gives the former an ascendant that is scarce supportable even without the additional weight of authority.'[86]

Over the years, the more Hastings studied Indian culture, the more respectful he became. Under his patronage, and under the guidance of the Persian scholar and pioneering Orientalist Sir William Jones, who was brought out to superintend the new legal system, an 'Asiatick Society' was founded in 1784 which, among other projects, sponsored the first translation of the *Bhagavad Gita*, for which Hastings composed a rightly celebrated introduction: 'It is not very long since the inhabitants of India were considered by many as creatures scarce elevated above the degree of savage life,' he wrote, 'nor, I fear, is that prejudice yet wholly eradicated, though surely abated. Every instance which brings their real character home will impress us with a more generous sense of feeling for their natural rights, and teach us to estimate them by the measure of our own. But such instances can only be obtained from their writings: and will survive when the British dominion in India shall long cease to exist, and when the sources which it once yielded of wealth and power are lost to remembrance ... In truth I love India a little more than my own country.'[87]

Under Jones and Hastings, the Asiatic Society became the catalyst for an outpouring of scholarship on the civilisation of what Jones called 'this wonderful country'. It formed enduring relations with the Bengali intelligentsia and led the way to uncovering the deepest roots of Indian history and civilisation. In India Jones wrote that he had found Arcadia. It was a moment, rare in the history of Empire, of genuine cross-cultural appreciation.[88]

Moreover, Hastings' interest in the *Gita* was not just antiquarian: aspects of its philosophy came to guide him in his personal life and he took as his own maxim the *sloka* [verse], 'Your entitlement is to the deed alone, never to its results. Do not make the results of an action your motive. Do not be attached to inaction. Having renounced rewards resulting from actions, wise men endowed with discrimination are freed from the bondage of birth and go to the Regions of Eternal Happiness.'[89]

Philip Francis, by contrast, took the Clive approach to India and wrote contemptuously of the 'ignorant and unimproved natives of Bengal', as well anticipating Macaulay by trying to insist on English becoming the language of government in India.[90] 'The baseness of the Bengali is proverbial,' he grumbled; you could not conceive a 'more refined depravity'. Such differing views left little neutral middle ground. Hastings came to loathe Francis – 'this man of levity, the vilest fetcher and carrier of tales ... without one generous or manly principle' – with the same intensity as he himself was hated by his nemesis. But though he might fume and fret, Hastings could not overrule the hostile majority on his council in Calcutta – 'We three are king,' crowed Francis – and, increasingly, Madras and Bombay began simply ignoring Hastings' orders, too.[91]

So began a period of intense political conflict and governmental paralysis in Bengal, generating what Ghulam Hussain Khan, who was baffled by the Company's methods of decision-making, called 'an infinity of disturbances and confusions which perpetually impeded the wheels of government'. There was no 'head over them all, with full power and authority'. Instead, authority was invested with the Council – 'what the English call a committee, four or five men ...

that are perpetually at variance with each other, and perpetually in suspense about their own staying, and their being succeeded by another'. The result was a 'constant failure' that now plagued 'every endeavour' of the Company ... 'This country seems to have no master,' concluded the historian.[92] Hastings would not have disagreed. As he himself wrote, 'All business stood still, for the Board is continually occupied in collecting proofs of my demerit, and of the virtues of my adversaries.'[93]

The political paralysis in Bengal soon became clear to all the Company's many enemies in India, and it was not long before two powers in particular decided to test the strength of their now divided and weakened adversary. Both courts had their capitals in the south: Company control of the north and east of the peninsula may now have been assured, but the same was far from true of the south and west.

The first power were the Marathas, who had been for nearly seventy years, since the death of Aurangzeb, by far the strongest military power in India, and largely responsible for the slow dismembering of the Mughal Empire. In 1761 the Marathas had received a major setback at the Battle of Panipat when, outmanoeuvred, poorly supplied, surrounded on all sides and hungry to the point of malnourishment, disease and weakness, they were catastrophically besieged on the plains outside Panipat by Ahmad Shah Durrani's invading Afghans. In the weeks leading up to their final annihilation, their commanders had slowly been killed one by one under an intensive Afghan artillery bombardment: first Balavant Rao Mehendale, then Govindpant Bundele: 'the earth trembled, people began to speak ill words, and they say thunderbolts fell to earth'.[94] Then, on the fateful day of 7 January 1761, the desperate and now starving Marathas tried to break out of their blockaded camp. Under their high yellow banner they were slaughtered by the camel-borne swivel guns and the massed cavalry charges of the well-provisioned Afghans. That day ended with 28,000 Maratha dead on the battlefield, including much of the younger Maratha leadership and the Peshwa's only heir, shot by a ball through the chest. The following day, a further 40,000 disarmed Maratha captives, who had surrendered and thrown themselves at the mercy of the Afghans, were to a man executed on Durrani's orders. The Peshwa Ballaji Rao died broken-hearted soon after: 'his mind had become confused and he began to revile and curse his people'.[95] But a decade later, Durrani was dead and the Marathas had begun to recover their strength. They were now back in control of much of central and western India, and ambitious to extend their influence from the Kaveri to the Indus.

The second power was a new force, which in the 1770s was just emerging and beginning to flex its military muscles: the Mysore Sultanate of Haidar Ali and his formidable warrior son, Tipu Sultan. Haidar, who was of Punjabi origin, had risen in the ranks of the Mysore army, where he introduced many of the innovations he had learned from observing French troops at work in the Carnatic Wars. In the early 1760s he deposed the reigning Wodiyar Raja of Mysore and seized control of his state in what today might be called a military coup, rapidly increasing the size of Mysore's army and using it to occupy the lands of a succession of small neighbouring rulers.

He imported French officers to train his troops and French engineers to rebuild the defences of the island fortress of Srirangapatnam. Haidar and Tipu even tried to create a navy, which by 1766 comprised two warships, seven smaller vessels and forty gallivats, all commanded by a European seaman named Stannett.[96]

Both the Marathas and Tipu's Mysore Sultanate would in time develop to be the two fiercest and most challenging military adversaries the Company would ever face, and the final obstacles to its seizure of peninsular India.

For some time the directors had been growing alarmed at how Indian military techniques were rapidly improving across the region: the easy victories of the Plassey era, a decade earlier, were now increasingly eluding the Company. It had taken Indian states some thirty years to catch up with the European innovations in military technology, tactics and discipline that had led to the Company's early successes; but by the mid-1760s there was growing evidence that that gap was fast being bridged: 'The progress that the natives make in the knowledge of the art of war, both in Bengal and on the Coast of Coromandel, is becoming a very alarming circumstance,' noted the directors, urging the Bengal Council to prevent 'letting any European officers or soldiers enter into the service of the country government', and 'discourage, as far as in your power, all military improvements among them'.[97]

The anxieties of the directors were shown to be fully justified when, in August 1767, Haidar Ali declared war on the Company and descended the ghats east of Bangalore with a huge force of around 50,000 men. Of these troops, 23,000 were cavalry, but 28,000 – some twenty battalions – were trained units of highly disciplined sepoy infantry. The Company was unaware that Haidar had modern infantry forces of such size and discipline, but this was not the only shock. The Mysore sepoys' rifles and cannon were found to be based on the latest French designs, and the Mysore artillery had a heavier bore and longer range than anything possessed by the Company's armies.

In many other respects, too, the Mysore troops were more innovative and tactically ahead of the Company armies. They had mastered the art of firing rockets from their camel cavalry to disperse hostile cavalry formations, for example, long before William Congreve's rocket system was adopted by the British army.[98] Haidar and Tipu had also developed a large bullock 'park' of white Deccani cattle to allow them rapidly to deploy infantry and their supplies through their kingdom, a logistical innovation later borrowed by the Company.

In September 1767, while Haidar was engaging the main Madras army near Trinomalee, the seventeen-year-old Tipu led a daring raid behind Company lines into the garden suburbs of Madras. He rode at speed across the plains of the Carnatic with his crack cavalry and, finding no opposition, began burning and looting the grand weekend Georgian villas of the Madras Council that covered the slopes of St Thomas Mount. He also came close to capturing the Governor of Madras, and might actually have done so had his cavalry not become distracted by their looting. 'I never saw black troops behave so bravely as Haidar's,' wrote a Company captain who saw them in action.[99]

In the end, the Company sued for peace. Haidar was successfully bought off: a treaty was signed and the Mysore forces returned home. But the fact that the Company could now be so easily surprised and defeated was a lesson noted with satisfaction in many courts in India, particularly that of Haidar in Mysore and the Marathas in Pune.

It was near Pune, twelve years later, in 1779, that the Company received its first major defeat since the victory at Plassey. In February, without consulting Hastings in Calcutta, the Bombay Council got itself entangled with internal Maratha politics and signed an agreement with one of the Marathas' ousted leaders, Raghunath Rao, offering to reinstate him on the throne of Pune as regent to the young Maratha Peshwa. On 24 November, this rogue expedition, unauthorised by Calcutta, left Bombay harbour and set off towards Pune with just 2,000 sepoys, a few hundred European cavalry and artillery, and a force of 7,000 of Raghunath Rao's Maratha cavalry. Commanding the expedition was the elderly Colonel Egerton. The second-in-command was Shah Alam's old adversary John Carnac, who had recently taken over a senior position in the Bombay Presidency.

Egerton's force made slow progress uphill. On 30 December it finally reached the top of the ghats, having marched only one mile a day, with 19,000 bullocks pulling the guns and supplies up the steep switchbacks. They then spent a further eleven days trying to reach Karle, site of some celebrated Buddhist cave monasteries, a distance of only eight miles. By this time they had almost run out of supplies, as well as giving the Marathas ample time to prepare their defences. On arrival at Karle, Egerton was horrified to find a vast force of 50,000 Marathas drawn up to oppose them under the young Maratha leader Mahadji Scindia.*

Carnac was the first to realise the hopelessness of their position and wrote back to Bombay in despair that 'Colonel Egerton's military ideas seem to be wholly derived from the mode of practice he has seen observed during the short time he was in Germany, and he proceeds

---

* Captain James Stewart was among those killed on 4 January 1779 near Karle, when he shinned up a tree to see where the Maratha army was and was promptly shot dead by a Maratha marksman. Two hundred years later Ishtur Phakda, as he is now known around Karle, has become a local Tantric deity, to whom the local police – among others – offer weekly blood sacrifice. The shrine to his head, which at some point seems to have become detached from his body, is in the local police station, just beyond the cells. If the station chief ignores him, according to the officer on duty, Ishtur Phakda 'gives him a good slap'. With many thanks to the great historian of the Marathas, Uday S. Kulkarni, who not only told me this story, but took me on a prolonged search for the obelisk marking the spot of his death, a second shrine – covered in goat's blood – where his body lies, and the third to his head in the local Wadgaon police lockup.

with the same precaution as if he had an European Enemy to deal with, whereas the only method of ensuring success in this country is to advance and be forward.'

> If we continue as we have hitherto done, moving on slowly from post to post, it is hard to say when the campaign may be at an end, for advantage will be all on their side, the ground being throughout broken into gullies and covered with bushes and underwood where they find many lurking places ... The Marathas hover about us and from the hours of 11 to three in the afternoon, playing their Artillery and Rockets upon us ... I do not think Colonel Egerton can hold out much longer.[100]

By 9 January 1779, Company forces had advanced as far as Talegaon, only eighteen miles from Pune. They arrived to find the place had been ransacked and stripped of all supplies. At dawn the following morning, they realised they were now surrounded and that their supply route had been cut off. Maratha cavalry picked off stragglers, rustled Company bullocks and deterred *banjara* (itinerant trader) bands from risking their herds by attempting to supply the Company force.[101] To compound the mess, Egerton was now seriously ill. Raghunath Rao begged them to continue their march, and said that if they only made it to the outskirts of Pune a few miles further on, his supporters would rise up to assist them. But the Company commanders had lost their nerve. Two days later, having run out of supplies, they threw their heavy cannon into a temple tank, burned what remained of their stores and at midnight began a chaotic, starving retreat. The Marathas soon detected their movements, surrounded them and fell on the column at first light: 350 were dead before noon. Egerton had no option but to surrender, and six days later signed the humiliating Treaty of Wadgaon. With this he handed over Raghunath Rao and several senior Company hostages and agreed to give up a swathe of Company territory to the Marathas.[102]

The reputation of the Company's army would never be the same again. But as well as exposing the limits of the Company's military power, the failed Pune expedition also revealed the degree to which the Company now had ambitions to reshape and interfere in the politics of the entire South Asian region. For the brilliant Maratha Prime Minister

Nana Phadnavis, 'the Maratha Machiavelli', this was the moment that he realised the urgent need for the various Indian powers, whatever their differences, to pull together and form an alliance against the alien intruders, and to attack them with a united front while their leadership was still weak and divided.[103]

On 7 February 1780, a year after the Treaty of Wadgaon, Nana Phadnavis picked up his pen and wrote a letter to his old enemy Haidar Ali, offering to bury the hatchet if the Mysore Sultan would join forces and together make war on the Company: 'The British,' he wrote, 'have grown intolerably belligerent. During these five years, their blind aggression has led them to violate solemn treaties.'

> They first make sweet promises in such an alluring tone, that one is led to believe that the only real faith and honesty in this world are to be found only among them. But it does not take long for one to be undeceived. One quickly realises their evil genius.
>
> They win over any disconnected member of the State and through him work its ruin. Divide and grab is their main principle. They are so blinded by selfish interest that they never observe written agreements. God alone can fathom their base intrigues. They are bent on subjugating the states of Pune, Nagpur, Mysore and Hyderabad one by one, by enlisting the sympathy of one to put down the others. They know best how to destroy Indian cohesion. They are adept at the art of creating insidious differences and destroying the harmony of any State.[104]

Haidar and Tipu responded positively, noting that 'the supremacy of the English was a source of evil to all God's creatures'.[105] Within a month, the Nizam of Hyderabad had joined the other two powers. By the coming of the summer heats in May, concrete plans were being formed for a Triple Alliance to oversee 'the expulsion of the English nation from India'. A month later, in June, news reached Madras that Haidar Ali had received a large shipment of arms and military stores from France. Other reports from Vellore brought the news that Haidar Ali was assembling a vast army in the plains around Bangalore.

Finally, on 17 July, Haidar Ali marched once again down into the plains of the Carnatic. This time he had twice the army he had gathered for his last invasion, thirteen years earlier: not much short of 100,000 men, including 60,000 cavalry, 35,000 European-style infantry and

100 guns. To his surprise, he found that yet again the Company had made no preparations for defence: what Company forces there were in the Carnatic lay scattered and dispersed in small groups around the country, and no preparations had been taken even to collect bullocks for transport or to gather supplies of food. Moreover, while on paper there were meant to be 30,000 Company men under arms guarding the Madras Presidency, it was quickly calculated that fewer than 8,000 could actually be gathered together in a month. The speed of Haidar's movement reduced the numbers still further: many sepoys had families living in Arcot. When it fell to Haidar's forces large numbers of sepoys deserted their regiments to attempt to protect their wives and children. Company efforts to organise defences in the Carnatic were completely ineffective. Garrisons willingly surrendered to Haidar's forces or opened their gates in exchange for bribes.[106]

A ship was immediately sent to Calcutta to request military assistance from Bengal, but the situation there was even more confused than that in Madras. For at the same time as Tipu was returning once more to loot the rich villas of St Thomas Mount and San Thome, and while Haidar was harrying the land around Madras, Vellore and Arcot, setting villages on fire and destroying what remained of the Company's food supplies, the feud between Hastings and Francis which had paralysed the Company's administration for six years was reaching its final embittered climax.

On 14 August, Hastings wrote a public minute in which he denounced Francis as a liar and braggard: 'I do not trust to his promise of candour,' he wrote, 'convinced that he is incapable of it, and that his sole purpose and wish is to embarrass and defeat every measure which I may undertake.'

Such has been the tendency and such the manifest spirit of all his actions from the beginning ... I judge of his public conduct by my experience of his private, which I have found to be void of truth and honour. This is a severe charge, but temperately and deliberately made from the firm persuasion that I owe this justice to the public and to myself as the only redress to both, of artifices of which I have been a victim, and which threaten to involve their interests with disgrace and ruin. The only redress for a fraud for which the law had made no provisions is the exposure of it.[107]

The following day, on 15 August 1780, Philip Francis challenged Warren Hastings to a duel.

The two duellists, accompanied by their seconds, met at 5.30 on the morning of 17 August at a clump of trees on the western edge of Belvedere, a former summer house of Mir Jafar, which had since been bought by Warren Hastings.*

Hastings had hardly slept. He spent much of the night composing a farewell letter to his beloved wife Marian, to be delivered in the event of his death. It began: 'My heart bleeds to think what your sufferings and feelings must be, if ever this letter be delivered into your hands … I shall leave nothing which I regret to lose but you. How much I have loved you, and how much, beyond all that life can yield, I still love you, He only knows. Do not, my Marian, forget me. Adieu, most beloved of women. My last thoughts will be employed on you. Remember and love me. Once more farewell.'[108] Hastings then slept fitfully on a couch until 4 a.m. when his second, Colonel Thomas Deane Pearse, came to collect him in his carriage.

'We arrived at Belvedere exactly at the time proposed, at 5.30,' wrote Hastings afterwards, 'and found Mr F[rancis] and Col Watson walking in the road. Some time was consumed looking for a private place. Our seconds proposed we should stand at a measured distance which both (taking a recent example in England) fixed at 14 paces, and Col Watson paced and marked 7. I stood to the southwards. There was, as I recollect, no wind. Our seconds (Col Watson I think) proposed that no advantage should be taken, but each choose his own time to fire.'

It was at this point that it became clear, as Pearse noted, 'that both gentlemen were unacquainted with the modes usually observed on these occasions'; indeed, neither of the two most powerful British intellectuals in Bengal seemed entirely clear how to operate their pistols. Francis

---

* The building still stands in Alipore, a few minutes' walk from the Taj Bengal Hotel, and now houses the National Library of India.

said he had never fired one in his life, and Hastings said he could only remember doing so once. So both had to have their weapons loaded for them by their seconds who, being military men, knew how to operate firearms.

Hastings, ever the gentleman, decided to let Francis fire first. Francis took aim and squeezed the trigger. The hammer snapped, but the pistol misfired. Again, Francis's second had to intervene, putting fresh priming in the pistol and chapping the flints. 'We returned to our stations,' wrote Hastings. 'I still proposed to receive the first fire, but Mr F twice aimed, and twice withdrew his pistol.' Finally, Francis again 'drew his trigger,' wrote Pearse, 'but his powder being damp, the pistol again did not fire. Mr Hastings came down from his present, to give Mr Francis time to rectify his priming, and this was done out of a cartridge with which I supplied him finding they had no spare powder. Again the gentlemen took their stands and both presented together.'[109]

'I now judged that I might seriously take my aim at him,' wrote Hastings. 'I did so and when I thought I had fixed the true direction, I fired.'

> His pistol went off at the same time, and so near the same instant that I am not certain which was first, but believe mine was, and that his followed in the instant. He staggered immediately, his face expressed a sensation of being struck, and his limbs shortly but gradually went under him, and he fell saying, but not loudly, 'I am dead.'
>
> I ran to him, shocked at the information, and I can safely say without any immediate sensation of joy for my own success. The Seconds also ran to his assistance. I saw his coat pierced on the right side, and feared the ball had passed through him; but he sat up without much difficulty several times and once attempted with our help to stand, but his limbs failed him, and he sank to the ground.
>
> Col. W[atson] then proposed that as we had met from a point of honour and not for personal rancour, we should join hands, or that Mr F should give me his. We did so; Mr F cheerfully, and I expressed my regret at the condition to which I saw him reduced. He found most ease lying on his back. A cot was brought from Major Tolley's, he having no palikeen, and he was conveyed upon it to Belvedere, where he remains. Col P[earse] and I returned to our house in town. We went to seek Dr Campbell and I desired Dr Francis [Hastings'

personal physician] to follow. Both immediately went. They found the wound not dangerous, having entered the side before the seam of the waistcoat a little below the shoulder, and passing through both muscles and within the skin which covers the backbone, was lodged within visible distance of the skin in the opposite side.

As soon as I returned home I sent Mr Markham to Sir E [Elijah Impey, the Chief Justice] to inform him of what had passed, and that I should wait the event, which if fatal I should instantly surrender myself to him, that the law might take its course against me.[110]

But there was no need for Hastings to be arrested. The doctor later reported that Hastings' musket ball 'pierced the right side of Mr Francis, but was prevented by a rib, which turned the ball, from entering the thorax. It went obliquely upwards, passed the backbone without injuring it, and was extracted about an inch to the left side of it. The wound is of no consequence and he is in no danger.'[111]

Ten days later, on 25 August 1780, the Company's largest concentration of troops in southern India finally marched out of Madras and headed south along the coast road towards Kanchipuram to confront Haidar. At their head was Sir Hector Munro, the Highland general who fifteen years earlier had snatched victory from the jaws of defeat when he broke Shuja ud-Daula's lines at Buxar. This time, however, he had only managed to muster 5,000 sepoys – they were unpaid and semi-mutinous – and they were facing a force 100,000 strong.

Twenty-five miles to the north, another Scot, Colonel William Baillie, had just received instructions to rendezvous with Munro at Kanchipuram with a second force of 2,800, most of whom were local sepoys, accompanied by a few hundred newly arrived Highlanders. If these two small armies were able to join up, they would only be outnumbered ten to one, and might have some chance of taking on the Mysore troops; but divided as they were, neither force stood much chance of success against so well trained and disciplined a force as Haidar had assembled, an army that, according to Ghulam Hussain Khan, 'covered the plains like waves of an angry sea, and with a trail of artillery that had no end'.[112] Munro should have waited for Baillie to join him, but, as impatient as ever, and hearing that there were ample provisions and a full magazine in Kanchipuram, which Haidar might otherwise have seized for himself, Munro headed off with his small force, when a single day's delay would have allowed the two armies to unite.

On the evening of 25 August, Baillie camped on the banks of the small river Kortalaiyar, north-west of Madras. That evening, the monsoon broke and it rained heavily and without a break for twelve hours. By first light, the Kortalaiyar had become a raging torrent, impossible to ford. It was eleven days before Baillie was able to move his troops across it, and, by the time he did so, Tipu had managed to interpose 11,000 of his best cavalry between Baillie and Munro.[113] He could now pick off Baillie's vulnerable column at his leisure.

The first engagement took place on 6 September, when a long-range artillery duel took place between the two armies. Baillie's small force 'wandering about in thick, drizzling rain, knee-deep in rice fields' was much more exposed and suffered heavy casualties, but neither army committed to close combat, and both called for reinforcements.[114] Haidar sent a large force to his son, but Munro refused to move from the principal temple at Kanchipuram, which he had now fortified sufficiently to resist a siege.

His one concession was to send a column of a thousand sepoys, along with nine camels carrying ammunition, to join Baillie's column and lead it back to the temple. The relief column moved swiftly at night, threw off the pursuing Mysore cavalry in the darkness and, making a wide detour to avoid running into Tipu's main army, managed successfully to make a junction with Baillie, bringing the number of his troops up to 3,800 and ten field pieces. The officer in charge of the relief column begged Baillie to move immediately, and to use the cover of darkness to rejoin Munro's force in the shelter of the Kanchipuram temple, now only nine miles away. But Baillie ignored the advice and did not move off until first light. It proved a fatal hesitation.

Baillie struck camp at dawn, and half an hour later, at around 5.30 a.m., while marching over an ascent that led down towards a river in the plain below, he found his way blocked by a small fortified village named Pollilur. It was full of Tipu's troops and artillery, with more artillery dug in to their left. Both had been waiting in ambush for several hours since being informed of Baillie's timing and exact route by Tipu's spies the night before. Both now began a fierce artillery barrage onto Baillie's exposed column. Baillie's troops were strung out along an avenue, raised up and exposed upon an embankment, with muddy paddy fields on both sides and a river at some distance to their right. Unable to advance, and with no real option of retreat, Baillie ordered his troops to form a hollow square, 'huddled one on the top of the other, three corps deep', with their baggage and ammunition in the middle. Within half an hour, Tipu's troops had fanned out from their entrenchments to block all the different paths to Kanchipuram.

The cannonade continued with growing intensity, with the front ranks of Baillie's square taking fire from around thirty of Tipu's guns. Baillie was among those wounded, hit in the leg by a cannon ball; but he continued to give orders from a palanquin. There was then a lull of half an hour, when all shooting stopped and an eerie silence fell.

Thirty minutes later, troops in the front ranks reported hearing the distant sound of beating kettledrums and blaring *nageshwaram* (long Tamil oboes). As the Company troops watched, a great cloud of dust rose up in the distance. This soon resolved into several long lines of scarlet columns advancing steadily towards them. The Scots assumed it was Munro coming to save them and gave out a loud cheer. It was only when the columns grew closer that they realised it was actually Haidar's main army – some 25,000 cavalry accompanied by thirty battalions of sepoys – closing in to seal their fate. 'We were quickly surrounded by Haidar's horse,' wrote one Highland officer. 'They were followed by his guns which joined a kind of semicircle round us, the number of about 50 at least, which opened upon us by degree.'[115]

In the course of the following hour, under Baillie's direction, the Scottish square repulsed thirteen successive charges from the Mysore cavalry. Failing to break the line, Haidar ordered a pause, and brought forward his biggest guns. Around 8 a.m., the heaviest cannonade of all began from close range, with grapeshot scything down the ranks of thickly packed redcoats. 'Our fate was for above an hour to be exposed to the hottest cannonade that ever was known in India,' wrote Baillie's younger brother John. 'We were mowed down by scores.'[116] Then two ammunition tumbrils were hit and both blew up simultaneously, making 'large openings in both lines, on which their Cavalry made the first impression. They were followed by the Elephants, which completed our overthrow.'[117]

After expending all the remaining gunpowder, Baillie tried to surrender and tied his handkerchief to his sword which he held aloft. He and his deputy, David Baird, both ordered their men to ground their arms; but straggling fire from some of his sepoys who had not heard the order meant that the Mysore cavalry disregarded the surrender and refused to give quarter. Instead the horsemen rode in and began to cut down the disarmed and defenceless troops; 'a most shocking massacre ensued ... It was in vain to ask for the quarter they offered readily enough, but cut you down the moment you laid down your arms.'[118]

According to a lieutenant in the 73rd Highland Regiment, 'The last and most awful struggle was marked by the clashing of arms and shields, the snorting and kicking of horses, the snapping of spears, the glistening of bloody swords, oaths and imprecations; concluded with the groans and cries of mutilated men, wounded horses tumbling to the ground amid dying soldiers, the hideous roaring of elephants as they trampled about and wielded their dreadful chains amongst both friends and foes.'

> Such as were saved from immediate death were so crowded together that it was only with difficulty they could stand; several were in a state of suffocation, while others from the weight of the dead bodies that had fallen upon them were fixed to the spot and therefore at the mercy of the enemy ... Some were trampled under the feet of elephants, camels and horses, and those who were stripped of their clothing lay exposed to the scorching sun, without water and died a lingering and miserable death, becoming the prey to ravenous wild animals.[119]

Out of eighty-six officers, thirty-six were killed, thirty-four were wounded and taken prisoner; only sixteen captured were unwounded. Baillie received a back and head wound, in addition to losing a leg. Baird received two sabre cuts on the head, a bullet in the thigh and a pike wound in the arm. His ADC and young cousin, James Dalrymple, received a severe back wound and 'two cuts in my head'.* Around 200 prisoners were taken. Most of the rest of the force of 3,800 was annihilated.[120]

The Mysore troops then began to strip the dead and dying, and looted what they could from the corpses. 'They began by pulling the buttons of my coat which they took for silver,' wrote the wounded John Baillie. 'They then tore the knee buckles out of my breeches & the coat off my back. One of them putting the butt end of his firelock to the back of my neck pinned me to the ground with it whilst another tried to pull off my boots.'

> He got off one with difficulty and enraged I suppose at not being able to pull off the other, he gave me a cut on my right thigh that laid it open to the bone. Shortly after another fellow, passing by, wantonly thrust his sword into my other thigh … After they were gone, one of Haidar's sepoys perceiving that I still lived, raised me up, placed me against a tree and gave me some water to drink.
>
> I lay there by an artillery man with his head shot off, with my face to the ground. By this time my wounds began to grow stiff, so that I was unable to move from the position I was in, or to defend myself from the swarms of flies which, getting into my wounds, seemed determined to suck the little blood that was left in me. I was covered with them from head to foot. It was a species of torture to the mind as well as to the body, keeping me continually in mind of my own helplessness.
>
> When I was beginning to give up all hopes of assistance, two Frenchmen looking out for those that were still alive, appeared in

---

* When Sir David Baird's Scottish mother heard that her son had been captured by Tipu, and that the prisoners had been led away handcuffed two by two, she remarked, 'I pity the man who was chained to oor Davie.' Quoted by Denys Forrest in *Tiger of Mysore: The Life and Death of Tipu Sultan*, London, 1970, p. 48. A letter of James Dalrymple to his father, Sir William Dalrymple, smuggled out of the prison of Seringapatam, survives in the India Office. According to a note written by James's Anglo-Indian grandson, G. Wemyss Dalrymple, 'The paper was rolled up, and put into a quill, then passed into the person of a native, and so brought into the prison. With the same quill, he wrote the letter, the ink was solid Indian ink, and was also in the quill, and the letter was brought out of the prison, by the same native in the same manner.' BL, OIOC, Eur Mss, E 330.

the avenue. I leaned upon one and was carried into their camp at 8 o'clock at night to the tent of the French surgeon. He had no other instruments than a knife, a pair of scissors and an iron spatula, and no other medicines than a large pot of ointment full of dirt and of the colour and consistence of hair oil; but they gave us half a bottle of arrack per day to wash our wounds which, though small the quantity amongst so many, was of infinite service to us. Our wounds were become very offensive: one officer who had received a bad cut across his ear had 26 maggots taken out of it by pouring a little arrack into it.[121]

Eventually, Baillie was brought before Haidar strapped to a gun carriage and made to sit at his feet in a semicircle with the other survivors, as the Sultan rewarded his officers in proportion to the number of heads or corpses of European soldiers they produced. 'Some had been dragged to his camp, so mangled and besmeared with blood and dust that they were unrecognisable; some had dropped speechless on the road and had been refused any water by their guards.'

Prisoners were beaten with their guards' rifles. Others were relieved from their excruciating tortures, which they endured by a succession of fainting fits, until, by total insensibility they finally eluded the persecution of their guards. The dismal fate of those around me, the dead bodies and distorted faces of the dying made me feel that I was also going to die shortly. As darkness came on, the horrors came with it: the groans of the dying, the ravages and howling of the jackals, coupled with the distant thunder and torrential rain.[122]

The tables were being turned. It was now Company troops who learned what it meant to be defeated, to be taken prisoner, to be mistreated. Munro, whose failure to rescue Baillie had been a major factor in the disaster, and who on his return to Madras with what was left of his panic-stricken army, was jeered and hooted at in the streets, called the Battle of Pollilur 'the severest blow that the English ever suffered in India'.[123]

Worse was to follow. There were so many Company amputees that there were not enough Indian medical orderlies to bear them away from the front lines. Surgeon Thomas Davis wrote, 'I have been as sparing of

Limbs as possible', but was compelled to remove many of them for lack of adequate medical supplies.[124] Of the 7,000 prisoners Tipu captured in the course of the next few months of warfare against the Company, around 300 were forcibly circumcised, forcibly converted to Islam and given Muslim names and clothes. By the end of the year, one in five of all the British soldiers in India were held prisoner by Tipu in his sophisticated fortress of Seringapatam. Even more humiliatingly, several British regimental drummer boys were made to wear dresses – *ghagra cholis* – and entertain the court in the manner of nautch (dancing) girls.[125]

At the end of ten years' captivity, one of these prisoners, James Scurry, found that he had forgotten how to sit in a chair or use a knife and fork; his English was 'broken and confused, having lost all its vernacular idiom', his skin had darkened to the 'swarthy complexion of Negroes' and he found he actively disliked wearing European clothes.[126]

This was the ultimate colonial nightmare, and in its most unpalatable form: the captive preferring the ways of his captors, the coloniser colonised.

Two days after Pollilur, a special vessel was sent off from Madras to Calcutta to tell Fort William of the disaster. The news arrived on 20 September. When Warren Hastings heard of the catastrophe, he realised immediately what the defeat meant: 'Our armies,' he wrote to London, 'which have been so long formed to habits of conquest, will not easily recover from the impression of the dreadful reverse, nor be brought to act with their former confidence under unsuccessful commanders.'[127] Lord Macartney wrote home in a similar vein from Madras: 'The Indians have less Terror of our Arms; we less Contempt for their opposition. Our future Advantages therefore are not to be calculated by past exploits.'[128]

The Company – now more than £10 million* in debt and unable to pay its own salaries – was now faced by a combination of all the

* £1,000 million today.

strongest powers in India, supported by the French.[129] Privately Hastings imagined himself 'on board a great leaky vessel, driving towards a Lee Shore with Shipwreck not to be avoided, except by a miracle'.[130]

Few would disagree. Never had the Company's position in India seemed so shaky. One early analysis of the defeat expressed surprise that the different Indian rivals of the Company did not take more advantage of the crucial opportunity Pollilur presented: 'Had the French sent timely assistance to the enemy,' he wrote, 'as there was every reason to expect, and had the Mahratta states, instead of remaining quiet spectators ... joined their confederate forces and acted with unanimity, there could not have been a doubt but the British must have been dispossessed of almost every settlement on the Peninsula. Had Haidar pursued his success after the defeat of Baillie considering the shattered and dispirited state of the rest of the army, there could scarcely have been a hope of it not falling, together with Fort St George, almost a defenceless prey into the hands of the enemy.'[131] Fortunately for the Company, Haidar was determined to preserve his forces. He avoided any further decisive engagements and focused on harassing Company supply lines by launching hit-and-run raids with his cavalry. The Company kept its toehold in the south only by the lack of confidence and initiative shown by its adversaries, and the quick supply of reinforcements from Calcutta. Over the months to come, with a mixture of imaginatively wide-ranging military action and deft diplomacy, Hastings managed to break both the Triple Alliance and the unity of the Maratha Confederacy when, on 17 May 1782, he signed the Treaty of Salbai, a separate peace with the Maratha commander Mahadji Scindia, who then became a British ally. For the Company's enemies it was a major missed opportunity. In 1780, one last small push could have expelled the Company for good. Never again would such an opportunity present itself, and the failure to take further immediate offensive action was something that the durbars of both Pune and Mysore would later both bitterly come to regret.

Elsewhere in the world, 1780 saw the British suffering other major reverses – and these were indeed followed through to their logical conclusion. In America, the Patriots had turned on the King, partly as a result of government's attempts to sell the stockpiles of East India Company tea, onto which was slapped British taxes: the Boston Tea Party, an event that built support for what would become the American War of Independence by dumping 90,000 pounds of EIC tea, worth £9,659 (over £1 million today), in Boston harbour, was in part provoked by fears that the Company might now be let loose on the thirteen colonies, much as it had been in Bengal.

One Patriot writer, John Dickinson, feared that the EIC, having plundered India, was now 'casting their eyes on America as a new theatre whereon to exercise their talents of rapine, oppression and cruelty ...'[132] Dickinson described the tea as 'accursed Trash', and compared the prospect of oppression by the corrupt East India Company in America to being 'devoured by Rats'. This 'almost bankrupt Company', he said, having been occupied in 'corrupting their Country', and wreaking 'the most unparalleled Barbarities, Extortions and Monopolies' in Bengal, now wished to do the same in America. 'But thank GOD, we are not Sea Poys, nor Marattas.' The American watchmen on their rounds, he said, should be instructed to 'call out every night, past Twelve o'Clock, "Beware of the East India Company."'[133]

After a horrendous war, the Patriots managed to see off the government troops sent to restore order after a series of standoffs. Even as Haidar was pursuing a terrified Munro back to Madras, British forces in America were already on their way to the final defeat by Washington at Yorktown, and the subsequent surrender of British forces in America in October. There was a growing sensation that everywhere the British Empire was in the process of falling apart. In Parliament, a year later, one MP noted that 'in Europe we have lost Minorca, in America 13 provinces, and the two Pensacolas; in the West Indies, Tobago; and some settlements in Africa'.[134] 'The British Empire,' wrote Edmund Burke, 'is tottering to its foundation.'[135]

Soon Parliament was publishing a six-volume report into these failures. 'The British purchase on India,' one senior Company military officer told Parliament, 'is more imaginary than real, to hold that vast territory in subjection with such a disparity of numbers. I fear the Indians will soon find out that we are but men like themselves.'[136]

Horace Walpole, as usual, put it more succinctly: 'India and America', he wrote, 'are alike escaping.'[137]

7

The Desolation of Delhi

On the morning of 12 April 1771, to a deafening fanfare of long-necked trumpets and the steady roll of camel-borne *nagara* drums, Shah Alam mounted his richly caparisoned elephant and set off through the vaulted sandstone gateway of the fort of Allahabad.

After an exile of more than twelve years, the Emperor was heading home. It was not going to be an easy journey. Shah Alam's route would take him through provinces which had long thrown off Mughal authority and there was every reason to fear that his enemies could attempt to capture, co-opt or even assassinate him. Moreover, his ultimate destination, the burned-out Mughal capital of Delhi, was further being reduced to ruins by rival Afghan and Maratha armies.

But the Emperor was not coming unprepared: following him were 16,000 of his newly raised troops and followers. A Mughal painting survives, showing the line of march: a long column of troops snakes in wide, serpentine meanders along the banks of the Yamuna, through a fertile landscape. At the front of the procession are the musicians. Then follow the macemen and the bearers of Mughal insignia – the imperial umbrellas, the golden *mahi maratib* fish standard, the face of a rayed sun and a Hand of Fatima, all raised on gilt staffs from which trail red silken streamers. Then comes the Emperor himself, high on his elephant and hedged around by a bodyguard armed with a thicket of spears.

The imperial princes are next, carried on a line of elephants with saffron headcloths, each embroidered with the Emperor's insignia. They are followed by the many women of the imperial harem in their covered carriages; then the heavy siege guns, dragged by foursomes of elephants. Behind, the main body of the army stretches off as far as the eye can see. The different cohorts of troops are divided into distinct battalions of sepoy infantry, cavalry, artillery and the camel corps with their swivel guns, each led by an elephant-mounted officer sitting high in a domed howdah. The expedition processes along the banks of the river, escorted by gilded royal barges, and heads on through woods and meadows, past islands dotted with temples and small towns whose skylines are punctuated with minarets.[1]

The moment was recorded, for it marked what was recognised, even at the time, as a crucial turning point in the politics of eighteenth-century India. Shah Alam had now finally given up on the Company ever honouring its many promises to give him an army, or even just an armed escort, to help him reconquer his capital. If the Company would not help him then he would have to look for new allies – and this, by default, meant his ancestral enemies, the Marathas. But whatever the dangers, the Emperor was determined to gamble everything in the hope of regaining his rightful place on the Peacock Throne of his ancestors.[2]

When they belatedly learned of the Emperor's plans, successive anxious Company officials in Calcutta wrote to Shah Alam that they 'could not in any way countenance His Majesty's impolitic enterprise', and that they did not 'think the present period opportune for so great and hazardous an undertaking, when disturbances are rife throughout the Empire'.[3] 'His Majesty should know that he has set himself a formidable task. If he regards the Marathas as friends he is greatly mistaken, since they are notoriously fickle and untrustworthy.' 'They will take pleasure in His Majesty's distress and the object of their intended loyalty is only to get you into their clutches in order to use your name to reach their own ends.'[4]

Behind this apparently benign concern for the Emperor lay a deep anxiety on the part of the Company. Shah Alam's announcement of his imminent departure had been entirely unexpected. Not only did the Emperor's keepers want him in their own hands to legalise and legitimate whatever decisions they made, they also feared the consequences if others should seize him with the same intention. The Marathas were the Company's most formidable rivals in India. They dominated almost the entire west coast of the subcontinent and much of the central interior, too. Too late, the Company was now contemplating 'the additional influence it must give to the Marathas having the Emperor's person in their hands, whose name will be made a sanction for their future depredations'.[5]

With a view to changing the Emperor's mind, one of the highest ranking Company officers, General Barker, was despatched to Allahabad to try and reason with him. Even Shah Alam's own senior advisers told him that he was 'throwing away the substance to grasp at a shadow ... and sacrificing his interests to the vain gratification of residing in the imperial palace'. They also warned him about the dangers of placing confidence in the Marathas, 'the very people whose perfidious conduct and insatiable ambition had proved so fatal to many of your august family'.[6]

But Shah Alam had made up his mind. Barker found him 'deaf to all arguments'.[7] The Emperor even went as far as threatening suicide if there was any attempt by the Company to thwart him. He had long found life in Allahabad as a puppet of the Company insupportable, and now he yearned to return home, whatever the risks. 'He sighed for the pleasures of the capital,' wrote William Francklin, a Company official who knew him well and who eventually wrote his first biography.[8]

The Council ultimately realised it had little option but to accept the Emperor's decision with the best grace possible: 'It was not in our power to prevent this step of the King's,' they wrote to the directors in London in January 1771, 'except by putting an absolute restraint on his person, which we judged would be as little approved by our Hon'ble masters, as it was repugnant to our own sentiments of Humanity.'[9] Barker wrote to the Emperor: 'since His Majesty has arranged all this with the Marathas secretly, the writer has received instructions neither to stand in the way of the royal resolution, nor to support it.'[10]

In fact, the Company had no one to blame but themselves for the Emperor's dramatic decision. The discourteous treatment he had received from EIC officers in Allahabad since he arrived there six years earlier was the principal reason he had decided to hazard everything on the gamble of the Delhi expedition: 'The English added to Shah Alam II's misfortunes by treating him with an insulting lack of respect,' wrote Jean-Baptiste Gentil, who had visited the Emperor in the Allahabad fort. 'They did this repeatedly, in a setting – the palace of his forebear Akbar – which constantly brought to mind the former power and glory of the House of Timur.'

These insults at length compelled him to abandon what little remained to him of this once-opulent inheritance, and to go back to Delhi to live in the squalid huts hastily put up there for his return.

Worse, they [the Company] increased his misery by refusing to pay him the full 26 lakhs Rupees* that had been agreed under the Treaty of Allahabad of 1765.

A mere battalion-officer, of his own accord, arrested and imprisoned one of Shah Alam's most senior liveried footmen. The Emperor duly requested the officer to release his servant, promising that in future his servant would be more careful, though the man had committed no offence deserving such treatment. Well, can you believe it? This officer immediately had the man brought out and horse-whipped in the presence of the Emperor's messenger, saying: 'This is how I punish anyone who fails to show me due respect!'

A short time after this, Brigadier Smith, who was staying in the imperial palace, forbade the Emperor's musicians to sound the traditional *naubat* trumpet fanfare which is always played in a chamber above the gateway to the palace, saying that it woke him too early in the morning. The musicians having played in spite of the Brigadier's orders, Smith sent guards to throw them and their instruments down from the upper chamber: luckily the musicians escaped in time, so it was only the instruments which were thrown down.

The uncouth and quarrelsome nature of this officer banished any peace of mind which the unfortunate Emperor might have enjoyed at Allahabad, till the humiliations inflicted on him daily compelled him, as said, to abandon his palace in Allahabad, to go and live on the

---

* £33.8 million today.

banks of the Yamuna in Delhi, exchanging a rich and fertile province for a township of ruins.[11]

These thoughtless insults by junior officers only added to the bitterness Shah Alam already felt towards their superiors. He had good reason to feel betrayed. In the course of his many attempts to get the Company to honour its promises, one exchange in particular with Clive still rankled.

In 1766 Shah Alam had gone as far as sending an envoy to his fellow monarch George III, one sovereign to another, to appeal to him for help, 'considering the sincerity of friendship and nobility of heart of my brother in England'. In his letter Shah Alam had offered to recognise the Hanoverian King's overlordship in return for being installed in Delhi by Company troops. But the Emperor's letters to the King had been intercepted by Clive, along with the *nazr* (ceremonial gift) of rare jewels worth Rs100,000,* and neither were ever delivered. Meanwhile, Shah Alam's presents to the King were given on his return to London by Clive, as if from himself, without any mention of the Emperor. Shah Alam's envoy did make it to Britain, and wrote a remarkable book about his travels, *The Wonders of Vilayet*, which revealed for the first time to an Indian audience the bleakness of the British winter and the quarrelsome nature of whisky-fuelled Scots; but the Company made sure he never succeeded in getting an audience with the King or near anyone in government.[12]

In December 1769, when Calcutta yet again refused to escort the Emperor to Delhi, this time allegedly 'owing to the unsuitability of the time', Shah Alam finally concluded that it was hopeless to rely on the Company: if he was ever to get to Delhi, he would have to do so protected by his own troops – and he would need to find new allies to convey him where he wished to go.[13]

Dramatic changes in the politics of Hindustan helped spur the Emperor into action. In the decade following the defeat of the Marathas at Panipat in 1761, and the death of 35,000 – an entire generation of Maratha warriors and leaders – the Afghans had had the upper hand in Hindustan from roughly 1761 until 1770.[14] In 1762 Ahmad Shah Durrani had ousted Shah Alam's teenage nemesis, Imad ul-Mulk, from the Red Fort, and installed as governor Najib ud-Daula, a Rohilla of

---

* Over £1 million today.

Afghan birth. Najib had started his Indian career as a humble Yusufzai horse dealer but had steadily risen thanks to his skills both as a fighter and as a political strategist.

Najib was the 'undefeated but not unchallenged master of Delhi for nine years', who succeeded in 'maintaining his position by a brilliant feat of poise and balance', between a viper's nest of contending forces.[15] In October 1770, however, Najib died, and rumours reached Allahabad that his unruly son and successor, Zabita Khan, 'had presumed to enter into the royal seraglio, to have connection with some of the ladies shut up in it. The king's own sister was one of the number.'[16] Mughal honour was now at stake, and the queen mother, Zeenat Mahal, wrote to her son to come immediately and take charge.

The main architect of the Afghan incursions into northern India, Ahmad Shah Durrani, had now returned to the mountains of his homeland to die. He was suffering the last stages of an illness that had long debilitated him, as his face was eaten away by what the Afghan sources call a 'gangrenous ulcer', possibly leprosy or some form of tumour. Soon after winning his greatest victory at Panipat, Ahmad Shah's disease began consuming his nose, and a diamond-studded substitute was attached in its place. By 1772, maggots were dropping from the upper part of his putrefying nose into his mouth and his food as he ate. Having despaired of finding a cure, he took to his bed in the Toba hills, where he had gone to escape the summer heat of Kandahar.[17] He was clearly no longer in any position to swoop down and assist his Rohilla kinsmen in India. The Afghans settled in India were now on their own.[18]

In May 1766, the Marathas launched their first, relatively modest, expedition north of the Chambal since Panipat five years earlier. By 1770, they were back again, this time with an 'ocean-like army' of 75,000, which they used to defeat the Jat Raja of Deeg and to raid deep into Rohilla territory east of Agra.[19] It was becoming increasingly clear that the future lay once again with the Marathas, and that the days of Afghan domination were now over.

In contrast to the failing and retreating Durrani monarchy, the Marathas had produced two rival young leaders who had showed both the determination and the military ability to recover and expand Maratha fortunes in the north. The first of these was the young Mahadji Scindia. Of humble origins, Scindia had been chased from the battlefield of Panipat by an Afghan cavalryman who rode him down, wounded him below the knee with his battle axe, then left him to bleed to death. Scindia had crawled to safety to fight another day but he would limp badly from the wound for the rest of his life. Unable to take exercise, Scindia had grown immensely fat. He was, however, a brilliant politician, capable, canny and highly intelligent.[20]

His great rival, Tukoji Holkar, had also narrowly survived death on the plains of Panipat, but was a very different man. A dashing bon viveur, with a fondness for women and drink, but with little of his rival's subtlety or intelligence, he and Scindia disagreed on most matters, and their nominal overlord, the Maratha Peshwa, had had to intervene repeatedly to warn the two rival warlords to stop squabbling and cooperate with each other. But both men did agree that this was the right moment to revive Maratha power in Hindustan, and that the best way of cementing this would be to install Shah Alam back in Delhi under their joint protection, and so secure control of his affairs.[21] The master of Delhi, they knew, was always the master of Hindustan.

In late 1770 a secret message from Scindia reached Allahabad, offering Shah Alam Maratha protection if he were to return home. In response the Emperor discreetly sent an envoy to both Maratha leaders to explore the possibility of an alliance. Both rival camps responded positively and an understanding was reached. On 15 February 1771, an agreement was settled between the Marathas and Shah Alam's son, the Crown Prince, who was in Delhi acting as Regent, that the Marathas would drive Zabita Khan and his Afghans out of Delhi, after which Scindia would escort Shah Alam to Delhi and hand over the palace to him. All this would be done in return for a payment by Shah Alam of Rs40 lakh.* The terms were secretly ratified by the Emperor on 22 March 1771.

By the middle of the summer, the Marathas had crossed the Yamuna in force and succeeded in capturing Delhi and expelling Zabita Khan's garrison. They then forded the upper Ganges and headed deep into Rohilkhand, burning and plundering as they went. Zabita Khan retreated in front of them to Pathargarh, his impregnable fortress in the badlands north-east of Meerut. All the pieces were now in place.[22]

Only one final matter remained to be decided: the commander of Shah Alam's new army. Here the Emperor had a rare stroke of luck. His choice fell on a man who would prove to be his greatest asset and most

* £52 million today.

loyal servant. Mirza Najaf Khan had only recently entered Shah Alam's service. He was the young Persian cavalry officer who had previously distinguished himself against the Company in the service of Mir Qasim.

Still in his mid-thirties, handsome, polished and charming, Najaf Khan had the blood of the royal Persian Safavid dynasty flowing in his veins and was allied through marriage with Nawab Shuja ud-Daula of Avadh. He was a refined diplomat, an able revenue manager and an even more accomplished soldier. He had carefully observed Company tactics and strategy while fighting with Mir Qasim, and learned the art of file-firing, modern European infantry manoeuvres and the finer points of artillery ballistics. The Company officers who met Najaf Khan were impressed: he was 'high spirited and an active and valiant commander, and of courteous and obliging manners', wrote William Francklin after meeting him. 'By his unremitting attention to business, he preserved regularity, and restored order throughout every department.' More unusually still for the times, he was 'a humane and benevolent man'.[23]

Few believed Shah Alam had much of a chance of getting safely back to Delhi. Fewer still believed he had any hope of re-establishing Mughal rule there, or of achieving any meaningful independence from the Marathas, who clearly wished to use him for their own ends, just as the Company had done. But if anyone could help Shah Alam succeed on all these fronts, Najaf Khan was the man.

As the historian Shakir Khan commented, 'A single courageous, decisive man with an intelligent grasp of strategy is better than a thousand ditherers.'[24]

Twenty miles on from Allahabad, the Emperor crossed into Avadh and that night arrived at Serai Alamchand. There, on 30 April, he was joined by Nawab Shuja ud-Daula.

The two had not come face to face since both had fled from the battlefield of Buxar seven years earlier. With Shuja came another veteran of that battle, the fearsome Naga commander, Anupgiri Gossain, now ennobled with the Persianate Mughal title, 'Himmat Bahadur' – or

'Great of Courage'. Like everyone else, Shuja tried to dissuade Shah Alam from progressing to Delhi, but 'finding that His Majesty was firm in his determination' he agreed to lend the Emperor the services of Anupgiri, along with his force of 10,000 Gossain horse and foot, as well as five cannon, numerous bullock carts full of supplies, tents and Rs12 lakh* in money, 'believing that if His Majesty joins the Marathas with insufficient troops he will be entirely in their hands'.[25] But he declined to come with the Emperor and warned him that he saw the expedition ending badly.[26]

Shuja's warnings continued to be echoed by General Barker. The general wrote to the Emperor: 'the rains have now set in, and the Royal March, if continued, will end in disaster. So long as His Majesty stops at Kora [on the western edge of Avadh] the English troops will be at his service. If, which God forbid, His Majesty goes beyond the boundaries of Kora, and sustains a defeat, we will not hold ourselves responsible.'[27]

But the Emperor kept his nerve. He stayed nearly three weeks at Serai Alamchand, sequestered in his tent with Mirza Najaf Khan, 'invisible to every person', planning every detail of their march and working out together how to overcome the different obstacles. They secretly sent a trusted eunuch ahead with Rs2.5 lakh** in bags of gold to buy influence among the Maratha nobles. His mission was to discover which of the rival young Maratha leaders was more open to Shah Alam's rule, and to begin negotiations about handing over the Red Fort back into Mughal hands.[28]

On 2 May, the Emperor packed up and headed westwards by a succession of slow marches until his army reached the last Company cantonment at Bithur, outside Kanpur. Here General Barker came and personally bade the Emperor farewell. He took with him all the British officers of Shah Alam's army, but as a goodwill gesture left him with two battalions of Company sepoys and a gift of four field guns.[29]

The following week, Shah Alam's army trudged in the heat past Kannauj and over the border into Rohilla territory. On 17 July, the monsoon broke in full force over the column, 'and the very heavy rains which have fallen impeded his progress' as the axles of his artillery foundered in the monsoon mud and the elephants waded slowly through roads that looked more like canals than turnpikes.[30] Towards the end of August, the Emperor's damp and bedraggled army finally

* Almost £16 million today.
** £3 million today.

reached Farrukhabad, dripping from the incessant rains. Here the Emperor faced his first real challenge.

The Rohilla Nawab of Farrukhabad, Ahmad Khan Bangash, had just died. Shah Alam decided to demonstrate his resolve by demanding that all the Nawab's estates should now escheat to the crown, in the traditional Mughal manner. His demands were resisted by the Nawab's grandson and successor, who gathered a Rohilla army, surrounded and cut off the Emperor's column, and prepared to attack the imperial camp. Shah Alam sent urgent messages to Mahadji Scindia, requesting immediate military assistance. This was the moment of truth: would the Marathas honour their promise and become imperial protectors, or would they stand by and watch their new protégé be attacked by their Afghan enemies?

Two days later, just as the Rohillas were preparing for battle, several thousand of Scindia's Marathas appeared over the horizon. The young Bangash Nawab saw that he was now outnumbered and appealed for peace, quickly agreeing to pay Shah Alam a *peshkash* (tribute) of Rs7 lakh* in return for imperial recognition of his inheritance. The Shah confirmed the young man in his estates, then moved with his winnings to Nabiganj, twenty miles from Farrukhabad, to spend the rest of the monsoon.[31]

On 18 November, Mahadji Scindia finally came in person to the imperial camp. He was led limping into the Emperor's durbar by Prince Akbar, as everyone watched to see whether the Maratha chieftain would conform to Mughal court etiquette and offer full submission to the Emperor. After a moment's hesitation, to the relief of the Mughals, Scindia prostrated himself before the Emperor, 'laid his head at the Emperor's feet, who raised him up, clasped him to his bosom and praised him. On account of his lameness, he was ordered to sit down in front of the Emperor's gold chair.'[32] Scindia then offered the Emperor *nazars* (ceremonial gifts), signifying obedience, after which the Emperor 'graciously laid the hands of favor upon his back. After two hours he received leave of absence and returned to his Encampment.'[33]

Two days later, Scindia returned for a second visit, and the two leaders, the Mughal and the Maratha, worked out their plans and strategy. On 29 November, the newly confederated armies struck camp and together headed on towards Delhi.[34]

Shah Alam marched out from his camp near Sikandra on New Year's Day 1772, and that evening, at Shahdara, on the eastern bank of the

* £9 million today.

Yamuna, he finally came within sight of the domes and walls of his capital rising across the river. The Maratha garrison rode out to greet him, bringing with them˜Zeenat Mahal, the Empress Mother, the Crown Prince Jawan Bakht and 'at least twenty-seven [of the Emperor's other] children.'[35] Shah Alam received them all in formal durbar.

Five days later, at quarter past eight in the morning, with his colours flying and drums beating, Shah Alam rode through the Delhi Gate into the ruins of Shahjahanabad. That day, the auspicious feast of Id ul-Fitr, marking the end of the holy fasting month of Ramadan, was remembered as his *bazgasht*, or homecoming.

This was the day on which he took his place in the palace of his fathers, ending twelve years in exile. The Mughals were back on the Peacock Throne.[36]

The mission before Shah Alam in January 1772 was now nothing less than to begin the reconquest of his lost empire – starting with the region around Delhi.

He and Mirza Najaf Khan had two immediate targets in sight: the Jat Raja of Deeg had usurped much of the territory immediately south of the capital, between Delhi and Agra. But more pressing than that was the need to bring to heel the rogue Rohilla leader Zabita Khan, who now stood accused of disobeying the Emperor's summons, as well as dishonouring his sister. This was a matter which could not wait. Leaving his army camped outside the city across the river, Shah Alam spent just over a week in the capital, leading Id prayers at the Id Gah, paying respects at his father's grave in Humayun's Tomb, surveying what remained of his old haunts and visiting long-lost relatives. Then, on 16 January, he returned to his camp at Shahdara. The following morning, the 17th, he set off with Mirza Najaf Khan and Mahadji Scindia to attack Zabita Khan's fortress.

The army first headed north towards the foothills of the Himalayas, then at Saharanpur swung eastwards. There they tried to find a ford across the Ganges at Chandighat, a day's march downstream from Haridwar. Zabita Khan's artillery guarded all the crossing places, and were entrenched on the far bank, firing canister over the river. But it was winter and the monsoon floods had long receded, while the spring Himalayan snowmelt had yet to begin. According to the Maratha newswriter who travelled with Shah Alam, an hour before sunrise, on 23 February, 'The Emperor reached the bank of the Ganges and said with urgency, "If sovereignty be my lot, then yield a path." Immediately, the river was found to be fordable, the water being deep only up to the knees and the lower half of the leg.' The imperial army crossed the river and as dawn came up, engaged in fighting at close quarters, swords in hand. 'Three miles to the right, Mahadji Scindia and his officers also crossed the river, then rode upstream and fell without warning on the Afghan rear.'[37]

The turning point came when Mirza Najaf Khan managed to get his camel cavalry onto an island halfway across the river, and from there they fired their heavy swivel guns at close quarters into the packed Afghan ranks on the far bank. One hour after sunrise, Zabita Khan gave up the fight and fled towards the shelter of the Himalayas. Several of his most senior officers were captured hiding in the reeds and rushes.[38]

The two armies, Mughal and Maratha, then closed in to besiege Zabita Khan's great stone fortress at Pathargarh, where he had lodged his family and treasure for safety. The fortress was newly built and well stocked with provisions; it could potentially have resisted a siege for some time. But Najaf Khan knew his craft. 'Najaf Khan closed the channel by which water comes from the river to this fort,' reported the Maratha newswriter. 'For four days cannon balls were fired by both sides like clouds of rain. At last one large bastion of the fort was breached. Immediately the garrison cried for quarter.'[39] The Qiladar sent an envoy to Najaf Khan offering to capitulate if the lives and honour of the garrison were assured. He accepted the offer.

On 16 March, the gates of Pathargarh were thrown open: 'The Marathas took their stand at the gate of the fort,' recorded Khair ud-Din. 'At first the poorer people came out; they were stripped and searched and let off almost naked. Seeing this, the rich people threw caskets full of gems and money down from the ramparts into the wet ditch to conceal them. Others swallowed their gold coins.'[40]

After this, the Marathas rushed in and began to carry away all the terrified Rohilla women and children to their tents, including those of Zabita Khan himself. All were robbed and many raped and dishonoured. In the chaos and bloodshed, the tomb of Zabita Khan's father, Najib ud-Daula, was opened, plundered and his remains scattered. The

Emperor and Najaf Khan intervened as best they could, and saved the immediate family of their adversary, whom they put under armed guard and sent on to Delhi. The families of other Afghans who wished to return to their mountains were marched back to Jalalabad under escort.[41] Among those liberated were a number of Maratha women who had been captive since the Battle of Panipat, more than a decade earlier.[42]

For two weeks the besiegers sacked Pathargarh, digging up buried treasure and draining the moat to find the jewels which had been thrown into it. The booty, collected by Najib over the thirty years he was Governor of Delhi, was allegedly worth an enormous Rs150 lakhs,* and included horses, elephants, guns, gold and jewels.

Zabita Khan's young son, Ghulam Qadir, was among the prisoners and hostages brought back to Shahjahanabad. There he was virtually adopted by the Emperor and brought up in style in the imperial gardens and palaces of Qudsia Bagh, north of Shahjahanabad. This was an act that Shah Alam would later come to regret. Even as his father continued to resist the Emperor and plot a series of rebellions against Shah Alam's rule, Ghulam Qadir was given the luxurious life of an imperial prince, and grew up, in the words of one Mughal prince, to be as arrogant 'as Pharaoh himself'.[43] One senior noble, whose brother had been killed by Zabita Khan, asked the Emperor for Ghulam Qadir's head in return, but Shah Alam protected the boy and insisted that no son should be responsible for the misdeeds of his father: 'If his father committed such crimes why should this innocent child be killed?' he asked. 'If you are bent on vengeance, then seize Zabita Khan and kill him.'[44]

Maybe it was this that gave rise to gossip of a strange bond between the boy and the Emperor. Before long, however, there were rumours spreading in the palace that the Emperor's affections for his young Rohilla protégé had crossed certain bounds. According to one gossipy Mughal princely memoir of the time, the *Waqi'at-i Azfari*, 'when His Majesty beheld this ungrateful wretch in his royal gaze, he showed remarkable compassion'.

After bringing him gently and peacefully to Shahjahanabad and installing him in Qudsia Bagh, he appointed him guards and sent him large trays of assorted foods three times a day. The Shah frequently

* £195 million today.

summoned him to the royal presence and would commiserate with him regarding his state, rubbing his blessed hand over the boy's back out of pity, and insisting on his learning how to read and write. He gave him the imperial title Raushan ud-Daula and, when the boy was missing his parents and weeping, the Shah promised that he would soon be sent home. However, due to the political expediencies of the time, certain senior nobles at court did not want Ghulam Qadir to be released and sent to his father's side. They prevented His Majesty from liberating the wretch.

At the time His Majesty greatly humoured Ghulam Qadir, allowing him intimate access, for he had designated his hostage as 'my beloved son'. The author recalls several lines of rekhta [Urdu] poetry His Majesty recited at a garden banquet held in honour of Ghulam Qadir. One of these [playing on Shah Alam's pen name of Aftab, the sun,] ran:

> He is my special son, and the others mere slaves,
> O God! Keep the house of my devotee ever inhabited.
> May his garden of desire continue blossoming,
> May Autumn never trespass amid his garden's borders.
> May he be reared in the shade of God's shadow,
> So long as Aftab (the sun) shines
> And the heavenly stars sparkle in the sky.[45]

It may well be that there is no firm basis for this story, nor for Azfari's homophobic joke that Ghulam Qadir suffered from *ubnah* – an itch in his arse. Homosexual relations were fairly acceptable between superiors and inferiors at this time and were not in themselves considered unusual or fodder for smutty jokes. Afzari's joke lay in Ghulam Qadir being the 'bottom' (which established his inferiority) rather than the 'top', apparently an important distinction at the time. But some later sources go further. According to *Najib-ul-Tawarikh*, compiled one hundred years later in 1865, Ghulam Qadir was very handsome and the Emperor Shah Alam II sensed or suspected that females of the royal harem were taking interest in him. So one day the Emperor had his young favourite drugged into unconsciousness and had him castrated. There is a widespread tradition supporting this, but the many contemporary accounts do not mention it and there is some later talk of the Rohilla prince as being bearded, presumably not something that would have been possible had he actually been a eunuch.*

Nevertheless, if the young captive Ghulam Qadir did suffer from unwanted imperial affections in his gilded Mughal cage, which is quite possible, it would certainly help explain the extreme, psychotic violence which he inflicted on his captors when the tables were turned a few years later.[46]

The Delhi Shah Alam returned to at the end of his campaign against Zabita Khan bore little resemblance to the magnificent capital in which he had grown up. Thirty years of incessant warfare, conquest and plunder since 1739 had left the city ruined and depopulated.

One traveller described what it was like arriving at Delhi in this period: 'As far as the eye can reach is one general scene of ruined buildings, long walls, vast arches, and parts of domes ... It is impossible to contemplate the ruins of this grand and venerable city without feeling the deepest impressions of melancholy ... They extend along the banks of the river, not less than fourteen miles ... The great Masjid, built of red stone, is greatly gone to decay. Adjacent to it is the [Chandni] Chowk, now a ruin; even the fort itself, from its having frequently changed its masters in the course of the last seventy years, is going rapidly to desolation ...'[47]

The Swiss adventurer Antoine Polier painted an equally bleak vision. Delhi, he wrote, was now a 'heap of ruins and rubbish'. The mansions were dilapidated, the gorgeously carved balconies had been sawn up for firewood by the Rohillas; the canals in the Faiz Bazaar and Chandni Chowk were clogged and dry. 'The only houses in good repair were those belonging to merchants or bankers,' noted the Comte de

---

* See Syed Mustafa Bareilwi, *Ghulam Qadir Ruhela*, Lahore, n.d., p. 55. Afzari and the *Ibratnama* both have Ghulam Qadir threatening to rape the women of the Mughal harem – 'to take them as concubines and fuck them at will' – additional evidence that at the time Ghulam Qadir was not thought of as a eunuch.

Modave.[48] A third of the city was completely wrecked. Polier blamed Zabita Khan's father, Najib ud-Daula, who he said had 'committed every kind of outrage in the city … the devastations and plunders of Nader Shah and Ahmad Shah Durrani were like violent tempests which carried everything before them but soon subsided; whereas the havoc made by the Rohillas over a decade resembled pestilential gales which keep up a continual agitation and destroy a country'.[49]

The great Urdu poet Mir returned to Delhi from exile around this time, full of hope that Delhi's downward trajectory might have been arrested after so many years of ill fortune. On arrival he could not believe the scale of the devastation he found. He wandered in despair around the abandoned and despoiled streets, searching for his old haunts, looking in vain for something familiar: 'What can I say about the rascally boys of the bazaar when there was no bazaar itself?' he wrote. 'The handsome young men had passed away, the pious old men had passed away. The palaces were in ruin, the streets were lost in rubble …'

Suddenly I found myself in the neighbourhood where I had lived – where I gathered friends and recited my verses; where I lived the life of love and cried many a night; where I fell in love with slim and tall beloveds and sang their praises. But now no familiar face came to sight so that I could spend some happy moments with them. Nor could I find someone suitable to speak to. The bazaar was a place of desolation. The further I went, the more bewildered I became. I could not recognize my neighbourhood or house … I stood there horrified.[50]

Here where the thorn grows, spreading over mounds of dust and ruins,
Those eyes of mine once saw gardens blooming in the spring.

Here in this city, where the dust drifts in deserted lanes
In days gone by a man might come and fill his lap with gold.

Only yesterday these eyes saw house after house,
Where now only ruined walls and doorways stands.

Sikhs, Marathas, thieves, pickpockets, beggars, kings, all prey on us
Happy he is who has no wealth, this is the one true wealth today.

The Age is not like the previous one, Mir,

The times have changed, the earth and sky have changed.

Tears flow like rivers from my weeping eyes.
My heart, like the city of Delhi, lies now in ruin.[51]

Nor was it clear that any sort of final peace had now come to the city. In the aftermath of the capture of Pathargarh, the fragile new alliance between the Mughals and the Marathas already appeared to be near collapse as the two sides fought over the division of the spoils: 'the faithless Marathas have seized all the artillery and treasures of Zabita Khan, as well as his elephants, horses and other property,' reported a palace newswriter, 'and have offered only a worthless fraction to the Emperor.'[52]

The Marathas countered that the Emperor had still to pay them the Rs40 lakh he had promised them, by treaty, for restoring him to the throne. In response the Emperor could do little more than chide his allies for their faithlessness: 'a harsh altercation broke out between him and the envoys of the Marathas, and the latter went away in anger.' In the end Scindia handed over to the Emperor just Rs2 lakh* of the 150 he had allegedly taken from Zabita's citadel. Shah Alam was rightly indignant: 'For six months not a dam has been paid to my soldiers as salary,' he said. 'My men only get their food after three or four days of fasting.'[53]

The matter was still unresolved when the two armies returned to Delhi. By December 1772 things had escalated to such a pitch of hostility that on Friday the 17th there was a full-scale Maratha attack on Shah Alam's small army, as his troops made a stand amid the ruins of the old fort of Purana Qila. During this skirmish, the newly recruited Breton adventurer René Madec, who had just been lured to Delhi by his friend Mirza Najaf Khan, took a bullet in the thigh. 'The Emperor proposed coming to terms,' wrote Madec in his *Mémoire*, 'but the Marathas wanted to extract every possible advantage from having won the recent battle, so now they forced this unfortunate prince to dance to their tune.'

They were determined not to allow him to increase his military strength, which would soon enough have been a counterbalance to their own armed forces. All they wanted was to keep Shah Alam dependent on themselves. Their terms were that the Emperor would

---

* The modern equivalences of these sums are: Rs40 lakh = £52 million; Rs2 lakh = £2.6 million.

keep only such troops as he strictly needed as a personal guard …
After this affair, the Emperor found himself reduced to a pitiable
condition. He had failed to pay his troops before the battle, and was
in even less of a position to pay them after. I could see that my troops
were on the point of rebellion.[54]

Things could easily have turned out very badly for Shah Alam, but at
the last minute he was saved. In early September 1773, an unexpected
message arrived by express courier from Pune, announcing the
premature death from consumption of the young Maratha Peshwa,
Narayan Rao. A violent succession dispute quickly followed, pitting the
many different factions in the Maratha Confederacy against each other.
As news arrived in Delhi of the fight for control, both Scindia and his
rival Holkar realised it was essential that they return south to Pune as
fast as they could in order to secure their interests. In their hurry to get
to Pune, they both departed within the week, leaving Shah Alam and
Mirza Najaf Khan in complete, unmediated control of Delhi.

So it was that Shah Alam's Delhi expedition ended in the one outcome
no one had foreseen. The Marathas, having helped install Shah Alam
back in power in Delhi, now withdrew for several years, while they
battled among themselves. By the monsoon of 1773, Shah Alam found
himself no longer the powerless puppet he had been for so much of his
life, but the surprised sovereign of his own dominions, with one of the
greatest generals of the eighteenth century as his commander.

Shah Alam was now forty-five, late middle age by Mughal standards.
For all his mixed fortunes in battle, he could still look back on many
aspects of his life with gratitude: he had successfully eluded assassination
at the hands of Imad ul-Mulk, and had survived four pitched battles with
the Company's sepoys, only to have the victors swear him allegiance.
He had made it back to Delhi and now occupied the Peacock Throne,
independent within his kingdom and beholden to no one. This was
for Shah Alam an almost miraculous outcome, and one that he had no
hesitation attributing to divine intervention.

The *Nadirat-i-Shahi, Diwan-e-Aftab* is a collection of 700 examples
of Shah Alam's best poetry and songs, ranging from *ghazals* (lyric poems)
to *nayika bheda*, verses that were compiled at his command in 1797. It
opens with a *ghazal* of supplication to his Creator, written around this
time, which shows the seriousness with which he took his royal duties,

and the degree to which he believed his role to be heaven-appointed, and guarded over by God:

> Lord! As You have bestowed by Your Grace, the Empire upon me
> Render obedient to my word the realm of hearts and minds
>
> In this world [*alam*] You have named me as King-of-the-World
> [*Shah Alam*]
> Strike a coin in my name for the benefit of this world and the next
>
> You have made me the sun [*aftab*] of the heaven of kingship
> Illuminate the world with the light of my justice
>
> At Your sacred court I am a beggar despite royal rank
> Admit unto Your Presence this hapless supplicant
>
> As You are the Most True and Supreme Judge, O God, I pray to You!
> Let the justice of my rule breathe life into rock and desert
>
> With Your help Moses prevailed over the tyrant Pharaoh
> Your divine aid made Alexander king of the kingdom of Darius
>
> As you have made shine in this world [*alam*] my name bright as the
> sun [*aftab*]
> From the sun of my benevolence, fill with light the hearts of friend
> and foe

There were new conquests to be made during the next fighting season, but first there was the monsoon to be enjoyed and thanks to be given. As the Emperor told the Maratha commanders just before they left, he could not come with them on their campaigns as he needed to be in 'Delhi for the marriage of my spiritual guide's sons and the *urs* [festival] of my *pir*', the great Sufi saint Qu'tb ud-Din Baktiar Khaki of Mehrauli.[55] Shah Alam had last been to the shrine of his *pir* when he went to seek his blessing and protection before fleeing Delhi twelve years earlier. Now he wished to thank the saint for bringing him safely back.

He first summoned Mirza Najaf Khan, and in full durbar formally rewarded him for his services with the post of Paymaster General, and the gift of estates in Hansi and Hissar, to the west of the capital.[56] He then decamped to the monsoon pleasure resort of Mehrauli, with its marble pavilions, swings, mango orchards and waterfalls, to celebrate his return in the traditional Mughal manner: with pilgrimages to Sufi shrines, music, songs, poetry recitations, fountains, feasting and love-making in the tented camps set up within the Mughal walled gardens of Mehrauli.

It was around this time that Shah Alam is thought to have written some of his most celebrated lyrics, a series of monsoon raags in the now lost musical mode of Raag Gaund, rain-tinged verses 'celebrating the imminent moment of joyful union between the clouds and the earth, the lover and the beloved'.[57] These were intended to be sung to celebrate the fecund beauty of the season, giving thanks to the patron saint of Mehrauli for his protection, and asking the saint for his blessing for what was to come:

The peafowl murmur atop the hills, while the frogs make noise as they gather
Turn your eyes to the beautiful waterfalls and spread the covering cloth fully!

I beg this of you, lord Qu'tb-ud Din, fulfil all the desires of my life
I worship you, please hear me, constantly touching your feet

Come on this beautiful day; take the air and delight in the garden,
Sate your thirst and take pleasure contemplating the beauties of Raag Gaund

Give riches and a country to Shah Alam, and fill his treasure house
As he strolls beneath the mango trees, gazing at the waterfalls.[58]

While Shah Alam relaxed and celebrated in Mehrauli, Najaf Khan was hard at work. He first secured the estates he had been granted in Hansi, and then used their revenues to pay his troops. He began to recruit and train further battalions, including one made up of destitute Rohillas, left penniless after the fall of Pathargarh, who were now driven by poverty to join the forces of their former enemies. As word spread of Shah Alam's ambition to reconquer his ancestral empire, veterans from across India flocked to Delhi looking for employment in the Mirza's new army.

Mirza Najaf was well aware that the new European military tactics that had already become well known in eastern and southern India were still largely unknown in Hindustan, where the old style of irregular cavalry warfare still ruled supreme; only the Jats had a few semi-trained battalions of sepoys. He therefore made a point of recruiting as many European mercenaries as he could to train up his troops. In the early 1770s, that meant attracting the French Free Lances who had been left unemployed and driven westwards by the succession of Company victories in Bengal, and their refusal to countenance the presence of any French mercenaries in the lands of their new ally, Avadh.[59]

Steadily, one by one, he pulled them in: first the Breton soldier of fortune René Madec; then Mir Qasim's Alsatian assassin, Walter Reinhardt, now widely known as Sumru and married to a remarkable and forceful Kashmiri dancing girl, Farzana. The Begum Sumru, as she later became celebrated, had become the mother of Sumru's son, and travelled across northern India with her mercenary husband; she would soon prove herself every bit as resilient and ruthless as he. While Sumru marched with Najaf Khan, the Begum pacified and settled the estates the couple had just been given by Shah Alam at Sardhana near Meerut.

Soon the pair created their own little kingdom in the Doab: when the Comte de Modave went to visit, he was astonished by its opulence. But Sumru, he noted, was not happy, and appeared to be haunted by the ghosts of those he had murdered: he had become 'devout, superstitious and credulous like a good German. He fasts on all set [Catholic feast] days. He gives alms and pays for as many masses as he can get. He fears the devil as much as the English ... Sometimes it seems he is disgusted by the life he leads, though this does not stop him keeping a numerous seraglio, far above his needs.'[60] Nor did this stop him arming against human adversaries as well as demonic ones, and the Comte reported that of all the mercenary chiefs, Sumru 'was the best equipped with munitions of war ... His military camp is kept in perfect order ... His artillery is in very good condition and he has about 1,200 Gujarati bulls in his park [to pull the guns.]'[61]

Then there was the Swiss adventurer Antoine Polier, a skilled military engineer, who had helped the Company rebuild Fort William in Calcutta after Siraj ud-Daula wrecked the old one. But he craved wilder frontiers and had found his way to Delhi, where he offered his military engineering skills and expertise in siege craft to Najaf Khan. Finally, there was also the suave and brilliant Comte de Modave himself, who, before bankruptcy propelled him eastwards, was a friend and aristocratic neighbour of Voltaire in Grenoble and a confidant of the French Foreign Minister, the Duc de Choiseul. Modave wrote and translated a number of books in the most elegant French, and his witty and observant memoirs of this period are by far the most sophisticated eyewitness account of the campaigns which followed.

A little later, the Mirza's army was joined by a very different class of soldiers: the dreadlocked Nagas of Anupgiri Gossain. Anupgiri had just defected from the service of Shuja ud-Daula and arrived with 6,000 of his naked warriors and forty cannon. These Nagas were always brilliant shock troops, but they could be particularly effective against Hindu opponents. The Comte de Modave records an occasion when the Company sent a battalion to stop the Nagas 'pillaging, robbing, massacring and causing havoc … [But] instead of charging the Nagas, the Hindu sepoys at once laid down their arms and prostrated themselves at the feet of these holy penitents – who did not wait to pick up the sepoys' guns and carry on their way, raiding and robbing.'[62]

By August, under these veteran commanders, Najaf had gathered six battalions of sepoys armed with rockets and artillery, as well as a large Mughal cavalry force, perhaps 30,000 troops in all. With these the Mughals were ready to take back their empire.

Najaf Khan began his campaign of reconquest close to home. On 27 August 1773, he surprised and captured the northernmost outpost of Nawal Singh, the Jat Raja of Deeg. This was a large mud fort named Maidangarhi which the Jat ruler Surajmal had built, in deliberate defiance of imperial authority, just south of Mehrauli, and within sight of the Qu'tb Minar. 'The rustic defenders fought long but at last could resist no longer. Najaf Khan captured the fort, and put to the sword all of the men found there.' Najaf Khan then took several other small mud forts with which the Jat Raja had ringed the land south of Delhi.[63]

Nawal Singh sued for peace, while actively preparing for war and seeking an alliance with Zabita Khan Rohilla, who had recently returned to his devastated lands and was now thirsting for revenge. But Najaf Khan moved too quickly to allow any pact to be stitched together. His swift advance crushed the troops of Nawal Singh. On 24 September, he marched deep into Jat country and on the evening of 30 October at Barsana, just north of Deeg, with the sun sinking fast into fields of high millet, he killed and beheaded the principal Jat general and defeated his army, leaving 3,000 of them dead on the battlefield. The Jat sepoys tried to fire in volleys, but did not understand how to file-fire. Najaf Khan's troops, who had worked out the rhythm of their loading and firing, fell to the ground during the volleys and then got up and rushed the Jat lines 'with naked swords' before they could reload. Najaf was himself wounded in the battle; but the immense plunder taken from the Jat camp paid for the rest of the campaign.[64]

As word spread of Najaf Khan's military prowess, his enemies began to flee in advance of his arrival, enabling Najaf to take in quick succession the fort of Ballabgarh, halfway to Agra, as well as a series of smaller Jat forts at Kotvan and Farrukhnagar.[65] By mid-December, Najaf Khan had laid siege to Akbar the Great's fort at Agra. He left Polier to direct siegeworks, and then headed further south with half the army to seize the mighty fortress of Ramgarh, which he took by surprise, then renamed Aligarh.

On 8 February 1774, after Polier had fired more than 5,000 cannonballs at the walls of Agra Fort, he finally succeeded in making a breach. Shortly afterwards, the Fort surrendered and was handed over to Sumru and his brigade to garrison.[66] Finally on 29 April 1776, after a siege of five months, the impregnable Jat stronghold of Deeg fell to Najaf Khan after the Raja fled and starvation had weakened the garrison. Madec records that three wives of Nawal Singh begged the palace eunuch to kill them after the capture of the city: 'They lay on the carpet and he cut off the heads of all three of them, one after another, and ended by killing himself on their corpses.'[67] The citadel was looted and the defenders put to the sword: 'Much blood was spilt and even women and children had their throats cut,' wrote the Comte de Modave. 'Women were raped and three widows of the former Raja committed suicide rather than endure this fate. Then the pillagers set fire to the town. The fire spread to the powder store, and on three consecutive days there were terrible explosions. Najaf tried to stop the plundering, but it took him three days to bring his troops under control.'[68]

Shah Alam later censured Najaf Khan for the sack: 'I have sent you to regulate the kingdom, not to plunder it,' he wrote. 'Don't do it again. Release the men and women you have captured.'[69]

Nevertheless, in less than four years, Najaf Khan had reconquered all the most important strongholds of the Mughal heartlands and brought to heel the Emperor's most unruly vassals. The Rohillas were crushed in 1772, again in 1774 and finally, in 1777, the Jats' strongholds were all seized. By 1778, the Sikhs had been driven back into the Punjab, and Jaipur had offered submission. A token suzerainty had been re-established over both Avadh and parts of Rajputana.

The Mughal imperium was beginning to emerge from its coma after forty years of incessant defeats and losses. For the first time in four decades, Delhi was once again the capital of a small empire.

While Mirza Najaf Khan was busy with the army, Shah Alam stayed in Delhi, re-establishing his court and trying to breathe life back into his dead capital. Imperial patronage began to flow and the artists and writers started to return: as well as the poets Mir and Sauda, the three greatest painters of the age, Nidha Mal, Khairullah and Mihir Chand, all came back home from self-exile in Lucknow.[70]

Inevitably, as the court became established, the usual court intrigue began to unfold, much of it directed at Najaf Khan, who was not only an immigrant outsider, but also a Persian Shia. Shah Alam's new Sunni minister, Abdul Ahad Khan, jealous of Najaf Khan's growing power and popularity, tried to convince the Emperor that his commander was conspiring to dethrone him. He whispered in Shah Alam's ears that Najaf Khan was plotting to join forces with his kinsman Shuja ud-Daula to found a new Shia dynasty which would replace the Mughals. 'Abdul Ahad was Kashmiri, over 60 years old, but as nimble and energetic as a man in the prime of life,' wrote the Comte de Modave. 'He had been trained to the intrigues of court life since his earliest youth, his father having occupied a similar position for Muhammad Shah Rangila.'

> On the surface, there could not be a more civil and decent person than this Abdul Ahad Khan, but all his political ambitions were nothing other than a tissue of disingenuous trickery, designed to extract money for himself, and to supplant anyone who gave him umbrage. He especially hated Najaf Khan, who was commanding the Emperor's troops, which depended only on him, and who was therefore in control of his game. That meant that Najaf Khan was also feared and oddly un-loved by the Emperor himself.[71]

Najaf Khan shrugged off the gossip, carrying on with his conquests with an equanimity that impressed observers: 'His perseverance is unparalleled,' wrote Polier. 'His patience and fortitude in bearing the reproaches and impertinence of this courtly rabble is admirable.'[72] Modave agreed: 'I have no words adequate to describe the phlegmatic poker-face which Najaf Khan kept up during all these intrigues directed against him,' he wrote. 'He was well-informed of their smallest details, and he would discuss them sardonically with his friends, frequently commenting that only the feeble fall back on such petty means.'

> He never betrayed any sign of unease and carried on his campaign against the Jats regardless ... He knew what power he could exercise in Delhi, and has often confided in one of his associates that he could, if he so wished, change matters in an instant, and send the Padshah back to the Princes' Prison, and put another one on the throne. But that he was held back from having recourse to such violent methods by the fear of making himself hateful and hated. He preferred patiently to suffer the petty frustrations and humiliations thrown in his way, secure in the knowledge that, as long as he had a strong army, he had little to fear from his impotent rivals.[73]

Inevitably in such circumstances, between the Emperor and his most brilliant commander, a polite and courtly coldness developed which manifested itself in subtle ways that Modave took great pleasure in noting down: 'It is a well-established custom in Delhi to send ready-cooked meals to the Emperor,' he wrote, 'to which the monarch responds by sending similar meals to those he wishes to honour.'

> The dishes selected to be sent to the Emperor are placed on large platters, then covered with a cloth bag sealed with the seal of the sender, and these are sent into the royal seraglio. The Padshah had any dishes coming from Najaf Khan's kitchen secretly thrown into the Yamuna; and when the compliment was returned, Najaf Khan would receive the royal gift with much ceremonious bowing, but, as soon as the royal servants carrying the meal had withdrawn, the cooked dishes were given to the *halal-khwar*s, who cheerfully feasted on them – these latter fine fellows are in charge of cleaning the privies in people's houses, so you can guess their status and function.[74]

Despite this, both Modave and Polier still found much to admire in Shah Alam. On 18 March 1773, soon after being taken into his service, Polier was formally received in the Diwan-i-Khas throne room by the Emperor. He was given fine living quarters in the haveli of Safdar Jung near the Kashmiri Gate, and presented with an elephant, a sword and a horse. The Emperor tied on his turban jewel himself, and he was sent food from the royal table. 'Shah Alum is now about 50 years of age,' Polier wrote in his diary soon afterwards, 'of a strong frame and good constitution, his size above the middling and his aspect, though generally with a melancholy cast, has a good deal of sweetness and benignity in it, which cannot but interest the beholder in his favour.'

> His deportment in public is grave and reserved, but on the occasion full of graciousness and condescension. Indulgent to his servants, easily satisfied with their services, he seldom finds fault with them, or takes notice of any neglect they may be guilty of. A fond father, he has the greatest affection for his children, whom yet he keeps agreeable to the usage of the court, under great subordination and restriction.
>
> He is always strictly devout and an exact observer of the ceremonies of his religion, though it must be owned, not without a strong scent of superstition. He is well versed in the Persic and Arabic languages, particularly the former, and is not ignorant of some of the dialects of India, in which he often amuses himself composing verses and songs.

That he wants neither courage nor spirit has been often put to the proof, and he has more than once had severe trials of his constancy and fortitude, all of which he bore with a temper that did him infinite credit. But from the first, he reposed too implicit confidence in his ministers, and generally suffered his own better opinion to give way to that of a servant, often influenced by very different motives from those which such a confidence should have dictated.

This has always been Shah Alum's foible, partly owing to indolence and partly to his unsuspecting mind, which prevents him from seeing any design in the flattery of a sycophant and makes him take for attachment to his person what is nothing more than a design to impose on him and obtain his confidence. Indeed two of the king's greatest faults are his great fondness of flattery, and the too unreserved confidence he places on his ministers. Though he cannot be called a great king, he must be allowed to have many qualities that would entitle him, in private life, to the character of a good and benevolent man ...[75]

The usually caustic Comte de Modave took a similar view of the Emperor. Modave thought him well-intentioned, gentle, courteous and lacking in neither wit nor wisdom. 'He is good to the point of weakness,' he wrote, 'and his physical appearance and demeanour radiate intelligence and kindness. I have often had the honour of being in close proximity to him, and I was able to observe on his face those expressions of restlessness which reveal a prince immersed in deep thoughts.'

The Padshah seems to be a tenderly affectionate father, cuddling his little children in public. I was told in Delhi that he has 27 male children, all in riotous good health. When he appears in public, he is often accompanied by three or four of his sons. I have seen him ride out from the Palace-Fort to gallop in the surrounding countryside, accompanied by several of these young princes similarly mounted on horses, and displaying to their father their skill and prowess in various sports and games. At other times, I have seen him within the Palace Fort, passing from one apartment to another, with his youngest sons aged from 3 to 6 years old carried in his train – eunuchs were the bearers of these noble burdens.

Travel and adventure have broadened the mind of this prince, and his dealings with the French and the English have exposed him to a general knowledge of the affairs of the world, which might have helped guide him in the pursuit of his ambitions. But once back in Delhi, his affairs were in such a mess, and the temptations of lazy leisure so strong as to render all the good qualities of this prince ineffectual, at least up till now ...

Though this prince has several good qualities – intelligence, gentleness, and a perceptive understanding – his occasional pettiness can ruin everything. Cossetted among his womenfolk, he lives out a flabby, effeminate existence. One of his daily pastimes is playing a board-game with his favourite concubines, with oblong dice about the length of the middle finger [*chaupar*] ... Each game the Padshah plays with his ladies involves 3 or 4 paisas, which he pays if he loses and insists that he receive if he wins, according to the rules.

He has the failings of all weak rulers, and that is to hate those he is constrained to promote, which is the case with his general Najaf Khan – they both mistrust each other, and are continually falling out ... Even though Shah Alam has taken part in war, he has never developed any taste for the military profession, even though the position he finds himself in would demand that he make fighting his principal occupation. One wastes one's time trying to persuade him to go on campaign; since his return to Delhi, he has either avoided or refused all proposals made to him on that subject.

His minister [Abdul Ahad Khan] is so avid for authority and riches that he uses his influence on the spirit of Shah Alam for the sole purpose of distancing the prince from the servants who were truly loyal, and then replacing them with his own creatures. The irritation that this conduct inspired in all at court, particular in Najaf Khan, the most important amongst them, has occasioned cabals and intrigues ... Jealous of his general [Najaf], and having little confidence in his ministers, who are without credit, Shah Alam always fears some petty revolution in the palace, which would put him back into the prison where he was born.[76]

But the most serious problem for the court was not internal divisions and intrigues so much as Shah Alam's perennial lack of funds. On 9 September 1773, Shah Alam wrote to Warren Hastings asking for the tribute of Bengal. He said he had received no money from the Company 'for the last two years and our distress is therefore very great now'. He reminded the Company of their treaty obligations – to remit revenue and to allow him the lands awarded to him at Kora and Allahabad.[77]

The appeal was unsuccessful. Hastings, appalled by the suffering of the Bengalis in the great famine, made up his mind to stop all payments to 'this wretched King of shreds and patches'.[78] 'I am entrusted with the care and protection of the people of these provinces,' he wrote, 'and their condition, which is at this time on the edge of misery, would be ruined past remedy by draining the country of the little wealth which remains in it.'[79] This did not, however, stop him from allowing his Company colleagues to remit much larger amounts of their savings back to England.

'I think I may promise that no more payments will be made while he is in the hands of the Marathas,' Hastings wrote to the directors a year later, 'nor, if I can prevent it, *ever more*. Strange that ... the wealth of the province (which is its blood) should be drained to supply the pageantry of a mock King, an idol of our own Creation! But how much more astonishing that we should still pay him the same dangerous homage whilst he is the tool of the only enemies we have in India, and who want but such aids to prosecute their designs even to our ruin.'[80] When his colleagues on the Council pointed out that the Company only held its land through the Emperor's charter, Hastings replied that he believed the Company held Bengal through 'the natural charter' of the sword. In 1774, Hastings finally made the formal decision to cease all payments to Shah Alam.[81]

The loss to Shah Alam's treasury was severe, and it meant he could rarely pay his troops their full salary. As a Company report noted, 'the expenses of his army are so greatly exceeding his Revenue that a considerable part of it remains for months together without any subsistence, except by Credit or Plunder. As a result, numerous Bodies of Troops are continually quitting his Service and others equally numerous engaging in it, as he indiscriminately receives all Adventurers.'[82]

All this was vaguely manageable while Najaf Khan was winning back the imperial demesne around Delhi and bringing back to the palace plunder from the Jats and the revenues of Hindustan. The real problems began when his health began to give way, and Najaf Khan retired, broken and exhausted, to his sickbed in Delhi.

Najaf Khan first became ill in the winter of 1775 and was confined to his
bed for several months. While he was unwell, the Jats rose in revolt and
it was not until he recovered in April that he was able to lead a second
campaign to re-establish imperial authority in Hariana.

In November 1779, the scheming Kashmiri minister Abdul Ahad Khan
finally lost the confidence of the Emperor when he led a catastrophic
campaign against the Sikhs of Patiala. In the aftermath of this debacle,
Shah Alam finally made Mirza Najaf Khan Regent, or Vakil-i-Mutlaq,
in place of his rival. He was forty-two. It was a promotion the Emperor
should have made years earlier: all observers were unanimous that the
Mirza was by far the most capable of all the Mughal officials. But no
sooner had Mirza Najaf Khan taken hold of the reins of government
than he began to be troubled by long spells of fever and sickness. 'The
gates of felicity seemed to open for the people of these times,' wrote
one observer. 'The citizens felt they were seeing promised happiness
in the mirror. Yet [after Najaf Khan retired to his bed] the bugles and
drums of marching troops approaching was like a poison dissolving
thoughts.'[83]

Many were still jealous of the meteoric rise of this Shia immigrant,
and to explain his marked absence from public life rumours were spread
that Mirza Najaf Khan had become a slave to pleasure who was spending
his days in bed with the dancing girls of Delhi. Khair ud-Din Illahabadi
claims in the *Ibratnama* that the great Commander was led astray by a
malevolent eunuch. 'One Latafat Ali Khan tricked his way into Mirza
Najaf's confidence,' he wrote, 'and gained great influence over him.'

Under the guise of being his well-wisher, he shamelessly encouraged
the Mirza, who till then had spent his time fighting and defeating
enemies of the state, to taste the hitherto unknown pleasures of
voluptuousness. Latafat Ali Khan was able to introduce into the
Mirza's own private quarters an experienced prostitute, who day
and night had slept with a thousand different men. He now had her
appear shamelessly at every intimate gathering, till the Mirza became

infatuated with her, and little by little became her sexual slave. By this channel, Latafat Ali Khan was able to receive endless sums of money and gifts; but the wine and the woman quickly sapped the Mirza's strength.

The Mirza spent all his time with this woman, worshipping her beauty, drinking wine to excess, his eyes enflamed and weakened, his body feverish and distempered, until he fell seriously ill. But he paid no attention to his health and carried on partying as long as he could manage it, ignoring doctors' advice to moderate his behaviour. Finally, his illness reached a stage where it could no longer be cured or treated: the bitter waters of despair closed over his head and Heaven decreed he should die suddenly in the full flower of his manhood.[84]

Whatever may have been the particulars of Najaf Khan's love life, the truth about his illness was far crueller. In reality, his time in bed was spent, not in sexual ecstasy, but in pain and suffering, spitting blood. The commander had contracted consumption. By August 1781 he was bedridden. He lingered for the first three months of 1782, gaunt and cadaverous, more dead than alive. 'From the Emperor to the meanest inhabitant of Delhi, Hindus and Musalmans alike became anxious for the life of their beloved hero,' wrote Khair ud-Din. 'When human efforts failed they turned to the heavenly powers and prayed for his recovery. A grand offering (*bhet*) was made at the shrine of the goddess Kalka Devi [near Oklah] in the night of 7th Rabi on behalf of the Mirza, and the blessings of the deity were invoked for his restoration to health. The Nawab distributed sweets to Brahmans and little boys, and released cows meant for slaughter by paying their price in cash to the butchers with a strong injunction to the effect that none should molest these animals. But all this was in vain.'[85] When the remorseful Emperor came to say goodbye at the beginning of April, Najaf Khan was 'too weak to stand or to perform the customary salutations':

On seeing the condition of the Mirza, His Majesty wept, and gently laid his hand on his shoulder to comfort him … Rumours of the Nawab's imminent death spread throughout the city. His womenfolk left the private quarters and, weeping and wailing, crowded around his bedside, which brought a last flicker of consciousness to his face. Then he called for his sister, sighing with regret, 'Sit by my pillow for a while, cast your merciful shadow on me, let me be your guest for a few moments'; and as he whispered this, he closed his eyes. They say one watch of the night was still left when the breath of life departed from his body's clay.[86]

Mirza Najaf Khan died on 6 April 1782, aged only forty-six. For ten years he had worked against all the odds, and usually without thanks, to restore to Shah Alam the empire of his ancestors. Thereafter, as one historian put it, 'The rays of hope for the recovery of the Mughal glory that had begun to shine were dissipated in the growing cloud of anarchy.'[87] Najaf Khan was remembered as the last really powerful nobleman of the Mughal rule in India and was given the honorific title of Zul-Fiqaru'd-Daula (the Ultimate Discriminator of the Kingdom).[88] He was buried in a modest tomb in a garden a short distance from that of Safdar Jung.* Like much of his life's work, it was never completed.

Almost immediately, the court disintegrated into rival factions as Najaf Khan's lieutenants scrambled for power. Afrasiyab Khan, Najaf Khan's most capable officer and his own choice of successor, was the convert son of a Hindu tradesman, and was supported by Anupgiri Gossain and his battalions of warrior ascetics; but because of his humble background he had little backing in the court.

His rise was strongly opposed by Najaf's grand-nephew, the urbanely aristocratic Mirza Muhammad Shafi, who organised a counter-coup on 10 September 1782, directing military operations from the top of the steps of the Jama Masjid. The two rival factions battled each other in the streets of Delhi, while outside the city the Sikhs, Jat and Rohillas all took the opportunity to rise as one in revolt. Shah Alam's attempt to reconcile both sides with marriage alliances came to nothing.[89] Within two years, both claimants had been assassinated and almost all of Mirza Najaf Khan's territorial gains had been lost. For the first time, jokes began to be made about how the empire of Shah Alam ran from Delhi to Palam – *Sultanat-i Shah Alam az Dilli ta Palam* – a distance of barely ten miles.

The Maratha newswriter reported to Pune that 'the city is again in a very ruinous condition. Day and night Gujars commit dacoity [violent robbery] and rob wayfarers. At night thieves break into houses and

---

* Najafgarh, a town in south-west Delhi, is named after him. So is the road next to his tomb south of Jor Bagh.

carry away shopkeepers and other rich people as captives for ransom. Nobody attempts to prevent these things.'[90] Sikh war parties began once again to raid the northern suburbs. As Polier noted, the Sikhs 'now set off after the rains and make excursions in bodies of 10,000 horses or more on their neighbours. They plunder all they can lay their hands on, and burn the towns.'[91]

Three successive failed monsoons, followed by a severe famine spreading across Hindustan, sweeping away around a fifth of the rural population, added to the sense of chaos and breakdown.[92] In Lucknow at the same time, the Nawab Asaf ud-Daula built his great Imambara mourning hall in order to provide employment for 40,000 people as famine relief work; but Shah Alam did not have the resources for anything like this.[93] The poet Sauda articulated in his letters the growing sense of despair: 'The royal treasury is empty,' he wrote. 'Nothing comes in from the crown lands; the state of the office of salaries defies description.'

Soldiers, clerks, all alike are without employment. Documents authorising payment to the bearer are so much waste paper: the pharmacist tears them up to wrap his medicines in. Men who once held jagirs or posts paid from the royal treasury are looking for jobs as village watchmen. Their sword and shield have long since gone to the pawn shop, and when they next come out, it will be with a beggar's staff and bowl. Words cannot describe how some of these once great ones live. Their wardrobe has ended up at the rag merchant ...

Meanwhile, how can I describe the desolation of Delhi? There is no house from which the jackal's cry cannot be heard. The mosques at evening are unlit and deserted, and only in one house in a hundred will you see a light burning. The lovely buildings, which once made the famished man forget his hunger, are in ruins now. In the once beautiful gardens, where the nightingale sang his love songs to the rose, the grass grows waist high around the fallen pillars and ruined arches.

In the villages round about, the young women no longer come to draw water at the wells and stand talking in the leafy shade of the trees. The villages around the city are deserted, the trees themselves are gone, and the well is full of corpses. Shahjahanabad, you never deserved this terrible fate, you were once vibrant with life and love and hope, like the heart of a young lover: you for whom men afloat upon the ocean of the world once set their course as to the promised shore, you from whose dust men came to gather pearls. Not even a lamp of clay now burns where once the chandelier blazed with light.

Those who once lived in great mansions, now eke out their lives among the ruins. Thousands of hearts, once full of hope, are sunk in despair. There is nothing to be said but this: we are living in the darkest of times.[94]

Unable to impose order on his court, and threatened by resurgent enemies on all sides, Shah Alam had no option but to reach out again to Mahadji Scindia, who had finally returned to Hindustan from the Deccan after an absence of eleven years: 'You must undertake the Regency of my house,' Shah Alam told him, 'and regulate my Empire.'[95] With the letter of supplication, he sent Scindia an Urdu couplet:

Having lost my kingdom and wealth, I am now in your hands,
Do Mahadji as you wish.[96]

In many ways Shah Alam made a canny decision when deciding to seek Mahadji Scindia's protection for the second time. Scindia's power had grown enormously since he left Delhi and headed south in 1772 to sort out affairs in the Deccan. He was now, along with Tipu, one of the two most powerful Indian commanders in the country. Moreover, his troops had just begun to be trained in the latest French military techniques by one of the greatest military figures of eighteenth-century India, Comte Benoît de Boigne, who would transform them beyond recognition. Before long they would be famed for their 'wall of fire and iron' which would wreak havoc on even the best-trained Indian armies sent against them.[97]

De Boigne was responsible for transferring to Scindia's Marathas sophisticated new European military technology including cannon armed with the latest sighting and aiming systems with adjustable heights and elevating screws, and the introduction of iron rods to their muskets that allowed the best-trained troops to fire three shots a minute. When used by infantry deployed in a three-row pattern, his Maratha sepoys could keep up a continuous fire at the enemy, deploying an unprecedented killing power: according to one calculation, a squadron of cavalry breaking into a gallop 300 metres from one of de Boigne's battalions would have to face around 3,000 bullets before they reached the sepoys' bayonets.

A decade hence, when Scindia's battalions were fully trained and reached their total strength, many would regard them as the most formidable army in India, and certainly the equal of that of the Company.[98] Already, Scindia's Rajput opponents were learning to surrender rather than attempt to defeat de Boigne's new battalions, and Ajmer, Patan and Merta all gave up the fight after a brief bombardment rather than face the systematic slaughter of man and horse that de Boigne inevitably unleashed on his enemies. One commander even advised his wife from his deathbed, 'Resist [Scindia] unless de Boigne comes. But if he comes, then surrender.'[99]

In November 1784, Scindia met Shah Alam at Kanua near Fatehpur Sikri. Scindia again prostrated himself, placing his head on the Emperor's feet and paying him 101 gold mohurs, so taking up the office of Vakil-i-Mutlaq vacated by Mirza Najaf's death. But as one British observer noted, 'Scindia was [now] the nominal slave, but [in reality] the rigid master, of the unfortunate Shah Alam.'[100]

The Maratha general, after all, had his own priorities, and protecting the Emperor had never been one of them. Visitors reported the imperial family occasionally going hungry, as no provision had been made to supply them with food.[101] When Scindia did visit, he gave insultingly cheap presents such as 'sesame sweets usually given to slaves and horses'. He ordered the Delhi butchers to stop killing cows, without even consulting the Emperor.[102] Finally, in January 1786, he took his forces off towards Jaipur in an attempt to raise funds and extend Maratha rule into Rajasthan, leaving the Red Fort unprotected but for a single battalion of troops under the command of Anupgiri Gossain.

It was while he was away in Rajasthan that Ghulam Qadir, now twenty years old, realised that the Red Fort, and its treasures, lay now almost undefended. Zabita Khan had recently died, and Ghulam Qadir had just succeeded not only to his father's estate, but also to those of his mother and paternal uncles, all of whom he had immediately imprisoned, seizing all their goods. 'The ungrateful wretch was behaving as if he was the Pharaoh himself,' wrote Azfari. 'He spoke much foolishness, and uttering obscenities in a loud voice, began to boast, "Soon I will come to Shahjahanabad and wreak my vengeance. In whatever way I can,

I will play the game of retribution and sink the Red Fort in the river Yamuna." Rumours of this spread like wildfire and on the tongue of plebeian and noble alike was the news that Ghulam Qadir would arrive and uproot the city from its foundations.'[103]

In mid-July 1788, Ghulam Qadir finally put his words into action. He saddled up and rode out with a Rohilla army towards Delhi, determined to avenge his father, take his retribution on the Emperor and make his former captors pay for what they had done to him and to his people.

On 17 July, the Rohillas arrived and camped at Shahdara, on the opposite bank of the Yamuna to the Red Fort. There was much nervousness in the palace, but the Emperor remained calm, insisting that there was no cause for alarm: 'I do not know why this young orphan should be an object of such hostility,' he said. 'This Ghulam Qadir is a child of His Majesty's house and has eaten his salt.* What possibility is there that he would take any rash or violent steps? This is all just calumny spread by the populace. Calm down, my children.'[104]

Over the course of the next few days, however, two things happened which made the presence of the Rohillas much more threatening. Firstly, Ghulam Qadir received a message from the elderly widow of the Emperor Ahmad Shah, the Dowager Empress, Malika-i-Zamani Begum, a former ally of Ghulam Qadir's grandfather, Najib ud-Daula. She offered twelve lakhs** to the Rohillas if they would depose Shah Alam and replace him on the throne with her grandson, the Emperor's young cousin, Bedar Bakht. Secondly, Anupgiri Gossain, who was encamped with his small battalion at Qudsia Bagh, took fright at the growing size of the Rohilla force on the opposite bank and on the night of the 28th decamped with his troops in the dark to look for reinforcements – or so he later said.[†]

---

* *Namak parvardah*: brought up and supported at the expense of Shah Alam.

† William Pinch in *Warrior Ascetics and Indian Empires*, Cambridge, 2006, p. 2, believes Anupgiri colluded with Ghulam Qadir and was already in correspondence with him.

** £15.6 million today.

At first light on the 29th, the Rohillas saw that there was no longer anyone guarding the Yamuna crossing and that even the city gates were unmanned. 'With the speed of lightning and wind', Ghulam Qadir quickly crossed with a boatload of men and military equipment.[105] He landed at his old home of Qudsia Bagh, and, before the Mughals could react, seized the Kashmiri Gate. He placed his own men on the parapet, while he waited for the ferries to bring across his siege guns and the rest of the troops.

When 2,000 Rohillas had crossed, he marched them down through the town, straight to the Red Fort where, finding the gates barred, he took up position at the Golden Mosque in front of the Delhi Gate, and sent a message inside: 'This house-born intimate of the court has suffered from the hands of fate and seeks refuge in the royal shadow, hoping for a kind reception!'[106]

'The Rohillas swore [on the Quran] that they had no intention of doing any harm,' wrote the Maratha newswriter. 'They said they only wanted that the Emperor should lay his gracious hand on their heads. After Ghulam Qadir had taken a formal oath swearing he came to his sovereign in peace and as an ally, the Emperor sent his eunuchs to tell him he would admit him to an audience, but only with ten or twenty followers.'[107] However, the Head Eunuch, Mansur Ali Khan, who was also the Nazer, or Overseer of the Fort Administration, had saved Ghulam Qadir's life at the fall of Pathargarh and now wished to reingratiate himself. Against the Emperor's orders, he opened the great double gates of the Fort and allowed the Afghan to march in all 2,000 of his men. 'The Nazer gave over the gates of the Fort into the hands of Ghulam Qader Khan's men,' wrote Khair ud-Din. 'Ghulam Qader Khan, now inside the Fort, posted his Rohilla military chiefs to keep watch over the thoroughfares and passages and gates, both external and internal, of the Fort and royal apartments.'[108]

The soldiers of Najaf Khan's Red Platoon were still eager to fight. In the Diwan-i-Khas throne room, Shah Alam's favourite son, Prince Akbar, gathered the other young Mughal shahzadas and asked for permission to engage: 'One choice is yet left,' he said. 'If you will allow us, we brothers will fall upon these traitors, and will bravely encounter martyrdom.' But the Emperor shook his head: 'No one can escape the decrees of the Almighty,' he said. 'There is no contending against doom. The power is now in the hands of others.'[109]

Ghulam Qadir moved quickly. The royal guards and the princes were immediately disarmed. The guards were expelled from the Fort and the princes locked up in Aurangzeb's white marble Moti Masjid. Then Ghulam Qadir, in what would at any other time be regarded as an unpardonable breach of etiquette, sat down on the cushions of the imperial throne next to the Emperor, 'passed an arm familiarly round his neck and blew tobacco smoke into his sovereign's face'.[110] So began what the Maratha newswriter described as a 'dance of the demons', a reign of terror which lasted for nine weeks.[111]

That evening, Ghulam Qadir retired to the camp he had set up in one of the palace gardens, the Hayat Baksh Bagh. The following morning, the 30th, the Rohilla returned to the throne chamber. 'When the King saw him trespassing onto the Privy Seat (*sarir-e khas*), he began reproaching him softly: "I trusted our verbal agreement and the oath you swore on the Holy Quran,"' said the Emperor. 'I see I was deceived.'

While he was still speaking, the Rohilla summoned Prince Bedar Bakht. Ghulam Qadir stepped forward, and took the Emperor's dagger from his girdle, then without a word sent the Emperor off to the imperial prison of Salimgarh, and placed Bedar Bakht on the throne. Drums were beaten and coins struck in the name of the new Emperor, Bedar Shah.[112] 'The Emperor could only bite the hand of astonishment with the teeth of reflection.'[113]

According to the newswriter's despatch, 'Ghulam Qadir then demanded from [the boy's grandmother] Malika-i-Zamani Begum the promised money.'

She came from her mansion in the city to the fort and said, 'after searching the people of the imperial mahals and the Begums, I shall provide you the money. If you act by my advice, all your affairs will flourish.' 'The money and the property in the fort now all belong to me,' replied Ghulam Qadir. 'You have to give me what you promised.'

Ghulam Qadir then confiscated all the money, furniture and wardrobes of Shah Alam, and the jewels and gold and silver vessels from the imperial stores. Then he searched the Begums and the princesses and seized whatever ornaments and clothes were found, so that even the clothes they wore were taken away and they were left with only their noses and ears intact. Then, stripping the male inhabitants of the fort, and the inhabitants of Delhi who had gone there for safety, he turned them out and seized all their property. He began to dig up the floors of the houses. He remarked, 'Shah Alam attempted to ruin my house, and in concert with the Marathas and Mirza Najaf Khan went to Pathargarh and dishonoured my women. Even now he wishes to summon Scindia and devastate my house. I have no option but to take retribution.'[114]

The cupola of the golden mosque was stripped of its gold leaf.[115] 'With the complicity of the Nazer Mansur Ali Khan, they stretched out the hand of oppression on the people of the city.'[116] Before long, Rs25 crore of jewels* had been disgorged from the city's jewellers and bankers. While he looted the city and the palace, according to Azfari, the Rohilla, 'day and night gave himself over to great quantities of various intoxicants, particularly to bhang, bauza [beer-like booze] and ganja'.[117]

Gradually, Ghulam Qadir became more and more savage. The servants began to be hung upside down and tortured over fires to reveal hiding places of the Emperor's treasure.[118] 'Some maid-servant dancing girls and providers of pleasure favoured by Shah Alam were brought in without veil or covering; they were taken to the *daira* camp where they were made to pleasure drunken louts.'[119] The Head Eunuch Mansur Ali was dragged through a latrine and left nearly to drown in the sewer beneath: 'Ghulam Qadir called out to his henchmen: "If this traitor (*namak-haram*) doesn't produce the seven lakhs rupees** within the next watch, stuff his mouth with excrement!"'[120] When the eunuch protested that he had saved Ghulam Qadir's life as a baby, the latter replied, 'Do you not know the old proverb, "to kill a serpent and spare its young is not wise".'

According to a report sent to Warren Hastings, 'the new King Bedar Shah was not allowed a change of raiment and was obliged to beg Ghulam Qadir for a rupee to buy a meal; but the Rohilla refused to see him when his Majesty went on foot to beg. The old Queens of Muhammed Shah [Rangila] who had seen Delhi in its utmost splendour before the invasion of Nader Shah, were forced from their Houses and their property ransacked. Shah Alam was seven days without any food but coarse bread & water.'[121]

---

* £3,250 million today.

** £9 million today.

Ghulam Qadir was convinced that the Emperor was still hiding many of his treasures from him, so on 10 August he summoned him and the princes back from the Salimgarh prison. According to Khair ud-Din, the Rohillas first 'ordered that Prince Akbar and Prince Sulaiman Shukoh should be bound and whipped by the carpet spreaders ... so that blood gushed from their mouths and noses. Shah Alam exclaimed, "whatever is to be done, do it to me! These are young and innocent." Then Ghulam Qadir said to some truculent Afghans, "Throw this babbler down and blind him."'[122]

Shah Alam looked straight at Ghulam Qadir and asked: 'What? Will you destroy those eyes that for a period of sixty years have been assiduously employed in perusing the sacred Quran?'[123] But the appeal to religion had no effect on the Afghan.

Those men threw him down, and passed the needle into his eyes. They kept him down on the ground by striking him with blows from sticks, and Ghulam Qadir asked derisively if he saw anything. He replied, 'Nothing but the Holy Koran between me and you.' All night long he and his children and the women of his palace kept up loud cries. Ghulam Qadir remained that night in the Moti Mahal and hearing these cries, he writhed like a snake, and directed his servants to beat and kill those who made them. But the men dreaded the questioning of the day of judgement, and held back their hands.

The next day, Ghulam Qadir said to Bedar Shah, 'Come out and I will show you a sight.' Ghulam Qadir then went to Shah Alam, and said, 'Find me some gold, or I will send you to join the dead.' Shah Alam reviled and reproached him, saying, 'I am in your power, cut off my head for it is better to die than to live like this.'

Ghulam Qadir Khan jumped up and, straddling his victim's chest, ordered Qandahari Khan and Purdil Khan to pinion his hands to his neck and hold down his elbows. With his Afghan knife [contrary to the usual practice of blinding with needles] Qandahari Khan first cut one of Shah Alam's eyes out of its socket, then the other eye was wrenched out by that impudent rascal. Shah Alam flapped on the ground like a chicken with its neck cut.

Ghulam Qadir then gave orders that the needle should be passed into the eyes of Prince Akbar, Suleiman Shikoh and Ahsan Bakht. The imperial ladies then came out from behind their curtains, and threw themselves at the feet of Ghulam Qadir; but he kicked them in the breasts and sent them away saying, 'Pinion all three and I will consider what to do with them another time.' He then ordered some followers to beat them until they were senseless and throw them back into prison. Then he called for a painter, and said, 'Paint my likeness at once, sitting, knife in hand, upon the breast of Shah Alam, digging out his eyes.' He then forbade his attendants to bring any food and water, either to Shah Alam or his sons.[124]

That night three valets and two water-carriers tried to relieve the Emperor's thirst. Ghulam Qadir ordered all five, in succession, to be killed, and their bodies left to rot where they had fallen, next to the sobbing Emperor.

On the 25th, Ghulam Qadir turned his attention to the imperial princes. Just as he may once have been turned into a catamite, so now it was his turn to humiliate the males of the royal house. Twenty of the princes, including the future Emperors Akbar Shah and his son, Bahadur Shah Zafar, were then forced to sing and dance for the Rohilla officers: 'However much they attempted to refuse his demands, he would not listen, merely commenting: "I've been hearing, for some time now, wonderful reports about your dancing and singing!"'

Then Ghulam Qadir turned to the guards and barked: 'If they dare to make any more excuses, have their beards shaven off, indeed, have their whole bodies clean shaven!' The princes and their sons had no choice but to obey the order, and so started making music and dancing, gyrating their hips and shoulders and necks. He was aroused and delighted by their performance and asked: 'What reward would you like me bestow on you?' They replied: 'Our father and our children have urgent need of food and water, we would be grateful for your permission to have these provided.'

He signed an order to that effect, dismissed his henchmen, and settled down to go to sleep with his head on the knees of the Crown Prince Mirza Akbar Shah, having taken off his sword and dagger and placed them within sight and reach of the princes. He closed his eyes for an hour, then got up and gave each of the princes a violent slap, calling out derisively: 'You are prepared so passively to swallow all this, and still you delude yourselves that you could become kings?

Huh! I was testing you: if you had one little spark of manly honour in your heart, you would have grabbed my sword and dagger and made quick work of me!' Heaping them with abuse, he dismissed them from his presence and sent them back to prison.[125]

In despair, a few of the princes threw themselves over the ramparts of the palace and were drowned in the Yamuna. In time, several others died from hunger: 'Salty the Eunuch (*Namakin Khwaja-sara*) entered to announce that a ten-year-old child of Shah Alam had just expired of thirst and hunger. But the Rohilla shouted: "Just dig a hole where it fell and throw it in, and don't bother to change the clothes it was wearing!"'[126]

In the days which followed, Ghulam Qadir broke the last remaining taboo as he turned his attention on the sacred, forbidden royal women. On 29 August, the Dowager Empress Malika-i-Zamani Begum was stripped of her clothes and left in the sun without food or water. The same day a number of the younger princesses were stripped naked, minutely searched 'in every orifice', fondled, flogged, then raped. Victorian translations of the sources have censored these passages, but the Persian original of Khair ud-Din tells the whole brutal story. One evening, Ghulam Qadir was told of 'the beautiful daughters of Mirza Hika and Mirza Jhaka; so that evening, he had those poor unfortunates brought to the Moti Mahal and had them placed before him without veil or covering, and lost himself in gazing on their beauty'.

He then invited in his like-minded most intimate henchmen into that private place to show them those peerless beauties and then gave them each to be enjoyed at leisure and in sin. When Bedar Shah heard what was going on, he beat his head and chest and sent a mace-bearer to that lying trickster to stop it. The official came back making excuses, saying: 'What can a servant like me say to a warlord like him?'

Bedar Shah then appealed to Ghulam Qadir in person, shouting: 'You cannot behave like this, it's outrageous, even to the daughters of your enemy! The sins of the fathers are not to be visited on their children! Not once did Shah Alam even look disrespectfully at your father's daughters or sisters! Stop behaving like this!' But Ghulam Qadir just threw a stone at him: 'I want to have these girls sent into my harem as my concubines, to fuck them at will! I want to give all the princes' daughters to my Afghans: from their sperm will arise a new generation of young men, manly and courageous! During the sack of Pathargarh, the royal officers behaved much worse than this with my father's serving-maids! Just think you are witnessing a return of those times when my henchmen grab the princesses and take them off to their own quarters to enjoy them without even a token marriage ceremony.'[127]

As Azfari put it: 'If even a fraction of the calamities and misfortunes of this time be described, if it be heard, anyone hearing it would go deaf. And if your hearing were to survive, and if you were still capable of compassion, your gall bladder would surely burst with sorrow.'[128]

It took until the middle of September for Mahadji Scindia to gather sufficient troops and war materiel to come to the Emperor's aid. It was again the monsoon and progress was slow for, as usual, the flooded roads made all movements impossibly difficult. It was not until the 21st that the Maratha force arrived at Shahdara. There they liaised with Anupgiri's warrior Gossains and a battalion of sepoys sent from Sardhana by the Begum Sumru and the man with whom she had taken up since the death of her husband in April 1778. This was an Irish mercenary called George Thomas, 'the Raja from Tipperary', a one-time cabin boy who had jumped ship in Madras and made a name for himself as a talented artilleryman and caster of cannon.

To lead his attack on Ghulam Qadir, Scindia had sent two of his most trusted lieutenants. One was Rana Khan, who seventeen years earlier had found Scindia bleeding to death in a ditch after the Battle of Panipat, and had carried him to safety. In thanks for saving his life and nursing him back to health, Scindia had trained up this Muslim former *bhisti*, or water-carrier; and his own talents and bravery led to his rapid promotion to be one of Scindia's most senior generals. The other leader of the rescue operation was the refined Savoyard mercenary Benoît de

Boigne, who had just been begun training up a modern infantry army for Scindia.

On 29 September, when the relief force crossed the river, to their surprise they found the city gates open. They made their way through the eerily deserted city, then took up position surrounding the Red Fort, besieging and blockading it as they waited for their artillery to make its slow progress through the monsoon-clogged roads.

Three days later, at noon on 2 October, just as Scindia's siege guns were nearing the city, the Delhi skies were rent asunder by a monumental explosion: 'The sound of it brought to mind the trumpet call of the angel of death on the Day of Judgment,' wrote Azfari. 'The darkening of the day from the explosion of the magazine, whose flying gunpowder, cannon, doors and walls blighted the air with dust and fumes, brought to mind the Quranic verse: "When the sun is shrouded in darkness." The toppling of the battlements of the fort, the breaking of the doors and walls and the collapse of sturdy roofs in the area – all could be rendered by the verse: "And the mountains will be like fluffy tufts of wool."'

> Inhabitants of my area of the fort, due to their great proximity to the magazine, were killed in large numbers; but several of my brothers and one of my aunts, by the grace of God, were still alive, though they had suffered heavy injuries. The sky was dark as cannon, rocks, bricks and plaster rained down from the air. The sound of groans and cries rose to the sky: we recognised the voices shrieking in distress, but could not see each other's faces for the dust and smoke. The sound of this terrifying explosion was audible as far away as Bahadur Garh, twenty miles from Delhi. Each man shook and asked: 'Has the sky fallen down on the earth?'[129]

As the clouds of smoke began to disperse the survivors peered down over the terrace of the Fort to see a succession of boats being rowed steadily upstream, while a single elephant loaded with treasure was lumbering up the riverbank. After almost three months, Ghulam Qadir had finally departed, taking with him everything he had plundered, along with nineteen of the senior princes, including Prince Akbar, as hostages. The badly wounded Shah Alam he left behind in the Red Fort, apparently hoping he would be incinerated by the explosion he set off as a final parting present to the Mughals.[130]

Anupgiri, perhaps guilt-stricken at having deserted his post nine weeks earlier, was one of the first into the Fort; with a small party of men, he shinned up a rope let down by one of the princes, opened the gates to the rest of the army and began extinguishing the fires. As they did so, the surviving members of the royal family began to emerge from their hiding places. The sight shocked even the most battle-hardened members of the relief force. Unkempt, smoke-blackened, skeletal and dirty, the princes and princesses gathered around their rescuers and sobbed with relief.

The sight of the Emperor was even more traumatic. He had somehow managed to barricade himself into his prison cell and had to be cajoled out by Rana Khan.[131] He initially refused all treatment. When a surgeon was sent to dress his wounds, he 'turned out the surgeon, and flung the ointment for his eyes on the ground, saying "many of my children and grandchildren have already died of hunger and thirst, and now we are also waiting for death."'[132]

While Rana Khan took charge of the Emperor and his fort, bringing in food and water, as well as a number of barbers to trim the imperial beards, the Begum Sumru and de Boigne set off in search of Ghulam Qadir and his treasure. The Rohilla was heading towards Pathargarh but had only made it as far as the fort of Meerut when, on 12 December, the pursuing forces caught up and surrounded him. Without the provisions to withstand a siege, he decided to abandon his hostages and try and break out that very night, 'attended by 500 horse, who were still attached to him. At their head, he rushed out of the fort and charged the enemy so vigorously that though every endeavour was made to take him prisoner, he made his way through the whole line, and accomplished his escape.'[133]

He did not get far. Like Siraj ud-Daula, he had made himself too notorious to slip away unnoticed. 'In the darkness of the night his companions lost him,' wrote Khair ud-Din. 'He went one way and they went another.'

> He endeavoured to find them but did not succeed. The road was full of water and mud, and the horse putting his foot into a hole, rolled Ghulam Qadir into a ditch. The night was dark, and the way bristled with thorny acacias, so that he knew not what way to turn. When morning came, seeing some inhabited place, he proceeded thither. On

reaching the habitation, he put his head into the house of a Brahmin. But the Brahmin, in days gone by, had suffered at the hands of the ruffian, and his village had been ravaged. His oppressor was now in his power, and having invited him in, he made the door fast.[134]

The Brahmin sent a message to his zamindar, who in turn alerted the Marathas. At noon, Scindia's men rode into the village and surrounded the house. They then seized Ghulam Qadir, bound him and locked him in a cage. They despatched him on a humble bullock cart, with chains on his legs and a collar around his neck, to Scindia's headquarters, 'guarded by two regiments of sepoys and a thousand horse'. For a while Ghulam Qadir was displayed in his cage, suspended in front of the army, to be jeered at and mocked.[135] Then, 'By the orders of Scindia, the ears of Ghulam Qadir were cut off and hung around his neck, his face was blackened, and he was carried around the city.'

> The next day his nose, tongue and upper lip were cut off, and he was again paraded. On the third day, he was thrown upon the ground, his eyes were scooped out, and he was once more carried round. After that his hands were cut off, then his feet, then his genitals and last of all, his head. The corpse was then hung, neck downwards, from a tree. A trustworthy person relates that a black dog, white around the eyes, came and sat under a tree and licked up the blood as it dripped. The spectators threw stones and clods at it, but still it kept there. On the third day, the corpse disappeared, and so did the dog.[136]

Mahadji Scindia sent the ears and eyeballs to the Emperor Shah Alam in a casket as a congratulatory gift. He then had Mansur Ali Khan, the head eunuch who had let the Afghans into the fort, 'trampled to death under the feet of an elephant'.[137] But by this stage, Shah Alam had ceased to worry about this world. When the Begum Sumru came to pay her respects, she found him sitting serenely amid the charred debris of the Shah Burj, quietly reciting from the Quran. He had already composed a couplet that he recited to her:

> The winds of calamity have been unleashed by our mutilation
> Our imperial rule has been cruelly laid waste

The exalted Sun (*Aftab*) of Kingship once illuminated the heavens,
Now we lament the darkness of our ruin as dusk descends upon us

That misbegotten son of an Afghan scattered our royal dignity
Who now, except God, could befriend us?

We suckled the spawn of a serpent, we nurtured him
But in the end, he became our executioner

Rife with danger are the riches and honours of this world
Now Fate has rendered our sufferings eternal

Now that this young Afghan has destroyed the dignity of my State,
I see none but thee, Most High!

Lord, have pity on me,
A sinner.

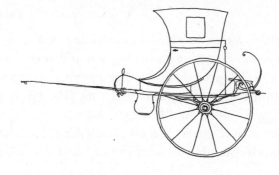

8

The Impeachment of Warren Hastings

At noon on 13 February 1788, while Ghulam Qadir was preparing for his assault on Delhi, in London huge crowds had gathered outside Parliament to witness the members of the House of Lords process into Westminster Hall to impeach Warren Hastings.

Tickets for the few seats reserved for spectators changed hands for as much as £50,* and even then so many people wished to attend that, as one of the managers of the impeachment noted, the audience 'will have to mob it at the door till nine, when the doors open, and then there will be a rush as there is at the pit of the Playhouse when Garrick plays King Lear ... The ladies are dressed and in the Palace Yard by six [in the morning], and they sit from nine to twelve, before the business begins ... Some people, and I believe, even ladies, have slept at the coffeehouses adjoining Westminster Hall, that they may be sure of getting in the door in time.'[1]

In addition to the 170 lords, there were bewigged and ermined judges, black-robed lawyers for both sides, and 200 members of the House of Commons. The Queen, 'dressed in fawn-coloured satin, her

---

* £5,250 today.

head dress plain, with a very slender sprinkling of diamonds', took her place in the Royal Box, along with her son and two of her daughters, the Duchess of Gloucester, and other attendants, among them the Dukes of Cumberland, Gloucester and York. The Prince of Wales was there with Charles James Fox. Among those who queued for admission were the great society actress and courtesan Sarah Siddons, the painter Joshua Reynolds, the diarist Fanny Burney and the historian Edward Gibbon.

For all the theatre of the occasion – indeed one of the prosecutors was the playwright Richard Brinsley Sheridan – this was not just the greatest political spectacle in the age of George III, it was the nearest the British ever got to putting the Company's Indian Empire on trial. They did so with one of their greatest orators at the helm – the Anglo-Irish Whig statesman and political theorist Edmund Burke, supported by his no less eloquent and much more radical rival, Charles James Fox.

Warren Hastings stood accused of nothing less than the rape of India – or as Burke put it in his opening speech, 'with injustice and treachery against the faith of nations':

> With various instances of extortion and other deeds of maladministration ... With impoverishing and depopulating the whole country ... with a wanton, and unjust, and pernicious, exercise of his powers ... in overturning the ancient establishments of the country ... With cruelties unheard of and devastations almost without name ... Crimes which have their rise in the wicked dispositions of men – in avarice, rapacity, pride, cruelty, malignity, haughtiness, insolence, ferocity, treachery, cruelty, malignity of temper – in short, nothing that does not argue a total extinction of all moral principle, that does not manifest an inveterate blackness of heart, a heart blackened to the very blackest, a heart corrupted, gangrened to the core ... We have brought before you the head, the Captain General of Iniquity – one in whom all the frauds, all the peculations, all the violence, all the tyranny in India are embodied.[2]

Hastings, Burke explained, was, quite simply, a criminal: 'He *is* a robber. He steals, he filches, he plunders, he oppresses, he extorts.' He was 'a professor, a doctor upon the subject' of crime.[3] Worse was to come. Hastings, said Burke, was also 'a rat', 'a weasel', 'a keeper of a pig stye, wallowing in corruption'. 'Like a wild beast, he groans in corners over the dead and dying.'[4]

Every bit as bad as the man was the institution he represented. Because it was a Company, a corporation, that was governing Bengal, there were, believed Burke, none of the usual checks and balances which could make national government just and legitimate: 'The East India Company in India is not the British nation,' he declaimed. 'When the Tartars entered China and into Hindoostan, when all the Goths and Vandals entered Europe, when the Normans came into England, they did so as a Nation.'

> The Company in India does not exist as a Nation. Nobody can go there that does not go in its service ... They are a Nation of Placemen. They are a Republic, a Commonwealth, without a people ... The consequence of which is that there are no people to control, to watch, to balance against the power of office ...
>
> Out of this has issued a species of abuse, at the head of which Mr Hastings has put himself against the authority of the East India Company at home and every authority in the Country ... He has corrupted his hands and sullied his government with bribes. He has used oppression and tyranny in place of legal government; and instead of endeavouring to find honest, honourable and adequate rewards for the persons who served the public, he has left them to prey upon it without the slightest degree of control.[5]

Burke then paused for effect, before launching into his thunderous climax:

> I impeach, therefore, Warren Hastings, Esquire, of High Crimes and Misdemeanours. I impeach him in the name of the Commons of Great Britain in Parliament assembled, whose Parliamentary trust he has betrayed. I impeach him in the name of the Commons of Great Britain, whose national character he has dishonoured. I impeach him in the name of the people of India, whose laws, rights and liberties he has subverted, whose properties he has destroyed, whose country he has laid waste. I impeach him in the name and by virtue of those eternal laws of justice which he has violated. I impeach him in the name of human nature itself, which he has cruelly outraged, injured and oppressed, in both sexes, in every age, rank, situation and condition of life.[6]

Burke's opening speech alone took four days. In it he alleged widespread use of torture by the Company in its ruthless search for plunder, and he accused Hastings of 'geographical morality ... as if when you have crossed the equatorial line all the virtues die'. Natural law, he said, meant that justice and human rights were universal: 'the laws of morality,' he declared, 'are the same everywhere, and there is no action which would pass for an act of extortion, of peculation, of bribery, and oppression in England which would not be an act of extortion, of peculation, of bribery, and oppression in Europe, Asia, Africa and the world over.'[7]

Company rule, he continued, had done nothing for India, except to asset-strip it: 'Every rupee of profit made by an Englishman is lost to India for ever. Every other conqueror ... has left some monument behind him. Were we to be driven out of India this day, nothing would remain to tell that it had been possessed, during the inglorious period of our domination, by anything better than an ouran-outang or the tiger ... [The Company appears] more like an army going to pillage the people under the pretence of commerce than anything else ... [Their business is] more like robbery than trade.'[8] Now, he argued, it was the duty of those gathered in judgement to ensure that corporations, like individuals, must be held accountable to Parliament.

When Burke began to describe the violation of Bengali virgins and their mothers by the Company's tax collectors – 'they were dragged out, naked and exposed to the public view, and scourged before all the people ... they put the nipples of the women into the sharp edges of split bamboos and tore them from their bodies' – several women in the audience fainted. According to Macaulay, 'the ladies in the galleries, unaccustomed to such displays of eloquence, were in a state of uncontrollable emotion. Handkerchiefs were pulled out; smelling bottles were handed around; hysterical sobs and screams were heard; and Mrs Sheridan was carried out in a fit.'[9]

Sheridan himself then took over, further outlining the prosecution case and holding forth for four more days. He too took a prolonged tilt at Hastings' alleged moral darkness which he compared to 'the writhing obliquity of the serpent ... shuffling, ambiguous, dark, insidious'. As for his employers, the Company, they combined 'the meanness of a pedlar and the profligacy of pirates ... wielding a truncheon in one hand, and picking a pocket with the other'.[10]

His speech was widely regarded as one of the greatest feats of oratory of his day. Even the Speaker was rendered speechless. At the end of his impassioned performance, Sheridan whispered, 'My lords, I have done', and swooned backwards, landing in Burke's arms. 'The whole house – the members, peers, strangers – involuntarily joined in a tumult of applause … There were few dry eyes in the assembly.'[11] Gibbon, alarmed at his friend's condition, went around the following day to check if Sheridan was all right: 'He is perfectly well,' he noted in his diary. 'A good actor.'[12]

Some of the Prosecution's charges and insights – such as the idea of universal human or 'natural' rights – were important, even profound.[13] Much of the rest was terrifically entertaining and scandalous. The only problem was that, thanks to the machinations of the ever-vindictive Philip Francis, Parliament had impeached the wrong man.

Earlier in his career, Burke had defended Robert Clive against parliamentary enquiry, and so helped exonerate someone who genuinely was a ruthlessly unprincipled plunderer. Now he directed his skills of oratory against Warren Hastings, a man who, by virtue of his position, was certainly the symbol of an entire system of mercantile oppression in India, but who had personally done much to begin the process of regulating and reforming the Company, and who had probably done more than any other Company official to rein in the worst excesses of its rule.

The impeachment had been Philip Francis's final revenge on the man who had shot him during their duel and whom he had continued to hate with an obsessional passion. As soon as he recovered from his duelling wound in October 1780, Francis had given in his resignation and caught ship to London. There he used his new Indian wealth to buy a parliamentary seat and begin lobbying to bring Hastings down.

In February 1782, he found a sympathetic ear in Edmund Burke, then a rising Whig star. Burke had never been to India, but part of his family had been ruined by unwise speculation in East India stock. Together Burke and Francis worked on a series of Select Committee reports exposing the Company's misdeeds in India. Before he met Francis, Burke had described himself as 'a great admirer' of Hastings' talents.[14] Francis quickly worked his dark magic to change that. By April 1782, he had drawn up a portentous list of twenty-two charges against Hastings which Burke then brought to the House.[15] In May

1787, after five years of obsessive campaigning to blacken Hastings' name and reputation, Burke and Francis persuaded Parliament that there was enough evidence to impeach him. On the 21st, the recently returned Hastings was taken into custody by the Serjeant-at-Arms, who passed him on to Black Rod. He was then made to kneel at the bar of the Lords, bow his head and hear the charges against him.

Hastings was certainly no angel; and the EIC under his rule was as extractive as ever. After Francis's departure, Hastings began to take a more old-fashioned, pseudo-monarchical and even despotic idea of his powers, something Burke particularly disliked.[16] Moreover, during the military crisis of the early 1780s, in the aftermath of victories by the armies of Tipu and the Marathas, when it looked as if the Company might easily be driven out of India, Hastings had been forced to raise money quickly to fight the war and to save Madras and Calcutta. He chose to raise it by pressuring the Company's princely allies to contribute, and he used some extremely dubious means to gather the sums he needed. These included bullying the Nawab of Lucknow, Asaf ud-Daula, forcefully to strip the wealth of his purdah-bound aunts, the Begums of Avadh. He also personally used strong-arm tactics on Chait Singh, the Raja of Benares, an intervention that caused a local uprising and nearly cost Hastings his life. There were other dubious decisions, too. In particular, Hastings had failed to intervene with a pardon to save the life of Nandakumar, a former Diwan of the Nawab of Bengal, who had faked evidence of Hastings' corruption which he handed to Philip Francis. Nandakumar had then been sentenced to death for forgery by Hastings' old Westminster schoolfriend, the Calcutta Chief Justice, Sir Elijah Impey. This opened Hastings up to charges of failing to prevent what Burke and Francis viewed as the convenient 'judicial murder' of a whistleblower.

All of these were potentially grave charges. But Hastings was nevertheless by far the most responsible and sympathetic of all the officials the Company had yet sent to India. From his early twenties, his letters had been full of outrage at the unprincipled way Company officials were exploiting India and mistreating Indians. He had many close Indian friends and regarded himself as an honourable champion of justice for the people of Bengal. He had railed and campaigned against those who were plundering the country and wrecking the Bengali economy and he did his best to set it on a more prosperous and sustainable path. He took concrete measures to make sure there was no repetition of the terrible famine of 1770, including building the great Gola in Patna, which survives to this day. His successor said that in Bengal he was by far the most popular of all the British officials in India, 'positively beloved of the people'.[17]

Nor did he even look the part: far from being an ostentatious and loud-mouthed new-rich 'Nabob', Hastings was a dignified, intellectual and somewhat austere figure. Standing gaunt at the bar in his plain black frock coat, white stockings and grey hair, he looked more Puritan minister about to give a sermon than some paunchy plunderer: nearly six feet tall, he weighed less than eight stone: 'of spare habit, very bald, with a countenance placid and thoughtful, but when animated, full of intelligence.'

As a result of Francis's influence, the Articles of Impeachment were full of demonstrable fantasies and distortions, which traded on the ignorance of the audience about the issues and personalities involved. They were also badly drafted and lacked the necessary legal detail. Many of the more entertaining speeches were little better than ad hominem rants, mixing falsified history and unproved innuendo. Hastings did not begin his career as 'as a fraudulent bullock contractor'. Chait Singh of Benares was not, as alleged, 'a sovereign prince'. Hastings had not been the one declaring war on the Marathas. He had never given orders 'to extirpate the Rohillas'. The Begum of Avadh's eunuchs were never scourged.[18] It took Hastings' defence many weeks even to begin correcting the multiple errors of basic facts which the prosecution had laid out.

If anything, the Impeachment demonstrated above all the sheer ignorance of the British about the subcontinent they had been looting so comprehensively, and profitably, for thirty years. Indeed, some of the charges were almost comically confused: the illiterate and piratical Rohilla Afghan warlord Hafiz Rehmat Khan, for example, was conflated by Burke with the fourteenth-century mystical Persian love poet Hafez, who had been dead in his grave for 400 years by the time of the Impeachment.[19]

Few were surprised when, after seven years, on 23 April 1795, Hastings was ultimately cleared of all charges. But it scarred the final decades of his life, leading to what he described as 'years of depression & persecution … Besides crimes of the most atrocious lies which were alleged against me, I was loaded by all the managers in succession, through the whole course of their pleadings in the trial, with language of the foulest abuse, aggravated by coarse and vulgar epithets, of which there had never been any examples in the jurisprudence of this or any other country.'[20]

The trial, however misconceived and misdirected, did have one useful outcome: to demonstrate that the Company's many misdeeds were answerable to Parliament, and it helped publicise the corruption, violence and venality of the EIC, so setting the stage for further governmental oversight, regulation and control. This was a process which had already begun with the 1773 Regulating Act and had been further enhanced by Pitt's India Act of 1784, which made the Company's political and military transactions subject to government supervision. It eventually culminated in the outright nationalisation of the Company seventy years later in 1858, but by 1784 the writing was already on the wall. In that year Alexander Dalrymple, the Company's now retired hydrographer, put it with utmost clarity and confidence: 'The East India Company must be considered in two lights', he wrote, 'as commercial and political; but the two are inseparable: and if the politics are not made subservient to the commerce, the destruction of the Company must ensue.'[21]

Amid all the spectacle of Hastings' trial, it made sense that the man sent out to replace him was chosen by Parliament specifically for his incorruptibility. General Lord Charles Cornwallis had surrendered the thirteen American Colonies of the British Empire over to George Washington, who then declared it a free and independent nation.

Cornwallis's mission was now to make sure that the same never happened in India.

On arrival in Calcutta in August 1786, Cornwallis inherited a far more flourishing Bengal than the famine-wrecked dustbowl which had greeted Hastings fourteen years earlier.

This was at least partly the result of the reforms Hastings had brought in. Calcutta itself had turned into a boomtown with a population of around 400,000, more than double that at the time of Plassey. Now known as the City of Palaces or the St Petersburg of the East to its British inhabitants, and the Paradise of Nations, *Zannat-al-Bilad* to the old Mughal aristocracy, the Company's bridgehead in Bengal was unquestionably the richest, largest and most elegant colonial city in the East: 'Imagine everything that is glorious in nature combined with everything that is beautiful in architecture,' wrote the newly arrived William Hunter, 'and you can faintly picture to yourself what Calcutta is.'[22]

The city was prosperous and fast growing. All it lacked was proper planning regulations: 'It is not without astonishment and some irritation that a stranger looks at the city of Calcutta,' wrote the Comte de Modave. 'It would have been so easy to turn it into one of the most beautiful cities in the world, by just following a regular planned layout; one cannot fathom why the English failed to take advantage of such a fine location, allowing everyone the freedom to build in the most bizarre taste, with the most outlandish planning. With the exception of two or three properly aligned streets, the rest is a labyrinth of winding narrow lanes. An effect, it is said, of British liberty, as if such liberty were incompatible with good order and symmetry.'[23]

Nor was it just the British who did well out of this new boom or who lived extravagantly: Bengali merchant and money-lending dynasties also flourished. The Mullick family, for example, had rambling baroque palaces strewn around the city and used to travel around Calcutta in an ornate carriage drawn by two zebras. But the boom reached down to benefit more humble Bengali labourers, too: by the end of the 1780s, their wages had risen by around 50 per cent in a decade.[24]

The finances of Bengal were in fact in a healthier state than they had been since the time of the Aliverdi Khan in the 1740s and 1750s: by the end of the decade, Cornwallis was able to report back to London that revenues exceeded expenditure by £2 million. After meeting deficits elsewhere, this left £1.3 million for the 'investment' to purchase export goods, which Cornwallis estimated would sell in London for £2.4 million.*[25] After a period on the edge, the Company was now back in business and making a healthy profit. Part of these profits came from

---

* The modern equivalences of these sums are: £2 million = £210 million; £1.3 million = £136 million; £2.4 million = £252 million.

the successful introduction of new cash crops like sugar, opium and indigo, but much was simply due to the natural fecundity of Bengal, which always produced large surpluses of rice each year. The same Bengali agricultural revenues which had once sustained the Mughal Empire now sustained the Company Raj.[26]

It was not just agriculture and land revenues which had turned around. Trade was flourishing, too. Since the low point of the Company's near bankruptcy in 1772, exports from Bengal had grown fivefold and now exceeded Rs15 million, or around £5 million. There was every sign that this looked likely to continue.[27] Fine Bengali textiles – especially cotton piece goods, muslins and fine silks – were selling well, to the tune of Rs28 million* annually, as was Malwa opium and Gujarati cotton; but the biggest success story was tea from China.[28] By 1795, tea sales had doubled in less than a decade to 20 million pounds (9,000 tons); one former director of the EIC wrote that it was as if tea had become 'the food of the whole people of Great Britain'.[29] The only thing holding back further growth was the question of supply: 'the demand for Bengal goods exceed double the quantity that can be procured,' Cornwallis reported back to London.

As a result, the shortages of bullion which had paralysed the Bengal economy in the 1770s were now long forgotten: the Calcutta mint was now striking Rs2.5 million** of coins each year.[30] In every way, the Company holdings in eastern India – the Three Provinces of Bengal, Bihar and Orissa – were now effectively the richest of all the regional post-Mughal successor states dotted around South Asia, with resources many times greater than any of their rivals.

All this meant that the Company state was able to keep building its army and apportion over £3 million annually to military expenditure, a sum no other South Asian power could possibly match.[31] From 2,900 sepoys in 1757 after Plassey, the Bengal army had grown to around 50,000 men by the arrival of Cornwallis.[32] The Company also had the pick of the best candidates in the military labour market since it paid its sepoys significantly more, and more regularly, than anyone else: Bengal army sepoys classed as 'gentlemen

---

* The modern equivalences of these sums are: £5 million = £525 million today; Rs28 million = £364 million.

** Rs2.5 million = £32.5 million today.

troopers' earned around Rs300 a year, while their equivalents in Mysore earned annually only Rs192 (four times the Rs48 Tipu paid an ordinary soldier); those in Avadh earned annually as little as Rs80.*[33] As Burton Stein nicely put it: 'The colonial conquest of India was as much bought as fought.'[34]

These sepoys were in turn supported by a sophisticated war machine, run out of the armouries of Fort William and the arms factories of Dumdum. When in 1787 the Hyderabadi minister Mir Alam spent several months in Calcutta he was amazed at the scale of the Company's Calcutta military establishments. He was particularly impressed by the arsenals he saw in Fort William: 'Three hundred thousand muskets hung up in good order and easy to collect, ammunitions factories hard at work, and two to three thousand cannons in place with five to six thousand more in reserve and ready for use.'[35] Forty years earlier, in 1750, the Company had been a trading corporation with a small security force and a few crumbling forts; by 1790 it had effectively transformed its Indian holdings into a tightly run fiscal-military state guarded by the most powerful army in Asia.

So when, in 1791, war once again loomed with Tipu Sultan of Mysore, Cornwallis's armies could now draw on unprecedented manpower, weaponry and military materiel. There was good reason for the Company generals to be confident: if war with Tipu was unavoidable they would now have a good opportunity of avenging their abject defeat at Pollilur twelve years earlier.

In 1783, Haidar Ali of Mysore had died of a suppurating tumour 'the size of a dinner plate' on his back. His son Tipu moved quickly to take over his father's throne.

The Governor of Madras called Tipu 'the youthful and spirited heir of Haidar, without the odium of his father's vices or his tyranny'.[36] According to one British observer, Tipu, now thirty-three, was 'about

---

* £3 million = £315 million; Rs300 = £3,900; Rs192 = £2,496; Rs48 = £624; Rs80 = £1,040.

5ft 7ins in height, uncommonly well-made, except in the neck, which was short, his leg, ankle and foot beautifully proportioned, his arms large and muscular, with the appearance of great strength, but his hands rather too fine and delicate for a soldier ... He was remarkably fair for a Mussulman in India, thin, delicately made, with an interesting, mild countenance, of which large animated black eyes were the most conspicuous feature.'[37]

On his deathbed, Haidar had written to Tipu with advice to his son on the art of good government. He warned him that the Company would attempt to exploit any weakness in the succession: 'The greatest obstacle you have to conquer is the jealousy of the Europeans,' he wrote. 'The English are today all-powerful in India. It is necessary to weaken them by war.'

He suggested that Tipu's best chance of doing this lay in dividing and ruling: 'The resources of Hindustan do not suffice to expel the English from the lands they have invaded. Put the nations of Europe one against the other. It is by the aid of the French that you could conquer the British armies, which are better trained than those of India. The Europeans have surer tactics; always use against them their own weapons.'

He then bade his son farewell and good luck: 'If God had allowed me a longer career, you need only have enjoyed the success of my enterprises.'

But I leave you for achieving them rich provinces, a population of twelve million souls, troops, treasures and immense resources. I need not awaken your courage. I have seen you often fight by my side, and you shall be the inheritor of my glory. Remember above all that valour can elevate us to the throne, but it does not suffice to keep it. While we may seize a crown owing to the timidity of the people, it can escape us if we do not make haste to entrust it to their love.[38]

Tipu was already one of the most feared and admired military commanders in India: able and brave, methodical and hard-working, he was above all innovative, determined to acquire the arsenal of European skills and knowledge, and to find ways to use them against his enemies. Tipu had already proved his capacity to do this on the battlefield, defeating the Company not only at Pollilur but also twice more since then: in 1782, he had annihilated another British army under Colonel John Braithwaite just outside Tanjore and then, a year later, immediately before his accession, ambushed and destroyed a third Company column on the banks of the Coleroon River. The surprise was that within a few years Tipu showed that he was just as imaginative in peace as he had been in war.

Tipu began to import industrial technology through French engineers and experimented with harnessing water power to drive his machinery. He sent envoys to southern China to bring back silkworm eggs and established sericulture in Mysore, something that still enriches the region today. He introduced irrigation and built dams so that even his British enemies had to admit that his kingdom was 'well cultivated, populous with industrious inhabitants, cities [including Bangalore] newly founded and commerce extended'.

More remarkably still, he created what amounted to a state trading company with its own ships and factories. Regulations issued to Tipu's 'commercial department' survive, providing details of a state trade in valuable commodities such as sandalwood, silk, spices, coconut, rice, sulphur, and elephants imported into and exported from Srirangapatnam. Trade centres were established in thirty places in Mysore and other places on the western coast as far north as Kutch, as well as in Pondicherry and Hyderabad. Officials were encouraged to recruit suitably trained assistants to run such markets, and each was to be placed under oath according to their religion. Capital for trade was to be provided from the revenue collected by state officials and provision was made for accepting deposits of private persons as investments in the state trade with fixed returns. Other factories were established at Muscat and dotted across the Persian Gulf. Tipu even asked his ambassadors to Ottoman Istanbul to secure for him the *ijara* – farm – of Basra so that, like the Europeans, he could establish an overseas settlement which would be a base for his vessels.[39]

Keeping in mind his father's advice to win the love of his subjects, Tipu went out of his way to woo and protect the Hindus of his own dominions. From the beginning of his reign he had loaded the temples of his realm with presents, honours and land. Few of his chancery records survive, but from the temple archives of the region we know, for example, that in 1784 he gave a land grant to one Venkatachala Sastri and a group of Brahmins, begging them 'to pray for the length of his life and prosperity'. A year later he sent the temple complex of Melkote twelve elephants and a kettledrum, while also sending a Sanskrit verse recording his grant of lands 'to the temples and Brahmins on the banks of the Tungabhadra'. So it continued at the rate of at least three or four major endowments or gifts of money, bells, pensions, villages, jewels or '*padshah lingams*' per year, for the rest of his reign, mostly in return for requests for prayers, *pujas* 'for the success of the King's armies' or temple processions.[40]

But it was the great temple of Sringeri that always received his most generous patronage, as a stash of correspondence discovered within the temple in the 1950s bears witness. Tipu put on record his horror at the damage done to the temple by a Maratha Pindari raiding party during a Maratha invasion of Mysore: 'People who have sinned against such a holy place are sure to suffer the consequences of their misdeeds,' wrote Tipu. 'Those who commit evil deeds smiling, will reap the consequences weeping. Treachery to gurus will undoubtedly result in the destruction of the line of descent.'[41]

Sending a large sum of cash and a consignment of grain 'for the consecration of the goddess Sarada', and to 'feed one thousand Brahmins', Tipu asked the Swami 'please to pray for the increase of our prosperity and the destruction of our enemies'. Shortly after this, he sent another note, along with a present of an elephant, writing that 'wrong-doers to gurus and our country will soon perish by the grace of God! Those who took away elephants, horses, palanquins and other things from your monastery will surely be punished by God. Cloth for the Goddess has been sent. Please consecrate the Goddess, and pray for our welfare and the destruction of our foes.'[42]

This was not just a matter of statecraft. Tipu, despite being a devout Muslim and viewing himself as a champion of Islam, thoroughly embraced the syncretic culture of his time and believed strongly in the power of Hindu gods. In his dreams, which he diligently recorded every morning in a dream book, Tipu encountered not only long-dead Sufi saints, but also Hindu gods and goddesses: in one dream sequence, there are references to him finding himself in a ruined temple with idols whose eyes moved: one talked to him and as a result Tipu ordered the temple rebuilt.[43] It is recorded that Tipu made all his troops, Hindu and Muslim, take ritual baths in holy rivers 'by the advice of his [Brahmin] augurs' in order to wash away cowardice and make them superior in battle to the Marathas. Tipu also strongly believed in the supernatural powers of holy men, both Hindu and Muslim. As he wrote in 1793 to the Swami of Sringeri: 'You are the *Jagatguru*, the preceptor of the world ... in whatever country holy personages like you may reside, that country will prosper with good showers and crops.'[44]

The British consistently portrayed Tipu as a savage and fanatical barbarian, but he was in truth a connoisseur and an intellectual, with a library containing some 2,000 volumes in several languages, mainly on law, theology and the secular sciences, as well as amassing a large collection of modern scientific instruments including thermometers and barometers.[45] When in the course of a raid on the outskirts of Madras, Tipu's troops captured some scholarly volumes on Indian botany, Tipu had the books rebound and added to his library. The culture of innovation Tipu fostered in Mysore stands record to a man very different from that imagined by Calcutta: a modernising technocrat who, as Christopher Bayly nicely put it, attempted to fight 'European mercantilist power with its own weapons: state monopoly and an aggressive ideology of expansion'. His imported French military technology was if anything more advanced than that of the Company; he failed only because the resources of the Company were now larger, and expanding significantly faster, than those of Mysore.

Tipu did, however, have some severe flaws which left him vulnerable to his enemies. For Tipu was prone, even by the standards of the time, to use unnecessary violence against his adversaries and those he defeated, creating many embittered enemies where conciliation would have been equally possible and much wiser. Rebels had their arms, legs, ears and noses cut off before being hanged. He routinely circumcised and brutally converted to Islam captive enemy combatants and internal rebels, both Hindu and Christians, Indian and British. More often than not he destroyed the temples and churches of those he conquered. He did this on a particularly horrific scale on his various campaigns in Malabar, Mangalore and Coorg. Huge numbers of people were forced to migrate from their homes: 60,000 Christians from the southern Carnatic to Mysore in one year alone.[46] Christian Portuguese missionaries wrote that 'he tied naked Christians and Hindus to the legs of elephants and made the elephants move around till the bodies of the helpless victims were torn to pieces'.

Allied to this often counter-productive aggression and megalomania was a fatal lack of diplomatic skills. When Cornwallis reached Calcutta in September 1786, Tipu was already at war with both the Maratha Peshwa and the Nizam of Hyderabad, both of whom had been allies of his father. Unlike Haidar, who joined the Triple Alliance coalition against the British, Tipu's aggressive attacks on his neighbours so alarmed both Marathas and Hyderabadis that, when courted by Cornwallis, they agreed to form a new Triple Alliance. This time the alliance would be with the Company, and it was aimed against Tipu's Mysore.

As if he had not made enough enemies, Tipu then decided to break off relations with Shah Alam, so becoming the first Indian ruler formally to disown even a nominal sovereignty to the Mughal Emperor. He ordered that the Friday sermon, the *khutbah*, should be read in his own name not that of the Emperor, observing that 'as to those idiots who introduce the name of Shah Alam into the *khutbah*, they act through ignorance, since the real condition of the so-called Emperor is this: that he is actually enslaved and a mere cypher, being the servant of Scindia at the monthly wages of Rs15,000.* Such being the case, to pronounce the name of a dependant of the infidels while reciting the sacred *khutbah* is a manifest sin.'[47]

Then, in December 1789, Tipu opened a new front. He had already conquered northern Malabar as far as Cochin; now he decided to bring to obedience the Raja of Travancore to its south. The Raja had protected himself with some remarkable fortifications known as the Travancore Lines: a forty-mile rampart flanked by a sixteen-foot ditch and topped by an impenetrable bamboo hedge. He had also signed a mutual defence pact with the Company.

So when, at daybreak on 29 December 1789, Tipu brought up his heavy artillery and blew a wide gap in the Travancore defences, sending in his crack Tiger Sepoys to massacre the unsuspecting Raja's troops, he suddenly found himself at war not only with the Marathas, the Hyderabadis and the people of Travancore – but also, yet again, with his oldest and bitterest enemy, the East India Company.

---

* £195,500 today.

The Third Anglo-Mysore War began, as had the previous two, with Tipu marching with unprecedented speed and violence into the Carnatic. He reached Trichinopoly in early December 1790, where he effortlessly outmanoeuvred a lumbering Company army. He then fell on the coast between Madras and Pondicherry, where his cavalry burned and devastated the undefended towns and villages. The great temple town of Tiruvannamalai was bloodily sacked in mid-January.

The Company had no ability to match the speed of Tipu's marches. One officer, Major James Rennell, recorded that the Mysore troops used to 'make three marches for one of ours ... The rapidity of Tippoo's marches was such that no army appointed like ours could ever bring it to action in the open country.'[48] This was partly because every Company officer travelled with at least six servants, a complete set of camp furniture, 'his stock of linens (at least 24 suits); some dozens of wine, brandy and gin; tea, sugar and biscuits; a hamper of live poultry and his milch goat'.[49] Tipu's troops had few such encumbrances.

But Cornwallis had no intention of allowing Tipu to run rings around him. He was also determined to redeem his military reputation, tarnished by his surrender to George Washington at Yorktown a decade earlier. So he decided to lead the counter-attack in person: 'We have lost time and our adversary has gained reputation, which are the two most valuable things in war,' wrote Cornwallis. 'I have no other part to take but to go myself ... and see whether I can do better.'[50]

In early February 1791, the portly figure of Marquess Cornwallis could be seen mounting his charger and trotting out of Madras at the head of an army of 19,000 sepoys. By 21 March he had climbed the Eastern Ghats and reached the plateau beyond without encountering opposition. He then seized by assault Tipu's second-largest city, Bangalore. Here he was joined by his Hyderabadi ally, Mir Alam, who brought with him 18,000 Mughal cavalry.

By May the combined force was ready and began the advance deep into Tipu's territory; but it was here that their problems began. Tipu had laid waste to the fields and villages on Cornwallis's line of march, so supplies of food were low and by the time they neared Tipu's island capital, Srirangapatnam, 10,000 Company transport bullocks had died; those that remained were so close to starvation they could hardly pull their loads. The dearth of carriage bullocks meant rank-and-file Europeans, sepoys and camp followers had to carry heavy ordnance for the artillery train on their backs. To add to Cornwallis's problems, sickness had broken out in the army and the monsoon arrived early, spoiling a large proportion of his rice rations and soaking his ailing troops. Low-caste followers were forced to survive on the decaying flesh of dead bullocks. Before long, smallpox was raging throughout the Company lines.[51] On 24 May, after a brief skirmish with Tipu, Cornwallis ordered his battering train and heavy guns to be destroyed and a muddy withdrawal to Bangalore to begin.

The retreating army had only marched for half a day when, near the temple town of Melkote, a troop of horses 2,000-strong appeared on the road in front of them. The alarm was raised and the first shots had been fired before it was realised that the cavalry were not Tipu's, but belonged to the Company's new Maratha allies. A much larger force came up soon after and was found to be carrying ample supplies for both Cornwallis's bullocks and his men.

After weeks of growing austerity and deprivation, the Company soldiers could hardly believe the profusion of goods available in the Maratha bazaar: 'English broadcloths, Birmingham pen-knives, the richest Kashmiri shawls, rare and costly jewellery together with oxen, sheep, poultry and all that the most flourishing towns could furnish.'[52] Famished sepoys and camp followers hurried into the Maratha camp to buy food at inflated prices. British officers bought up all the carriage bullocks they could and pressed them into service.[53] Together, the three allied armies marched back to Bangalore to sit out the rains and make preparations for a fresh attack when the monsoon subsided and the rivers had ebbed.

After two months of resting, feasting and military parades with their Maratha and Hyderabadi allies, Cornwallis sent his men off to begin besieging Tipu's mountain fortresses that guarded the remaining passes through the ghats. They started with those commanding the Nandi Hills, overlooking Bangalore, and the fearsome fort of Savandurga, perched on a near-vertical peak and believed to be one of the most impregnable fortresses in the Deccan. By New Year, Cornwallis had secured the safety of his supply routes and made sure that there would be no repetition of May's logistical failures.

Finally, on 26 January 1792, the three armies marched out of Bangalore for a second attempt to corner the Tiger of Mysore in his lair. Cornwallis now had 22,000 sepoys, plus 12,000 Marathas and a slightly larger number of Hyderabadis.[54]

Tipu had a larger army than this – more than 50,000 sepoys and cavalry troopers – but he was too careful a general to risk open battle against such a formidable force. Instead he stayed within the magnificent fortifications of Srirangapatnam which had been designed for him by French engineers on the latest scientific principles, following Sébastian de Vauban's research into artillery-resistant fortification designs, as adapted by the Marquis de Montalembert in his book *La Fortification Perpendiculaire*. These provided the most up-to-date defences that the eighteenth century could offer, and took into account the newly increased firepower of cannon, bombs and mines, as well as the latest developments in tactics for storming and laying siege to forts.[55] Penetrating these defences was the challenge now facing Cornwallis's army.

Late on 5 February 1792, the three armies arrived in front of the formidable walls of Srirangapatnam island for the second time. Without waiting for Tipu to make the first move, and without telling his allies of his plans, Cornwallis launched an immediate attack, taking advantage of the moonless night. He concentrated his initial fire on Tipu's fortified encampment on the high ground opposite the island which overlooked and guarded the bridges and fords over the Kaveri. Tipu, who had thought Cornwallis would wait until his entire force had assembled, was taken completely by surprise. He led a brave resistance for two hours, but by midnight had retreated onto the island and into the walls of his citadel.

Once Tipu had abandoned the encampment, and the fords were left unguarded, Cornwallis unleashed a second column towards the fortress at the eastern end of the island. By daybreak, the beautiful Lal Bagh, the Red Garden, was in Cornwallis's hands. James Kirkpatrick, who was in the second column, had gazed across the river and seen Tipu's magnificent Mughal-style garden palace, 'Lall Baug, in all its glory', the day before: 'Alas!' he wrote to his father, 'it fell sacrifice to the emergencies of war.' The palace was made a hospital for the wounded and the beautiful garden 'toppled to supply materials for the siege. Whole avenues of tall and majestic cypresses were in an instant laid low, nor was the orange, apple, sandal tree or even the fragrant bowers of rose and jasmine spared in this indiscriminate ruin. You might have seen in our batteries fascines of rose bushes, bound with jasmine and picketed with pickets of sandal wood. The very pioneers themselves became scented ...'[56]

Even the 'alarming mortality' among the European troops and the 'infectious exhalations from millions of putrid carcases that cover the whole surface of the earth for twenty miles around the capital', he wrote, could not blind him to the astonishing loveliness of the city he was engaged in besieging: 'The palaces and gardens both upon the island and without the city as far exceed the palace and gardens at Bangalore in extent, taste and magnificence, as they are said to fall short of the principal ones within the city.'[57]

The following day, Tipu made a series of ineffectual counter-attacks, but, as the hopelessness of his position became apparent, more and more of his troops deserted and he was forced to send a message to Cornwallis, through some captured Company officers, suggesting peace negotiations. Cornwallis accepted, but his terms were severe: Tipu must surrender half his kingdom, and pay an indemnity of 30 million rupees,* release all his prisoners of war, and give his two eldest sons as hostages to guarantee full payment. The borderlands next to the Marathas were to be handed over to the Peshwa; those next to Hyderabad to the Nizam; and the Company was to receive his territories in the Eastern Ghats as well as those in Coorg and spice-rich Malabar.

The treaty was finally signed, and the two young princes – Abdul Khaliq, who was eight, and Muizuddin, aged five – handed over to Cornwallis on 18 March 1792. The boys were taken off by elephant to Madras, which they appeared in general to like, though they clearly did not enjoy being made to sit through entire performances of Handel's *Messiah* and *Judas Maccabaeus*.[58] Having created a sensation in Madras society with their dignity, intelligence and politeness, they were sent back two years later when Tipu delivered the final tranche of his indemnity payment.

All this was a crushing blow to Tipu. Over the course of the war he had already lost 70 forts and 800 guns, and sustained 49,340 casualties. Now he stood to lose one entire half of the kingdom he had inherited from his father. But even as negotiations over the peace treaty were wrangling on, it was clear that Tipu was unbowed even by his defeat.

Around this time he reached out to Nizam Ali Khan of Hyderabad: 'Know you not the custom of the English?' he wrote. 'Wherever they fix their talons they contrive little by little to work themselves into the whole management of affairs.' One night just before the treaty was signed, according to Maratha sources, Tipu appeared

* £390 million today.

secretly in the Maratha camp, and asked to be taken to the tent of the 'lordly old Brahmin' general, Haripant Phadke: 'You must realise I am not at all your enemy,' he said. 'Your real enemy is the Englishman, and it is he of whom you must beware.'[59]

In many ways 1792 was the major turning point for the East India Company in India: before this, the Company was often on the defensive and always insecure. After this year, the Company appeared increasingly dominant. Up to this point, too, the EIC was still, in terms of land, a relatively small Indian power, controlling only 388,500 out of 4.17 million square kilometres – about 9.3 per cent of the Indian land mass, almost all in the north and east.[60] But with the great chunks of land it had just seized from Tipu in the south, the Company Raj was now on its way to becoming a major territorial, as well as a military and economic, power.

The reforms Cornwallis initiated on his return to Calcutta further consolidated this position. In America, Britain had lost its colonies not to Native Americans, but to the descendants of European settlers. Cornwallis was determined to make sure that a settled colonial class never emerged in India to undermine British rule as it had done, to his own humiliation, in America. By this period one in three British men in India were cohabiting with Indian women, and there were believed to be more than 11,000 Anglo-Indians in the three Presidency towns.[61] Now Cornwallis brought in a whole raft of unembarrassedly racist legislation aimed at excluding the children of British men who had Indian wives, or *bibis*, from employment by the Company.

In 1786 an order had already been passed banning the Anglo-Indian orphans of British soldiers from qualifying for service in the Company army. In 1791 the door was slammed shut when an order was issued that no one with an Indian parent could be employed by the Civil, Military or Marine branches of the Company. A year later, this was extended to 'officers of the Company ships'. In 1795, further legislation was issued, again explicitly disqualifying anyone not descended from European parents on both sides from serving in the Company's armies except as 'pipers, drummers, bandsmen and farriers'. Yet, like their British fathers, the Anglo-Indians were also banned from owning land. Thus excluded from all the most obvious sources of lucrative employment, the Anglo-Indians quickly found themselves at the beginning of a long slide down the social scale. This would continue until, a century later, the Anglo-Indians had been reduced to a community of minor clerks, postmen and train drivers.[62]

It was under Cornwallis, too, that many Indians – the last survivors of the old Murshidabad Mughal administrative service – were removed from senior positions in government, on the entirely spurious grounds that centuries of tyranny had bred 'corruption' in them.[63] Increasingly, all non-Europeans began to be treated with disdain by the exclusively white officials at the Company headquarters of Fort William. Around this time, Warren Hastings' Military Secretary, Major William Palmer, who was married to a Mughal princess, wrote expressing his dismay at the new etiquette regarding Indian dignitaries introduced to Calcutta by Cornwallis: 'They are received,' he wrote, 'in the most cold and disgusting style, and I can assure you that they observe and feel it, and no doubt they will resent it whenever they can.'[64]

Cornwallis then set about making a series of land and taxation reforms guaranteeing a steady flow of revenue, particularly in time of war, as well as reinforcing the Company's control of the land it had conquered. The Permanent Settlement, introduced in 1793, gave absolute rights to land to zamindar landowners, on the condition that they paid a sum of land tax which Company officials now fixed in perpetuity. So long as zamindars paid their revenues punctually, they had security over the land from which the revenue came. If they failed to pay up, the land would be sold to someone else.[65]

These reforms quickly produced a revolution in landholding in Company Bengal: many large old estates were split up, with former servants flocking to sale rooms to buy up their ex-masters' holdings. In the ensuing decades, draconian tax assessments led to nearly 50 per cent of estates changing hands. Many old Mughal landowning families were ruined and forced to sell, a highly unequal agrarian society was produced and the peasant farmers found their lives harder than ever. But from the point of view of the Company, Cornwallis's reforms were a huge success. Income from land revenues was both stabilised and enormously increased; taxes now arrived punctually and in full. Moreover, those who had bought land from the old zamindars were in many ways throwing in their lot with the new Company order. In this way, a new class of largely Hindu pro-British Bengali bankers and traders began to emerge as moneyed landowners to whom the Company could devolve local responsibility.

So even as the old Mughal aristocracy was losing high office, a new Hindu service gentry came to replace them at the top of the social ladder in Company-ruled Bengal. This group of emergent Bengali *bhadralok* (upper-middle classes) represented by families such as the Tagores, the Debs and the Mullicks, tightened their grip on mid-level public office in Calcutta, as well as their control of agrarian peasant production and the trade of the bazaars. They participated in the new cash crop trades to Calcutta – Dwarkanath Tagore, for example, making a fortune at this time in indigo – while continuing to lend the Company money, often for as much as 10–12 per cent interest. It was loans from this class which helped finance colonial armies and bought the muskets, cannon, horses, elephants, bullocks and paid the military salaries which allowed Company armies to wage and win their wars against other Indian states. The Company's ever-growing Indian empire could not have been achieved without the political and economic support of regional power groups and local communities. The edifice of the East India Company was sustained by the delicate balance that the Company was able to maintain with merchants and mercenaries, its allied nawabs and rajas, and above all, its tame bankers.[66]

In the end it was this access to unlimited reserves of credit, partly through stable flows of land revenues, and partly through the collaboration of Indian moneylenders and financiers, that in this period finally gave the Company its edge over their Indian rivals. It was no longer superior European military technology, nor powers of administration that made the difference. It was the ability to mobilise and transfer massive financial resources that enabled the Company to put the largest and best-trained army in the eastern world into the field. The biggest firms of the period – the houses of Lala Kashmiri Mal, Ramchand-Gopalchand Shahu and Gopaldas-Manohardas – many of them based in Patna and Benares, handled the largest military remittances, taking charge of drawing bills of exchange in Bombay or Surat or Mysore, as well as making large cash loans, all of which made possible the regular payment, maintenance, arming and provisioning of the Company's troops. The Company in turn duly rewarded these invaluable services in 1782 when they announced that the house of Gopaldas would henceforth be the government's banker in the place of the Jagat Seths. Support from the Company then enabled the house to break into western India from where they had previously been absent.[67]

As Rajat Kanta Ray put it, 'With regard to the indigenous systems of commercial credit, the Company was better placed than the Indian powers by virtue of its reputation as an international capitalist corporation with a developed sense of the importance of paying its debts. It was known, moreover, to have the biggest revenue surplus available in the country to offer as collateral for large contract loans obtained from *sahukaras* [moneylenders].'[68] The Company was perceived as the natural ally of Indian traders and financiers; the British, wrote Hari Charan Das, did not 'interfere with the wealth of any rich men, bankers and merchants, and other people who reside in their cities, but on the contrary they are kind to those who are wealthy.'[69]

As the Jagat Seths had discovered forty years earlier, the East India Company spoke a language Indian financiers understood, and offered a higher degree of security to Indian capital than its rivals.[70] In the end, it all came down to money. By the end of the century, Bengal was annually yielding a steady revenue surplus of Rs25 million at a time when Scindia struggled to net Rs1.2 million* from his territories in Malwa.[71] No wonder that Scindia reflected anxiously that 'without money it was impossible to assemble an army or prosecute a war'.[72]

Ultimately it was the East India Company, not the Marathas or the Sultans of Mysore, that the financiers across India decided to back.[73] Moreover, for all the rapacity of the Company, it was an increasingly easy decision for them to make. By 1792, there was little credible opposition. Tipu had just been defeated and had lost half his kingdom. For all his valour and determination, it would take a miracle for him ever again to muster sufficient resources to defeat the Company as he once did at Pollilur.

Meanwhile, the great Maratha Confederacy, the power which controlled the most land and fielded the largest and most formidable armies, was slowly beginning to unravel. On 1 June 1793, at the Battle

---

* The modern equivalences of these sums are: Rs25 million = £325 million; Rs1.2 million = £15.6 million.

of Lakheri, after many years of open rivalry and increasingly strained relations, Tukoji Holkar was comprehensively defeated by Mahadji Scindia. When the result of the battle was reported to the blind Shah Alam in Delhi, he chuckled and commented, 'the power of the Marathas will soon be destroyed'.[74] He was right. In the next round of internecine bloodshed that followed, 'the Maratha princes bore less resemblance to a confederacy than to a bag of ferrets'.[75]

It was no longer difficult to predict the future. By the 1790s the Comte de Modave, for one, had no doubt what lay in store for India. 'I am convinced that the English will establish themselves in the Mughal empire only precariously and with much uncertainty,' he wrote, 'and they will no doubt, eventually, in due course of time, lose it.'

But they will certainly control it for long enough to extract prodigious amounts of money from it, which will enable them to maintain the role they have arrogated to themselves of being the principal, or rather the one and only, power, exclusive of all others, among the trading nations of Europe.

Who can stop them? In Hindustan, anarchy smothers the hope of anything good germinating or sprouting: the people live in want and misery, even though they have so many possibilities of living well. The English in Bengal are watching this curious situation attentively, hoping to profit by it, for their lust for gain is as voracious as their mania for conquest.

I have no doubt that these ever-recurring disturbances, which pin down all the armed forces of this empire, are welcomed by the English as a sure means of taking over the empire itself, bit by bit. It strikes me that their behaviour corresponds exactly to this long-term strategy as they carefully stoke the fires of civil discord, which they then offer to resolve, backing up such mediation with a show of military strength as soon as they well can.

This pattern of behaviour, from which they have not deviated for several years, has allowed them to seize control of many areas beyond the limits of Bengal, so much so that they will soon be masters of the Ganges from Allahabad to the Ocean. They play the game of advancing without ever being seen to make any step forward … In brief, they assiduously practise that old maxim followed by the Romans in their politics, that is, in the words of Tacitus, everywhere to keep in place [local hereditary] rulers, in order to use them as instruments to reduce the people to slavery.

The English Company stands alone, today, on this vast stage, preparing secretly and silently to extend immeasurably the major role they are playing here. All their schemes, their plans, their initiatives, all tend to this one great object. One by one, all the powers of India are being reduced by terror, intrigues, flattery, promises or threats. Every day the English Company takes a step closer to that goal. I have no doubt at all that, for some years now, the plan of invading Hindustan and taking over the trade of all the East Indies has been the object of their speculations and calculations, a profitable compensation for what they have lost in America. If you also consider the power of the English navy, the strength of their military establishments on the coast of India, you will realise that, given the means already in their hands, they need make only a small effort to achieve this grand and magnificent project.

When the moment comes to act, their plan, however vast and complex, will be fully formed, down to its last details, with all necessary preliminary information ready gathered: then their operations will be carried out with a rapidity and success which will astonish the whole of Europe.[76]

The Company, he believed, now looked unassailable. But he was overlooking one thing. There was in fact one force which could still stop the Company in its tracks. Modave's own homeland, now in the grip of revolution and led by a heavily accented Corsican colonel named Napoleon Bonaparte, had just declared war against Britain on 1 February 1793. Four years later, in December 1797, Tipu despatched an embassy seeking Napoleon's help against the Company. What the Sultan of Mysore did not know was that the army he needed was already being prepared in Toulon. By the time Tipu's embassy arrived in Paris, in April 1798, Napoleon was waiting for an opportunity to sail his 194 ships, carrying 19,000 of his best men, out of Toulon, and across the Mediterranean to Egypt. Napoleon was quite clear as to his plans.

In a book about Turkish warfare he had scribbled in the margin before 1788 the words, 'Through Egypt we shall invade India, we shall re-establish the old route through Suez and cause the route by the Cape of Good Hope to be abandoned.' Nor did he anticipate many problems: 'The touch of a French sword is all that is needed for the framework of mercantile grandeur to collapse.'[77] From Cairo in 1798 he sent a letter to Tipu, answering the latter's pleas for help and outlining his grand strategy:

You have already been informed of my arrival on the borders of the Red Sea, with an innumerable and invincible army, full of the desire of releasing and relieving you from the iron yoke of England. I eagerly embrace this opportunity of testifying to you the desire I have of being informed by you, by the way of Muscat and Mocha, as to your political situation. I wish you could send some sort of intelligent person to Suez or Cairo, possessing your confidence, with whom I may confer. May the Almighty increase your power, and destroy your enemies!

Yours &c &c

Bonaparte[78]

9

The Corpse of India

On 17 May 1798, two days before Napoleon's fleet slipped out of Toulon and sailed swiftly across the Mediterranean towards Alexandria, a single tall-masted ship, this time a sleek East Indiaman, was tacking into the River Hooghly after seven months at sea. On board was a man who would change the history of India as much as Napoleon would change that of France; indeed, though his name is largely forgotten today, in the next seven years he would conquer more territory in India, and more quickly, than Napoleon conquered in Europe.

When Robert Clive had turned into the same river in December 1756, noting in his letters the point where the waters of the Bay of Bengal took on the distinctive colour of Ganges silt, the only Company men left in Bengal had been the beaten and malaria-stricken refugees from Calcutta, dying in droves amid the Sunderban mangrove swamps at Fulta. Calcutta itself was a ruin. Now, only forty-two years later, Calcutta was one of the largest cities in Asia, the Company completely dominated eastern and southern India and had successfully encircled the entire peninsula. As the passenger looked out from his berth in the roundhouse, he was conscious that he was being sent east specifically to bring this work of corporate conquest and consolidation to its climax.

This was his first glimpse of Bengal and he was excited by what he saw: 'Nothing could equal the magnificence of my approach,' he wrote to his wife on his arrival. 'For nearly three miles the river, which is as large as the Thames at London, is bordered by lovely, well-built country houses with porticoes and colonnades. The town is a mass of superb palaces in the same style, with the finest fortress in the world. The green of the lawns surpasses anything you have ever seen ... an extraordinary effect in so hot a country. The trees are more beautiful, their foliage more luxuriant, than in any European country ... Arthur met us a few miles from the town, and on arrival at the fort I was saluted with a salvo of artillery.'[1]

The passenger was the new Governor General, Richard, Marquess Wellesley;[2] 'Arthur' was his younger brother, who had also recently been posted to India, and who would, in time, eclipse Richard and be ennobled as the Duke of Wellington. Between them, the two would transform both India and Europe.

There was nothing inevitable about this. The brothers were neither great noblemen nor distinguished politicians and they possessed no great fortune. They came from minor, provincial Anglo-Irish Protestant stock; their main assets were their steely self-confidence, quick brains and extraordinary chutzpah. Like Clive before them, they were both aggressive and autocratic pragmatists who believed that offence was the best form of defence; like him they seemed to lack self-doubt and managed to remain undaunted by odds which would terrify more anxious, or sensitive, men.

At this stage in their lives, it was Richard, not Arthur, who was the star of the family. He had entered the House of Commons at twenty-four, was soon made a Lord of the Treasury and became close friends with the Prime Minister, William Pitt. Now, at the age of thirty-seven, when he stepped ashore at Calcutta to succeed Lord Cornwallis as Governor General of the Company's possessions in India, Richard Wellesley was an unusually self-possessed young man with a high forehead, thick, dark eyebrows and a prominent Roman nose. He had deep-set, compelling blue eyes and a firm chin, the prominence of which was emphasised by his three-quarter-length sideburns. There was a purposeful set to his small mouth and an owlish gleam in his expression that hinted at his brilliance, and perhaps also at his ruthlessness. But there was also a look of suspicion, and even a paranoia there, too, apparent in all his portraits. It was a flaw that he increasingly came to disguise with a mask of extreme arrogance.

Where Wellesley differed quite markedly from his predecessors as Governor General was in his attitude to the Company he was expected to serve. For just as Calcutta was now quite different from the small, battered town familiar to Clive, so the Company was a very different beast from that which Clive had served. In India it might be immeasurably more powerful, with an army now roughly twenty times the size of that commanded by Clive; but in London, Parliament had been steadily chiselling away at its powers and independence, first with Lord North's Regulating Act of 1773 and then with Pitt's India Act of 1784. Between them, the two bills had done much to take control of political and military affairs of British India out of the hands of the Company directors in Leadenhall Street and into those of the Board of Control, the government body set up in 1784 to oversee the Company, across town in Whitehall.

Wellesley was, unrepentantly, a government man, and unlike his predecessors made no secret of his 'utter contempt' for the opinions of 'the most loathsome den of the India House'.[3] Though he would win the directors a vast empire, he came within a whisker of bankrupting their Company to do so, and it was clear from the beginning that he had set his sights on far more ambitious goals than maintaining the profit margins of the Company he was supposed to serve, but whose mercantile spirit he actually abhorred.

Unknown to the Company's directors, Wellesley had come out east with two very clear goals in his mind. He was determined to secure India for British rule and was equally determined to oust the French from their last footholds on the subcontinent. In this he was following the bidding of Henry Dundas, the Board of Control's president, whose Francophobia was transmitted to a receptive Wellesley at a series of lengthy briefings before the new Governor General embarked for India.

In particular Dundas had instructed Wellesley to 'cleanse' those pockets of Indian princely power that had been 'contaminated' by French influence – namely the courts of Tipu Sultan of Mysore, Nizam Ali Khan of Hyderabad and those of that network of rival chiefs that ruled the great Maratha Confederacy – all of whom had raised sepoy armies trained by French mercenaries and renegades, and all of which could, potentially, be used against the British and in favour of the French. At a time of national crisis, when Britain was at war not only with France but also with Holland and Spain; when its last ally – Austria – had just laid down her arms; when a naval mutiny had broken out in the Channel Fleet; and when Napoleon was drawing up plans for seaborne invasions of both Ireland, then on the verge of rebellion, and the English south coast, this was not something the British government was prepared to tolerate.[4]

Wellesley's ideas about the renewed French threat to the Company in India came into much closer focus when, halfway through his outward voyage, his ship docked on the Cape to refit. There, at the end of January 1798, he had met a senior Company diplomat who was taking the waters at the Cape mineral baths to treat his gout and attempt to recover his shattered health. Major William Kirkpatrick was as much a Francophobe as Wellesley, but unlike the new Governor General knew India intimately, having spent all his adult life there, latterly serving as Company Resident in both Delhi and Hyderabad. There he had come into direct contact with the French mercenaries Wellesley was determined to defeat and expel.

Wellesley had initially asked Major Kirkpatrick to provide written answers to a range of questions about the French troops employed by the Nizam of Hyderabad, notably a battalion 'commanded by a Frenchman by the name of Raymond' and officered by 'Frenchmen of the most virulent and notorious principles of Jacobinism ... an armed French party of great zeal, diligence and activity ... The basis of a permanent French faction in India.'[5] The answers he received so impressed him, that he not only forwarded them, unedited, to Dundas, he also begged Kirkpatrick to abandon the plans he had been making to return to England, and to take up a job at his side in Calcutta, as his Military Secretary.

Over the course of Wellesley's days in the Cape, the two remained cloistered as Kirkpatrick briefed his new boss on his perceptions of the French threat, and what steps the new Governor General could take to contain it. He told him of the well-equipped French-commanded Maratha sepoy battalions which had been trained up for Scindia by the brilliant Savoyard general Benoît de Boigne. De Boigne had now retired to Europe and handed over his battalions to a far less formidable commander named General Pierre Perron, but Kirkpatrick had witnessed the skills of the army he had created, and particularly its ruthlessly efficient artillery divisions. Three years earlier, in March 1795, he had been present when the Nizam of Hyderabad's army had disintegrated under their fire at the Battle of Khardla. Kirkpatrick was under no illusions about the formidable nature of Scindia's new army, which was now almost indistinguishable from that of the Company in uniform, drill, weaponry and even in its sepoys' ethnic and caste backgrounds.

Wellesley was especially alarmed to hear about the degree to which the army of Tipu Sultan, the Company's most implacable and relentless enemy, had fallen into the hands of a body of 500 Revolutionary French mercenaries, advisers, technicians and officers. Kirkpatrick told him how, in May 1797, Tipu's French troops had gone as far as establishing a Revolutionary Jacobin club in Srirangapatnam: 'The National Flag [the Tricolour] was hoisted to the sound of artillery and musketry of the camp', while symbols of the pre-Revolutionary Bourbon monarchy were burned. Republican hymns were sung during the subsequent planting of 'the Liberty Tree' – a sort of Jacobin maypole – and while the tree was crowned with a 'Cap of Equality', the assembly 'swore hatred of all Kings, except Tipoo Sultan, the Victorious, the Ally of the Republic of France, to make war on tyrants and to love towards the motherland as well as the land of Citizen Prince Tipoo'. Finally, they took a solemn oath to support the Republican constitution, 'or die at arms … to live free or die!'[6]

At the end of the ceremony, the French corps marched to the Srirangapatnam parade ground, where the Citizen Prince awaited them. As they approached, Tipu ordered a salute from 2,300 cannon, 500 rockets and all the musketry his troops could muster. 'Behold,' announced Citizen Tipu, 'my acknowledgement of the Standard of your country, which is dear to me and to which I am allied; it shall always be carried aloft in my country, as it has been in our sister Republic! Go, conclude your festival!'[7]

Wellesley's greatest fear was that the different French mercenary units could unite to challenge the Company if war broke out again with Tipu. He wrote to London how

in the present weak state of the Nizam of Hyderabad's Government, the French corps in his service would openly join with Tipu Sultan, and by a sudden blow, endeavour to seize the Nizam's territories, and to secure them to the dominion of France, under an alliance with Tipu Sultan. The interest and inclination of Scindia, who also entertains a large army in his service under the command of a French officer, would lead him to engage with Tipu Sultan and the French. The junction which might thus be effected between the French officers, with their several corps in the respective services of the Nizam, Scindia and Tipu, might establish the power of France upon the ruin of the states of Pune and of the Deccan.[8]

As soon as he arrived in Calcutta, Wellesley began drawing up plans to send troops south to take on this threat. But his plans greatly accelerated when, on 8 June, he read in a Calcutta newspaper of a declaration, issued in Mauritius by the island's French Governor General, M. Malartic. This publicised the intention of Tipu to conclude an offensive and defensive alliance with the French and 'that he only waits for the moment when the French shall come to his assistance to declare war on the English, whom he ardently wishes to expel from India'.[9]

From that moment, Tipu's fate was sealed. Wellesley's priority was now to eradicate all traces of French influence before any French military expedition could arrive. In June he wrote to General Harris, the Commander-in-Chief at Madras, who was a veteran of Cornwallis's campaign against Tipu, announcing his decision to 'call upon our allies without delay and assemble the army on the coast with all possible expedition', with a view to 'striking a sudden blow against Tippoo before he can receive foreign aid'.[10]

By early August, Wellesley had completed his war plan. This he transmitted to Dundas in London, outlining 'measures ... most advisable for the purpose of frustrating the united efforts of Tippoo Sultan and of France'.[11] As far he was concerned, Tipu was now a proven enemy and predator and must be immediately crushed: 'The evidence of meditated hostility is complete,' he wrote. 'While professing the most amicable disposition, bound by subsisting treaties of peace and friendship, and unprovoked by an offence on our part, Tipu Sultan has manifested a design to effect our total destruction.'[12]

First, however, Wellesley decided to deal with Raymond's French Revolutionary force in Hyderabad.

Although many of Wellesley's writings at this period have an air of Francophobe paranoia to them, the new Governor General was in fact quite correct about the potential threat posed to the Company by Raymond. As a recently discovered cache of papers has shown, Raymond was indeed in correspondence both with the French officers of de Boigne's corps in Scindia's service and those working for Tipu at Srirangapatnam, where Raymond had himself been employed before entering the Nizam's service.

Raymond's ambitions are revealed in the series of passionately patriotic letters he wrote in the early 1790s to the French headquarters at Pondicherry, pledging his loyalty to France and the Revolution: 'I am ready to sacrifice all,' he wrote to the Governor of Pondicherry, 'if I am so fortunate that circumstances may ever put it in my power to prove the zeal for my country which animates me.' To the Governor of Mauritius, he was even more explicit about his intentions: 'I shall always follow as my first duty whatever [orders] you wish to give me ... If ever I can be useful to France I am ready to pour my blood once more for her. I labour only to discharge this duty and gain your good opinion.'[13]

James Achilles Kirkpatrick, the new British Resident in Hyderabad, upon whom the job of ousting the French corps devolved, was the younger brother of Wellesley's new Military Secretary. His task was far from easy. Raymond's personal income was vast – his estates on their own yielded Rs500,000 a year* – and in the early months of 1798 Raymond had persuaded the Nizam again to increase the size of his force, this time to over 14,000 men, with their own bespoke gun foundry and a complete train of artillery, drawn by a force of 5,000 of its own bullocks. The corps manufactured its own swords, muskets and pistols, besides its excellent artillery; there was even a small cavalry group numbering 600. To make matters worse Raymond was personally very popular with the Hyderabad court. The heir apparent, Sikander Jah, was so taken with the Frenchman that he went as far as swearing 'by the head of Raymond'.[14]

---

* £6.5 million today.

Then, on the morning of 25 March 1798, Raymond was found dead, aged only forty-three; there was gossip that the cause may have been poison, possibly administered by the pro-Company faction in the durbar. Whatever the truth, the sudden death of Raymond gave Kirkpatrick his chance. It helped that one of the Nizam's ministers, Mir Alam, had recently visited Calcutta and been astonished by the size and scale of the Company's barracks and arms factories, and that other senior officials in the Hyderabad durbar were equally convinced that the Company was the rising power in India. They argued that an alliance was essential for the safety of Hyderabad, surrounded as it was by two much more powerful neighbours, Tipu's Mysore to the south and the Marathas in Pune, immediately to the west.

Six months later, after weeks of hard negotiation, a secret treaty was signed, bringing Hyderabad and the Company into a close military alliance: 6,000 Company troops were to be resident in Hyderabad and available for the Nizam's protection. In return the Nizam was to pay the Company an annual subsidy of £41,710,* and to dismiss the French corps. Exactly how or when this was to be done, however, was not made clear in the Treaty.

Following the signing, an uneasy month passed as the new Company force of four battalions, along with a train of artillery, made its way slowly up the 150 miles from the coast near Guntur. This was the nearest Company-controlled town, where Wellesley had ordered them to collect two months earlier, in readiness to march on Hyderabad.[15]

Before first light on 22 October, the EIC troops quietly encircled the French cantonments, arranging their guns on the ridge above the French lines, not far from where a classical Greek temple and obelisk had just been raised as a memorial for Raymond. They achieved complete surprise. When dawn broke, the French corps woke up to find itself surrounded. At nine o'clock Kirkpatrick offered the mutineers payment of all salaries owing if they would surrender. They had 'one quarter of an hour to stack their arms and march off to a protection flag, which was pitched about half a mile to the right of the camp. If they did not comply, they were immediately to be attacked.'[16]

For thirty minutes the French corps remained undecided. Two thousand Company cavalry massed on the right flank of the French

* £4,379,550 today.

camp; 500 more waited on the right. In the centre were 4,000 East India Company infantry. There was complete silence. Then, just after 9.30 a.m., to Kirkpatrick's great relief, the sepoys finally sent out word that they accepted the terms.

The Company cavalry rode in and quickly took possession of the French magazine, store houses, powder mills, gun foundries and cannon, while the French sepoys fled to the flag under which they were to surrender themselves: 'at once a glorious and piteous sight', thought Kirkpatrick.[17] Within a few hours, the largest French corps in India, more than 14,000-strong, was disarmed by a force of less than a third that number. Not a single shot had been fired, not a single life lost.

Kirkpatrick watched the soldiers laying down their arms all afternoon from the roof of the British Residency. That evening, in a state of mixed exhaustion and elation, he wrote to his brother William that the 'turning adrift of thousands of Raymond's troops, all of which I saw this evening from the roof of my house with my spy glasses as plain as if it had been on the spot, was the finest sight I ever saw in my life.'

In a postscript written two hours later, there came even better news: had William heard yet the news, which had just arrived post-haste from Bombay, 'of Admiral Nelson's glorious naval action'? In the Battle of the Nile on 1 August, Nelson had sunk almost the entire French fleet in Aboukir Bay, wrecking Napoleon's hopes of using Egypt as a secure base from which to attack India. It was an amazing turn of events. Ever since news had arrived of Napoleon's expedition to Egypt, it had looked quite possible that India would be next and might even become a French colony. Now that threat was greatly diminished.[18]

The operation had been carried out with great skill and Wellesley was delighted. 'You will enjoy my gentle conquest of an army of 14,000 men under the command of French officers in the service of the Nizam,' he wrote to Dundas later that month. 'My despatches do not mention a curious fact, that the standard of this army was the Tricolour flag: the first of that description erected on the Continent of India. This standard has fallen into my hands; and I shall send it home as the best comment upon the whole policy of making an effort to crush the French influence in India.'[19]

Now with Hyderabad secured, Wellesley was ready to move directly against his principal adversary, Tipu Sultan.

On 4 November 1798, Wellesley wrote a sarcastic letter to Tipu, telling him of the cataclysmic defeat of his French allies at the Battle of the Nile: 'Confident that from the union and attachment subsisting between us that this intelligence will afford you sincere satisfaction, I could not deny myself the pleasure of communicating it.'[20] Tipu replied in kind, penning an apparently friendly but equally disingenuous letter back, telling Lord Wellesley: 'I am resident at home, at times taking the air, and at times amusing myself with hunting at a spot which is used as a pleasure ground.'[21]

When Wellesley next wrote, the Company's alliance with Hyderabad had been secured and the French corps rounded up, and the Governor General was now much more confident of the strength of his position. This time his tone was very different: 'It is impossible that you should suppose me ignorant of the intercourse between you and the French, whom you know to be inveterate enemies of the Company,' he wrote. 'Nor does it appear necessary or proper that I should any longer conceal from you the surprise and concern with which I perceived you disposed to involve yourself in all the ruinous consequences of a connection which threatens to subvert the foundations of friendship between you and the Company, and to introduce into your kingdom the principles of anarchy and confusion and ... to destroy the religion which you revere.'[22] But Tipu refused to be drawn: 'Being frequently disposed to make excursions and hunt,' he wrote back, 'I am accordingly proceeding on another hunting expedition ... Always continue to gratify me by friendly letters, notifying your welfare.'[23]

Wellesley was now busy putting the final touches to his invasion plans. The finances to fight the war were now secure and, having won the support of the Marwari bankers of Bengal, Wellesley sent to Bombay and Madras the vast sum of Rs10 million (£1 million, £130 million today), which he had managed to raise on the Calcutta money market.[24] More money came in a timely injection of treasure from Europe.[25]

He wrote to the Resident in Pune, William Palmer, that he must at all costs get the Marathas to break off relations with Mysore and join

Sepoys of the Madras Infantry, by Yellapah of Vellore.

Following pages: *The Battle of Pollilur*. A copy of the mural Tipu Sultan had painted
on the walls of his garden palace, Darya Daulat Bagh, commemorating his greatest
victory in 1780. At the centre, Colonel William Baillie can be seen in his palanquin,
touching his finger to his mouth in astonishment as Tipu blows up his ammunition
wagon and the Mysore cavalry assault the Company square on all sides.

Edmund Burke, from the studio of Sir Joshua Reynolds. Burke was an Anglo-Irish Whig statesman and political theorist. He had never been to India, but part of his family had been ruined by unwise speculation in East India stock. Together Burke and Francis worked on a series of Select Committee reports exposing the Company's misdeeds in India. Before he met Philip Francis, Burke had described himself as 'a great admirer' of Hastings' talents. Francis quickly worked to change that. By April 1782, Francis had drawn up a list of twenty-two charges against Hastings, which Burke then brought to the House. After five years of obsessive campaigning, Burke and Francis persuaded Parliament that there was enough evidence to impeach him.

Philip Francis by James Lonsdale, c. 1806. Wrongly convinced that Hastings was the source of all corruption in Bengal, and ambitious to replace him as Governor General, Francis pursued Hastings from 1774 until his death. Having failed to kill Hastings in a duel, and instead receiving a pistol ball in his own ribs, he returned to London, where his accusations eventually led to the impeachment of both Hastings and his Chief Justice, Elijah Impey. Both were ultimately acquitted.

Portrait of the elderly Warren Hastings by Lemuel Francis Abbott, 1796. Far from being an ostentatious and loud-mouthed new-rich 'Nabob', Hastings was a dignified, intellectual and somewhat austere figure. Standing gaunt at the bar during his impeachment in his plain black frock coat, white stockings and grey hair, he looks more Puritan minister about to give a sermon than some paunchy plunderer. Nearly six feet tall, he weighed less than eight stone: 'of spare habit, very bald, with a countenance placid and thoughtful, but when animated, full of intelligence.'

Following pages: *The Impeachment of Warren Hastings in Westminster Hall*, 1788. This was not just the greatest political spectacle in the age of George III, it was the nearest the British ever got to putting the Company's Indian Empire on trial. Tickets for the few seats reserved for spectators changed hands for as much as £50, and even then so many people wished to attend that, as one of the managers of the impeachment noted, the audience 'will have to mob it at the door till nine, when the doors open, and then there will be a rush as there is at the pit of the Playhouse when Garrick plays King Lear'.

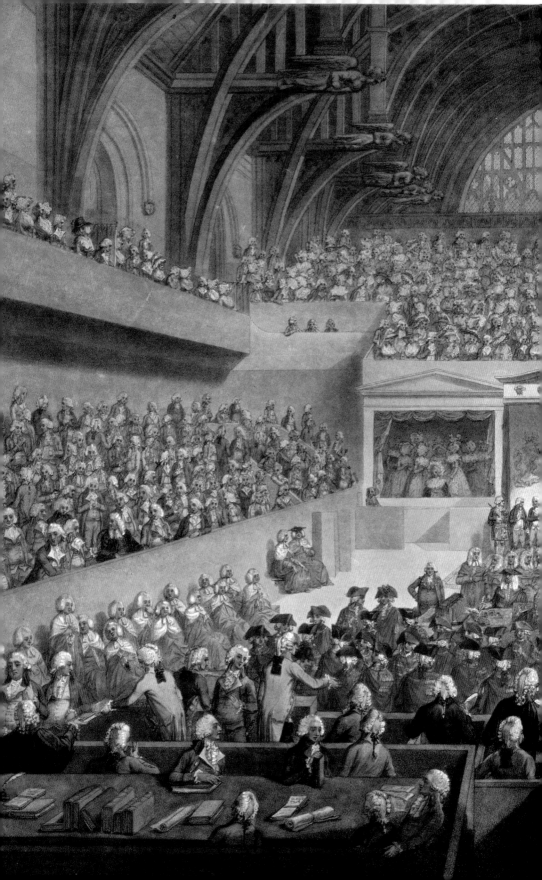

Mahadji Scindia in Delhi Entertaining a British Naval Officer and a Young British Military Officer with a Nautch, c. 1790.

Qudsia Bagh palace where Ghulam Qadir was brought up during his time at the court of Shah Alam.

The blind Shah Alam II on a wooden replica of the Peacock Throne, c. 1790, by Khairullah. Now in his seventies, the old king sat amid his ruined palace, the sightless ruler of a largely illusory empire.

Tipu Sultan on his elephant commanding his forces at the Battle of Pollilur.

Lord Cornwallis receiving the sons of Tipu Sultan after his 1792 invasion of Mysore, by Mather Brown.

Tipu succeeded his father in 1782 and ruled with great efficiency and imagination during peace, but with great brutality in war. He was forced to cede half his kingdom to Lord Cornwallis's Triple Alliance with the Marathas and Hyderabadis in 1792 and was finally defeated and killed by Lord Wellesley in 1799.

A View of the East India Docks, c. 1808 by William Daniell, seen from what is now East India Dock, London.

In less than fifty years since the 1750s the Company had seized control of almost all of what had once been Mughal India and encircled the globe. It had also created a sophisticated administration and civil service, built much of London's docklands and come close to generating nearly half of Britain's trade. Its annual spending within Britain alone – around £8.5 million – equalled about a quarter of total British government annual expenditure. No wonder, then, that the Company now referred to itself as 'the grandest society of merchants in the Universe'.

The Scindias

Above: Mahadji Scindia was a shrewd Maratha politician who took Shah Alam under his wing from 1771 onwards and turned the Mughals into Maratha puppets. He created a powerful modern army under the Savoyard General Benoît de Boigne, but towards the end of his life his rivalry with Tukoji Holkar and his unilateral peace with the East India Company at the Treaty of Salbai both did much do undermine Maratha unity.

Below: When Mahadji Scindia died in 1794, his successor, Daulat Rao, was only fifteen. The boy inherited the magnificent army that Benoît de Boigne had trained up for his predecessor, but he showed little vision or talent in its deployment. His rivalry with the Holkars and failure to present a common front against the East India Company led to the disastrous Second Anglo-Maratha war of 1803. This left the East India Company the paramount power in India and paved the way for the British Raj.

The Wellesleys

Above: Richard Wellesley conquered more of India than Napoleon did of Europe. Despising the mercantile spirit of the East India Company, he used its armies and resources successfully to wage the Fourth Anglo-Mysore War, which ended with the killing of Tipu Sultan and the destruction of his capital in 1799, then the Second Anglo-Maratha War, which led to the defeat of the armies of both Scindia and Holkar, 1803. By this time he had expelled the last French units from India and given the East India Company control of most of the subcontinent south of the Punjab.

Below: Arthur Wellesley was fast promoted by his elder brother to be Governor of Mysore and 'Chief Political and Military Officer in the Deccan and Southern Maratha Country'. He helped defeat the armies of Tipu in 1799 and those of the Marathas in 1803, most notably at the Battle of Assaye. Later famous as the Duke of Wellington.

The Duke of Wellington on Campaign in the Deccan, 1803. After the Battle of Assaye one of Wellesley's senior officers wrote: 'I hope you will not have occasion to purchase any more victories at such a high price.'

Two armies drawn up in combat, with artillery in front, cavalry in the wings and elephants bringing up the rear.

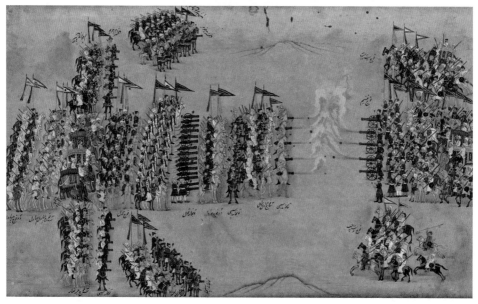

the war against Tipu, in accordance with the Triple Alliance signed by Cornwallis. In due course a reluctant Peshwa promised Palmer that the Marathas would honour their commitments and send the Company 25,000 troops – though after much foot-dragging in Pune, these failed to arrive in time for action.[26] A message was also sent to the Nizam to call up his troops to assist his new British allies, as had been agreed in the Treaty he and Kirkpatrick had signed five months earlier

In a process of vilification familiar from more recent Western confrontations with assertive Muslim leaders, Wellesley now stepped up his propaganda against Tipu, who he depicted as 'a cruel and relentless enemy', 'a beast of the jungle', an 'intolerant bigot' with 'a rooted hatred of Europeans' who had 'perpetually on his tongue the projects of Jihad'. This tyrant was also deemed to be an 'oppressive and unjust ruler ... [a] sanguinary tyrant, a perfidious negociator', and, above all, a 'furious fanatic'.[27]

At the same time he wrote to reassure the Court of Directors that he was not engaged in some vainglorious adventure at their expense: 'Although I have deemed it my duty to call your armies into the field in every part of India,' he wrote, 'my views and expectations are all directed to the preservation of the peace, which in the present crisis cannot otherwise be secured than by a state of forward preparations for war.'[28]

This letter was as insincere as anything he had ever written to Tipu. For Wellesley had, in reality, absolutely no intention whatsoever of keeping the peace. Instead, he was hugely enjoying the prospect of using the directors' private army to wage his entirely avoidable war against the French-led forces in India.

On Christmas Day, 25 December 1798, Lord Wellesley embarked from Calcutta for Madras, so that he could better control affairs from his southern base. He arrived on the last day of 1798, to be greeted by the new Governor of Madras. This was Edward, Lord Clive, the slightly slow-witted son of Robert Clive, whose victory at Plassey thirty-five years earlier had begun the East India Company's transformation from a trading company to a privately owned imperial power with a standing army and territorial possessions far larger than that of its parent country. After their first meeting, Wellesley wrote that the younger Clive was 'a worthy, zealous, obedient & gentlemanlike man of excellent temper; but neither of talents, knowledge, habits of business, or firmness equal to his present situation. How the devil did he get here?'[29] Henceforth Wellesley more or less ignored his host and busied himself with managing the detail of his onslaught against Tipu without involving Edward Clive in any way.

By this stage, General Harris's heavy siege train, with its battering rams and mining gear, had already reached Vellore, the last British-held fort before the Mysore frontier. There 20,000 East India Company sepoys, 1,400 elite British grenadiers under Arthur Wellesley, the future Duke of Wellington, and a battalion of kilted Scottish Highlanders engaged in training exercises, while Harris waited for his orders to advance.[30]

Tipu had an extremely efficient network of spies and knew exactly what was happening beyond his borders: 'It has lately come to my ears from report,' he wrote, 'that, in consequence of the talk of interested persons, military preparations are on foot.'[31] While Lord Wellesley finessed his military plans, Tipu tried, with equal energy, to raise support from the last indigenous armies capable of taking on the Company, warning them that whatever differences they may have had in the past, this was their chance to unite and defeat the British.

On 8 January, James Kirkpatrick reported from Hyderabad that Tipu had written to the Nizam begging forgiveness if he had infringed any treaty and asking for an alliance, claiming that the English 'intended extirpating all Mussulmans and establishing hat-wearers in their place'.[32] Two days later, on 10 January, despatches from Pune reached Wellesley announcing the intelligence that a delegation of Tipu's ambassadors had also presented themselves at the Maratha court, seeking military assistance.[33]

Wellesley's spies reported that Tipu Sultan had even written to Ahmad Shah Durrani's grandson, Zaman Shah, the ruler of Afghanistan. 'It ought to be the duty of faithful chiefs to extirpate the infidels by uniting together,' wrote Tipu, before proposing that, 'after deposing the pathetic King [Shah Alam,] who has reduced the faith to such a state of feebleness', they should divide India between them.[34] But it was all too late.

Wellesley was now ready and there would be no time for Tipu to create the alliances he needed to protect himself.[35] When he was dying, Tipu's father, Haidar Ali, had advised his son always to make sure he took on the Company in alliance with other Indian rulers; only that way could he be sure of victory. Ambitious and self-confident, Tipu had ignored that advice. Now, when he most needed that assistance, he would fight alone.

Tipu must have known how slim the odds now were of success: his dream book records one about the last-minute arrival of a rescue force 'of 10,000 Franks [Frenchmen]', while on 20 December the Sultan was awoken by a nightmare of a vast army of regiments of English Christians with the heads of pigs marching on his capital.[36] But he had no intention of backing down. As he is alleged to have said when he heard the news that Wellesley's invasion of his kingdom had begun, 'I would rather live a day as a lion than a lifetime as a sheep ... Better to die like a soldier, than to live a miserable dependant on the infidels, in their list of pensioned rajas and nabobs.'[37]

On 3 February 1799, General Harris was ordered to mobilise his troops and 'with as little delay as possible ... enter the territory of Mysore and proceed to the siege of Seringapatam'. The Governor General sent characteristically detailed instructions on how to proceed and ordered that, whatever the circumstances, there were to be no negotiations until the army was standing in front of the walls of Srirangapatnam.[38]

On 19 February, the four East India Company battalions in Hyderabad under Colonel James Dalrymple, along with the four further battalions of Hyderabadi sepoys and more than 10,000 Hyderabadi cavalry, joined up with General Harris's Company army. On 5 March, with some 30,000 sheep, huge stocks of grain and 100,000 carriage bullocks trailing behind them, the two armies crossed the frontier into Mysore.[39] There followed at least 100,000 camp followers, who outnumbered the combatants by at least four to one. Wellesley believed his army to be 'the finest which ever took the field in India'; but it was a huge and unwieldy force, and it trundled towards Srirangapatnam at the agonisingly slow place of five miles a day, stripping the country bare 'of every article of subsistence the country can afford' like some vast cloud of locusts.[40]

Having surrendered half his kingdom in 1792, Tipu's resources were much more limited than they had been during Cornwallis's campaign, and he realised that his best chance of success lay in concentrating all his troops on his island fortress-capital. He made only two brief sorties, one against a small British force from Bombay as it passed through the mountains from Coorg, and another against Harris's main force near Bangalore, where Tipu personally led a spirited cavalry charge. Then he retired behind the great walls of Srirangapatnam to begin strengthening the defences and preparing for the siege.

With only 37,000 troops, he was slightly outnumbered by the allies, but remained a formidable opponent. No one forgot that, in the three previous Anglo-Mysore Wars, Tipu's forces had frequently defeated the Company. Indeed, two of the most prominent Company commanders in the campaign, Sir David Baird and his cousin James Dalrymple, had both been prisoners of Tipu, having been captured and imprisoned for forty-four long months after the disastrous British defeat at Pollilur in 1780, 'the most grievous disaster which has yet befallen British arms in India'.[41]

By 14 March, Harris's force had passed Bangalore and taken several key forts in the surrounding hills. Three weeks later, on 5 April, the army finally came within sight of Srirangapatnam. On 6 April, Arthur Wellesley led a failed night attack on some of the outer defences; a party of thirteen Company sepoys was captured by Tipu's forces and then tortured to death. On the 7th, the siege began.[42]

With his characteristic ingenuity and tenacity, Tipu showed every sign of resisting. As one British soldier wrote, he 'gave us gun for gun … [and night-time skirmishes were] made with desperate exertion … Soon the scenes became tremendously grand; shells and rockets of uncommon weight were incessantly poured upon us from the SW side, and fourteen pounders and grape from the North face of the Fort continued their havoc in the trenches; while the blaze of our batteries, which frequently caught fire … was the signal for the Tiger sepoys [Tipu's elite forces dressed in tiger-striped uniforms] to advance, and pour in galling vollies of musketry.' In all, around 120 Frenchmen were taken prisoner, including twenty officers.[43]

The small French corps, around 450-strong, all wearing Republican cockades and sprigs of laurel, also 'behaved with great spirit', sallying out on 22 April to the British positions on the north bank of the island: 'some of them fell within the entrenchment upon our bayonets, and others were killed close to it.'[44]

Tipu put up a brave and skilful defence and for some time it appeared that the Company troops were making little headway: 'the enemy continued during the night to repair their dismantled parapets,' wrote one officer, 'and in the morning surprised us with the production of several guns in a new work, embracing the N.W cavalier … Something akin to despondence was now beginning to steal upon the mind; and unless this aspect of affairs soon changed our calculations went to determine that this truly formidable place, manfully defended as it was, would not change masters without extensive blood-shedding.'[45]

But Wellesley's army was equipped with unprecedented quantities of heavy artillery, and deployed forty 18-pounders for breaching the walls and seven 8-inch and 5.5-inch howitzers for plunging fire inside the fort's walls. In addition, there were fifty-seven 6-pounders for fire support for the besieging army against Tipu's infantry.[46] By the end of April, most of Tipu's guns on the northern and western end of the island had been disabled. By 3 May, the artillery of the Hyderabad contingent felt secure enough to move forward to within 350 yards of the weakest corner of the walls, and by evening a substantial breach was made. Harris set the following day for the assault.[47]

That morning, after inspecting the breach and bathing, Tipu consulted his Brahmin astrologers. They warned the Sultan of particularly bad omens. Tipu gave them 'three elephants, two buffaloes, a bullock and a she-goat', as well as an iron pot full of oil, used for divination, asking them to 'pray for the prosperity of the Empire'. He now suspected himself doomed.[48]

At 1 p.m., in the heat of the day, most of Tipu's sepoys went off to rest for the afternoon. In the Company trenches, David Baird roused himself and gave his troops 'a cheering dram and a biscuit, and drew his sword saying, "Men are you ready?" "Yes," was the reply. "Then forward my lads!"'[49] He then jumped out of the trench and led a storming party 4,000-strong into the River Kaveri and across the shallows into the breach. His two columns scrambled over the glacis and into the city, swinging right and left along the ramparts, amid fierce hand-to-hand fighting.

When he heard the news that the assault had finally been launched, Tipu left his lunch in the palace and rode straight to the breach, accompanied by a bodyguard from his elite Lion of God battalion. But by the time he arrived, the Company troops were already well within the walls. There was nothing for him to do but to climb on the battlements and fight for his life. Outnumbered, bravely taking on the overwhelming incoming rush of Company sepoys, he quickly received two bayonet wounds and a glancing musket shot in the left shoulder. His attendants called on him to surrender, but he replied, 'Are you mad? Be silent.'

Here, between the water gate and the inner ramparts of the fort, Tipu stood to make what even his most hostile British opponents acknowledged was 'his gallant last stand'.[50] A party of redcoats had forced their way between the gates, and one grenadier, seeing a gold buckle sparkling on the waist of the wounded man, tried to grab at it, and received a last fatal sword slash from the Sultan in return. Seconds later, one of his companions shot Tipu at point-blank range, through the temple. After four wars against the Company, over a period of thirty-two years, the Tiger of Mysore finally fell, sword in hand, among the heaps of dead and dying men.[51]

Within a few hours, the city was in Company hands. That evening, after sunset, Baird was taken to Tipu's body by one of his courtiers, Raja Khan. 'The scene was altogether shocking,' wrote an eyewitness. 'The numbers of bodies so great, and the place so dark, that it was impossible to distinguish one person from another.' They had to roll the bodies off the pile, one at a time, checking each face by the flickering light of a lamp. Eventually Baird found Tipu; as chance would have it, his body was only 300 yards from the gate of the prison where Baird had spent his captivity.[52]

The Sultan's body lay at the bottom of a heap of dead and wounded, stripped of its jewels. Tipu's eyes were open and the body was so warm that for a few moments, in the lamplight, Baird wondered whether the Sultan was still alive; but feeling his pulse, he declared him dead: 'His countenance was in no ways distorted, but had an expression of stern composure,' wrote Baird.[53] 'His dress consisted of jackets of fine white linen,' remembered another eyewitness. Below, he wore 'loose drawers of flowered silk, with a crimson cloth of silk and cotton round his waist; a handsome pouch with a red and green silk belt hung over his shoulder;

his head was uncovered, his turban being lost in the confusion of the fall; he had an amulet on his arm, but no ornament whatsoever.'* The corpse was placed in a palanquin and taken to the palace. There its identity was confirmed by Tipu's captured family.[54]

Already, the Mysore casualties hugely outnumbered those of the allies: some 10,000 of Tipu's troops were dead as opposed to around 350 of the Company and Hyderabadi sepoys: 'It would be scarcely possible,' wrote one British observer, 'to describe, in adequate terms, the objects of horror, the ghastly spectacle, presented to the senses by the bodies of the slain, in every attitude, and in every direction; lying in the verandas and along the principal street.'[55] But the horrors had barely begun.

That night the city of Srirangapatnam, home to 100,000 people, was given over to an unrestrained orgy of rape, looting and killing. Arthur Wellesley told his mother, 'Scarcely a house in the town was left unplundered, and I understand that in camp jewels of the greatest value, bars of gold etc etc have been offered for sale in the bazaars of the army by our soldiers, sepoys and followers. I came in to take command of the army of the morning of the 5th and with the greatest exertion, by hanging, flogging etc etc, in the course of that day I restored order …'[56]

At 4.30 that afternoon, the Sultan's funeral procession wound its way slowly and silently through crowds of weeping survivors. People lined the streets, 'many of whom prostrated themselves before the body, and expressed their grief by loud lamentations'.[57] Eventually the cortège reached the white, onion-domed tomb of Haidar Ali in the Lal Bagh garden.

Here Tipu was laid to rest next to his father, 'immediately consecrated by his Mahomedan followers as a Shahid, or Martyr of the Faith … with the full military honours due to his exalted rank'.[58] The British, all of whom had during the campaign been force-fed on Wellesley's propaganda that Tipu was a brutal tyrant, were surprised to discover

---

*Some secondary sources erroneously have Tipu's body being discovered by Arthur Wellesley. That it was Baird who found Tipu is made quite clear in the letter Baird wrote to General Harris; it can be found in Montgomery Martin (ed.), *The Despatches, Minutes and Correspondence of Marquis Wellesley*, vol. I, 1836, pp. 687–9. Arthur Wellesley's role in the taking of Seringapatam has in general been exaggerated by some historians who have inflated his importance with the benefit of hindsight and in view of his subsequent European triumphs. Baird and Harris were the two ranking officers who at the time were credited with defeating Tipu.

how much his people, both Hindu and Muslim, clearly loved him, just as they had been surprised to see how prosperous his kingdom was – 'well-cultivated, populous with industrious inhabitants, cities newly founded and commerce extending' – and how popular he was with his personal staff: 'numbers of his confidential Hindoo servants who during the war fell into our hands, acknowledged him to be a lenient and indulgent master.'[59]

Meanwhile, the Prize Committee, whose job it was to distribute the booty, began to amass what was left of Tipu's possessions and the contents of his treasury. They were astonished by what they found: 'The wealth of the palace, which was sufficiently dazzling to the eyes of many who were much more habituated to the sight of hoarded treasure than we were, seemed, at that moment, in specie, and jewels, and bullion, and bales of costly stuff, to surpass all estimate.'[60]

In all, around £2 million* of gold plate, jewellery, palanquins, arms and armour, silks and shawls were accumulated: 'everything that power could command, or money could purchase.'[61] The most magnificent object of all was Tipu's gold throne, inlaid with precious stones and with bejewelled tiger head finials 'superbly decorated ... [It took the form of a] howdah supported on the back of a Tyger, the solid parts made of black wood, and entirely covered by a sheet of purest gold, about as thick as a guinea, fastened on with silver nails, and wrought in tiger stripes, curiously indented, and most beautifully and highly polished.'[62]

Unable to decide who to award it to, the Prize Agents cut it up into small pieces, so destroying one of the great wonders of eighteenth-century India. Arthur Wellesley was the first to lament its loss, writing to the directors that 'it would have given me pleasure to have been able to send the whole throne entire to England but the indiscreet zeal of the prize agents of the army had broken that proud monument of the Sultan's arrogance into fragments before I had been appraised even of the existence of such a trophy.'[63]

Such was the notoriety of the bloody looting of Srirangapatnam that it later inspired Wilkie Collins' pioneering detective novel, *The Moonstone*. This opens at the fall of the city when the narrator's cousin, John Herncastle, seizes 'the Yellow Diamond ... a famous gem in the native annals of India [once] set in the forehead of the four-handed

---

* £200 million today.

Indian God who typifies the Moon'. To do this Herncastle, 'a torch in one hand, and a dagger dripping with blood in the other', murders the Moonstone's three guardians, the last of whom tells him as he dies that the diamond's curse will follow Herncastle to his grave: 'The Moonstone will have its vengeance yet on you and yours!' In the course of the novel, the diamond brings death and bad luck to almost everyone who comes into contact with the gem, before being seized back by the stone's mysterious Hindu guardians – something that has yet to happen with the real loot of Srirangapatnam.[64]

For the cream of Tipu's treasures were later collected by Clive's daughter-in-law, Henrietta, Countess of Powis, when she made a pleasure trip through southern India the following year. She was bored by the company of her husband, Edward Clive, the dim new Governor of Madras, and she left him to his new job at Governors House while she toured Tipu's former lands of Mysore. Whenever she came to a Company cantonment, she found herself surrounded by infantrymen longing to swap their share of the jewelled loot of Srirangapatnam for cash. She was happy to oblige. In this way, with very little outlay, she casually accumulated one of Europe's most impressive collections of Indo-Islamic art. In due course it made its way back to the Clive seat of Powis, where it was put on display beside the loot collected, forty years earlier, from the Murshidabad palace of Siraj ud-Daula. There it remains.

In the political settlement that followed, Tipu's sons were despatched to exile in the fort of Vellore and most of the best lands of the state of Mysore were divided between the Company and the Nizam of Hyderabad. The rump was returned to the Hindu Wadyar dynasty whose throne Haidar and Tipu had usurped. A five-year-old child from the dynasty was found living 'in a state of misery ... in kind of stable with sheds attached to it'.[65] The boy was informed he was now Raja, and, after a brief ceremony, was given charge of a reduced Mysore state, carefully watched over by a British Resident. The Wadyars in due course moved their capital back to Mysore and Srirangapatnam was left a ruin. It never recovered.

Today a small village squats beside the foundations of Tipu's former palace, and goats graze in his once magnificent pleasure grounds. Other than the majestic French-designed fortifications, the best-preserved building in Tipu's former capital is, ironically, the ancient Hindu Sri Ranganatha temple, after which Tipu's capital was named, and which was not just protected by Tipu but loaded with the valuable gifts which are still on display today, as are all its beautiful Vijayanagara-era images. Not one of these has suffered from the iconoclast's chisel, despite standing in the middle of the capital of a ruler denounced by his British enemies as a fanatical 'intolerant bigot'.

Today most of Tipu's capital is grazing land, and very little remains as witness of the former splendour of the kingdom of the Tiger of Mysore, the single Indian ruler who did more than any other to resist the onslaught of the Company.

'Ladies and gentlemen,' said Lord Wellesley, raising a glass, when the news of Tipu's death was brought to him, 'I drink to the corpse of India.'[66]

In less than two years, Wellesley had managed to disarm the largest French force in India, and to defeat and destroy the second largest. Now only the French-commanded corps of the Marathas stood between him and complete mastery of peninsular India. Further conflict was, sooner or later, inevitable.

The Marathas still controlled great swathes of western, central and southern India – very much more of the country than was then held by the Company. Had they been able to form a united front they could yet have re-emerged as the pre-eminent power in India; but their forces were now more hopelessly divided than ever, and this was something Wellesley took the greatest pleasure in exploiting.

The final act of the great Maratha Confederacy opened with the death, on 13 March 1800, of its veteran Prime Minister, the brilliant Nana Phadnavis, who had controlled Maratha diplomacy and administration for a quarter of a century.[67] Nana, 'the Maratha Machiavelli', had been one of the first to realise the existential threat posed by the Company to all independent Indian rulers and it was he who in the 1780s had stitched together the first Triple Alliance with a view to expelling the Company from India.

He had worked equally hard to keep the different parts of the Confederacy together. Tragically for the Marathas, he was the last of the talented generation that came to prominence after the catastrophic Maratha defeat at the Battle of Panipat in 1761, and his death came at the end of a five-year period, 1795–1800, which had also seen the loss of the Peshwa and the senior members of the houses of Scindia and Holkar. 'With the death of the great Minister Nana Phadnavis,' wrote the British Resident at Pune, General Palmer, 'all the wisdom and moderation of the Maratha government departed.'[68] Wellesley needed to do very little: he could just sit back in Calcutta and watch as the great Confederacy fell apart.

In Nana's absence, the three ambitious but quarrelsome and inexperienced teenagers who had between them inherited the leadership of Confederacy – the new Peshwa, Baji Rao II; the new head of the house of Scindia, Daulat Rao; and the new chief of the house of Holkar, Jaswant Rao – were now free to conspire and intrigue against each other unchecked. Just as Wellesley was beginning to move the troops of the increasingly well-armed, well-financed and aggressively militaristic Company with great subtlety around the subcontinental chessboard, the Marathas found themselves hopelessly stuck deep in a swamp of internal conflict. They could only hope to win against the Company if they stood united. With every passing day, however, that unity was becoming more and more elusive.[69]

The politics of north India had long been dominated by the old, hereditary feud between the Scindia and Holkar dynasties; now it passed down a generation, growing in bitterness and violence as it did so. When Mahadji Scindia had died in 1794, his successor, Daulat Rao, was only fifteen. The boy inherited the magnificent army that Benoît de Boigne had trained up for his predecessor, but he showed little vision or talent in its deployment. General Palmer, who was the Company's most experienced observer of Maratha politics, had greatly admired Mahadji Scindia; but he was not impressed by his successor. He described him as a 'profligate young man … weak [and] totally destitute of decency or principle'.

His revenues have declined rapidly, while his army has been unnecessarily augmented & he is now more than a crore [10 million rupees, £130 million today] in arrears to his troops, though he has received five crores by the most shameless oppression and robbery since he came to the *musnud* [throne]. The fidelity of his European officers & their corps have so far prevented his deposal, but they cannot save him much longer ... He is totally ignorant of his own affairs & incapable of understanding his own true interests, has not the smallest regard to honour or character, nor the least benevolence of mind. His servants take every advantage of these defects, and his government is a scene of confusion, fraud & rapine.[70]

It did not help that the new Peshwa, Baji Rao II, was equally young and inexperienced: his character, thought Palmer, 'is not better than Scindia's, but he wants the power to do as much mischief. In his private demeanour, however, he is decent while Scindia is quite abandoned. I have had a very troublesome and mortifying part to act here [in Pune] with two young men who neither understand their own good, nor the rights of others.'[71]

Baji Rao, a slight, timid, unconfident-looking boy of twenty-one with a weak chin and a downy upper lip, quickly showed himself comprehensively unequal to the challenge of holding together the different factions that made up his power base. Moreover, both he and Scindia were on irreconcilably hostile terms with the third principal Maratha power broker, Jaswant Rao Holkar, the one-eyed 'Bastard of Indore'.

The Peshwa's traditional role was to act as mediator between the different Maratha warlords and to bring them together. But in April 1802, Baji Rao managed instead, quite unnecessarily, to initiate a new blood feud with the Holkars. When Jaswant Rao's elder brother Vitoji was unexpectedly captured by the Peshwa's troops, the gleeful Baji Rao hung him in chains and sentenced him to suffer a flogging of 200 strokes, followed by a lingering death, tied to the foot of an elephant. In this manner, Vitoji was dragged screaming around the palace, while Baji Rao looked on, giggling, from a palace terrace.[72] Shortly afterwards Baji Rao invited Nana Phadnavis's former allies and supporters to the palace and there charged them with conspiracy and had them all arrested.[73]

As the epithet suggests, Jaswant Rao was the illegitimate son of Tukoji Holkar by a concubine. On the accession of his legitimate half-brother, Jaswant Rao had become a fugitive and set off into the jungle with a band of similarly desperate armed outlaws, living hard and moving fast in the badlands surrounding Indore. Following Vitoji's murder, having invoked the assistance of the family deity at Jejuri, and buoyed by his reputation as a courageous and resourceful leader, with the help of a tribe of 200 loyal Bhil warriors, Jaswant marched on his brother's fortress of Maheshwar, and had himself crowned as his successor.

There, on 31 May, Jaswant Rao Holkar vowed vengeance on those he held responsible for his brother's murderers. He first turned his attention to Scindia, setting off almost immediately to raid his enemy's territory and plunder and burn down his palaces. The two rivals spent much of 1801 fighting each other to a standstill across the hills and battlefields of central India as their armies marched and counter-marched between Ujjain and Burhanpur, haemorrhaging men with every inconclusive engagement. According to the chronicler Munna Lal, 'The other commanders of the Deccan, who could see things as they really were, strove to make peace with Jaswant Rao, saying that mutual hatred between us Marathas is a disgrace: prosperity arises from unity, while discord will bring about our ruin. But as the times were not favourable, their good advice made no impact. Day by day, the flames of discord burned ever more violently.'[74]

Finally, Jaswant Rao crossed the Godavari, marched south and headed for Pune with his army. The Peshwa, desperate for allies, turned to the only force still in play after the death of Tipu. He summoned the British Resident and asked for an alliance.

This was Wellesley's chance further to divide the Maratha Confederacy and to paralyse its war machine. He offered Baji Rao the same terms he had just offered the Nizam: a defensive alliance and a permanent garrison of Company sepoys to be stationed for his protection in Pune, in return for a large annual cash payment. The Peshwa accepted the terms; but before any Company troops could arrive to protect him, he and Scindia had to face Holkar's army, which was now rapidly advancing on Pune.

On Sunday 25 October 1802, the feast of Diwali, the two armies faced each other across a wide wooded valley at Hadaspur, a few miles from the Maratha capital. The battle began at half past nine in the morning with a prolonged artillery duel. It continued indecisively until, soon after one o'clock, Jaswant Rao personally led a massed cavalry charge on Scindia's guns, 'like a tiger on a herd of deer'. He was seriously wounded in the charge, but won a decisive victory.[75] Long before the battle was finally lost, and 5,000 of his men were killed, the frightened and bewildered Baji Rao had fled.

For a month, the young Peshwa moved with his bodyguard from one hillfort to another, avoiding Jaswant Rao's patrols. For a while he hid in the fortress of Sinhagarh, south of Pune, before making his way to the spectacular and craggily inaccessible hilltop fort of Raigad, where the first great Maratha, Shivaji, had been crowned and from where he had defied the Mughal armies of Aurangzeb. All the while, Baji Rao kept in close touch with his new Company allies, who soon put into action a rescue operation.

From Raigad, the Peshwa was instructed to make his way towards the sea coast, where he took shelter in the old pirate stronghold of Suvarnadurg. Shortly afterwards, he was picked up by the HMS *Herculean*, commanded by Wellesley's emissary, Captain Kennedy. Baji Rao and his men were fed and entertained, and two lakh rupees* in gold provided for their personal use. A fortnight later, on 16 December, the sloop docked, to artillery salutes, at Bassein – modern Vassai – the former Portuguese trading post a little to the north of Bombay: an extraordinary crumbling city full of decaying Jesuit churches and overgrown Dominican convents, all slowly beginning to return to the jungle, with mighty banyan trees corkscrewing through the broken baroque pediments and collapsing cloisters.

Here Baji Rao signed a treaty of alliance with the Company, which he now acknowledged to be the Marathas' overlord. A large British garrison would be installed in a new barracks to overlook the Peshwa's palace in Pune, where British arms would now reinstall him.

The document, known as the Treaty of Bassein, was ratified on the last day of the year, 31 December 1802. When Holkar learned the details of the terms, he declared, simply: 'Baji Rao has destroyed the Maratha state. Now the British will deal the same blow to it that they did to Tipu Sultan.'[76]

With the Treaty of Bassein, Wellesley believed he had succeeded, bloodlessly, in turning the Marathas into dependants of the Company, just as he had the Nizam. Other more experienced observers were less sure. As soon as he heard the details of the treaty, the Resident in Hyderabad,

* £2.6 million today.

James Kirkpatrick, wrote an official despatch from Hyderabad warning that not one of the Maratha warlords – the real powers in the Peshwa's dominions – would sit back and allow the English to control Baji Rao as their puppet. He predicted that Wellesley's actions, instead of bringing peace, would succeed in uniting the Marathas where Baji Rao himself had failed, and that together the Maratha armies would now mass in a 'hostile confederacy' to fight the Company.

Wellesley was predictably furious at what he regarded as Kirkpatrick's impertinence. He wrote an intemperate reply to Hyderabad, saying that any sort of united Maratha resistance was now 'categorically impossible' and that the Resident was guilty of 'ignorance, folly, and treachery' in suggesting otherwise. But Kirkpatrick held his ground, replying that his sources of intelligence indicated that 'such a confederacy was highly probable', that Holkar was even now on his way to occupy Pune, and that another of the leading Maratha chieftains, Raghuji Bhosle, the Raja of Berar, was planning to join him there.

Kirkpatrick was correct. Within months, the Company would once again be at war, and this time against the largest, best armed and most tightly trained forces they had ever faced.

The last survivor of the older generation of rulers was the Emperor Shah Alam. Now seventy-five, the old, blind king still sat on the gilt replica of the Peacock Throne amid his ruined palace, the sightless ruler of a largely illusory empire.

The Emperor had outlived all his enemies – Nader Shah, Imad ul-Mulk, Clive, Carnac, Shuja ud-Daula, Ghulam Qadir – but this was really his only victory. In old age, he was at least realistic about his failures, telling his heir apparent, Akbar Shah, that from the day that he arrived back in Delhi he was a ruler in name only. He was merely a high-class prisoner, he said, and his sons should not consider themselves more than that.[77]

Mahadji Scindia, who had at least showed an intermittent interest in the welfare of the Emperor, had died in 1794 and his successor, Daulat

Rao, was completely indifferent to his nominal position as Mughal Vakil-i-Mutlaq, or Vizier. He had still less interest in maintaining the Mughal court which lay in the far north of his dominions, and which he never visited after ascending the *musnud*. So while the Emperor remained under nominal Maratha protection, with a Maratha garrison resident within the Red Fort, the imperial family lived in poverty, neglected by their keepers.

These were a group of French officers led by Louis Guillaume François Drugeon, a Savoyard aristocrat who was given charge of the Emperor's person and command of the Emperor's bodyguard, and Louis Bourquien, a French mercenary of humble origins, who one historian of the Marathas has described as a 'pastry cook, pyrotechnic and poltroon'. Overall command lay with Scindia's Commander-in-Chief, General Pierre Perron, the son of a Provençal weaver, who lived with his troops a hundred miles to the south-east in the great fortress of Aligarh.[78]

Several volumes of the palace diary from the period, the *Roznamcha-i-Shah Alam*, survive in the British Library and they reveal as no other source the degree to which Mughal court life had been diminished by sheer lack of resources. We hear how one prince was caught stripping out pieces of marble and inlaid semi-precious stones from the floor of the Asad Burj tower 'for the purpose of sale. He was summoned by His Majesty and warned against committing such malicious activities.' A princess got into a dispute with the king over the interest on some jewels she had been forced to mortgage. A concubine was accused of stealing the ornaments of Nawab Mubarak Mahal. The royal children complained their salaries had not been paid; the more distant royal cousins made a bid to escape from the Salatin Cage, claiming they were not receiving adequate food and were near starvation. The king replied that 'due to the infirm state of the Empire, it was necessary for the Princes to be contented with whatever the Masters of Pune [the Marathas] provide for expenditure'.

On one especially telling occasion, the blind king had to reprimand the royal servants when a visiting Maratha chief threw a handful of coins on the floor of the audience hall, and all the attendants, abandoning court decorum, scrambled to grab them, some even breaking into fist fights within the Diwan-i-Am. Meanwhile, petitioners from the city complained about raids by Gujjars within the walls, and by the Sikhs on the outer suburbs.[79]

Shah Alam was also alarmed by the reports he heard of the violence and instability generated by the Maratha civil war, and blamed Daulat Rao: 'His Majesty expressed deep regret at these developments,' reported his biographer, Munna Lal, 'saying "this ill-omened one now strives to sow disunity among his companions. With such ugly and inappropriate behaviour, he saws off the branch he's sitting on. It will all end in scandal and disaster."'[80]

Frustrated by the ways of this world, the Emperor looked more and more to the world of the spirit. When a celebrated dervish arrived from Lahore, the imperial princes were sent out to the gates of the city to welcome him. On one occasion, it was reported that a concubine 'saw in a dream that if His Majesty paid a visit to Qadam Sharif and ordered a red cow to be released to wander free, the situation in the Empire would improve'. The Emperor gave orders that both should be done.[81]

Shah Alam's one remaining pleasure was his literary work. He spent much of his free time in his seventies editing his lifetime's poetic composition, from which he produced a single volume of his favourite verses, and the *Nadirat-i-Shahi, Diwan-i-Aftab*. He also dictated what scholars hold to be the first full-length novel in Delhi Urdu, a massive and ambitious 4,000-page work called the *Ajaib ul-Qasas*. This *dastan* (story) is a meditation on kingship and tells the story of a prince and princess tossed back and forth by powers beyond their control, from India to Constantinople via various magical islands and fairy and demonic realms. While the prince's sense of helplessness in the hands of fate reflects Shah Alam's experience, the lavish courtly settings of the *dastan* contrast with the impoverished reality of Shah Alam's daily life under the neglectful regime of the younger Scindia.

Daulat Rao may not have realised the value of controlling the elderly Mughal Emperor, but Lord Wellesley certainly did. He understood the vital distinction that, while Shah Alam may not have commanded any significant military power, he still held substantial symbolic authority, and that his decisions instantly conferred legality. 'Notwithstanding His Majesty's total deprivation of real power, dominion, and authority,' he wrote, 'almost every state and every class of people in India continue to acknowledge his nominal sovereignty. The current coin of every established power is struck in the name of Shah Alam ...'[82]

As it became clear by the end of June 1803 that Scindia was not going to accept the Treaty of Bassein, and that war was now unavoidable, Wellesley began drawing up detailed plans to invade Hindustan and seize both its ancient Mughal capital and its emperor. Having brought about 'the destruction of M. Perron's force', he would, he wrote, 'invade Scindia's possessions and make alliances with the Rajputs'.[83] 'I will seize Agra and Delhi,' he told his brother Arthur, and thus 'take the person of the Mogul into British protection … at the earliest practical moment.'[84] This would be the moment when the Company finally, both symbolically and in substance, came to replace the Mughals and the Marathas as the paramount rulers of India.

The British had long used Shah Alam's confidant, Sayyid Reza Khan, as a discreet channel of communication with the Emperor, and now Wellesley decided to send a secret letter to Shah Alam, offering him asylum and opening negotiations to take the Mughals back under Company care for the first time since the Emperor had left Allahabad thirty years earlier, in 1772: 'Your Majesty is fully apprised of the sentiments of respect and attachment which the British Government has invariably entertained towards your Royal Person and Family,' he began in his usual style, mixing flattery, sarcasm and half-truths. 'The injuries and indignities to which your Majesty and your illustrious family have been exposed since the time when your Majesty unhappily transferred the Protection of your person to the Power of the Maratha State, have been a subject of unceasing concern to the Honourable Company.'

> I have deeply regretted that the Circumstances of the times have hitherto not been conducive to the interposition of British Power for the purpose of affording your Majesty effectual relief from injustice, rapacity and inhumanity. In the present Crisis of Affairs, it is probable that your Majesty may have the opportunity of again placing yourself under the Protection of the British Government, and I shall avail myself of any event which may enable me to obey the Dictates of my Sincere respect and Attachment to your Royal House.[85]

Wellesley's Commander-in-Chief, Lord Lake, was instructed to 'show His Majesty every demonstration of reverence, respect and attention and every degree of regard for the comfort of His Majesty and the Royal Family', and to assure him 'that adequate Provision will be made for the support of your Majesty and of your family and Household'. It sounded generous, although the following paragraph hinted at Wellesley's actual intentions, when he suggested that the Emperor might prefer to leave the Red Fort and reside closer to Calcutta, at the modestly provincial fort of Monghyr near Patna.[86] But the chivalrous Lord Lake, misunderstanding Wellesley's meaning, went beyond his superior's intentions and assumed the tone of a subject rather than that of a friendly protector: 'I am cordially disposed to render your Majesty every demonstration of my loyalty and attachment,' he wrote, 'and I consider it to be a distinguished honour, as it is a peculiar privilege, to execute your Majesty's commands.'

The subtle difference in tone was not lost on the Emperor.

Two Company armies, one in the north, the other in the south, were now actively preparing for the coming conflict. In the north, Lake was drilling his men at his forward post, 'the vast ruins of the ancient city of Kannauj'. This lay close to the Company's western border with the Marathas, 'amidst lofty grass, covering the remains of splendid edifices and the tombs of princes, concealing a variety of game, such as wolves, jackals and tigers'.[87]

At the age of only seventeen, Lake had served close to Frederick the Great, and from him had learned the effectiveness of fast, light, horse-drawn artillery, or, as he called them, 'galloper guns'. Now he brought this military novelty to India: 'Two of these guns, six-pounders, were attached to each regiment of horse,' wrote Major William Thorn, 'and nothing could exceed the speed and exactness of the manoeuvres made with them at full speed by this large body of cavalry, whose combined movements were conducted with the most perfect order', something which would soon provoke 'terror among the Maratha horse'.[88] Lake worked his troops hard, but also charmed his army with his lavish evening hospitality. Once war broke out, he would soon need all these reserves of trust and popularity to persuade his troops to face down the magnificent Maratha artillery.

In the south, Lord Wellesley's younger brother, the newly promoted Major General Arthur Wellesley, was also deep in preparations for the forthcoming war: busy gathering in troops, rice and other provisions at Tipu's old capital of Srirangapatnam. Here he had earlier absorbed some of Tipu's troops, artillery and, most important of all, his vast transport machine – 32,000 bullocks and 250,000 strong white Mysore cattle – into his army.[89] Like Lake, he put his men through a rigorous training programme, practising crossing fast-flowing rivers with coracles, while in the hills round about he 'manoeuvred his future army, and taught us that uniformity of movement, which afterwards would enable him to conquer foes twenty times as numerous'.[90]

In early March 1803 Arthur Wellesley set off to march Peshwa Baji Rao II back into Pune and return him to his throne, now under British protection and the Wellesleys' own firm control. This he achieved in early April, without firing a shot, as Holkar cautiously withdrew his army north-east, across the Deccan to Aurangabad. Baji Rao resumed his palace life, now less as a Maratha leader than a British puppet, but apparently 'happy with his routine of baths and prayers, eating, drinking and making merry, having no bother of any outside concern ... Sumptuous dinners with profuse decorations for plates are arranged daily. Hot discussion takes place on the selection of dishes ...'[91]

The ease with which Arthur Wellesley achieved this success later led him to underestimate the bravery and skill of the Marathas, laughing at the former Resident, Lieutenant Colonel John Ulrich Collins, who warned him that 'their infantry and guns will astonish you'. This was a serious mistake; it would not be long before the Maratha armies proved themselves by far the most formidable enemy ever tackled by the Company. One of the major general's officers, who later remembered Collins' warning, wrote in his memoirs how 'riding home afterwards we amused ourselves, the General among the rest, in cutting jokes at the expense of "little King Collins." We little thought how true his words would soon prove.'[92]

While his generals were busy with drilling and training their troops, the Governor General himself was in Calcutta, engaged in finalising the financial and diplomatic support for his forthcoming war.

The Company's army had expanded very quickly under Wellesley's rule and within a few years its muster roll had gone up by nearly half from 115,000 to 155,000 men; in the next decade its numbers would rise again to 195,000, making it one of the largest standing European-style armies in the world, and around twice the size of the British army. It had also belatedly recruited an impressive new cavalry arm, mounted on strong European and South African horses. Their job it was to protect the slow-moving and cumbersome infantry and artillery columns from flanking attacks by irregular Indian light horse, as had happened with fatal consequences at Talegaon and Pollilur. This was a form of warfare in which the Marathas were especially skilled.[93]

Unlike the perennially cash-strapped Warren Hastings, Wellesley had no problem paying for this vastly increased military establishment. After the rural upheavals of Cornwallis's land reforms had settled down, the Company in Bengal found it had a considerable annual revenue surplus of Rs25 million. In contrast, Scindia was able to realise only Rs1.2 million* from his poorly irrigated home base in Malwa. This dependable surplus in turn allowed the Company easy access to credit from the Bengal money market, so much so that under Wellesley, between 1798 and 1806, the Company's debt in India more than tripled.

The Company was also able efficiently to redistribute these financial resources around India. The bankers of Benares and the west coast house of Gopaldas-Manohardas, both of whom were given the protection of the Company's army, now began to send representatives to travel with it, supplying cash as required both to the troops themselves and their army paymasters. Indeed, bankers from across India began to compete among themselves to supply the Company army with finance. Two Benares banking houses, Mannu Lal and Beniparshad, went as far as asking for assurances that the Company 'would honour them with a preference on being permitted to furnish supplies of cash that may be required for the use of the army'.[94]

---

* The modern equivalences of these sums are: Rs25 million = £325 million; Rs1.2 million = £15.6 million.

Ultimately the East India Company succeeded in war precisely because it had found a way to provide a secure financial base for its powerful mercenary army, and always found it easier than any of its rivals to persuade Indian *seths*, *sahukaras* and *shroffs* quickly to realise the cash needed to pay the army's salaries and feed its hungry troops. In contrast, as the young Arthur Wellesley noted, 'there is not a Maratha in the whole country, from the Peshwa down to lowest horseman, who has a shilling'. This was hardly surprising as, by 1801, Arthur had noted that after the devastations of the Maratha civil war, there was 'not a tree or an ear of corn standing for 150 miles around Pune'.[95]

Things were just as bad at the Mughal court where a Maratha envoy reported that 'money is nowhere to be seen'.[96] As a result Scindia and Holkar, both enormously in arrears to their troops and with their *sahukaras* often refusing further loans, found themselves in the same position as an earlier Maratha Peshwa who described himself as having 'fallen into that hell of being beset by creditors ... I am falling at their feet till I have rubbed the skin from my forehead.'[97]

But Richard Wellesley was far too cunning and ruthless an adversary to rely merely on brute military force or indeed the power of the Company's money alone. His greatest pleasure always lay in moving his pieces on the chessboard in such a way as to frustrate or hopelessly entrap his enemies.

Messages were sent out to seduce, corrupt and buy the frequently unpaid mercenaries in Maratha service; the Commander-in-Chief of Scindia's northern forces, General Pierre Perron, who had already invested his life savings of £280,000* in Company stock, was one of the first to show an interest in coming to a mutually beneficial financial arrangement.[98] Lake was given authority 'to conclude any arrangement with M. Perron for the security of his personal interests and property accompanied by any reasonable renumeration which shall induce him to deliver up the whole of his military resources and power into your hands'.[99]

The gnarled old warrior ascetic Anupgiri Gossain, now known as Himmat Bahadur, was also persuaded to come to terms with his former adversaries and ally his Bundelkhand-based Naga warriors with the Company. This happened despite warnings from one of Wellesley's intelligence men that 'Himmat Bahadur is not to be trusted ... A native

---

* Over £29 million today.

speaking of him said he was like a man who in crossing a river kept a foot in two boats, ready to abandon the one that was sinking.'[100]

Wellesley also worked hard to keep the warring Maratha armies from patching up their differences. In particular, adopting the old Roman maxim *divide et impera*, divide and rule, Wellesley did all he could to keep Scindia and Holkar from reconciling. In this he was especially successful.

By the end of June 1803, Holkar had gathered his entire army near Aurangabad but still equivocated about joining the coalition with his brother's murderers to fight the Company. Here Wellesley's masterstroke was to send Holkar a captured letter from Scindia in which the latter plotted with Peshwa Baji Rao to overthrow Holkar after the war was over: 'Let us make a show of satisfying his demands,' wrote Daulat Rao. 'After the war is over, we shall both wreak our full vengeance upon him.'[101]

After receiving this, Holkar, who had just made the first two days' march towards Scindia, turned back, and firmly declined to join the coalition. Shortly afterwards, he recrossed the Narmada and set off back towards his central Indian base at Maheshwar.[102] This allowed Wellesley first to pick off Scindia and his ally Raghuji Bhosle, Raja of Berar, and only later to move his forces against Holkar. This, perhaps more than any other factor, gave the Company its most overwhelming advantage against its still militarily powerful but politically fractured Maratha adversaries.

Behind all these manoeuvres, Wellesley was developing an aggressive new conception of British Empire in India, not as a corporate but as a state enterprise; and it was a vision that was markedly more nationalist and nakedly expansionist than anything his Company predecessors could have dreamed of. On 8 July Sir George Barlow first articulated it in an official memorandum: 'It is absolutely necessary,' he wrote, 'that no Native State should be left to exist in India which is not upheld by the British power, or the political conduct of which is not under its absolute control.'[103] It was from this idea of total British government control over the entire Indian peninsula that would grow the British Raj – and with it a future in which Mughal, Maratha and finally even the Company itself would all, in time, give way to the control of the British Crown.

As usual, Wellesley neglected to tell his nominal employers, the Company directors, what he was planning. Already there was growing nervousness in Leadenhall Street about Wellesley's grandiose style of ruling. When the traveller Lord Valentia arrived in Calcutta he applauded Wellesley's imperial style, writing that it was better that 'India be ruled from a palace than a counting house'; but it was Wellesley's increasingly wasteful and spendthrift use of Company funds that was steadily eroding his support among the directors, and provoking the first discussions about his eventual recall.[104] Already the directors were sending shots across Wellesley's bow, making it quite clear that 'It by no means appears to us essential to the well-being of our Government in India that pomp, magnificence and ostentation of the Native Governments should be adopted by the former; the expense that such a system would naturally lead must prove highly injurious to our commercial interests.'[105]

In his usual spirit of dissimulation to his employers, well into 1803 Lord Wellesley was still promising the directors a 'speedy and hasty conclusion of the late arrangements with His Highness the Peshwa, and of the amicable adjustment of the differences existing among the Maratha chieftains, through the mediation and influence of the British power'.[106] Maybe that spring Wellesley really did still hope that Scindia could be intimidated into recognising the Treaty of Bassein, and, like the Nizam and the Peshwa Baji Rao before him, be bullied into accepting the protection of the Company. But as spring gave way to the summer of 1803, such dreams quickly faded, as the increasingly gloomy despatches from his envoy Colonel John Collins confirmed. In July, Wellesley sent Scindia an ultimatum to withdraw north of the Narmada or to face the consequences.

In the end, Daulat Rao Scindia did not back down; instead, like Tipu, he began making preparations for hostilities. On 1 August 1803, he gave Collins a formal declaration of war and dismissed him from his camp.

It took a week for express couriers to carry the news to Calcutta; but only a few hours for Lord Wellesley to give the order for his carefully laid war plans to be immediately put into action on no less than four fronts – with minor thrusts along the coasts of Orissa and Gujarat as well as the two main assaults which were designed to take control of the entire Deccan and all of Hindustan.[107]

To Scindia and Bhosle, the Governor General wrote a brief note: 'While we have no desire to open war against you, you two chiefs have given a clear indication of your intention to attack us, since you have collected large forces on the Nizam's frontiers and you have refused to move away from your positions. You have rejected the hand of friendship I have offered you, and I am now starting hostilities without further parleys. The responsibility is entirely yours.'[108]

Major General Arthur Wellesley heard the news of Scindia's declaration of war on 4 August. On the 6th he broke camp and with 40,000 troops headed off north towards the mighty fortress of Ahmadnagar which he captured on the 11th after a brief bombardment and the payment of a large bribe to the French and Arab mercenaries holding the fort for Scindia. Inside was found large amounts of gunpowder, part of Scindia's remaining treasure and ample food supplies. Arthur Wellesley garrisoned the fort as his base while he sent scouts out to search for the main Maratha army.

Scindia and Bhosle, meanwhile, had succeeded in bringing their forces together; they then marched their confederated army south to plunder the Nizam's territories around Aurangabad and draw Wellesley out of the safety of his fortifications. In this they succeeded. Leaving a large garrison behind to guard Ahmadnagar, Wellesley moved eastwards to defend his allies' territory and stop the Maratha advance. The two armies finally came within sight of one another in the dusty alluvial plain to the north of the Ajanta Pass, in the early morning of 23 September, after Wellesley's troops had just marched eighteen miles through the night.

The major general had broken his force in two the day before to avoid the delay that would have taken place in sending his whole army through the narrow Ajanta defile; half he had sent off to the west under his deputy, Colonel Stevenson. He therefore had less than 5,000 men – half of them Madrasi sepoys, the other half kilted Highlanders – when he heard from his scouts that Scindia's camp was only five miles away and that the Marathas were about to move off. His small army was exhausted from their night march. But, worried that his quarry might escape if he waited, Wellesley made an immediate decision to head straight into the attack, without giving his troops time to rest or waiting for the other half of his force.

Reaching the crest of a low hill, the major general saw the two Maratha armies spread out before him, next to the fortified village of Assaye. Their tents and *qanats* (tented enclosures) extended for as much as six miles along the banks of the shallow Khelna River to near where it reached a confluence with another smaller stream, the Juah. He calculated that there were around 10,000 infantry and around five times that number of irregular cavalry. They were clearly not expecting an attack and their artillery bullocks were out grazing along the riverbank.

Leaving his baggage and stores behind him under guard, Wellesley marched straight forward, as if to make an immediate frontal attack over the river. Then at the last moment he turned eastwards to cross the meandering Khelna at an unguarded ford whose position he had guessed at due to the proximity of two small villages just before it. His guess was a lucky one: the water was between knee and waist high, and Wellesley just managed to get all his troops across without them getting their powder wet. Even so, his artillery had trouble crossing, and several guns got stuck in the mud, leaving his infantry to form up and face the opening salvos of the Maratha bombardment without the protection of artillery cover.

Arthur Wellesley had hoped that the speed and surprise of his movement would leave the Marathas in disarray and allow him to attack their unguarded right flank; but to his surprise he found that Scindia's troops had managed not only to get themselves into full battle formation but had also skilfully wheeled around to the left in order to face his new direction of attack, all the while maintaining perfect order. This was a difficult manoeuvre that he presumed they would be incapable of, but which they instantly effected with parade-ground precision.

This was only the first in a whole series of surprises in a battle that Arthur Wellesley would later remember as one of the hardest he had ever fought, and altogether tougher than his later confrontation with Napoleon at Waterloo. 'Their infantry is the best I have ever seen in India, excepting our own,' he wrote afterwards to his friend John Malcolm. 'I assure you that their fire was so heavy that I doubted at one time if I should be able to induce our troops to advance. All agree that the battle was the fiercest that has ever been seen in India. Our troops behaved admirably; the sepoys astonished me.'[109]

A particular shock was Scindia's heavy field guns which proved just as deadly as Collins had warned: 'The fire of the enemy's artillery became most dreadful,' remembered Major John Blakiston. 'In the space of less than a mile, 100 guns worked with skill and rapidity, vomited forth death into our feeble ranks. It cannot then be a matter of surprise if our sepoys should have taken advantage of any irregularities in the ground to shelter themselves from the deadly shower, or that even, in some few instances, not all the endeavours of the officers could persuade them to move forward.'[110] Major Thorn concurred: 'It was acknowledged by all the officers present, who had witnessed the power of the French artillery in the wars of Europe, that the enemy's guns at the Battle of Assaye were equally well-served.'[111]

The major general himself had two horses shot under him and had several of his immediate staff killed around him by the clouds of grape the Maratha gunners sent in his direction. One large round shot just missed Wellesley as he was crossing the Khelna but decapitated his dragoon orderly as he paused midstream. The horrifying sight of the headless horseman features in many accounts of the battle, 'the body being kept in its seat by the valise, holsters, and other appendages of a cavalry saddle, and it was some time before the terrified horse could rid himself of the ghastly burden'.[112]

The Madras infantry sepoys in the centre and the Highlanders on the right wing of Wellesley's front line were targeted with particular violence, as the Maratha gunners tried to blow away the core of Wellesley's formation with large canisters of anti-personnel chain and grapeshot, fired at short range and at close quarters: whirring through the air with a terrifying screeching noise, 'it knocked down men, horses and bullocks, every shot'.[113]

Nevertheless, Wellesley's infantry continued to advance at a steady pace, through the smoke. They fired a single volley, then charged the Maratha guns with bayonets, killing the gunners as they stood at the gun muzzles 'and none quitted their posts until the bayonets were at their breasts ... nothing could surpass the skill or bravery displayed by their *golumdauze* [gunners]'.[114]

A final surprise awaited the British as they marched forward to drive Scindia's men from their fallback position. Once the British infantry lines had safely passed by, many of the Maratha 'dead' around the cannons 'suddenly arose, seized the cannon which had been left behind by the army, and began to reopen a fierce fire upon the rear of our troops, who, inattentive to what they were doing, were eagerly bent upon the pursuit of the flying enemy before them'. The British lines were raked with yet more canister shot until the major general personally led a desperate cavalry charge 'against the resuscitated foe', during which he had his second horse shot beneath him.[115]

Two hours later, after a final stand in the village fort, Scindia's Marathas were driven from the field and back over the Juah, leaving ninety-eight of their guns in British hands; but the casualties on both sides were appalling. The Marathas lost around 6,000 men. Wellesley lost fewer, but as the smoke cleared the major general found he had just left fully one-third of his army dead on the battlefield: 1,584 out of 4,500 of his troops were later burned or buried on the plains of Assaye.[116] Indeed, so battered were his forces that Wellesley declared pursuit of Scindia and his fleeing men impossible, writing to his elder brother, 'Scindia's French[-trained] infantry were far better than Tipu's, his artillery excellent, and his ordnance so good, and so well equipped, that it answers for our service. We never could use Tipu's. Our loss is great, but the action, I believe, was the most severe that ever was fought in this country.'[117] As one of Wellesley's senior officers wrote to the major general soon afterwards: 'I hope you will not have occasion to purchase any more victories at such a high price.'[118]

Because of Arthur Wellesley's later celebrity after Waterloo, Assaye has long come to be regarded as the crucial victory of the Maratha War; but at the time, most eyes were actually on the north, where, long before Assaye, the Commander-in-Chief, Lord Lake, was already advancing rapidly on the Mughal capital, in what was seen at the time as the final chapter of the Company's conquest of what had once been the Mughal Empire.

As Richard Wellesley wrote unequivocally to Lake: 'The defeat of Perron is certainly the first object of the campaign.' Lake, he stressed, must understand the crucial 'importance of securing the person and nominal authority of the Mogul against the designs of France, and the increase in reputation to the British name which would result from offering an honourable asylum to the person and family of that injured and unfortunate monarch'.[119]

Lord Lake, who liked to claim descent from the Arthurian hero Lancelot of the Lake, was not a man who admired diplomacy or who liked being told what to do: 'Damn your writing,' he is alleged to have cried at an army book-keeper. 'Mind your fighting!' The phrase became his maxim. Although sixty years old, and a veteran of the Seven Years War and, more recently, the American War of Independence, where he fought against Washington at Yorktown, he was still famous for his boyish charm and immense energy, often rising at 2 a.m. to be ready to lead the march, blue eyes flashing.[120]

Determined to take the offensive, Lake left Kanpur on 7 August, a day after he heard about the declaration of war, even though it was in the middle of the monsoon and the roads were awash with mud. He headed due west towards Perron's fortress at Aligarh. Intent on fighting a fast-moving campaign, Lake brought with him a small but highly trained Grand Army of 10,000 men, including a cavalry division armed with his light galloper guns; but he deliberately brought little heavy artillery and no siege equipment.

His intention to lead a small and mobile force was, however, somewhat challenged by Indian reality. By the early nineteenth century, East India Company armies had accumulated a huge establishment of attendants and assistants and support staff. In the end, the total body heading west amounted to more than 100,000 people, including mahouts and coolies, grass-cutters and horse-keepers, tent lascars and bullock-men, Banjarrah grain-collectors and money-changers, 'female quacks, jugglers, groups of dancing girls, and votaries of pleasure'. These numbers did not, of course, include the thousands of elephants, camels, horses, poultry and flocks of goats and sheep which followed close on their heels: 'The march of our army had the appearance of a moving town or citadel,' remembered Major Thorn, 'in the form of an oblong square, whose sides were defended by ramparts of glittering swords and bayonets.'[121]

After three weeks of difficult marching through heavy rain, wading through mud and badly flooded roads with carefully sealed ammunition boxes carried aloft on men's heads, on 29 August Lake's army crossed into Maratha territory and advanced swiftly on the mighty polygonal fortress of Aligarh, with its massive French-designed walls, reinforced corner towers and deep moat.

Aligarh was regarded as one of the strongest and best-provisioned forts in Hindustan; a siege could have taken months. Throughout the march, however, Lake had been in negotiations with General Perron over what he would charge to deliver the fortress into the hands of the British.[122] Through intermediaries, the two commanders had eventually come to an understanding, and when Lake's army advanced on his headquarters, Perron obediently withdrew, along with his bodyguard, after only the briefest of skirmishes with Lake and a few salvoes from his galloper guns.

Perron told his men he was off to gather reinforcements from Agra and Delhi, and to his deputy, Colonel Pedron, 'a stout, elderly man with a green jacket with gold lace and epaulettes', he sent a remarkably disingenuous letter: 'Remember you are a Frenchman,' he wrote, 'and let no action of yours tarnish the character of your nation. I hope in a few days to send back the English general as fast, or faster, than he came. Make yourself perfectly easy on the subject. Either the Emperor's army or General Lake shall find a grave before Allyghur. Do your duty, and defend the fort while one stone remains upon another. Once more remember your nation. The eyes of millions are fixed upon you!'[123]

These brave words were belied by the last conversation he had before fleeing up the Delhi road. One of his junior cavalry officers, of mixed Scottish and Rajput blood, attempted to ride with him, but was waved away, 'Ah, no, no! It is all over!' Perron shouted over his shoulder, 'in confusion and without his hat', at the young James Skinner. 'These fellows [the cavalry] have behaved ill: do not ruin yourself, go over to the British; it is all up with us!'[124]

Distrusted by the French, all the Anglo-Indians among the Maratha forces, including Skinner himself, crossed the battle lines at this point: 'We went to General Lake and were kindly received,' wrote Skinner later.[125] Pedron and many of Perron's French mercenary colleagues were equally happy to surrender if they were assured of a safe passage home with their lifetimes' savings intact. But Lake had not reckoned with the honour of Scindia's Rajput and Maratha officers, who stoutly refused all inducements to drop their weapons and quickly withdrew behind the walls to begin their defence. There they deposed and imprisoned Pedron, elected a Maratha commander of their own, and prepared to fight to the death.

For three days Lake continued to negotiate, making the men a variety of extravagant promises, but the defenders remained firm. 'I tried every method to prevail upon these people to give up the fort,' wrote Lake, 'and offered a very large sum of money, but they were determined to hold out, which they did most obstinately, and, I may say, most gallantly.'[126]

Lake was daunted by the challenge now lying in front of him: 'The strength of the place cannot be described,' he wrote to Wellesley. 'A Seventy-Four [gun ship] might sail in the ditch.'[127] But ever the hyperactive sexagenarian, Lake was temperamentally incapable of conducting a patient siege, and anyway had left his siege equipment in Kanpur. So, on 4 September he opted for the only alternative: a frontal assault on the main gate of a fortress long considered impregnable. An Irish deserter from Scindia's garrison, Lieutenant Lucan, offered to lead the storming party, under the supervision of Lake's deputy, Colonel Monson.

Two hours before dawn, the storming party set off and shortly after that had their first stroke of luck. Had the Marathas withdrawn behind the moat and destroyed the bridge, there was very little Lake could have done. But the defenders had stationed a piquet of fifty men with a 6-pounder gun behind a breastwork in front of the fort, leaving the bridge undamaged and the wicket gate open. Lucan and his storming party edged up in the dark and found the men smoking at their post. 'They ran at them like lions,' wrote Skinner, and slit the throats of as many as stood their ground. The rest 'ran away to the wicket, and got in. The assaulting party attempted to get in along with them, but were shut out.'

> Instead, however, of retreating, these brave fellows stood upon the *goonjus* [bridge] under one of the heaviest fires of musketry and great guns I have seen ... [attempting to scale the walls.] Only at sunrise did they fall back about one hundred yards ... and in going back they carried with them the [abandoned] Maratha gun.[128]

They fired the gun twice, then a third time, but failed to blow open the heavily reinforced gate. While waiting for a new and larger cannon to be hauled up, the attackers continued their attempts to mount the walls with scaling ladders. As before, they were driven down by the Marathas on the battlements, who had long pikes waiting for them. A heavy 12-pounder cannon was finally wheeled forward to the gate, but just before it could be fired its weight broke through a mine gallery that the defenders had skilfully tunnelled under the area in front of the wicket gate, leaving the gun half in, half out of the tunnel beneath.

As Monson and Lucan tried to lever the cannon out, the attackers were raked with musketry from above and exposed to the fire from two heavy mortars filled with grape that the defenders had prepared and positioned for just this moment. To add to the chaos, the defenders then began to climb down the scaling ladders that the British troops had left propped against the walls. One of them wounded Monson in the thigh with a thrust of his pike; four of his officers were also killed.[129] 'This misfortune detained us considerably, and at this time it was that we lost so many of our officers and men. Never did I witness such a scene. The sortie became a perfect slaughter house, and it was with the greatest difficulty that we dragged the gun over our killed and wounded.'[130]

In the Company camp, Lake was on the verge of blowing the bugle to call off the attack. But at the last minute the cannon was righted, pressed against the wood of the gate and fired. It was a muzzle-blast containing no shot, but the pressure from the powder charge at close quarters finally buckled one of the great doors open.[131] 'I was close to Lord Lake,' wrote Skinner, 'and saw and heard everything that passed.'

> The God of Heaven certainly looked down upon those noble fellows ... for they blew open half the gate, and giving three shouts, they rushed in. The Rajputs stood their ground, like brave soldiers, and from the first to the second gate the fight was desperately maintained on both sides, and the carnage was very great ... Then spurring his horse [Lake] galloped to the gate. When he saw his heroes lying thick there, tears came to his eyes. 'It is the fate of good soldiers!' he said; and turning round, he galloped back to the camp, and gave up the fort to plunder.[132]

In the hours that followed, the garrison of 2,000 was massacred. No quarter was asked for and none was given. 'Many of the enemy were killed in attempting to escape by swimming the ditch after we got in, and I remarked an artilleryman to snap his piece at a man who at the same instance dived to save himself,' wrote John Pester, Lake's quartermaster. 'The soldier coolly waited his coming up and shot him through the head.'

> As the heat of the business was over, I remonstrated with him on putting them to death at that time, but the man declared he had lost some of his oldest comrades that morning, and that he wished to be revenged, reminding me also that we had received orders to spare none ... Guards were disposed over the different magazines, and at each gate as soon as we had possession, and the enemy were all disposed of; scarcely a man of them escaped for those who swam the ditch were cut up by the troopers on the plain, and all we found in the place were bayonetted.[133]

At midnight on the night of 1 September, the Qu'tb Minar, built in the twelfth century as a symbol of the establishment of Islamic rule in India, was hit by a massive earthquake and its top storey collapsed to the ground: 'In Delhi and all around many buildings were toppled from their foundations,' wrote Shah Alam's biographer, Munna Lal. 'In several places the earth cracked wide open. Had it lasted a moment longer, it would have ushered in the Day of Resurrection. The wise interpreted it as a bad omen, signifying that disasters would appear in these times.'[134]

Shah Alam, always sensitive to omens and premonitions, was alarmed. He was, after all, in a difficult position. For much of his adult life he had had no option but to choose between the protection of the Marathas and that of the Company. Both had used him for their own ends, and both had, at crucial junctures in his life, let him badly down. But when the news arrived that Perron had finally surrendered himself to Lord Lake, and been given safe passage to Calcutta with his family, his diamonds and his fortune, the Emperor took the view that the Company was now clearly in the ascendant, and it was time to reopen negotiations.

Shah Alam calculated that his best chance lay in covertly reaching out to Wellesley, while appearing to obey his French and Maratha masters who still garrisoned his fort and staffed his bodyguard. Thus, while putting his seal to proclamations that he would fight against the Company which had 'seized of the whole country and laid aside allegiance to the throne', he authorised Sayyid Reza Khan to enter into renewed correspondence with Lake, explaining that 'the public letter which the Emperor has written and the announcement of his taking to the field are not voluntary acts but arise from compulsion and are directly contrary to his own wishes ... He says, "I shall resist it to the utmost, but as I am in their power, I am helpless."'[135]

Shah Alam nevertheless could not forget the way that Hastings had unilaterally cut the promised payment of the Diwani revenue from Bengal due to him under the terms of the Treaty of Allahabad, and he asked for written assurances that his allowances would be properly paid before he committed to throwing his lot in with the Company: 'Conceiving therefore that when the English gain possession of the Country they may prove forgetful of me, it becomes necessary for the General [Lake] to settle this point with the Governor General, that hereafter there be no want of obedience or cause of dissatisfaction to me.'[136] At the same time the Emperor firmly refused to allow Scindia's men to take his heir apparent, Akbar Shah, with them into battle.

Since Perron's defection, military authority in the Red Fort had devolved to Lieutenant Colonel Louis Bourquien, who had once earned his living by making both fireworks and tartlets in Calcutta, 'his craft in culinary matters being superior to his skill in military ones'.[137] But wherever his true talents lay, Scindia's troops remained loyal to him, and were determined to revenge the massacre of their brothers-in-arms in Aligarh.

When news came that Lake was advancing rapidly up from Aligarh and had decided to skirt Agra with a view to capturing Delhi and 'liberating' the Emperor as soon as possible, Bourquien ferried his army of 19,000 troops across the Yamuna from the ghats under the Red Fort over to Shahdara. The area was flat and, in places, marshy, but he found a low hill commanding the approach to the city and prepared an ambush near the Hindan River, at a point where two swampy lakes flanked the road. This meant that any force coming towards the city from Aligarh would have to funnel themselves into a narrow causeway between the bogs. He then hid his one hundred heavy guns in a semicircle behind tall fans of elephant grass at the base of the hill and waited for Lake to approach.

On the afternoon of 10 September, Lake had camped his men to the north of Akbar's Tomb at Sikandra. Towards evening his spies brought news that Scindia's army had crossed the Yamuna and were preparing to block his crossing; but they brought little specific information about the whereabouts of the army. Word quickly circulated that the final battle for the control of Mughal Delhi would be fought the following day: 'We drank an extra bottle of claret upon this intelligence,' wrote Quartermaster Pester, 'and without much reflection on the fate of a battle enjoyed ourselves until after nine.'[138]

Lake woke his troops at 2 a.m., as was his habit, and the final march towards the Mughal capital began an hour later, at 3 a.m. At 10 a.m., after marching eighteen miles, with the sun beginning to beat down on the column, Lake ordered a halt for breakfast beside a marshy lake on the banks of the Hindan. Tents were erected, boots were removed, fires lit and the sepoys began to cook their parathas. The general sent a dram around his officers.

Quite suddenly there was a series of bright flashes and the thunder crash of heavy artillery, 'shattering not only the tranquillity of the day but the eardrums of men closest to the guns ... The accompanying pressure wave generated by the explosive muzzle-blasts, which flattened the obstructing grass, was immediately followed by other, unnatural and far more eerie auditory sensations that played upon deafened ears. Grape shot tore and chain shot scythed through the grass with a shearing sound which was followed by a metallic clatter or muffled thuds depending on whether the projectiles struck equipment or the flesh of men and horses.'[139]

It was a massacre. Among the many casualties was Pester, who was hit by some of the first volleys: 'A grapeshot passed through the housing of my pistols, and shattered the stock of one of them, and I felt my horse stagger under me; another grape had grazed his side and lodged under the skin; a third went through him. It entered at his near quarter and passed out at the other. He staggered and fell onto me.'[140]

Chaos broke out, but the Marathas remained at their defensive position on the raised ground, failing to advance and scatter the terrified

Company sepoys. This gave Lake time to rally his men. Deciding to lure Bourquien off his strong position, Lake gave the order for the infantry to fall back in a feint, and they did so, between two wings of cavalry who lay hidden behind the tall grass. The Marathas took the bait and rushed forward, only to find themselves caught in a pincer movement. The Company infantry then turned and advanced methodically forward with bayonets, supported by the galloper guns. 'We drove them into the Yamuna,' wrote the badly bruised Pester, 'and hundreds of them were destroyed in endeavouring to cross it.'

> The Flying Artillery was up, and the river appeared boiling by the fire of grape kept up on those of the enemy who had taken to the river. It was literally, for a time, a stream of blood, and presented such a scene as at another period would freeze a man's very soul. When this was past, we faced about, and returned to the field of battle to collect our wounded men and officers …
>
> There the scene was truly shocking … About thirty surgeons were absolutely covered in blood, performing operations on the unfortunate soldiers who had had their legs and arms shattered in the action, and death in every shape seemed to preside in this assembly of human misery. Their exclamations were enough to pierce the hardest heart. Numbers were fainting, and even dying under the operation; others bore the pain with as much fortitude as they could … In one corner of the tent stood a pile of legs and arms, from which the boots and clothes of many were not yet stripped off.[141]

That night, five French commanders gave themselves up, and Lord Lake wrote to tell Wellesley what had passed.[142] He added: 'Your Lordship will perceive that our loss has been very great … under as heavy a fire as I have ever been witness to …'[143] Later he expanded on the bravery and skill shown by his Maratha opponents. 'Their battalions are uncommonly well appointed,' he wrote, 'have a most numerous artillery, as well served as they possibly can be.'

> All the sepoys of the enemy behaved exceedingly well, the gunners standing to their guns until killed by the bayonet … I was never in so severe a business in my life, and I pray to God I may never be in

such a situation again. Their army is better appointed than ours; no expense is spared, and they have three times the number of men to a gun we have. These fellows fought like devils, or rather heroes, and had we not made a disposition for attack in a style that we should have done against the most formidable army we could have been opposed to, I verily believe, from the position they had taken, we might have failed.[144]

Terrible as it was, the Battle of Delhi was the last time British troops faced French officers in South Asia, ending more than a century of rivalry which had caused so much bloodshed, mostly of non-Europeans, across the subcontinent. It also brought to a close Hindustan's unhappy century of being fought over, and plundered, by rival armies. As Khair ud-Din put it shortly afterwards, 'the country is now flourishing and at peace. The deer lies down with the leopard, the fish with the shark, the pigeon with the hawk, and the sparrow with the eagle.'[145] Khair ud-Din was, of course, writing to flatter his British patrons, but there was a measure of truth in what he wrote: in comparison with the horrors of the last century – 'the Great Anarchy' – the next fifty years would be remembered as 'the Golden Calm'.

Most importantly, the Battle of Delhi decided the future fate of India. The Marathas were the last indigenous Indian power that was militarily capable of defeating the Company and driving it out of South Asia. There were other battles still to be fought against both Scindia and Holkar before they surrendered, but after Assaye and Delhi the outcome of the war was quite clear. The last power who could have ousted the Company had been humbled and was about to be conquered.

Company Bengal, Madras and Bombay were now linked up as a continuous unit, joined with the Deccan and much of Hindustan, so consolidating a land empire that controlled over half a million square miles of territory and which, fifty years later, would become the British Raj.[146] Before long, the Company would conclude treaties with all the Rajput states that had been fiefs of Scindia: Jodhpur, Jaipur, Macheri, Bundi and the Jat Raja of Bharatpur. All the major regimes of peninsular India had now either been annexed or become allies of the Company through a process of conquest, collaboration and co-option. As Arthur

Wellesley told his delighted brother: 'Your policy and our power have reduced all the powers in India to the state of mere cyphers.'[147]

Around 600 well-trained Company civil servants, guarded by 155,000 Indian sepoys, were to administer most of peninsular India.[148] Here the Company's army was now unequivocally the dominant military force, and the Governor General who controlled it the real Emperor. Not only had Lord Wellesley gained many more subjects than Britain had lost a decade earlier in North America – around 50 million – he had also created a cadre of young men committed to his imperial project, and who would carry it forward after he had gone.[149] Wellesley's ambitious protégés were working for the establishment and spread of an Anglicised colonial state that would provide an efficiently regimented but increasingly remote and alien administrative infrastructure for this new empire. As one of them, the young Company diplomat Charles Metcalfe, wrote, 'Sovereigns you are, and as such must act.'[150]

In London there was surprisingly little awareness as yet of what had been achieved. The country was still obsessed with the struggle with Napoleon, and despite the swathe of territories Lord Wellesley had conquered, there was little interest in what had taken place in India outside those organisations or people directly concerned with it. Even Wellesley's ultimate boss, the Foreign Secretary, Lord Grenville, declared himself 'totally unacquainted with every part of this subject' when Lord Wellesley's aggressively expansionist Indian policy was briefly discussed in a half-empty House of Lords.[151]

But within India everyone knew that a major revolution had just taken place. Many Muslims, led by the puritanical Delhi imam Shah Abdul Aziz, saw this as the moment that India had slipped out of their hands for the first time since the twelfth century: 'From here to Calcutta, the Christians are in complete control,' wrote Shah Abdul Aziz in an 1803 fatwa of jihad. 'India is no longer *Dar ul-Islam*.'[152] Company officials realised it with equal clarity: 'We are now complete masters of India,' wrote Thomas Munro, 'and nothing can shake our power if we take proper measures to confirm it.'[153]

The sinews of British supremacy were now established. With the exception of a few months during the Great Uprising of 1857, for better or worse, India would remain in British hands for another 144 years, finally gaining its freedom only in August 1947.

Shah Alam and the royal family watched the battle anxiously from the roof of the Red Fort. Towards late afternoon they had a grandstand view of the Company lancers chasing fleeing Maratha sepoys immediately opposite their marble pavilions and 'cutting them up on the banks of the river which runs immediately under the fort of Delhi. The Emperor had sent out instantly to congratulate the Commander-in-Chief on our victory and declared that "he waited to receive the General as his saviour in his arms."'[154]

The following day, 15 September, according to the *Shah Alam Nama*,

General Lake proceeded to pitch his tents on the far side of the Yamuna and sent Sayyid Reza Khan, who had for a long time been the Company's representative at the Imperial Court, to humbly request an audience at the Celestial Threshold. He also asked that boats should be provided for crossing the river. The Universal Monarch gave the order to his Commander of the River to send boats without delay. The General crossed the Yamuna and lodged in the vicinity of the old fort, Purana Qila. The next day, Sayyid Reza Khan presented the Governor General's letter to His Majesty expressing good wishes and loyal friendship. His Majesty honoured the messenger with gifts of robes.[155]

On 16 September, the Crown Prince, Akbar Shah, was meant to have presented himself at Lord Lake's camp in Purana Qila at noon, but with the usual Mughal sense of time-keeping, did not appear until 3 p.m., when the sepoys had been on parade for a full three hours. Major William Thorn was among those standing to attention, sweating in his fustian red coat in the claggy monsoon heat. 'By the time that the usual ceremonies had been gone through,' he wrote, 'his Highness had remounted his elephant, and the cavalcade had formed, it was past four o'clock.'

The distance being four miles, His Excellency [Lake] did not arrive at the palace until sunset. So great, indeed, was the pressure of the crowd

through which the procession had to pass, that it was with difficulty
that the line could be preserved; for the population of Delhi was in
a manner concentrated into a solid mass: and even the courts of the
palace were filled with spectators, anxious to witness the revival of the
House of Timur, which had so long been under a cloud.[156]

Memories of earlier Maratha sieges and lootings were not easily
forgotten and Scindia's troops had always been unpopular in Delhi; no
one, it seems, was sad to see them go. As for what might be expected
from the Emperor's new protectors, the people of the Mughal capital
kept, for the time being, an open but curious mind:

> At length, after a slow progress, amidst this immense assemblage, all
> eager to behold the deliverer of their sovereign, the Commander-in-
> Chief reached the palace, and was ushered into an apartment where
> the eyes of beholders had formerly been dazzled by the splendour of
> oriental magnificence …
>
> But now, such is the vanity of earthly grandeur, and the uncertainty
> of mortal power, the descendant of the great Akbar, and the victorious
> Aurangzeb, was found, an object of pity, blinded and aged, stripped of
> authority, and reduced to poverty, seated under a small tattered canopy,
> the fragment of regal state, and the mockery of human pride. Such a
> scene could not fail to make a deep impression on the minds of those
> who beheld it.[157]

According to the *Shah Alam Nama*, Lake nevertheless 'bowed his
head at the feet of the imperial throne', then conversed with the
blind Emperor through his deputy, Colonel Sir David Ochterlony.
Ochterlony's father was a Highland Scot who had settled in
Massachusetts. When the American Revolution broke out, his
loyalist family fled to Canada, and David entered the Company's
army in 1777. He never returned to the New World, and, having
made India his home, vowed never to leave it. He had collected a
variety of Indian wives, to each of whom he gave an elephant, and
through whom he learned to speak fluent Urdu and Persian. This was
something that impressed and surprised the chronicler Munna Lal,
who noted that Da'ud Akhtar-Luni Bahadur (as he called him) 'was
unrivalled for understanding and penetration and very well-versed

in Persian letters. At the Emperor's request, he was left at Court to advise on political and financial negotiations with His Majesty.'[158]

Ochterlony read to Shah Alam the carefully worded letters sent for the occasion by Wellesley, in which the Governor General described himself as 'the happy instrument of your Majesty's restoration to a state of dignity and tranquillity, under the power of the British Crown'.[159] In return, wrote Munna Lal, 'His Majesty, in order to show his appreciation of Kampani Sahib Bahadur, bestowed on the two men rich robes and awarded the title Nawab Samsam al-Daula, Khan Dauran Khan, to General Gerard Lake. The Colonel [Ochterlony] also received a gift of suitably fine robes, and the title Nasir al-Daula, Muzaffar Jang.'[160]* Ochterlony, in turn, announced Wellesley's gift of 600,000 rupees to be made available for Shah Alam's immediate expenses, and undertook to provide 64,000 rupees** monthly 'for the costs of the servants of the Imperial Household, the Princes and the chief courtiers, the Pillars of the State'.[161]

In the days that followed, Lord Lake held a durbar in Delhi for all the nobles of the Mughal court, and some others 'who declared themselves to be attached to the English'.[162] These included the Begum Sumru, who had sent a battalion of her troops to fight with the Marathas, and was anxious that this, in addition to her husband's role in the Patna Massacre, might mean that her estates would now be confiscated. During the dinner that followed the durbar, she however charmed Ochterlony, who would in time become a close friend.

She also introduced herself to Lord Lake. This proved more problematic. Lake was deep in his cups, and clearly surprised to be approached by a woman once celebrated as one of Delhi's most beautiful courtesans; 'instead of some well-bearded chief, and,' wrote Skinner, 'being a little elevated by the wine which had just been drunk, he gallantly advanced, and, to the utter dismay of her attendants, took her in his arms and kissed her'. This broke every rule of Mughal etiquette and a ghastly silence descended on the dinner. 'The mistake might have been awkward, but the lady's presence of mind put all right. Receiving courteously the proffered attention, she turned calmly

---

* The Rajasthani town of Nasirabad is, perhaps surprisingly, named after the Scottish Bostonian.

** The modern equivalences of these sums are: 600,000 rupees = almost £8 million; 64,000 rupees = £832,000.

round to her astonished attendants – "It is," said she, "the salute [of forgiveness and reconciliation] of a padre to his daughter." The Begum professed Christianity, and thus the explanation was perfectly in character, though more experienced spectators might have smiled at the appearance of the jolly red-coated clergyman, exhibited in the person of his Lordship.'[163]

Shortly afterwards, Lake set off to Agra to capture the fort, mop up remaining Maratha resistance and win his final great victory over Scindia at Laswari. Ochterlony, who had just been appointed the new Company Resident, took up residence in the ruins of an old Mughal building which had once been the library of the Sufi prince Dara Shukoh, eldest son of Shah Jahan, and more recently the house from which the young prince Shah Alam had escaped Imad ul-Mulk nearly fifty years earlier.[164] Meanwhile, a hospital and accommodation for the cavalry and artillery were set up near the Kashmiri Gate, while Qamar al-Din's haveli near the Ajmeri Gate became the new Custom House. Several other old mansions were taken over for official use by the new Company administration, and a twin Anglo-Mughal court system was set up.[165] A new joint Anglo-Mughal administration quickly fell into place.

The Company conquest of Delhi was, by any standards, a hugely significant moment. For the sightless and powerless Shah Alam, described by the poet Azad as 'only a chessboard king', it represented a final resolution to the conundrum that had been haunting him all his life: how to rule the Empire of his Timurid ancestors, from where, and under whose protection.[166] He was now in his seventy-seventh year. As a boy he had seen Nader Shah ride into Delhi, and leave carrying away the Peacock Throne, into which was embedded the great Koh-i-Noor diamond. He had escaped Imad ul-Mulk's attempt to assassinate him and survived repeated battles with Clive. He had fought the Company at Patna and Buxar, awarded the Diwani to Clive at Allahabad and defied the Company with his cross-country trek back to Delhi. There, with Mirza Najaf Khan, against all the odds he had nearly succeeded in rebuilding the empire of his ancestors; only to see it vanish like a mirage after the premature death of the last great Mughal general. Finally, at his lowest point, the Emperor had been assaulted and blinded by his psychotic former favourite, Ghulam Qadir. Now under the wings of Wellesley's protection, and with a Company pension, he could at least spend his last years on the throne of his ancestors, in his beloved Red Fort, in comfort and safety, and with some measure of dignity.

Three years later, on 1 April 1806, Ochterlony's deputy, the newly arrived William Fraser, one of the first graduates of Lord Wellesley's new Fort William College, wrote home to his father in Inverness about his impressions of the old Emperor and his court: 'On one of the late Mussulman festivals,' he wrote, 'I accompanied the King to the Mosque, and was much struck by the dignity and humility with which the whole court offered their prayers to the Almighty.'

> At this time, I was constantly by the side of the King; and could not but admire the extreme of nobility in his gait, aspect and mien. The loss of his eyes does not at all disfigure his countenance; but the history of their loss and his misfortune exalts to the highest our pity and veneration. On his death, and not till then, we may say, the Line of Timour is extinct as a Dynasty; beginning with the lame, and ending with the blind.[167]

It had hardly been a glorious reign, but his was, nonetheless, a life marked by kindness, decency, integrity and learning at a time when all such qualities were in short supply. Above all, Shah Alam showed an extraordinary determination through successive horrific trials. Throughout his life, he had suffered a long series of repeated reverses; but he never gave up, and only briefly – after the rape of his family and his blinding by the Rohillas – did he allow himself to give way to despair. In the most adverse circumstances imaginable, that of the Great Anarchy, he had ruled over a court of high culture, and as well as writing fine verse himself he had been a generous patron to poets, scholars and artists.

Moreover, he had guided his dynasty through its lowest moments and managed to keep the Mughal flame alive through the worst of the Great Anarchy. He also succeeded in creating a new model of Mughal rule, where the absence of real power lay well disguised beneath the aura of divinely appointed kingship and the gilt screen of high culture and courtly manners, both of which were derived from his Timurid ancestors. It was a vision that was still sufficiently inspiring, some half a century later, for the court of his grandson to become the centre of the greatest anti-colonial revolt in history. This uprising very nearly ended British rule and might well have initiated a new phase of Mughal rule.[168]

For the Company, too, this was an historic occasion, the final denouement of its long struggle to defeat the Marathas and seize from them control of the erstwhile Mughal Empire. At the same time, it also represented the final act in the gradual penetration by the Company of the Mughal system, in which a joint stock company from the City of London slowly appropriated the power of the mighty Mughal Empire, and to some extent, under Wellesley, also took on the trappings of Mughal grandeur.

In the end, the Company established its paramountcy by imposing itself on the Mughal Emperor as Regent, so finding a measure of legitimacy for itself in the eyes of India under the Mughal umbrella. As late as 1831, the Bengali reformer Raja Rammohan Roy dwelt 'on the greater stability to the power of the British government attained by securing the grateful friendship of a monarch, who though without territorial possession, was still regarded by the nations of Hindustan as the only legitimate foundation of either honour or dominion'.[169] The Company understood the importance of infiltrating the Mughal system rather than simply blowing it apart or abolishing it.

Wellesley would protest to the directors that he 'recoiled from the thought of it being suspected in England' that he wished to 'place the East India Company, substantially or vicariously, on the throne of the Mughals'.[170] But this, of course, was exactly what he had done. In less than fifty years, a multinational corporation had seized control of almost all of what had once been Mughal India. It had also, by this stage, created a sophisticated administration and civil service, built much of London's docklands and come close to generating half of Britain's trade. Its annual spending within Britain alone – around £8.5 million* – equalled about a quarter of total British government annual expenditure.[171] No wonder the Company now referred to itself as 'the grandest society of merchants in the Universe'. Its armies were larger than those of almost all nation states and its power now encircled the globe; indeed, its shares were by now a kind of global reserve currency. As Burke wrote: 'The Constitution of the Company began in commerce and ended in Empire;' or rather, as one of its directors admitted, 'an empire within an empire'.[172]

Nevertheless, for all its vast resources, to finance his six years of incessant warfare Wellesley had come close to bankrupting the

* £890 million today.

Company, hugely increasing its annual deficits to around £2 million* a year. The Company's overall debt, which had stood at £17 million when Wellesley first arrived in India, was now rising towards £31.5 million.† Between 1800 and 1806, £3.9 million of silver** had to be shipped from London to Bengal to help begin repaying the enormous debts that Wellesley had run up.[173] The news of the cost of the palatial new Government House in Calcutta, which Lord Wellesley had begun to build on a truly Mughal scale, was the final straw for the directors. Under Wellesley, the Government of India, they declared, had 'simply been turned into a despotism'.

On 6 November 1803 the Court of Directors wrote to the government's Board of Control listing their objections to Wellesley. They accused him of

> making various inroads upon the constitution established for the governance of British India, and when they so far expressed their feelings in the hope of his effecting great promised retrenchments in the public expenditure ... instead of answering their views he embarked, unnecessarily as they think, those extensive plans of foreign policy inevitably leading to wars which ... have, in the opinion of the Court, been productive of many serious evils, have removed further than ever the prospect of reducing the debt and expenses of the country, and have exchanged the secure state and respected character of British power for an uncertain supremacy, and it is to be feared, the disaffection of all the states in India.[174]

By the end of 1803, the final decision had been taken: Wellesley, the Empire-building government cuckoo in the Company's corporate nest, was to be recalled.

---

* Say, £210 million a year in today's currency.

† Say, £3.3 billion in today's currency.

** Over £400 million today.

In 1803 the directors got their way, but in the end it was the British government that prevailed over the Company. Even as the Company grew daily stronger and more invincible than it had ever been in India, as the first half of the nineteenth century progressed it became ever more closely overseen and restricted by the British state; and the idea that the corporation should be running what had now become the country's most important colony began to be seen as more and more of an anomaly.

An anonymous writer in the *Edinburgh Review*, probably James Mill, put it well a few months after Wellesley's recall: 'Among all the visionary and extravagant systems of policy that have been suggested,' he wrote, 'no one has been absurd enough to maintain that the most advisable way to govern an empire was by committing it to the care of a body of merchants residing at a distance of many thousands of miles.'[175] In 1813, Parliament abolished the Company's monopoly of trade with the East, allowing other, merchants and agency houses to set up shop in Bombay and Calcutta.[176]

By 1825 there was growing opposition in Parliament to the continuing existence of the East India Company at all. One MP remarked that the power and influence of the Company were so great that 'were it not, indeed, that the locality of its wealth is at so remote a distance, the very existence of such a body would be dangerous, not merely to the liberty of the subject, but to the stability of the state'. Five years later another MP raged against politicians allowing 'a gigantic power to exist in opposition to the welfare of the kingdom, and over which Parliament has a most *feeble* and *indirect* control'.[177] In Parliament, James Silk Buckingham went even further: 'The idea of consigning over to a joint stock association ... the political administration of an Empire peopled with 100 million souls were so preposterous that if it were now for the first time to be proposed it would be deemed not merely an absurdity, but an insult to the meanest understanding of the realm.'[178]

In 1833, Parliament finally took action. They passed the East India Company Charter Bill, which removed the East India Company's right to trade and so turned it into a sort of governing corporation. The Company, which had once presided over a vast empire of business – and which even at this stage was annually making £1 million* from the tea

---

* Over £100 million today.

trade alone – entered its final phase devoted exclusively to the business of Empire.[179]

Finally, on 10 May 1857, the EIC's own private army rose up in revolt against its employer. On crushing the rebellion, after nine uncertain months, the Company distinguished itself for a final time by hanging and murdering many tens of thousands of suspected rebels in the bazaar towns that lined the Ganges, probably the bloodiest episode in the entire history of British colonialism. In the aftermath of the Great Uprising – the Indian Mutiny as it is known in Britain, or the First War of Independence as it is called in India – Parliament finally removed the Company from power altogether.

Enough was enough. The Victorian state, alerted to the dangers posed by corporate greed and incompetence, successfully tamed history's most voracious corporation. The Company's navy was disbanded and its army passed to the Crown. In 1859, it was within the walls of Allahabad Fort – the same space where Clive had first turned the Company into an imperial power by signing the Diwani – that the Governor General, Lord Canning, formally announced that the Company's Indian possessions would be nationalised and pass into the control of the British Crown. Queen Victoria, rather than the directors of the EIC, would henceforth be ruler of India.

The East India Company limped on in its amputated form for another fifteen years when its charter expired, finally quietly shutting down in 1874, 'with less fanfare,' noted one commentator, 'than a regional railway bankruptcy'.[180]

Its brand name is now owned by two brothers from Kerala who use it to sell 'condiments and fine foods' from a showroom in London's West End.

Epilogue

The red sandstone Mughal fort where the Diwani was extracted from Shah Alam, and where the Company was finally dispossessed of its empire – a much larger fort than those visited by tourists in Lahore, Agra or Delhi – is still a closed-off military zone. When I visited it late last year, neither the guards at the gate nor their officers knew anything of the events that had taken place there; none of the sentries had even heard of the Company whose cannons still dot the parade ground where Clive's Diwani tent was once erected.

On the evening of my visit, I hired a small dinghy from beneath the fort's walls and asked the boatman to row me upstream. It was an hour before sunset, that beautiful moment north Indians call *godhulibela* – cow-dust time – and the Yamuna glittered in the evening light as brightly as a scattering of Mughal gems. Egrets picked their way along the banks, past pilgrims taking a dip near the auspicious point of confluence, where the Yamuna meets the Ganga. Ranks of little boys with fishing lines stood among the holy men and the pilgrims, engaged in the less mystical task of trying to hook catfish. Parakeets swooped out of cavities in the battlements; mynahs called to roost.

For forty minutes we drifted slowly, the water lapping against the sides of the boat, past the mile-long succession of mighty towers and projecting bastions of the fort, each decorated with superb Mughal kiosks, lattices and finials. It seemed impossible to imagine that a single London corporation, however ruthless and aggressive, could have conquered a Mughal Empire that was so magnificently strong, so confident in its own strength and brilliance and beauty.

In both India and Britain, people still talk about the British conquering India, but, as this book has attempted to show, that phrase disguises a much more ominous and complex reality. Because it was not the British government that seized India in the middle of the eighteenth century, but a private company. India's transition to colonialism took place through the mechanism of a for-profit corporation, which existed entirely for the purpose of enriching its investors.

The Company's conquest of India almost certainly remains the supreme act of corporate violence in world history. For all the power wielded today by the world's largest corporations – whether ExxonMobil, Walmart or Google – they are tame beasts compared with the ravaging territorial appetites of the militarised East India Company. Yet if history shows anything, it is that in the intimate dance between the power of the state and that of the corporation, while the latter can be regulated, the corporation will use all the resources in its power to resist.

Today we are back to a world that would be familiar to Britain's first envoy to India, Sir Thomas Roe, where the wealth of the West has begun again to drain eastwards, in the way it did from Roman times until the birth of the East India Company. Now when a Western prime minister visits India, he no longer comes, as Clive did, to dictate terms. In fact, negotiation of any kind has passed from the agenda. Like Roe, he comes as a supplicant begging for contracts and business, and with him come the CEOs of his country's biggest corporations.

The corporation – the idea of a single integrated business organisation stretching out across the seas – was a revolutionary European invention contemporaneous with the beginnings of European colonialism that upended the trading world of Asia and Europe, and which helped give Europe its competitive edge. It is, moreover, an idea that has continued to thrive long after the collapse of European imperialism. When historians debate the legacy of British colonialism in India, they usually mention democracy, the rule of law, railways, tea and cricket. Yet the idea of the joint stock company is arguably one of Britain's most important exports to India, and the one that has for better or worse changed South Asia as much any other European idea. Its influence certainly outweighs that of communism and Protestant Christianity, and possibly even that of democracy.

Companies and corporations now occupy the time and energy of more Indians than any institution other than the family. This should come as no surprise: as Ira Jackson, the former director of Harvard's Center for Business and Government, recently noted, corporations and their leaders have today 'displaced politics and politicians as ... the new high priests and oligarchs of our system'. Covertly, companies still govern the lives of a significant proportion of the human race.

The 300-year-old question of how to cope with the power and perils of large multinational corporations remains today without a clear answer: it is not obviously apparent how a nation state can adequately protect itself and its citizens from corporate excess. No contemporary corporation could get away with duplicating the violence and sheer military might of the East India Company, but many have attempted to match its success at bending state power to their own ends.

As the international subprime bubble and bank collapses of 2007–9 have so recently demonstrated, just as corporations can enrich, mould and positively shape the destiny of nations, so they can also drag down their economies. In all, US and European banks lost more than $1 trillion on toxic assets from January 2007 to September 2009. What Burke feared the East India Company would do to England in 1772 – potentially drag the government 'down into an unfathomable abyss' – actually happened to Iceland in 2008–11, when the systemic collapse of all three of the country's major privately owned commercial banks brought the country to the brink of complete bankruptcy. In the twenty-first century, a powerful corporation can still overwhelm or subvert a state every bit as effectively as the East India Company did in Bengal in the eighteenth.

Corporate influence, with its fatal blend of power, money and unaccountability, is particularly potent and dangerous in frail states where corporations are insufficiently or ineffectually regulated, and where the purchasing power of a large company can outbid or overwhelm an underfunded government. This would seem to have been the case, for example, with the Congress government that ruled India from 2009 until 2014 and which was embroiled in a succession of corruption scandals that ranged from land and mineral giveaways to the corrupt sale of mobile phone spectrum at a fraction of its real value.

In September 2015, the then governor of India's central bank, Raghuram Rajan, made a speech in Mumbai expressing his anxieties about corporate money eroding the integrity of parliament: 'Even as our democracy and our economy have become more vibrant,' he said, 'an important issue in the recent election was whether we had substituted the crony socialism of the past with crony capitalism, where the rich and the influential are alleged to have received land, natural resources and spectrum in return for payoffs to venal politicians. By killing transparency and competition, crony capitalism is harmful to free enterprise, and economic growth. And by substituting special interests for the public interest, it is harmful to democratic expression.' His anxieties were remarkably similar to those expressed by Horace Walpole and many others in Britain more than 300 years earlier, when the East India Company had become synonymous with ostentatious wealth and political corruption.

The East India Company has, thankfully, no exact modern equivalent. Walmart, which is the world's largest corporation in revenue terms, does not number among its assets a fleet of nuclear submarines; neither Facebook nor Shell possesses regiments of infantry. Yet the East India Company – the first great multinational corporation, and the first to run amok – was the ultimate model and prototype for many of today's joint stock corporations. The most powerful among them do not need their own armies: they can rely on governments to protect their interests and bail them out.

Today, the site of the company's headquarters in Leadenhall Street lies underneath Richard Rogers' glass and metal Lloyd's building. No blue plaque marks the site of what Macaulay called 'the greatest corporation in the world', and certainly the only power to equal the Mughals by seizing political power across wide swathes of South Asia. But anyone seeking a monument to the company's legacy in the City need only look around them.

This book has attempted to study the relationship between commercial and imperial power. It has looked at how corporations can impact on politics, and vice versa. It has examined how power and money can corrupt, and the way commerce and colonisation have so often walked in lock-step. For Western imperialism and corporate capitalism were born at the same time, and both were to some extent the dragons' teeth that spawned the modern world.

Such was the disruption caused in eighteenth-century India by the advent of the East India Company that a whole new literary genre was invented to deal with it. This is the genre of moralising histories known as The Book of Admonition, or 'Ibrat-Nâma. The admonitory purpose of these histories was put succinctly by Khair ud-Din Illahabadi, the author of the best known such volume: 'Az farâ-dîd-i sar-guzasht-i guzashtagân, bar khud 'ibrat pazîrad' – By considering these past lives, take heed for your own future.[1]

The East India Company remains today history's most ominous warning about the potential for the abuse of corporate power – and the insidious means by which the interests of shareholders can seemingly become those of the state. For as recent American adventures in Iraq have shown, our world is far from post-imperial, and quite probably never will be. Instead Empire is transforming itself into forms of global power that use campaign contributions and commercial lobbying, multinational finance systems and global markets, corporate influence and the predictive data harvesting of the new surveillance-capitalism rather than – or sometimes alongside – overt military conquest, occupation or direct economic domination to effect its ends.

Four hundred and twenty years after its founding, the story of the East India Company has never been more current.

Glossary

Aftab	the Sun
Akhbars	Indian court newsletters
Alam	the world. It also means a standards used by Shias as focuses for their *Muharram* venerations. Usually tear-shaped or fashioned into the shape of a hand, they are stylised representations of the standards carried by Imam Hussain at the Battle of Kerbala in AD 680
Amir	nobleman
Arrack	Indian absinthe
Arzee	Persian petition
Atashak	gonorrhea
Bagh	a formal Mughal garden, often a *char bagh*, named after its division into four (*char*) squares by a cross of runnels and fountains
Banjara	nomadic trading community
Bazgasht	return or homecoming
Begum	Indian Muslim noblewoman. A title of rank and respect: 'Madam'
Betel	nut used as a mild narcotic in India, and eaten as *paan*
Bhadralok	the prosperous and well-educated upper middle class of Bengal
Bhang	cannabis preparation
Bhet	an offering
Bhisti	water carrier
Bibi	an Indian wife or mistress

Bibi ghar	'Women's House' or *zenana*
Brahmin	the Hindu priestly caste and the top rung of the caste pyramid
Charpoy	Rope-strung bed (literally, 'four feet')
Chattri	a domed kiosk supported on pillars, often used as a decorative feature to top turrets and minarets (literally, 'umbrella')
Chaupar	a cross-shaped board game very similar to pachisi
Chhatrapati	royal title – literally, 'Lord of the Umbrella'. Equivalent of Emperor
Choli	short (and at this period often transparent) Indian bodice
Chowkidar	guard, gatekeeper
Coss	Mughal measurement of distance amounting to just over three miles
Crore	10 million (or 100 lakh)
Cuirassier	armoured cavalry officer armed with a musket
Dacoit	outlaw; a member of a robber gang
Daftar	office, or in the Nizam's palace, chancellery
Dak	post (sometimes spelled '*dawke*' in the eighteenth and early nineteenth centuries)
Dargah	Sufi shrine, usually built over the grave of a saint
Dar ul-Islam	the lands or house of Islam
Dastak	a pass
Dastan	story, epic or oral history
Deorhi	courtyard house or *haveli*
Derzi	tailor
Dharamasala	resthouse
Dharma	duty
Dhobi	laundryman
Dhoolie	covered litter
Dhoti	loincloth
Divan	book of collected poetry
Diwan	Prime Minister, or the vizier in charge of administrative finance
Dubash	an interpreter
Dupatta	shawl or scarf, usually worn with a *salvar kemise* (literally, 'two leaves or widths'). Also known as a *chunni*

Durbar	court
Fakir	literally, 'poor'. Sufi holy man, dervish or wandering Muslim ascetic
Faujdar	fort keeper or garrison commander
Firangi	foreigner
Firman	an order of the Emperor in a written document
Gagra Choli	Indian bodice and skirt
Ghat	steps leading to a bathing place or river
Ghazal	Urdu or Persian love lyric
Godhulibela	'cow-dust time' – the golden hour before sunset
Golumdauze	artillery gunners
Gomasta	agent or manager
Goonjus	bridge
Hakim	physician
Hamam	Turkish-style steam bath
Haveli	courtyard house or traditional mansion
Harkarra	literally, 'all-doo-er'. Runner, messenger, newswriter or spy. In eighteenth-century sources the word is sometimes spelled *hircarrah*
Havildar	a sepoy non-commissioned officer corresponding to a sergeant
Holi	the Hindu spring festival in which participants sprinkle red and yellow powder on one another
Hookah	waterpipe or hubble-bubble
Id	the two greatest Muslim festivals: Id ul-Fitr marks the end of Ramadan, while Id ul-Zuha commemorates the delivery of Isaac. To celebrate the latter a ram or goat is slaughtered, as on the original occasion recorded in both the Old Testament and Koran
Iftar	the evening meal to break the Ramadan fast
Ijara	rental contract
Jagatguru	guru of the Universe
Jagir	landed estate, granted for service rendered to the state and whose revenues could be treated as income by the *jagirdar*
Jali	a latticed stone or wooden screen
Jazair	swivel gun, usually mounted on camelback
Jharoka	projecting balcony

Jizya	Islamic tax on non-believers
Kalawant	singer or chanter
Kar-khana	workshop or factory
Khanazad	palace-born princes
Khansaman	in the eighteenth century the word meant butler. Today it more usually means cook
Kharita	sealed Mughal brocade bag used to send letters as an alternative to an envelope
Khilat	symbolic court dress
Khutba	the sermon during which the Islamic prayer for the ruler is said at Friday prayers
Kotla	fortress or citadel
Kotwal	the Police Chief, Chief Magistrate or City Administrator in a Mughal town
Lakh	a hundred thousand
Langar	free distribution of food during a religious festival
Lathi	truncheon or strick
Lota	water pot
Lingam	the phallic symbol associated with Lord Shiva in his role as Creator
Lungi	Indian-type sarong; longer version of the *dhoti* (QV)
Mahal	literally, 'palace' but often used to refer to sleeping apartments or the *zenana* wing of a palace or residence
Mahi maratib	the Order of the Fish; a Mughal standard
Majlis	assembly (especially the gatherings during *Muharram* – QV)
Mandapa	the gateway of a temple
Mansabadar	a Mughal nobleman and office holder, whose rank was decided by the number of cavalry he would supply for battle, for example a *mansabdar* of 2,500 would be expected to provide 2,500 horsemen when the Nizam went to war
Masnavi	Persian or Urdu love lyric
Mehfil	an evening of courtly Mughal entertainment, normally including dancing, the recitation of poetry and the singing of *ghazals* (QV)
Mihrab	the niche in a mosque pointing in the direction of Mecca

Mir	the title 'Mir' given before a name usually signifies that the holder is a Sayyed (QV)
Mirza	a prince or gentleman
Mohalla	a distinct quarter of a Mughal city, i.e. a group of residential lanes, usually entered through a single gate
Muharram	the great Shia Muslim festival commemorating the defeat and death of Imam Hussain, the Prophet's grandson. Celebrated with particular gusto in Hyderabad and Lucknow.
Munshi	Indian private secretary or language teacher
Mushairas	poetic symposia
Marqanas	stalactite-type decoration over mosque or palace gateways
Musnud	the low arrangement of cushions and bolsters that forms the throne of Indian rulers at this period
Nabob	English corruption of the Hindustani *Nawab*, literally 'deputy', which was the title given by the Mughal Emperors to their regional governors and viceroys. In England it became a term of abuse directed at returned 'Old Indian hands', especially after Samuel Foote's 1768 play *The Nabob* brought the term into general circulation and in England was soon reduced to 'nob'
Nagara	Indian ceremonial kettledrum
Nageshwaram	long Tamil oboe-like wind instrument
Namak-haram	traitor, literally 'bad to your salt'
Naqqar Khana	ceremonial drum house
Naubat	drum used for welcoming dignitaries and festivities
Naubat Khana	drum house above the gateway of a fort
Nautch	an Indian dance display
Nazr/Nazar	symbolic gift given in Indian courts to a feudal superior
Nizam	title of the hereditary ruler of Hyderabad
Omrah	nobleman
Padshahnama	the history of the Emperor
Palanquin	Indian litter
Peshkash	an offering or present given by a subordinate to a superior. The term was used more specifically by the

	Marathas as the money paid to them by 'subordinate' powers such as the Nizam
Peshwaz	a long high-waisted gown
Pir	Sufi holy man
Pikdan	spittoon
Prasad	temple sweets given to devotees in exchange for offerings; a tradition transferred from Hindu to Islamic practice at the Sufi shrines of the Deccan
Puja	prayer
Pukhur	pond
Pukka	proper, correct
Purdah	literally, 'a curtain'; used to signify the concealment of women within the *zenana*
Qanat	portable shelter of canvas or tenting
Qawal	a singer of *Qawalis*
Qawalis	rousing hymns sung at Sufi shrines
Qiladar	fort keeper
Qizilbash	literally, 'redheads'. Name given to Safavid soldiers (and later traders) due to the tall red cap worn under their turbans
Raja	king
Ryott	peasant or tenant farmer
Sahukara	moneylender
Salatin	palace-born princes
Sanad	charter or warrant
Sanyasi	a Hindu ascetic
Sarir-e khas	the Privy Seat
Sarpeche	turban jewel or ornament
Sati	the practice of widow burning, or the burned widow herself
Sawaree	elephant stables (and the whole establishment and paraphernalia related to the keeping of elephants)
Sayyed	(or f. *Sayyida*) a lineal descendant of the Prophet Mohammed. Sayyeds often have the title 'Mir'
Sepoy	Indian soldier
Seth	trader, merchant, banker or moneylender
Shadi	marriage feast or party
Shamiana	Indian marquee, or the screen formed around the perimeter of a tented area

Shia	one of the two principal divisions of Islam, dating back to a split immediately after the death of the Prophet, between those who recognised the authority of the Medinian Caliphs and those who followed the Prophet's son-in-law Ali (*Shiat Ali* means 'the Party of Ali' in Arabic). Though most Shiites live in Iran, there have always been a large number in the Indian Deccan, and Hyderabad was for much of its history a centre of Shi'ite culture
Shikar	hunting
Shroff	trader, merchant, banker or moneylender
Sirdar	nobleman
Sloka	Sanskrit couplet
Strappado	Portuguese form of torture involving dropping the victim from a height while bound with a rope
Subadhar	governor
Takhta	wooden frame for keeping shawls
Tawaif	the cultivated and urbane dancing girls and courtesans who were such a feature of late Mughal society and culture
Thali	tray
Ubnah	gay male sex
Ulama	Muslim clerics
Unani	Ionian (or Byzantine Greek) medicine, originally passed to the Islamic world through Byzantine exiles in Persia and still practiced in India today
'Urs	festival day
Ustad	master, teacher or expert
Vakil	ambassador or representative (though in modern usage the word means merely lawyer)
Vilayat	province, homeland
Zenana	harem, or women's quarters
Zamindar	landholder or local ruler

Notes

BL   British Library
CPC   *Calendar of Persian Correspondence*
IOR   India Office Records
NAI   National Archives of India
OIOC Oriental and India Office Collections

INTRODUCTION

1 Philip Stern has shown brilliantly how much earlier than was previously understood the Company acquired real and tangible political power. See Philip J. Stern., *The Company State: Corporate Sovereignty & the Early Modern Foundations of the British Empire in India.* Cambridge, 2011.

2 'The Muzaffarnama of Karam Ali', in *Bengal Nawabs,* translated into English by Jadunath Sarkar, Calcutta, 1952, p. 63.

3 Ghulam Hussain Khan, *Seir Mutaqherin*, Calcutta, 1790– 94, vol. 3, pp. 9–10.

4 Quoted by Emma Rothschild in her unpublished essay, 'The East India Company and the American Revolution'.

5 More recent research is represented by historians like Richard Barnett's pioneering *North India Between Empires: Awadh, the Mughals and the British, 1720–1801*, Berkeley, 1980 and Christopher Bayly's *Rulers, Townsmen and Bazaars*, and Alam, who, in his *The Crisis of Empire in Mughal North India*, demonstrates economic growth in north India during the first half of the eighteenth century. There has been a considerable literature devoted to this new understanding. For collections of essays espousing these 'revisionist' views see Seema Alavi (ed.), *The Eighteenth Century in India*, New Delhi,

2002; P. J. Marshall (ed.), *The Eighteenth Century in Indian History. Evolution or Revolution*, New Delhi, 2003. See also; Stewart Gordon, *Marathas, Marauders and State Formation in Eighteenth-Century India*, Delhi, 1998; Rajat Datta, *The Making of the Eighteenth Century in India: Some Reflections on Its Political and Economic Processes*. Jadunath Sarkar Memorial Lecture, Bangiya Itihas Samiti, Kolkatta, April 2019; Karen Leonard, 'The Hyderabad Political System and Its Participants', *Journal of Asian Studies*, 30(3) (1971); Tilottama Mukherjee, *Political Culture and Economy in Eighteenth-Century Bengal. Networks of Exchange, Consumption and Communication*, New Delhi, 2013; John F. Richards, *The Seventeenth-Century Crisis in South Asia* in *Modern Asian Studies*, 24, 4,(1990), pp625-638; M. Athar Ali, *The Passing of an Empire: The Mughal Case,* Modern Asian Studies, Vol 9. No.13 (1975), pp385-396; Stewart Gordon, *Legitimacy and Loyalty in some Successor States of the Eighteenth Century. In John F Richards, Kingship and Authority in South Asia,* [New Delhi, 1998], pp327-347 Madhu Trivedi, *The Making of the Awadh Culture*, New Delhi, 2010; Stephano Pelò, '*Drowned in the Sea of Mercy. The Textual Identification of Hindu Persian Poets from Shi'i Lucknow in the Tazkira of Bhagwan Das 'Hindi'*, in Vasudha Dalmia and Munis D. Faruqui (eds), *Religious Interactions in Mughal India*, New Delhi, 2014; Sanjay Subrahmanyam, '*Connected Histories: Notes Towards a Reconfiguration of Early Modern Eurasia*', *Modern Asian Studies*, 31(3) (1997); J. F. Richards, '*Early Modern India and World History*', *Journal of World History*, 8(2) (1997), C. A. Bayly, 'Indian Merchants in a 'Traditional' Setting. Banaras, 1780–1830', in Clive Dewey and A. J. Hopkins (eds), *The Imperial Impact. Studies in the Economic History of India and* Africa, London, 1978; Philip Calkins, 'The Formation of Regionally Oriented Ruling Group in Bengal, 1700–1740', *Journal of Asian Studies*, 29(4) (1970).

6 Fakir Khair-al Din Illahabadi, Fakir, '*Ibrat Nama*, BL, OIOC, Or. 1932. fiv

CHAPTER I: 1599

1 James Shapiro, *1599: A Year in the Life of William Shakespeare*, London, 2005, pp. 303–8.

2 Henry Stevens, *The Dawn of British Trade to the East Indies, as Recorded in the Court Minutes of the East India Company 1599–1603, Containing an Account of the Formation of the Company*, London, 1866, pp. 1–10.

3 Marguerite Eyer Wilbur, *The East India Company and the British Empire in the Far East*, New York, 1945, pp. 18–24.

4 Robert Brenner, *Merchants and Revolution: Commercial Change, Political Conflict, and London's Overseas Traders, 1550–1653*, Princeton, 2003, pp. 19–23, 61–4; James Mather, *Pashas: Traders and Travellers in the Islamic World*, London, 2009, pp. 4, 40–2.

5 Stevens, *The Dawn of British Trade*, pp. 1–10.

6 Sir William Foster, 'The First Home of the East India Company', in *The Home Counties Magazine*, ed. W. Paley Baildon, FSA, vol. XIV, 1912, pp. 25–7; Beckles Willson, *Ledger and Sword: The Honourable Company of Merchants of England Trading to the East Indies 1599–1874*, 2 vols, London, 1903, vol. I, pp. 19–23.

7 Stevens, *The Dawn of British Trade*, pp. 5–6; P. J. Marshall, 'The English in Asia to 1700', in Nicholas Canny, *The Oxford History of the British Empire*, vol. I, *The Origins of Empire*, Oxford, 1998, pp. 267–9.

8 A pauper in comparison to Mughal prosperity, England was not however impoverished by north European Standards, and conducted a large and growing textile trade, largely through the Netherlands.

9 Kenneth R. Andrews, *Trade, Plunder and Settlement: Maritime Enterprise and the Genesis of the British Empire, 1430–1630*, Cambridge, 1984, pp. 12, 33, 256.

10 Niall Ferguson, *Empire: How Britain Made the Modern World*, London, 2003, pp. 6, 7, 9; G. L. Beer, *The Origins of the British Colonial System, 1578–1660*, London, 1908, pp. 8–9.

11 Giles Milton, *Nathaniel's Nutmeg or, The True and Incredible Adventures of the Spice Trader Who Changed the Course of History*, London, 1999, pp. 15–20.

12 Andrews, *Trade, Plunder and Settlement*, pp. 176, 200–22, 309, 314; Ferguson, *Empire*, p. 58.

13 *National Archives of India Calendar of Persian Correspondence, intro. Muzaffar Alam & Sanjay Subrahmanyam*, vol. I, New Delhi, 2014 (henceforth *CPC*), p. xxxi.

14 William Foster (ed.), *Early Travels in India 1583–1619*, London, 1921, pp. 1–47; G. V. Scammell, *The World Encompassed: The First European Maritime Empires*, London, 1981, p. 474.

15 Brenner, *Merchants and Revolution*, pp. 20–1; Milton, *Nathaniel's Nutmeg*, pp. 7, 42–52; Holden Furber, 'Rival Empires of Trade in the Orient, 1600–1800', in *Maritime India*, intro. Sanjay Subrahmanyam, New Delhi, 2004, p. 31, 343n.

16 Furber, 'Rival Empires of Trade in the Orient', pp. 31–2; Shapiro, *1599*, p. 303; Andrews, *Trade, Plunder and Settlement*, p. 260.

17 K. N. Chaudhuri, *The English East India Company: The Study of an Early Joint-Stock Company 1600–1640*, London, 1965, p. 11; Mather, *Pashas*, p. 40.

18 Willson, *Ledger and Sword*, pp. 19–21.

19 Stevens, *The Dawn of British Trade*, pp. 5–6.

20 Sir William Foster, *England's Quest of Eastern Trade*, London, 1933, pp. 144–50.

21 Mather, *Pashas*, p. 41.

22 Philip J. Stern, *The Company State: Corporate Sovereignty & the Early Modern Foundations of the British Empire in India*, Cambridge, 2011, pp. 6–9.
23 John Micklethwait and Adrian Wooldridge, *The Company: A Short History of a Revolutionary Idea*, London, 2003, p. 26.
24 Brenner, *Merchants and Revolution*, pp. 12–13.
25 Willson, *Ledger and Sword*, p. 31.
26 John Keay, *The Honourable Company: A History of the English East India Company*, London, 1991, p. 13; Milton, *Nathaniel's Nutmeg*, p. 77.
27 Keay, *The Honourable Company*, p. 9.
28 Stern, *The Company State*, pp. 12, 56–8.
29 Philip Stern has shown brilliantly how much earlier than was previously understood the Company acquired real and tangible political power. See stem, *The Company State*.
30 Stevens, *The Dawn of British Trade*, p. 13.
31 Ibid., pp. 14–20, 42–3.
32 Ibid., pp. 30–46, 52.
33 Sir William Foster, *John Company*, London, 1926, p. 5.
34 Milton, *Nathaniel's Nutmeg*, pp. 77–80.
35 Keay, *The Honourable Company*, p. 15; Milton, *Nathaniel's Nutmeg*, pp. 80–2.
36 Keay, *The Honourable Company*, p. 23.
37 Furber, 'Rival Empires of Trade in the Orient', pp. 38–9.
38 Marshall, *The English in Asia to 1700*, p. 268; Scammell, *The World Encompassed*, pp. 480–1.
39 Cited in H. Love, *Vestiges of Old Madras*, 2 vols, London, 1913, vol. I, p. 533, vol. II, p. 299.
40 Scammell, *The World Encompassed*, p. 479.
41 Furber, 'Rival Empires of Trade in the Orient', p. 42.
42 Ferguson, *Empire*, p. 21.
43 *CPC*, p. xxxi; Brenner, *Merchants and Revolution*, p. 49; Furber, 'Rival Empires of Trade in the Orient', p. 39; Marshall, *The English in Asia to 1700*, pp. 270–1; Andrews, *Trade, Plunder and Settlement*, p. 270.
44 Richard M. Eaton, *India in the Persianate Age, 1000–1765*, London, 2019, p. 373.

The Cambridge historian Angus Maddison shows that around 1700 India briefly overtook China as the largest economy in the world. This was due to many factors: Sher Shah Suri and the Mughals had encouraged trade by developing roads, river transport, sea routes, ports and abolishing many inland tolls and taxes. Their aesthetic obsessions also helped bring Indian textile manufacturing to a new height of beauty and brilliance.

As the French traveller François Bernier wrote around 1700: 'Gold and silver come from every quarter of the globe to Hindostan,' words echoed by Sir Thomas Roe, who remarked that: 'Europe bleedeth to enrich Asia.' Maddison's exact figures show than in 1600 Britain was creating 1.8 per cent of world GDP, while India was creating 22.5 per cent. The figures for 1700 are 2.88 per cent vs 22.44 per cent.

On the other hand, Maddison also shows that from 1600 onwards GDP per head was already higher in England than in India, which implies that the wealth in India in this period, as today, was concentrated in the ruling and business classes, and very unevenly distributed. European travellers constantly remarked on the wealth of the rulers and the bankers and the poverty of the agricultural classes. Maddison's work does show, however, that GDP per head was higher in seventeenth-century India than in any previous period.

Shireen Moosvi, who did her dissertation under the supervision of Irfan Habib, undertook a detailed study of Ain-i-Akbari in the 1980s. Her conclusion was that the Mughal state was unusually extractive and appropriated 56.7 per cent of the total produce. Her research focused on five north Indian provinces: Agra, Delhi, Lahore, Allahabad and Avadh. The total population of these provinces was estimated at 36 million. She estimated the average income per peasant family to be 380 dams per annum – roughly 1 dam per day (a 'dam' was the standard copper coin in Mughal India. Roughly 40 dams made a rupee).

According to W. W. Hunter, in 1882 the total revenue of Aurangzeb in 1695 was estimated at £80 million. The gross taxation levied by British India between 1869 and 1879 was £35.3 million. So the Mughal Empire under Aurangzeb (circa 1700) collected twice as much land revenue as the British Raj (circa 1880), though the economy size was about the same in both periods. See W. W. Hunter, *The Indian Empire* (London, 1882). With thanks to Śrīkānta Kṛṣṇamācārya for bringing this to my attention.

45 D. A. Washbrook, 'Progress and Problems: South Asian Economic and Social History c. 1720–1860', *Modern Asian Studies*, vol. 22, no. 1 (1988), pp. 57–96.

46 Angus Maddison, *Contours of the World Economy, 1–2030 AD: Essays in Macro-Economic History*, Oxford, 2007, pp. 116–20, 309–11, 379; Shashi Tharoor, *Inglorious Empire: What the British Did in India*, New Delhi, 2016, pp. 2–3.

47 Shireen Moosvi, *Economy of the Mughal Empire, c1595: A Statistical Study*, New Delhi, 1987, p. 376; Foster (ed.), *Early Travels*, p. 112; Eaton, *India in the Persianate Age*, p. 371.

48 Furber, 'Rival Empires of Trade in the Orient', p. 45.

49 Geoffrey Parker, *The Military Revolution*, Oxford, 1988, p. 135. The figure may not be correct: Parker probably gets this from Irvine, who got it from Abu'l Fazl's *Ain-i Akbari*. Dirk Kolff's *Naukar, Rajput, and Sepoy*, London, 1992, makes a compelling case that this number by Abu'l Fazl was actually an estimation of the 'military labour market' of the twelve subahs of the empire in the 1590s (essentially northern India) and should not be understood as the actual size of the Mughal army. See pp. 3ff (basically the whole chapter on the 'armed peasantry').

50 Milo Cleveland Beach and Ebba Koch (eds), *King of the World – the Padshahnama: an Imperial Mughal Manuscript from the Royal Library, Windsor Castle*, London, 1997, pp. 56–7, 58–60, 179–80; Sanjay Subrahmanyam, *The Portuguese Empire in Asia: A Political and Economic History 1500–1700*, New York, 1993, pp. 165–6, 201; Tirthankar Roy, *The East India Company: The World's Most Powerful Corporation*, New Delhi, 2012, p. 83.

51 Furber, 'Rival Empires of Trade in the Orient', p. 40.

52 The best biography is Michael Strachan, *Sir Thomas Roe 1581–1644*, Salisbury, 1989.

53 Bernard Cohn, *Colonialism and Its Forms of Knowledge*, Princeton, 1996, p. 17.

54 Sir Thomas Roe and Dr John Fryer, *Travels in India in the 17th Century*, London, 1873, pp. 26–9, 38–9.

55 Ibid., pp. 103–4. See also Sir William Foster, *The Embassy of Sir Thomas Roe to India 1615–9, as Narrated in his Journal and correspondence*, New Delhi, 1990.

56 Roe wrote a wonderful love letter to Elizabeth, Lady Huntingdon, from 'Indya' on 30 October 1616. I would like to thank Charlotte Merton for sending me this reference. Pasadena Library, Hastings Collection, 5 Box 7 (1612 to 1618, Thomas Roe to Elizabeth, Countess of Huntingdon, HA10561).

57 Roe and Fryer, *Travels in India*, p. 74. See William Pinch's brilliant essay, 'Same Difference in India and Europe', *History and Theory*, vol. 38, no. 3 (October 1999), pp. 389–407.

58 Strachan, *Sir Thomas Roe*, pp. 86–7.

59 Samuel Purchas, *Hakluytus Posthumus or Purchas His Pilgrimes, Contayning a History of the World*, 20 vols, Glasgow, 1905, part 1, IV, pp. 334–9.

60 This is certainly the argument of Beni Prasad in his *History of Jahangir*, Allahabad, 1962.

61 Roe and Fryer, *Travels in India*, pp. 83–4.

62 *Jahangir Preferring a Shaykh to Kings*, by Bichitr, c.1615–18. Opaque watercolour and gold on paper. Freer Gallery of Art, Smithsonian Institution. Purchase F1942.15. I am in debt here to Simon Schama's brilliant

and witty analysis of the painting in BBC/PBS *Civilisations*, Episode 5. Jahangir's dream pictures are all enigmatic and difficult to decode. In this case the painting reflects one of Jahangir's own dreams which revealed how the pious Emperor was actually the Millennial Sovereign of Islamic thought: master of time as well as space, ushering in the new millennium in which all other kings are beneath him and of little account; instead the Emperor turns his gaze towards the inner mysteries of Sufi wisdom. See A. Azfar Moin's brilliant *The Millennial Sovereign: Sacred Kingship & Sainthood in Islam*, Columbia, 2014, and Kavita Singh's perceptive *Real Birds in Imagined Gardens: Mughal Painting between Persia and Europe*, Los Angeles, 2017.

63 C. A. Bayly, *Indian Society and the Making of the British Empire*, Cambridge, 1988, p. 16.

64 *CPC*, p. xxxiii.

65 Quoted in G. J. Bryant, *The Emergence of British Power in India 1600–1784: A Grand Strategic Interpretation*, Woodbridge, 2013, p. 4.

66 Marshall, 'The English in Asia to 1700', pp. 272–3.

67 Eaton, *India in the Persianate Age*, p. 373.

68 Rupali Mishra: *A Business of State: Commerce, Politics and the Birth of the East India Company*, Harvard, 2018, p. 6.

69 Keay, *The Honourable Company*, pp. 112–13.

70 Mather, *Pashas*, p. 53.

71 Thomas Mun, *A Discourse of Trade, from England unto the East Indes By T.M.*, London, 1621, quoted in Mishra, *A Business of State*, p. 3.

72 *CPC* I, p. xi; Stern, *The Company State*, p. 19.

73 Stern, *The Company State*, p. 19; Keay, *Honourable Company*, p. 68; *CPC* I, p. xi; Furber, 'Rival Empires of Trade in the Orient', p. 71.

74 Furber, 'Rival Empires of Trade in the Orient', pp. 71–2.

75 Stern, *Company State*, pp. 35–6.

76 Ibid., pp. 22–3; Keay, *Honourable Company*, pp. 130–1; Bruce P. Lenman, *Britain's Colonial Wars 1688–1783*, New York, 2001, p. 85; Roy, *East India Company*, p. 77.

77 Lenman, *Britain's Colonial Wars*, pp. 86–8.

78 Sir William Foster (ed.), *The English Factories in India 1618–1669*, 13 vols, London, 1906–27, vol. 3, p. 345.

79 Stern, *Company State*, p. 109, for the Bombay witchcraft trials.

80 Keay, *The Honourable Company*, pp. 136–7.

81 William Letwin, *The Origin of Scientific Economics*, London, 1963, p. 37.

82 Richard Carnac Temple, *The Diaries of Streynsham Master, 1675–1680*, 2 vols, London, 1911, vol. 2, p. 28; Foster, *English Factories*, vol. 4, p. 308; John R. McLane, *Land and Local Kingship in Eighteenth-Century Bengal*,

Cambridge, 1993, p. 112; Jon Wilson, *India Conquered: Britain's Raj and the Chaos of Empire*, London, 2016, p. 39.

83 Bryant, *Emergence of British Power*, p. 3.

84 Wilson, *India Conquered*, p. 49.

85 Ibid., p. 47.

86 Ibid., p. 53.

87 Alexander Hamilton, *A New Account of the East Indies*, 2 vols, London, 1930, vol. I, pp. 8–9, 312–15.

88 Wilson, *India Conquered*, p. 53; Maya Jasanoff, *Edge of Empire: Conquest and Collecting in the East, 1750–1850*, London, 2005, p. 25.

89 François Bernier, *Travels in the Mogul Empire, 1656–68*, ed. Archibald Constable, trans. Irving Brock, Oxford, 1934, pp. 437, 442; McLane, *Land and Local Kingship*, pp. 29–30; Om Prakash, *The Dutch East India Company and the Economy of Bengal, 1630–1720*, Princeton, 1985, pp. 75, 162–3.

90 Audrey Truschke, *Aurangzeb: The Man and the Myth*, New Delhi, 2017, pp. 66, 105.

91 C. A. Bayly, *Rulers, Townsmen and Bazaars: North Indian Society in the Age of British Expansion*, Cambridge, 1983, pp. 20–1; Satish Chandra, 'Social Background to the Rise of the Maratha Movement During the 17th Century', *Indian Economic and Social History Review*, x (1973), pp. 209–18.

92 Dr John Fryer, *A New Account of East India & Persia 1672–81*, ed. W. Crooke, Hakluyt Society, 3 vols, London, 1909–15, vol. I, p. 341; Irfan Habib, 'The Agrarian Causes of the Fall of the Mughal Empire', in *Enquiry*, 2, September 1958, pp. 81–98 and *Enquiry*, 3, 3 April 1960, pp. 68–80. See also Meena Bhargava, *The Decline of the Mughal Empire*, New Delhi, 2014, p. 43.

93 Fryer, *A New Account of East India & Persia*, vol. II, pp. 67–8.

94 Truschke, *Aurangzeb*, p. 66.

95 Kaushik Roy, 'Military Synthesis in South Asia: Armies, Warfare, and Indian Society, *c*.1740–1849', in *Journal of Military History*, vol. 69, no. 3 (July 2005), pp. 651–90; V. G. Dighe and S. N. Qanungo, 'Administrative and Military System of the Marathas', in R. C. Majumdar and V. G. Dighe (eds), *The Maratha Supremacy*, Mumbai, 1977, pp. 567–8. For Shivaji's two coronation ceremonies the best source is the *Sivarajyabhiṣekakalpataru* (*The Venerable Wish-Fulfilling Tree of Śiva's Royal Consecration*) dated 30 September 1596 Saka era (= 1674 AD). See Bihani Sarkar, *Traveling Tantrics and Belligerent Brahmins: the Sivarajyabhiṣekakalpataru and Sivaji's Tantric consecration*, for the conference on 'Professions in motion: culture,

power and the politics of mobility in 18th-century India', St Anne's, Oxford, 2 June 2017; available at www.academica.edu; James W. Laine, *Shivaji: Hindu King in Islamic India*, Oxford, 2003.

96 Quoted in Velcheru Narayana Rao, David Shulman and Sanjay Subrahmanyam, *Textures of Time: Writing History in South India 1600–1800*, New York, 2003, p. 232. Shivaji's reputation as a warrior hero against Islam is still alive and even growing today in modern Maharashtra, especially Bombay, where the airport, the railway station and even the Prince of Wales Museum have all recently been named after him. Here the far right-wing Hindutva Shiv Sena party, Shivaji's Army, is one of the most powerful political forces on the streets of the city and set the city ablaze in 1992 following the destruction of the Babri Masjid.

97 Truschke, *Aurangzeb*, p. 69.

98 Syed Ghulam Hussain Khan Tabatabai, *Seir Mutaqherin*, Calcutta, 1790–94, vol. 1, pp. 310–11. For Ghulam Hussain Khan see Iqbal Ghani Khan, 'A Book With Two Views: Ghulam Husain's "An Overview of Modern Times"', in Jamal Malik, ed., *Perspectives of Mutual Encounters in South Asian History, 1760–1860*, Leiden, 2000, pp. 278–97, and Kumkum Chatterjee, 'History as Self-Representation: The Recasting of a Political Tradition in Late Eighteenth Century Eastern India', *Modern Asian Studies*, vol. 32, no. 4 (1998), pp. 913–48.

99 Truschke, *Aurangzeb*, p. 120.

100 Ibid., p. 65, quoting Giovanni Gemelli Careri, *Indian Travels of Thevenot and Careri*, ed. S. N. Sen, New Delhi, 1949, p. 216. Originally published as *Giro del Mondo*, Rome, 1699.

101 *Ahkam-i Alamgiri*, f 61b quoted in Bhargava, *The Decline of the Mughal Empire*, p. 43.

102 Quoted in Waldemar Hansen, *The Peacock Throne*, New Delhi, 1986, p. 28.

103 Uday Kulkarni's *The Era of Baji Rao: An Account of the Empire of the Deccan*, Pune, 2017, is both popular and exhaustively researched and makes for an excellent introduction to this period of Maratha rule.

104 Fakir Khair ud-Din Illahabadi, '*Ibrat Nama*, BL Or. 1932. 2v.

105 Jean-Baptiste Gentil, *Mémoires sur l'Indoustan*, Paris, 1822, p. 76.

106 See Stewart Gordon, 'The Slow Conquest: Administrative Integration of Malwa into the Maratha Empire, 1720–1760', in *Modern Asian Studies*, vol. 11, no. 1 (1977), pp. 1–40. Also Andre Wink, 'Maratha Revenue Farming', in *Modern Asian Studies*, vol. 17, no. 4 (1983), pp. 591–628; Stewart Gordon, *Marathas, Marauders and State Formation in Eighteenth Century India*, Delhi, 1994.

107 *Voyage en Inde du Comte de Modave, 1773–1776*, ed. Jean Deloche, Pondicherry, 1971, pp. 400–1.

108 Roy, 'Military Synthesis in South Asia'; R. C. Majumdar et al., *An Advanced History of India*, 1978, reprint, Madras, 1991, pp. 536–46; Eaton, *India in the Persianate Age 1000–1765*, p. 354; Stewart Gordon, *The Marathas, 1600–1818*, Cambridge, 1993, pp. 127–9, 140–3.

109 Munis D. Faruqui, 'At Empire's End: The Nizam, Hyderabad and Eighteenth Century India', in *Modern Asian Studies*, 43, 1 (2009), pp. 5–43; Sanjay Subrahmanyam, 'Un Grand Derangement: Dreaming An Indo-Persian Empire in South Asia, 1740–1800', *Journal of Early Modern History*, 4, 3–4 (2000), pp. 337–78; Muzaffar Alam, *The Crisis of Empire in Mughal North India: Awadh and the Punjab 1707–1748*, New Delhi, 1986.

110 Salim Allah, *A Narrative of the Transactions in Bengal*, trans. Francis Gladwin, Calcutta, 1788; McLane, *Land and Local Kingship*, p. 72. See also Tilottama Mukherjee, 'The Co-ordinating State and Economy: The Nizamat in Eighteenth-Century Bengal', *Modern Asian Studies*, vol. 43, no. 2 (2009), pp. 389–436.

111 Ghulam Hussain Khan, *Seir Mutaqherin*, vol. 2, p. 450; J. H. Little, *The House of Jagat Seth*, Calcutta, 1956, p. 3.

112 BL, IOR, Orme Mss India, VI, f. 1455.

113 Ibid., f. 1525.

114 For the Jagat Seths the best source remains Little, *The House of Jagat Seth*. See also Sushil Chaudhury, 'The banking and mercantile house of Jagat Seths of Bengal', in *Studies in People's History*, 2, 1 (2015), pp. 85–95; Lakshmi Subramanian, 'Banias and the British: the role of indigenous credit in the Process of Imperial Expansion in Western India in the second half of the Eighteenth century', *Modern Asian Studies*, 21, 3 (1987); Kumkum Chatterjee, 'Collaboration and Conflict: Bankers and Early Colonial Rule in India: 1757–1813', *Indian Economic and Social History Review*, vol. 30, 3 (1993); Thomas A. Timberg, *The Marwaris: From Jagat Seth to the Birlas*, New Delhi, 2014, p. 22; Lokanatha Gosha, *The Modern History of the Indian Chiefs, Rajas, Zamindars, & C.*, Calcutta, 1881. For the wider Indian economy at this time see also Rajat Datt, 'Commercialisation, Tribute and the Transition from late Mughal to Early Colonial in India', *Medieval History Journal*, vol. 6, no. 2 (2003), pp. 259–91; D. A. Washbrook, 'Progress and Problems: South Asian Economic History c.1720–1860', in *Modern Asian Studies*, vol. 22, no. 1 (1988), pp. 57–96; K. N. Chaudhuri, 'India's International Economy in the Nineteenth Century: A Historical Survey', in *Modern Asian Studies*, vol. 2, no. 1 (1968), pp. 31–50.

115 Sanjay Subrahmanyam, *Penumbral Visions: Making Politics in Early Modern South India*, Michigan, 2001, p. 106; Muzaffar Alam and Sanjay Subrahmanyam, *Writing the Mughal World*, New York, 2012, pp. 353–5; Niccolao Manucci, *Storia do Mogor, or Mogul India, 1653–1708*, trans. William Irvine, London, 1907, vol. 3, pp. 369–70.

116 *CPC* I, p. xxi; Stern, *The Company State*, p. 176; Alam and Subrahmanyam, *Writing the Mughal World*, pp. 358–9, 394.

117 Brijen K. Gupta, *Sirajuddaullah and the East India Company, 1756–7*, Leiden, 1966, p. 44.

118 Stephen P. Blake, *Shahjahanabad: The Sovereign City in Mughal India, 1639–1739*, Cambridge, 1991, p. 162.

119 Ishrat Haque, *Glimpses of Mughal Society and Culture*, New Delhi, 1992, p. 21.

120 William Dalrymple and Yuthika Sharma, *Princes and Poets in Mughal Delhi 1707–1857*, Princeton, 2012, pp. 4–5; Zahir Uddin Malik, *The Reign of Muhammad Shah 1719–1748*, Aligarh, 1977.

121 Gentil, *Mémoires sur l'Indoustan*, pp. 123–4.

122 Subrahmanyam, *Penumbral Visions*, pp. 15–16.

123 Sayid Athar Abbas Rizvi, *Shah Walli-Allah and His Times*, Canberra, 1980, p. 141; Gordon, *The Marathas 1600–1818*, pp. 124–5; Zahir Uddin Malik, *The Reign of Muhammad Shah*, p. 133; Michael Axworthy, *The Sword of Persia: Nader Shah from Tribal Warrior to Conquering Tyrant*, London, 2006, p. 189; Govind Sakharam Sardesai, *A New History of the Marathas*, 3 vols, Poona, 1946, vol. 2, p. 154; Bhargava, *The Decline of the Mughal Empire*, p. xv; Jadunath Sarkar, *Fall of the Mughal Empire, 1739–54*, 4 vols, New Delhi, 1991, vol. 1, pp. 2, 135.

124 Ghulam Hussain Khan, *Seir Mutaqherin*, vol. 1, p. 302; Subrahmanyam, *Un Grand Derangement*, pp. 356–7; Malik, *The Reign of Muhammad Shah*, p. 135; Blake, *Shahjahanabad*, p. 150.

125 Malik, *The Reign of Muhammad Shah*, p. 111.

126 C. A. Bayly, *Indian Society and the Making of the British Empire*, pp. 8–9.

127 Malik, *The Reign of Muhammad Shah*, p. 265; Rizvi, *Shah Walli-Allah and His Times*, p. 141; Gordon, *Marathas*, pp. 125, 128, 129, 135; Sardesai, *New History of the Marathas*, vol. 2, p. 159.

128 Père Louis Bazin, 'Memoires sur dernieres annees du regne de Thamas Kouli-Kan et sa mort tragique, contenus dans un letter du Frere Bazin', 1751, in *Lettres Edifiantes et Curieuses Ecrites des Mission Etrangeres*, Paris, 1780, vol. IV, pp. 277–321. This passage, pp. 314–18.

129 Willem Floor, 'New Facts on Nadir Shah's Indian Campaign', in *Iran and Iranian Studies: Essays in Honour of Iraj Afshar*, ed. Kambiz Eslami, Princeton, 1998, pp. 198–220, p. 200.

130 Anand Ram Mukhlis, 'Tazkira', in Sir H. M. Elliot and John Dowson, *The History of India as Told by its Own Historians*, London, 1867, vol. VIII, pp. 82–3.

131 Subrahmanyam, *Un Grand Derangement*, pp. 357–8.

132 Axworthy, *The Sword of Persia*, p. 207.

133 Mukhlis, 'Tazkira', in Elliot and Dowson, *The History of India*, vol. VIII, p. 85.

134 Michael Edwards, *King of the World: The Life and Times of Shah Alam, Emperor of Hindustan*, London, 1970, p. 15.

135 Floor, 'New Facts on Nadir Shah's Indian Campaign', p. 217.

136 Ghulam Hussain Khan, *Seir Mutaqherin*, vol. 1, pp. 315–17.

137 Mukhlis, 'Tazkira', in Elliot and Dowson, *The History of India*, vol. VIII, p. 86.

138 Floor, 'New Facts on Nadir Shah's Indian Campaign', p. 217.

139 Mukhlis, 'Tazkira', in Elliot and Dowson, *The History of India*, vol. VIII, p. 87.

140 Mahdi Astarabadi, *Tarikh-e Jahangosha-ye Naderi: The official history of Nader's reign*, Bombay lithograph 1849/1265), p. 207.

141 Sarkar, *Fall of the Mughal Empire, 1739–54*, vol. 1, pp. 2–3, 4, 13.

142 BL, Add 6585, Shakir Khan, *Tarikh-i Shakir Khani*, ff. 34–6.

143 Dirk H. A. Kolff, *Naukar, Rajput & Sepoy*, Cambridge, 1990.

144 Washbrook, 'Progress and Problems: South Asian Economic and Social History c.1720–1860', p. 67.

145 Ghulam Hussain Khan, *Seir Mutaqherin*, vol. 3, pp. 160–1.

146 Subrahmanyam, *Un Grand Derangement*, p. 344.

147 S. P. Sen's book, *The French in India, 1763–1816*, Calcutta, 1958; Arvind Sinha, *The Politics of Trade: Anglo-French Commerce on the Coromandel Coast, 1763–1793*, New Delhi, 2002; Ferguson, *Empire*, pp. 30–2.

148 Jean Marie Lafont and Rehana Lafont, *The French & Delhi, Agra, Aligarh and Sardhana*, New Delhi, 2010, pp. 41–4.

149 The introduction of infantry drill to India occurred on a small scale before Dupleix. See David Harding's *Small Arms of the East India Company 1600–1856*, London, 1997, vol. 4, pp. 150–65, and Randolf Cooper's important essay, 'Culture, Combat and Colonialism in Eighteenth and Nineteenth Century India', *International History Review*, vol. 27, no. 3 (September 2005), pp. 534–49 esp. pp. 537–8.

150 Henry Dodwell, *Dupleix and Clive: The Beginning of Empire*, London, 1920, pp. 1–9.

151 Ferguson, *Empire*, p. 31.

152 *The Private Diary of Ananda Ranga Pillai, Dubash to Joseph François Dupleix*, ed. J. F. Price and K. Rangachari, 12 vols, Madras, 1922, vol. 3, p. 90.

153 Ibid., p. 9; Subrahmanyam, *Penumbral Visions*, p. 14; Geoffrey Parker, *The Military Revolution*, Oxford, 1988, p. 133.

154 *The Private Diary of Ananda Ranga Pillai*, p. 96; Subrahmanyam, *Penumbral Visions*, p. 14; Parker, *The Military Revolution*, p. 133; Bert S. Hall and Kelly De Vries, 'Essay Review – The "Military Revolution" Revisited', *Technology and Culture*, 31 (1990), p. 502; Knud J. V. Jespersen, 'Social Change and Military Revolution in Early Modern Europe: Some Danish Evidence', *Historical Journal*, 26 (1983), pp. 1–2; Michael Howard, *War in European History* (1976, reprint), Oxford, 1977, pp. 61, 78; Hew Strachan, *European Armies and the Conduct of War* (1983, reprint), London, 1993, p. 33; Roy, 'Military Synthesis in South Asia'.

155 Sir Penderel Moon, *The British Conquest and Dominion of India*, London, 1989, p. 19.

156 Partha Chatterjee, *The Black Hole of Empire: History of a Global Practice of Power*, New Delhi, 2012, p. 11.

157 Subrahmanyam, *Penumbral Visions*, p. 19.

158 Gupta, *Sirajuddaullah and the East India Company*, p. 36.

159 Bryant, *Emergence of British Power*, p. 9.

160 *Voyage en Inde*, pp. 67–8. Modave's thoughts were echoed by his old friend Voltaire: 'Finally there remained with the French, in this part of the world, only the regret that they had spent, over the course of more than forty years, immense sums of money in the upkeep of a Company which never provided the least profit, which never paid anything from its trade profits to its shareholders and its creditors, which in its Indian administration survived only by means of secret brigandry, and which has been upheld only by the share of the farming of tobacco accorded to it by the king: a memorable and perhaps useless example of the lack of intelligence which the French nation has had up to now in the grand ruinous trade with India', Voltaire, *Précis du siècle de Louis XV*, p. 1507, in *Oeuvres historiques*, ed. R. Pomeau, Paris, 1962, pp. 1297–572.

161 Daniel Baugh, *The Global Seven Years War, 1754–63*, New York, 2014, pp. 52–4.

162 Ibid., pp. 59–60.

CHAPTER 2: AN OFFER HE COULD NOT REFUSE

1 NAI, Bengal Select Committee, *Letters from Court*, 25 May 1756, vol. 23 (1756–71), 13 February 1756

2 Ibid.

3 Daniel Baugh, *The Global Seven Years War, 1754–63*, New York, 2014, p. 462.

4 John Keay, *The Honourable Company: A History of the English East India Company*, London, 1991, pp. 111–12.

5 K. N. Chaudhuri, *The English East India Company in the 17th and 18th Centuries: A Pre-Modern Multinational Organisation*, The Hague, 1981, p. 29.

6 Sir William Foster, *The East India House: Its History and Associations*, London, 1924, pp. 132–3.

7 Holden Furber, 'Rival Empires of Trade in the Orient, 1600–1800', in *Maritime India*, intro. Sanjay Subrahmanyam, New Delhi, 2004, pp. 128–9; Tirthankar Roy, *East India Company: The World's Most Powerful Corporation*, New Delhi, 2012, pp. 116–17.

8 Tillman W. Nechtman, *Nabobs: Empire and Identity in Eighteenth Century Britain*, Cambridge, 2010.

9 P. J. Marshall, 'The British in Asia: Trade to Dominion, 1700–1765', in P. J. Marshall (ed.), *The Oxford History of the British Empire*, vol. 2, *The Eighteenth Century*, Oxford, 1998, pp. 267–9; Keith Feiling, *Warren Hastings*, London, 1954, p. 13; Burton Stein, 'Eighteenth Century India: Another View', *Studies in History*, vol. 5, 1 n.s. (1989), p. 20.

10 George Forrest, *The Life of Lord Clive*, 2 vols, London, 1918, vol. 1, pp. 232–3; Percival Spear, *Master of Bengal: Clive and his India*, London, 1975, pp. 62–3.

11 Mark Bence-Jones, *Clive of India*, London, 1974, p. 3; A. M. Davies, *Clive of Plassey*, London, 1939, p. 7.

12 Forrest, *The Life of Lord Clive*, vol. 1, pp. 4–5.

13 Feiling, *Warren Hastings*, p. 31.

14 Sir Penderel Moon, *The British Conquest and Dominion of India*, London, 1989, p. 29.

15 Spear, *Master of Bengal*, p. 61.

16 Bruce Lenman, *Britain's Colonial Wars, 1688–1783*, Harlow, 2001, pp. 99–100.

17 Moon, *The British Conquest and Dominion of India*, pp. 30–1; Baugh, *The Global Seven Years War*, p. 67; G. J. Bryant, *Emergence of British Power Power in India 1600–1784: A Grand Strategic Interpretation*, Woodbridge, 2013, p. 59; Forrest, *The Life of Lord Clive*, vol. 1, pp. 194–201; Bence-Jones, *Clive of India*, pp. 65–7.

18 Forrest, *The Life of Lord Clive*, vol. 1, p. 218.

19 Ibid., p. 233.

20 P. J. Marshall, *The Making and Unmaking of Empires: Britain, India and America c. 1750–1783*, Oxford, 2005, pp. 84–5.

21 Quoted in John Keay, *India Discovered*, London, 1981, p. 21.

22 Feiling, *Warren Hastings*, p. 10.

23 Marshall, *The Making and Unmaking of Empires*, p. 148.

24 Brijen K. Gupta, *Sirajuddaullah and the East India Company, 1756–7*, Leiden, 1966, p. 14. But at this stage it was still the Asians and not the Europeans who were the major importers of bullion into Bengal in the early eighteenth century. One of the responsible officials of the EIC who lived in Bengal in the 1750–60s writes that it was the Asian merchants and not the Europeans who were the major importers of bullion into Bengal and that their imports of precious metals far exceeded those of the Europeans. Another Company official, Luke Scrafton, corroborates this finding. See Sushil Chaudhury, *Companies Commerce and Merchants: Bengal in the Pre-Colonial Era*, Oxford, 2017, pp. 389–95. According to Richard Eaton, 'Even as late as the mid-eighteenth century, Asian traders – especially Gujaratis, Armenians, and Punjabis – played a more important role in Bengal's commercial economy than did Europeans.' Eaton points out that in exchange for manufactured textiles both Asian and European merchants poured into the delta substantial amounts of silver, which, minted into currency, fuelled the booming agrarian frontier by monetising the local economy. Relying on Mughal documents, Eaton has done excellent work on the Bengal delta, the long-term expanding agrarian frontier and the changing courses of rivers in the eighteenth century which allowed the Mughal rulers to extend a rich and fertile agrarian base of rice cultivation – a process which was disrupted with the Company's intervention in Bengal by the late eighteenth century. See Richard M. Eaton, *Essays on Islam and Indian History*, Oxford, 2000, p. 263.

25 Mrs Jemima Kindersley, *Letters from the East Indies*, London, 1777, p. 17. Also very good for Calcutta at this period is Farhat Hasan, 'Calcutta in the Early Eighteenth Century', in J. S. Grewal, *Calcutta: Foundation and Development of a Colonial Metropolis*, New Delhi, 1991, and Rajat Datta, 'From Medieval to Colonial: Markets, Territoriality and the Transition in Eighteenth-Century Bengal', in *Medieval History Journal*, vol. 2, no. 1 (1999).

26 K. N. Chaudhuri, *The Trading World of Asia and the English East India Company 1660–1760*, Cambridge, 1978, p. 253.

27 Kaushik Roy, 'Military Synthesis in South Asia: Armies, Warfare, and Indian Society, c.1740–1849', in *Journal of Military History*, vol. 69, no. 3 (July 2005), pp. 651–90; V. G. Dighe and S. N. Qanungo, 'Administrative and Military System of the Marathas', in R. C. Majumdar and V. G. Dighe (eds), *The Maratha Supremacy*, Mumbai, 1977, pp. 567–8; Jadunath Sarkar, *Fall of the Mughal Empire, 1789–1803*, 4 vols, 1950; reprint, New Delhi, 1992, p. 85. The English factory records graphically described the anarchy: 'The

Marathas are plundering Birbhum (1742) which has put a stop to all businesses, the merchants and weavers flying whenever they can.' Some of their reports are quoted in Sarkar, *Fall of the Mughal Empire*, vol. 1, p. 43.

28 Quoted in Sarkar, *Fall of the Mughal Empire*, vol. 1, p. 44.

29 Velcheru Narayana Rao, David Shulman and Sanjay Subrahmanyam, *Textures of Time: Writing History in South India 1600–1800*, New York, 2003, pp. 236–7.

30 John R. McLane, *Land and Local Kingship in Eighteenth-Century Bengal*, Cambridge, 1993, pp. 163–5; *The Maharahtra Purana: An Eighteenth Century Bengali Historical Text*, trans. and ed. Edward C. Dimock Jr and Pratul Chandra Gupta, Honolulu, 1965, pp. 28–32. There are many other accounts that corroborate Ganga Ram's account. The historians Salimullah and Ghulam Husain Salim, for example, also endorse these accounts. They write, 'The *Bargis* cut off the ears, noses and hands of multitudes of people, or killed them with many kinds of torture and suffering – by gagging their mouths with bags of dust and destroying them' (i.e. outraged their women); see Sarkar, *Fall of the Mughal Empire*, vol. 1, p. 44. Sarkar provides a long narrative of Vidyalankar's account. The letters from the French factory at Chandernagar and the English settlement of Calcutta narrate the same story of oppression and destruction.

31 Sarkar, *Fall of the Mughal Empire*, vol. 1, p. 8.

32 Francis Gladwin, trans., *The Memoirs of Khojeh Abdulkurreem*, Calcutta, 1788, pp. 147–8.

33 Roy, *East India Company*, p. 165.

34 Ibid., pp. 25, 141–2, 165–7.

35 C. A. Bayly, *Indian Society and the Making of the British Empire*, Cambridge, 1988, p. 49.

36 Roy, *East India Company*, p. 23. The problem with seeing Calcutta as a kind of shelter or tax haven for Indian merchants is that these merchants were not only operating in Calcutta, but instead depended on far-flung networks of merchants and suppliers throughout eastern and northern India. Calcutta's status as a flourishing port, and the Company's deep pockets, made it a magnet, but it's also true that the city could only flourish in symbiosis with large sectors of the late Mughal economy. Calcutta was not the only city with a 'legal system', and it is possible Roy may have overestimated the distinctiveness of the Company in this regard.

37 Abdul Latif Shushtari, *Kitab Tuhfat al-'Alam*, written Hyderabad 1802 and lithographed Bombay 1847, p. 427.

38 Ibid., p. 434.

39 P. J. Marshall, *East India Fortunes: The British in Bengal in the Eighteenth Century*, Oxford, 1976, pp. 218–19.

40 See Andrew Ward, *Our Bones Are Scattered*, London, 1996, p. 8.

41 Marshall, *East India Fortunes*, p. 159.

42 Scottish Records Office, Hamilton-Dalrymple Mss, bundle 56, GD 110, folios 1021,1021. Stair Dalrymple to Sir Hew Dalrymple, 3 Jan 1754; Marshall, *East India Fortunes*, pp. 159, 215.

43 *Causes of the Loss of Calcutta 1756*, David Renny, August 1756, OIOC, BL, O.V. 19, pp. 147–61; OIOC, HM vol. 66, pp. 821–4.

44 Jean Law de Lauriston, *A Memoir of the Mughal Empire 1757–61*, trans. G. S. Cheema, New Delhi, 2014, p. 59.

45 OIOC, Bengal Correspondence, Court of Directors to the Fort William Council, 16 January 1752; Gupta, *Sirajuddaullah and the East India Company, 1756–7*, p. 37.

46 Watts to Drake and the Fort William Council, BL, OIOC, Bengal Public Consultations, 15 August 1755; Gupta, *Sirajuddaullah and the East India Company, 1756–7*, p. 38.

47 Philip B. Calkins, 'The Role of Murshidabad as a Regional and Subregional Centre in Bengal', in Richard L. Park, *Urban Bengal*, East Lansing, 1969, pp. 25–6.

48 J. P. Losty, 'Murshidabad Painting 1750–1820', in Neeta Das and Rosie Llewellyn Jones, *Murshidabad: Forgotten Capital of Bengal*, Mumbai, 2013, pp. 82–105; J. P. Losty, 'Towards a New Naturalism: Portraiture in Murshidabad and Avadh, 1750–80', in Barbara Schmitz (ed.), *After the Great Mughals: Painting in Delhi and the Regional Courts in the 18th and 19th Centuries*, Mumbai, 2002; J. P. Losty, 'Eighteenth-century Mughal Paintings from the Swinton Collection', in *The Burlington Magazine*, CLIX, October 2017, pp. 789–99; Tilottama Mukherjee, 'The Coordinating State and the Economy: the Nizamat in Eighteenth Century Bengal', in *Modern Asian Studies*, 43, 2 (2009), p. 421.

49 The miniature shows the Delhi exile Natthu Khan heading the band on his great rabab, the beautiful young Muhammad Khan with his astonishing blue eyes singing, while his elders Chajju Khan and Dindar Khan accompany him, one on either side, on the tambura, with Taj Khan strumming the been and Sita Ram on the pakhawaj; 1755 is the date of Shahamat Jang's death. See also 'Eighteenth-century Mughal Paintings from the Swinton Collection', in *The Burlington Magazine*, CLIX, October 2017, pp. 789–99, fig. 29. Thanks to Katherine Butler Schofield for explaining this image for me.

50 Syed Ghulam Hussain Khan Tabatabai, *Seir Mutaqherin*, Calcutta, 1790–4, vol. 2, pp. 156–62; Mukherjee, 'The Coordinating State and the Economy: The Nizamat in Eighteenth Century Bengal', p. 412.

51 Sir Jadunath Sarkar (ed.), *The History of Bengal*, vol. II, *The Muslim Period 1200 A.D.–1757 A.D.*, New Delhi, 1948, p. 448.

52 NAI, Home Dept, Public Branch, vol. 1, 9 January 1749, p. 73; Mukherjee, 'The Coordinating State and the Economy: The Nizamat in Eighteenth Century Bengal', pp. 389–436.

53 Gupta, *Sirajuddaullah and the East India Company, 1756–7*, p. 45.

54 Ghulam Hussain Khan, *Seir Mutaqherin*, vol. 2, p. 164. Another good account of this period is *Waqa-i-Mahabat Jang [The Full History of Aliverdi Khan] or Ahwal-i-Mahabat Jang of Yusuf Ali*, English translation by Sir Jadunath Sarkar, published by Asiatic Society of Bengal as *Nawabs of Bengal*, Calcutta, 1952.

55 Robert Travers, *Ideology and Empire in Eighteenth Century India: The British in Bengal*, Cambridge, 2007, p. 3; McLane, *Land and Local Kingship*, p. 6; Marshall, *East India Fortunes*, p. 34.

56 BL, OIOC, IOR, Bengal Public Consultations, 10 June 1753, Range 1, vol. 26, f. 169. Despite the overwhelming evidence from contemporary sources of Siraj behaving rather like Uday Hussain in pre-9/11 Baghdad, there have been several spirited post-Colonial attempts to resuscitate his reputation, for example see Sushil Chaudhury, who argues that Sira ud-Daula's villainous character is a misrepresentation. See Sushil Chaudhury, *The Prelude to Empire: Plassey Revolution of 1757*, New Delhi, 2000, pp. 29–36.

57 Law, *A Memoir of the Mughal Empire 1757–61*, pp. 65–6.

58 Ghulam Hussain Khan, *Seir Mutaqherin*, vol. 2, pp. 122, 183–4, 188.

59 J. H. Little, *The House of Jagat Seth*, Calcutta, 1956, p. 165.

60 Ghulam Hussain Khan, *Seir Mutaqherin*, vol. 2, p. 225. See also the excellent discussion in Lakshmi Subramanian and Rajat K. Ray, 'Merchants and Politics: From the Great Mughals to the East India Company', in Dwijendra Tripathi, *Business and Politics in India: A Historical Perspective*, New Delhi, 1991, pp. 19–45.

61 Ghulam Hussain Khan, *Seir Mutaqherin*, vol. 2, p. 95.

62 Law, *A Memoir of the Mughal Empire 1757–61*, p. 52.

63 Ghulam Hussain Khan, *Seir Mutaqherin*, vol. 2, p. 163.

64 Gupta, *Sirajuddaullah and the East India Company, 1756–7*, pp. 39, 51; S. C. Hill, Indian Records Series, *Bengal in 1756–7*, 3 vols, London, 1905, vol. 1, p. 147.

65 'The Muzaffarnama of Karam Ali', in *Bengal Nawabs*, trans. Jadunath Sarkar, Calcutta, 1952, p. 58.

66 Ibid., p. 63.

67 Gupta, *Sirajuddaullah and the East India Company, 1756–7*, p. 54.

68 *Narrative of the Capture of Calcutta from April 10 1756 to November 10 1756*, William Tooke, BL, OIOC, O.V. 19, Bengal 1756, pp. 5–46; Rajat Kanta Ray, *The Felt Community: Commonality and Mentality before the Emergence of Indian Nationalism*, New Delhi, 2003, p. 233.

69 *Narrative of the Capture of Calcutta from April 10 1756 to November 10 1756*, pp. 5–46.

70 Feiling, *Warren Hastings*, p. 21.

71 Gupta, *Sirajuddaullah and the East India Company, 1756–7*, pp. 14, 53; Hill, *Bengal in 1756–7*, vol. I, p. 3.

72 *Voyage en Inde du Comte de Modave, 1773–1776*, ed. Jean Deloche, Pondicherry, 1971, pp. 67–8.

73 Law, *A Memoir of the Mughal Empire 1757–61*, pp. 218–19.

74 *CPC* ii, no. 1101; Sarkar, *Fall of the Mughal Empire*, vol. 2, pp. 315, 328.

75 Ghulam Ali Khan alias Bhikhari Khan, *Shah Alam Nama*, BL, Add 24080, f. 21.

76 Khurshidul Islam and Ralph Russell, *Three Mughal Poets: Mir, Sauda, Mir Hasan*, New Delhi, 1991, pp. 30, 59.

77 Sarkar, *Fall of the Mughal Empire*, vol. I, p. 222.

78 Law, *A Memoir of the Mughal Empire 1757–61*, p. 126.

79 Ghulam Hussain Khan, *Seir Mutaqherin*, vol. 3, p. 334.

80 Law, *A Memoir of the Mughal Empire 1757–61*, p. 126; Manna Kai, 'Imad ul-Mulk', in *The Encyclopedia of Islam – Three*, ed. Kate Fleet and Gudrun Krämer, Brill, 2018, pp. 110–13.

81 Law, *A Memoir of the Mughal Empire 1757–61*, p. 125.

82 Muzaffar Alam and Sanjay Subrahmanyam, *Writing the Mughal World: Studies on Culture and Politics*, New York, 2012, pp. 434–4.

83 This section derives from a remarkable essay by Katherine Schofield and David Lunn, 'Delight, Devotion and the Music of the Monsoon at the Court of Emperor Shah Alam II', in Margit Pernau, Imke Rajamani and Katherine Schofield, *Monsoon Feelings*, New Delhi, 2018, pp. 185–218.

84 Ibid. It may be a little reductive to draw too strong a contrast between Shah Alam as a 'Sufi' and his father, who had many Sufi connections, as a 'puritan'. There was a distinction, but Nile Green's work has convincingly argued that Mughal Sufism should be seen less as a distinct branch of 'mystical Islam' than as a many-headed and multi-faceted group of scholarly and sacred lineages which had in fact become over the early modern period the Muslim 'establishment'. Nile Green, *Sufism: A Global History*, London, 2012.

85 Ghulam Ali Khan alias Bhikhari Khan, *Shah Alam Nama*, BL, Add 24080, f. 18.

86 Fakir Khair ud-Din Illahabadi, *'Ibrat Nama*, BL Or. 1932, 17v–18r.

87 *Tarikh-i-Alamgir Sani*, BL Mss Or. 1749, f. 166 verso.

88 Ibid., f. 167 recto.

89 Fakir Khair ud-Din Illahabadi, 'Ibrat Nama, BL Or. 1932, 17v–18r. I have added several details from the related and slightly earlier account of the same event in the *Tarikh-i-Alamgir Sani*, BL Mss Or. 1749, f. 166 verso.

90 Ghulam Hussain Khan, *Seir Mutaqherin*, vol. 3, pp. 365–8.

91 Law, *A Memoir of the Mughal Empire 1757–61*, p. 254.

92 Fakir Khair ud-Din Illahabadi, 'Ibrat Nama, BL Or. 1932, 17v–18r. I have added a line of dialogue here from Ghulam Hussain Khan's closely related account of the same event.

93 Ghulam Ali Khan alias Bhikhari Khan, *Shah Alam Nama*, BL, Add 24080, f. 30.

94 K. K. Dutta, *Shah Alam II & The East India Company*, Calcutta, 1965, pp. 1–2.

95 Ghulam Hussain Khan, *Seir Mutaqherin*, vol. 2, pp. 286–9, vol. 3, pp. 189–90; Ray, *The Felt Community*, p. 333.

CHAPTER 3: SWEEPING WITH THE BROOM OF PLUNDER

1 William Tooke, *Narrative of the Capture of Calcutta from April 10, 1756 to November 10, 1756*, BL, OIOC, O.V. 19, Bengal 1756, pp. 5–46.

2 John Zephaniah Holwell, quoted in John Keay, *The Honourable Company: A History of the English East India Company*, London, 1991, p. 301.

3 William Watts and John Campbell, *Memoirs of the Revolution in Bengal, Anno. Dom. 1757*, p. 14.

4 John Zephaniah Holwell, quoted in Bruce P. Lenman, *Britain's Colonial Wars 1688–1783*, New York, 2001, p. 106.

5 *An Account Of The Capture Of Calcutta By Captain Grant*, BM Add Mss 29200, f. 38.

6 Ibid.

7 *Concerning the Loss of Calcutta*, BL, OIOC, HM vol. 66, pp. 821–4.

8 *An Account Of The Capture Of Calcutta By Captain Grant*, BM Add Mss 29200, f. 39.

9 Ibid.

10 *Account of the loss of Calcutta by David Renny*, BL, OIOC, HM vol. 66, pp. 821–4.

11 *Cooke's Evidence before the Select Committee of the House of Commons*, in W. K. Firminger (ed.), *Great Britain, House of Commons, Report on East India Affairs, Fifth report from the Select Committee*, vol. III, p. 299.

12 Quoted in Sir Penderel Moon, *The British Conquest and Dominion of India*, London, 1989, p. 42.

13 Syed Ghulam Hussain Khan Tabatabai, *Seir Mutaqherin*, Calcutta, 1790–4, vol. 2, p. 190.

14 *Concerning the Loss of Calcutta*, BL, OIOC, HM vol. 66, pp. 821–4.

15 *Narrative of the loss of Calcutta, with the Black Hole by Captain Mills, who was in it, and sundry other particulars, being Captain Mills pocket book, which he gave me*, BL, OIOC, O.V. 19, pp. 77–92.

16 Ibid.

17 *Account of the loss of Calcutta by John Cooke Esq. who was in the Black Hole, June 1756*, in *Cooke's Evidence before the Select Committee of the House of Commons*, in W. K. Firminger (ed.), *Great Britain, House of Commons, Report on East India Affairs, Fifth report from the Select Committee*, vol III, p. 299.

18 Ghulam Husain Salim, *Riyazu-s-salatin: A History of Bengal, Translated from the original Persian by Maulvi Abdus Salam*, Calcutta, 1902, p. 366.

19 S. C. Hill, Indian Records Series, *Bengal in 1756–7*, 3 vols, Calcutta, 1905, vol. 1, p. 51, French letter from Chandernagar.

20 *Account of the loss of Calcutta by John Cooke Esq. who was in the Black Hole, June 1756*, in *Cooke's Evidence before the Select Committee of the House of Commons*, in W. K. Firminger (ed.), *Great Britain, House of Commons, Report on East India Affairs, Fifth report from the Select Committee*, vol. III, p. 299.

21 Yusuf Ali Khan, *Tarikh-i-Bangala-i-Mahabatjangi*, trans. Abdus Subhan, Calcutta, 1982, pp. 120–2.

22 John Zephaniah Holwell, *A Genuine Narrative of the Deplorable Deaths of the English Gentlemen, and others, who were suffocated in the Black Hole in Fort William, in Calcutta, in the Kingdom of Bengal; in the Night Succeeding the 20th June 1756*, London, 1758.

23 There is a large literature on the Black Hole. The best forensic examination of the primary evidence is to be found in Brijen K. Gupta, *Sirajuddaullah and the East India Company, 1756–7*, Leiden, 1966, pp. 70–81. There are also good discussions in Partha Chatterjee, *The Black Hole of Empire: History of a Global Practice of Power*, Ranikhet, 2012, p. 255; Jan Dalley, *The Black Hole: Money, Myth and Empire*, London, 2006; Rajat Kanta Ray, *The Felt Community: Commonality and Mentality before the Emergence of Indian Nationalism*, New Delhi, 2003, pp. 235–7; Linda Colley, *Captives: Britain, Empire and the World 1600–1850*, London, 2002; Ian Barrow, 'The many meanings of the Black Hole of Calcutta', in *Tall Tales and True: India, Historiography and British Imperial Imaginings*, ed. Kate Brittlebank, Clayton, Vic., 2008, pp. 7–18. Betty Joseph has argued that the Black Hole helped the Company avoid much public and political scrutiny of the crucial shift that had taken place in its role in India, and as a result, the Company moved from being a commercial power to a territorial power

and began the conquest of India without criticism. Betty Joseph, *Reading the East India Company*, New Delhi, 2006, pp. 70–1.

24 *Concerning the Loss of Calcutta*, BL, OIOC, HM vol. 66, pp. 821–4.

25 *Causes of the Loss of Calcutta 1756*, David Renny, August 1756, BL, OIOC, O.V. 19, pp. 147–61.

26 G. J. Bryant, *Emergence of British Power in India 1600–1784: A Grand Strategic Interpretation*, Woodbridge, 2013, pp. 118–21.

27 Hill, Indian Records Series, *Bengal in 1756–7*, vol. 1, p. 233, Extract of a letter from Colonel Clive to the Secret Committee, London, dated Fort St George, 11 October, 1756.

28 George Forrest, *The Life of Lord Clive*, 2 vols, London, 1918, vol. 1, p. 278.

29 Mark Bence-Jones, *Clive of India*, London, 1974, p. 94.

30 Daniel Baugh, *The Global Seven Years War, 1754–63*, New York, 2014, p. 286.

31 Ghulam Hussain Khan, *Seir Mutaqherin*, vol. 2, p. 220.

32 Bence-Jones, *Clive of India*, p. 98; Keith Feiling, *Warren Hastings*, London, 1954, p. 23.

33 Captain Edward Maskelyne, *Journal of the Proceedings of the Troops commanded by Lieutenant Colonel Robert Clive on the expedition to Bengal*, BL, OIOC, Mss Eur Orme, vol. 20, p. 19.

34 Edward Ives, *A Voyage From England to India in the Year 1754*, London, 1733, quoted in Keay, *The Honourable Company*, p. 307.

35 Ghulam Hussain Khan, *Seir Mutaqherin*, vol. 2, p. 221.

36 Ives, *A Voyage From England to India in the Year 1754*, p. 102.

37 Feiling, *Warren Hastings*, p. 23.

38 Ghulam Husain Salim, *Riyazu-s-salatin*, pp. 369–70.

39 Captain Edward Maskelyne, *Journal of the Proceedings of the Troops commanded by Lieutenant Colonel Robert Clive on the expedition to Bengal*, BL, OIOC, Mss Eur Orme, vol. 20, pp. 23–4; Watts and Campbell, *Memoirs of the Revolution in Bengal, Anno. Dom. 1757*, p. 18.

40 Watts and Campbell, *Memoirs of the Revolution in Bengal, Anno. Dom. 1757*, p. 20.

41 Clive's Evidence – First Report of the Committee of the House of Commons; Forrest, *The Life of Lord Clive*, vol. 1, pp. 354–5.

42 Captain Edward Maskelyne, *Journal of the Proceedings of the Troops commanded by Lieutenant Colonel Robert Clive on the expedition to Bengal*, BL, OIOC, Mss Eur Orme, vol. 20, pp. 28–30.

43 Forrest, *The Life of Lord Clive*, vol. 1, pp. 359–60.

44 Ghulam Hussain Khan, *Seir Mutaqherin*, vol. 2, p. 222.

45 P. J. Marshall (ed.), *The Eighteenth Century in Indian History. Evolution or Revolution*, New Delhi, 2003, p. 362.

46 Ray, *The Felt Community*, p. 244.

47 The three British players in this story – the Crown, the Company and Parliament – rarely worked as a unified force. For a good analysis of the tensions between them see Lucy Sutherland's classic, *The East India Company in Eighteenth-Century Politics*, Oxford, 1952.

48 Baugh, *The Global Seven Years War*, p. 291. Cuba was a Spanish colony, only involved in the war at the very end, when Spain joined in.

49 Hill, Indian Records Series, *Bengal in 1756–7*, vol. 1, pp. 180–1, Letter to M Demontorcin, Chandernagar, August 1, 1756.

50 Jean Law de Lauriston, *A Memoir of the Mughal Empire 1757–61*, trans. G. S. Cheema, New Delhi, 2014, p. 87.

51 Keay, *The Honourable Company*, p. 314.

52 Quoted by Sir Jadunath Sarkar (ed.), *The History of Bengal*, vol. II, *The Muslim Period 1200 A.D.–1757 A.D.*, New Delhi, 1948, pp. 484–5.

53 Law, *A Memoir of the Mughal Empire 1757–61*, p. 98.

54 Ghulam Husain Salim, *Riyazu-s-salatin*, pp. 373–4; BL, OIOC, HM 193, p. 88.

55 Ghulam Hussain Khan, *Seir Mutaqherin*, vol. 2, p. 193.

56 Law, *A Memoir of the Mughal Empire 1757–61*, p. 66.

57 Ghulam Hussain Khan, *Seir Mutaqherin*, vol. 2, pp. 211, 213.

58 Law, *A Memoir of the Mughal Empire 1757–61*, pp. 82–3.

59 Hill, Indian Records Series, *Bengal in 1756–7*, vol. 2, pp. 368–9, Letter from Colonel Clive to Mr Pigot, dated 30 April 1757.

60 This is why the eminent Indian scholar K. M. Pannikar famously called the Battle of Plassey a 'transaction, not a battle, a transaction by which the compradors of Bengal, led by Jagat Seth, sold the Nawab to the East India Company', K. M. Pannikar, *Asia and Western Dominance*, New York, 1954, p. 100. See also Sushil Chaudhury, *Companies, Commerce and Merchants: Bengal in the Pre-Colonial Era*, New Delhi, 2015, pp. 336–52.

61 Fort William Select Committee Proceedings of May 1, 1757, in Hill, Indian Records Series, *Bengal in 1756–7*, vol. 2, p. 370.

62 In an effort to declutter an already complicated narrative, I have omitted the important role in the conspiracy of another banker, this time a Punjabi, named Amir Chand, known to the Company as Omichand. He played a major role in the Plassey conspiracy. Clive made full use of Omichand as a negotiator and he also accompanied Watts to Murshidabad following the conclusion of the February treaty. Omichand wanted his share in the spoils of Plassey and demanded 5 per cent on all the Nawab's treasure, threatening to reveal the conspiracy to Siraj. However, when the Select Committee met on 17 May Clive deviously persuaded it to draw up a

double treaty to be signed by Mir Jafar and the British, in one the article in favour of Omichand's 'cut' being inserted and in the other left out. See Sushil Chaudhury, *The Prelude to Empire: Plassey Revolution of 1757*, p. 127 and passim.

63 Letter from Petrus Arratoon to the Court of Directors, dated 25 January 1759, quoted in Forrest, *The Life of Lord Clive*, vol. 1, p. 432.

64 Watts and Campbell, *Memoirs of the Revolution in Bengal, Anno. Dom. 1757*, pp. 98–9.

65 BL, OIOC, Mss Eur Orme India XI, no. 153.

66 BL, OIOC, IOR, HM 193, no. 158.

67 Ibid., no. 159.

68 Spear, *Master of Bengal*, p. 87.

69 Forrest, *The Life of Lord Clive*, vol. 1, p. 440.

70 BL, OIOC, IOR, HM 193, no. 161.

71 Ibid., no. 162.

72 Ibid., no. 167.

73 Ibid., no. 169.

74 Ibid.

75 BL, OIOC, Orme Papers, O.V., CLXIV-A, f. 115.

76 NAI, Home Misc of Ancient Records, 1757, vol. 19, pp. 120–8, 26 July 1757.

77 Ghulam Hussain Khan, *Seir Mutaqherin*, vol. 2, pp. 230–1.

78 *The Muzaffarnama of Karam Ali*, in *Bengal Nawabs*, trans. Jadunath Sarkar, Calcutta, 1952, p. 76.

79 Ghulam Husain Salim, *Riyazu-s-salatin*, pp. 375–6.

80 Captain Edward Maskelyne, *Journal of the Proceedings of the Troops commanded by Lieutenant Colonel Robert Clive on the expedition to Bengal*, BL, OIOC, Mss Eur Orme, vol. 20, p. 30.

81 NAI, Home Misc of Ancient Records, 1757, vol. 19, pp. 120–8, 26 July 1757.

82 BL, OIOC, IOR, HM 193, no. 172.

83 Moon, *The British Conquest and Dominion of India*, p. 55.

84 Hill, Indian Records Series, *Bengal in 1756–7*, vol. 2, p. 437, Clive to Select Committee, Fort William June 30th 1757.

85 BL, OIOC, IOR, HM 193, no. 194.

86 Ghulam Hussain Khan, *Seir Mutaqherin*, vol. 2, pp. 235–42.

87 *The Muzaffarnama of Karam Ali*, p. 78.

88 P. J. Marshall, *The Making and Unmaking of Empires: Britain, India and America c. 1750–1783*, p. 150; John R. McLane, *Land and Local Kingship in Eighteenth-Century Bengal*, Cambridge, 1993, p. 150.

89 Forrest, *The Life of Lord Clive*, vol. 2, p. 35.

90 Philip Stern has shown how much earlier than was previously understood the Company acquired political power, but there can be no doubt that Plassey hugely augmented this. See Philip J. Stern, *The Company State: Corporate Sovereignty & the Early Modern Foundations of the British Empire in India*, Cambridge, 2011.

91 Ray, *The Felt Community*, pp. 245–6.

92 Keay, *The Honourable Company*, pp. 317–18.

93 Alexander Dow, *History of Hindostan*, 3 vols, Dublin, 1792, vol. 3, p. xxiv.

94 P. J. Marshall, *East India Fortunes: The British in Bengal in the Eighteenth Century*, Oxford, 1976, p. 8.

CHAPTER 4: A PRINCE OF LITTLE CAPACITY

1 Percival Spear, *Master of Bengal: Clive and his India*, London, 1975, p. 97.

2 Ibid.

3 Clive to Mir Jafar, 15 July 1757, OIOC, HM 193, 180; Mark Bence-Jones, *Clive of India*, London, 1974, p. 157.

4 Clive to John Payne, 11 November 1758, National Library of Wales, Clive Mss 200 (2), pp. 102–4.

5 George Forrest, *The Life of Lord Clive*, New Delhi, 1986, vol. 2, pp. 119–22.

6 Abdul Majed Khan, *The Transition in Bengal 1756–1775*, Cambridge, 1969, pp. 10–11.

7 J. Price, *Five Letters from a Free Merchant in Bengal, to Warren Hastings Esq*, London, 1778, p. 136; Peter Marshall, *Problems of Empire: Britain and India 1757–1813*, London, 1968, p. 26.

8 Forrest, *The Life of Lord Clive*, vol. 2, p. 179; Tillman W. Nechtman, 'A Jewel in the Crown? Indian Wealth in Domestic Britain in the Late Eighteenth Century', *Eighteenth Century Studies*, 41:1 (2007), pp. 71–86, p. 74; Spear, *Master of Bengal*, p. 119.

9 Sir Penderel Moon, *Warren Hastings and British India*, London, 1947, p. 35; Abdul Majed Khan, *The Transition in Bengal 1756–1775*, pp. 28–9.

10 Syed Ghulam Hussain Khan Tabatabai, *Seir Mutaqherin*, Calcutta, 1790–94, vol. 2, pp. 262, 270.

11 Sir Penderel Moon, *The British Conquest and Dominion of India*, London, 1989, p. 62.

12 Ghulam Hussain Khan, *Seir Mutaqherin*, vol. 2, p. 241.

13 Ibid., vol. 2, p. 351.

14 Ibid., vol. 2, pp. 262, 250–1, 373; Henry Vansittart, *A Narrative of the Transactions in Bengal from the Year 1760, to the year 1764, during the Government of Mr Henry Vansittart*, London, 1766, vol. 1, pp. 151–3.

15 Moon, *The British Conquest and Dominion of India*, p. 86.

16 OIOC, Bengal Secret Consultations, 30 April, 25, 26, 30 July, 27 Aug 1764, Range A, vol. 5, pp. 156–61, 408–21, 444–58; P. J. Marshall, *East India Fortunes: The British in Bengal in the Eighteenth Century*, Oxford, 1976, pp. 118, 128; Bence-Jones, *Clive of India*, p. 156.

17 Vansittart, *A Narrative of the Transactions in Bengal*, vol. 1, p. 25.

18 Marshall, *East India Fortunes*, p. 120.

19 Quoted in Bence-Jones, *Clive of India*, p. 156.

20 *Voyage en Inde du Comte de Modave, 1773–1776*, ed. Jean Deloche, Pondicherry, 1971, p. 48.

21 Ibid., pp. 282–7.

22 Quoted by Vansittart, *A Narrative of the Transactions in Bengal*, vol. 2, pp. 79–84.

23 Hastings to Vansittart, 25 April 1762, OIOC, BL Add Mss 29,098, f. 7–8. See also Walter K. Firminger and William Anderson, *The Diaries of Three Surgeons of Patna*, Calcutta, 1909, p. 16.

24 Keith Feiling, *Warren Hastings*, London, 1954, pp. 1–11; Jeremy Bernstein, *Dawning of the Raj: The Life & Trials of Warren Hastings*, Chicago, 2000, pp. 32–5.

25 Feiling, *Warren Hastings*, pp. 39, 66. The portrait is now in the National Portrait Gallery, London, NPG 81.

26 Ibid., pp. 28, 41.

27 Kumkum Chatterjee, *Merchants, Politics & Society in Early Modern India Bihar: 1733–1820*, Leiden, 1996, pp. 118–23. For other complaints about Pearkes see Vansittart, *A Narrative of the Transactions in Bengal*, vol. 1, p. 28.

28 For the Jagat Seths writing to Shah Alam see Forrest, *The Life of Lord Clive*, vol. 2, p. 126. For Mir Ashraf's support for Shah Alam see BL, Or. 466, *Tarikh-i Muzaffari* of Muhammad 'Ali Khan Ansari of Panipat, pp. 635–6.

29 Ghulam Ali Khan alias Bhikhari Khan, *Shah Alam Nama*, BL, Add 24080.

30 The historiography of the period usually contrasts the old thesis of Mughal decline against which are aligned revisionist claims of provincial autonomy and growth. Shah Alam's story reveals a more complex story than just a case study of decentralisation, and reveals instead the fluidity of the situation and the shifting political allegiances and interests which are not incorporated in either of these linear positions.

31 Sayid Athar Abbas Rizvi, *Shah Walli-Allah And His Times*, Canberra, 1980, p. 170.

32 Fakir Khair ud-Din Illahabadi, '*Ibrat Nama*, BL Or. 1932, 20r–21v.

33 Ghulam Ali Khan alias Bhikhari Khan, *Shah Alam Nama*, BL, Add 24080.

34 Krishna Dayal Bhargava, *Browne Correspondence*, Delhi, 1960, p. 1.

35 Jean Law de Lauriston, *A Memoir of the Mughal Empire 1757–61*, trans. G. S. Cheema, New Delhi, 2014, p. 297.

36 Jadunath Sarkar, *Fall of the Mughal Empire*, 4 vols, New Delhi, 1991, vol. 2, p. 315.

37 *Tarikh-i Shakir Khani*, British Library Oriental manuscripts, Add. 6568, f. 14r.

38 Law, *A Memoir of the Mughal Empire 1757–61*, pp. 265, 280, 290–1.

39 Ghulam Ali Khan alias Bhikhari Khan, *Shah Alam Nama*, BL, Add 24080. Also John R. McLane, *Land and Local Kingship in Eighteenth-Century Bengal*, Cambridge, 1993, p. 181.

40 Ghulam Hussain Khan, *Seir Mutaqherin*, vol. 2, pp. 338–41.

41 Ibid., vol. 2, p. 342.

42 Hastings to Vansittart, BL, OIOC, Add Mss 29132, f. 103–11; also Moon, *Warren Hastings and British India*, p. 37.

43 John Caillaud, *A Narrative of What Happened in Bengal in the Year 1760*, London, 1764, p. 15.

44 Ghulam Hussain Khan, *Seir Mutaqherin*, vol. 2, pp. 344–5.

45 *Tarikh-i Muzaffari* of Muhammad 'Ali Khan Ansari of Panipat, pp. 634–6. Also McLane, *Land and Local Kingship*, p. 181.

46 Caillaud, *A Narrative of What Happened in Bengal in the Year 1760*, p. 25.

47 *Tarikh-i Muzaffari* of Muhammad 'Ali Khan Ansari of Panipat, pp. 634–5.

48 Ghulam Hussain Khan, *Seir Mutaqherin*, vol. 3, p. 180.

49 Law, *A Memoir of the Mughal Empire 1757–61*, p. 297.

50 K. K. Dutta, *Shah Alam II & The East India Company*, Calcutta, 1965, p. 15. Shah Alam also lost some of his baggage and his writing desk, which was seized by Archibald Swinton and is now in the Royal Scottish Museum in Edinburgh.

51 Jean-Baptiste Gentil, *Mémoires sur l'Indoustan*, Paris, 1822, pp. 203–4.

52 Ghulam Hussain Khan, *Seir Mutaqherin*, vol. 2, p. 404.

53 Ibid., vol. 2, p. 403.

54 Ibid., vol. 2, pp. 401–3.

55 Caillaud, *A Narrative of What Happened in Bengal in the Year 1760*, p. 35.

56 Ghulam Hussain Khan, *Seir Mutaqherin*, vol. 2, pp. 371–2.

57 Ibid., vol. 2, p. 374.

58 Hastings to Vansittart, BL, OIOC, Add Mss 29132, f. 103–11.

59 Hastings to Vansittart, 10 July 1760, BL, OIOC, Add Mss 29132, f. 103–11.

60 Moon, *The British Conquest and Dominion of India*, p. 88; Moon, *Warren Hastings and British India*, p. 39; Nicholas B. Dirks, *The Scandal of Empire: India and the Creation of Imperial Britain*, Harvard, 2006, p. 50.

61 Ghulam Husain Salim, *Riyazu-s-salatin: A History of Bengal. Translated from the original Persian by Maulvi Abdus Salam*, Calcutta, 1902, pp. 385–6.

62 Caillaud, *A Narrative of What Happened in Bengal in the Year 1760*, p. 50.

63 Lushington to Clive, 3 December 1760, cited in John Malcolm, *Life of Robert, Lord Clive*, London, 1836, vol. II, p. 268.

64 *Tarikh-i Muzaffari* of Muhammad 'Ali Khan Ansari of Panipat, p. 681.

65 Ibid., pp. 681–9.

66 P. J. Marshall, *Bengal: The British Bridgehead – Eastern India 1740–1828*, Cambridge, 1987, p. 86.

67 *Tarikh-i Muzaffari* of Muhammad 'Ali Khan Ansari of Panipat, pp. 683, 685.

68 All details on Sumru from *Voyage en Inde*, pp. 420–2.

69 Ghulam Hussain Khan, *Seir Mutaqherin*, vol. 2, pp. 500–3.

70 Ibid., vol. 2, pp. 421, 434.

71 Ibid., vol 2, pp. 427, 433.

72 Ibid., vol. 2, p. 427.

73 *Tarikh-i Muzaffari* of Muhammad 'Ali Khan Ansari of Panipat, pp. 683, 688.

74 Carnac's Letter to the Select Committee, 5 March 1761, Vansittart, *A Narrative of the Transactions in Bengal*, vol. 1, p. 185.

75 Dutta, *Shah Alam II & The East India Company*, p. 18.

76 Ghulam Hussain Khan, *Seir Mutaqherin*, vol. 2, pp. 406–7.

77 Recently given by the Swinton family to the Royal Scottish Museum in Edinburgh.

78 Ghulam Hussain Khan, *Seir Mutaqherin*, vol. 2, p. 407.

79 Moon, *The British Conquest and Dominion of India*, pp. 92–3.

80 Dutta, *Shah Alam II & The East India Company*, p. 21.

81 G. J. Bryant, *The Emergence of British Power in India, 1600–1784: A Grand Strategic Interpretation*, Woodbridge, 2013, p. 161 n; Dutta, *Shah Alam II & The East India Company*, p. 47.

82 Nandalal Chatterji, *Mir Qasim, Nawab of Bengal, 1760–1763*, Allahabad, 1935.

83 Gentil, *Mémoires sur l'Indoustan*, p. 205.

84 Feiling, *Warren Hastings*, p. 42.

85 Moon, *Warren Hastings and British India*, p. 39.

86 Vansittart, *A Narrative of the Transactions in Bengal*, vol. 1, pp. 300–7, 322–3.

87 Ibid., vol. 2, pp. 97–102; Forrest, *The Life of Lord Clive*, vol. 2, pp. 227–8.

88 Vansittart, *A Narrative of the Transactions in Bengal*, vol. 2, pp. 97–102; Feiling, *Warren Hastings*, pp. 46–7; G. S. Cheema, *The Ascent of John Company: From Traders to Rulers (1756–1787)*, New Delhi, 2017, p. 66.

89 Moon, *The British Conquest and Dominion of India*, pp. 98–9.

90 Moon, *Warren Hastings and British India*, pp. 50–1.

91 Gentil, *Mémoires sur l'Indoustan*, p. 210.

92 Ghulam Husain Salim, *Riyazu-s-salatin*, pp. 387–8.

93 Vansittart, *A Narrative of the Transactions in Bengal*, vol. 2, pp. 164–8; also Rajat Kanta Ray, *The Felt Community: Commonality and Mentality before the Emergence of Indian Nationalism*, New Delhi, 2003, pp. 282–7.

94 Ghulam Hussain Khan, *Seir Mutaqherin*, vol. 2, pp. 465–6.

95 Ibid.

96 Moon, *The British Conquest and Dominion of India*, p. 100.

97 Firminger and Anderson, *The Diaries of Three Surgeons of Patna*, p. 38.

CHAPTER 5: BLOODSHED AND CONFUSION

1 BL, Or. 466, *Tarikh-i Muzaffari* of Muhammad 'Ali Khan Ansari of Panipat, pp. 700–2.

2 Walter K. Firminger and William Anderson, *The Diaries of Three Surgeons of Patna*, Calcutta, 1909, p. 40.

3 Ibid., p. 24.

4 Syed Ghulam Hussain Khan Tabatabai, *Seir Mutaqherin*, Calcutta, 1790–94, vol. 2, pp. 473–4.

5 *Tarikh-i Muzaffari* of Muhammad 'Ali Khan Ansari of Panipat, p. 703.

6 Ibid., p. 704.

7 Rajat Kanta Ray, *The Felt Community: Commonality and Mentality before the Emergence of Indian Nationalism*, New Delhi, 2003, p. 277; Nicholas Shreeve, *Dark Legacy*, Crossbush, 1996, pp. 11–12.

8 Jean-Baptiste Gentil, *Mémoires sur l'Indoustan*, Paris, 1822, pp. 216–18.

9 Luke Scrafton, *Observations on Vansittart's Narrative*, London, 1770, pp. 48–9.

10 *Tarikh-i Muzaffari* of Muhammad 'Ali Khan Ansari of Panipat, pp. 710–13.

11 Ghulam Hussain Khan, *Seir Mutaqherin*, vol. 2, p. 496.

12 *Tarikh-i Muzaffari* of Muhammad 'Ali Khan Ansari of Panipat, p. 710.

13 Ibid., p. 711.

14 Ibid.

15 Ibid., p. 715.

16 Gentil, *Mémoires sur l'Indoustan*, pp. 218–21.

17 *Tarikh-i Muzaffari* of Muhammad 'Ali Khan Ansari of Panipat, p. 708.

18 Gentil, *Mémoires sur l'Indoustan*, pp. 226–7. I have gone with Gentil's account as he seems to have been an eyewitness. There are, however, conflicting accounts of the deaths of the Jagat Seth: for example, Ghosha says that they were mercilessly killed by the Nawab himself. 'They were attended by their faithful servant (*Khidmatgar*) Chuni who could not be persuaded on any account to leave them, and when Kasim Ali [Mir Qasim] was shooting them with arrows he stood before them,

so that, he fell first and then the two cousins.' See Lokanatha Ghosha, *The Modern History of the Indian Chiefs, Rajas, Zamindars, &c*, Calcutta, 1881, p. 346.

19 Firminger and Anderson, *The Diaries of Three Surgeons of Patna*, p. 1.

20 Sir Penderel Moon, *Warren Hastings and British India*, London, 1947, p. 54.

21 Shreeve, *Dark Legacy*, p. 16.

22 Ibid.

23 Gentil, *Mémoires sur l'Indoustan*, pp. 227–34.

24 Shreeve, *Dark Legacy*, p. 18.

25 Julia Keay, *Farzana: The Woman Who Saved an Empire*, London, 2014, p. 48.

26 *Tarikh-i Muzaffari* of Muhammad 'Ali Khan Ansari of Panipat, p. 713.

27 Unlike the Black Hole, the Patna Massacre is almost forgotten. We hardly read about it in history books in Britain and it is completely absent from Indian history books.

28 Ghulam Hussain Khan, *Seir Mutaqherin*, vol. 2, p. 518.

29 Gentil, *Mémoires sur l'Indoustan*, p. 35.

30 Ghulam Hussain Khan, *Seir Mutaqherin*, vol. 2, p. 514.

31 Gentil, *Mémoires sur l'Indoustan*, p. 35.

32 Ghulam Hussain Khan, *Seir Mutaqherin*, vol. 2, p. 512.

33 The *Bhausahebanci Bhakar*, quoted in Velcheru Narayana Rao, David Shulman and Sanjay Subrahmanyam, *Textures of Time*, Delhi, 2003, pp. 232–3.

34 Quoted by Jadunath Sarkar, *Fall of the Mughal Empire*, 4 vols, New Delhi, 1991, vol. 2, p. 316.

35 Ghulam Hussain Khan, *Seir Mutaqherin*, vol. 2, pp. 528, 558.

36 Fakir Khair ud-Din Illahabadi, '*Ibrat Nama*, BL Or. 1932, 38v–39r.

37 Ibid., 39r.

38 Ibid., 40v–41r.

39 Naga Gossains were not unfamiliar with musketry and some even fought on horseback, according to Ghulam Hussain Khan, describing Rajendragiri's defence of Allahabad in 1751, though it is true that they excelled at close-quarter combat. William Pinch details the evolution of their military style in chapter two of *Warrior Ascetics and Indian Empires*, Cambridge 2006. It is difficult to get a firm sense of the distribution of arms among Naga soldiers, but see the description of the prolonged sanyasi/fakir insurgency in Bengal in David N. Lorenzen, 'Warrior Ascetics in Indian History', in *Journal of the American Oriental Society*, vol. 98, no. 1 (January–March 1978), pp. 61–75.

40 *CPC* I, items 2130–1, 2136; Ashirbadi Lal Srivastava, *Shuja ud-Daula*, vol. I, *1754–1765*, Calcutta, 1939, p. 182; Rajat Kanta Ray, 'Indian Society and the Establishment of British Supremacy, 1765–1818', in Peter Marshall, *The Eighteenth Century*, Oxford, 1998, pp. 518–19.

41 Fakir Khair ud-Din Illahabadi, '*Ibrat Nama*, BL Or. 1932, 41v.

42 Ghulam Hussain Khan, *Seir Mutaqherin*, vol. 2, p. 530.

43 Ibid., vol. 2, p. 531.

44 Fakir Khair ud-Din Illahabadi, '*Ibrat Nama*, BL Or. 1932. 42v.

45 Ghulam Hussain Khan, *Seir Mutaqherin*, vol. 2, p. 530.

46 Fakir Khair ud-Din Illahabadi, '*Ibrat Nama*, BL Or. 1932. 42v.

47 Ibid., 43v.

48 Ibid., 43v–44r.

49 Ibid., 44r.

50 Ibid.

51 René-Marie Madec, *Mémoire*, ed. Jean Deloche, Pondicherry 1983, p. 71.

52 Ghulam Hussain Khan, *Seir Mutaqherin*, vol. 2, p. 565.

53 Fakir Khair ud-Din Illahabadi, '*Ibrat Nama*, BL Or. 1932, 44r.

54 Ibid., 45v.

55 Ibid.

56 Ibid., 45r.

57 Ashirbadi Lal Srivastava, *Shuja ud-Daula*, vol. I, p. 232.

58 Sir Penderel Moon, *The British Conquest and Dominion of India*, London, 1989, p. 111.

59 Gentil, *Mémoires sur l'Indoustan*, p. 258–9.

60 Ibid.

61 Madec, *Mémoire*, p. 74.

62 Fakir Khairud-Din Illahabadi, '*Ibrat Nama*, BL Or. 1932, 45v.

63 Ghulam Hussain Khan, *Seir Mutaqherin*, vol. 2, p. 530.

64 Ibid.

65 The Late Reverend John Entick et al., *The Present State of the British Empire*, 4 vols, London, 1774, vol. IV, p. 533.

66 Philip J. Stern, *The Company State: Corporate Sovereignty & the Early Modern Foundations of the British Empire in India*, Cambridge, 2011, p. 3.

67 Thomas Twining, *Travels in India One Hundred Years Ago*, London, 1983, pp. 144–5.

68 For the domestic political background at this time, see James Vaughn, *The Politics of Empire at the Accession of George III*, Princeton, 2009.

69 Keay, *Farzana*, pp. 53, 89.

70 Ghulam Hussain Khan, *Seir Mutaqherin*, vol. 2, pp. 583–4.

71 Gentil, *Mémoires sur l'Indoustan*, p. 259.

72 Sadasukh Dihlavi, *Munkatab ut-Tawarikh*, trans. Sir H. M. Elliot and John Dowson, *The History of India Told By Its Own Historians*, London, 1867, vol. VIII, p. 408.

73 Richard B. Barnett, *North India Between Empires: Awadh, the Mughals, and the British 1720–1801*, Berkeley, 1980, p. 73.

74 Amar Farooqui, *Zafar, and the Raj: Anglo-Mughal Delhi, c. 1800–1850*, New Delhi, 2013, pp. 8–9.

75 Ghulam Hussain Khan, *Seir Mutaqherin*, vol. 2, p. 571.

76 Shah Alam II to the Council, n.d., received in Calcutta 6 Dec 1764, NAI, Foreign Department Secret Consultations, 1764, 2A, 738; *CPC* I, lv, p. 353.

77 K. K. Dutta, *Shah Alam II & The East India Company*, Calcutta, 1965, pp. 28–9.

78 Bengal Despatches, February 1764, quoted in Mark Bence-Jones, *Clive of India*, London, 1974, p. 205.

79 Percival Spear, *Master of Bengal: Clive and his India*, London, 1975, pp. 130–1.

80 Clive to Carnac, 7 May 1762, quoted in Bence-Jones, *Clive of India*, p. 208.

81 Bence-Jones, *Clive of India*, p. 208.

82 H. V. Bowen, 'Lord Clive and speculation in East India Company stock, 1766', *Historical Journal*, 30 (1987), pp. 905–20. For two other excellent essays on Clive's loot and its fallout back home: Bruce Lenman and Philip Lawson, 'Robert Clive, the "Black Jagir" and British Politics', in *Historical Journal*, vol. 26, no. 4 (December 1983), pp. 801–29, and C. H. Philips, 'Clive in the English Political World, 1761–64', in *Bulletin of the School of Oriental and African Studies*, University of London, vol. 12, no. 3/44, *Oriental and African Studies Presented to Lionel David Barnett by His Colleagues, Past and Present* (1948), pp. 695–702.

83 BL, OIOC, BL G37/4/1, f. 42; Barnett, *North India Between Empires*, p. 74.

84 Dutta, *Shah Alam II & The East India Company*, p. 38.

85 Clive and Carnac to Council, 14 July, quoted in Ashirbadi Lal Srivastava, *Shuja ud-Daula*, vol. 2, *1765–1775*, Calcutta, 1939, p. 10; Barnett, *North India Between Empires*, p. 75.

86 Quoted in Bence-Jones, *Clive of India*, p. 219.

87 Clive to Sykes, 3 August 1765, quoted in Barnett, *North India Between Empires*, p. 74.

88 Ghulam Hussain Khan, *Seir Mutaqherin*, vol. 3, pp. 9–10. Sheikh Itesamuddin, who was involved in writing the text of the Treaty of Allahabad with another munshi, reported that Shah Alam with tears in his eyes told Clive and Carnac, who were getting ready to leave after the signing of the Treaty, that they were abandoning him among his enemies

without a thought for his safety (*Shigurf Namah* 1825:5). See Mirza Itesamuddin, *Shigurf Namah-i-Velaet*, translated from Persian to English by James Edward Alexander (London, 1827). Itesamuddin travelled from the subcontinent to England in 1767 to place Shah Alam's request before King George III of England. Quoted in Jeena Sarah Jacob, 'The travellers' tales: The travel writings of Itesamuddin and Abu Taleb Khan', in William A. Pettigrew and Mahesh Gopalan, *The East India Company, 1600–1857: Essays on Anglo-Indian Connection*, London and New York, 2017, p. 141.

89 Ghulam Husain Salim, *Riyazu-s-salatin*, pp. 398, 413–14.

90 George Forrest, *The Life of Lord Clive*, New Delhi, 1986, vol. 2, p. 335.

91 The question of the relative importance of Company imports of bullion to the Bengal economy is contested – see Rajat Datta, *Society, Economy and the Market: Commercialisation in Rural Bengal, c1760–1800*, New Delhi, 2000. So is the question of to what degree the Company ruthlessly asset-stripped Bengal. As Peter Marshall put in a letter to me, 'You can certainly make a case that "India would henceforth be treated as if it were a vast plantation to be milked and exploited, with all its profits shipped overseas." But I do not think you cannot ignore that there was a rhetoric of just rule in the EIC going back to the seventeenth century and that the directors try, however ineffectually, to enforce it after 1757. Their failure to do so is the ostensible reason for increasing state intervention. Unrelenting plunder would ruin Bengal and, a maxim endlessly repeated, kill the goose that laid the golden eggs. The [directors tried to ensure that the] goose must be carefully looked after. Many of the articulate servants in India certainly shared this rhetoric, Hastings most obviously. You can say, reasonably, that considerations of good governance repeatedly gave way, especially in times of emergency, to the imperatives to maximise resources, but I do not think that you can deny that they existed.' With many thanks to PJM for his kindness in looking over my manuscript and for all his encouragement and assistance over many years.

92 Bowen, *Revenue and Reform*, pp. 111–12; Moon, *The British Conquest and Dominion of India*, p. 125.

93 Bence-Jones, *Clive of India*, p. 221.

94 Om Prakash, 'From Market-Determined to Coercion-based: Textile Manufacturing in Eighteenth-Century Bengal', in Giorgio Riello and Tirthankar Roy (eds), *How India Clothed the World: The World of South Asian Textiles, 1500–1800*, Leiden, 2013, pp. 224–41.

95 Dutta, *Shah Alam II & The East India Company*, p. 45; Moon, *The British Conquest and Dominion of India*, p. 125; Jon Wilson, *India Conquered: Britain's Raj and the Chaos of Empire*, London, 2016, p. 115.

96 Quoted in John R. McLane, *Land and Local Kingship in Eighteenth-Century Bengal*, Cambridge, 1993, p. 195.

97 Ghulam Hussain Khan, *Seir Mutaqherin*, vol. 3, pp. 3, 46, 192–3, 202–4. See also the brilliant analysis of Khan's observations in Rajat Kanta Ray, 'Indian Society and the Establishment of British Supremacy, 1765–1818', in Marshall, *The Eighteenth Century*, pp. 514–15. Also P. J. Marshall, *The Making and Unmaking of Empires: Britain, India and America c. 1750–1783*, Oxford, 2007, p. 260.

98 Ghulam Hussain Khan, *Seir Mutaqherin*, vol. 3, pp. 158–213. Talking about the annual drain of wealth from Bengal, the Company's whistleblower Alexander Dow wrote: 'They [the Company] began to drain the reservoir without turning into it any stream to prevent it from being exhausted', quoted in Ranajit Guha, *A Rule of Property for Bengal: An Essay on the Idea of Permanent Settlement*, Durham, NC, 1983, p. 33.

99 Ghulam Hussain Khan, *Seir Mutaqherin*, vol. 3, pp. 158–213.

100 Ibid., vol. 3, pp. 32, 181, 194–5.

101 Moon, *The British Conquest and Dominion of India*, p. 224.

CHAPTER 6: RACKED BY FAMINE

1 OIOC, SCC, P/A/9, 29 November 1769. There is a large body of scholarship on the terrible Bengal famine of 1769–79. The best work on the Bengal famine and its effects in rural Bengal can be found in Rajat Datta, *Society, Economy and the Market: Commercialisation in Rural Bengal, c1760–1800*, New Delhi, 2000, chapter five, pp. 238–84. Rajat Datta argues that while military conquests, political dislocations and Company exactions certainly contributed to the vulnerability of peasants, there had been a major shift in agriculture and the economy under the Company which contributed to the intensity of the famine. Bengal's prosperity was vulnerable and ecologically it was undergoing major changes. The flow of the rivers was moving eastward and cultivation was spreading eastward too. While the west of Bengal was drying out, which made it desperately vulnerable to famine if the rains failed, the east was flourishing. It escaped the 1769–70 famine, although as Datta shows, flooding was to devastate it later.

Bengal had witnessed a long intensification of wet rice cultivation under the Nawabs. This was a long-drawn-out process of ecological transformation whereby the eastern Bengal delta constituted an agrarian frontier where provincial Mughal officials had directly encouraged forest clearing, water control and wet rice cultivation from the later sixteenth century up to the middle of the eighteenth century. See J. F. Richards,

The Unending Frontier: An Environmental History of the Early Modern World, Berkeley, 2003, p. 33.

The pioneering work in this field has been done by Richard Eaton who, in his study of the Bengal frontier, argues that the provincial Mughal officials deepened the roots of their authority in the countryside through encouraging intensive wet rice cultivation at a time when the Mughal power in Delhi was steadily diminishing. This patronage system, introduced by the Nawabs, which had played a decisive role in the steady growth of food grains, ended in 1760 with the paramountcy of the East India Company in the Bengal region. See Richard M. Eaton, *The Rise of Islam and the Bengal Frontier 1204–1760*, Berkeley, 1993, p. 5.

Datta's account emphasises the expansion of the regional market in grains which may have made peasants more exposed to price shocks. He also makes an important point about the geographical imbalance of the famine, which he believes was more severe in western Bengal and Bihar and practically non-existent in eastern Bengal. Therefore to speak of all-Bengal mortality and to peg it at 10 million is not possible. The veteran historian of the EIC, Peter Marshall, largely agrees with Datta's account. In a letter to me he wrote: 'The entrenched assumption, from contemporary polemics to our own times, is that British conquest ruined Bengal. I suppose that I belong to a minority opinion, most authoritatively expounded by Rajat Datta, which is sceptical of the decisive influence of the British, let alone of specific individuals, on the fortunes of the province. There of course can be no doubt that Bengal was potentially a highly fertile and productive province. It had developed a sophisticated commercialised economy … The British stimulated commercialisation by the growth of their export trades and of the great conurbation at Calcutta. Did their access to political power have adverse affects? Probably. They may well have taxed more severely, even if they had no capacity to extract directly from the mass of peasants. They regulated some trades, such as high-quality textiles or salt, to their own advantage and to the disadvantage of indigenous merchants and artisans, but the huge grain trade was surely beyond their capacity to interfere in significantly. On the whole, I doubt whether the British either "caused" the famine or what you seem to see in Chapter Eight as the recovery of Bengal under Hastings and Cornwallis … I think Bengalis largely made their own history … I would not credit Hastings with the recovery of Bengal, since I do not think it was in his or any other British individual's capacity to bring about such a thing.'

These are clearly complicated matters, involving ecological as well as economic history, and the jury remains out. I have tried to argue here, however, that whether or not the Company was directly responsible for the famine, or whether ecological factors played a more important role, its incompetent response made the famine in West Bengal much more deadly, while its excessive tax collecting hugely exacerbated the sufferings of the Bengalis under its rule – which was certainly the opinion of many observers, both Indian and British, who wrote accounts of the disaster at the time.

2 OIOC, Bengal Public Consultations, 23 October 1769.

3 Datta, *Society, Economy and the Market*, p. 244.

4 Abdul Majed Khan, *The Transition in Bengal 1756–1775*, Cambridge, 1969, p. 218.

5 Datta, *Society, Economy and the Market*, p. 244.

6 Quoted in John R. McLane, *Land and Local Kingship in Eighteenth-Century Bengal*, Cambridge, 1993, p. 196.

7 For Richard Becher's Report on Cannibalism, see OIOC, SCC, P/A/10.

8 Datta, *Society, Economy and the Market*, p. 252; Robert Travers, *Ideology and Empire in Eighteenth-Century India*, Cambridge, 2007, p. 72.

9 I am going here with the figures of Datta, *Society, Economy and the Market*, p. 264, who has done the most intensive and detailed work on the famine. He rejects the widely quoted figure given by Warren Hastings (who was in London at the time) that 10 million, one-third of the population, died based on detailed village-by-village study of tax returns in the years before and after the famine. Data has shown that the famine was at its worst in West Bengal, and that large parts of Eastern Bengal were unaffected. See also Jon Wilson, *India Conquered: Britain's Raj and the Chaos of Empire*, London, 2016, p. 114, and Abdul Majed Khan, *The Transition in Bengal 1756–1775*, Cambridge, 1969, p. 219.

10 Joseph Price, *The Saddle Put on the Right Horse*, London, 1783, vol. 1, p. 33. See also Wilson, *India Conquered*, p. 114.

11 OIOC, HM, vol. 102, p. 94. Also Wilson, *India Conquered*, p. 113.

12 Khan, *The Transition in Bengal*, p. 219.

13 Datta, *Society, Economy and the Market*, p. 259.

14 Syed Ghulam Hussain Khan Tabatabai, *Seir Mutaqherin*, Calcutta, 1790–94, vol. 3, p. 56.

15 W. W. Hunter, *The Annals of Rural Bengal*, London, 1868, pp. 43–5.

16 Khan, *The Transition in Bengal*, p. 219; S. C. Mukhopadhyay, *British Residents at the Darbar of Bengal Nawabs at Murshidabad 1757–1772*, Delhi [n.d.], p. 388.

17 Jeremy Bernstein, *Dawning of the Raj: The Life & Trials of Warren Hastings*, Chicago, 2000, p. 11.

18 Datta, *Society, Economy and the Market*, p. 259.

19 Dean Mahomet, *The Travels of Dean Mahomet*, Berkeley, 1997, pp. 35–6.

20 Mukhopadhyay, *British Residents at the Darbar of Bengal Nawabs at Murshidabad*, p. 388.

21 Datta, *Society, Economy and the Market*, pp. 256–60; Nick Robins, *The Corporation That Changed the World: How the East India Company Shaped the Modern Multinational*, London, 2006, p. 90.

22 Romesh Chunder Dutt, *The Economic History of India under Early British Rule, 1757–1837*, London, 1908, p. 52.

23 P. J. Marshall, *Bengal: The British Bridgehead – Eastern India 1740–1828*, Cambridge, 1987, p. 134.

24 Mukhopadhyay, *British Residents at the Darbar of Bengal Nawabs at Murshidabad*, p. 378; Khan, *The Transition in Bengal*, p. 217.

25 Khan, *The Transition in Bengal*, p. 222.

26 *Gentleman's Magazine*, September 1771. The author signed himself merely as 'JC', but some passages closely mirror those in John Debrit's memoirs.

27 Robins, *The Corporation That Changed the World*, p. 94.

28 *Gentleman's Magazine*, September 1771.

29 Mukhopadhyay, *British Residents at the Darbar of Bengal Nawabs at Murshidabad*, p. 399.

30 Quoted in George Forrest, *The Life of Lord Clive*, New Delhi, 1986, vol. 2, p. 383.

31 Quoted in H. V. Bowen, *The Business of Empire: The East India Company and Imperial Britain, 1756–1833*, Cambridge, 2006, p. 16.

32 H. V. Bowen, *Revenue and Reform: The Indian Problem in British Politics, 1757–1773*, Cambridge, 1991, p. 95.

33 *Gentleman's Magazine*, April 1767, p. 152; Robins, *The Corporation That Changed the World*, p. 17.

34 P. J. Marshall, *The Making and Unmaking of Empires: Britain, India and America c. 1750–1783*, Oxford, 2007, p. 199.

35 John Micklethwait and Adrian Wooldridge, *The Company: A Short History of a Revolutionary Idea*, London, 2003, p. 42.

36 Quoted in Tillman W. Nechtman, *Nabobs: Empire and Identity in Eighteenth-Century Britain*, Cambridge, 2010, p. 87.

37 Jack Green, *Arenas of Asiatic Plunder*, London, 1767, Robins, *The Corporation That Changed the World*, p. 103.

38 Extract from Act II of *The Nabob*, a play by Samuel Foote, quoted in P. J. Marshall, *Problems of Empire: Britain and India, 1757–1813*, London, 1968.

39 Arthur Young, *Political Essays concerning the present state of the British Empire*, London, 1772, p. 518.

40 Alexander Dow, *History of Hindostan*, 3 vols, Dublin, 1792, vol. 3, p. v; Ranajit Guha points out that long before R. C. Dutt and Digby and later nationalists, the phrase 'drain of wealth' had come into common use through the Company officials such as Dow. Ranajit Guha, *A Rule of Property for Bengal: An Essay on the Idea of Permanent Settlement*, Durham, NC, 1983, pp. 33–4.

41 William Bolts, *Considerations on Indian Affairs; Particularly Respecting the Present State of Bengal and its Dependencies*, 3 vols, London, 1772–5.

42 N. L. Hallward, *William Bolts: A Dutch Adventurer Under John Company*, Cambridge, 1920; Willem G. J. Kuiters, *The British in Bengal 1756–1773: A Society in Transition seen through the Biography of a Rebel: William Bolts (1739–1808)*, Paris, 2002. Lucy Sutherland cites Bolts as being responsible for turning public opinion against Clive. Lucy S. Sutherland, *The East India Company in Eighteenth-Century Politics*, Oxford, 1952, p. 221.

43 This story is the origin of the later nationalist myth that the British themselves cut off the thumbs of workers in order to break Indian textile production and so assist the import of Lancashire cotton.

44 There is a good analysis of Bolts' writings in Nicholas B. Dirks, *The Scandal of Empire: India and the Creation of Imperial Britain*, Harvard, 2006, pp. 250–4. See also Travers, *Ideology and Empire in Eighteenth-Century India*, pp. 61–2.

45 Ralph Leycester to Warren Hastings, March 1772, BL, Add Mss 29133, f. 72.

46 Quoted in Dirks, *The Scandal of Empire*, p. 15.

47 *The Monthly Review* (1772); see also Robins, *The Corporation That Changed the World*, pp. 78, 96.

48 Bowen, *Revenue and Reform*, p. 127; H. Hamilton, 'The Failure of the Ayr Bank, 1772', *Economic History Review*, 2nd series, VIII (1955–6), pp. 405–17.

49 *The Correspondence of Adam Smith*, ed. E. C. Mossner and I. S. Ross, 2nd edn, Oxford, 1987, p. 162, quoted by Emma Rothschild in her brilliant unpublished essay, 'The East India Company and the American Revolution'.

50 Marshall, *The Making and Unmaking of Empires*, p. 212.

51 Bowen, *Revenue and Reform*, p. 117.

52 BL, Add Mss, 29133, f. 534, quoted in Bowen, *Revenue and Reform*, pp. 119–21.

53 Bernstein, *Dawning of the Raj*, p. 81. Robins, *The Corporation That Changed the World*, pp. 90–5.

54 Bowen, *Revenue and Reform*, p. 127.

55 Quoted in Wilson, *India Conquered*, p. 129.

56 Anon, *The Present State of the British Interest in India,* quoted in *Monthly Review*, vol. XLVIII (1773), p. 99.

57 Thomas Pownall, *The Right, Interest and Duty of Government, as concerned in the affairs of the East India Company,* revised edn, 1781, p. 4. Quoted in Bowen, *The Business of Empires*, p. 17.

58 George III to Grafton, 9 Dec 1766, in J. Fortescue, *Correspondence of George III, 1760–1783,* 6 vols (1927–8), vol. I, pp. 423–4. Quoted in Marshall, *The Making and Unmaking of Empires*, p. 209.

59 Bowen, *Revenue and Reform*, p. 85.

60 Forrest, *The Life of Lord Clive*, vol. 2, pp. 404–5.

61 Ibid., vol. 2, pp. 408–9.

62 Nechtman, *Nabobs*, p. 84.

63 28 May 1773, BL, Egerton Mss, 249, ff. 84–6.

64 BL, Egerton Mss, 240, pp. 221, 225–6.

65 For the case in support of Francis as 'Junius', see *The Letters of Junius*, ed. John Cannon, Oxford, 1978.

66 See Linda Colley's brilliant article: 'Gendering the Globe: The Political and Imperial Thought of Philip Francis', *Past & Present*, no. 209 (November 2010), pp. 117–48. See also Sophia Weitzman, *Warren Hastings and Philip Francis*, Manchester, 1929; Keith Feiling, *Warren Hastings*, London, 1954, p. 138.

67 W. S. Lewis et al., *The Yale Edition of Horace Walpole's Correspondence*, 48 vols, New Haven, CT, 1937–83, vol. 32, pp. 61–2.

68 Quoted in Mark Bence-Jones, *Clive of India*, London, 1974, pp. 300, 356. Patty Ducarel was a sister of General Gustavus Ducarel (1745–1800).

69 Nechtman, *Nabobs*, p. 87; Bence-Jones, *Clive of India*, p. 299.

70 Travers, *Ideology and Empire in Eighteenth-Century India*, pp. 150–1.

71 Feiling, *Warren Hastings*, p. 133.

72 Ibid.

73 Sophia Weitzman, *Warren Hastings and Philip Francis*, Manchester, 1929, p. 227.

74 Ibid., pp. 221–2.

75 Ibid., p. 224.

76 Feiling, *Warren Hastings*, pp. 232–3.

77 Ghulam Hussain Khan, *Seir Mutaqherin*, vol. 3, p. 168.

78 Sir Penderel Moon, *The British Conquest and Dominion of India*, London, 1989, p. 148.

79 Travers, *Ideology and Empire in Eighteenth-Century India*, p. 139.

80 Sir Penderel Moon, *Warren Hastings and British India*, London, 1947, p. 113.

81 G. R. Gleig, *Memoirs of the Life of the Rt Hon Warren Hastings, First Governor General of Bengal*, 3 vols, London, 1841, vol. 1, p. 317.

82 Hastings to J. Dupre, 11 November 1772, BL, Add Mss 29,127, f. 63v. Hastings to L. Sullivan, Kasimbazar, 7 September 1772, ibid., f. 38v.

83 Bernstein, *Dawning of the Raj*, pp. 89–90.

84 Quoted in ibid., p. 57.

85 Moon, *The British Conquest and Dominion of India*, p. 149.

86 Moon, *Warren Hastings and British India*, p. 87.

87 Quoted in Bernstein, *Dawning of the Raj*, p. 147. For Jones see S. N. Mukherjee, *Sir William Jones: A Study of Eighteeth-Century Attitudes to India*, Cambridge, 1968.

88 Feiling, *Warren Hastings*, p. 138.

89 *Bhagavad Gita*, 2, 47–51, translated for me by Sir James Mallinson. For Hastings' attachment to these verses, see Feiling, *Warren Hastings*, p. 238.

90 Colley, *Gendering the Globe*, p. 121; Moon, *Warren Hastings and British India*, p. 348.

91 Some post-colonial historians have taken a more benign attitude to Francis, notably Ranajit Guha, one of the founders of Subaltern Studies, who has written admiringly of his wide reading of radical French thinkers and the intellectual rigour which he channelled into projects for agrarian, administrative and monetary reform in Bengal. See Guha, *A Rule of Property for Bengal*, especially chapters 3–4.

92 Ghulam Hussain Khan, *Seir Mutaqherin*, vol. 3, pp. 184–6.

93 Feiling, *Warren Hastings*, p. 160.

94 Velcheru Narayana Rao, David Shulman and Sanjay Subrahmanyam, *Textures of Time: Writing History in South India 1600–1800*, New York, 2003, p. 230, quoting the *Bhausahebanci Bhakar*.

95 Ibid., p. 231. See also the always excellent Uday S. Kulkarni, 'Solstice at Panipat: An Authentic Account of the Panipat Campaign', Pune, 2012; Jadunath Sarkar, 'Events Leading up to Panipat and Panipat, 1761', in *India Historical Quarterly* (June 1934), pp. 258–73 and pp. 547–58.

96 Irfan Habib (ed.), *Resistance and Modernisation under Haidar Ali & Tipu Sultan*, New Delhi, 1999, Introduction, p. xxii.

97 Letter from the Court of Directors to the Council in Bengal, 27 April 1765, in *Fort William-India House Correspondence*, London, 1949–58, vol. 4, p. 96.

98 For the bore of the Mysore artillery see Jean-Marie Lafont, *Indika: Essays in Indo-French Relations 1630–1976*, Delhi, 2000, p. 157. For the rockets see Linda Colley, 'Going Native, Telling Tales: Captivity, Collaborations and Empire', in *Past & Present*, no. 168 (August 2000), p. 190.

99 Captain Mathews, cited in Partha Chatterjee, *The Black Hole of Empire: History of a Global Practice of Power*, Princeton, 2012, p. 85.

100 John Carnac to the Bombay Council, 1 January 1779, BL, OIOC, P/D/63, f. 132.

101 Replies to Resolutions, 24/01/1782, BL, IOR, bscc P/D/68, ff. 617–18, 24, quoted in Mesrob Vartavarian, 'An Open Military Economy: The British Conquest of South India Reconsidered, 1780–1799', *Journal of the Economic and Social History of the Orient*, vol. 57, no. 4 (2014), pp. 486–510, p. 494.

102 Stewart Gordon, *The Marathas: 1600–1818*, Cambridge, 1993, p. 164.

103 For Nana Phadnavis and his celebrated intelligence network, see C. A. Bayly, *Empire & Information: Intelligence Gathering and Social Communication in India 1780–1870*, Cambridge, 1996, pp. 31–2.

104 Govind Sakharam Sardesai, *A New History of the Marathas*, 3 vols, Baroda, 1948, vol. 3, pp. 97–8.

105 Rajat Kanta Ray, 'Indian Society and the Establishment of British Supremacy, 1765–1818', in Peter Marshall, *The Eighteenth Century*, Oxford, 1998, p. 519.

106 Mark Wilks, *Historical sketches of the south of India*, vol. 2, 1820, pp. 261–2; Vartavarian, 'An Open Military Economy', pp. 486–510, p. 491.

107 Bernstein, *Dawning of the Raj*, p. 134.

108 Ibid.

109 Ibid., pp. 113–14.

110 BL, Add Mss 39, 878, f. 36; Moon, *Warren Hastings and British India*, p. 249.

111 Bernstein, *Dawning of the Raj*, p. 82.

112 Ghulam Hussain Khan, *Seir Mutaqherin*, vol. 3, p. 125.

113 Captain Muat's *Account of the Defeat at Pollilur*, BL, IOR, HM 223, p. 117.

114 Ibid.

115 John Baillie's *Account of Pollilur*, BL, IOR, HM 223, pp. 160–6.

116 Ibid.

117 Captain Wood's *Account of Pollilur*, BL, IOR, HM 211, f. 246.

118 Captain Muat's *Account of the Defeat at Pollilur*, BL, IOR, HM 223, pp. 83–5.

119 A lieutenant of the 73rd Highland Regiment, in Alan Tritton, *When the Tiger Fought the Thistle*, London, 2013, pp. 271–2.

120 Tritton, *When the Tiger Fought the Thistle*, pp. 243, 248–53, 262–3.

121 John Baillie's *Account of Pollilur*, BL, IOR, HM 223, pp. 160–6.

122 Tritton, *When the Tiger Fought the Thistle*, pp. 272–4.

123 Quoted by Mohibbul Hasan, *History of Tipu Sultan*, Calcutta, 1951, p. 15.

124 Ross to Macartney, 07/06/1781, IOR, HM 330, ff. 259–61; Davis to Coote, 02/07/1781, Add. Mss 22439, f. 9, quoted in Vartavarian, 'An Open Military Economy', p. 507.

125 It was actually the job of boys and young men from some hereditary drummer castes to dance as girls. From the Mysore perspective, this may not have been anywhere near as extraordinary or outrageous as it sounds, though of course the British would have found it hugely humiliating. Linda Colley, *Captives: Britain, Empire and the World, 1600–1850*, London, 2002, pp. 276–91; Colley, 'Going Native, Telling Tales: Captivity, Collaborations and Empire', in *Past & Present*, no. 168 (August 2000).

126 James Scurry, *The Captivity, Sufferings and Escape of James Scurry, who was detained a prisoner during ten years, in the dominions of Haidar Ali and Tippoo Saib*, London, 1824, pp. 252–3.

127 G. J. Bryant, *The Emergence of British Power in India, 1600–1784: A Grand Strategic Interpretation*, Woodbridge, 2013, p. 291.

128 BL, OIOC, HM 246, f. 335.

129 Feiling, *Warren Hastings*, p. 246.

130 Moon, *Warren Hastings and British India*, p. 5.

131 *Incomplete Draft (1785) of an account of the Mysore War (1780–84)*, BL, OIOC, Mss Eur K 116, f. 84. Quoted in Maya Jasanoff, *Edge of Empire: Conquest and Collecting in the East, 1750–1850*, London, 2005, p. 158.

132 Marshall, *The Making and Unmaking of Empires*, pp. 330–2.

133 Quoted by Emma Rothschild in her unpublished essay, 'The East India Company and the American Revolution'.

134 *Narrative of all the Proceedings and Debates ... on East India Affairs* (1784), p. 89, quoted in Colley, *Captives*, p. 272.

135 Feiling, *Warren Hastings*, p. 230.

136 *Parliamentary History*, 21 (1780–81), pp. 1201–2, quoted in Colley, *Captives*, p. 275.

137 Lewis et al., *The Yale Edition of Horace Walpole's Correspondence*, 48 vols, vol. 29, p. 123.

CHAPTER 7: THE DESOLATION OF DELHI

1 Victoria & Albert Museum (V&A), IS.38–1957.

2 Even if the jewelled Peacock Throne of Shah Jahan had long been stolen and destroyed and what remained was only a wooden replica, sitting in a half-ruined palace.

3 NAI, Select Committee Proceedings, 2 Jan to 6 Dec, 1771, No. 18; Headquarters, Allahabad, 20 April 1771, pp. 177–81.

4 *CPC* 3, pp. 134–5, no. 504, 14 Dec 1770; *CPC* 3, p. 98, no. 329, 11 Aug, to the King; *CPC* 3, p. 194, no. 719, 22 April, to the King; K. K. Dutta, *Shah Alam II & The East India Company*, Calcutta, 1965, p. 57.

5 NAI, Select Committee Progs, 2 Jan to 6 Dec, 1771, No. 18; Fort William, 20 April 1771, pp. 177–81.

6 William Francklin, *The History of Shah Alam*, London, 1798, p. 36.

7 NAI, Select Committee Progs, 2 Jan to 6 Dec, 1771, No. 18; Fort William, 17 May, pp. 184–7.

8 Francklin, *The History of Shah Alam*, pp. 27–8.

9 NAI, Select Committee Progs, 2 Jan to 6 Dec, 1771, No. 18; Fort William, 17 May, pp. 184–7.

10 *CPC* 3, pp. 190–1, no. 702, 14 Dec 1770, General Barker to Nawab Shuja ud-Daula; *CPC* 3, p. 189, no. 698, General Barker to the King.

11 Jean-Baptiste Gentil, *Mémoires sur l'Indoustan*, pp. 257–9.

12 Michael H. Fisher, 'Diplomacy in India 1526–1858', in H. V. Bowen, Elizabeth Mancke and John G. Reid, *Britain's Oceanic Empire: Atlantic and Indian Ocean Worlds, c. 1550–1850*, Cambridge, 2012, pp. 276–7. I'tisam al-Din's book, *Shigrif-namah-i Vilayet* is at BL, Or. 200. For a full translation, via Bengali, see *The Wonders of Vilayet, being a memoir, originally in Persian, of a visit to France and Britain*, trans. Kaiser Haq, Leeds, 2001.

13 Nandalal Chatterji, *Verelst's Rule in India*, 1939, p. 129.

14 There is a fascinating popular ballad on the Battle of Panipat which gives a sense of the scale of the upheaval it caused. K. R. Qanungo, 'Fragment of a Bhao Ballad in Hindi', *Historical Essays*, Calcutta, 1968, pp. 81–113.

15 Percival Spear, *The Twilight of the Moghuls*, Cambridge, 1951, p. 16.

16 Jadunath Sarkar, *The Fall of the Mughal Empire*, 4 vols, New Delhi, 1991, vol. 2, p. 329.

17 Ganga Singh, *Ahmed Shah Durrani*, p. 326. See also Gulfishan Khan, *Indian Muslim Perceptions of the West during the Eighteenth Century*, Karachi, 1998, pp. 72–8, and K. K. Dutta, *Shah Alam II & The East India Company*, pp. 49–50.

18 Ganga Singh, *Ahmad Shah Durrani*, Patiala, 1959, p. 326.

19 Jadunath Sarkar (ed.), *Persian Records of Maratha History*, 1: *Delhi Affairs (1761–1788)*, Bombay, 1953, p. 21.

20 Michael Edwardes, *King of the World: The Life of the Last Great Moghul Emperor*, London, 1970, p. 172.

21 Govind Sakharam Sardesai, *A New History of the Marathas*, 3 vols, Baroda, 1948, vol. 3, p. 138.

22 Iqbal Husain, *The Rise and Decline of the Ruhela Chieftaincies in 18th Century India*, Aligarh, 1994, p. 138.

23 Francklin, *The History of Shah Alam*, pp. 50, 70.

24 BL, Add 6585, Shakir Khan, *Tarikh-i Shakir Khani*, f. 91.

25 *CPC* 3, p. 216, no. 798, from Nawab Shuja ud-Daula, 22 June 1771.

26 Ibid.

27 *CPC* 3, p. 215, no. 795, General Barker to the King, 20 June 1771.

28 *CPC* 3, p. 225, no. 828, 22 May; from Raja Shitab Ray, 20 July; NAI, Select Committee Progs, 2 Jan to 6 Dec, 1771, No. 18; Fort William, 6 July 1771, pp. 266–9.

29 Dutta, *Shah Alam II & The East India Company*, pp. 58–9.

30 NAI, Select Committee Progs, 2 Jan to 6 Dec, 1771, No. 18; Allahabad, 17 July 1771, pp. 258–9.

31 Sarkar (ed.), *Persian Records of Maratha History*, 1, p. 36; Sarkar, *Fall of the Mughal Empire*, vol. 2, pp. 330–1.

32 Sarkar (ed.), *Persian Records of Maratha History*, 1, p. 47.

33 NAI, Foreign Select Committee Progs, 1772–3, vol. 20, 10 Jan 1772.

34 Dutta, *Shah Alam II & The East India Company*, p. 59.

35 *Voyage en Inde du Comte de Modave, 1773–1776*, ed. Jean Deloche, Pondicherry, 1971.

36 Sarkar (ed.), *Persian Records of Maratha History*, 1, p. 55; Sarkar, *Fall of the Mughal Empire*, vol 2, p. 331.

37 Sarkar (ed.), *Persian Records of Maratha History*, 1, p. 57.

38 Sarkar, *Fall of the Mughal Empire*, vol. 3, p. 32.

39 Sarkar (ed.), *Persian Records of Maratha History*, 1, p. 58.

40 Sarkar, *Fall of the Mughal Empire*, vol. 3, p. 34; Fakir Khair ud-Din Illahabadi, '*Ibrat Nama*, BL Or. 1932, f. 207–8.

41 Husain, *The Rise and Decline of the Ruhela Chieftaincies in 18th Century India*, p. 144.

42 Sardesai, *A New History of the Marathas*, vol. 2, p. 516.

43 Mirza 'Ali Bakht, *Waqi'at-i Azfari*, ed. T. Chandrasekharan and Syed Hamza Hussain Omari, Madras, 1957, p. 5.

44 Ibid.

45 Ibid., pp. 5–6.

46 This section is derived from a brilliant essay by Muzaffar Alam and Sanjay Subrahmanyam in *Writing the Mughal World*, New York, 2012, pp. 433–44.

47 Quoted in Dutta, *Shah Alam II & The East India Company*, p. 81.

48 *Voyage en Inde*, p. 231.

49 Stephen P. Blake, *Shahjahanabad: The Sovereign City in Mughal India, 1639–1739*, Cambridge, 1991, p. 167.

50 C. M. Naim (translated, annotated and introduced), *Zikr-I Mir: The Autobiography of the Eighteeenth Century Mughal Poet, Mir Muhammad Taqi 'Mir'*, New Delhi, 1998, pp. 83–5, 93–4.

51 Khurshidul Islam and Ralph Russell, *Three Mughal Poets: Mir, Sauda, Mir Hasan*, New Delhi, 1991, pp. 221–2, 247–8.

52 Sarkar (ed.), *Persian Records of Maratha History*, 1, p. 45.

53 Sarkar, *Fall of the Mughal Empire*, vol. 3, p. 35.

54 René-Marie Madec, *Mémoire*, ed. Jean Deloche, Pondicherry, 1983, p. 170.

55 Sarkar (ed.), *Persian Records of Maratha History*, 1, p. 61.

56 Sarkar, *Fall of the Mughal Empire*, vol. 3, p. 55.

57 These translations are taken from a beautiful essay by David Lunn and Katherine Butler Schofield, 'Delight, Devotion and the Music of the Monsoon at the Court of Emperor Shah 'Alam II', in Imke Rajamani, Margrit Pernau and Katherine Butler Schofield (eds), *Monsoon Feelings: A History of Emotions in the Rain*, New Delhi, 2018, pp. 219–54.

58 Lunn and Butler Schofield, 'Delight, Devotion and the Music of the Monsoon at the Court of Emperor Shah 'Alam II', pp. 219–54.

59 Modave writes well on this. See *Voyage en Inde*, pp. 427–8.

60 Ibid., pp. 420–2.

61 Ibid., p. 422.

62 Ibid., p. 103.

63 Sarkar (ed.), *Persian Records of Maratha History*, 1, pp. 68–9. 'This victory proved,' as Khair ud-Din writes, 'the title page of Mirza Najaf Khan's record of victories and the first rung in the ladder of his fortune.' Quoted in K. R. Qanungo, *History of the Jats*, Calcutta, 1925, pp. 145–6.

64 Sarkar (ed.), *Persian Records of Maratha History*, pp. 72–3. On the battle of Barsana see F. S. Growse, *Mathura: A District Memoir*, 1883.

65 The fort of Ballabhgarh was captured on 20 April 1774, and Farukhnagar 6 May 1774. See Sarkar, *Fall of the Mughal Empire*, vol. 3, p. 64.

66 Ibid., p. 83.

67 Emile Barbé, *Le Nabob René Madec*, Paris, 1894, Sec. 48.

68 *Voyage en Inde*, p. 438. Khair ud-Din captures the valour of the Jats during their war with Mirza Najaf Khan. He says, 'Not a single man tried to save his life. If they had fought unitedly they would have slain many more and safely made their way out [of the fort].' Qanungo adds that 'no *johar* seems to have been lighted at Deeg; women and children were put to sword.' See Qanungo, *History of the Jats*, p. 174, fn. 15.

69 Sarkar (ed.), *Persian Records of Maratha History*, 1, p. 75.

70 Yuthika Sharma, 'From Miniatures to Monuments: Picturing Shah Alam's Delhi (1771–1806)', in Alka Patel and Karen Leonard (eds), *Indo-Muslim Cultures in Transition*, Leiden, 2002, pp. 126–30.

71 *Voyage en Inde*, pp. 434–5.

72 Antoine Polier, *Shah Alam II and his Court*, Calcutta, 1947, p. 99.

73 *Voyage en Inde*, pp. 432–4.

74 Ibid., pp. 217–18.

75 Polier, *Shah Alam II and his Court*, pp. 67–9.

76 *Voyage en Inde*, pp. 254–69.

77 *CPC* 4, p. 95, no. 506, 9 Sept 1773, from the King.

78 Sir Penderel Moon, *The British Conquest and Dominion of India*, London, 1989, p. 158.

79 Dutta, *Shah Alam II & The East India Company*, p. 69.

80 Sir Penderel Moon, *Warren Hastings and British India*, London, 1947, pp. 158–9.

81 Sir John Strachey, *Hastings and the Rohilla War*, Oxford, 1892, p. 97.

82 BL, IOR, HM/336, f. 1–8.

83 Fakir Khair ud-Din Illahabadi, '*Ibrat Nama*, BL Or. 1932, 116v.

84 Ibid., 117r–120v.

85 Quoted in Qanungo, *History of the Jats*, pp. 185–6.

86 Fakir Khair ud-Din Illahabadi, '*Ibrat Nama*, BL Or. 1932, 120v.

87 Sayid Athar Abbas Rizvi, *Shah 'Abd al'Aziz: Puritanism, Sectarianism and Jihad*, Canberra, 1982, p. 29.

88 *Urdu Letters of Mirza Asadu'llah Khan Ghalib*, New York, 1987, p. 435.

89 Sarkar (ed.), *Persian Records of Maratha History*, 1, pp. 105–6.

90 Ibid., p. 146.

91 Ibid., p. 124; Ganda Singh, 'Colonel Polier's Account of the Sikhs', *The Panjab Past and Present*, 4 (1970), pp. 239, 24.

92 Spear, *The Twilight of the Moghuls*, p. 21.

93 C. A. Bayly, *Rulers, Townsmen and Bazaars: North Indian Society in the Age of British Expansion*, Cambridge, 1983, p. 102.

94 Islam and Russell, *Three Mughal Poets*, pp. 62–3.

95 Dutta, *Shah Alam II & The East India Company*, p. 86.

96 Sayid Athar Abbas Rizvi, *Shah 'Abd al'Aziz: Puritanism, Sectarianism and Jihad*, p. 47.

97 Quoted in Jean-Marie Lafont, *Indika: Essays in Indo-French Relations 1630–1976*, Delhi, 2000, p. 179.

98 Ibid.

99 Herbert Compton, *The European Military Adventurers of Hindustan*, London, 1943, pp. 8–9; Lafont, *Indika*, p. 185.

100 Sayid Athar Abbas Rizvi, *Shah 'Abd al'Aziz: Puritanism, Sectarianism and Jihad*, pp. 29–30.

101 Sarkar (ed.), *Persian Records of Maratha History*, 1, p. 127.

102 Muzaffar Alam and Sanjay Subrahmanyam, in *Writing the Mughal World*, New York, 2012, pp. 416–23.

103 Mirza 'Ali Bakht, *Waqi'at-i Azfari*, ed. T. Chandrasekharan and Syed Hamza Hussain Omari, Madras, 1957, p. 6.

104 Ibid., p. 8.

105 Fakir Khair ud-Din Illahabadi, '*Ibrat Nama*, BL, Or. 1932, f. 212.

106 Ibid.

107 Sarkar (ed.), *Persian Records of Maratha History*, 1, p. 195.

108 Fakir Khair ud-Din Illahabadi, '*Ibrat Nama*, BL, Or. 1932, f. 214.

109 Ibid., f. 213. This section is translated in Sir H. M. Elliot and John Dowson, *A History of India as Told By Its Own Historians*, 8 vols, London, 1867–77, vol. VIII, p. 246.

110 Fakir Khair ud-Din Illahabadi, '*Ibrat Nama*, BL, Or. 1932. f. 214. Also Sarkar, *Fall of the Mughal Empire*, vol. 3, p. 270.

111 Dutta, *Shah Alam II & The East India Company*, p. 101.

112 Fakir Khair ud-Din Illahabadi, '*Ibrat Nama*, BL, Or. 1932, v. This section is translated in Elliot and Dowson, *A History of India as Told By Its Own Historians*, vol. VIII, pp. 246–7.

113 Fakir Khair ud-Din Illahabadi, '*Ibrat Nama*, BL, Or. 1932, f. 214.

114 Sarkar (ed.), *Persian Records of Maratha History*, 1, p. 199.

115 Sarkar appears to have got the wrong mosque when he writes 'Qadir removed the golden coating of the Jami Masjid and sold it but he was prevented from similarly stripping the remainder by Maniyar Singh who warned him that such an outrage on the holy edifice would rouse the entire city population in arms against him.' See Sarkar, *Fall of the Mughal Empire*, vol. 3, p. 273.

116 Fakir Khair ud-Din Illahabadi, '*Ibrat Nama*, BL, Or. 1932, f. 214.

117 Mirza 'Ali Bakht, *Waqi'at-I Azfari*, ed. Chandrasekharan and Syed Hamza Hussain Omari, p. 9.

118 Fakir Khair ud-Din Illahabadi, '*Ibrat Nama*, BL, Or. 1932, f. 214.

119 Ibid., f. 215.

120 Ibid., f. 216.

121 BL, Add Mss 29171, ff 319–20, Jonathan Scott to Warren Hastings.

122 Fakir Khairud-Din Illahabadi, '*Ibrat Nama*, BL, Or. 1932, ?v. This section is translated in Elliot and Dowson, *A History of India as Told By Its Own Historians*, vol. VIII, p. 248.

123 Francklin, *The History of Shah Alam*, p. 127.

124 Fakir Khair ud-Din Illahabadi, '*Ibrat Nama*, BL Or. 1932, f. 216. This section is translated in Elliot and Dowson, *A History of India as Told By Its Own Historians*, vol. VIII, p. 249, but I have added a few details censored by those Victorians.

125 Fakir Khair ud-Din Illahabadi, '*Ibrat Nama*, BL, Or. 1932, f. 217r. Previously untranslated.

126 Ibid.

127 Ibid. This section was heavily bowdlerised by Elliot and Dowson. The Persian language is brutal: '*Mi-khwaham ke in-ha-ra dar zomra-ye parastaran-e khod dakhel nemayam wa dad-e mobasherat deham! wa hama dokhtaran-e salatin be Afghana separam, ke az notfa-ye an-ha farzandan-e jawan-mard be-ham-resad.*'

128 Mirza 'Ali Bakht, *Waqi'at-I Azfari,* ed. Chandrasekharan and Syed Hamza Hussain Omari, p. 8.

129 Ibid., p. 9.

130 Julia Keay, *Farzana: The Woman Who Saved an Empire*, London, 2014, pp. 183–4.

131 Ibid., p. 184.

132 Sarkar (ed.), *Persian Records of Maratha History*, 1, p. 200.

133 Francklin, *The History of Shah Alam*, p. 189.

134 Fakir Khair ud-Din Illahabadi, '*Ibrat Nama*, BL, Or. 1932, ?v. This section is translated in Elliot and Dowson, *A History of India as Told By Its Own Historians*, vol. VIII, p. 253.

135 Francklin, *The History of Shah Alam*, p. 190.

136 Fakir Khair ud-Din Illahabadi, '*Ibrat Nama*, BL, Or. 1932, ?v. This section is translated in Elliot and Dowson, *A History of India as Told By Its Own Historians*, vol. VIII, p. 254.

137 Francklin, *The History of Shah Alam*, p. 190.

CHAPTER 8: THE IMPEACHMENT OF WARREN HASTINGS

1 Quoted in Tillman W. Nechtman, *Nabobs: Empire and Identity in Eighteenth-Century Britain*, Cambridge, 2010, p. 104.

2 Edmund Burke, *The Writings and Speeches of Edmund Burke*, ed. P. J. Marshall, 6 vols, Oxford, 1991, vol. 6, pp. 275–6, 457.

3 Edmund Burke, *Speeches on the Impeachment of Warren Hastings*, ed. George Bell, Calcutta, 1906, vol. 1, p. 361, vol. 6, pp. 275–6.

4 Keith Feiling, *Warren Hastings*, London, 1954, p. 355.

5 Burke, *Speeches on the Impeachment of Warren Hastings*, vol. 1, p. 361, vol. 6, pp. 285–7.

6 V. K. Saxena (ed.), *Speeches on the Impeachment of Warren Hastings*, 2 vols, Delhi, 1987, vol. 1, pp. 13–14.

7 Burke, *The Writings and Speeches of Edmund Burke*, 6 vols, vol. 5, pp. 401–2.

8 Burke, *Speeches on the Impeachment of Warren Hastings*, vol. 1, p. 79.

9 Thomas Babington Macaulay, 'Warren Hastings', in *The Historical Essays of Macaulay*, ed. Samuel Thurber, Boston, 1892, p. 362.

10 Quoted in Nick Robins, *The Corporation That Changed the World: How the East India Company Shaped the Modern Multinational*, London, 2006, p. 133.

11 Quoted in the *Oxford Dictionary of National Biography*, vol. XVIII, p. 81.

12 Feiling, *Warren Hastings*, p. 357.

13 Jennifer Pitts, 'Edmund Burke's peculiar Universalism', in Jennifer Pitts, *A Turn to Empire: The Rise of Imperial Liberalism in Britain and France*, Princeton, 2005.

14 Ibid., p. 285.

15 Ibid., p. 339.

16 The more despotic character of the final phase of Hastings' period as Governor General is well explored in Andrew Otis's fascinating study, *Hicky's Bengal Gazette: The Untold Story of India's First Newspaper*, Chennai, 2018.

17 Sir Penderel Moon, *The British Conquest and Dominion of India*, London, 1989, p. 222.

18 Feiling, *Warren Hastings*, p. 354.

19 Ibid., p. 111.

20 BL, Add Mss 39903, f. 34r.

21 Alexander Dalrymple, *A Retrospective View of the Antient System of the East India Company, with a Plan of Regulation*, London, 1784, p. 73.

22 Denis Kincaid, *British Social Life in India up to 1938*, London, 1938, pp. 22, 95.

23 *Voyage en Inde du Comte de Modave, 1773–1776*, ed. Jean Deloche, Pondicherry, 1971, p. 77.

24 Rajat Datta, 'The Commercial Economy of Eastern India under British Rule', in H. V. Bowen, Elizabeth Mancke and John G. Reid, *Britain's Oceanic Empire: Atlantic and Indian Ocean Worlds, c. 1550–1850*, Cambridge, 2012, p. 361.

25 Moon, *The British Conquest and Dominion of India*, p. 245.

26 P. J. Marshall, *The Making and Unmaking of Empires: Britain, India and America c. 1750–1783*, Oxford, 2007, p. 243.

27 P. J. Marshall, *Bengal: The British Bridgehead – Eastern India 1740–1828*, Cambridge, 1987, p. 114; Datta, 'The Commercial Economy of Eastern India under British Rule', p. 346.

28 H. V. Bowen, 'British India, 1765–1813: The Metropolitan Context', in Peter Marshall, *The Eighteenth Century*, Oxford, 1998, p. 535; C. A. Bayly, *Indian Society and the Making of the British Empire*, Cambridge, 1988, p. 35; Datta, 'The Commerical Economy of Eastern India under British Rule', p. 358.

29 Quoted in H. V. Bowen, *The Business of Empire: The East India Company and Imperial Britain, 1756–1833*, Cambridge, 2006, pp. 241–2; Holden Furber, 'Rival Empires of Trade in the Orient, 1600–1800', in *Maritime India*, intro. Sanjay Subrahmanyam, New Delhi, 2004, p. 175.

30 Datta, 'The Commercial Economy of Eastern India under British Rule', p. 346.

31 Marshall, *The Making and Unmaking of Empires*, pp. 248–51.

32 Datta, 'The Commercial Economy of Eastern India under British Rule', p. 363.

33 Ibid., pp. 362–3; Bayly, *Indian Society and the Making of the British Empire*, p. 85. See also Seema Alavi, *The Sepoys and the Company: Tradition and Transition in Northern India 1770–1830*, Delhi, 1995.

34 Burton Stein, 'Eighteenth Century India: Another View', *Studies in History*, vol. 5, 1 n.s. (1989), p. 21.

35 Abdul Latif Shushtari: *Kitab Tuhfat al-'Alam*, written Hyderabad 1802 & lithographed Bombay 1847, p. 427.

36 Moon, *The British Conquest and Dominion of India*, p. 247.

37 Quoted in Denys Forrest, *Tiger of Mysore: The Life and Death of Tipu Sultan*, London, 1970, p. 205.

38 J. Michaud, *History of Mysore Under Haidar Ali and Tippoo Sultan*, trans. V. K. Raman Menon, Madras, 1924, pp. 47–8.

39 Burton Stein, 'State Formation and Economy Reconsidered', *Modern Asian Studies*, vol. 19, no. 3, Special Issue: Papers Presented at the Conference on Indian Economic and Social History, Cambridge University, April 1984 (1985), pp. 387–413, p. 403. See also Irfan Habib (ed.), *Resistance and Modernisation under Haidar Ali & Tipu Sultan*, New Delhi, 1999, Introduction, p. xxxi.

40 A. Subbaraya Chetty, 'Tipu's Endowments to Hindus and Hindu institutions', in Habib (ed.), *Resistance and Modernisation under Haidar Ali & Tipu Sultan*, pp. 101–11.

41 B. A. Saletore, 'Tipu Sultan as a Defender of Hindu Dharma', in Habib (ed.), *Resistance and Modernisation under Haidar Ali & Tipu Sultan*, p. 125.

42 Ibid., p. 126.

43 Habib (ed.), *Resistance and Modernisation under Haidar Ali & Tipu Sultan*, Introduction, p. xxvii. See also Mahmud Husain, *The Dreams of Tipu Sultan*, Karachi, n.d.

44 Habib (ed.), *Resistance and Modernisation under Haidar Ali & Tipu Sultan*, Introduction, p. xxvi.

45 Maya Jasanoff, *Edge of Empire: Conquest and Collecting in the East, 1750–1850*, London, 2005, pp. 184–5; Habib (ed.), *Resistance and Modernisation under Haidar Ali & Tipu Sultan*, Introduction, p. xxxiv.

46 T. Venkatasami Row, *A Manual of the District of Tanjore in the Madras Presidency*, Madras, 1883, pp. 812–13. See also Stein, 'Eighteenth Century India: Another View', *Studies in History*, vol. 5, 1 n.s. (1989).

47 Moon, *The British Conquest and Dominion of India*, p. 248.

48 James Rennell, *The Marches of the British Armies in the Peninsula of India*, London, 1792, p. 33.

49 Moon, *The British Conquest and Dominion of India*, p. 251.

50 Quoted in Forrest, *Tiger of Mysore*, p. 149.

51 Cornwallis to Malet, 25 March 1791, BL IOR, MMC P/252/60, ff. 2005–6; Cornwallis to Oakeley, 30 April 1791, MMC P/252/61, ff. 2318–2319; Letter from Madras, 15 July 1791, BL IOR, HM 251, ff. 9–11; Cornwallis to Oakeley, 24 May 1791, BL IOR, MMC P/252/62, ff. 2827–9; Cockburn to Jackson, 12 July 1791, BL IOR, MMC P/252/63, ff. 3317, 3321; Torin to Cornwallis, 21 October 1791, National Archives, PRO 30/11/45, f. 5. Quoted in Mesrob Vartavarian, 'An Open Military Economy: The British Conquest of South India Reconsidered, 1780–1799', *Journal of the Economic and Social History of the Orient*, vol. 57, no. 4 (2014), pp. 486–510, p. 496.

52 Quoted in Govind Sakharam Sardesai, *A New History of the Marathas*, 3 vols, Baroda, 1948, vol. 3, p. 193.

53 Military Operations BL, IOR, HM251, ff. 746–7, quoted in Vartavarian, 'An Open Military Economy', p. 497.

54 BL, OIOC, Eur Mss F228/52 Dec 1791, f. 1.

55 Jean-Marie Lafont, *Indika: Essays in Indo-French Relations 1630–1976*, Delhi, 2000, p. 186.

56 BL, OIOC, Eur Mss F228/52 Dec 1791, f. 2.

57 Ibid.

58 Forrest, *Tiger of Mysore*, p. 200.

59 Sardesai, *A New History of the Marathas*, vol. 3, p. 192.

60 Datta, 'The Commerical Economy of Eastern India under British Rule', p. 342.

61 Durba Ghosh, *Sex and the Family in Colonial India: The Making of Empire*, Cambridge, 2006; William Dalrymple, *White Mughals: Love and Betrayal in Eighteenth-Century India*, London, 2002.

62 R. B. Saksena, *Indo-European Poets of Urdu and Persian*, Lucknow, 1941, p. 21; Christopher J. Hawes, *Poor Relations: The Making of a Eurasian Community in British India, 1773–1833*, London, 1996, ch. 4; William Dalrymple, *White Mughals: Love and Betrayal in Eighteenth-Century India*, London, 2002, pp. 50–2; Bayly, *Indian Society and the Making of the British Empire*, p. 70.

63 C. A. Bayly, *The Birth of the Modern World 1780–1914*, Oxford, 2004, p. 111.

64 Anderson Correspondence, BL, Add Mss 45, 427, Wm Palmer to David Anderson, 12 November 1786, f. 196.

65 Marshall, *Bengal: The British Bridgehead*, pp. 122–5.

66 Bayly, *The Birth of the Modern World*, p. 111; Marshall, *Bengal: The British Bridgehead*, pp. 122–5; C. A. Bayly, *Rulers, Townsmen and Bazaars: North Indian Society in the Age of British Expansion*, Cambridge, 1983, pp. 466–7, 474, 479; Bayly, *Indian Society and the Making of the British Empire*, pp. 108, 150.

67 Kumkum Chatterjee, 'Collaboration and Conflict: Bankers and Early Colonial Rule in India: 1757–1813', *Indian Economic and Social History Review*, 30, 3 (1993), pp. 296–7. This whole argument was first made in the 1980s by Christopher Bayly in *Rulers, Townsmen and Bazaars* and by Karen Leonard in her groundbreaking essay 'The Great Firm Theory of the Decline of the Mughal Empire', *Comparative Studies in Society and History*, 21, 2 (1979), and in 'Banking Firms in Nineteenth-Century Hyderabad Politics', *Modern Asian Studies*, 15, 2 (1981). See also the dissent of J. F. Richards in 'Mughal State Finance and the Premodern World Economy', *Comparative Studies in Society and History*, vol. 23, no. 2 (1981).

68 Rajat Kanta Ray, 'Indian Society and the Establishment of British Supremacy, 1765–1818', in Marshall, *The Eighteenth Century*, pp. 516–17.

69 'Chahar Gulzar Shuja' of Hari Charan Das in Sir H. M. Elliot and John Dowson, *A History of India as Told By Its Own Historians*, 8 vols, London, 1867–77, vol. VIII, p. 229.

70 At the cost, according to Washbrook, Bayly and more recently – in a different vein – Parthasarathi, of rendering the Indian economy relatively static, and unable to respond effectively to the new challenges of British industrialisation – though this is disputed: Tirthakar Roy offers a more optimistic account.

71 Ray, 'Indian Society and the Establishment of British Supremacy, 1765–1818', in Marshall, *The Eighteenth Century*, p. 517.

72 Jadunath Sarkar, *Fall of the Mughal Empire*, 4 vols, New Delhi, 1991, vol. 3, p. 254.

73 The Company was, of course, not only dependent on 'local money' – it could also draw on the resources of the Company at home and the domestic state. See J. R. Ward's important older article 'The Industrial Revolution and British Imperialism, 1750–1850', in *Economic History Review*, n.s., vol. 47, no. 1 (February 1994), pp. 44–65 on the role of domestic consumers in financing the tea trade.

74 Sayid Athar Abbas Rizvi, *Shah 'Abd al'Aziz: Puritanism, Sectarianism and Jihad*, Canberra, 1982, p. 44.

75 In the lovely words of Ferdinand Mount, *Tears of the Rajas: Mutiny, Money and Marriage in India 1805–1905*, London, 2016, p. 185.

76 *Voyage en Inde*, pp. 549–550.

77 Napoleon to Tipu, 7 Pluviôse VII [26 January 1799], OIOC, P/354/38. The second quotation, which is quoted by Andrew Roberts in *Napoleon and Wellington*, London, 2001, pp. 16–17, in fact dates from 1812 when Napoleon was flirting with launching a second Eastern expedition; but it reflected the ease with which he saw India falling into his hands on the earlier expedition. Maya Jasanoff is especially good on Napoleon's Egyptian expedition in her brilliant *Edge of Empire*.

78 Quoted in Sir John Malcolm, *Political History of India*, 2 vols, London, 1826, vol. 1, p. 310.

CHAPTER 9: THE CORPSE OF INDIA

1 Quoted in Iris Butler, *The Elder Brother: The Marquess Wellesley 1760–1842*, London, 1973, p. 134.

2 When he first arrived in India, Richard Wellesley was still known as the 2nd Earl of Mornington. For ease of comprehension I have called him Marquis Wellesley, his title after 1799, throughout.

3 Quoted by Sir Penderel Moon, *The British Conquest and Dominion of India*, London, 1989, p. 341.

4 Butler, *The Elder Brother*, p. 134.

5 Richard Wellesley, *Two Views of British India: The Private Correspondence of Mr Dundas and Lord Wellesley: 1798–1801*, ed. Edward Ingram, London, 1970, p. 16.

6 Quoted by Anne Buddle in *The Tiger and the Thistle: Tipu Sultan and the Scots in India*, Edinburgh, 1999, p. 33.

7 The ultimate source for this is the *Proceedings of a Jacobin Club formed at Seringapatam by the French soldiers in the Corps commanded by M Domport*. Paper C in *Official Documents Relating the Negotiations Carried on by Tippoo Sultan with the French Nation*, Calcutta, 1799; J. Michaud, *History of Mysore Under Hyder Ali and Tippoo Sultan*, trans. V. K. Raman Menon, Madras, 1924, pp. 108–9. See also Denys Forrest, *Tiger of Mysore: The Life and Death of Tipu Sultan*, London, 1970, pp. 250–2; Maya Jasanoff, *Edge of Empire: Conquest and Collecting in the East, 1750–1850*, London, 2005, pp. 150–1, 159–60.

8 Quoted in Herbert Compton, *The European Military Adventurers of Hindustan*, London, 1943, pp. 8–9.

9 Forrest, *Tiger of Mysore: The Life and Death of Tipu Sultan*, p. 254.

10 Ibid., p. 259.

11 Richard Wellesley, Marquess Wellesley, *The Despatches, Minutes and Correspondence of the Marquess Wellesley KG during his Administration of India*, ed. Montgomery Martin, 5 vols, London, 1840, vol. 1, p. 159.

12 Mark Wilks, *Historical Sketches of the South Indian History*, 2 vols, London, 1817, vol. 2, p. 689.

13 The full translations of Raymond's correspondence can be found in Jadunath Sarkar, 'General Raymond of the Nizam's Army', in Mohammed Taher, *Muslim Rule in Deccan*, Delhi, 1997, pp. 125–44.

14 Compton (ed.), *The European Military Adventurers of Hindustan*, pp. 382–6.

15 Wellesley, *The Despatches, Minutes and Correspondence of the Marquess Wellesley KG*, 5 vols, vol. 1, p. 209. See also Jac Weller, *Wellington in India*, London, 1972, pp. 24–5.

16 Rt Hon. S. R. Lushington, *The Life and Services of Lord George Harris GCB*, London, 1840, p. 235.

17 J. W. Kaye, *The Life and Correspondence of Sir John Malcolm GCB*, London, 1840, vol. 1, p. 78.

18 Ibid., vol. 1, p. 78n.

19 Quoted by Moon, *The British Conquest and Dominion of India*, p. 281.

20 Quoted in Butler, *The Elder Brother*, p. 166.

21 Quoted by Moon, *The British Conquest and Dominion of India*, p. 284.

22 Quoted in Butler, *The Elder Brother*, p. 167.

23 Quoted by Moon, *The British Conquest and Dominion of India*, p. 285.

24 Amales Tripathi, *Trade and Finance in the Bengal Presidency, 1793–1833*, Calcutta, 1979, pp. 4, 46–7, 72, 80–1; Rajat Kanta Ray, 'Indian Society and the Establishment of British Supremacy, 1765–1818', in Peter Marshall, *The Eighteenth Century*, Oxford, 1998, pp. 516–17.

25 Burton Stein, 'Eighteenth Century India: Another View', *Studies in History*, vol. 5, 1 n.s. (1989), p. 21. Also see D. Peers, 'State, Power and Colonialism', in *India and the British Empire*, ed. Douglas Peers and Nandini Gooptu, Oxford, 2012, p. 33.

26 Pratul C. Gupta, *Baji Rao II and the East India Company*, New Delhi, 1939, p. 57. The politics of the period are extremely complex, even by Maratha standards. The death (whether by accident or suicide) in October 1795, had thrown the Peshwa's succession wide open as the only surviving members of the Peshwa family, Baji Rao and his brother Chimaji, were in prison (being sons of the disgraced Raghunath Rao) and no love was lost between them and Nana Phadnavis. Daulat Rao, who was still in Pune, and Nana began a long drawn-out struggle to be in control of the next Peshwa. Baji Rao was a master in guile, behind an apparently sweet-natured exterior. He eventually promised Scindia money, obtained Nana's

concurrence and after fourteen months rose to be a Peshwa with no money, dependent on Scindia for arms and Nana for administrative experience. However, mutual suspicions were deep and Nana and Daulat Rao were at loggerheads. Nana wanted Scindia to go north. Scindia wanted money which he believed Nana alone had. By a clever deception using the 'word of a European officer' named Filose, Scindia lured Nana to his camp for a farewell meeting and arrested him. Nana was kept in the Scindia camp for three months but refused to disgorge any money. He was then sent as a prisoner to Ahmednagar. The administration collapsed and Nana had to be released and restored. But the suspicions remained and none of the advice that Nana gave was accepted. The British attack on Tipu had Nana pleading for an army to be sent, and finally, at the end April 1799, he wrote to the British that he would lead an army himself. However, it was too late. The British offer of a part of Tipu's province in exchange for a humiliating treaty was rejected by Nana in 1799. He died in 1800.

27 Quoted in William Kirkpatrick, *Select Letters of Tipoo Sultan to Various Public Functionaries*, London, 1811. See also Kate Brittlebank, *Tipu Sultan's Search for Legitimacy*, New Delhi, 1997, p. 11.

28 Quoted in Butler, *The Elder Brother*, p. 162.

29 Quoted by Moon, *The British Conquest and Dominion of India*, p. 277.

30 Forrest, *Tiger of Mysore*, pp. 270–1.

31 Quoted in Butler, *The Elder Brother*, p. 166.

32 OIOC, India Office Library, Kirkpatrick letters, Mss Eur F228/11 f. 10.

33 Gupta, *Baji Rao II and the East India Company*, p. 58.

34 Michaud, *History of Mysore Under Hyder Ali and Tippoo Sultan*, pp. 100–3.

35 Ibid., p. 129.

36 Mahmud Husain, *The Dreams of Tipu Sultan*, Karachi, n.d.; Michaud, *History of Mysore Under Hyder Ali and Tippoo Sultan*, pp. 165–7.

37 Quoted by Moon, *The British Conquest and Dominion of India*, p. 285; C. A. Bayly, *Indian Society and the Making of the British Empire*, Cambridge, 1988, p. 97.

38 Butler, *The Elder Brother*, p. 170.

39 Organising the carriage bullocks and sheep for feeding the army was one of James Kirkpatrick's main concerns at this period. See OIOC, Kirkpatrick papers, Mss Eur F228/11, pp. 14, 15, 28, etc.

40 Wellesley's remark quoted by Moon, *The British Conquest and Dominion of India*, p. 286; the subsistence remark quoted by Buddle, *The Tiger and the Thistle*.

41 Quoted by Buddle, *The Tiger and the Thistle*, p. 15.

42 David Price, *Memoirs of the Early Life and Service of a Field Officer on the Retired List of the Indian Army*, London, 1839, p. 430.

43 Quoted by Buddle, *The Tiger and the Thistle*, p. 34.

44 Alexander Beatson, *A View of the Origin and Conduct of the War with Tippoo Sultan*, London, 1800, pp. 97, 139–40; Price, *Memoirs of the Early Life and Service of a Field Officer*, pp. 434–5.

45 Price, pp. 418–21.

46 Captain G. R. P. Wheatley, 'The Final Campaign against Tipu', *Journal of the United Service Institution of India*, 41 (1912), p. 255.

47 Weller, *Wellington in India*, p. 73.

48 Michaud, *History of Mysore Under Hyder Ali and Tippoo Sultan*, p. 169; Forrest, *Tiger of Mysore*, p. 290.

49 Captain W. H. Wilkin, *The Life of Sir David Baird*, London, 1912, p. 68.

50 Price, *Memoirs of the Early Life and Service of a Field Officer*, p. 427.

51 Forrest, *Tiger of Mysore*, p. 291.

52 Beatson, *A View of the Origin and Conduct of the War with Tippoo Sultan*, p. civ.

53 Wilkin, *The Life of Sir David Baird*, p. 73.

54 Beatson, *A View of the Origin and Conduct of the War with Tippoo Sultan*, p. 123.

55 Edward Moor, *A Narrative of the Operations of Captain Little's Detachment*, London, 1874, pp. 24–32.

56 Quoted by Moon, *The British Conquest and Dominion of India*, p. 288.

57 Beatson, *A View of the Origin and Conduct of the War with Tippoo Sultan*, p. 148.

58 Price, *Memoirs of the Early Life and Service of a Field Officer*, p. 432.

59 Edward Moore, 1794, cited in A. Sen, 'A Pre-British Economic Formation in India of the Late Eighteenth Century', in Barun De (ed.), *Perspectives in Social Sciences*, Calcutta, 1977, I, *Historical Dimensions*, p. 46.

60 Price, *Memoirs of the Early Life and Service of a Field Officer*, pp. 434–5.

61 See Forrest, *Tiger of Mysore*, p. 299. Also Buddle, *The Tiger and the Thistle*, p. 37.

62 Anon, *Narrative Sketches of the Conquest of Mysore*, London, 1800, p. 102; Anne Buddle, *Tigers Around the Throne: The Court of Tipu Sultan (1750–1799)*, London, 1990, p. 36.

63 Arthur Wellesley to the Court of Directors, January 1800. Quoted in Buddle, *Tigers Around the Throne*, p. 38.

64 Wilkie Collins, *The Moonstone*, London, 1868.

65 Quoted by Butler, *The Elder Brother*, p. 188.

66 Quoted in Abdus Subhan, 'Tipu Sultan: India's Freedom-Fighter par Excellence', in Aniriddha Ray (ed.), *Tipu Sultan and his Age: A Collection of Seminar Papers*, Calcutta, 2002, p. 39.

67 For Nana Phadnavis see Grant Duff's *A History of the Mahrattas*, London, 1826, at A. L. Srivastava, *The Mughal Empire, 1526–1803 A.D.* (Agra, 1964); S. N. Sen, *Anglo-Maratha Relations during the Administration of Warren Hastings*, Madras, 1974.

68 Moon, *The British Conquest and Dominion of India*, p. 314.

69 Quoted by Moon, *The British Conquest and Dominion of India*, p. 314. See also Sir Jadunath Sarkar, ed. Raghubir Singh, *Mohan Singh's Waqai-Holkar*, Jaipur, 1998.

70 *Archives Departmentales de la Savoie, Chambery, De Boigne Archive, bundle AB IV*, Wm Palmer to de Boigne, Poona, 13 Dec 1799.

71 Ibid.

72 Govind Sakharam Sardesai, *A New History of the Marathas*, 3 vols, Baroda, 1948, vol. 3, p. 371.

73 Gupta, *Baji Rao II and the East India Company*, p. 23.

74 Munshi Munna Lal, *Shah Alam Nama*, Tonk Mss 3406, Oriental Research Library, p. 536.

75 Jadunath Sarkar, *Fall of the Mughal Empire*, 4 vols, New Delhi, 1991, vol. 3, pp. 173–5.

76 Sardesai, *A New History of the Marathas*, vol. 3, p. 371.

77 Sayid Athar Abbas Rizvi, *Shah 'Abd al'Aziz: Puritanism, Sectarianism and Jihad*, Canberra, 1982, p. 43.

78 Compton, *The European Military Adventurers of Hindustan*, pp. 346–7; Amar Farooqui, *Zafar and the Raj: Anglo-Mughal Delhi c1800–1850*, Delhi, 2013, p. 31.

79 *Roznamcha-i-Shah Alam*, BL, Islamic 3921. All examples are from the months of Sha'ban and Ramazan, November–December 1791.

80 Lal, *Shah Alam Nama*, Tonk Mss 3406, p. 535.

81 *Roznamcha-i-Shah Alam*, BL, Islamic 3921. Both examples are from the months of Sha'ban and Ramazan, November–December 1791.

82 Governor General in Council to the Secret Committee of the Court of Directors, 13 July 1804, Wellesley, *The Despatches*, vol. IV, p. 153.

83 Wellesley, *The Despatches*, vol. III, pp. 230–3.

84 Ibid., vol. III, no. xxxv, 27 June 1803.

85 BL, IOR, H/492 ff. 251–2, Wellesley to Shah Alam, 27 June (Political Consultations, 2 March 1804).

86 BL, IOR, H/492 f. 241, Wellesley to Shah Alam, 27 June (Political Consultations, 2 March 1804). See also Percival Spear, *The Twilight of the*

Moghuls, Cambridge, 1951, p. 35. Monghyr was the former capital of Mir Qasim.

87 Colonel Hugh Pearse, *Memoir of the Life and Military Services of Viscount Lake*, London, 1908, p. 150.

88 Major William Thorn, *Memoir of the War in India Conducted by Lord Lake and Major General Sir Arthur Wellesley on the Banks of the Hyphasis*, London, 1818, p. 80.

89 Bayly, *Indian Society and the Making of the British Empire*, p. 86.

90 James Welsh, *Military Reminiscences Extracted from a Journal of Nearly Forty Years Active Service in the East Indie*s, 2 vols, London, 1830, vol. 1, p. 147. Also Sarkar, *Fall of the Mughal Empire*, vol. 4, p. 227.

91 Sardesai, *A New History of the Marathas*, vol. 3, pp. 398–9.

92 John Blakiston, *Twelve Years Military Adventure in Three Quarters of the Globe*, 2 vols, London, 1829, vol. 1, p. 145. Quoted in Randolph G. S. Cooper, *The Anglo-Maratha Campaigns and the Contest for India: The Struggle for the Control of the South Asian Military Economy*, Cambridge, 2003, p. 81.

93 Bayly, *Indian Society and the Making of the British Empire*, p. 85; Jon Wilson, *India Conquered: Britain's Raj and the Chaos of Empire*, London, 2016, p. 187; H. V. Bowen, *The Business of Empire: The East India Company and Imperial Britain, 1756–1833*, Cambridge, 2006, p. 47; John Micklethwait and Adrian Wooldridge, *The Company: A Short History of a Revolutionary Idea*, London, 2003, p. 4.

94 Letters issued by Agent to Governor General. Extract from volumes (Registers) 1–21 Commissioner Banares pre-Mutiny Agency Records. See also the excellent discussion in Lakshmi Subramanian and Rajat K. Ray, 'Merchants and Politics: From the Great Mughals to the East India Company', in Dwijendra Tripathi, *Business and Politics in India*, New Delhi, 1991, pp. 19–85, esp. pp. 57–9.

95 Cited in Bayly, *Indian Society and the Making of the British Empire*, p. 102.

96 Ibid., pp. 102–3, 106, 108; Rajat Kanta Ray, 'Indian Society and the Establishment of British Supremacy, 1765–1818', in Marshall, *The Eighteenth Century*, pp. 516–17; C. A. Bayly, *Rulers, Townsmen and Bazaars: North Indian Society in the Age of British Expansion*, Cambridge, 1983, pp. 211–12.

97 Quoted in James Duff, *A History of the Mahrattas*, Calcutta, 1912, vol. 1, p. 431.

98 Compton, *The European Military Adventurers of Hindustan*, p. 328.

99 Sardesai, *A New History of the Marathas*, vol. 3, pp. 413–14.

100 William Pinch in *Warrior Ascetics and Indian Empires*, Cambridge, 2006, pp. 106–7, 114. Thomas Brooke to Major Shawe, Secretary to Lord Wellesley. BL, Add Mss 37, 281 ff. 228b–229f.

101 Sardesai, *A New History of the Marathas*, vol. 3, pp. 403–5.

102 Ibid., vol. 3, p. 397.

103 Memorandum of 8 July 1802, quoted by Michael H. Fisher, 'Diplomacy in India, 1526–1858', in H. V. Bowen, Elizabeth Mancke and John G. Reid, *Britain's Oceanic Empire: Atlantic and Indian Ocean Worlds, c. 1550–1850*, Cambridge, 2012, p. 263.

104 For an excellent account of Wellesley's grandiose style, see Mark Bence-Jones, *Palaces of the Raj*, London, 1973, ch. 2.

105 Quoted in Philip Davies, *Splendours of the Raj: British Architecture in India 1660–1947*, London, 1985, p. 35.

106 Butler, *The Elder Brother*, p. 306.

107 Sarkar, *Fall of the Mughal Empire*, vol. 4, p. 229.

108 Sardesai, *A New History of the Marathas*, vol. 3, p. 402.

109 26 Sept AW to JM, *Supplementary Despatches of Arthur, Duke of Wellington, KG, 1797–1818*, vol. IV, p. 160. See also Major Burton, 'Wellesley's Campaigns in the Deccan', *Journal of the United Services Institution India*, 29 (1900), p. 61.

110 John Blakiston, *Twelve Years Military Adventure in Three Quarters of the Globe*, 2 vols, London, 1829, vol. 1, pp. 164–5. Quoted in Cooper, *The Anglo-Maratha Campaigns and the Contest for India*, p. 108.

111 Major William Thorn, *Memoir of the War in India*, p. 279.

112 Cooper, *The Anglo-Maratha Campaigns* contains much the best account of the battle. I visited the site of the battle with the current Duke of Wellington and found Cooper's maps invaluable. A single East India Company lead musket ball that I picked up at Pipalgaon while walking the battleground sits in front of me as I write.

113 Sir T. E. Colebrook, *The Life of Mountstuart Elphinstone*, 2 vols, London, 1884, vol. 1, pp. 63–9.

114 Quoted by Sarkar, *Fall of the Mughal Empire*, vol. 4, p. 276. Also Wilson, *India Conquered*, p. 173.

115 Thorn, *Memoir of the War in India*, pp. 276–7.

116 Cooper, *The Anglo-Maratha Campaigns*, p. 116.

117 Antony Brett-James (ed.), *Wellington at War, 1794–1815: A Selection of his Wartime Letters*, London, 3 October 1803, pp. 84–5.

118 Sir Thomas Munro, quoted in Moon, *The British Conquest and Dominion of India*, p. 321.

119 Compton, *The European Military Adventurers of Hindustan,* p. 204; Ray, 'Indian Society and the Establishment of British Supremacy, 1765–1818', in Marshall, *The Eighteenth Century,* p. 522.

120 Pearse, *Memoir of the Life and Military Services of Viscount Lake,* p. 1; Moon, *The British Conquest and Dominion of India,* p. 323.

121 Thorn, *Memoir of the War in India,* pp. 87–9.

122 Compton, *The European Military Adventurers of Hindustan,* pp. 299–301.

123 James Baillie Fraser, *Military Memoirs of Lt. Col. James Skinner C.B.,* 2 vols, London, 1851, vol. 1, p. 265; Compton, *The European Military Adventurers of Hindustan,* pp. 302–3. Compton calls the letter 'a surely characteristic letter, with its vainglorious vauntings and its ineffable French vanity'.

124 Fraser, *Military Memoirs of Lt. Col. James Skinner C.B.,* vol. 1, pp. 253–4; Compton, *The European Military Adventurers of Hindustan,* p. 301.

125 Fraser, *Military Memoirs of Lt. Col. James Skinner C.B.,* vol. 1, p. 251.

126 Compton, *The European Military Adventurers of Hindustan,* pp. 303–4.

127 Ibid., p. 231.

128 Fraser, *Military Memoirs of Lt. Col. James Skinner C.B.,* vol. 1, p. 266.

129 Thorn, *Memoir of the War in India,* pp. 96–7.

130 Ibid.

131 The best modern account of the attack on Aligarh can again be found in Randolph G. S. Cooper's wonderful *Anglo-Maratha Campaigns,* pp. 161–3.

132 Fraser, *Military Memoirs of Lt. Col. James Skinner C.B.,* vol. 1, pp. 266–7.

133 John Pester, *War and Sport in India 1802–6,* London, 1806, pp. 156–7.

134 Lal, *Shah Alam Nama,* Tonk Mss 3406, 46th Year of the Auspicious Reign, p. 535; Maulvi Zafar Hasan, *Monuments of Delhi,* New Delhi, 1920, vol. 3, p. 7.

135 BL, OIOC, IOR/H/492 f. 301, f. 305, Proclamation by Shah Alam.

136 BL, OIOC, IOR/H/492 f. 292, Proclamation by Shah Alam.

137 Sardesai, *A New History of the Marathas,* vol. 3, p. 419; Compton: *The European Military Adventurers of Hindustan,* pp. 340–1, Cooper *Anglo-Maratha Campaigns,* p. 188.

138 Pester, *War and Sport in India 1802–6,* p. 163.

139 This bravura passage by Randolph G. S. Cooper is taken from *Anglo-Maratha Campaigns,* p. 172, and is derived from the Journal of Captain George Call, vol. 1. p. 22, National Army Museum, Acc. No. 6807–150.

140 Pester, *War and Sport in India,* p. 166.

141 Ibid., p. 169.

142 Sarkar, *Fall of the Mughal Empire,* vol. 4, p. 246.

143 Pearse, *Memoir of the Life and Military Services of Viscount Lake,* p. 197.

144 Martin, *Despatches of Marquess Wellesley*, vol. III, p. 445. Commander-in-Chief General Lake's Secret Despatch to Governor General Richard Wellesley.

145 Fakir Khair ud-Din Illahabadi, '*Ibrat Nama*, BL Or. 1932, f. 1r.

146 Bowen, *Business of Empire*, p. 5.

147 Wilson, *India Conquered*, p. 176.

148 Ibid., pp. 122, 187. Lord Wellesley opened Fort William College to train a new generation of covenanted civil servants in July 1800.

149 Bowen, *Business of Empire*, p. 5.

150 Moon, *The British Conquest and Dominion of India*, pp. 328, 343.

151 Butler, *The Elder Brother*, p. 333.

152 Rajat Kanta Ray, *The Felt Community: Commonality and Mentality before the Emergence of Indian Nationalism*, New Delhi, 2003, p. 327; Ray, 'Indian Society and the Establishment of British Supremacy, 1765–1818', in Marshall, *The Eighteenth Century*, p. 526.

153 Moon, *The British Conquest and Dominion of India*, pp. 328, 343.

154 Pester, *War and Sport in India*, p. 174.

155 Lal, *Shah Alam Nama*, Tonk Mss 3406, 46th Year of the Auspicious Reign, p. 542.

156 Thorn, *Memoir of the War in India*, p. 125.

157 Ibid., pp. 125–6.

158 Lal, *Shah Alam Nama*, Tonk Mss 3406, 46th Year of the Auspicious Reign, p. 544.

159 K. K. Dutta, *Shah Alam II & The East India Company*, Calcutta, 1965, p. 115.

160 Lal, *Shah Alam Nama*, Tonk Mss 3406, 46th Year of the Auspicious Reign, p. 544.

161 BL, OIOC, IOR H/492, f. 349.

162 Dutta, *Shah Alam II & The East India Company*, pp. 114–15.

163 Fraser, *Military Memoirs of Lt. Col. James Skinner C.B.*, vol. 1, pp. 293–4.

164 K. N. Pannikar, *British Diplomacy in Northern India: A Study of the Delhi Residency 1803–1857*, New Delhi, 1968, p. 7.

165 Stephen P. Blake, *Shahjahanabad: The Sovereign City in Mughal India, 1639–1739*, Cambridge, 1991, pp. 170, 181; Spear, *The Twilight of the Moghuls*, p. 92.

166 Quoted in Frances W. Pritchett, *Nets of Awareness*, Berkeley and Los Angeles, 1994, p. 3.

167 Fraser of Reelig Archive, Inverness, vol. 29, Wm Fraser letterbook, 1 April 1806, to Edward S. Fraser.

168 See William Dalrymple, *The Last Mughal: The Fall of a Dynasty, Delhi, 1857*, London, 2006.

169 Ray, *The Felt Community*, pp. 301–3, 334.

170 Quoted in J. K. Majumdar, *Raja Rammohun Roy and the Last Moghuls: A Selection from Official Records (1803–1859)*, Calcutta, 1939, pp. 4, 319–20.

171 Bowen, *Business of Empire*, p. 277.

172 See Joseph Sramek, *Gender, Morality, and Race in Company India, 1765–1858*, New York, 2011, p. 17.

173 Ibid., p. 229.

174 P. J. Marshall, *Problems of Empire: Britain and India, 1757–1813*, London, 1968, pp. 142–4.

175 Quoted in Tillman W. Nechtman, *Nabobs: Empire and Identity in Eighteenth-Century Britain*, Cambridge, 2010, p. 225.

176 Micklethwait and Wooldridge, *The Company*, p. 36.

177 Bowen, *Business of Empire*, pp. 16–17.

178 Ibid., p. 297.

179 Tirthankar Roy, *The East India Company: The World's Most Powerful Corporation*, New Delhi, 2012, p. xxiii.

180 Micklethwait and Wooldridge, *The Company*, p. 36.

EPILOGUE

1 Fakir Khair ud-Din Illahabadi, '*Ibrat Nama*, BL, OIOC, Or. 1932, f. iv.

Bibliography

I. MANUSCRIPT SOURCES IN EUROPEAN LANGUAGES

Oriental and India Office Collections, British Library (Formerly India Office Library) London

MSS EUR

'Incomplete Draft (1785) of an account of the Mysore War (1780–84)', Mss Eur K 116

James Dalrymple Papers, Mss Eur E 330

Elphinstone Papers, Mss Eur F.88

Fowke Papers, Mss Eur E 6.66

Kirkpatrick Papers, Mss Eur F.228

Sutherland Papers, Mss Eur D.547

Orme Mss

Causes of the Loss of Calcutta 1756, David Renny, August 1756, Mss Eur O.V. 19

Narrative of the Capture of Calcutta from April 10 1756 to November 10 1756, William Tooke, Mss Eur O.V. 19

'Narrative of the loss of Calcutta, with the Black Hole by Captain Mills, who was in it, and sundry other particulars, being Captain Mills' pocket book, which he gave me', Mss Eur O.V. 19

Journal of the Proceedings of the Troops commanded by Lieutenant Colonel Robert Clive on the expedition to Bengal, Captain Edward Maskelyne, Mss Eur O.V. 20
Home Miscellaneous
Bengal Correspondence
Bengal Public Considerations
Bengal Secret Consultations
Bengal Wills 1780–1804 L/AG/34/29/4-16
Bengal Regimental Orders IOR/P/BEN/SEC
Bengal Political Consultations IOR/P/117/18

British Library

'An Account Of The Capture Of Calcutta By Captain Grant', Add Mss 29200
Warren Hastings Papers, Add Mss 29,098–29,172
Anderson Papers, Add Mss 45,427
Brit Mus Egerton MS 2123
Wellesley Papers, Add Mss 37,274–37,318

Devon Records Office, Exeter

Kennaway Papers B 961M ADD/F2

Archives Départementales de la Savoie, Chambéry, France

De Boigne archive

National Army Museum Library, London

The Gardner Papers, NAM 6305–56

National Library of Wales

Robert Clive Papers, GB 0210 ROBCL1

Pasadena Library

Letters of Thomas Roe to Elizabeth, Countess of Huntingdon, Hastings Collection

Punjab Archives, Lahore

Delhi Residency Papers

Scottish Records Office, Registrar House, Edinburgh

The Will of Lieut. Col. James Dalrymple, Hussein Sagar, December 8
    1800: GD 135/2086
Letters of Stair Dalrymple, Hamilton-Dalrymple Mss

National Library of Scotland

The Papers of Alexander Walker, NLS 13,601–14,193

National Archives of India, New Delhi

Secret Consultations
Political Consultations
Foreign Consultations
Foreign Miscellaneous
Letters from Court
Secret Letters to Court
Secret Letters from Court
Political Letters to Court
Political Letters from Court
Hyderabad Residency Records

Private Archives

The Fraser Papers, Inverness
The Kirkpatrick Papers, London

2. UNPUBLISHED MSS AND DISSERTATIONS

Chander, Sunil, *From a Pre-Colonial Order to a Princely State: Hyderabad in
    Transition, c1748–1865*, unpublished Ph.D., Cambridge University, 1987
Ghosh, Durba, *Colonial Companions: Bibis, Begums, and Concubines of the
    British in North India 1760–1830*, unpublished Ph.D., Berkeley, 2000
Kaicker, Abhishek, *Unquiet City: Making and Unmaking Politics in Mughal
    Delhi*, 1707–39, unpublished Ph.D., Columbia, 2014
Rothschild, Emma, 'The East India Company and the American Revolution',
    unpublished essay

3. PERSIAN, URDU, BENGALI & TAMIL SOURCES

A. MANUSCRIPTS

Oriental and India Office Collections, British Library (Formerly India Office Library) London

Tarikh-i-Alamgir Sani, Mss Or. 1749
   (This manuscript has apparently no author name, nor date of
   composition, nor introduction)
Fakir Khair ud-Din, '*Ibrat Nama*, Mss Or. 1932
Ghulam Ali Khan alias Bhikhari Khan, *Shah Alam Nama*, Mss Add 24080
I'tisam al-Din, *Shigrif-namah-i Vilayet*, Mss Or. 200
Muhammad 'Ali Khan Ansari of Panipat, *Tarikh-i Muzaffari*, Mss Or. 466
Roznamcha-i-Shah Alam, Islamic 3921
Shakir Khan, *Tārikh-i Shākir Khānī*, Mss Add. 6585

Private Collection, Hyderabad

Tamkin Kazmi, edited and expanded by Laeeq Salah, *Aristu Jah*
   (unpublished Urdu biography, written c. 1950 and re-edited by Laeeq
   Salah, c. 1980)

MAAPRI Research Institute Library, Tonk, Rajasthan

Munshi Mohan Lal, *Shah Alam Nama*, Tonk Mss 3406

B. PUBLISHED TEXTS

Abu'l Fazl, *Ain-I-Akbari*, 3 vols, trans. H. Blochman and H. S. Jarrett,
   written c. 1590, Calcutta, 1873–94
Ali, Karam, 'The *Muzaffarnama of Karam Ali*', in *Bengal Nawabs*, trans.
   Jadunath Sarkar, Calcutta, 1952
Allah, Salim, *A Narrative of the Transactions in Bengal*, trans. Francis
   Gladwin, Calcutta, 1788
Anon., *The Chronology of Modern Hyderabad from 1720 to 1890*, Hyderabad,
   1954
Astarabadi, Mirza Mahdi, *Tarikh-e Jahangosha-ye Naderi: The official history
   of Nader's reign*, Bombay lithograph, 1265 AC/AD 1849

Azad, Muhammed Husain, trans. and ed. Frances Pritchett and Shamsur Rahman Faruqi, *Ab-e Hayat: Shaping the Canon of Urdu Poetry*, New Delhi, 2001

Beach, Milo Cleveland, and Koch, Ebba, eds, *King of the World – the Padshahnama: An Imperial Mughal Manuscript from the Royal Library, Windsor Castle*, London, 1997

Begley, W. E., and Desai, Z. A., eds, *The Shah Jahan Nama of Inayat Khan*, New Delhi, 1990

Bidri, Mohammed Qadir Khan Munshi, *Tarikh I Asaf Jahi*, trans. Dr Zaibunnisa Begum, written 1266 AH/AD 1851, Hyderabad, 1994

Das, Hari Charan, 'Chahar Gulzar Shuja' *of Hari Charan Das*, in Sir H. M. Elliot and John Dowson, *A History of India as Told By Its Own Historians*, 8 vols, London, 1867–77, vol. VIII

'Firaqi', Kunwar Prem Kishor, *Waqa'i-i Alam Shahi*, Calcutta, 1949

Ganga Ram, *The Maharashtra Purana: An Eighteenth-Century Bengali Historical Text*, trans. and ed. Edward C. Dimock Jr and Pratul Chandra Gupta, Honolulu, 1965

Ghalib, *Urdu Letters of Mirza Asadu'llah Khan Ghalib*, New York, 1987

Gholam Ali Khan, *Shah Alam Nama*, ed. A. A. M. Suhrawardy and A. M. K. Shiirazi, Calcutta, 1914

Ghulam Husain Salim, *Riyazu-s-salatin: A History of Bengal. Translated from the original Persian by Maulvi Abdus Salam*, Calcutta, 1902

Gladwin, Francis (trans.), *The Memoirs of Khojeh Abdulkurreem*, Calcutta, 1788

Hasan, Mehdi, Fateh Nawaz Jung, *Muraqq-Ibrat*, Hyderabad, 1300 AH/AD 1894

Husain, Saiyyad Iltifat, *Nagaristan i-Asafi*, written c. 1816, printed in Hyderabad, 1900

Islam, Khurshidul, and Russell, Ralph, *Three Mughal Poets: Mir, Sauda, Mir Hasan*, New Delhi, 1991

I'tisam al-Din, *The Wonders of Vilayet, being a memoir, originally in Persian, of a visit to France and Britain*, trans. Kaiser Haq, Leeds, 2001

Jehangir, *The Tuzuk-i Jehangiri or Memoirs of Jehangir*, trans. Alexander Rodgers, ed. Henry Beveridge, London, 1909–14

Kamran, Mirza, 'The Mirza Name: The Book of the Perfect Gentleman', trans. Mawlavi M. Hidayat Husain, *Journal of the Asiatic Society of Bengal*, New Series, vol. IX, 1913

Kashmiri, Abd ol-Karim, *Bayan-e-Waqe'*, trans H. G. Pritchard, BM Mss Add 30782

Khair ud-Din Illahabadi, Fakir, '*Ibrat Nama*, BL Or. 1932

Khan, Dargah Quli, *The Muraqqa' e-Dehli*, trans. Chander Shekhar, New
    Delhi, 1989
Khan, Ghulam Hussain, Khan Zaman Khan, *Tarikh e-Gulzar e-Asafiya*,
    Hyderabad, 1302 AH/AD 1891
Khan, Ghulam Iman, *Tarikh i-Khurshid Jahi*, Hyderabad, 1284 AH/AD 1869
Khan, M. Abdul Rahim, *Tarikh e-Nizam*, Hyderabad, 1311 AH/AD 1896
Khan, Mirza Abu Taleb, *The Travels of Mirza Abu Taleb Khan in Asia, Africa,
    and Europe during the years 1799, 1800, 1801, 1802, and 1803*, trans. Charles
    Stewart, London, 1810
Khan, Mohammed Najmul Ghani, *Tarikh-e-Riyasat-e-Hyderabad*, Lucknow,
    1930
Khan, Saqi Must'ad, *Maasir-i-Alamgiri*, trans. as *The History of the Emperor
    Aurangzeb-Alamgir 1658–1707*, Jadunath Sarkar, Calcutta, 1946
Khan, Syed Ghulam Hussain Tabatabai, *Seir Mutaqherin or Review of
    Modern Times*, 4 vols, Calcutta, 1790
Lal, Makhan, *Tarikh i-Yadgar-i-Makhan Lal*, Hyderabad, 1300 AH/AD 1883
Mansaram, Lala, *Masir i-Nizami*, trans. P. Setu Madhava Rao, *Eighteenth
    Century Deccan*, Bombay, 1963
Marvi, Mohammad Kazem, *Alam Ara-ye Naderi*, 3 vols, ed. Mohammad
    Amin Riyahi, Tehran, 3rd edn, 1374 AH/AD 1995
Mirza 'Ali Bakht, *Waqi'at-i Azfari*, ed. T Chandrasekharan and Syed Hamza
    Hussain Omari, Madras, 1957
Muhammad, Fayz, *Siraj ul-Tawarikh* (The Lamp of Histories), Kabul, 1913,
    trans. R. D. McChesney (forthcoming)
Mukhlis, Anand Ram, *Tazkira*, in Sir H. M. Elliot and John Dowson, *A
    History of India as Told By Its Own Historians*, 1867–77, vol. VIII
C. M. Naim (translated, annotated and introduced), *Zikr-I Mir: The
    Autobiography of the Eighteenth-Century Mughal Poet, Mir Muhammad
    Taqi 'Mir'*, New Delhi, 1998
National Archives of India Calendar of Persian Correspondence, intro. Muzaffar
    Alam and Sanjay Subrahmanyam, vols 1–9, New Delhi, 2014 reprint
Pillai, A. R., *The Private Diary of Ananda Ranga Pillai, Dubash to Joseph
    François Dupleix*, ed. J. F. Price and K. Rangachari, 12 vols, Madras, 1922
*Proceedings of a Jacobin Club formed at Seringapatam by the French soldiers
    in the Corps commanded by M. Domport*, Paper C in Official Documents
    Relating the Negotiations Carried on by Tippoo Sultan with the French
    Nation, Calcutta, 1799
Ruswa, Mirza Mohammed Hadi Ruswa, *Umrao Jan Ada*, trans. from the
    original Urdu by Khuswant Singh and M. A. Hussani, Hyderabad, 1982

Sadasukh Dihlavi, *Munkatab ut-Tawarikh*, trans. Sir H. M. Elliot and
John Dowson, *A History of India as Told By Its Own Historians*, 1867–77,
vol. VIII

Salim, Allah, *A Narrative of the Transactions in Bengal*, trans. Francis
Gladwin, Calcutta, 1788

Shustari, Seyyed Abd al-Latif Shushtari, *Kitab Tuhfat al-'Alam*, written
Hyderabad, 1802 and lithographed Bombay, 1847

Talib, Mohammed Sirajuddin, *Mir Alam*, Hyderabad

Talib, Mohammed Sirajuddin, *Nizam Ali Khan*, Hyderabad

Tuzuk-i-Jahangiri or Memoirs of Jahanagir, trans. Alexander Rogers, ed.
Henry Beveridge, London, 1919

Yusuf Ali Khan, *Tarikh-i-Bangala-i-Mahabatjangi*, trans. Abdus Subhan,
Calcutta, 1982

4. CONTEMPORARY WORKS AND PERIODICAL ARTICLES IN EUROPEAN LANGUAGES

Anon., *Narrative Sketches of the Conquest of Mysore*, London, 1800

Andrews, C. F., *Zakaullah of Delhi*, Cambridge, 1929

Archer, Major, *Tours in Upper India*, London, 1833

Barnard, Anne, *The Letters of Lady Anne Barnard to Henry Dundas from
the Cape and Elsewhere 1793–1803*, ed. A. M. Lewin Robinson, Cape
Town, 1973

Barnard, Anne, *The Cape Journals of Lady Anne Barnard 1797–98*, ed. A. M.
Lewin Robinson, Cape Town, 1994

Bayley, Emily, *The Golden Calm: An English Lady's Life in Moghul Delhi*,
London, 1980

Bazin, Père Louis, 'Mémoires sur dernieres années du regne de Thamas
Kouli-Kan et sa mort tragique, contenus dans une lettre du Frere Bazin',
1751, in *Lettres Edifiantes et Curieuses Ecrites des Mission Etrangères*, Paris,
1780, vol. IV

Beatson, Alexander, *A View of the Origin and Conduct of the War with Tippoo
Sultan*, London, 1800

Bernier, François, *Travels in the Mogul Empire, 1656–68*, ed. Archibald
Constable, trans. Irving Brock, Oxford, 1934

Bhargava, Krishna Dayal, *Browne Correspondence*, Delhi, 1960

Blakiston, John, *Twelve Years Military Adventure in Three Quarters of the
Globe*, 2 vols, London, 1829

Blochmann, H., trans. and ed., *The A'in-i Akbari by Abu'l Fazl 'Allami*, New
Delhi, 1977

Bolts, William, *Considerations on Indian Affairs; Particularly Respecting the Present State of Bengal and its Dependencies,* 3 vols, London, 1772–5

Bourquien, Louis, 'An Autobiographical Memoir of Louis Bourquien translated from the French by J.P. Thompson', in *Journal of the Punjab Historical Society,* vol. IX, part 7, 1923

Burke, Edmund, *The Writings and Speeches of Edmund Burke,* ed. P. J. Marshall, 6 vols, Oxford, 1991

Caillaud, John, *A Narrative of What Happened in Bengal in the Year 1760,* London, 1764

Colebrook, Sir T. E., *The Life of Mountstuart Elphinstone,* 2 vols, London, 1884

'Cooke's Evidence before the Select Committee of the House of Commons', in W. K. Firminger, ed., Great Britain, House of Commons, *Report on East India Affairs,* Fifth Report from the Select Committee, vol. III, 1812

Dalrymple, Alexander, *A Retrospective View of the Antient System of the East India Company, with a Plan of Regulation,* London, 1784

Dalrymple, James, *Letters &c Relative To The Capture of Rachore* by Capt. James Dalrymple, Madras, 1796

D'Oyly, Charles, *The European in India,* London, 1813

Dow, Alexander, *History of Hindostan,* 3 vols, Dublin, 1792

Duff, Grant, *A History of the Mahrattas,* 2 vols, London, 1826

Entick, The Late Reverend John, et al., *The Present State of the British Empire,* 4 vols, London, 1774

Fenton, Elizabeth, *The Journal of Mrs Fenton,* London, 1901

Firminger, Walter K., and Anderson, William, *The Diaries of Three Surgeons of Patna,* Calcutta, 1909

Foster, William, ed., *The English Factories in India 1618–1669,* 13 vols, London, 1906–27

Foster, William, ed., *Early Travels in India 1583–1619,* London, 1921

Foster, Sir William, *The Embassy of Sir Thomas Roe to India 1615–9, as Narrated in his Journal and Correspondence,* New Delhi, 1990

Francklin, William, *The History of Shah Alam,* London, 1798

Francklin, William, *Military Memoirs of Mr George Thomas Who by Extraordinary Talents and Enterprise rose from an obscure situation to the rank of A General in the Service of Native Powers in the North-West of India,* London, 1805

Fraser, James, *The History of Nadir Shah,* London, 1742

Fraser, James Baillie, *Military Memoirs of Lt. Col. James Skinner C.B.,* 2 vols, London, 1851

Fryer, Dr John, *A New Account of East India and Persia Letters Being Nine Years Travels Begun 1672 and finished 1681,* 3 vols, London, 1698

Gentil, Jean-Baptiste, *Mémoires sur l'Indoustan*, Paris, 1822

George III, ed. J. Fortescue, *Correspondence of George III, 1760–1783*, 6 vols, 1927–8

Green, Jack, *Arenas of Asiatic Plunder*, London, 1767

Hamilton, Alexander, *A New Account of the East Indies*, 2 vols, London, 1930

Hanway, Jonas, *An Historical Account of the British Trade over the Caspian Sea ... to which are added The Revolutions of Persia during the present Century, with the particular History of the great Userper Nadir Kouli*, 4 vols, London, 1753

Hastings, Warren, ed. G. R. Gleig, *Memoirs of the Life of the Rt Hon Warren Hastings, First Governor General of Bengal*, 3 vols, London, 1841

Heber, Reginald, *A Narrative of a Journey Through the Upper Provinces of India from Calcutta to Bombay, 1824–1825*, 3 vols, London, 1827

Hickey, William, *The Memoirs of William Hickey*, ed. Alfred Spencer, 4 vols, London, 1925

Hill, S. C., *Bengal in 1756–7*, 3 vols, Indian Records Series, Calcutta, 1905

Hollingbery, William, *A History of His Late Highness Nizam Alee Khaun, Soobah of the Dekhan*, Calcutta, 1805

Holwell, John Zephaniah, *A Genuine Narrative of the Deplorable Deaths of the English Gentlemen, and others, who were suffocated in the Black Hole in Fort William, in Calcutta, in the Kingdom of Bengal; in the Night Succeeding the 20th June 1756*, London, 1758

Hunter, W. W., *The Annals of Rural Bengal*, London, 1868

Jones, Sir William, *The Letters of Sir William Jones*, ed. Garland Canon, 2 vols, Oxford, 1970

Jourdain, John, *Journal of John Jourdain 1608–17*, ed. W. Foster, London, 1905

Kaye, John W., *The Life and Correspondence of Sir John Malcolm GCB*, 2 vols, London, 1856

Kindersley, Mrs Jemima, *Letters from the East Indies*, London, 1777

Kirkpatrick, William, *Diary and Select Letters of Tippoo Sultan*, London, 1804

Lauriston, Jean Law de, *A Memoir of the Mughal Empire 1757–61*, trans. G. S. Cheema, New Delhi, 2014

Linschoten, J. H. Van, *The Voyage of John Huyghen Van Linschoten to the East Indies*, 2 vols, London, 1885 (original Dutch edn 1598)

Lockyer, Charles, *An Account Of The Trade With India Containing Rules For Good Government In Trade, And Tables: With Descriptions Of Fort St. George, Aheen, Malacca, Condore, Anjenjo, Muskat, Gombroon, Surat, Goa, Carwar, Telicherry, Panola, Calicut, The Cape Of Good Hope, And St Helena Their Inhabitants, Customs, Religion, Government Animals, Fruits &C.*, London, 1711

Lushington, Rt Hon. S. R., *The Life and Services of Lord George Harris GCB*, London, 1840

Macaulay, Thomas Babington, 'Warren Hastings', in *The Historical Essays of Macaulay*, ed. Samuel Thurber, Boston, 1892

Madec, René-Marie, *Mémoire*, ed. Jean Deloche, Pondicherry, 1983

Majumdar, J. K. (ed.), *Raja Rammohun Roy and the Last Moghuls: A Selection from Official Records (1803–1859)*, Calcutta, 1939

Malcolm, Sir John, *Sketch of the Political History of India from the Introduction of Mr Pitts Bill*, London, 1811

Malcolm, Sir John, *Political History of India*, 2 vols, London, 1836

Malcolm, Sir John, *Life of Robert, Lord Clive*, London, 1836

Mandelslo, J. A. de, *The Voyages and Travels of J. Albert de Mandelslo The Voyages & Travels of the Ambassadors sent by Frederick Duke of Holstein, to the Great Duke of Muscovy, and the King of Persia*, trans. John Davis, London, 1662

Manucci, Niccolao, *Storia do Mogor, or Mogul India, 1653–1708*, 2 vols, trans. William Irvine, London, 1907

Methwold, William, 'Relations of the Kingdome of Golchonda and other neighbouring Nations and the English Trade in Those Parts, by Master William Methwold', in W. H. Moreland, *Relations of Golconda in the early Seventeenth Century*, London, 1931

Modave, Comte de, *Voyage en Inde du Comte de Modave, 1773–1776*, ed. Jean Deloche, Pondicherry, 1971

Moor, Edward, *A Narrative of the Operations of Captain Little's Detachment*, London, 1794

Nugent, Lady Maria, *Journal of a Residence in India 1811–15*, vol. 2, London, 1839

Parkes, Fanny, *Wanderings of a Pilgrim in Search of the Picturesque*, London, 1850

Pellow, Thomas, *The Adventures of Thomas Pellow, of Penryn, Mariner*, ed. Robert Brown, London, 1890

Polier, Antoine, *Shah Alam II and his Court*, Calcutta, 1947

Pownall, Thomas, *The Right, Interest and Duty of Government, as concerned in the affairs of the East India Company*, revised edn, 1781

Price, David, *Memoirs of the Early Life and Service of a Field Officer on the Retired List of the Indian Army*, London, 1839

Price, Joseph, *Five Letters from a Free Merchant in Bengal, to Warren Hastings Esq*, London, 1778

Price, Joseph, *The Saddle Put on the Right Horse*, London, 1783

Purchas, Samuel, *Hakluytus Posthumus or Purchas His Pilgrimes, Contayning a History of the World*, 20 vols, Glasgow, 1905

Rennell, James, *The Marches of the British Armies in the Peninsula of India*, London, 1792

Roe, Sir Thomas, and Fryer, Dr John, *Travels in India in the 17th Century*, London, 1873

Row, T. Venkatasami, *A Manual of the District of Tanjore in the Madras Presidency*, Madras, 1883

Sarker, Jadunath, ed., *English Records of Mahratta History: Poona Residency Correspondence*, vol. 1, *Mahadji Scindhia and North Indian Affairs 1785–1794*, Bombay, 1936

Sarkar, Jadunath, trans. and ed., 'Haidarabad and Golkonda in 1750 Seen Through French Eyes: From the Unpublished Diary of a French Officer Preserved in the Bibliothèque Nationale, Paris', in *Islamic Culture*, vol. X, p. 24

Saxena, V. K., ed., *Speeches on the Impeachment of Warren Hastings*, 2 vols, Delhi, 1987

Scrafton, Luke, *Observations on Vansittart's Narrative*, London, 1770

Scurry, James, *The Captivity, Sufferings and Escape of James Scurry, who was detained a prisoner during ten years, in the dominions of Haidar Ali and Tippoo Saib*, London, 1824

Sen, S., *Indian Travels of Thevenot and Careri*, New Delhi, 1949

Sleeman, Major General Sir W. H., *Rambles and Recollections of an Indian Official*, Oxford, 1915

Smith, Adam, *The Correspondence of Adam Smith*, ed. E. C. Mossner and I. S. Ross, 2nd edn, Oxford, 1987

Sramek, Joseph, *Gender, Morality, and Race in Company India, 1765–1858*, New York, 2011

Srinivasachari, C. S., ed., *Fort William–India House Correspondence*, vol. 4, London, 1949–58

Stevens, Henry, *The Dawn of British Trade to the East Indies, as Recorded in the Court Minutes of the East India Company 1599–1603, Containing an Account of the Formation of the Company*, London, 1866

Tavernier, Jean-Baptiste, *Travels in India*, trans. V. Ball, ed. Wm Crooke, 2 vols, Oxford, 1925

Temple, Richard Carnac, *The Diaries of Streynsham Master, 1675–1680*, 2 vols, London, 1911

Thorn, Major William, *Memoir of the War in India Conducted by Lord Lake and Major General Sir Arthur Wellesley on the Banks of the Hyphasis*, London, 1818

Vansittart, Henry, *A Narrative of the Transactions in Bengal from the Year 1760, to the year 1764, during the Government of Mr Henry Vansittart*, 3 vols, London, 1766

Walpole, Horace, ed. W. S. Lewis et al., *The Yale Edition of Horace Walpole's Correspondence*, 48 vols, New Haven, CT, 1937–83

Watts, William, and Campbell, John, *Memoirs of the Revolution in Bengal, Anno. Dom. 1757*, London, 1758

Welsh, James, *Military Reminiscences Extracted from a Journal of Nearly Forty Years Active Service in the East Indies*, 2 vols, London, 1830

Wellesley, Arthur, Duke of Wellington, *Supplementary Despatches and Memoranda of Field Marshal Arthur Duke of Wellington*, edited by his son, the 2nd Duke of Wellington, 15 vols, London, 1858–72

Wellesley, Richard, Marquess Wellesley, *The Despatches, Minutes and Correspondence of the Marquess Wellesley KG during his Administration of India*, 5 vols, ed. Montgomery Martin, London, 1840

Wellesley, Richard, Marquess Wellesley, *Two Views of British India: The Private Correspondence of Mr Dundas and Lord Wellesley: 1798–1801*, ed. Edward Ingram, London, 1970

Wilkin, Captain W. H., *The Life of Sir David Baird*, London, 1912

Wilks, Mark, *Historical Sketches of the South of India*, vol. 2, 1820

Williamson, Captain Thomas, *The East India Vade Mecum*, 2 vols, London, 1810, 2nd edn, 1825

Young, Arthur, *Political Essays concerning the present state of the British Empire*, London, 1772

Yule, Henry, *Hobson-Jobson: A Glossary of Colloquial Anglo-Indian Words and Phrases*, London, 1903

5. SECONDARY WORKS AND PERIODICAL ARTICLES

Ahmed Aziz, *Studies in Islamic Culture in the Indian Environment*, Oxford, 1964

Alam, Muzaffar, *The Crisis of Empire in Mughal North India: Awadh and the Punjab 1707–1748*, New Delhi, 1986

Alam, Muzaffar, and Alavi, Seema, *A European Experience of the Mughal Orient: The I'jaz-I Arslani (Persian Letters, 1773–1779) of Antoine-Louis Henri Polier*, New Delhi, 2001

Alam, Muzaffar, and Subrahmanyam, Sanjay, *Writing the Mughal World*, New York, 2012

Alam, Shah Manzur, 'Masulipatam: A Metropolitan Port in the Seventeenth Century', in Mohamed Taher, ed., *Muslim Rule in Deccan*, New Delhi, 1997

Alavi, Seema, *The Sepoys and the Company: Tradition and Transition in Northern India 1770–1830*, Delhi, 1995

Alavi, Seema, ed., *The Eighteenth Century in India*, New Delhi, 2002

Ali, M. Athar, 'The Passing of an Empire: The Mughal Case', *Modern Asian Studies*, vol. 9, no. 13 (1975)

Arasaratnam, Sinnappah, and Ray, Aniruddha, *Masulipatam and Cambay: A History of Two Port Towns 1500–1800*, New Delhi, 1994

Archer, Mildred, *Company drawings in the India Office Library*, London, 1972

Archer, Mildred, and Falk, Toby, *India Revealed: The Art and Adventures of James and William Fraser 1801–35*, London, 1989

Avery, Peter, Hambly, Gavin, and Melville, Charles, *The Cambridge History of Iran*, vol. 7, *From Nadir Shah to the Islamic Republic*, Cambridge, 1991

Axworthy, Michael, *The Sword of Persia: Nader Shah from Tribal Warrior to Conquering Tyrant*, New York, 2006

Axworthy, Michael, *Iran: Empire of the Mind: A History from Zoroaster to the Present Day*, London, 2007

Ballhatchet, Kenneth, *Race, Sex and Class under the Raj: Imperial Attitudes and Policies and their Critics 1793–1905*, London, 1980

Barnett, Richard, *North India Between Empires: Awadh, the Mughals and the British, 1720–1801*, Berkeley, 1980

Barrow, Ian, 'The many meanings of the Black Hole of Calcutta', in *Tall Tales and True: India, Historiography and British Imperial Imaginings*, ed. Kate Brittlebank, Clayton, Vic., 2008

Baugh, Daniel, *The Global Seven Years War, 1754–63*, New York, 2014

Bayly, C. A., 'Indian Merchants in a "Traditional" Setting. Banaras, 1780–1830', in Clive Dewey and A. J. Hopkins, eds, *The Imperial Impact: Studies in the Economic History of India and Africa*, London, 1978

Bayly, C. A., *Rulers, Townsmen and Bazaars: North Indian Society in the Age of British Expansion*, Cambridge, 1983

Bayly, C. A., *Indian Society and the Making of the British Empire*, Cambridge, 1988

Bayly, C. A., *Imperial Meridian: the British Empire and the World 1780–1830*, London, 1989

Bayly, C. A., *Empire &Information: Intelligence Gathering and Social Communication in India 1780–1870*, Cambridge, 1996

Bence-Jones, Mark, *Palaces of the Raj*, London, 1973

Bence-Jones, Mark, *Clive of India*, London, 1974

Bernstein, Jeremy, *Dawning of the Raj: The Life & Trials of Warren Hastings*, Chicago, 2000

Bhargava, Meena, *The Decline of the Mughal Empire*, New Delhi, 2014

Blake, Stephen P., *Shahjahanabad: The Sovereign City in Mughal India, 1639–1739*, Cambridge, 1991

Bowen, H. V., 'Lord Clive and speculation in East India Company stock, 1766', *Historical Journal*, vol. 30, no.4 (1987)

Bowen, H. V., *Revenue and Reform: The Indian Problem in British Politics, 1757–1773*, Cambridge, 1991

Bowen, H. V., 'British India, 1765–1813: The Metropolitan Context', in P. J. Marshall, *The Eighteenth Century*, Oxford, 1998

Bowen, H. V., *The Business of Empire: The East India Company and Imperial Britain, 1756–1833*, Cambridge, 2006

Brenner, Robert, *Merchants and Revolution: Commercial Change, Political Conflict, and London's Overseas Traders, 1550–1653*, Princeton, 2003

Brett-James, Antony, ed., *Wellington at War, 1794–1815: A Selection of His Wartime Letters*, London, 1961

Briggs, Henry, *The Nizam: His History and Relations with the British Government*, London, 1861

Brittlebank, Kate, *Tipu Sultan's Search for Legitimacy: Islam and Kingship in a Hindu Domain*, New Delhi, 1997

Bryant, G. J., *The Emergence of British Power in India 1600–1784: A Grand Strategic Interpretation*, Woodbridge, 2013

Buchan, James, *John Law: A Scottish Adventurer of the Eighteenth Century*, London, 2019

Buddle, Anne, *The Tiger and the Thistle: Tipu Sultan and the Scots in India*, Edinburgh, 1999

Burton, David, *The Raj at Table: A Culinary History of the British in India*, London, 1993

Butler, Iris, *The Elder Brother: The Marquess Wellesley 1760–1842*, London, 1973

Calkins, Philip, 'The Formation of a Regionally Oriented Ruling Group in Bengal, 1700–1740', *Journal of Asian Studies*, vol. 29, no. 4, (1970)

Calkins, Philip B., 'The Role of Murshidabad as a Regional and Subregional Centre in Bengal', in Richard L. Park, *Urban Bengal*, East Lansing, 1969

Carlos, Ann M. and Nicholas, Stephen, 'Giants of an Earlier Capitalism: The chartered trading companies as modern multinationals', *Business History Review*, vol. 62, no. 3 (Autumn 1988), pp. 398–419

Chandra, Satish, *Parties and Politics at the Mughal Court, 1717–1740*, New Delhi, 1972

Chandra, Satish, 'Social Background to the Rise of the Maratha Movement During the 17th Century', *The Indian Economic & Social History Review*, x, (1973)

Chatterjee, Indrani, *Gender, Slavery and Law in Colonial India*, New Delhi, 1999

Chatterjee, Kumkum, 'Collaboration and Conflict: Bankers and Early Colonial Rule in India: 1757–1813', *The Indian Economic and Social History Review*, vol. 30, no. 3 (1993)

Chatterjee, Kumkum, *Merchants, Politics & Society in Early Modern India, Bihar: 1733–1820*, Leiden, 1996

Chatterjee, Kumkum, 'History as Self-Representation: The Recasting of a Political Tradition in Late Eighteenth Century Eastern India', *Modern Asian Studies*, vol. 32, no. 4 (1998)

Chatterjee, Partha, *The Black Hole of Empire: History of a Global Practice of Power*, New Delhi, 2012

Chatterji, Nandlal, *Mir Qasim, Nawab of Bengal, 1760–1763*, Allahabad, 1935

Chatterji, Nandlal, *Verelst's Rule in India*, 1939

Chaudhuri, K. N., *The English East India Company: The Study of an Early Joint-Stock Company 1600–1640*, London, 1965

Chaudhuri, K. N., 'India's International Economy in the Nineteenth Century: A Historical Survey', in *Modern Asian Studies*, vol. 2, no. 1 (1968)

Chaudhuri, K. N., *The Trading World of the Asia and the English East India Company 1660–1760*, Cambridge, 1978

Chaudhuri, Nani Gopal, *British Relations with Hyderabad*, Calcutta, 1964

Chaudhury, Sushil, *The Prelude to Empire: Plassey Revolution of 1757*, New Delhi, 2000

Chaudhury, Sushil, 'The banking and mercantile house of Jagat Seths of Bengal', in *Studies in People's History*, vol. 2, no. 1 (2015)

Chaudhury, Sushil, *Companies, Commerce and Merchants: Bengal in the Pre-Colonial Era*, Oxford, 2017

Cheema, G. S., *The Forgotten Mughals: A History of the Later Emperors of the House of Babar, 1707–1857*, New Delhi, 2002

Chetty, A. Subbaraya, 'Tipu's Endowments to Hindus and Hindu institutions', in I. H. Habib, ed., *Resistance and Modernisation under Haidar Ali & Tipu Sultan*, New Delhi, 1999

Colley, Linda, 'Britain and Islam: Perspectives on Difference 1600–1800' in *Yale Review*, LXXXVIII (2000)

Colley, Linda, 'Going Native, Telling Tales: Captivity, Collaborations and Empire', *Past & Present*, no. 168 (August 2000)

Colley, Linda, *Captives: Britain, Empire and the World 1600–1850*, London, 2002

Colley, Linda, 'Gendering the Globe: The Political and Imperial Thought of Philip Francis', *Past & Present*, no. 209 (November 2010)

Collingham, E. M., *Imperial Bodies: The Physical Experience of the Raj c.1800–1947*, London, 2001

Compton, Herbert, ed., *The European Military Adventurers of Hindustan*, London, 1943

Cooper, Randolph G. S., *The Anglo-Maratha Campaigns and the Contest for India: The Struggle for the Control of the South Asian Military Economy*, Cambridge, 2003

Cooper, Randolph, 'Culture, Combat and Colonialism in Eighteenth and Nineteenth Century India', *International History Review*, vol. 27, no. 3 (September 2005)

Cruz, Maria Augusta Lima, 'Exiles and Renegades in Early Sixteenth-Century Portuguese India', in *Indian Economic and Social History Review*, vol. XXIII, no. 3 (1986)

Dalley, Jan, *The Black Hole: Money, Myth and Empire*, London, 2006

Dalmia, Vasudha, and Faruqui, Munis D., eds, *Religious Interactions in Mughal India*, New Delhi, 2014

Dalrymple, William, *City of Djinns*, London, 1993

Dalrymple, William, *White Mughals: Love and Betrayal in Eighteenth-Century India*, London, 2002

Dalrymple, William, *The Last Mughal: The End of a Dynasty, Delhi, 1857*, London, 2006

Dalrymple, William, and Sharma, Yuthika, *Princes and Poets in Mughal Delhi 1707–1857*, Princeton, 2012

Das, Neeta, and Llewellyn-Jones, Rosie, *Murshidabad: Forgotten Capital of Bengal*, Mumbai, 2013

Datta, Rajat, 'Commercialisation, Tribute and the Transition from late Mughal to Early Colonial in India', *Medieval History Journal*, vol. 6, no. 2 (2003)

Datta, Rajat, *Society, Economy and the Market: Commercialisation in Rural Bengal, c.1760–1800*, New Delhi, 2000

Datta, Rajat, 'The Commercial Economy of Eastern India under British Rule', in H. V. Bowen, Elizabeth Mancke and John G. Reid, *Britain's Oceanic Empire: Atlantic and Indian Ocean Worlds, c. 1550–1850*, Cambridge, 2012

Datta, Rajat, *The Making of the Eighteenth Century in India: Some Reflections on Its Political and Economic Processes*, Jadunath Sarkar Memorial Lecture, Bangiya Itihas Samiti, Kolkatta, April 2019

Davies, Philip, *Splendours of the Raj: British Architecture in India 1660–1947*, London, 1985

Dewey, Clive, and Hopkins, A. J., eds, *The Imperial Impact: Studies in the Economic History of India and Africa*, London, 1978

Dighe, V. G., and Qanungo, S. N., 'Administrative and Military System of the Marathas', in R. C. Majumdar and V. G. Dighe, eds, *The Maratha Supremacy*, Mumbai, 1977

Dirks, Nicholas B., *The Scandal of Empire: India and the Creation of Imperial Britain*, Harvard, 2006

Disney, A. R., *Twilight of the Pepper Empire: Portuguese Trade in South West India in the Early Seventeenth Century*, Harvard, 1978

Dodwell, Henry, *Dupleix and Clive: The Beginning of Empire*, London, 1920

Dodwell, Henry, *The Nabobs of Madras*, London, 1926

Dutt, Romesh Chunder, *The Economic History of India under Early British Rule, 1757–1837*, London, 1908

Dutta, K. K., *Shah Alam II & The East India Company*, Calcutta, 1965

Eaton, Richard M., *The Rise of Islam and the Bengal Frontier 1204–1760*, Berkeley, 1993

Eaton, Richard M., *Essays on Islam and Indian History*, Oxford, 2000

Eaton, Richard M., *India in the Persianate Age, 1000–1765*, London, 2019

Edwards, Michael, *King of the World: The Life and Times of Shah Alam, Emperor of Hindustan*, London, 1970

Farooqui, Amar, *Zafar, and the Raj: Anglo-Mughal Delhi, c. 1800–1850*, New Delhi, 2013

Faruqi, Munis D., 'At Empire's End: The Nizam, Hyderabad and Eighteenth-Century India', in *Modern Asian Studies*, vol. 43, no. 1 (2009)

Feiling, Keith, *Warren Hastings*, London, 1954

Ferguson, Niall, *Empire: How Britain Made the Modern World*, London, 2003

Findly, Ellison Banks, *Nur Jehan: Empress of Mughal India*, New Delhi, 1993

Fisher, Michael H., *Beyond the Three Seas: Travellers' Tales of Mughal India*, New Delhi, 1987

Fisher, Michael, *The Travels of Dean Mahomet: An Eighteenth-Century Journey Through India*, Berkeley, 1997

Fisher, Michael, *Counterflows to Colonialism*, New Delhi, 2005

Fisher, Michael H., 'Diplomacy in India 1526–1858', in H. V. Bowen, Elizabeth Mancke and John G. Reid, *Britain's Oceanic Empire: Atlantic and Indian Ocean Worlds, c. 1550–1850*, Cambridge, 2012

Floor, Willem, 'New Facts on Nader Shah's Indian Campaign', in *Iran and Iranian Studies: Essays in Honour of Iraj Afshar*, ed. Kambiz Eslami, Princeton, 1998

Forrest, Denys, *Tiger of Mysore: The Life and Death of Tipu Sultan*, London, 1970

Forrest, George, *The Life of Lord Clive*, 2 vols, London, 1918

Foster, Sir William, 'The First Home of the East India Company', in *The Home Counties Magazine*, ed. W. Paley Baildon, FSA, vol. XIV (1912)

Foster, Sir William, *John Company*, London, 1926

Foster, Sir William, *England's Quest of Eastern Trade*, London, 1933

Furber, Holden, 'Rival Empires of Trade in the Orient, 1600–1800', in *Maritime India*, intro. Sanjay Subrahmanyam, New Delhi, 2004

Ghosh, Durba, *Sex and the Family in Colonial India: The Making of Empire*, Cambridge, 2006

Ghosh, Suresh Chandra, *The Social Condition of the British Community in Bengal*, Leiden, 1970

Goetzmann, William N., *Money Changes Everything: How Finance Made Civilisation Possible*, London, 2016

Gommans, Jos J. L., *The Rise of the Indo-Afghan Empire c.1710–1780*, New Delhi, 1999

Gordon, Stewart, 'The Slow Conquest: Administrative Integration of Malwa into the Maratha Empire, 1720–1760', in *Modern Asian Studies*, vol. 11, no. 1 (1977)

Gordon, Stewart, *The Marathas 1600–1818*, Cambridge, 1993

Gordon, Stewart, *Marathas, Marauders and State Formation in Eighteenth-Century India*, Delhi, 1998

Gordon, Stewart, 'Legitimacy and Loyalty in some Successor States of the Eighteenth Century', in John F. Richards, *Kingship and Authority in South Asia*, New Delhi, 1998

Gosha, Lokanatha, *The Modern History of the Indian Chiefs, Rajas, Zamindars, &C.*, Calcutta, 1881

Green, Nile, *Sufism: A Global History*, London, 2012

Grewal, J. S., *Calcutta: Foundation and Development of a Colonial Metropolis*, New Delhi, 1991

Grey, C., and Garrett, H. L. O., *European Adventurers of Northern India 1785–1849*, Lahore, 1929

Guha, Ranajit, *A Rule of Property for Bengal: An Essay on the Idea of Permanent Settlement*, Durham, NC, 1983

Gupta, Brijen K., *Sirajuddaullah and the East India Company, 1756–7*, Leiden, 1966

Gupta, Narayani, *Delhi Between Two Empires 1803–1931*, New Delhi, 1981

Gupta, Pratul C., *Baji Rao II and the East India Company*, New Delhi, 1939

Habib, Irfan, ed., *Resistance and Modernisation under Haidar Ali & Tipu Sultan*, New Delhi, 1999

Hall, Bert S., and De Vries, Kelly, 'Essay Review – The "Military Revolution" Revisited', *Technology and Culture*, no. 31 (1990)

Hallward, N. L., *William Bolts: A Dutch Adventurer Under John Company*, Cambridge, 1920

Hamilton, H., 'The Failure of the Ayr Bank, 1772', *Economic History Review*, 2nd series, vol. VIII (1955–6)

Hansen, Waldemar, *The Peacock Throne*, New Delhi, 1986

Haque, Ishrat, *Glimpses of Mughal Society and Culture*, New Delhi, 1992

Harding, David, *Small Arms of the East India Company 1600–1856*, 4 vols, London, 1997

Harris, Jonathan Gil, *The First Firangis*, Delhi, 2014

Harris, Lucian, 'Archibald Swinton: A New Source for Albums of Indian Miniature in William Beckford's Collection', *Burlington Magazine*, vol. 143, no. 1179 (June 2001), pp. 360–6

Hasan, Maulvi Zafar, *Monuments of Delhi*, New Delhi, 1920

Hasan, Mohibbul, *History of Tipu Sultan*, Calcutta, 1951

Hawes, Christopher, *Poor Relations: The Making of the Eurasian Community in British India 1773–1833*, London, 1996

Howard, Michael, *War in European History* (1976, reprint), Oxford, 1977

Husain, Ali Akbar, *Scent in the Islamic Garden: A Study of Deccani Urdu Literary Sources*, Karachi, 2000

Husain, Iqbal, *The Rise and Decline of the Ruhela Chieftaincies in 18th Century India*, Aligarh, 1994

Hutchinson, Lester, *European Freebooters in Moghul India*, London, 1964

Ives, Edward, *A Voyage From England to India in the Year 1754*, London, 1733

Jacob, Sarah, 'The Travellers' Tales: The travel writings of Itesamuddin and Abu Taleb Khan', in William A. Pettigrew and Mahesh Gopalan, *The East India Company, 1600–1857: Essays on Anglo-Indian Connection*, New York, 2017

Jasanoff, Maya, *Edge of Empire: Conquest and Collecting in the East, 1750–1850*, London, 2005

Jespersen, Knud J. V., 'Social Change and Military Revolution in Early Modern Europe: Some Danish Evidence', *Historical Journal*, vol. 26, no. 1 (1983)

Joseph, Betty, *Reading the East India Company*, New Delhi, 2006

Keay, John, *India Discovered*, London, 1981

Keay, John, *The Honourable Company: A History of the English East India Company*, London, 1991

Keay, Julia, *Farzana: The Woman Who Saved an Empire*, London, 2014

Khan, *Indian Muslim Perceptions of the West during the Eighteenth Century*, Karachi, 1998

Khan, Abdul Majed, *The Transition in Bengal 1756–1775*, Cambridge, 1969

Khan, Iqbal Ghani, 'A Book With Two Views: Ghulam Husain's "An Overview of Modern Times"', in Jamal Malik, ed., *Perspectives of Mutual Encounters in South Asian History, 1760–1860*, Leiden, 2000

Kincaid, Denis, *British Social Life in India up to 1938*, London, 1938

Kolff, Dirk, *Naukar, Rajput, and Sepoy*, London, 1992

Kuiters, Willem G. J., *The British in Bengal 1756–1773: A Society in Transition seen through the Biography of a Rebel: William Bolts (1739–1808)*, Paris, 2002

Kulkarni, G., and Kantak, M. R., *The Battle of Khardla: Challenges and Responses*, Pune, 1980

Kulkarni, Uday S., *Solstice at Panipat, 14 January 1761*, Pune, 2011

Kulkarni, Uday, *The Era of Baji Rao: An Account of the Empire of the Deccan*, Pune, 2017

Kumar, Ritu, *Costumes and Textiles of Royal India*, London, 1998

Lafont, Jean-Marie, 'Lucknow in the Eighteenth Century', in Violette Graff, ed., *Lucknow: Memories of a City*, Delhi, 1997

Lafont, Jean-Marie, *Indika: Essays in Indo-French Relations 1630–1976*, Manohar, Delhi, 2000

Lafont, Jean-Marie, and Lafont, Rehana, *The French & Delhi, Agra, Aligarh and Sardhana*, New Delhi, 2010

Laine, James W., *Shivaji: Hindu King in Islamic India*, Oxford, 2003

Lal, John, *Begam Samru: Fading Portrait in a Gilded Frame*, Delhi, 1997

Lal, K. Sajjun, *Studies in Deccan History*, Hyderabad, 1951

Lal, K. S., *The Mughal Harem*, New Delhi, 1988

Lane-Poole, Stanley, *Aurangzeb and the Decay of the Mughal Empire*, London, 1890

Leach, Linda York, *Mughal and Other Paintings from the Chester Beatty Library*, London, 1995

Lenman, Bruce, and Lawson, Philip, 'Robert Clive, the "Black Jagir" and British Politics', in *Historical Journal*, vol. 26, no. 4 (December 1983)

Lenman, Bruce P., *Britain's Colonial Wars 1688–1783*, New York, 2001

Leonard, Karen, 'The Hyderabad Political System and Its Participants', *Journal of Asian Studies*, vol. 30, no. 3 (1971)

Leonard, Karen, 'The Great Firm Theory of the Decline of the Mughal Empire', *Comparative Studies in Society and History*, vol. 21, no. 2 (1979)

Leonard, Karen, 'Banking Firms in Nineteenth-Century Hyderabad Politics', *Modern Asian Studies*, vol. 15, no. 2 (1981)

Little, J. H., *The House of Jagat Seth*, Calcutta, 1956

Llewellyn-Jones, Rosie, *A Fatal Friendship: The Nawabs, the British and the City of Lucknow*, Delhi, 1982

Llewellyn-Jones, Rosie, *A Very Ingenious Man: Claude Martin in Early Colonial India*, Delhi, 1992

Llewellyn-Jones, Rosie, *Engaging Scoundrels: True Tales of Old Lucknow*, New Delhi, 2000

Lockhardt, Laurence, *Nadir Shah*, London, 1938

Losty, J. P., 'Towards a New Naturalism: Portraiture in Murshidabad and Avadh, 1750–80', in Barbara Schmitz, ed., *After the Great Mughals: Painting in Delhi and the Regional Courts in the 18th and 19th Centuries*, Mumbai, 2002

Losty, J. P., 'Murshidabad Painting 1750–1820', in Neeta Das and Rosie Llewellyn-Jones, *Murshidabad: Forgotten Capital of Bengal*, Mumbai, 2013

Losty, J. P., 'Eighteenth-century Mughal Paintings from the Swinton Collection', *Burlington Magazine*, vol. 159, no. 1375, October 2017

Losty, J. P., and Roy, Malini, *Mughal India: Art, Culture and Empire*, London, 2012

Love, H. D., *Vestiges of Old Madras*, 2 vols, London, 1913

Maddison, Angus, *Contours of the World Economy, 1–2030 AD: Essays in Macro-Economic History*, Oxford, 2007

Malik, Jamaled, *Perspectives of Mutual Encounters in South Asian History, 1760–1860*, Leiden, 2000

Malik, Zahir Uddin, *The Reign of Muhammad Shah, 1719–1748*, Aligarh, 1977

Mansingh, Gurbir, 'French Military Influence in India', in *Reminiscences: The French in India*, New Delhi, 1997

Marshall, P. J., *Problems of Empire: Britain and India 1757–1813*, London, 1968

Marshall, P. J., ed., *The British Discovery of Hinduism*, Cambridge, 1970

Marshall, P. J., *East India Fortunes: The British in Bengal in the Eighteenth Century*, Oxford, 1976

Marshall, P. J., *Bengal: The British Bridgehead – Eastern India 1740–1828*, Cambridge, 1987

Marshall, P. J., 'Cornwallis Triumphant: War in India and the British Public in the Late Eighteenth Century', in Lawrence Freeman, Paul Hayes and Robert O'Neill, eds, *War, Strategy and International Politics*, Oxford, 1992

Marshall, P. J., 'British Society under the East India Company', in *Modern Asian Studies*, vol. 31, no. 1 (1997)

Marshall, P. J., 'The British in Asia: Trade to Dominion, 1700–1765', in P. J. Marshall, ed., *The Oxford History of the British Empire*, vol. 2, *The Eighteenth Century*, Oxford, 1998

Marshall, P. J., 'The English in Asia to 1700', in Nicholas Canny, *The Oxford History of the British Empire*, vol. 1, *The Origins of Empire*, Oxford, 1998

Marshall P. J., ed., *The Eighteenth Century in Indian History: Evolution or Revolution?*, New Delhi, 2003

Marshall, P. J., *The Making and Unmaking of Empires: Britain, India and America c. 1750–1783*, Oxford, 2005

Matar, Nabil, *Turks, Moors & Englishmen in the Age of Discovery*, New York, 1999

Mather, James, *Pashas: Traders and Travellers in the Islamic World*, London, 2009

McLane, John R., *Land and Local Kingship in Eighteenth-Century Bengal*, Cambridge, 1993

Michaud, J., *History of Mysore Under Haidar Ali and Tippoo Sultan*, trans. V. K. Raman Menon, Madras, 1924

Micklethwait, John, and Wooldridge, Adrian, *The Company: A Short History of a Revolutionary Idea*, London, 2003

Milton, Giles, *Nathaniel's Nutmeg or, The True and Incredible Adventures of the Spice Trader Who Changed the Course of History*, London, 1999

Mishra, Rupali, *A Business of State: Commerce, Politics and the Birth of the East India Company*, Harvard, 2018

Moin, A. Azfar, *The Millennial Sovereign: Sacred Kingship & Sainthood in Islam*, Columbia, 2014

Moon, Sir Penderel, *Warren Hastings and British India*, London, 1947

Moon, Sir Penderel, *The British Conquest and Dominion of India*, London, 1989

Moosvi, Shireen, *Economy of the Mughal Empire, c.1595: A Statistical Study*, New Delhi, 1987

Moreland, W. H., 'From Gujerat to Golconda in the Reign of Jahangir', in *Journal of Indian History*, vol. XVII (1938)

Morris, James, *Heaven's Command: An Imperial Progress*, London, 1973

Mount, Ferdinand, *Tears of the Rajas: Mutiny, Money and Marriage in India 1805–1905*, London, 2016

Moynihan, Elizabeth B., *Paradise as a Garden in Persia and Mughal India*, New York, 1979

Mukherjee, S. N., *Sir William Jones: A Study in Eighteenth-Century Attitudes to India*, Cambridge, 1968

Mukherjee, Tilottama, 'The Coordinating State and the Economy: the Nizamat in Eighteenth-Century Bengal', in *Modern Asian Studies*, vol. 43, no. 2 (2009)

Mukherjee, Tilottama, *Political Culture and Economy in Eighteenth-Century Bengal: Networks of Exchange, Consumption and Communication*, New Delhi, 2013

Mukhopadhyay, S. C., *British Residents at the Darbar of Bengal Nawabs at Murshidabad 1757–1772*, Delhi (n.d.)

Nayeem, M. A., *Mughal Administration of the Deccan under Nizamul Mulk Asaf Jah (1720–48)*, Bombay, 1985

Nechtman, Tillman W., 'A Jewel in the Crown? Indian Wealth in Domestic Britain in the Late Eighteenth Century', *Eighteenth-Century Studies*, vol. 41, no. 1 (2007)

Nechtman, Tillman W., *Nabobs: Empire and Identity in Eighteenth-Century Britain*, Cambridge, 2018

Nilsson, Sten, *European Architecture in India 1750–1850*, London, 1968

Otis, Andrew, *Hicky's Bengal Gazette: The Untold Story of India's First Newspaper*, Chennai, 2018

Owen, Sidney J., *The Fall of the Mughal Empire*, London, 1912

Pannikar, K. N., *British Diplomacy in Northern India: A Study of the Delhi Residency 1803–1857*, New Delhi, 1968

Parker, Geoffrey, *The Military Revolution*, Oxford, 1988

Pearse, Colonel Hugh, *Memoir of the Life and Military Services of Viscount Lake*, London, 1908

Pearson, M. N., *The New Cambridge History of India*, 1.1, *The Portuguese in India*, Cambridge, 1987

Peers, D., 'State, Power and Colonialism', in Douglas Peers and Nandini Gooptu, eds, *India and the British Empire*, Oxford, 2012

Pelò, Stephano, 'Drowned in the Sea of Mercy. The Textual Identification of Hindu Persian Poets from Shi'i Lucknow in the Tazkira of Bhagwan Das "Hindi"', in Vasudha Dalmia and Munis D. Faruqui, eds, *Religious Interactions in Mughal India*, New Delhi, 2014

Pemble, John, 'Resources and Techniques in the Second Maratha War', *Historical Journal*, vol. 19, no. 2 (June 1976), pp. 375–404

Pernau, Margrit, Rajamani, Imke, and Schofield, Katherine, *Monsoon Feelings*, New Delhi, 2018

Philips, C. H., 'Clive in the English Political World, 1761–64', in *Bulletin of the School of Oriental and African Studies, University of London*, vol. 12, no. 3/44, Oriental and African Studies Presented to Lionel David Barnett by His Colleagues, Past and Present (1948)

Phillips, Jim, 'A Successor to the Moguls: The Nawab of the Carnatic and the East India Company, 1763–1785', *International History Review*, vol. 7, no. 3 (August 1985), pp. 364–89

Pinch, William, *Warrior Ascetics and Indian Empires*, Cambridge, 2006

Pitts, Jennifer, *A Turn to Empire: The Rise of Imperial Liberalism in Britain and France*, Princeton, 2005

Prakash, Om, *The Dutch East India Company and the Economy of Bengal, 1630–1720*, Princeton, 1985

Prakash, Om, 'Manufacturing in Eighteenth-Century Bengal', in Giorgio Riello and Tirthankar Roy, eds, *How India Clothed the World: The World of South Asian Textiles, 1500–1800*, Leiden, 2013

Pritchett, Frances W. P., *Nets of Awareness: Urdu Poetry and Its Critics*, Berkeley and Los Angeles, 1994

Qanungo, K. R., *History of the Jats*, Calcutta, 1925

Qanungo, K. R., 'Fragment of a Bhao Ballad in Hindi', *Historical Essays*, Calcutta, 1968

Rao, P. Setu Madhava, *Eighteenth Century Deccan*, Bombay, 1963

Rao, Velcheru Narayana, Shulman, David, and Subrahmanyam, Sanjay, *Textures of Time: Writing History in South India 1600–1800*, New York, 2003

Ray, Aniriddha, ed., *Tipu Sultan and his Age: A Collection of Seminar Papers*, Calcutta, 2002

Ray, Rajat Kanta, 'Race, Religion and Realm', in M. Hasan and N. Gupta, *India's Colonial Encounter*, Delhi, 1993

Ray, Rajat Kanta, 'Indian Society and the Establishment of British Supremacy, 1765–1818', in P. J. Marshall, *The Eighteenth Century*, Oxford, 1998

Ray, Rajat Kanta, *The Felt Community: Commonality and Mentality before the Emergence of Indian Nationalism*, New Delhi, 2003

Regani, Sarojini, *Nizam-British Relations 1724–1857*, New Delhi, 1963

Richards, J. F., 'Early Modern India and World History', *Journal of World History*, vol. 8, no. 2 (1997)

Richards, J. F., 'Mughal State Finance and the Premodern World Economy', in *Comparative Studies in Society and History*, vol. 23, no. 2 (1981)

Richards, J. F., 'The Seventeenth-Century Crisis in South Asia', in *Modern Asian Studies*, vol. 24, no. 4 (1990)

Richards, John F., *Kingship and Authority in South Asia*, New Delhi, 1998

Richards, J. F., *The Unending Frontier: An Environmental History of the Early Modern World*, Berkeley, 2003

Rizvi, Sayid Athar Abbas, *Shah Walli-Allah And His Times*, Canberra, 1980

Rizvi, Sayid Athar Abbas, *Shah 'Abd al'Aziz: Puritanism, Sectarianism and Jihad*, Canberra, 1982

Robb, Peter, *Clash of Cultures? An Englishman in Calcutta*, Inaugural Lecture, 12 March 1998, London, 1998

Roberts, Andrew, *Napoleon and Wellington*, London, 2001

Robins, Nick, *The Corporation That Changed the World: How the East India Company Shaped the Modern Multinational*, London, 2006

Roy, Kaushik, 'Military Synthesis in South Asia: Armies, Warfare, and Indian Society, c. 1740–1849', in *Journal of Military History*, vol. 69, no. 3 (July 2005)

Roy, Tirthankar, *The East India Company: The World's Most Powerful Corporation*, New Delhi, 2012

Russell, Ralph, *Hidden in the Lute: An Anthology of Two Centuries of Urdu Literature*, New Delhi, 1995

Saksena, Ram Babu, *European & Indo-European Poets of Urdu & Persian*, Lucknow, 1941

Sardesai, Govind Sakharam, *A New History of the Marathas*, 3 vols, Poona, 1946

Sarkar, Bihani, 'Traveling Tantrics and Belligerent Brahmins: The Sivarajyabhiṣekakalpataru and Sivaji's Tantric consecration', for the conference on *Professions in motion: culture, power and the politics of mobility in 18th-century India*, St Anne's College, Oxford, 2 June 2017 (forthcoming)

Sarkar, Jadunath, ed., *The History of Bengal*, vol. II, *The Muslim Period 1200 AD–1757 AD*, New Delhi, 1948

Sarkar, Jadunath, *Bengal Nawabs*, trans. Jadunath Sarkar, Calcutta, 1952

Sarkar, Jadunath, ed., *Persian Records of Maratha History*, 1, *Delhi Affairs (1761–1788)*, Bombay, 1953

Sarkar, Jadunath, *Nadir Shah in India*, Calcutta, 1973

Sarkar, Jadunath, *Fall of the Mughal Empire*, 4 vols, New Delhi, 1991

Sarkar, Jadunath, 'General Raymond of the Nizam's Army', in Mohammed Taher, ed., *Muslim Rule in Deccan*, Delhi, 1997

Saroop, Narindar, *A Squire of Hindoostan*, New Delhi, 1983

Scammell, G. V., *The World Encompassed: The First European Maritime Empires*, London, 1981

Scammell, G. V., 'European Exiles, Renegades and Outlaws and the Maritime Economy of Asia c.1500–1750', in *Modern Asian Studies*, vol. 26, no. 4 (1992)

Schimmel, Annemarie, *Islam in the Indian Subcontinent*, Leiden-Köln, 1980

Schmitz, Barbara, ed., *After the Great Mughals: Painting in Delhi and the Regional Courts in the 18th and 19th Centuries*, Mumbai, 2002

Schofield, Katherine, and Lunn, David, 'Delight, Devotion and the Music of the Monsoon at the Court of Emperor Shah Alam II', in Margit Pernau, Imke Rajamani and Katherine Schofield, *Monsoon Feelings*, New Delhi, 2018

Scott, William Robert, *The Constitution and Finance of English, Scottish and Irish Joint Stock Companies to 1720*, 3 vols, Cambridge, 1912

Sen, A., 'A Pre-British Economic Formation in India of the Late Eighteenth Century', in Barun De, ed., *Perspectives in Social Sciences*, I, *Historical Dimensions*, Calcutta, 1977

Sen, S. N., *Anglo-Maratha Relations during the Administration of Warren Hastings*, Madras, 1974

Sen, S. P., *The French in India, 1763–1816*, Calcutta, 1958

Shapiro, James, *1599: A Year in the Life of William Shakespeare*, London, 2005

Shreeve, Nicholas, *Dark Legacy*, Arundel, 1996

Singh, Ganda, *Ahmed Shah Durrani*, Delhi, 1925

Singh, Ganda, 'Colonel Polier's Account of the Sikhs', *The Panjab Past and Present*, 4 (1970)

Singh, Kavita, *Real Birds in Imagined Gardens: Mughal Painting between Persia and Europe*, Los Angeles, 2017

Spear, Percival, *The Twilight of the Moghuls*, Cambridge, 1951

Spear, Percival, *The Nabobs*, Cambridge, 1963

Spear, Percival, *Master of Bengal: Clive and his India*, London, 1975

Spear, T. G. P., 'The Mogul Family and the Court in 19th-Century Delhi', in *Journal of Indian History*, vol. XX (1941)

Srivastava, Ashirbadi Lal, *Shuja ud-Daula*, vol. 1, *1754–1765*, Calcutta, 1939

Stein, Burton, 'State Formation and Economy Reconsidered', *Modern Asian Studies*, vol. 19, no. 3, Special Issue: Papers Presented at the Conference on Indian Economic and Social History, Cambridge University, April 1984 (1985)

Stein, Burton, 'Eighteenth Century India: Another View', *Studies in History*, vol. 5, issue 1 (1989)

Stern, Philip J., *The Company State: Corporate Sovereignty & the Early Modern Foundations of the British Empire in India*, Cambridge, 2011

Strachan, Hew, *European Armies and the Conduct of War* (1983; reprint), London, 1993

Strachan, Michael, *Sir Thomas Roe 1581–1644*, Salisbury, 1989

Strachey, Edward, 'The Romantic Marriage of James Achilles Kirkpatrick, Sometime British Resident at the Court of Hyderabad', in *Blackwood's Magazine*, July 1893

Strachey, Sir John, *Hastings and the Rohilla War*, Oxford, 1892

Subrahmanyam, Sanjay, *Improvising Empire: Portuguese Trade and Settlement in the Bay of Bengal 1500–1700*, Delhi, 1990

Subrahmanyam, Sanjay, *The Portuguese Empire in Asia: A Political and Economic History*, London, 1993

Subrahmanyam, Sanjay, 'Connected Histories: Notes Towards a Reconfiguration of Early Modern Eurasia', *Modern Asian Studies*, vol. 31, no. 3 (1997)

Subrahmanyam, Sanjay, 'Un Grand Derangement: Dreaming An Indo-Persian Empire in South Asia, 1740–1800', *Journal of Early Modern History*, vol. 4, nos. 3–4 (2000)

Subrahmanyam, Sanjay, *Penumbral Visions: Making Politics in Early Modern South India*, Michigan, 2001

Subramanian, Lakshmi, 'Banias and the British: the role of indigenous credit in the Process of Imperial Expansion in Western India in the second half of the Eighteenth century', *Modern Asian Studies*, vol. 21, no. 3 (1987)

Subramanian, Lakshmi, and Ray, Rajat K., 'Merchants and Politics: From the Great Mughals to the East India Company', in Dwijendra Tripathi, *Business and Politics in India*, New Delhi, 1991

Subramanian, Lakshmi, 'Arms and the Merchant: The Making of the Bania Raj in Late Eighteenth-Century India', *South Asia*, vol. XXIV, no. 2 (2001), pp. 1–27

Sutherland, Lucy, *The East India Company in Eighteenth-Century Politics*, Oxford, 1952

Teltscher, Kate, *India Inscribed: European and British Writing on India 1600– 1800*, Oxford, 1995

Tharoor, Shashi, *Inglorious Empire: What the British Did in India*, New Delhi, 2016

Timberg, Thomas A., *The Marwaris: From Jagat Seth to the Birlas*, New Delhi, 2014

Travers, Robert, *Ideology and Empire in Eighteenth Century India: The British in Bengal*, Cambridge, 2007

Tripathi, Amales, *Trade and Finance in the Bengal Presidency, 1793–1833*, Calcutta, 1979

Trivedi, Madhu, *The Making of the Awadh Culture*, New Delhi, 2010

Truschke, Audrey, *Aurangzeb: The Man and the Myth*, New Delhi, 2017

Vartavarian, Mesrob, 'An Open Military Economy: The British Conquest of South India Reconsidered, 1780–1799', *Journal of the Economic and Social History of the Orient*, vol. 57, no. 4 (2014)

Ward, Andrew, *Our Bones Are Scattered*, London, 1996

Washbrook, D. A., 'Progress and Problems: South Asian Economic and Social History c. 1720–1860', in *Modern Asian Studies*, vol. 22, no. 1 (1988)

Weitzman, Sophia, *Warren Hastings and Philip Francis*, Manchester, 1929

Weller, Jac, *Wellington in India*, London, 1972

Wheatley, Captain G. R. P., 'The Final Campaign against Tipu', *Journal of the United Services Institute*, no. 41 (1912)

Wilbur, Marguerite Eyer, *The East India Company and the British Empire in the Far East*, New York, 1945

Wilkinson, Theon, *Two Monsoons*, London, 1976

Willson, Beckles, *Ledger and Sword: The Honourable Company of Merchants of England Trading to the East Indies 1599–1874*, 2 vols, London, 1903

Wilson, Jon, 'A Thousand Countries to go to: Peasants and rulers in late eighteenth-century Bengal', *Past and Present*, no. 189, November 2005

Wilson, Jon, *India Conquered: Britain's Raj and the Chaos of Empire*, London, 2016

Wink, André, 'Maratha Revenue Farming', in *Modern Asian Studies*, vol. 17,
    no. 4 (1983)
Young, Desmond, *Fountain of Elephants*, London, 1959
Zaidi, S. Inayat, 'European Mercenaries in the North Indian armies
    1750–1803 AD', in *The Ninth European Conference on Modern South Asian
    Studies*, Heidelberg, 9–12 July 1986
Zaidi, S. Inayat, 'French Mercenaries in the Armies of South Asian States
    1499–1803', in *Indo-French Relations: History and Perspectives*, Delhi, 1990

Image Credits

SECTION I

The first subscription list: © British Library Board. All Rights Reserved/Bridgeman Images

Sir Thomas Smythe by Simon de Passe: © British Library Board. All Rights Reserved/Bridgeman Images

Sir James Lancaster: © National Maritime Museum, Greenwich, London

Sir Thomas Roe: © National Maritime Museum, Greenwich, London

Jahangir as the Millennial Sultan: © Freer Gallery of Art, Smithsonian Institution, USA/Bridgeman Images

New East India House: © London Metropolitan Archives, City of London/Bridgeman Images

East India Company ships at Deptford, 1660: © National Maritime Museum, Greenwich, London

Headquarters of the Dutch East India Company at Hughli: CC0 1.0 Universal/Courtesy of Rijksmuseum, Amsterdam

Fort William, Calcutta: © British Library Board. All Rights Reserved/ Bridgeman Images

Mughal Emperor Alamgir Aurangzeb: © Ashmolean Museum, University of Oxford

Shivaji Bhonsle: © The Trustees of the British Museum

Nader Shah: © The Bodleian Libraries, The University of Oxford MS. Ouseley Add. 173, fol. 29v

SECTION 2

The Duke of Wellington on Campaign in the Deccan: © Private Collection

Two armies drawn up in combat: © The Trustees of the Chester Beatty Library, Dublin CBL In 64.17

Index

A Note on the Author

William Dalrymple is one of Britain's great historians and the bestselling author of the Wolfson Prize-winning *White Mughals*, *The Last Mughal*, which won the Duff Cooper Prize, and the Hemingway and Kapuściński Prize-winning *Return of a King*. In 2018 he was presented with the prestigious President's Medal by the British Academy for his outstanding literary achievement and for co-founding the Jaipur Literature Festival. He was named one of the world's top 50 thinkers for 2020 by *Prospect*. William lives with his wife and three children on a farm outside Delhi.

A Note on the Type

The text of this book is set Adobe Garamond. It is one of several versions of Garamond based on the designs of Claude Garamond. It is thought that Garamond based his font on Bembo, cut in 1495 by Francesco Griffo in collaboration with the Italian printer Aldus Manutius. Garamond types were first used in books printed in Paris around 1532. Many of the present-day versions of this type are based on the Typi Academiae of Jean Jannon cut in Sedan in 1615.

Claude Garamond was born in Paris in 1480. He learned how to cut type from his father and by the age of fifteen he was able to fashion steel punches the size of a pica with great precision. At the age of sixty he was commissioned by King Francis I to design a Greek alphabet, and for this he was given the honourable title of royal type founder. He died in 1561.

A Note on the Type